Fixing the Euro Within the National Constitutional Guardrails

European Monographs Series Set

VOLUME 117

Editor

Prof. Andrea Biondi is Professor of European Law and Director of the Centre of European Law at King's College London

Introduction & Contents/Subjects

As the process of European integration assumes an increasingly complex character, the EU legal system continues to undergo sweeping changes. The European Monographs series offers a voice to thoughtful, knowledgeable, cutting edge legal commentary on the now unlimited field of European law. Its emphasis on focal and topical issues makes the series an invaluable tool for scholars, practitioners, and policymakers specializing or simply interested in EU law.

Objective

The aim is to publish innovative work appealing to academics and practitioners alike. The result is an original and ongoing library of detailed analyses, theories, commentaries, practical guides, and proposals, each of which furthers the cause of meaningful European integration. Cumulatively, the series may be regarded as a 'work in progress' engaged in building a sharply defined representation of law in Europe.

Readership

Academics and practitioners dealing with EU law.

The titles published in this series are listed at the end of this volume.

Fixing the Euro Within the National Constitutional Guardrails

A Comparative Assessment of the National Constitutional Space for EU (Fiscal) Integration

Frederik Behre

Wolters Kluwer

Published by:
Kluwer Law International B.V.
PO Box 316
2400 AH Alphen aan den Rijn
The Netherlands
E-mail: lrs-sales@wolterskluwer.com
Website: www.wolterskluwer.com/en/solutions/kluwerlawinternational

Sold and distributed by:
Wolters Kluwer Legal & Regulatory U.S.
920 Links Avenue
Landisville, PA 17538
United States of America
E-mail: customer.service@wolterskluwer.com

ISBN 978-94-035-3586-9

e-Book: ISBN 978-94-035-4126-6
web-PDF: ISBN 978-94-035-4136-5

Table of Contents

Preface xiii

Acknowledgements xv

CHAPTER 1
Introduction 1
A Setting the Stage: EU Fiscal Integration and National Constitutional Law 1
B Making the Case for EU Fiscal Integration 3
C EU Fiscal Integration Between a Fiscal Rock and a Constitutional Hard Place? 7
D Framework and Structure of the Book 9
I Comparative Framework 10
II Concept of Constitutional Flexibility 13
III Resulting Structure of the Book 15
E Constructing a Resilient Euro Within the National Constitutional Guardrails 16

PART I
Charting the National Constitutional Space 17

SECTION I
Macro-comparative Assessment of Finland and Germany 19

CHAPTER 2
Macro-comparative Assessment of Finland 21
A Finland and EU Integration 21
B Introducing the Finnish Constitutional Order 23
I Finnish Constitutional Reforms to Accommodate EU Cooperation 25
II The Finnish Constitutional Law Committee 26
III Interim Conclusion: Constitutional Embracement of EU Membership 28

C Procedural and Institutional Framework Applicable to EU Fiscal Integration 28
I Transferring Budgetary and Fiscal Competences to the EU 29
1 Preliminary Step: Scope for EU Cooperation 29
2 Conferral of Competences under Section 94 Finnish Constitution 30
3 Constitutional Amendments According to Section 73 Finnish Constitution 33
a Fiscal Integration via Exceptive Enactment? 33
b Fiscal Integration via Constitutional Amendments? 34
4 Application of the Framework During the Eurocrisis 35
II The Finnish Model of National Engagement in EU Matters 38
III *Ex Ante* Constitutional Review and *Ex Post* Judicial Scrutiny 41
IV Applicable Procedural and Institutional Framework to EU Fiscal Integration 42
D Substantive Framework Applicable to EU Fiscal Integration 43
I Finnish Sovereignty: An Evolutionary Conception 43
1 The Historic Origin of Finnish Sovereignty 43
2 A New Conception of Finnish Sovereignty 44
3 Application During the Eurocrisis and Implications for EU Fiscal Integration 46
II Finnish Democracy 51
1 A Normative Core of Finnish Democracy? 51
2 Implications for EU Fiscal Integration Steps 52
III Section 94(3) Finnish Constitution: A Finnish *Eternity Clause*? 53
IV Conclusive Appraisal: Substantive Flexibility Towards European Fiscal Integration 54
E Resulting Constitutional Space: The Finnish Road to EU Fiscal Integration 55

CHAPTER 3
Macro-comparative Assessment of Germany 57
A Germany and EU Integration 57
B Setting the Stage: EU Membership and the German Constitution 59
I Origin of the German Constitution and Its EU Features 59
II The German Constitutional Court 60
C Procedural and Institutional Framework for EU Cooperation 61
I Conferral of Additional Competences to the EU under Article 23 GG 62
II Participation of Parliament in the Exercise of Conferred Powers 64
III The Involvement of the German Federal Council 65
IV Constitutional Oversight: Proceedings Before the *Bundesverfassungsgericht* 66
1 Individuals Initiating Constitutional Proceedings 66

a Possible Violation of Individual Constitutional Rights 67
b Application of Subjective Gravamen in EU Matters 68
c Emerging Constitutional Double Standard 69
2 Institutional Actors Initiating Constitutional Proceedings 72
a Constitutional Requirements for Initiating Inter-institutional Proceedings 72
b Application of Adversarial Nature of Proceedings in EU Matters 72
c Possible Constitutional Double Standard 74
3 Apparent Procedural Double Standard 75
V Applicable Procedural and Institutional Framework for EU Fiscal Integration 75
D Substantive Framework Applicable to EU Fiscal Integration 76
I Underpinning Mechanisms 76
1 Eternity Clause 76
2 The Different Limits Employed by the German Constitutional Court 79
a Fundamental Rights Review 79
b *Ultra Vires* Review 80
c Constitutional Identity Review 82
d Overlap of *Ultra Vires* and Identity Review 82
3 Guiding Concepts for Constitutional Jurisprudence on EU Integration 83
II Constitutional Principles 84
1 Democracy 85
a Legitimizing Subject ('Volkssouveränität') 85
b Elections as a Mechanism to Determine Representation 86
c Legitimizing Object: Components Allowing for a Political Process 87
d Delegation of Public Authority 88
e Resulting Challenge for EU (Fiscal) Integration 89
2 Overall Budgetary Responsibility 92
a Underpinning Democracy-Theoretical Considerations 92
b Requirements of Budgetary Responsibility 94
c Application of These Requirements by the Bundesverfassungsgericht 96
d Conclusion on Overall Budgetary Responsibility 101
e Possible Double Standard in the Conception of Overall Budgetary Responsibility 101
i Constitutional Scrutiny of the German Budget 102
3 German Sovereignty 105

E Resulting German Constitutional Space for EU Fiscal Integration Steps 106
F Additional Constitutional Space by Applying Consistent Constitutional Standard 107

CHAPTER 4
Comparative Conclusions on Finland and Germany 111
A Comparing Finland and Germany 111
B Comparing the National Constitutional Review 111
C Comparing the National Procedural Framework for EU Fiscal Integration 113
D Comparing the National Substantive Benchmark for EU Fiscal Integration 116
E Overall Comparative Conclusion 119

SECTION II
Micro-comparative Assessment of Selected National Material Limits to EU Fiscal Integration 121

CHAPTER 5
Micro-comparative Assessment of French, German, Polish and Spanish Limit to EU Fiscal Integration 123
A Introduction 123
B The French Constitutional Approach to EU Fiscal Integration 124
I Identifying the Relevant French Constitutional Limits 125
1 Relevant Constitutional Limits for EU Primary Law 127
2 Relevant Constitutional Limits for EU Secondary Law 128
II Essential Conditions for the Exercise of National Sovereignty 129
1 Institutional Actor Enforcing the Limit 130
2 Procedural Framework: Or How to Trigger the Limit 131
3 Constitutional Basis of the Employed Limit 133
4 Substantive Core Protected by the Limit 134
a The Conception of the French Sovereignty Doctrine 134
b Sovereignty as a Limit to EU Integration: A Competence-Based Approach 137
i Union Citizenship, AFJS and Free Movement 137
ii EMU and Single Currency 139
c Interim Conclusion: A Substantive Limit to EU Fiscal Integration? 142
5 Longevity and Absoluteness of the Constitutional Limit 142
III Particularity of the French Constitutional Identity Limit 143
1 Scope of Application of the Constitutional Identity Limit 144
2 Substantive Content Covered by the French Constitutional Identity Limit 145
3 Interim Conclusion: No Immediate Limit for EU Fiscal Integration 147
IV Conclusion on the French Constitutional Identity Limit(s) 147

C The Spanish Constitutional Perspective: An Emerging *Constitutional Identity?* 149
I Identifying the Core Constitutional Limit to EU Fiscal Integration in Spain 151
II Spanish Constitutional Identity Limit 153
1 Institutional Actor Enforcing the Limit 153
2 Procedural Framework: Or How to Trigger the Limit 154
3 Constitutional Basis of the Employed Limit 156
4 Substantive Core Protected by the Limit 157
a Protecting Spanish Sovereignty and Its Statehood 158
b Protecting the Hierarchical Position of the Spanish Constitution 160
c The Tribunal's Concrete Assessment 162
d Interim Conclusion on the Spanish Substantive Core 163
5 Longevity and Absoluteness of the Constitutional Limit 164
III Conclusion 166
D The Polish Perspective on EU Fiscal Integration 167
I Identifying the Core Constitutional Limits to EU Fiscal Integration in Poland 170
II The Polish *Constitutional Identity* Limit: Protecting a *Sovereign* Poland? 171
1 Institutional Actor Enforcing the Limit 171
2 Procedural Framework: Or How to Trigger the Limit 172
3 Constitutional Basis of the Employed Limit 174
4 Substantive Core Protected by the Limit 175
a Constitutional Identity Limit: General Characteristics 176
b Polish Sovereignty 178
i General Conception of Polish Sovereignty 178
ii Specific Material Dimension of Sovereignty Covered by Constitutional Identity Limit 181
c Interim Conclusion 183
5 Longevity and Absoluteness of the Constitutional Limit 183
III Rule of Law at Risk in Poland: The Independence of the Constitutional Tribunal 185
IV Conclusion 188
E Research Findings on German Constitutional Identity Limit 191

CHAPTER 6
Comparing the Different National *Constitutional Identity Limits* and Their Implications for EU Fiscal Integration Proposals 193
A Introducing the Comparative Evaluation 193
B What National Constitutional Space for EU Fiscal Integration? 195

C Institutional and Procedural Framework of National *Constitutional Identity* Limits 203
D Implications of the Comparative Findings for EU Fiscal Integration 205

PART II
Testing the Charted National Constitutional Space 207

CHAPTER 7
Deconstructing EU Fiscal Integration Proposals 213
A Introduction 213
B Creating a Eurozone Fiscal Capacity 213
I Eurozone-Budget 214
II Emergency Budgetary Instruments 216
C Funding Options for Fiscal Integration 218
I The Required Funding 218
II Funding Sources 220
1 Treaty-Based Funding Sources 220
2 Extending the Current Treaty-Framework 222
3 Interim Conclusion on Possible Funding Sources 223
D EU Ministry of Finance: Creating Administrative-Executive Capacity 224
E Enhanced Supervision of National Budgeting 227
F Conclusion: The Envisaged EU Fiscal Integration 229

CHAPTER 8
The Compatibility of EU Fiscal Integration Proposals with National Constitutional Concerns 231
A Introduction 231
B Compatibility of Fiscal Integration with Current National Constitutional Space 232
I Compatibility of an EU Fiscal Capacity with National Constitutional Space 232
1 A Fiscal Capacity or Instrument Based on the Existing Treaty-Framework 233
a Compatibility with the Charted Macro-comparative Constitutional Space 233
b Compatibility with the Charted Micro-comparative Constitutional Space 241
c Interim Conclusion 243
2 A Budgetary Capacity or Instrument Introduced by EU Treaty Amendment 243
a Compatibility with the Charted Macro-comparative Constitutional Space 244
b Compatibility with the Charted Micro-comparative Constitutional Space 247
c Interim Conclusion 253

3 Conclusion on the Feasibility of EU Budgetary Capacity or Instrument 253

II Compatibility of Funding Options with National Constitutional Space 259

1 Introducing New Tax-Based Own Resources for the EU 259

2 Genuine EU Taxation Competence 263

a Compatibility with the Charted Macro-comparative Constitutional Space 263

b Compatibility with the Charted Micro-comparative Constitutional Space 266

c Interim Conclusion 269

3 EU Debts and Shared Liabilities 269

a Compatibility with the Charted Macro-comparative Constitutional Space 269

b Compatibility with the Charted Micro-comparative Constitutional Space 274

c Interim Conclusion 279

4 Conclusion: Altering Constitutional Appraisal of Eurozone Budgetary Tool 280

III Compatibility of Proposals Envisaging an EU Ministry of Finance with National Constitutional Space 284

1 Structural-Institutional Dimension of the Proposed Eurozone Ministry 284

a Compatibility with the Charted Macro-comparative Constitutional Space 284

b Compatibility with the Charted Micro-comparative Constitutional Space 288

c Interim Conclusion 290

2 Conferring New Competences to the Eurozone Ministry 290

a Compatibility with the Charted Macro-comparative Constitutional Space 290

b Compatibility with the Charted Micro-comparative Constitutional Space 292

c Interim Conclusion 294

3 Conclusion on the Creation of an EU Ministry of Finance 294

IV Compatibility of Tightened EU Supervision with National Constitutional Space 296

1 Compatibility with the Charted Macro-comparative Constitutional Space 297

2 Compatibility with the Charted Micro-comparative Constitutional Space 298

3 Conclusion on Tightened EU Fiscal Supervision 299

V Interim Conclusion: Compatibility of Fiscal Integration with Current Constitutional Space 300

C Compatibility Through *Constitutional Flexibility* 301

I Consistent Constitutional Standards in Germany 301
1 Actual German Contributions to the EU Budget 303
2 Net Contribution of Germany 303
3 Wider EU Advantages and German Interest in a Functioning Euro 304
4 Focus on the Procedural Dimension of Overall Budgetary Responsibility 305
5 Interim Conclusion on the German Constitutional Approach 306
II Best Practice Examples 307
III Re-conception of National Approach and EU Benefits 308
IV Interim Conclusion: EU Integration as a Two-Way Street 310
D Final Conclusions on the *Constitutional Feasibility* of EU Fiscal Integration 310

CHAPTER 9
Overall Conclusions and Outlook 317
A Tackling the Dilemma: Constitutional Concerns and EU Fiscal Integration 317
B Charted Comparative Constitutional Space for EU Fiscal Integration 319
C Constitutionally Attainable EU Fiscal Integration Steps 322
D Transforming National Constitutional Limits Through *Constitutional Flexibility* 323
I Consistent Application of the National Constitutional Framework 323
II Creating Constitutional Flexibility Through Domestic Best Practices 325
III Immediate and Indirect Benefits of EU Cooperation 327
E Transforming the Design of Fiscal Integration Proposals 329
F EU Cooperation as a National Constitutional Duty in the Twenty-First Century 330

Bibliography 335

Table of Constitutional Decisions and Case-Law 363

Index 371

Preface

This book is the result of comprehensive PhD research conducted at the Europa Institute of Leiden University. The idea for it was born after many thought-provoking discussions with Professor Armin Cuyvers and subsequently Professor Stefaan Van den Bogaert during the author's LLM studies at the Europa Institute. The PhD research was executed between 2016 and 2021. It involved a research stay with Professor Juha Raitio, Professor Tuomas Ojanen and Professor Kaarlo Tuori at Helsinki University. And it also included a research exchange with Professor Martin Nettesheim, as COVID-19 prevented a research stay in Germany. The final manuscript was reviewed and approved by Professor Ojanen and Professor Nettesheim as well as Professor Christa Tobler and Professor Ben Smulders. The author successfully defended his PhD manuscript on 21 October 2021 at Leiden University.

After completing his PhD research, the author started as an official in the Legal Service of the European Commission. The following disclaimer must thus be added: The book is based on the PhD research conducted between 2016 and 2021 at Leiden University and it has only been updated in light of recent developments. The book represents the author's own, personal views. The expressed views do not in any way bind the European Commission.

Acknowledgements

Thanking people and acknowledging their contribution and help in writing this book is a pleasant and impossible task. I want to thank everybody who was part of this process over the years – you motivated me to complete the research and publish this book.

I am extremely grateful to my PhD supervisors Professor Armin Cuyvers and Professor Stefaan Van den Bogaert for their continuous support and for inspiring me. Your detailed and constructive feedback was vital for drafting, refining and finishing this book. I also want to thank my former colleagues at the Europa Institute for providing a forever-stimulating working environment. I am particularly grateful to Dr Vicky Kosta and Barbora Budinská for listening to and discussing with me various ideas that are a part of this book. I must also thank the Meijers Institute and the Graduate School of Leiden Law School for awarding my PhD project with a Meijers research grant.

My parents have been a steady source of inspiration and unconditional backing. They taught me to stay curious and committed, which has greatly benefited me during my research. Finally, I want to thank Simón Ballen Botero for constantly supporting me, for broadening my thinking, for providing creative input on the included figures and for encouraging me to complete this book, for which I will always be grateful.

CHAPTER 1
Introduction

A SETTING THE STAGE: EU FISCAL INTEGRATION AND NATIONAL CONSTITUTIONAL LAW

The EU financial and sovereign debt crisis - better known as the Eurocrisis - erupted in late 2009 with destructive force. It threatened the survival of the EU's single currency and thereby endangered the entire European integration process.[1] The crisis revealed that the Euro suffers from major structural deficiencies, formally embedded into the Economic and Monetary Union's (EMU) legal framework.[2] Despite emergency fixes undertaken - including reinforced budgetary constraints,[3] the creation of the Eurozone loan facility European Stability Mechanism (ESM),[4] and the initiation of the Banking Union[5] - it is largely acknowledged that comprehensive reforms are necessary to remedy the deficient EMU structure.[6]

1. Matthias Ruffert, 'The Future of the European Economic and Monetary Union: Issues of Constitutional Law' in Francesca Bignami (ed.), *EU Law in Populist Times: Crises and Prospects* (Cambridge University Press 2020) 33-34; Damian Chalmers, Damian Jachtenfuchs and Christian Joerges, 'The Retransformation of Europe' in Damian Chalmers, Damian Jachtenfuchs and Christian Joerges (eds), *The End of the Eurocrats' Dream: Adjusting to European Diversity* (Cambridge University Press 2016) 1-2.
2. Paul Craig, *The Lisbon Treaty: Law, Politics, and Treaty Reform*, vol. Revisited (Oxford University Press 2013) 458; Alicia Hinarejos, 'The Euro Area Crisis and Constitutional Limits to Fiscal Integration' (2012) 14 Cambridge Yearbook of European Legal Studies 243, 244.
3. Under the 'European Semester', cf. Kaarlo Tuori and Klaus Tuori, *The Eurozone Crisis:A Constitutional Analysis* (Cambridge University Press 2014) 108; and the Fiscal Compact, cf. Mark Dawson and Floris De Witte, 'Constitutional Balance in the EU after the Euro-Crisis' (2013) 76 The Modern Law Review 817, 826.
4. Rosa M. Lastra and Jean-Victor Louis, 'European Economic and Monetary Union: History, Trends, and Prospects' (2013) 32 Yearbook of European Law 57, 143, 192.
5. Luca Lionello, *The Pursuit of Stability of the Euro Area as a Whole: The Reform of the European Economic Union and Perspectives of Fiscal Integration* (Springer 2020) 172-175.
6. Apparent from political proposals, cf. Jean-Claude Juncker et al., *The Five Presidents' Report: Completing Europe's Economic and Monetary Union* (European Commission 2015); and the academic debate: Mark Dawson, Henrik Enderlein and Christian Joerges, 'Introduction: The

According to the most authoritative reform proposals, any structural remedy to improve the resilience of the EMU has to comprise EU fiscal integration, which could entail the creation of a specific Eurozone-budget and the establishment of a centralized economic governance directed by a Eurozone Ministry of Finance.[7] These proposals imply that EU fiscal integration is *indispensable* for the Euroarea to effectively tackle macroeconomic imbalances and stimulate economic convergence. The reform imperative for EU fiscal integration is accentuated by the persisting economic impact of COVID-19 and Russia's war of aggression against Ukraine resulting in changing global trade patterns, high inflation and a European energy emergency. The EU's economy is thus navigating turbulent water, which could leave the Euroarea more divided economically, politically and fiscally.[8] Swiftly addressing the underlying structural EMU deficiencies is thus not an elitist reform vision of the '*Brussels-bubble*'. Instead, it is a matter of general concern as only a reinforced Euro can pre-empt future Eurozone-crises (with their associated high socio-economic and sovereignty costs) and thereby secure the continuation of sustainable EU cooperation.[9]

At the same time, the available space for EU fiscal integration steps is increasingly delimited by national constitutional law, as illustrated by the German Public Sector Purchase (PSP)-Programme judgment[10] or the critical evaluation of *Next Generation EU* (NGEU) by the Finnish Constitutional Law Committee[11] and the German Constitutional Court.[12] These constitutional decisions are the tip of the *iceberg* of sceptical national constitutional views on the conferral of core state powers – especially budgetary and

Governance of the Transformation of Europe's Economic, Political, and Constitutional Constellation Since the Euro-Crisis' in Mark Dawson, Henrik Enderlein and Christian Joerges (eds), *Beyond the Crisis: The Governance of Europe's Economic, Political, and Legal Transformation* (Oxford University Press 2015) 3.

7. Juncker et al., *The Five Presidents' Report: Completing Europe's Economic and Monetary Union* 14-15; cf. for example as well: George Pagoulatos, 'EMU and the Greek Crisis: Testing the Extreme Limits of an Asymmetric Union' (2020) 42 Journal of European Integration 363, 367, 373; Charles Wyplosz, 'The Six Flaws of the Eurozone' (2016) 31 Economic Policy 559, 561-562, 572, 592-594.
8. Oscar Arce, Gerrit Koester and Christiane Nickel, 'One Year since Russia's Invasion of Ukraine: The Effects on Euro Area Inflation' (2023), https://www.ecb.europa.eu/press/blog/date/2023/html/ecb.blog20230224~3b75362af3.en.html, accessed 5 April 2023; Alfred Kammer, 'Europe Must Address a Toxic Mix of High Inflation and Flagging Growth' (2022), https://www.imf.org/en/Blogs/Articles/2022/10/23/europe-must-address-a-toxic-mix-of-high-inflation-and-flagging-growth, accessed 5 April 2023.
9. German chancellor Angela Merkel prominently stressed: 'Scheitert der Euro, dann scheitert Europa' ('A collapse of the Euro entails a collapse of Europe', cf. Herman van Rompuy, *Europe in the Storm: Promise and Prejudice* (Davidsfonds Uitgeverij nv 2014) 31.
10. 2 BvR 859/15, 2 BvR 1651/15, 2 BvR 2006/15, 2 BvR 980/15 *Quantitative Easing (PSPP) Final Judgment* (German Federal Constitutional Court) paras 163, 178; cf. as well: Christian Calliess, 'Konfrontation statt Kooperation zwischen BVerfG und EuGH? Zu den Folgen des Karlsruher PSPP-Urteils' (2020) 39 Neue Zeitschrift für Verwaltungsrecht (NVwZ) 897, 898; Paul Kirchhof, 'Die Rechtsarchitektur der Europäischen Union' (2020) 73 Neue Juristische Wochenschrift (NJW) 2057, 2057.
11. PeVL 14/21 vp *Ratification of the Own Resources Decision (II.)* (Finnish Constitutional Law Committee); PeVL 16/2020 vp *Commission's Draft EU Recovery Plan and MFF Planning* (Finnish Constitutional Law Committee) 18; cf. as well: Päivi Leino-Sandberg and Matthias Ruffert, 'Next Generation EU and Its Constitutional Ramifications: A Critical Assessment' (2022) 59 Common Market Law Review 433, 447.
12. 2 BvR 547/21; 2 BvR 798/21 *Final Decision on the Ratification of the Own Resources Decision (NGEU)* (German Federal Constitutional Court); cf. as well: Mattias Wendel, 'The Fog of Identity

fiscal prerogatives – to the EU.[13] On the basis of national sovereignty and democracy,[14] national constitutional actors increasingly reduce the available constitutional space for EU integration, which renders the *legal-constitutional* attainability of the required EMU-reforms questionable.

The reform of the Euro is thus running into a fundamental dilemma: effective EU fiscal integration is both necessary to stabilize the single currency and legally impossible given the limits that national constitutional systems set. In the following chapters, this book critically evaluates and deconstructs the dilemma's *legal-constitutional* parameter comparatively, and it hypothesizes: First, seemingly strict national constitutional limits to EU fiscal integration can be reinterpreted in a more flexible manner thereby offering additional leeway for EMU-reforms. And second, the resulting more flexible protection of the national constitutional core cannot be equated with weaker constitutional safeguards, but it offers more effective contemporary protection of the underlying national constitutional values.

B MAKING THE CASE FOR EU FISCAL INTEGRATION

The Eurocrisis demonstrated that the EMU suffers from serious structural flaws, specifically imbalances that result from a centralized EU monetary policy with no corresponding fiscal-economic competences at EU level. These structural deficiencies result in an inability to effectively contain and manage macroeconomic imbalances across Member States – as for example, visible in the different levels of economic competitiveness and the sharply diverging national unemployment rates,[15] the EU

and Judicial Contestation: Preventive and Defensive Constitutional Identity Review in Germany' (2021) 27 European Public Law 465, 479-480.

13. Apparent in the various national *constitutional identity limits*, cf. Luke Dimitrios Spieker, 'Framing and Managing Constitutional Identity Conflicts: How to Stabilize *Modus Vivendi* Between the Court of Justice and Constitutional Courts' (2020) 57 Common Market Law Review 361, 362; Gerhard Van der Schyff, 'Exploring Member State and European Union Constitutional Identity' (2016) 22 European Public Law 227, 228.
14. On democracy, cf. for example, the German concept of *overall budgetary responsibility* is based on German democracy, cf. Christian Calliess, '70 Jahre Grundgesetz und europäische Integration: "Take back control" oder "Mehr Demokratie wagen"?' (2019) 38 Neue Zeitschrift für Verwaltungsrecht (NVwZ) 684, 688; on sovereignty, cf. for example France, where the *Conseil Constitutionnel* identified economic and fiscal competences as particularly important *sovereign* competences, cf. Erich Vranes, 'Constitutional Foundation of, and Limitations to, EU Integration in France' (2013) 19 European Public Law 525, 540; or the Polish Constitutional Tribunal, which equally protects certain competence areas against EU integration based on the concept of Polish sovereignty, cf. Anna Śledzińska-Simon and Michał Ziółkowski, 'Constitutional Identity in Poland: Is the Emperor Putting on the Old Clothes of Sovereignty' in Christian Calliess and Gerhard Van der Schyff (eds), *Constitutional Identity in a Europe of Multilevel Constitutionalism* (Cambridge University Press 2019) 253; Andrzej Wróbel, 'Die Grenzen der europäischen Integration im Lichte jüngerer Entscheidungen des polnischen Verfassungsgerichts' (2013) 13 ERA Forum – Journal of the Academy of European Law 491, 499.
15. Michael Hume, 'Macroeconomic Imbalances in the Euro Area: Can They Be Managed?' in Nauro F. Campos, Paul De Grauwe and Yuemei Ji (eds), *Economic Growth and Structural Reforms in Europe* (Cambridge University Press 2020) 141-142; Pagoulatos, 'EMU and the Greek Crisis: Testing the Extreme Limits of an Asymmetric Union' 366; Wyplosz, 'The Six Flaws of the Eurozone' 561-562, 592-594.

lacking the capacity to tackle large asymmetric macroeconomic shocks[16] or persistently fragile national public finances which entail a contagious risk for the Eurozone.[17] Contrary to the initial assumption that centralized EU monetary policy could operate without centralized economic powers, the Eurocrisis exposed the need for Eurozone fiscal integration to foster economic convergence and shield the single currency against asymmetric macro-economic shocks.[18] Experiences during the Eurocrisis indicate that the centralized monetary policy conducted by the European Central Bank (ECB) cannot sustainably operate without attributing at least limited fiscal competences to the Eurozone.[19] The prevailing structural EMU-deficiencies leave the Eurozone vulnerable to future crises and illustrate the imperative to swiftly initiate EMU-reforms that increase budgetary, fiscal and economic capacities within the Eurozone.

However, instead of implementing concrete new and solid foundations for a stronger Euro, the political debate has so far mainly introduced draft proposals, even as the outlined new existential challenges for the Eurozone materialize. In fact, COVID-19 did not only constitute an immediate global health emergency but has also triggered serious economic disruption that culminated in a severe recession within the Eurozone.[20] In spring 2020, the European Economic Forecast warned that Member States might recover at different speeds leaving economies in the EU's geographical *South* highly exposed.[21] Although the EU arguably addressed this immediate risk by adopting NGEU, the recovery strategy does not remedy the persisting problematic economic and structural differences.[22] Since February 2022, the Eurozone is confronted with the

16. Paul Craig and Menelaos Markakis, 'EMU Reform' in Fabian Amtenbrink and Christopf Herrmann (eds), *The EU Law of Economic and Monetary Union* (Oxford University Press 2020) 1420; Federico Fabbrini, 'Fiscal Capacity' in Federico Fabbrini and Marco Ventoruzzo (eds), *Research Handbook on EU Economic Law* (Edward Elgar Publishing Limited 2019) 107; Juncker et al., *The Five Presidents' Report: Completing Europe's Economic and Monetary Union* 15.
17. Hume, 'Macroeconomic Imbalances in the Euro Area: Can They Be Managed?' 142; Ruffert, 'The Future of the European Economic and Monetary Union: Issues of Constitutional Law' 35-36; Lionello, *The Pursuit of Stability of the Euro Area as a Whole: The Reform of the European Economic Union and Perspectives of Fiscal Integration* 161-163; Fabbrini, 'Fiscal Capacity' 107-109; Wyplosz, 'The Six Flaws of the Eurozone' 572; Juncker et al., *The Five Presidents' Report: Completing Europe's Economic and Monetary Union* 14.
18. Lionello, *The Pursuit of Stability of the Euro Area as a Whole: The Reform of the European Economic Union and Perspectives of Fiscal Integration* 180-181; European Commission, *Reflection Paper on the Deepening of the Economic and Monetary Union* (European Commission 2017) 23; Tuori and Tuori, *The Eurozone Crisis: A Constitutional Analysis* 77.
19. Pagoulatos, 'EMU and the Greek Crisis: Testing the Extreme Limits of an Asymmetric Union' 364, 373; Lastra and Louis, 'European Economic and Monetary Union: History, Trends, and Prospects' 90-91.
20. Eszter Zalan, 'EU Set for Record Recession, Putting Euro at Risk' *EU-Observer* (Brussels 7 May 2020), https://euobserver.com/coronavirus/148283, accessed 5 April 2023; after France already entered into a recession in the first quarter of 2020, cf. Martin Arnold and Valentina Romei, 'Eurozone Economy Shrinks by Fastest Rate on Record' *Financial Times* (London 30 April 2020), https://www.ft.com/content/dd6cfafa-a56d-48f3-a9fd-aa71d17d49a8, accessed 5 April 2023.
21. European Commission, 'European Economic Forecast: Spring 2020' (*Publication Office of the European Union*, 2020),https://ec.europa.eu/info/sites/info/files/economy-finance/ip125_en.pdf, accessed 5 April 2023, 31-32.
22. Problematic according to Mundell's optimum currency area theory, cf. Jennifer Jager and Kurt A. Hafner, 'The Optimum Currency Area Theory and the EMU: An Assessment in the Context of

humanitarian, political and economic consequences of the Russian war of aggression against Ukraine.[23] Economically speaking, the war resulted in extremely high inflation rates, supply shortages and increased energy prices which generate overall uncertainty, significantly reduce the purchasing power of households and affect (industrial) production costs.[24] Hence, the Eurozone economy faces again uncertain times rendering a reform of the single currency even more urgent. Yet, how to make the Euro stronger and remedy the existing structural weaknesses?

One central element which features in various reform plans is deeper EU *fiscal* integration, which could result in the creation of a fully-fledged EU Fiscal Union, as advocated by the EU Five Presidents' Report.[25] According to this authoritative EU proposal, the Eurozone must be equipped with a genuine budgetary capacity by 2025 in order to achieve economic cohesion and effectively tackle future macro-economic shocks. The Fiscal Union would be administered by a Eurozone Ministry of Finance that would thoroughly monitor and possibly even veto national budgeting. These ambitious reform steps were supplemented by recommendations of the EU high-level group on own resources (HLGOR), which emphasized the importance of establishing an independent Eurozone revenue stream that could sustain the proposed budgetary capacity.[26] Subsequently, the reform ideas were reaffirmed by the European Commission in its 2017 White Paper on the Future of Europe[27] and its Reflection Paper on the deepening of EMU.[28] Similar reform proposals were formulated at the national level, most notably by the Franco-German axis that suggested the creation of a separate Eurozone budget as part of the Multiannual Financial Framework (MFF) from 2021 onwards[29] under the administration of the Euro

the Eurozone Crisis' (2013) 48 Intereconomics – Review of European Economic Policy 315, 316; Barry Eichengreen, *European Monetary Unification: Theory, Practice, and Analysis* (MIT Press 1997) 51-52.

23. Andrew Walker, 'Eurozone Suffers Double-Dip Recession as Pandemic Impact Continues' (2021), https://www.bbc.com/news/business-56940720, accessed 5 April 2023.
24. Impacting significantly the financial and price stability in the Eurozone, cf. Drazen Rakic, 'Monetary Policy Issues in the Context of the War in Ukraine (Briefing ECON in Focus)' (2022), http://www.europarl.europa.eu/RegData/etudes/BRIE/2022/703361/IPOL_BRI(2022)703361_EN.pdf, accessed 5 April 2023.
25. Juncker et al., *The Five Presidents' Report: Completing Europe's Economic and Monetary Union.*
26. Mario Monti et al., *Future Financing of the EU: Final Report and Recommendations of the High Level Group on Own Resources December 2016* (EU High Level Group on Own Resources (HLGOR), 2016) 67-69; cf. as well: Fabbrini, 'Fiscal Capacity' 116; Peter Becker, 'Haushaltspolitik' in Werner Weidenfeld and Wolfgang Wessels (eds), *Jahrbuch der Europäischen Integration 2017* (Nomos 2017) 272.
27. Reforming the EMU as envisaged by the EU Five Presidents' Report is part of Scenario 5 presented by the Commission, cf. European Commission, *White Paper on the Future of Europe: Reflections and Scenarios for the EU27 by 2025* (European Commission 2017) 24-25.
28. Commission, *Reflection Paper on the Deepening of the Economic and Monetary Union*; cf. as well: Craig and Markakis, 'EMU Reform' 1414.
29. As announced in the *Meseberg Declaration*, Franco-German Ministerial Meeting, *Erklärung von Meseberg: Das Versprechen Europas für Sicherheit und Wohlstand erneuern* (German Government 2018); cf. as well: Lionello, *The Pursuit of Stability of the Euro Area as a Whole: The Reform of the European Economic Union and Perspectives of Fiscal Integration* 164, 186; Marijn van der Sluis, 'A Euro Area Budget: Another Seedling?' (2019) Maastricht Law – Faculty of Law Working Paper Series 18, 23.

Summit.[30] With this proposal, both Member States lay the basis for the subsequently adopted NGEU. Taken together, the multitude of submitted supranational and national reform proposals illustrates a widely shared understanding that EU fiscal integration steps are an essential building block for the reform of the single currency.

Despite the necessity of and political support for fiscal integration across some Member States, other Member States remain less receptive to such integration steps.[31] This national political reluctance concerns in particular the conferral of *re-distributive* and taxation competences which could lead to permanent fiscal transfers across Eurozone Member States with far-reaching consequences for domestic political decision-making.[32] Therefore, the adoption of EU fiscal integration steps remains politically contested, as apparent from the European Council's discussions on *NGEU*.[33] Notably, Member States initially disagreed on the ratio of grants and favourable loans under the recovery instrument as well as the potential rebates for 'net-contributors', thereby underscoring the sensitivity of any form of *redistribution* or *transfer*.[34] Although the Member States ultimately adopted the EUR 750 billion recovery plan financed through EU borrowing, which signals the feasibility of EU action with large budgetary implications for Member States, the design, the volume and the permanence of fiscal integration remains politically contested, particularly in an increasingly Eurosceptical political climate[35] and in economically uncertain times.

30. Fabbrini, 'Fiscal Capacity' 122; Sluis, 'A Euro Area Budget: Another Seedling?' 23.
31. In relation to Next Generation EU, cf. Cinzia Alcidi and Daniel Gros, 'Next Generation EU: A Large Common Response to the COVID-19 Crisis' (2020) 55 Intereconomics – Review of European Economic Policy 202, 203; on the more general opposition against a fiscally more integrated EMU, cf. Magnus G. Schoeller, 'Preventing the Eurozone Budget: Issue Replacement and Small State Influence in EMU' (2020) Journal of European Public Policy 1, 11-12.
32. Erik Oddvar Eriksen, *Contesting Political Differentiation: European Division and the Problem of Dominance* (Palgrave Macmillan – Springer 2019) 249-250; Stefan Oeter, 'Bundesstaat, Föderation, Staatenverbund: Trennlinien und Gemeinsamkeiten föderaler Systeme' (2015) 75 Zeitschrift für ausländisches öffentliches Recht und Völkerrecht (ZaöRV) 733, 750; Albrecht Weber, 'Die Reform der Wirtschafts- und Währungsunion in der Finanzkrise' (2011) 22 Europäische Zeitschrift für Wirtschaftsrecht 935, 938; on the notion of '(re-) distributive policy' cf. Tom Sefton, 'Distributive and Redistributive Policy' in Robert E. Goodin, Michael Moran and Martin Rein (eds), *The Oxford Handbook of Public Policy* (Oxford University Press 2008) 607.
33. European Council, *Conclusions Special Meeting of the European Council (17, 18, 19, 20 and 21 July 2020): EUCO 10/20* (General Secretariat of the Council 2020) 2-3; cf. as well: Alcidi and Gros, 'Next Generation EU: A Large Common Response to the COVID-19 Crisis' 203.
34. Notably, this political opposition was formulated by the 'frugal four', cf. Mehreen Khan and Michael Peel, '"Frugal Four" Fight to Protect EU Budget Rebates' *Financial Times* (London 18 August 2020), https://www.ft.com/content/55f6796e-4a9f-43b2-8d94-da0804d1f83b, accessed 5 April 2023; cf. as well: Alcidi and Gros, 'Next Generation EU: A Large Common Response to the COVID-19 Crisis' 203.
35. Francesca Bignami, 'Introduction: EU Law, Sovereignty, and Populism' in Francesca Bignami (ed.), *EU Law in Populist Times: Crises and Prospects* (Cambridge University Press 2020) 3-5; Luuk Van Middelaar, 'Taking Decisions or Setting Norms? EU Presidencies Between Executive and Legislative Power in a Crisis-Driven Union' in Bernard Steunenberg, Wim Voermans and Stefaan Van den Bogaert (eds), *Fit for the Future? Reflections from Leiden on the Functioning of the EU* (Eleven International Publishing 2016) 11-12.

C EU FISCAL INTEGRATION BETWEEN A FISCAL ROCK AND A CONSTITUTIONAL HARD PLACE?

In addition, the attainment of EU fiscal integration is increasingly restricted by national constitutional law. At least since the failed EU Constitutional Treaty and the then-adopted Lisbon Treaty, national constitutional authorities started to engage in a comprehensive review of EU integration steps. Based on national constitutional (identity) limitations,[36] these national actors restrict the available domestic legal space for EU integration. The result is a unidirectional dependency of EU integration on the legal space that national constitutional systems allow for EU cooperation.[37] Given that fundamental EU reforms generally depend on unanimous adoption,[38] a constitutional conflict in one Member State blocks the adoption of the reform in the entire EU. Consequently, EU reform proposals have to fit within the legal space that national constitutions offer. Ambitious EMU-reforms can therefore only be adopted with full respect for Member States' constitutional frameworks.[39]

The disruptive impact of national constitutional opposition to EU integration was forcefully demonstrated by the German Constitutional Court's PSP-Programme judgment. In this decision, the German Court declared the ECB's PSP-Programme, and the connected CJEU's preliminary ruling, a manifest and structurally relevant excesses of power.[40] In addition to constituting a concrete threat to the exercise of the ECB's monetary policy mandate, the German PSP-Programme judgment forms part of a larger body of cross-EU constitutional decisions that challenge an increasing supranationalization of the national space.[41] This national constitutional contestation is rooted in the

36. Spieker, 'Framing and Managing Constitutional Identity Conflicts: How to Stabilize *Modus Vivendi* Between the Court of Justice and Constitutional Courts' 362; Schyff, 'Exploring Member State and European Union Constitutional Identity' 228; Alejandro Saiz Arnaiz and Carina Alcoberro Llivina, 'Why Constitutional Identity Suddently Matters: A Tale of Brave States, a Mighty Union and the Decline of Sovereignty' in Alejandro Saiz Arnaiz and Carina Alcoberro Llivina (eds), *National Constitutional Idenity and European Integration* (Intersentia Ltd 2013) 3.
37. Monica Claes, 'Luxembourg, Here We Come? Constitutional Courts and the Preliminary Reference Procedure' (2015) 16 German Law Journal 1331, 1334; namely, in case the legislator intends to confer 'non-transferable competences' to the EU, cf. Mattias Wendel, 'Lisbon Before the Courts: Comparative Perspectives' (2011) 7 European Constitutional Law Review 96, 100.
38. Referring to EU reforms that require Treaty amendment in the sense of Article 48 TEU, cf. Lucia Serena Rossi, 'A New Revision of the EU Treaties After Lisbon?' in Lucia Serena Rossi and Federico Casolari (eds), *EU after Lisbon: Amending or Coping with the Existing Treaties?* (Springer 2014) 12.
39. Monica Claes, 'National Idenity: Trump Card or up for Negotiation?' in Alejandro Saiz Arnaiz and Carina Alcoberro Llivina (eds), *National Constitutional Idenity and European Integration* (Intersentia Ltd 2013) 110.
40. And thus, an *ultra vires* act, cf. *Quantitative Easing (PSPP) Final Judgment* paras 163, 178; cf. as well: Ulrich Haltern, 'Ultra-vires-Kontrolle im Dienst europäischer Demokratie' (2020) 39 Neue Zeitschrift für Verwaltungsrecht (NVwZ) 817, 818.
41. *Germany: Quantitative Easing (PSPP) Final Judgment*; 2 BvR 2728/13, 2 BvR 2729/13, 2 BvR 2730/13, 2 BvR 2731/13, 2 BvE 13/13 *Final OMT-Judgment* (German Federal Constitutional Court); cf. as well: Ruffert, 'The Future of the European Economic and Monetary Union: Issues of Constitutional Law' 40-42; *Poland:* K 32/09 *Treaty of Lisbon* (Polish Constitutional Tribunal) section III.2.1. and section III.3.; cf. as well: Śledzińska-Simon and Ziółkowski, 'Constitutional Identity in Poland: Is the Emperor Putting on the Old Clothes of Sovereignty' 253; *Denmark:* Mikael Rask Madsen, Henrik Palmer Olsen and Urška Šadl, 'Competing Supremacies and

importance of the affected competences for national democracy[42] and sovereignty.[43] Furthermore, budgetary and fiscal decision-making powers are traditionally referred to as the 'crown jewels' of modern national parliaments.[44] Decisions on expenditure and revenue, including the level of taxation, social welfare benefits, or the funding of education, are not just shaping national political debates, but they equally have a direct (financial) impact on citizens. Political leaders compete in elections on fiscal policy decisions, such as tax breaks or high-income taxation. The result is a close link between budgetary and fiscal competences on the one hand, and democratic self-determination of the people and sovereign (political) discretion of state institutions on the other hand, which national constitutional actors protect against EU (fiscal) integration.[45]

The precise formulation of these constitutional limitations against conferring fiscal competences to the EU varies per Member State. Whereas the Finnish Constitutional Law Committee characterized EU cooperation as an important exercise of national sovereignty in a globalizing world,[46] the German Constitutional Court concluded that too far-reaching competence conferrals undermine German democracy.[47] What is more, the legal-constitutional barriers erected against EU fiscal integration differ in their nature and intensity. In Germany, the legislator is prevented from overcoming a conflict between the German Constitution and EU integration, if an

---

Clashing Institutional Rationalities: The Danish Supreme Court's Decision in the Ajos Case and the National Limits of Judicial Cooperation' (2017) 23 European Law Journal 140, 147-148; *Czech Republic:* Michal Bobek, 'Landtová, Holubec, and the Problem of an Uncooperative Court: Implications for the Preliminary Rulings Procedure' (2014) 10 European Constitutional Law Review 54, 54-55.

42. The concept of *overall budgetary responsibility* is, for example, based on German democracy, cf. Calliess, '70 Jahre Grundgesetz und europäische Integration: "Take Back Control" oder "Mehr Demokratie wagen"?' 688.
43. *See* for example in France, where the *Conseil Constitutionnel* identified economic and fiscal competences as particularly important sovereign competences, cf. Vranes, 'Constitutional Foundation of, and Limitations to, EU Integration in France' 540; the Polish Constitutional Tribunal protects certain competence areas against EU integration based on Polish sovereignty, cf. Wróbel, 'Die Grenzen der europäischen Integration im Lichte jüngerer Entscheidungen des polnischen Verfassungsgerichts' 499.
44. Given their historic and contemporary constitutional importance, cf. Sonja Puntscher Riekmann and Doris Wydra, 'Representation in the European State of Emergency: Parliaments Against Governments?' (2013) 35 Journal of European Integration 565, 567; Dawson and De Witte, 'Constitutional Balance in the EU after the Euro-Crisis' 827.
45. As highlighted by the German Constitutional Court, cf. *Final Decision on the Ratification of the Own Resources Decision (NGEU)* paras 84-85; 2 BvR 859/15, 2 BvR 1651/15, 2 BvR 2006/15, 2 BvR 980/15 *Quantitative Easing (PSPP) Reference* (German Federal Constitutional Court) para. 56; cf. as well: Christoph Herrmann, 'Die Bewältigung der Euro-Staatsschulden-Krise an den Grenzen des deutschen und europäischen Währverfassungsrechts' (2012) 23 Europäische Zeitschrift für Wirtschaftsrecht (EuZW) 805, 808.
46. Framed as 'qualified sovereignty', cf. Tuomas Ojanen, 'The EU at the Finnish Constitutional Arena' (2013) 4 Tijdschrift voor Constitutioneel Recht 242, 246; Tuomas Ojanen, 'EU Law and the Response of the Constitutional Law Committee of the Finnish Parliament' (2007) 52 Scandinavian Studies in Law 203, 217.
47. *Quantitative Easing (PSPP) Final Judgment* paras 99-101; cf. as well: Nicolas De Sadeleer, 'The New Architecture of European Economic Governance' in Niels Philipsen and Guangdong Xu (eds), *The Role of Law and Regulation in Sustaining Financial Markets* (Routledge 2015) 36.

interference with the so-called *eternity clause* in Article 79(3) Basic Law is established.[48] In contrast, the French legislator can remedy constitutional conflicts identified by the *Conseil Constitutionnel* by amending the French Constitution,[49] and similarly, the Finnish Parliament can approve EU integration steps that challenge Finnish constitutional principles by a two-thirds majority.[50]

EU fiscal integration proposals are, thus, confronted with a diverse, multi-layered national constitutional space that includes (seemingly) insurmountable limitations.[51] The result of an increasing national constitutional opposition against competence conferrals is the identified dilemma: The reform of the single currency is stuck between an *EU fiscal integration* rock and a *national constitutional* hard place.

D FRAMEWORK AND STRUCTURE OF THE BOOK

The book examines this dilemma through a comparative assessment of a selection of national constitutional limits applicable to EU fiscal integration. It thereby determines first how similarly – or differently – national constitutional systems address the very same EU integration ambition in order to then determine what EU integration steps are compatible with national constitutional law. The book is hence divided into two different parts: In the first part, the available national constitutional space for EU fiscal integration is *charted* and *deconstructed*. The chosen comparative setting allows to focus on a selection of representative national constitutional approaches and to identify national constitutional *best practices* that can be employed to locate constitutional space for EU fiscal integration while enhancing the protection of core constitutional principles. In the second part, this charted national constitutional space is tested against the most authoritative fiscal integration reform proposals debated within the EU in order to *evaluate* and *determine* their national constitutional attainability.

Drawing from this assessment, the book develops two *transformative propositions* that can reduce the friction between EU fiscal integration ambitions and national constitutional concerns. First, the direct and implicit benefits resulting from EU fiscal integration steps have to be included in the national constitutional appraisal, thereby

48. For example, in case EU integration violates the core of German democracy, cf. *Quantitative Easing (PSPP) Final Judgment* paras 103-104; 2 BvE 2/08 *Lisbon-judgment* (German Federal Constitutional Court) paras 252, 256; cf. as well: Christian Calliess, 'Constitutional Identity in Germany: One for Three or Three in One?' in Christian Calliess and Gerhard Van der Schyff (eds), *Constitutional Identity in a Europe of Multilevel Constitutionalism* (Cambridge University Press 2019) 164-165.
49. As explicitly emphasized by the *Conseil Constitutionnel* itself, cf. Decision 92-308 DC *Review of Maastricht Treaty (Maastricht I)* (French Conseil Constitutionnel) paras 36-44; cf. as well: Jaques Ziller, 'European Union Law in the Jurisprudence of French Supreme Courts: Europe-Friendliness with a French Touch' (2015) 21 European Public Law 765, 772.
50. Päivi Leino and Janne Salminen, 'The Euro Crisis and Its Constitutional Consequences for Finland: Is There Room for National Politics in EU Decision-Making?' (2013) 9 European Constitutional Law Review 451, 463; Ojanen, 'The EU at the Finnish Constitutional Arena' 247.
51. As for example the case in Germany, Calliess, 'Constitutional Identity in Germany: One for Three or Three in One?' 164-165; Mattias Wendel, 'Exceeding Judicial Competence in the Name of Democracy: The German Federal Constitutional Court's OMT Reference' (2014) 10 European Constitutional Law Review 263, 285.

replacing the prevailing state-or competence-centric interpretation of national constitutional principles. And second, the design of EU fiscal integration has to take national constitutional concerns into account and integration steps have to be devised *in tandem* with the national constitutional debate. As demonstrated throughout this book, these two *transformative propositions* ultimately allow for the implementation of the required EU fiscal integration steps to stabilize the single currency by equally guaranteeing effective protection of national constitutional values.

I Comparative Framework

Confronted with 27 national constitutional strategies to manage EU integration, the book works with a representative sample of national constitutional approaches. Despite an inherent element of uniqueness, national constitutional approaches bear similarities and draw in fact inspiration from one another. National constitutional courts reference the constitutional jurisprudence employed in other Member States to support their own findings,[52] which results in a transnational exchange of legal-constitutional arguments.[53] A conceptual convergence of national constitutional reasoning results from this exchange. Moreover, national constitutional approaches fulfil the same function, namely to provide a domestic constitutional framework for *engaging* with EU cooperation while *protecting* core constitutional elements from EU integration.[54]

The book distinguishes between two main *archetypes* of national constitutional approach to EU integration. A range of national constitutional systems developed more *rigid*[55] or *stable*[56] constitutional approaches to EU integration. These approaches are characterized by substantive limits that formulate legal *red-lines* for EU integration.[57] These *red-lines* are traditionally determined by strong and independent constitutional courts on the basis of the national constitution.[58] An important element when establishing constitutional *red-lines* is the procedural framework for enacting

52. Wendel, 'Lisbon Before the Courts: Comparative Perspectives' 136-137; cf., for example, the French *Conseil Constitutionnel*, cf. Vranes, 'Constitutional Foundation of, and Limitations to, EU Integration in France' 546; or the Polish Constitutional Tribunal, cf. *Treaty of Lisbon* section III.3.3; cf. as well: Joël Rideau, 'The Case-Law of the Polish, Hungarian and Czech Constitutional Courts on National Idenity and the "German Model"' in Alejandro Saiz Arnaiz and Carina Alcoberro Llivina (eds), *National Constitutional Idenity and European Integration* (Intersentia Ltd 2013) 253.
53. Tom Ginsburg and Rosalind Dixon, 'Introduction' in Tom Ginsburg and Rosalind Dixon (eds), *Comparative Constitutional Law* (Edward Elgar Publishing Limited 2011) 4.
54. Claes, 'Luxembourg, Here We Come? Constitutional Courts and the Preliminary Reference Procedure' 1334-1335.
55. Referring to constitutions that limit the 'substantive scope of constitutional amendments', cf. Aalt Willem Heringa, *Constitutions Compared: An Introduction to Comparative Constitutional Law* (4th edn, Intersentia Ltd 2016) 7-8.
56. Terminology employed as opposite term to *constitutional mutability* cf. Rosalind Dixon, 'Constitutional Amendment Rules: A Comparative Perspective' in Tom Ginsburg and Rosalind Dixon (eds), *Comparative Constitutional Law* (Edward Elgar Publishing Limited 2011) 102.
57. Wendel, 'Lisbon Before the Courts: Comparative Perspectives' 123.
58. The Polish Constitutional Tribunal: Rideau, 'The Case-Law of the Polish, Hungarian and Czech Constitutional Courts on National Idenity and the "German Model"' 252-253; or the German

constitutional amendments.[59] In case the domestic constitution either restricts the available scope or imposes high parliamentary majority requirements for constitutional amendments, these can also not be circumvented via EU integration.[60]

These constitutional *red-line* limits are increasingly framed as *national constitutional identity* concerns.[61] Commonly, the concept of *constitutional identity* refers to core principles or structural characteristics of the Member State that characterize its constitutional order, including sovereignty, democracy, respect for fundamental rights or the rule of law.[62] These *stricter* limits to EU integration can be, *inter alia*, found in the Czech Republic,[63] France,[64] Germany,[65] Italy,[66] Poland,[67] and Spain.[68] In these Member States, the constitution limits the *substantive* constitutional space that is available for EU integration steps. Consequently, EU integration is increasingly becoming (also) a question of legal-constitutional feasibility.

Constitutional Court: Tilman Rademacher, 'Die "Verfassungsidentität" als Grenze der Kompetenzübertragung auf die Europäische Union?' (2018) 53 Europarecht (EuR) 140, 144-146.

59. Such 'rigidity' can relate to the prescribed national constitutional amendment procedures, cf. Constance Grewe, 'Methods of Identification of National Constitutional Identity' in Alejandro Saiz Arnaiz and Carina Alcoberro Llivina (eds), *National Constitutional Idenity and European Integration* (Intersentia Ltd 2013) 40; even within rigid systems one can distinguish between '*red-line*'-limits and amendable limits, cf. Wendel, 'Lisbon Before the Courts: Comparative Perspectives' 123.
60. Cf. Article 79(3) Basic Law in Germany or Article 89(5) French Constitution in France, cf. Samuel Edward Finer, Vernon Bogdanor and Bernard Rudden, *Comparing Constitutions* (Clarendon Press 1995) 13, 15-16.
61. The national *constitutional identity* logic can be traced back to the *Italian Constitutional Court*: Judgment of 27 December 1973 – No. 183 *Frontini* (Italian Constitutional Court); Judgment of 8 June 1984 *Granital* (Italian Constitutional Court); cf. as well: Schyff, 'Exploring Member State and European Union Constitutional Identity' 228; and the German Constitutional Court: BvL 52/71 *Solange I-Decision* (German Federal Constitutional Court) paras 43-44; cf. as well: Monika Polzin, 'Constitutional Identity, Unconstitutional Amendments and the Idea of Constituent Power: The Development of the Doctrine of Constitutional Identity in German Constitutional Law' (2016) 14 International Journal of Constitutional Law 411, 426-427.
62. Claes, 'National Idenity: Trump Card or up for Negotiation?' 129.
63. Zdenek Kühn, 'Ultra Vires Review and the Demise of Constitutional Pluralism: The Czecho-Slovak Pension Saga, and the Dangers of State Court's Defiance of EU Law' (2016) 23 Maastricht Journal of European and Comparative Law 185, 186-187.
64. François-Xavier Millet, 'Constitutional Identity in France: Vices and – Above All – Virtues' in Christian Calliess and Gerhard Van der Schyff (eds), *Constitutional Identity in a Europe of Multilevel Constitutionalism* (Cambridge University Press 2019) 134-135; Gary J. Jacobsohn, 'The Formation of Constitutional Idenities' in Tom Ginsburg and Rosalind Dixon (eds), *Comparative Constitutional Law* (Edward Elgar Publishing Limited 2011) 130.
65. *Final Decision on the Ratification of the Own Resources Decision (NGEU)* paras 134-137; *Quantitative Easing (PSPP) Final Judgment* para 101; cf. as well: Calliess, 'Constitutional Identity in Germany: One for Three or Three in One?' 156-157.
66. Diana-Urania Galetta, 'European Union Law in the Jurisprudence of Italian High Courts: Is the Counter-Limits Doctrine a Dog That Barks but Does Not Bite?' (2015) 21 European Public Law 747, 750.
67. *Treaty of Lisbon* section III.2.1.; cf, as well: Śledzińska-Simon and Ziółkowski, 'Constitutional Identity in Poland: Is the Emperor Putting on the Old Clothes of Sovereignty' 249-251.
68. Declaration 1/2004 *Treaty Establishing a Constitution for Europe* (Spanish Constitutional Tribunal) section II.2.; cf. as well: Rafael Bustos Gisbert, 'National Constitutional Identity in European Constitutionalism: Revisiting the Tale of the Emperor's New Clothes in Spain?' in Alejandro Saiz Arnaiz and Carina Alcoberro Llivina (eds), *National Constitutional Idenity and European Integration* (Intersentia Ltd 2013) 77.

However, not all EU Member States adopt a rigid constitutional approach. As a conceptual opposite to constitutional rigidity, some Member States adopted *flexible*[69] or *mutable*[70] constitutional approaches to EU integration.[71] In contrast to rigid systems, these flexible approaches refrain from imposing substantive *red-line* limits to EU integration, thereby offering a wider and less restricted legal-constitutional space for EU cooperation by at the same time allowing for effective protection of core constitutional values. The main *hurdle* for EU integration is political-procedural in nature, as the emphasis rests on attaining the prescribed constitutional majority-thresholds to confirm the conferral of competences.[72] Examples of flexible constitutional approaches include the Netherlands[73] and Finland.[74]

Based on this framework, the book examines in detail one representative example per archetype from a general, macro-comparative[75] perspective. The German constitutional order is analysed as an example of constitutional rigidity. Germany provides an excellent basis for a case study given its constitutional structure with a protected constitutional core and a strong constitutional court as well as its overall prominence in the EU constitutional debate.[76] The Finnish constitutional order is studied as an example of a flexible constitutional approach. Finland does not have a constitutional court, but instead, the parliamentary Constitutional Law Committee decides on the constitutionality of legislative action.[77] As visualized in Figure 1.1, both countries can be positioned at opposite ends on a linear scale that distinguishes between flexible and rigid national constitutional approaches towards the EU. Therefore, the resulting research findings on Germany and Finland offer representative insights into a wider range of national constitutional limitations against EU fiscal integration ambitions.

69. Referring to constitutions that are more open to amendments and that do not contain substantive limits, cf. Heringa, *Constitutions Compared: An Introduction to Comparative Constitutional Law* 9.
70. Dixon, 'Constitutional Amendment Rules: A Comparative Perspective' 102.
71. Based on the previous outline of national constitutional amendment procedures, systems that do not contain material obstacles to constitutional amendments, but that rather have a 'formal' conception of constitutional amendments, cf. Grewe, 'Methods of Identification of National Constitutional Identity' 43.
72. Heringa, *Constitutions Compared: An Introduction to Comparative Constitutional Law* 9.
73. Schyff, 'Exploring Member State and European Union Constitutional Identity' 230.
74. Grewe, 'Methods of Identification of National Constitutional Identity' 43.
75. The term 'macro-comparison' refers to a *wider, general* research into the legal system, cf. Gerhard Dannemann, 'Comparative Law: Study of Similarities or Differences?' in Mathias Reimann and Reinhard Zimmermann (eds), *The Oxford Handbook of Comparative Law* (2nd edn, Oxford University Press 2019) 394; Mark Van Hoecke, 'Methodology of Comparative Legal Research' (2015) Law and Method 1, 21-22.
76. Arthur Dyevre, 'The German Federal Constitutional Court and European Judicial Politics' (2011) 34 West European Politics 346, 346-347.
77. Juha Lavapuro, Tuomas Ojanen and Martin Scheinin, 'Finland: Intermediate Constitutional Review in Finland: Promising in Theory, Problematic in Practice' in John Bell and Marie-Luce Paris (eds), *Rights-Based Constitutional Review: Constitutional Courts in a Changing Landscape* (Edward Elgar Publishing Limited 2016) 219.

Figure 1.1 Underpinning Comparative Conceptualization of the Constitutional System

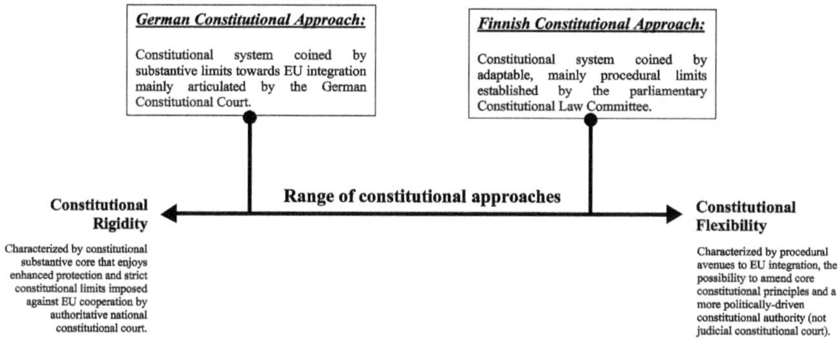

In a second comparative step, the book turns to a detailed *micro-comparison*[78] of the most significant constitutional limits that EU fiscal integration faces. Resulting from the findings in the *macro-comparison*, such obstacles are mainly the substantive *constitutional identity limits* apparent in rigid constitutional systems. The underlying claim is that the national constitutional system contains a stable core which may not be affected or altered by EU integration.[79] Effectively, these limits reduce the powers that can be transferred to the EU. Therefore, the *micro-comparison* focuses on strict *constitutional identity limits* that formulate obstacles to the attainment of EU fiscal integration steps in a representative sample of Member States. Based on constitutional and political relevance as well as geographical considerations, the comparative assessment includes the French, Spanish, Polish and German *constitutional identity* limits. The *micro-comparison* provides insights into how the *constitutional identity limit* is employed across different constitutional systems and what implications it has for EU fiscal integration steps.

II Concept of Constitutional Flexibility

The book illustrates that rigid constitutional limitations formulated against EU fiscal integration can be construed and interpreted in a more receptive and adapted manner. This adaptability of national limits is conceptualized through the concept of *constitutional flexibility*. It operates as a research tool to showcase how national constitutional limits – in particular *constitutional identity limits* – can be more receptive to EU fiscal

78. The term 'micro-comparison' refers to a more targeted comparative assessment of a specific rule – in this specific case national *identity clauses*, cf. Dannemann, 'Comparative Law: Study of Similarities or Differences?' 394; Ralf Michaels, 'The Functional Method of Comparative Law' in Mathias Reimann and Reinhard Zimmermann (eds), *The Oxford Handbook of Comparative Law* (2nd edn, Oxford University Press 2019) 381.
79. Defined by the German Constitutional Court as 'integrationsfeste Verfassungsidentität der Mitgliedstaaten', cf. *Lisbon-judgment* para. 239; cf. as well: Rademacher, 'Die "Verfassungsidentität" als Grenze der Kompetenzübertragung auf die Europäische Union?' 148.

integration while protecting the underlying constitutional concern in an effective manner. The two major strategies employed to locate and activate *constitutional flexibility* are a constitutional consistency assessment and a comparative identification of national *best practices*.

Considering the prior, national *constitutional identity limits* seem to constitute the most severe hurdle for EU fiscal integration steps. Especially when considering the absolute German *constitutional identity limit*, it seems questionable whether this limit could be transformed through a transnational exchange of constitutional arguments[80] or through the application of constitutional *best practices*. In fact, a possible flexibilization of the national constitutional approach depends on the receptiveness of the competent national actors[81] and the ability of the national system to accommodate it. Therefore, the book conducts a consistency assessment of the German constitutional approach in an exemplary manner to demonstrate how *constitutional flexibility* can be generated even within highly rigid constitutional approaches. The proposed consistency assessment is rooted in the assumption that judicial decisions in a constitutional system based on the rule of law are not taken arbitrarily. In order to pre-empt arbitrariness, courts employ established legal methods when interpreting legal provisions.[82] The reliance on accepted interpretive methods renders the judicial decision objectively comprehensible.[83] The constitutional consistency assessment departs from this rule-of-law-requirement, arguing that the same (constitutional) rule may in principle not be interpreted differently based on the particular case before the constitutional authority, as the judicial methods employed for interpreting the rule cannot depend on the concrete proceedings. Although the application of a rule may be influenced by concrete circumstances, which allow courts to distinguish based on justified grounds, the general interpretation and the conception of the rule may not. Therefore, the argument put forward here is that the constitutional scrutiny based on the same constitutional provisions, and with it the respective interpretation of the constitutional legal framework, may not differ, given that the constitutional authority would otherwise introduce a constitutional double standard.

Considering national *best practices*, the book explores how national constitutional authorities perceive and portray the EU in their respective constitutional approaches. The identified *best practices* are national approaches, interpretations or concepts that do not conceptualize EU integration steps as an outright threat to national constitutional law but rather emphasize the advantages EU integration offers for

80. Mattias Wendel, 'Comparative Reasoning and the Making of a Common Constitutional Law: EU-Related Decisions of National Constitutional Courts in a Transnational Perspective' (2013) 11 International Journal of Constitutional Law 981, 984; Heiko Sauer, 'Verfassungsvergleichung durch das Bundesverfassungsgericht – Zur Bedeutung der Verfassungsvergleichung für die Auslegung des Grundgesetzes' (2010) 18 Journal für Rechtspolitik 194, 199.
81. Wendel, 'Comparative Reasoning and the Making of a Common Constitutional Law: EU-Related Decisions of National Constitutional Courts in a Transnational Perspective' 986-987; Ginsburg and Dixon, 'Introduction' 4.
82. Dominik Schäfers, 'Einführung in die Methodik der Gesetzesauslegung' (2015) 55 Juristische Schulung (JuS) 875, 876.
83. Reinhold Zippelius, *Juristische Methodenlehre* (JuS Schriftreihe, 11th edn, C.H. Beck 2012) 17-19, 35-37.

domestic priorities. The research argues that national *best practices* can function as comparative inspiration across other Member States.[84] Notably, when considering national constitutional decisions, the different accentuation of constitutional benefits and risks stemming from EU integration becomes obvious. For example, some national constitutional authorities construe EU integration measures as an *increase* in the impact of sovereign powers, given that a union of 27 Member States can more effectively defend shared interests in a globalized world.[85] In contrast, other national constitutional authorities primarily focus on the loss of autonomous, independent decision-making in the competence areas conferred at EU level.[86] The perception of advantages and risks for constitutional principles stemming from EU cooperation is a crucial element for the resulting national constitutional approaches and possible *constitutional flexibility* towards EU integration. By focusing on the constitutional advantages that EU cooperation offers, as displayed by some approaches, *constitutional flexibility* can be located and activated to accommodate EU fiscal integration.

III Resulting Structure of the Book

The book is divided into two conceptually different parts. The first part *maps* and *deconstructs* the national constitutional space for EU fiscal integration following a two-tiered comparison (Part I). In *Section I* a wide mapping of how constitutional systems with fundamentally different characteristics – notably Finland and Germany – approach EU fiscal integration is conducted. *Section II* then conducts a narrow mapping centring around the strictest national constitutional limits formulated against EU fiscal integration.

Once this comparative exercise is completed, Part II *evaluates* and *determines* what form of EU fiscal integration is compatible with the charted national constitutional space. This requires the identification and deconstruction of the most relevant EU fiscal integration proposals. Subsequently, the deconstructed EU fiscal integration steps are tested against the charted national constitutional space to determine their attainability. The resulting overview outlines possible constitutional conflicts and remedies to address these both at the national constitutional level as well as when devising EMU-reform plans.

84. Ginsburg and Dixon, 'Introduction' 4; which can be, for example, observed in Poland, where the Polish Constitutional Tribunal extensively refers to constitutional arguments from other constitutional orders, cf. *Treaty of Lisbon* section III.3.3.
85. As, for example, the case in Finland, cf. Ojanen, 'The EU at the Finnish Constitutional Arena' 246; similarly, the Polish Constitutional Tribunal developed a *modern* interpretation of sovereignty that considers the benefits of EU integration for national sovereignty, cf. Jacek Czaputowicz, 'Sovereignty in Theories of European Integration and the Perspective of the Polish Constitutional Tribunal' (2014) 17 Yearbook of Polish European Studies 15, 32.
86. Cf. Germany: *Quantitative Easing (PSPP) Final Judgment* paras 99-101; *Lisbon-judgment* paras 233, 264; cf. as well: De Sadeleer, 'The New Architecture of European Economic Governance' 36; or Poland: Grewe, 'Methods of Identification of National Constitutional Identity' 38.

E CONSTRUCTING A RESILIENT EURO WITHIN THE NATIONAL CONSTITUTIONAL GUARDRAILS

The unfolding disastrous economic consequences of COVID-19 and the Russian war of aggression against Ukraine have once again put the Eurozone in the limelight; the current situation might even evolve into a new breaking-test for the single currency. The adopted financial remedies, including NGEU, may operate as temporary breathing aid; however, they cannot provide the cure required to correct the structural flaws in the current design of the Euro.[87] Hence, EU fiscal integration is indispensable to establish a stable single currency in the long run, which is however ever more difficult in light of increasing national constitutional opposition. To refute the apparent dilemma between EU fiscal integration and national constitutional limits, this book provides a structured, comparative overview and outlook on how the available national constitutional space can be adapted to the political aspirations aiming at implementing EU fiscal integration steps at the same time effectively protecting the national constitutional values at stake.

87. Ruffert, 'The Future of the European Economic and Monetary Union: Issues of Constitutional Law' 44-45; Fabbrini, 'Fiscal Capacity' 114-115.

PART I Charting the National Constitutional Space

SECTION I

Macro-comparative Assessment of Finland and Germany

Introducing the macro-comparative assessment

The national constitutional reception of the measures enacted during the Eurocrisis such as the Fiscal Compact, the ESM or the Six-Pack-Legislation varied considerably across Member States. For example, the Finnish Constitutional Law Committee established that all Eurocrisis-measures could be adopted by a simple parliamentary majority[1] – although the Committee required a two-third majority for the adoption of the more recent NGEU and the underpinning Own Resources Decision.[2] The Finnish Parliament was ultimately able to overcome the constitutional concerns by following the prescribed procedures. In contrast, the German Federal Constitutional Court raised severe constitutional concerns over an increasing EU influence on national budgetary and fiscal decision-making.[3] These concerns were confirmed in the PSP-Programme judgment, where the Court declared that the challenged EMU-related EU acts constituted a transgression of the conferred mandate and were hence unconstitutional,[4] and in the appraisal of NGEU.[5]

---

1. Although the Constitutional Law Committee already raised concerns in relation to a draft ESM-Treaty, Leino and Salminen, 'The Euro Crisis and Its Constitutional Consequences for Finland: Is There Room for National Politics in EU Decision-Making?' 464; Ojanen, 'The EU at the Finnish Constitutional Arena' 247.
2. *Ratification of the Own Resources Decision (II.)*; cf. as well: Leino-Sandberg and Ruffert, 'Next Generation EU and Its Constitutional Ramifications: A Critical Assessment' 447.
3. *Quantitative Easing (PSPP) Final Judgment* para. 104; *Final OMT-Judgment* para. 212; cf. as well: Calliess, '70 Jahre Grundgesetz und europäische Integration: "Take Back Control" oder "Mehr Demokratie wagen"?' 688.
4. *Quantitative Easing (PSPP) Final Judgment* paras 163, 234; cf. as well: Haltern, 'Ultra-vires-Kontrolle im Dienst europäischer Demokratie' 818.
5. *Final Decision on the Ratification of the Own Resources Decision (NGEU)*, in particular paras 134-137; cf. as well: Wendel, 'The Fog of Identity and Judicial Contestation: Preventive and Defensive Constitutional Identity Review in Germany' 479.

Both national constitutional approaches can be placed at two opposite points on the linear scale of flexible and rigid constitutional approaches to EU integration. On that scale, Finland is a more flexible constitutional system,[6] which stems from its institutional design[7] and an absence of substantive constitutional limitations to EU integration.[8] Notably, the Eurocrisis-related and the NGEU decisions of the Constitutional Law Committee indicate a particular focus on procedural safeguards that secure the comprehensive participation of the Finnish Parliament in EU decision-making.[9] By contrast, Germany can be located on the other end of that scale, given the authoritative institutional position of the Constitutional Court in the appraisal of EU law as well as the highlighted *eternity clause* that formulates an absolute restriction to the available space for EU integration steps.[10] Based on this clause, the Constitutional Court developed its *constitutional identity* review,[11] which gained particular importance since the Eurocrisis.[12] Especially the financial implications of these measures triggered constitutional concerns regarding their compatibility with German democracy.[13]

The subsequent analysis *charts, deconstructs,* and *contrasts* the Finnish and German constitutional framework for EU fiscal integration steps from a holistic perspective. Specifically, the institutional and procedural framework applicable to EU integration measures as well as possible substantive limitations to such fiscal integration ambitions are evaluated. The assessment includes the localization and activation of *constitutional flexibility*. The result of this initial *macro-comparative* assessment is a clear overview of the respective Finnish constitutional approach to EU fiscal integration in Chapter II and of the German one in Chapter III. Chapter IV compares and contrasts both constitutional approaches in order to identify the opportunities and risks that each representative system entails for EU fiscal integration proposals, including the determination of potential national *best practices*.

6. Grewe, 'Methods of Identification of National Constitutional Identity' 43; Markku Suksi, 'Finland' in Oliver Dawn and Carlo Fusaro (eds), *How Constitutions Change: A Comparative Study* (Hart Publishing 2011) 114.
7. Maartje De Visser, *Constitutional Review in Europe: A Comparative Analysis* (Hart Publishing 2015) 76.
8. Anu Mutanen, *Towards a Pluralistic Constitutional Understanding of State Sovereignty in the European Union? The Concept, Regulation and Constitutional Practice of Sovereignty in Finland and Certain Other EU Member States* (Hansaprint Oy 2015) 324-325.
9. Leino and Salminen, 'The Euro Crisis and Its Constitutional Consequences for Finland: Is There Room for National Politics in EU Decision-Making?' 463; Ojanen, 'The EU at the Finnish Constitutional Arena' 247.
10. *Lisbon-judgment* para. 230; cf. as well: Alexander Thiele, 'Die Integrationsidentität des Art. 23 Abs. 1 GG als (einzige) Grenze des Vorrangs des Europarechts' (2017) 52 Europarecht (EuR) 367, 371; Stephan Jaggi, 'Revolutionary Constitutional Lawmaking in Germany: Rediscovering the German 1989 Revolution' (2016) 17 German Law Journal 579, 619.
11. Rademacher, 'Die "Verfassungsidentität" als Grenze der Kompetenzübertragung auf die Europäische Union?' 144-146; Matthias Kottmann and Christian Wohlfahrt, 'Der gespaltene Wächter? Demokratie, Verfassungsidentität und Integrationsverantwortung im Lissabon-Urteil' (2009) 69 Zeitschrift für ausländisches öffentliches Recht und Völkerrecht (ZaöRV) 443, 447-448.
12. A tendency that can be observed across different EU Member States, cf. Hinarejos, 'The Euro Area Crisis and Constitutional Limits to Fiscal Integration' 14.
13. Calliess, 'Constitutional Identity in Germany: One for Three or Three in One?' 164-165.

CHAPTER 2

Macro-comparative Assessment of Finland

A FINLAND AND EU INTEGRATION

The Eurocrisis can be described as a drastic turning point in the Finnish political debate on EU integration. Since Finnish accession to the EU in 1995, the country was praised as a commendable EU Member State.[1] From its inception, EU membership was perceived as beneficial and supported by a cross-party, political consensus.[2] This consensus translated into a positioning at the centre of the EU, which made possible opt-outs from integration steps politically undesired[3] and which explains the introduction of the Euro in 2002.[4] An apparent underlying motive of this strong commitment to EU cooperation is to compensate for Finland's geographical position at the EU's periphery as well as to obtain political insurance against possible interferences from neighbouring Russia[5] – an objective that has obviously become more important recently.

1. Tapio Raunio, 'Refusing to Be Sidelined: The Engagement of the Finnish *Enduskunta* in Foreign Affairs' (2016) 39 Scandinavian Political Studies 312, 316; Juha Jokela, *Finland and the Eurozone Crisis* (Palgrave Macmillan 2014) 29.
2. Sanna Salo and Jens Rydgren, 'Politicisation of the Eurozone Crisis in Finland: Adaptation Toward the Radical Right?' (2018) 34 Journal of International and Comparative Social policy 234, 243; Leino and Salminen, 'The Euro Crisis and Its Constitutional Consequences for Finland: Is There Room for National Politics in EU Decision-Making?' 451.
3. J. Jokela, 'Finland: Towards a More Cautious Europeanization' in C. Bretherton and M. Mannin (eds), *The Europeanization of European Politics* (Palgrave Macmillan 2013) 39-40; Teija Tiilikainen, 'Finland: An EU Member State with a Small State Identity' (2006) 28 Journal of European Integration 73, 77-78.
4. Jokela, *Finland and the Eurozone Crisis* 29; Leino and Salminen, 'The Euro Crisis and Its Constitutional Consequences for Finland: Is There Room for National Politics in EU Decision-Making?' 455.
5. Salo and Rydgren, 'Politicisation of the Eurozone Crisis in Finland: Adaptation Toward the Radical Right?' 243; Mark C. Miller, 'Finnish Judges and the European Union: An American Perspective' (2016) 24 Michigan State International Law Journal 495, 498.

At the national constitutional level, EU membership coincided with and contributed to a more general process of fundamental constitutional transformation which, *inter alia*, established the Finnish Parliament as the central national actor in all EU-related decisions.[6] Notably, under the amended constitutional framework the Finnish Parliament has to approve the conferral of competences to the EU and it is subsequently involved in the domestic *ex ante* preparation of EU secondary law.[7] The Finnish Constitution thus extends internal parliamentary prerogatives to international and EU cooperation. Moreover, this constitutional transformation enabled a more flexible interpretation of substantive constitutional principles, most prominently Finnish sovereignty.[8] The Finnish constitutional system hence actively addressed the constitutional challenges stemming from increasing supranational cooperation and thereby prepared the Finnish Constitution for an increasingly globalized reality.

However, the eruption of the Eurocrisis changed this unconditional dedication to EU cooperation. It triggered an intense national debate on how to best react to the then unfolding crisis which prominently featured in the 2011 Finnish parliamentary election[9] and which resulted in a clear electoral success of the Eurosceptical 'Finns'-party.[10] The 'Finns' obtained 39 out of the 200 parliamentary seats, a share the party could largely defend in the 2015, 2019 and 2023 parliamentary elections.[11] This implies that significantly more Eurosceptical voices have been represented in the Finnish Parliament since 2011, which obviously alter the political debate and impacts the EU agenda of the established political parties.[12] Given that the Eurocrisis was the most important

6. As now enshrined in sections 94, 95 and 96 Finnish Constitution, cf. Leino and Salminen, 'The Euro Crisis and Its Constitutional Consequences for Finland: Is There Room for National Politics in EU Decision-Making?' 459; Tuomas Ojanen, 'Constitutional Amendment in Finland' in Xenophon Contiades (ed.), *Engineering Constitutional Change: A Comparative Perspective on Europe, Canada and the USA* (Routledge 2013) 102.
7. Leino and Salminen, 'The Euro Crisis and Its Constitutional Consequences for Finland: Is There Room for National Politics in EU Decision-Making?' 456-457; Tuomas Ojanen, 'The Europeanization of Finnish Law' in Paul Luif (ed.), *Österreich, Schweden, Finland: Zehn Jahre Mitgliedschaft in der Europäischen Union* (Böhlau Verlag 2007) 168-171; Tuomas Ojanen, 'The Impact of EU Membership on Finnish Constitutional Law' (2004) 10 European Public Law 531, 554-556.
8. Mutanen, *Towards a Pluralistic Constitutional Understanding of State Sovereignty in the European Union? The Concept, Regulation and Constitutional Practice of Sovereignty in Finland and Certain Other EU Member States* 334-335; Tuomas Ojanen, 'The Europeanization of Finnish Law: Observations on the Transformations of the Finnish Scene of Constitutionalism' in Kimmo Nuotio, Melander Sakari and Merita Huomo-Kettunen (eds), *Introduction to Finnish Law and Legal Culture* (University of Helsinki 2012) 101.
9. Salo and Rydgren, 'Politicisation of the Eurozone Crisis in Finland: Adaptation Toward the Radical Right?' 243; Jokela, *Finland and the Eurozone Crisis* 36.
10. Note, the political party was previously called the 'True Finns'.
11. The party received 19.1 % of the votes in 2011 compared to 4.05 % in 2007, cf. Salo and Rydgren, 'Politicisation of the Eurozone Crisis in Finland: Adaptation Toward the Radical Right?' 243; Jokela, *Finland and the Eurozone Crisis* 33; Ojanen, 'Constitutional Amendment in Finland' 95.
12. Tuomas Iso-Markku, 'Finland: Pro-European Arguments Prevail Despite the Rise of Euroscepticism' in Karlis Bukovskis (ed.), *Euroscepticism in Small EU Member States* (Zinatne 2016) 65, 73; Leino and Salminen, 'The Euro Crisis and Its Constitutional Consequences for Finland: Is There Room for National Politics in EU Decision-Making?' 455.

non-domestic matter fuelling the electoral success of the 'Finns' in 2011,[13] other political parties altered their positions and embraced a more critical stance towards the EU as well. Despite the changed political climate, which was for example showcased in the negotiations of NGEU,[14] the constitutional system itself remains open for EU integration. This enabled the Finnish Parliament to play an influential role in the drafting of the various Eurocrisis-measures[15] and allowed the Constitutional Law Committee to refrain from imposing substantive limitations on EU integration ambitions.[16] This confirms the identified flexible legal-constitutional nature of the Finnish constitutional order, which proved adaptive towards EU cooperation.[17]

The following assessment maps this apparent *constitutional flexibility* by analysing the general constitutional framework for EU cooperation (B) as well as the specific procedural (C) and substantive constitutional rules (D) that EU fiscal integration proposals are confronted with. A particular focus rests on charting the flexible constitutional handling of the Eurocrisis. Contouring the high degree of *constitutional flexibility* will subsequently facilitate determining whether and to what extent Finnish flexibility can be a *best practice* example for other constitutional systems.

B INTRODUCING THE FINNISH CONSTITUTIONAL ORDER

Finnish accession to the EU entailed a firm political commitment to the EU's values and an economic orientation towards the EU single market. It required a renunciation of the policy of 'active neutrality' that Finland followed during the Cold War.[18] Therefore, the

13. Salo and Rydgren, 'Politicisation of the Eurozone Crisis in Finland: Adaptation Toward the Radical Right?' 243.
14. As Finland partly sided with the *frugal four*, cf. Dolores Utrilla, 'Insight: "The European Deal for Post-Pandemic Economic Recovery: Content and Meaning"' (*EU Law Live*, 21 July 2020), https://eulawlive.com/the-european-deal-for-post-pandemic-economic-recovery-content-and-meaning/, accessed 5 April 2023.
15. Tuomas Ojanen and Janne Salminen, 'Finland: European Integration and International Human Rights Treaties as Sources of Domestic Constitutional Change and Dynamism' in Anneli Albi and Samo Bardutzky (eds), *National Constitutions in European and Global Governance: Democracy, Rights, the Rule of Law* (T.M.C. Asser Press 2019) 391-392; Leino and Salminen, 'The Euro Crisis and Its Constitutional Consequences for Finland: Is There Room for National Politics in EU Decision-Making?' 458, 478.
16. Mutanen, *Towards a Pluralistic Constitutional Understanding of State Sovereignty in the European Union? The Concept, Regulation and Constitutional Practice of Sovereignty in Finland and Certain Other EU Member States* 324-325; De Visser, *Constitutional Review in Europe: A Comparative Analysis* 26-27.
17. Lavapuro, Ojanen and Scheinin, 'Finland: Intermediate Constitutional Review in Finland: Promising in Theory, Problematic in Practice' 222; Ojanen, 'The EU at the Finnish Constitutional Arena' 242; Pekka Länsineva, 'Fundamental Principles of the Constitution of Finland' in Kimmo Nuotio, Melander Sakari and Merita Huomo-Kettunen (eds), *Introduction to Finnish Law and Legal Culture* (Univeristy of Helsinki 2012) 111.
18. Coined by the term 'active neutrality', cf. Frank Emmert and Siniša Petrović, 'The Past, Present, and Future of EU Enlargement' (2014) 37 Fordham International Law Journal 1349, 1372; Tiilikainen, 'Finland: An EU Member State with a Small State Identity' 76.

Finnish commitment to EU integration is a genuine political decision, confirmed by public referendum,[19] which translated into a highly constructive approach to EU cooperation.[20]

Furthermore, Finland acceded in 1995 to a highly integrated EU. Constitutionally contentious concepts such as the direct effect or primacy of EU law were (judicially) established.[21] In short, EU cooperation was politically, economically and legally advanced, which challenged the Finnish Constitution – as it stood during accession. Specifically, the doctrine of absolute sovereignty then proclaimed in section 1(1) Finnish Constitution, excluded the competence conferrals and thus rendered EU membership incompatible with the constitutional text.[22] Finnish EU membership was only constitutionally achievable by adopting a limited constitutional derogation, so-called 'exceptive enactment'.[23] Nevertheless, it has to be emphasized that accession to such a highly integrated EU entailed a constitutional ad hoc adaptation for Finland which was confirmed by a firm political decision in favour of EU membership.[24] This experience is fundamentally different to that of the EU founding Member States, whose constitutional systems had to evolve alongside EU integration.[25] Subsequently, it enabled the Finnish constitution-amending legislator to reform the Finnish Constitution in light of the new EU obligations.[26] This process of the 'Europeanization' of Finnish constitutional law,[27] is outlined below in order to investigate the adaptability of the Finnish Constitution.

19. In a public referendum 56.9% voted in favour of EU accession, cf. Emmert and Petrović, 'The Past, Present, and Future of EU Enlargement' 1373; A. Rosas, 'Finland: Finland's Accession to the European Union: Constitutional Aspects' (1995) 1 European Public Law 166, 166.
20. Characterized as most constructive approach to EU integration of all Nordic countries, cf. Jokela, *Finland and the Eurozone Crisis* 26, 30; also referred to as 'community-centred approach', cf. Tiilikainen, 'Finland: An EU Member State with a Small State Identity' 78.
21. Miller, 'Finnish Judges and the European Union: An American Perspective' 519.
22. As section 1(1) Finnish Constitution proclaimed absolute sovereignty, cf. Mutanen, *Towards a Pluralistic Constitutional Understanding of State Sovereignty in the European Union? The Concept, Regulation and Constitutional Practice of Sovereignty in Finland and Certain Other EU Member States* 331-332; Ojanen, 'The EU at the Finnish Constitutional Arena' 245-246.
23. Ojanen and Salminen, 'Finland: European Integration and International Human Rights Treaties as Sources of Domestic Constitutional Change and Dynamism' 364; Rosas, 'Finland: Finland's Accession to the European Union: Constitutional Aspects' 168.
24. Miller, 'Finnish Judges and the European Union: An American Perspective' 519; Tapio Raunio and Teija Tiilikainen, *Finland in the European Union* (Frank Cass Publishers 2003) 2-3.
25. Notably, new Member States are required to accept a fully developed legal framework, cf. Gerda Falkner, 'How Pervasive Are Euro-Politics? Effects of EU Membership on a New Member State' (2000) 38 Journal of Common Market Studies 223, 224.
26. Leino and Salminen, 'The Euro Crisis and Its Constitutional Consequences for Finland: Is There Room for National Politics in EU Decision-Making?' 456-457; Ojanen, 'The Europeanization of Finnish Law: Observations on the Transformations of the Finnish Scene of Constitutionalism' 100-101; Ojanen, 'The Impact of EU Membership on Finnish Constitutional Law' 563.
27. Jaakko Husa, *The Constitution of Finland: A Contextual Analysis* (Hart Publishing 2011) 24; a process, which however already started before EU membership with the accession to the ECHR and the EEA, cf. Juha Lavapuro, Tuomas Ojanen and Martin Scheinin, 'Rights-Based Constitutionalism in Finland and the Development of Pluralist Constitutional Review' (2011) 9 International Journal of Constitutional Law 505, 512-513.

I Finnish Constitutional Reforms to Accommodate EU Cooperation

When Finland acceded to the EU, the Constitutional Act of 1919 was still in force. The Act was adopted following Finnish independence from Russia,[28] which was reflected in its design. Notably, the Constitutional Act focused on the internal organization of state power. The apparent constitutional introversion cumulated in the conception of Finnish sovereignty as an absolute constitutional principle established in section 1(1) Constitutional Act.[29] Historically, section 1(1) Constitutional Act constituted the constitutional confirmation of Finnish independence from Russia and it anticipated Finland's new international role among other sovereign states.[30] The absolute conception of Finnish sovereignty, however, collided with Finnish EU membership[31] and triggered comprehensive constitutional reforms.[32] This thorough reform process was initiated after Finnish accession to the European Convention of Human Rights (ECHR) in 1989 as well as Finnish EU membership in 1995, and it was completed in 2012 with the explicit acknowledgement of EU membership in section 1(3) Finnish Constitution.[33]

The current constitutional text qualifies Finnish sovereignty and explicitly mentions the possibility to engage in international and EU cooperation (section 1(3) Finnish Constitution).[34] Furthermore, it establishes a specific procedural framework for the conferral of competences to the EU (sections 94 and 95 Finnish Constitution) and it lays down a procedural framework for parliamentary involvement in the national preparation of EU matters (section 96 Finnish Constitution), including a parliamentary right to be informed on EU developments (section 97 Finnish Constitution). The reform also introduced a limited *ex post* judicial review of legislative acts (section 106 Finnish

28. Mutanen, *Towards a Pluralistic Constitutional Understanding of State Sovereignty in the European Union? The Concept, Regulation and Constitutional Practice of Sovereignty in Finland and Certain Other EU Member States* 276.
29. Ojanen, 'The EU at the Finnish Constitutional Arena' 245-246; Ojanen, 'The Europeanization of Finnish Law: Observations on the Transformations of the Finnish Scene of Constitutionalism' 100.
30. Mutanen, *Towards a Pluralistic Constitutional Understanding of State Sovereignty in the European Union? The Concept, Regulation and Constitutional Practice of Sovereignty in Finland and Certain Other EU Member States* 280.
31. Ojanen and Salminen, 'Finland: European Integration and International Human Rights Treaties as Sources of Domestic Constitutional Change and Dynamism' 364; Rosas, 'Finland: Finland's Accession to the European Union: Constitutional Aspects' 168.
32. In particular the acknowledgement of the 'specificity of the EU' and the conception of EU membership as 'exercising Finland's sovereign powers', cf. Miller, 'Finnish Judges and the European Union: An American Perspective' 501; Mutanen, *Towards a Pluralistic Constitutional Understanding of State Sovereignty in the European Union? The Concept, Regulation and Constitutional Practice of Sovereignty in Finland and Certain Other EU Member States* 301.
33. Ojanen and Salminen, 'Finland: European Integration and International Human Rights Treaties as Sources of Domestic Constitutional Change and Dynamism' 366; Leino and Salminen, 'The Euro Crisis and Its Constitutional Consequences for Finland: Is There Room for National Politics in EU Decision-Making?' 456.
34. Note also the 'special status' that the Constitutional Law Committee awards to the EU in its decisions, cf. Mutanen, *Towards a Pluralistic Constitutional Understanding of State Sovereignty in the European Union? The Concept, Regulation and Constitutional Practice of Sovereignty in Finland and Certain Other EU Member States* 301; Ojanen, 'The Europeanization of Finnish Law: Observations on the Transformations of the Finnish Scene of Constitutionalism' 101.

Constitution). In addition, it modified the power balance between the Finnish President and the Finnish Government, as the Finnish Constitution now explicitly characterizes EU affairs as governmental prerogatives (section 93(2) Finnish Constitution).[35] Thus, the reform cemented the departure from a 'presidential democracy' to an increasing dominance of the Finnish Parliament and the Finnish Government.[36]

II The Finnish Constitutional Law Committee

The most authoritative Finnish actor in constitutional matters is the parliamentary Constitutional Law Committee.[37] This *quasi-judicial* authority assesses the compatibility of proposed national legislation and EU law with the Finnish Constitution.[38] The Committee's precise mandate is enshrined in section 74 Finnish Constitution, which establishes:

> The Constitutional Law Committee shall issue statements on the constitutionality of legislative proposals and other matters brought for its consideration, as well as on their relation to international human rights treaties.

Although its institutional mandate can be compared to other constitutional authorities in the EU, the Constitutional Law Committee is peculiar in several regards. It is a standing committee of the Finnish Parliament composed of 17 parliamentarians.[39] Therefore, its composition changes after every parliamentary election.[40] Furthermore, the Committee's members are not required to have any legal qualifications.[41] To ensure continuity and legal expertise, the Committee is assisted by a permanent secretary, composed of civil servants with constitutional expertise.[42] In addition, the Committee

35. Suksi, 'Finland' 112.
36. Mutanen, *Towards a Pluralistic Constitutional Understanding of State Sovereignty in the European Union? The Concept, Regulation and Constitutional Practice of Sovereignty in Finland and Certain Other EU Member States* 285; Ojanen, 'The EU at the Finnish Constitutional Arena' 247-248; Ojanen, 'The Impact of EU Membership on Finnish Constitutional Law' 547-548.
37. In Finnish: *Perustuslakivaliokunta*.
38. Lavapuro, Ojanen and Scheinin, 'Finland: Intermediate Constitutional Review in Finland – Promising in Theory, Problematic in Practice' 219; De Visser, *Constitutional Review in Europe: A Comparative Analysis* 26; Leino and Salminen, 'The Euro Crisis and Its Constitutional Consequences for Finland: Is There Room for National Politics in EU Decision-Making?' 453; Ojanen, 'Constitutional Amendment in Finland' 96.
39. As established in sections 35(1) and 74 Finnish Constitution, cf. Lavapuro, Ojanen and Scheinin, 'Finland: Intermediate Constitutional Review in Finland – Promising in Theory, Problematic in Practice' 226; De Visser, *Constitutional Review in Europe: A Comparative Analysis* 29; Ojanen, 'The Impact of EU Membership on Finnish Constitutional Law' 532.
40. Although, members are often re-elected into the Committee, cf. De Visser, *Constitutional Review in Europe: A Comparative Analysis* 29.
41. Kaarlo Tuori, '§ 98: Verfassungsgerichtsbarkeit in Finnland' in Armin von Bogdandy, Christoph Grabenwarter and Peter Michael Huber (eds), *Handbuch Ius Publicum Europaeum: Band VI (Verfassungsgerichtsbarkeit in Europa: Institutionen)* (C.F. Müller 2016) 172 para. 33; Lavapuro, Ojanen and Scheinin, 'Finland: Intermediate Constitutional Review in Finland – Promising in Theory, Problematic in Practice' 226.
42. De Visser, *Constitutional Review in Europe: A Comparative Analysis* 27.

consults constitutional law experts, which provide it with legal arguments and which have a major impact on the final decision of the 17 Committee members.[43]

As the Constitutional Law Committee is a parliamentary committee, its constitutional review is embedded in the parliamentary process. Upon referral by either the plenary[44] or by a specialized parliamentary committee,[45] the Constitutional Law Committee engages with the constitutional questions put before it.[46] Hence, the Committee cannot act *ex officio* or request a referral.[47] Furthermore, its statements are embedded in the parliamentary process, which results in the adoption of a 'final' parliamentary decision. Given that the considered matters are not yet enacted laws when assessed by the Committee, the Committee's review is only exercised in an abstract, anticipatory *ex ante* manner, which prevents the materialization of a constitutional conflict.

Traditionally, the Committee formulates its statements in a formalistic fashion in order to minimize political debates and to allow for unanimous support.[48] In its statements, the Committee includes a general assessment of the matter as well as suggestions for potential amendments and the applicable procedural requirements.[49] Overall, the statements are widely respected and considered constitutionally binding, although formally lacking legally binding force.[50] At the same time, the statements are not intended to establish strict constitutional limits. Instead, the Finnish Parliament can employ the *flexibility* offered by the Finnish Constitution in order to overcome possible constitutional concerns and adopt an exceptive enactment or a constitutional amendment.[51]

43. Tuomas Ojanen, '§ 296: Grundrechte in Finland' in Detlef Merten and Hans-Jürgen Papier (eds), *Handbuch der Grundrechte in Deutschland und Europa: Band X (Grundrechte in West-, Nord- und Südeuropa)* (C.F. Müller 2018) 380, para. 122; Tuori, '§ 98: Verfassungsgerichtsbarkeit in Finnland' 172, para. 35; Ojanen, 'The EU at the Finnish Constitutional Arena' 252.
44. Following section 6 No. 2 Rules of Procedure and subsequently approved by the parliament's plenary according to section 32(1)(2) Rules of Procedure, cf. De Visser, *Constitutional Review in Europe: A Comparative Analysis* 27; Suksi, 'Finland' 102.
45. Suksi, 'Finland' 102; for example, as part of the procedure established in section 96 Finnish Constitution, cf. Ojanen, 'Constitutional Amendment in Finland' 109; Ojanen, 'The Impact of EU Membership on Finnish Constitutional Law' 555.
46. As established in section 38(2) Rules of Procedure, cf. Tuori, '§ 98: Verfassungsgerichtsbarkeit in Finnland' 177 paras 45-46.
47. Mutanen, *Towards a Pluralistic Constitutional Understanding of State Sovereignty in the European Union? The Concept, Regulation and Constitutional Practice of Sovereignty in Finland and Certain Other EU Member States* 325.
48. De Visser, *Constitutional Review in Europe: A Comparative Analysis* 29.
49. Mutanen, *Towards a Pluralistic Constitutional Understanding of State Sovereignty in the European Union? The Concept, Regulation and Constitutional Practice of Sovereignty in Finland and Certain Other EU Member States* 325; De Visser, *Constitutional Review in Europe: A Comparative Analysis* 27-28.
50. Leino and Salminen, 'The Euro Crisis and Its Constitutional Consequences for Finland: Is There Room for National Politics in EU Decision-Making?' 459-460.
51. Ojanen and Salminen, 'Finland: European Integration and International Human Rights Treaties as Sources of Domestic Constitutional Change and Dynamism' 364; Ojanen, 'The Impact of EU Membership on Finnish Constitutional Law' 537.

Overall, this indicates that the Constitutional Law Committee is peculiar regarding its composition, its embedment in the parliamentary process and the effect of its decisions.[52] This institutional design appears to reflect the strong constitutional position of the Finnish Parliament within the Finnish constitutional order.[53] Hence, the review of the Constitutional Law Committee is not intended to limit parliamentary action within certain preordained substantive boundaries, including in EU matters, but instead to ensure the sound exercise of the parliament's constitutionally secured prerogatives, which includes altering the substantive interpretation of constitutional provisions by, for example, exceptive enactment.[54]

III Interim Conclusion: Constitutional Embracement of EU Membership

Taken together, the implemented national constitutional reforms transformed the Finnish constitutional order into an outward-looking constitutional system that embraces EU membership. The constitutional text provides for comprehensive parliamentary involvement in EU decisions, which ensures that the conferral of powers to the EU level is not equated with a loss of influence for the Finnish Parliament. The open outlook of the Finnish constitutional system on EU cooperation is also fostered by the decisions of the Constitutional Law Committee. Given that this parliamentary committee considers the constitutionality of EU commitments *ex ante*, possible constitutional obstacles can be identified and removed in the parliamentary process.

C PROCEDURAL AND INSTITUTIONAL FRAMEWORK APPLICABLE TO EU FISCAL INTEGRATION

The Finnish Constitution contains different procedures to engage with EU cooperation. These distinguish between the conferral of new competences to the EU (sections 94-95 Finnish Constitution) and the exercise of already conferred competences (sections 96-97 Finnish Constitution), as illustrated in Figure 2.1. As the precise design of future EU fiscal integration may either require new EU competences or the use of conferred competences, the subsequent analysis outlines the procedural framework for the conferral of budgetary and fiscal competences (I), the adoption of EU secondary law (II) and the conducted constitutional review (III).

52. De Visser, *Constitutional Review in Europe: A Comparative Analysis* 26.
53. Ojanen, 'The EU at the Finnish Constitutional Arena' 254; Lavapuro, Ojanen and Scheinin, 'Rights-Based Constitutionalism in Finland and the Development of Pluralist Constitutional Review' 509.
54. As showcased during the Eurocrisis, cf. Klaus Tuori and Juha Raitio, 'Finland' in Ulla Neergaard, Catherine Jacqueson and Jens Hartig Danielsen (eds), *The Economic and Monetary Union: Constitutional and Institutional Aspects of the Economic Governance within the EU (The XXVI FIDE Congress in Copenhagen)*, vol. 1 (DJØF Publishing Copenhagen 2014) 331.

Figure 2.1 Finnish Procedural Framework for EU Fiscal Integration Steps

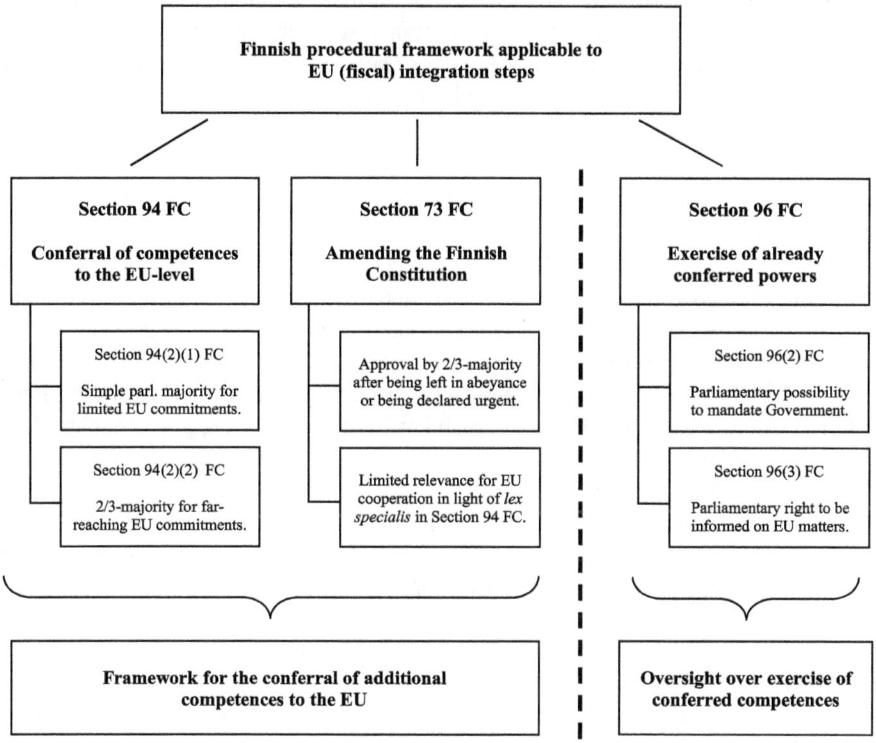

I Transferring Budgetary and Fiscal Competences to the EU

Section 94 Finnish Constitution explicitly regulates the transfer of competences to the EU.[55] This procedure can be classified as a *lex specialis* to section 73 Finnish Constitution, which governs constitutional amendments. While section 94 Finnish Constitution seems to constitute the most relevant basis for the conferral of powers to the EU, the subsequent assessment will equally consider section 73 Finnish Constitution as a possible alternative.

1 Preliminary Step: Scope for EU Cooperation

As a preliminary step, section 1(3)(1) Finnish Constitution prescribes that Finland only participates in international cooperation that serves '[…] the protection of peace and

55. Ojanen, 'The EU at the Finnish Constitutional Arena' 247; Ojanen, 'EU Law and the Response of the Constitutional Law Committee of the Finnish Parliament' 206.

human rights and [...] the development of society'.[56] Thus, international cooperation is connected to the attainment of broader constitutional aims. However, section 1(3)(2) Finnish Constitution now explicitly mentions Finnish EU membership, which might render the application of this scope restriction ultimately superfluous. In any case, fiscal integration proposals aim to stabilize the Eurozone and therefore clearly contribute to the development of society, which corresponds to the requirements listed in section 1(3)(2) Finnish Constitution.

2 *Conferral of Competences under Section 94 Finnish Constitution*

The primary basis for conferring competences to the EU is section 94 Finnish Constitution.[57] The scope of the provision is restricted to three situations: First, it applies in case the envisaged conferral contains provisions of a 'legislative nature'. Although the Finnish Constitution does not explicitly define this concept, its meaning can be deduced systematically. Section 3(1) Finnish Constitution establishes that all legislative power is exercised by the Finnish Parliament, which suggests that legislative power is a parliamentary prerogative. This legislative power is exercised by adopting 'acts' following the prescribed procedure in section 70 Finnish Constitution. In addition, section 2(3) Finnish Constitution clarifies that the exercise of all public power has to be based on parliamentary acts. This extends in particular to measures that affect 'the rights and obligations of private individuals', which have to be established in their core content by a legislative act according to section 80(1)(2) Finnish Constitution.[58] Overall, this suggests that EU integration steps, which provide the supranational level with the ability to enact directly applicable, binding rules concerning the exercise of public power, are legislative in nature and require parliamentary approval. Second, the provision applies in case the EU commitment affects matters that require parliamentary approval according to the Finnish Constitution. An example is the parliamentary prerogative to establish the annual budget according to sections 3(1) and 83(1) Finnish Constitution.[59] And third, it applies in case the EU commitment contains provisions

56. The Constitutional Law Committee has adopted a lenient interpretation of this provision, cf. Mutanen, *Towards a Pluralistic Constitutional Understanding of State Sovereignty in the European Union? The Concept, Regulation and Constitutional Practice of Sovereignty in Finland and Certain Other EU Member States* 336; Ojanen and Salminen, 'Finland: European Integration and International Human Rights Treaties as Sources of Domestic Constitutional Change and Dynamism' 366.
57. Mutanen, *Towards a Pluralistic Constitutional Understanding of State Sovereignty in the European Union? The Concept, Regulation and Constitutional Practice of Sovereignty in Finland and Certain Other EU Member States* 307-308, 344; Ojanen, 'The EU at the Finnish Constitutional Arena' 244.
58. Leino and Salminen, 'The Euro Crisis and Its Constitutional Consequences for Finland: Is There Room for National Politics in EU Decision-Making?' 458.
59. Section 3(1) Finnish Constitution establishes firstly that the parliament exercises legislative power and, subsequently, that it decides on the State finances – which suggests that both matters are different in nature.

that are otherwise significant, which is broadly interpreted by the Constitutional Law Committee as a *catch-all-clause*.[60]

Considering this wide framing, it is likely that EU fiscal integration proposals that involve competence conferrals require parliamentary approval under section 94 Finnish Constitution. Specifically, budgetary and fiscal competences are assigned to the Finnish Parliament, following section 3(1) in conjunction with Chapter 7 Finnish Constitution.[61] These matters concern decisions that require parliamentary approval under the second-mentioned alternative, which also prompted the application of section 94 Finnish Constitution in relation to various Eurocrisis-measures.[62]

Once it is established that parliamentary approval is required, the significance of the envisaged competence transfer is crucial to determine the applicable majority requirement.[63] Section 94(2) Finnish Constitution imposes a two-thirds majority requirement for EU commitments that conflict with fundamental constitutional doctrines, whereas, all other obligations merely require approval by a simple majority. Section 94(2)(2) Finnish Constitution states:

> However, if the proposal concerns the Constitution or an alteration of the national borders, or such transfer of authority to the European Union, an international [organization] or an international body that is of significance with regard to

60. During the Eurocrisis, the Committee considered EU obligations under section 94 Finnish Constitution to secure wide parliamentary involvement despite their (partly) intergovernmental nature, cf. Ojanen and Salminen, 'Finland: European Integration and International Human Rights Treaties as Sources of Domestic Constitutional Change and Dynamism' 391.
61. For example highlighted by the Constitutional Law Committee in: PeVL 13/2012 vp *Final Assessment Draft ESM-Treaty (III.)* (Finnish Constitutional Law Committee) 2; Christian Tomuschat, 'Lisbon: Terminal of the European Integration Process? The Judgment of the German Constitutional Court of 30 June 2009' (2010) 70 Zeitschrift für ausländisches öffentliches Recht und Völkerrecht (ZaöRV) 251 3; cf. as well: Leino and Salminen, 'The Euro Crisis and Its Constitutional Consequences for Finland: Is There Room for National Politics in EU Decision-Making?' 463; Ojanen, 'The EU at the Finnish Constitutional Arena' 247.
62. For the opinions of the Committee in chronological order: Tomuschat, 'Lisbon: Terminal of the European Integration Process? The Judgment of the German Constitutional Court of 30 June 2009'; PeVL 1/2011 vp *First Assessment Draft ESM-Treaty (I.)* (Finnish Constitutional Law Committee); PeVL 5/2011 vp *Amendment to the EFSF (Increase in State Guarantee)* (Finnish Constitutional Law Committee); PeVL 6/2011 vp *Amendment of Article 136 (3) TFEU* (Finnish Constitutional Law Committee); PeVP 11/2011 vp *Protocol on the EFSF* (Finnish Constitutional Law Committee); PeVL 22/2011 vp *Second Assessment Draft ESM-Treaty (II.)* (Finnish Constitutional Law Committee); PeVL 24/2011 vp *Preliminary Assessment of Fiscal Compact (I.)* (Finnish Constitutional Law Committee); PeVL 3/2012 vp *Additional Amendment to the EFSF* (Finnish Constitutional Law Committee); *Final Assessment Draft ESM-Treaty (III.)*; PeVL 37/2012 vp *Final Assessment of Fiscal Compact (II.)* (Finnish Constitutional Law Committee); on the ESM-Treaty assessment, which triggered the widest constitutional concerns, cf. Ojanen and Salminen, 'Finland: European Integration and International Human Rights Treaties as Sources of Domestic Constitutional Change and Dynamism' 391-392; Leino and Salminen, 'The Euro Crisis and Its Constitutional Consequences for Finland: Is There Room for National Politics in EU Decision-Making?' 464.
63. Cf. the different thresholds established by section 94(2) Finnish Constitution, Ojanen and Salminen, 'Finland: European Integration and International Human Rights Treaties as Sources of Domestic Constitutional Change and Dynamism' 366-367; Leino and Salminen, 'The Euro Crisis and Its Constitutional Consequences for Finland: Is There Room for National Politics in EU Decision-Making?' 458; Ojanen, 'The EU at the Finnish Constitutional Arena' 247.

> Finland's sovereignty, the decision shall be made by at least two-thirds of the votes cast.

The provision determines three cases that trigger the stricter parliamentary threshold. First, a qualified majority is required in case an EU obligation directly affects the Finnish Constitution. Such conflict is given in case constitutional principles or constitutional provisions are altered or modified by the envisaged EU obligations,[64] which hence extends the requirements formulated by section 73(1) Finnish Constitution to the EU context.[65] Second, an alteration of the Finnish border has to be approved by a qualified majority. And third, competence transfers that are significantly affecting Finnish sovereignty require approval by a two-thirds majority.

A thorough assessment of the principle of sovereignty will be conducted further below.[66] Here, it can be concluded that under the current understanding of Finnish sovereignty, a transfer of authority is significant in case it either transfers decision-making abilities to the EU level, which can be exercised independently from any Finnish control or in case the EU would be transformed into an entirely new entity.[67] Considering the third and the first qualification, significant overlap can be observed, as the principle of sovereignty is established in section 1(1) Finnish Constitution, and an alteration of this principle would therefore equally 'concern the Constitution'. Consequently, the separate mentioning of sovereignty might indicate, on the one hand, that the principle of sovereignty enjoys elevated constitutional importance. On the other hand, it might indicate that EU cooperation involves a particular risk for national sovereignty, which is explicitly recognized by the constitutional legislator.

Hence, the extent and significance of the envisaged conferral are important to determine the applicable majority threshold, which is conducted by the Constitutional Law Committee.[68] As indicated, EU fiscal integration steps will likely alter parliamentary budgetary and fiscal prerogatives, which are constitutionally assigned to the Finnish Parliament, as well as particularly relevant under the Finnish sovereignty doctrine. Therefore, it seems likely that the Constitutional Law Committee would

64. Ojanen, 'EU Law and the Response of the Constitutional Law Committee of the Finnish Parliament' 224.
65. Cf. section 73(1) Finnish Constitution establishes an even higher threshold, given that the matter has to be either approved by two consecutive parliaments or declared urgent by a five-sixths majority; however, under the 1919 Finnish Constitution, a special threshold for accepting international cooperation was recognized under section 69(1) Parliament Act of 1928, merely imposing a two-thirds threshold for constitutionally relevant international obligations, cf. Mutanen, *Towards a Pluralistic Constitutional Understanding of State Sovereignty in the European Union? The Concept, Regulation and Constitutional Practice of Sovereignty in Finland and Certain Other EU Member States* 291; Rosas, 'Finland: Finland's Accession to the European Union: Constitutional Aspects' 168.
66. Cf. within this chapter under section D.I.
67. *Commission's Draft EU Recovery Plan and MFF Planning* 18; Päivi Leino-Sandberg, 'Who Is Ultra Vires Now? The EU's Legal U-Turn in Interpreting Article 310 TFEU' (*Verfassungsblog*, 18 June 2020), https://verfassungsblog.de/who-is-ultra-vires-now-the-eus-legal-u-turn-in-interpreting-article-310-tfeu/, accessed 5 April 2023; this threshold was not met with regard to the Eurocrisis measures, which were not perceived as to significantly alter Finnish sovereignty, cf. Leino and Salminen, 'The Euro Crisis and Its Constitutional Consequences for Finland: Is There Room for National Politics in EU Decision-Making?' 458-459.
68. Cf. section 74 Finnish Constitution.

consider several forms of EU fiscal integration, for example, the creation of a Eurozone budget, the introduction of new EU funding streams, the establishment of a Eurozone government, or additional supervisory competences on national budgeting, as significant encroachments on the Finnish parliamentary prerogative to establish and administer the state budget, as laid down in section 3(1) in conjunction with section 83(1) Finnish Constitution. The resulting potential constraints on the Finnish Parliament regarding the exercise of its budgetary prerogatives and on Finnish sovereignty would likely require the approval of a qualified majority following section 94(2)(2) Finnish Constitution. This seems to be further confirmed by the Constitutional Law Committee's opinion on NGEU, which identified a particular risk for Finnish (budgetary) responsibility due to the potential (long-term) impact of the made financial commitments on the Finnish budget.[69]

Overall, this underscores that the Finnish Parliament is the central actor when considering a transfer of additional competences to the EU. Although it might prove practically difficult to attain a qualified majority threshold on EMU reforms given the outlined national political controversy on the EU, it should be emphasized that the constitutional text explicitly allows for the transfer of core constitutional competences by a qualified majority - even if these could fundamentally alter the Finnish constitutional order. The (narrow) Finnish adoption of the Own Resources Decision and with it NGEU[70] has showcased the potential - as well as the related risks - of these flexible rules that primarily rely on political support.

3 *Constitutional Amendments According to Section 73 Finnish Constitution*

In addition to the special procedure for the transfer of competences to the EU enshrined in section 94 Finnish Constitution, the Finnish Parliament could amend the constitutional text itself in order to accommodate EU fiscal integration steps. Such amendment can be either adopted as an exceptive enactment, which introduces a limited constitutional derogation or as an explicit modification of the constitutional text.

a *Fiscal Integration via Exceptive Enactment?*

Exceptive enactments are a distinct instrument of the Finnish constitutional order. The underlying idea is that the Finnish Parliament can enact derogations to the Finnish Constitution, without altering the constitutional text. The instrument originated during the Russian occupation and has to be seen in this specific historic context. At that time, exceptive enactments were employed by the Finnish Parliament to adapt the Finnish

69. *Ratification of the Own Resources Decision (II.)*; cf. as well: Päivi Leino-Sandberg, 'Between European Commitment and "Taking the Law Seriously"' (*Verfassungsblog*, 2021), https://verfassungsblog.de/between-european-commitment-and-taking-the-law-seriously/, accessed 5 April 2023.
70. *Ratification of the Own Resources Decision (II.)*; cf. as well: Leino-Sandberg and Ruffert, 'Next Generation EU and Its Constitutional Ramifications: A Critical Assessment' 447.

Constitution to changing socio-economic realities, while at the same time preserving the integrity of the constitution, which was used as a shield against too far-reaching Russian interferences.[71] Subsequently, the constitutional practice was preserved under the 1919 Constitutional Act[72] and frequently employed.[73] Under the reformed Finnish Constitution, the legislator and the Constitutional Law Committee emphasized that exceptive enactments should be restricted to, as the wording in section 73(1) Finnish Constitution suggests, 'a limited derogation of the Constitution'.[74]

Therefore, it seems unlikely that (far-reaching) EU fiscal integration could be based on an exceptive enactment. Section 94 Finnish Constitution provides for a special procedure to enact EU commitments which largely resembles an exceptive enactment. An exceptive enactment under section 73 Finnish Constitution seems not to offer additional leeway to parliament and it would even impose higher majority requirements.

b ***Fiscal Integration via Constitutional Amendments?***

Consequently, only an explicit constitutional amendment could constitute an alternative to section 94 Finnish Constitution. Section 73 Finnish Constitution does not restrict the extent or scope for an envisaged constitutional amendment.[75] Thus, the constitution-amending legislator can alter any section of the Finnish Constitution either following the ordinary or the expedited amendment procedure.

Under the ordinary procedure, a constitutional amendment proposal is forwarded to the Finnish Parliament and left in abeyance after the second parliamentary reading, confirmed by a simple majority. Only after the newly elected parliament convenes, the amendment process can resume.[76] Then, the Constitutional Law Committee issues a statement on the proposed amendments, which is subsequently

71. Ojanen and Salminen, 'Finland: European Integration and International Human Rights Treaties as Sources of Domestic Constitutional Change and Dynamism' 360; Ojanen, 'The Europeanization of Finnish Law: Observations on the Transformations of the Finnish Scene of Constitutionalism' 98.
72. Tuori, '§ 98: Verfassungsgerichtsbarkeit in Finnland' 180-181, para. 57.
73. Notably, 888 exceptive enactments were enacted between 1919 and 2000, cf. Ojanen, 'The Impact of EU Membership on Finnish Constitutional Law' 535.
74. Ojanen and Salminen, 'Finland: European Integration and International Human Rights Treaties as Sources of Domestic Constitutional Change and Dynamism' 369-370; Mutanen, *Towards a Pluralistic Constitutional Understanding of State Sovereignty in the European Union? The Concept, Regulation and Constitutional Practice of Sovereignty in Finland and Certain Other EU Member States* 307-308; the Constitutional Law Committee emphasized the 'principle of avoidance of exceptive enactments', cf. Tuori, '§ 98: Verfassungsgerichtsbarkeit in Finnland' 181-182, para. 60; Juha Lavapuro, 'Constitutional Review in Finland' in Kimmo Nuotio, Melander Sakari and Merita Huomo-Kettunen (eds), *Introduction to Finnish Law and Legal Culture* (University of Helsinki 2012) 133; and it is equally emphasized by the *travaux preparatoires* to the reformed section 73 Finnish Constitution, cf. Suksi, 'Finland' 104.
75. Different to the German *eternity clause*, which explicitly restricts the scope for constitutional amendments, cf. Calliess, 'Constitutional Identity in Germany: One for Three or Three in One?' 164-165.
76. Ojanen and Salminen, 'Finland: European Integration and International Human Rights Treaties as Sources of Domestic Constitutional Change and Dynamism' 368; Suksi, 'Finland' 91.

debated in the parliamentary plenary. Finally, the originally proposed amendment - without any changes to the content of the amendment - has to be confirmed by a two-thirds parliamentary majority. Hence, the ordinary constitutional amendment procedure is lengthy, and its success remains uncertain, as two consecutive parliaments have to support it. Obtaining such wide and lasting parliamentary support for EU fiscal integration measures might prove challenging in Finland.[77] Illustrative of this is the ESM-Treaty, for which the Finnish Government negotiated an amendment to the international commitment in order to escape the two-thirds requirement at home.[78] Similarly, the Own Resources Decision was only narrowly adopted by the required two-thirds majority.[79] Although both acts were adopted under section 94 Finnish Constitution, they illustrate the practical difficulty of uniting a two-thirds majority for EU fiscal matters.

In the alternative, the Finnish Parliament could employ the expedited procedure. Following section 73(2) Finnish Constitution, a five-sixths parliamentary majority can declare an envisaged constitutional amendment urgently and approve the amendment with a two-thirds majority after the second reading.[80] The required almost consensual parliamentary support seems hardly achievable for EU fiscal integration proposals. For instance, the Eurosceptical 'Finns'-party currently occupies 38 of the 200 seats in the Finnish Parliament. This means that the 'Finns'-party alone could block any 'urgent' constitutional amendment. Consequently, an expedited procedure to accommodate EU fiscal integration proposals seems highly uncertain.

Therefore, only the ordinary constitution-amending procedure provides an alternative to section 94 Finnish Constitution. However, section 94 Finnish Constitution constitutes the *lex specialis* and it imposes *lighter* procedural requirements. As a result, section 94 Finnish Constitution constitutes the preferable constitutional basis for accommodating EU fiscal integration both from a conceptual and from a practical-political point of view.

4 *Application of the Framework During the Eurocrisis*

The outlined procedural framework was used to address the different Eurocrisis-measures, which have high indicative value for further EU fiscal integration proposals. To start, the Fiscal Compact required parliamentary approval following section 94

77. Leino and Salminen, 'The Euro Crisis and Its Constitutional Consequences for Finland: Is There Room for National Politics in EU Decision-Making?' 454; Ojanen, 'Constitutional Amendment in Finland' 95.
78. Ojanen and Salminen, 'Finland: European Integration and International Human Rights Treaties as Sources of Domestic Constitutional Change and Dynamism' 391-392.
79. *Ratification of the Own Resources Decision (II.)*; cf. as well: Leino-Sandberg and Ruffert, 'Next Generation EU and Its Constitutional Ramifications: A Critical Assessment' 447.
80. Ojanen and Salminen, 'Finland: European Integration and International Human Rights Treaties as Sources of Domestic Constitutional Change and Dynamism' 368; Suksi, 'Finland' 91.

Finnish Constitution as it altered Finnish parliamentary prerogatives. The Constitutional Law Committee noted that the proposed measures affected the budgetary decision-making and the state budget, both prerogatives of the Finnish Parliament following section 3(1) in conjunction with Chapter 7 Finnish Constitution. Although the Fiscal Compact mainly reiterated existing EU commitments of the EU Stability and Growth Pact, the Committee emphasized that new reference values for the cyclically adjusted deficit of public finances were to be introduced.[81] The Committee saw these new values as a modification of the original commitment, which required anew approval following section 94(1) Finnish Constitution.[82] However, as the Fiscal Compact largely reiterated existing EU commitments and as the Finnish Parliament could decide how to implement the balanced budget rule in Article 3(2) Fiscal Compact, a simple majority was sufficient for its adoption.[83]

Similarly, the amendment of Article 136(3) TFEU required parliamentary approval under section 94 Finnish Constitution.[84] From the outset, the Constitutional Law Committee stressed that the proposed Treaty amendment was merely of declaratory and clarifying nature, as required under the employed simplified revision procedure in Article 48(6) TFEU[85] – as the CJEU would later also confirm in its *Pringle*-judgment.[86] Given its declaratory nature, it was questioned whether parliamentary approval would be at all required. The Committee concluded that the envisaged Treaty amendment did neither entail additional legislative obligations nor affect parliamentary prerogatives. However, the amendment was 'otherwise significant' under the third alternative of section 94(1) Finnish Constitution,[87] as it amended the Lisbon Treaty, which was

81. *Final Assessment of Fiscal Compact (II.)* 3; cf. as well: Leino and Salminen, 'The Euro Crisis and Its Constitutional Consequences for Finland: Is There Room for National Politics in EU Decision-Making?' 472.
82. Already highlighted in the first decision on the matter: *Preliminary Assessment of Fiscal Compact (I.)* 2; *Final Assessment of Fiscal Compact (II.)* 3; cf. as well: Leino and Salminen, 'The Euro Crisis and Its Constitutional Consequences for Finland: Is There Room for National Politics in EU Decision-Making?' 472-473.
83. *Final Assessment of Fiscal Compact (II.)* 3; cf. as well: Tuori and Raitio, 'Finland' 330; as Finland is a dualist system, EU obligations require implementation following the procedure established in section 95 Finnish Constitution, thus Article 3 Fiscal Compact did not impose additional obligation, cf. generally Mutanen, *Towards a Pluralistic Constitutional Understanding of State Sovereignty in the European Union? The Concept, Regulation and Constitutional Practice of Sovereignty in Finland and Certain Other EU Member States* 288.
84. *Amendment of Article 136 (3) TFEU* 2; Päivi Leino and Janne Salminen, *Constitutional Change Through Euro Crisis Law: 'Finland'* (European University Institute – Law Department Project 2014) V.2.; Leino and Salminen, 'The Euro Crisis and Its Constitutional Consequences for Finland: Is There Room for National Politics in EU Decision-Making?' 469.
85. *Amendment of Article 136 (3) TFEU* 2; cf. as well: Leino and Salminen, *Constitutional Change Through Euro Crisis Law: 'Finland'* V.2.
86. C-370/12 *Pringle* (CJEU) paras 61-76; cf. on the findings of the CJEU: Vestert Borger, 'The ESM and the European Court's Predicament in Pringle' (2013) 14 German Law Journal 113, 122.
87. *Amendment of Article 136 (3) TFEU* 2; cf. as well: Leino and Salminen, *Constitutional Change Through Euro Crisis Law: 'Finland'* V.2.; Leino and Salminen, 'The Euro Crisis and Its Constitutional Consequences for Finland: Is There Room for National Politics in EU Decision-Making?' 469.

adopted by the Finnish Parliament.[88] Given the highlighted declaratory nature of the amendment, a simple parliamentary majority was applicable.[89]

In contrast, the adoption of the European Financial Stability Facility (EFSF)-and ESM-Treaty triggered wider constitutional concerns.[90] From the outset, it was clear that the EFSF- and ESM-Treaty required parliamentary approval under section 94 Finnish Constitution.[91] The Constitutional Law Committee concluded that both intergovernmental Treaties affected parliamentary budgetary prerogatives established in section 3(1) in conjunction with Chapter 7 Finnish Constitution.[92] In its statement, the Committee further highlighted that the Treaties could constitute State guarantees, which require parliamentary approval under section 82(2) Finnish Constitution.[93] The subsequent question was whether a simple or qualified parliamentary majority applied.[94] The Constitutional Law Committee was particularly concerned that the ESM-Board could initially increase the Member States' financial commitment under emergency voting procedure by a qualified majority – and thus against Finnish opposition. The Committee considered that such a mechanism could have far-reaching consequences for parliamentary prerogatives and sovereignty, requiring approval by a qualified majority.[95] However, given that the attainment of a two-thirds majority was uncertain,[96] the Finnish Government successfully re-negotiated the ESM-Treaty. In its final appraisal of the amended ESM-Treaty, the Constitutional Law Committee concluded that the new voting arrangement safeguarded parliamentary prerogatives and that the budgetary commitment was sufficiently limited. Therefore, a simple majority

88. *Amendment of Article 136 (3) TFEU* 2; cf. as well: Leino and Salminen, *Constitutional Change Through Euro Crisis Law: 'Finland'* V.2.; Leino and Salminen, 'The Euro Crisis and Its Constitutional Consequences for Finland: Is There Room for National Politics in EU Decision-Making?' 469.
89. *Amendment of Article 136 (3) TFEU* 2; cf. as well: Leino and Salminen, 'The Euro Crisis and Its Constitutional Consequences for Finland: Is There Room for National Politics in EU Decision-Making?' 469.
90. For the opinions of the Committee: *First Assessment Draft ESM-Treaty (I.)*; *Second Assessment Draft ESM-Treaty (II.)*; *Final Assessment Draft ESM-Treaty (III.)*; on the ESM-Treaty, cf. Ojanen and Salminen, 'Finland: European Integration and International Human Rights Treaties as Sources of Domestic Constitutional Change and Dynamism' 391-392; Leino and Salminen, *Constitutional Change Through Euro Crisis Law: 'Finland'* VIII.1; Leino and Salminen, 'The Euro Crisis and Its Constitutional Consequences for Finland: Is There Room for National Politics in EU Decision-Making?' 464; Ojanen, 'The EU at the Finnish Constitutional Arena' 247.
91. As already indicated in relation to the EFSF, cf. *Amendment to the EFSF (Increase in State Guarantee)* 3; and the first draft ESM-Treaty, cf. *First Assessment Draft ESM-Treaty (I.)*.
92. Leino and Salminen, 'The Euro Crisis and Its Constitutional Consequences for Finland: Is There Room for National Politics in EU Decision-Making?' 465.
93. *Final Assessment Draft ESM-Treaty (III.)* 2; *First Assessment Draft ESM-Treaty (I.)*; cf. as well: Tuori and Raitio, 'Finland' 328; Leino and Salminen, 'The Euro Crisis and Its Constitutional Consequences for Finland: Is There Room for National Politics in EU Decision-Making?' 465.
94. *Final Assessment Draft ESM-Treaty (III.)* 4; *Second Assessment Draft ESM-Treaty (II.)* 2; *First Assessment Draft ESM-Treaty (I.)*.
95. *Second Assessment Draft ESM-Treaty (II.)* 2; cf. as well: Ojanen and Salminen, 'Finland: European Integration and International Human Rights Treaties as Sources of Domestic Constitutional Change and Dynamism' 391-392; Leino and Salminen, 'The Euro Crisis and Its Constitutional Consequences for Finland: Is There Room for National Politics in EU Decision-Making?' 467.
96. Tuori, '§ 98: Verfassungsgerichtsbarkeit in Finnland' 174-175, para. 39.

was sufficient to adopt the ESM-Treaty. In this instance, the continuous involvement of the Constitutional Law Committee illustrates the advantages of the Finnish *ex ante* constitutional review, as the issued statements *informed* the EU negotiations instead of merely *scrutinizing* the final legislative outcome – as is the case with (German) judicial *ex post* appraisal.

Finally, in the Committee's ultimate appraisal of the latest Own Resources Decision – and implicitly also NGEU – the Constitutional Law Committee found that the Own Resources Decision was an 'otherwise significant' commitment in the sense of section 94(1) Finnish Constitution that required parliamentary approval. The Constitutional Law Committee had subsequently to answer whether a qualified majority would be applicable. In its assessment, the Committee established that the required conferral had to be considered significant for Finnish sovereignty, as NGEU in the Finnish view altered core principles of the EU's constitutional framework which were comparable with a significant transfer of competences.[97] As a result, the Committee deemed the approval of a two-thirds majority necessary following section 94(2)(2) Finnish Constitution.

II THE FINNISH MODEL OF NATIONAL ENGAGEMENT IN EU MATTERS

The Finnish Constitution provides for the *ex ante* involvement of the Finnish Parliament in the preparation of EU secondary law. The parliamentary involvement is based on a comprehensive right to receive information enshrined in section 97(1) Finnish Constitution.[98] This obligation extends to the Finnish Prime Minister, who has to inform parliament about the deliberations of the European Council following section 97(2) Finnish Constitution. In addition, section 96 Finnish Constitution introduces a mandating practice for EU decisions that affect the constitutional prerogatives of the Finnish Parliament.[99]

Considering the EU Council of Ministers, section 96(1) Finnish Constitution applies to all envisaged EU 'acts, agreements [or] other measures' that affect parliamentary prerogatives. This shows that the Finnish procedure is not restricted to

97. *Ratification of the Own Resources Decision (II.)*; cf. as well: Leino-Sandberg and Ruffert, 'Next Generation EU and Its Constitutional Ramifications: A Critical Assessment' 465; Leino-Sandberg, 'Between European Commitment and "Taking the Law Seriously"'.
98. Ojanen and Salminen, 'Finland: European Integration and International Human Rights Treaties as Sources of Domestic Constitutional Change and Dynamism' 365; Leino and Salminen, 'The Euro Crisis and Its Constitutional Consequences for Finland: Is There Room for National Politics in EU Decision-Making?' 459; Ojanen, 'The Impact of EU Membership on Finnish Constitutional Law' 555.
99. Ojanen and Salminen, 'Finland: European Integration and International Human Rights Treaties as Sources of Domestic Constitutional Change and Dynamism' 365; Leino and Salminen, 'The Euro Crisis and Its Constitutional Consequences for Finland: Is There Room for National Politics in EU Decision-Making?' 452; Husa, *The Constitution of Finland: A Contextual Analysis* 47; Ojanen, 'The Impact of EU Membership on Finnish Constitutional Law' 554-555.

specific EU acts.[100] The EU matter has to fall within the constitutional competences of the Finnish Parliament, which include legislative acts as well as budgetary and fiscal competences.[101] This suggests that the Finnish Parliament would likely be involved in the national preparation of EU secondary law required by some EU fiscal integration proposals. This corresponds to the view of the Constitutional Law Committee. In its review of the proposed EU Six-Pack legislation, the Committee illustrated that the legislation contained provisions that limit government spending, fiscal planning, and the overall government debt level.[102] The proposed legislation thus impacted parliamentary prerogatives and warranted the involvement of the Finnish Parliament under section 96(1) Finnish Constitution.[103] An interesting aspect of this decision is the *implied ultra vires* assessment, as the Committee considered whether the Six-Pack legislation required approval under section 94 Finnish Constitution.[104] In its assessment, the Committee pointed out that the legislation did not widen the Finnish EU commitment and that section 96 Finnish Constitution thus applied.[105] Implicitly, the Committee evaluated whether the proposed secondary law corresponded to the conferred competences. However, different to the German *ultra vires* assessment,[106] the conclusion that EU law (significantly) exceeds the EU-Treaties does not automatically lead to the illegality of such acts in Finland, but it would trigger a different procedure.

100. In line with the interpretation of the Constitutional Law Committee to ensure the 'effective participation' of the Finnish Parliament, cf. Ojanen, 'The Europeanization of Finnish Law' 169; Ojanen, 'The Impact of EU Membership on Finnish Constitutional Law' 554-555.
101. For example established by the Constitutional Law Committee in: *Final Assessment Draft ESM-Treaty (III.)* 2; Tomuschat, 'Lisbon: Terminal of the European Integration Process? The Judgment of the German Constitutional Court of 30 June 2009' 3; cf. as well: Leino and Salminen, 'The Euro Crisis and Its Constitutional Consequences for Finland: Is There Room for National Politics in EU Decision-Making?' 457.
102. Tomuschat, 'Lisbon: Terminal of the European Integration Process? The Judgment of the German Constitutional Court of 30 June 2009' 4; cf. as well: Leino and Salminen, 'The Euro Crisis and Its Constitutional Consequences for Finland: Is There Room for National Politics in EU Decision-Making?' 471.
103. Tomuschat, 'Lisbon: Terminal of the European Integration Process? The Judgment of the German Constitutional Court of 30 June 2009' 4-5; cf. as well: Ojanen and Salminen, 'Finland: European Integration and International Human Rights Treaties as Sources of Domestic Constitutional Change and Dynamism' 391; Leino and Salminen, 'The Euro Crisis and Its Constitutional Consequences for Finland: Is There Room for National Politics in EU Decision-Making?' 458; Ojanen, 'The EU at the Finnish Constitutional Arena' 247.
104. Tomuschat, 'Lisbon: Terminal of the European Integration Process? The Judgment of the German Constitutional Court of 30 June 2009' 4; cf. as well: Leino and Salminen, 'The Euro Crisis and Its Constitutional Consequences for Finland: Is There Room for National Politics in EU Decision-Making?' 471.
105. Tomuschat, 'Lisbon: Terminal of the European Integration Process? The Judgment of the German Constitutional Court of 30 June 2009' 4-5; cf. as well: Leino and Salminen, 'The Euro Crisis and Its Constitutional Consequences for Finland: Is There Room for National Politics in EU Decision-Making?' 470-472.
106. On the German *ultra vires* review, cf. for example: *Quantitative Easing (PSPP) Final Judgment* para. 110; 2 BvR 2661/06 *Honeywell Judgment* (German Federal Constitutional Court) paras 54-61; cf. as well: Angela Schwerdtfeger, 'Europäisches Unionsrecht in der Rechtsprechung des Bundesverfassungsgerichts: Grundrechts-, ultra-vires- und Identitätskontrolle im gewaltenteiligen Mehrebenensystem' (2015) 50 Europarecht (EuR) 290, 292-293.

Once established that section 96 Finnish Constitution applies, the matter has to be immediately referred to the Finnish Parliament in order to allow for sufficient time for parliamentary assessment. The procedure is initiated by an official communication of the Finnish Government (section 96(2)(1) Finnish Constitution). It is referred to the Grand Committee, generally charged with EU matters, and, if necessary, to other specialized committees.[107] For example, the Constitutional Law Committee is consulted when proposed EU measures raise constitutional concerns.[108] The specialized committees issue reports and forward these to the lead committee, which takes them into account when drafting the overall appraisal. The final position is forwarded to the Finnish Government if deemed necessary in the form of an official statement, as provided for in section 96(2)(4) Finnish Constitution. Particularly important matters can also be considered by the plenary,[109] which takes, however, no final decision.

Although the final parliamentary position is not legally binding,[110] practice shows that the Finnish Government tends to follow the communicated positions[111] given the government's institutional dependency on continuous parliamentary support. Notably, if the Finnish Parliament is dissatisfied, it can consider taking additional *internal* steps, including the initiation of a motion of no confidence following section 43(2) Finnish Constitution. Thus, parliamentary positions have a politically *binding force* that nevertheless awards the government with certain leeway for EU negotiations.[112] Section 97 Finnish Constitution provides for similar parliamentary scrutiny of the Finnish vote in the European Council.[113] Overall, this shows that the Finnish Parliament occupies a pivotal position in the exercise of conferred competences, which is constitutionally secured by a right to be informed on EU policies and the outlined 'mandating' system. Through such a mandate, parliament is able to influence EU decision-making of the Finnish representative at EU level and it vests the adopted

107. As established in section 96(2)(2) Finnish Constitution, the speaker of the Finnish Parliament assigns the matter to the committee, cf. section 30(1)(2) Rules of Procedure, which will be announced during plenary session, cf. section 30(2) Rules of Procedure.
108. Miller, 'Finnish Judges and the European Union: An American Perspective' 503; Ojanen, 'Constitutional Amendment in Finland' 96-97; Ojanen, 'The Impact of EU Membership on Finnish Constitutional Law' 555.
109. Following section 96(2)(5) Finnish Constitution; note that particularly during the Eurocrisis, matters were frequently referred to the plenary, cf. Katrin Auel and Tapio Raunio, 'Debating the State of the Union? Comparing Parliamentary Debates on EU Issues in Finland, France, Germany and the United Kingdom' (2014) 20 The Journal of Legislative Studies 13, 19.
110. Section 96(2) Finnish Constitution does not specify the status of the statement, cf. Ojanen, 'The Europeanization of Finnish Law' 170; Ojanen, 'The Impact of EU Membership on Finnish Constitutional Law' 556.
111. Ojanen, 'The Europeanization of Finnish Law' 170; Raunio and Tiilikainen, *Finland in the European Union* 86.
112. Ojanen, 'The Europeanization of Finnish Law' 170; Ojanen, 'The Impact of EU Membership on Finnish Constitutional Law' 556.
113. Ojanen and Salminen, 'Finland: European Integration and International Human Rights Treaties as Sources of Domestic Constitutional Change and Dynamism' 365; Ojanen, 'The Impact of EU Membership on Finnish Constitutional Law' 555.

Finnish position with additional democratic authority. Furthermore, the early involvement of the Finnish Parliament in the adoption of EU law can trigger a greater politicization of EU matters and stimulate a public debate.[114]

Although such a mandating system entails the risk that parliaments focus merely on national benefits, the overall involvement of the Finnish Parliament provides an interesting example of how to enhance the position of national parliaments in the EU decision-making process. Given the extensive, continuous involvement and the strong procedural tools available to the Finnish Parliament, this model constitutes a *best practice* example. The Finnish model addresses democratic concerns against EU fiscal integration by guaranteeing thorough national parliamentary involvement in EU decision-making. Ultimately, the better national parliaments are involved - and connected among each other - the more legal-constitutional, political and normative space may be available for EU fiscal integration.

III *EX ANTE* CONSTITUTIONAL REVIEW AND *EX POST* JUDICIAL SCRUTINY

The Finnish system relies on *ex ante* constitutional review *in abstracto* conducted by the Constitutional Law Committee upon referral.[115] Given the Committee's institutional position within the Finnish Parliament, the Finnish constitutional order does not provide for a comprehensive *ex post* review of legislation. This affects judicial review in Finland, which is traditionally based on formalistic and rule-based reasoning,[116] relying on the authority of the contested measure and legislative supremacy.[117] The initial outright prohibition of judicially reviewing parliamentary acts was lifted during the constitutional reform process. Currently, section 106 Finnish Constitution allows for the review of legislative acts by Finnish courts under strict conditions.[118] Notably, section 106 Finnish Constitution limits the judicial review to an 'evident conflict [of a legislative act] with the Constitution'.[119] Such 'evident conflict' is given in case no

114. Antti Suvanto et al., *Improving the Resilience of Europe's Economic and Monetary Union (37b/2015)* (Finnish Ministry of Finance Publications 2015) 17-18, 22; Tapio Raunio, 'The Finnish Eduskunta and the European Union: The Strengths and Weaknesses of a Mandating System' in Claudia Hefftler et al. (eds), *The Palgrave Handbook of National Parliaments and the European Union* (Palgrave Macmillan 2015) 407.
115. Tuori, '§ 98: Verfassungsgerichtsbarkeit in Finnland' 176, para. 44; Ojanen, 'The Europeanization of Finnish Law' 146.
116. Ojanen and Salminen, 'Finland: European Integration and International Human Rights Treaties as Sources of Domestic Constitutional Change and Dynamism' 361-362; Ojanen, 'EU Law and the Response of the Constitutional Law Committee of the Finnish Parliament' 205
117. Ojanen, 'Constitutional Amendment in Finland' 109; Lavapuro, Ojanen and Scheinin, 'Rights-Based Constitutionalism in Finland and the Development of Pluralist Constitutional Review' 509.
118. Cf. parallel to the British doctrine of parliamentary sovereignty, Miller, 'Finnish Judges and the European Union: An American Perspective' 503.
119. Ojanen and Salminen, 'Finland: European Integration and International Human Rights Treaties as Sources of Domestic Constitutional Change and Dynamism' 361-362; Veli-Pekka Hautamäki, 'Novel Rules in the Finnish Constitution: The Question of Applicability' (2007) 52 Scandinavian Studies in Law 133, 136, 140.

available interpretative method could resolve the conflict and the Constitutional Law Committee has not confirmed the constitutionality of the act.[120] Furthermore, the respective court can only declare the act of parliament inapplicable to the case at hand and not generally invalidate it,[121] which illustrates the limited mandate of Finnish courts vis-à-vis the Finnish legislator.[122] Hence, *ex post* judicial challenges against EU fiscal integration measures are unlikely in Finland.

IV APPLICABLE PROCEDURAL AND INSTITUTIONAL FRAMEWORK TO EU FISCAL INTEGRATION

EU integration triggered a comprehensive reform of the Finnish constitutional order, which introduced a specific procedural framework to interact with the EU. This framework applies to EU fiscal integration proposals. As outlined, the Finnish Parliament can confer budgetary and fiscal competences to the EU (section 94 Finnish Constitution). Given the possible impact on Finnish sovereignty and parliamentary budgetary prerogatives, a qualified two-thirds majority could apply.[123] Once conferred, section 96 Finnish Constitution extends internal parliamentary prerogatives to EU matters and the Finnish Parliament can mandate governmental action at EU level. Thus, even if (fiscal) competences are conferred to the EU, the Finnish Parliament retains an active role in the domestic preparation of such EU decisions.[124]

The centrality of parliament in the Finnish constitutional system is underscored by the mode of constitutional review. Notably, constitutional review is conducted by a parliamentary committee. This review is conducted *ex ante* and *in abstracto*. When considering EU integration, the Constitutional Law Committee emphasized the specificity of EU law and that Finnish and EU law worked 'in tandem'.[125] As a result, the Committee traditionally refrains from declaring open conflicts between Finnish and EU law[126] and emphasizes parliament's discretion when taking EU integration steps. Once adopted, no additional constitutional challenge can be initiated. Therefore, it appears that the special Finnish constitutional set-up – which enables comprehensive constitutional reform and underscores parliamentary discretion – is the main source of Finnish *constitutional flexibility*.

---

120. De Visser, *Constitutional Review in Europe: A Comparative Analysis* 29; Ojanen, 'The Europeanization of Finnish Law: Observations on the Transformations of the Finnish Scene of Constitutionalism' 108.
121. Ojanen and Salminen, 'Finland: European Integration and International Human Rights Treaties as Sources of Domestic Constitutional Change and Dynamism' 361.
122. Hautamäki, 'Novel Rules in the Finnish Constitution: The Question of Applicability' 146.
123. Ojanen, 'The EU at the Finnish Constitutional Arena' 247.
124. Leino and Salminen, 'The Euro Crisis and Its Constitutional Consequences for Finland: Is There Room for National Politics in EU Decision-Making?' 460
125. Lavapuro, Ojanen and Scheinin, 'Finland: Intermediate Constitutional Review in Finland: Promising in Theory, Problematic in Practice' 238.
126. Miller, 'Finnish Judges and the European Union: An American Perspective' 533.

D SUBSTANTIVE FRAMEWORK APPLICABLE TO EU FISCAL INTEGRATION

The Finnish Constitution contains substantive principles in Chapter 1. These 'fundamental principles' represent core characteristics of the Finnish Constitution and they function as substantive reference points when interpreting the Finnish Constitution[127] The principle of sovereignty and the recognition of Finnish EU membership are such 'fundamental principles' (section 1 Finnish Constitution). Similarly, the principle of democracy in section 2 Finnish Constitution and parliamentary responsibility for budgetary decisions in section 3(1) Finnish Constitution form part of these fundamental principles. For EU fiscal integration steps, Finnish sovereignty (I)[128] and parliamentary budgetary prerogatives (II)[129] are of significance. Finally, section 94(3) Finnish Constitution might evolve into a supra-constitutional limit potentially preventing EU fiscal integration (III).[130]

I Finnish Sovereignty: An Evolutionary Conception

Given the systematic importance of Finnish sovereignty,[131] the transformation over the past decades triggered to accommodate EU cooperation is remarkable. It can be traced back to statements of the Constitutional Law Committee on Finnish EU accession. Although section 1(1) Constitutional Act then proclaimed absolute sovereignty, the Committee considered the factual benefits stemming from EU membership when evaluating its impact on Finnish sovereignty.[132] This *qualified understanding* of Finnish sovereignty was codified by the 2000 constitutional reform which introduced section 1(3) Finnish Constitution and with it the principle of internationality as a counterbalance to sovereignty.[133]

1 The Historic Origin of Finnish Sovereignty

Initially, section 1(1) of the 1919 Constitutional Act declared the sovereignty of the Finnish Republic without providing for any derogation. This absolute conception is

127. Länsineva, 'Fundamental Principles of the Constitution of Finland' 115.
128. In particular, 'budgetary sovereignty', cf. Ojanen and Salminen, 'Finland: European Integration and International Human Rights Treaties as Sources of Domestic Constitutional Change and Dynamism' 391-392.
129. Reflected in prevailing legislative sovereignty, cf. Ojanen, 'The EU at the Finnish Constitutional Arena' 254; Lavapuro, Ojanen and Scheinin, 'Rights-Based Constitutionalism in Finland and the Development of Pluralist Constitutional Review' 509.
130. Leino and Salminen, 'The Euro Crisis and Its Constitutional Consequences for Finland: Is There Room for National Politics in EU Decision-Making?' 463.
131. Mutanen, *Towards a Pluralistic Constitutional Understanding of State Sovereignty in the European Union? The Concept, Regulation and Constitutional Practice of Sovereignty in Finland and Certain Other EU Member States* 281; Ojanen, 'The Impact of EU Membership on Finnish Constitutional Law' 540-541.
132. Ojanen, 'The EU at the Finnish Constitutional Arena' 245.
133. Ojanen, 'The Europeanization of Finnish Law: Observations on the Transformations of the Finnish Scene of Constitutionalism' 101.

historically rooted.[134] Based on the unambiguous wording of section 1 Constitutional Act, Finnish sovereignty was traditionally construed as an absolute, unconditional principle. Consequently, the Constitutional Law Committee initially considered any form of international cooperation as conflicting with Finnish sovereignty.[135] The Constitutional Law Committee followed a highly formalistic interpretation of section 1 Constitutional Act and with it a formalistic conception of Finnish sovereignty, which focused on whether international cooperation limited internal decision-making abilities. At the same time, this strict conception of sovereignty could be remedied under the Finnish Constitution by adopting the outlined exceptive enactments.[136] Although exceptive enactments had to be adopted following the constitutional amendment procedure, section 69(1) Finnish Parliament Act established a simplified procedure for implementing international obligations into Finnish law via exceptive enactment.[137] This special procedure rendered the implementation of international obligations more feasible compared to ordinary constitutional amendments.

This formalistic conception of Finnish sovereignty partially prevailed after Finnish accession to the EU. When confronted with the Finnish EU Accession Treaty, the Constitutional Law Committee identified a conflict with Finnish sovereignty, given the significant transfer of responsibility involved. Although a change in the understanding of Finnish sovereignty emerged, as the Committee reflected on wider constitutional implications of EU membership beyond sovereignty, the Accession Treaty was found in conflict with Finnish sovereignty, which was overcome by exceptive enactment.[138] Taken together, this constitutes the starting point of a changed understanding of Finnish sovereignty and a subsequent diversification in the substantive constitutional review of EU commitments.[139]

2 *A New Conception of Finnish Sovereignty*

The qualified interpretation of Finnish sovereignty was embedded in the new constitutional text, which entered into force in 2000. Section 1(3) Finnish Constitution now provides:

134. Ojanen and Salminen, 'Finland: European Integration and International Human Rights Treaties as Sources of Domestic Constitutional Change and Dynamism' 360.
135. Ojanen, 'The EU at the Finnish Constitutional Arena' 245; Ojanen, 'The Europeanization of Finnish Law' 151.
136. Ojanen and Salminen, 'Finland: European Integration and International Human Rights Treaties as Sources of Domestic Constitutional Change and Dynamism' 364.
137. So-called 'narrow procedure of constitutional enactment', cf. Mutanen, *Towards a Pluralistic Constitutional Understanding of State Sovereignty in the European Union? The Concept, Regulation and Constitutional Practice of Sovereignty in Finland and Certain Other EU Member States* 291; Rosas, 'Finland: Finland's Accession to the European Union – Constitutional Aspects' 168.
138. Rosas, 'Finland: Finland's Accession to the European Union – Constitutional Aspects' 168.
139. Mutanen, *Towards a Pluralistic Constitutional Understanding of State Sovereignty in the European Union? The Concept, Regulation and Constitutional Practice of Sovereignty in Finland and Certain Other EU Member States* 331-332.

> Finland participates in international co-operation for the protection of peace and human rights and for the development of society.

Hence, today section 1 Finnish Constitution explicitly recognizes the possibility to engage in international cooperation. The *travaux preparatoires* of the constitutional reform process suggest that the legislator intentionally qualified Finnish sovereignty in light of international and EU obligations.[140] This codification resonated with the Constitutional Law Committee, which concluded that the new section 1(3) Finnish Constitution established the principle of internationality, which systematically qualifies Finnish sovereignty embedded in section 1(1) Finnish Constitution.[141] Despite the fact that the text in section 1(1) Finnish Constitution remained unchanged ('Finland is a sovereign republic.'), the new constitutional context and the legislator's intention resulted in the qualification of Finnish sovereignty.

Following these changes, the Committee now departs in its reasoning from the constitutional assumption that Finnish sovereignty is indeed qualified in light of EU membership[142] and it employs the concept of 'specificity of EU cooperation'.[143] Based on this principle, the Constitutional Law Committee appears to be more readily accepting limitations to Finnish sovereignty stemming from EU commitments given the particularly close cooperation between EU Member States, which differs from other international cooperation.[144] Furthermore, the Committee construes Finnish participation in EU affairs as an exercise of sovereign powers together with other sovereign countries secured by procedural arrangements at EU level.[145] Moreover, given the increasing need for international cooperation, states are required to take decisions jointly to retain control.[146] Overall, the Constitutional Law Committee appears to accept EU-related limitations of Finnish sovereignty more readily, given the specific safeguards of EU law and the factual benefits of acting jointly as a Union in a globalized world. Since 2012, the special status of EU cooperation is reflected in section 1(3), which acknowledges EU membership.

The new constitutional approach to sovereignty is spelt out in the Committee's opinion on the Lisbon Treaty.[147] The Committee acknowledged the qualified status of sovereignty in light of EU membership, highlighting that the Lisbon Treaty is a

140. Ojanen, 'The Europeanization of Finnish Law' 154.
141. Mutanen, *Towards a Pluralistic Constitutional Understanding of State Sovereignty in the European Union? The Concept, Regulation and Constitutional Practice of Sovereignty in Finland and Certain Other EU Member States* 335.
142. Ojanen, 'EU Law and the Response of the Constitutional Law Committee of the Finnish Parliament' 217.
143. Mutanen, *Towards a Pluralistic Constitutional Understanding of State Sovereignty in the European Union? The Concept, Regulation and Constitutional Practice of Sovereignty in Finland and Certain Other EU Member States* 301.
144. Ojanen, 'The EU at the Finnish Constitutional Arena' 246.
145. Ojanen, 'The Europeanization of Finnish Law' 156.
146. PeVL 13/2008 vp *Adoption of the Lisbon Treaty* (Finnish Constitutional Law Committee) 4-5; cf. as well: Mutanen, *Towards a Pluralistic Constitutional Understanding of State Sovereignty in the European Union? The Concept, Regulation and Constitutional Practice of Sovereignty in Finland and Certain Other EU Member States* 334.
147. *Adoption of the Lisbon Treaty* 4-5.

consolidation of the EU legal order and not an entirely new form of agreement.[148] Yet, due to the abolishment of the three pillar structure, the consequential wider reach of the CJEU's jurisprudence and changes to the institutional structure with the formal introduction of the European Council as an EU institution, the Committee nevertheless required a qualified majority for the approval of the Lisbon Treaty.[149]

Overall, this illustrates the fundamental transformation from absolute to qualified sovereignty. As *Ojanen* points out, the introduction of section 1(3) Finnish Constitution offered the opportunity to break with the traditional, formalistic conception of Finnish sovereignty.[150] The current approach centres around Finnish participation at EU level as an exercise of sovereign powers among sovereign states. This conception underscores the derived nature of EU cooperation as a shared exercise of sovereign powers.[151] In addition, the constitution-amending legislator was able to initiate these changes by introducing the mentioned section 1(3) Finnish Constitution. Put differently, despite the overall importance of the principle of sovereignty from a systematic and historic point of view, the made changes were constitutionally permissible. Thus, the principle of sovereignty is not an insurmountable object for constitutional reforms.[152]

3 *Application During the Eurocrisis and Implications for EU Fiscal Integration*

Finnish sovereignty was an important constitutional benchmark in the assessment of the various Eurocrisis-measures. As indicated, the Constitutional Law Committee was particularly concerned about the compatibility of the ESM-Treaty with Finnish sovereignty. In a first assessment, the Committee concluded that the draft ESM-Treaty could be approved by a simple parliamentary majority, given that the proposed agreement did neither modify the Finnish Constitution nor significantly alter Finnish sovereignty in the sense of section 94(2) Finnish Constitution.[153] In particular, the Committee considered that the budgetary implications of the ESM-Treaty were limited without undermining parliamentary budgetary prerogatives and sovereignty. The Committee had already emphasized in its EFSF-assessment that all major decisions had to be taken unanimously by the then EFSF board of governors composed of the Member States' finance ministers. Given that parliament could mandate the Finnish Finance Minister under section 96 Finnish Constitution, the Committee concluded that the Finnish

148. Mutanen, *Towards a Pluralistic Constitutional Understanding of State Sovereignty in the European Union? The Concept, Regulation and Constitutional Practice of Sovereignty in Finland and Certain Other EU Member States* 357.
149. *Adoption of the Lisbon Treaty* 4, 11; cf. as well: Ojanen, 'The EU at the Finnish Constitutional Arena' 244.
150. Ojanen, 'The Impact of EU Membership on Finnish Constitutional Law' 540-541.
151. Ojanen and Salminen, 'Finland: European Integration and International Human Rights Treaties as Sources of Domestic Constitutional Change and Dynamism' 371-372.
152. Ojanen, 'The EU at the Finnish Constitutional Arena' 247.
153. *First Assessment Draft ESM-Treaty (I.)*; cf. as well: Ojanen and Salminen, 'Finland: European Integration and International Human Rights Treaties as Sources of Domestic Constitutional Change and Dynamism' 391-392.

Parliament retained full control over EFSF-decisions.[154] The general structure of the EFSF was replicated by the first draft ESM-Treaty. Based on its prior constitutional reasoning, the Constitutional Law Committee emphasized the possibility to veto ESM-decisions and concluded that the proposed ESM-Treaty neither transformed the Finnish EU commitment as such nor fundamentally altered parliamentary budgetary prerogatives. Therefore, the first draft ESM-Treaty could be approved by a simple majority.

In the following assessment of an altered version of the ESM-Treaty, the Committee was concerned about the changed emergency voting procedure in the ESM board of governors (Article 4(4) draft ESM-Treaty). According to this emergency voting, the Member States' financial commitments could be increased by a qualified majority vote.[155] The Committee found that the conditions and scope of emergency voting were not sufficiently limited. It feared that financial commitments could be increased against the explicit will of the Finnish Parliament which would significantly affect parliamentary budgetary prerogatives and sovereignty. Notably, Finland would have been bound by a majority decision of Eurozone Member States. According to the Constitutional Law Committee, this would have fundamentally modified the relationship between the Member States and the EU.[156] In addition, an increase in the Finnish financial commitment could ultimately impact the state's ability to fulfil its constitutionally enshrined obligations.[157] Therefore, the Committee established that the second ESM-Treaty draft could only be approved by a qualified parliamentary majority.[158]

Given that the Finnish Government feared it could not achieve the required parliamentary majority,[159] Finnish representatives at EU level successfully renegotiated the ESM-Treaty to escape the stricter majority requirement. Subsequently, the Constitutional Law Committee was confronted with a final draft version of the ESM-Treaty. In its assessment, the Committee reiterated that the envisaged Treaty needed parliamentary approval under section 94 Finnish Constitution. Specifically, the

154. *Amendment to the EFSF (Increase in State Guarantee)* 4; cf. as well: Leino and Salminen, 'The Euro Crisis and Its Constitutional Consequences for Finland: Is There Room for National Politics in EU Decision-Making?' 468.
155. Ojanen and Salminen, 'Finland: European Integration and International Human Rights Treaties as Sources of Domestic Constitutional Change and Dynamism' 391.
156. *Second Assessment Draft ESM-Treaty (II.)* 2; cf. as well: Ojanen and Salminen, 'Finland: European Integration and International Human Rights Treaties as Sources of Domestic Constitutional Change and Dynamism' 391-392; this reasoning features equally in subsequent decisions, cf. *Commission's Draft EU Recovery Plan and MFF Planning* 17-18; cf. as well: Leino-Sandberg, 'Who Is Ultra Vires Now? The EU's Legal U-Turn in Interpreting Article 310 TFEU'.
157. Cf. for example: PeVL 12/2018 vp *On the Establishment of a European Monetary Fund* (Finnish Constitutional Law Committee) 3-4.
158. In the sense of section 94(2)(2) Finnish Constitution: *Second Assessment Draft ESM-Treaty (II.)* 2; cf. as well: Ojanen and Salminen, 'Finland: European Integration and International Human Rights Treaties as Sources of Domestic Constitutional Change and Dynamism' 391-392; Leino and Salminen, 'The Euro Crisis and Its Constitutional Consequences for Finland: Is There Room for National Politics in EU Decision-Making?' 467.
159. Tuori and Raitio, 'Finland' 328; Jokela, *Finland and the Eurozone Crisis* 35-36.

Committee considered the possible impact of the financial commitments under the envisaged ESM-Treaty on the Finnish state budget. In order to determine this impact, the Constitutional Law Committee conducted a detailed assessment of the financial commitments (roughly EUR 12.5 billion callable capital, thereof EUR 1.44 billion paid-in capital) in relation to the overall volume of the Finnish state budget - which, as an orientation, amounted to around EUR 54 billion in 2015[160] - and the Finnish state debt level - which, to put it in perspective, amounted to 63.2% of the Finnish GDP in 2016.[161] It concluded that although the financial commitment was considerable compared with both indicators, the commitment was sufficiently limited and that the Finnish Parliament could influence ESM-decisions. The most important question for the Committee appeared to be to determine whether the Finnish budget remained 'under the control' of the Finnish Parliament.[162] Different to the previous draft, national financial commitments could no longer be increased by a qualified majority.[163] The Constitutional Law Committee also pointed out that the financial commitment of up to EUR 12.5 billion could potentially negatively impact the ability of the Finnish State to fulfil its constitutional obligations, including providing for social welfare.[164] Although this risk did ultimately not manifest in relation to the ESM-Treaty, future financial commitments at EU level will have to comply with this constitutional benchmark - or would otherwise have to be approved by a qualified parliamentary majority.

In addition to considering the extent of the financial commitments, the Committee focused extensively on the question of whether the modified ESM-Treaty involved a competence conferral of relevance for Finnish sovereignty.[165] In a first step, it examined again the voting procedure applicable to decisions by the ESM board of governors.[166] As outlined, given that the final ESM-Treaty did not provide for a possible increase in the Member States' financial commitments by a qualified majority vote, the Constitutional Law Committee concluded that the Finnish financial commitment was

160. Ojanen and Salminen, 'Finland: European Integration and International Human Rights Treaties as Sources of Domestic Constitutional Change and Dynamism' 392; Leino and Salminen, 'The Euro Crisis and Its Constitutional Consequences for Finland: Is There Room for National Politics in EU Decision-Making?' 466.
161. Eurostat Online Publications, 'Government Finance Statistics' (*Eurostat*, 2020), https://ec.europa.eu/eurostat/statistics-explained/pdfscache/1137.pdf, accessed 5 April 2023.
162. *Final Assessment Draft ESM-Treaty (III.)* 4; *Second Assessment Draft ESM-Treaty (II.)* 2; *First Assessment Draft ESM-Treaty (I.)*.
163. *Final Assessment Draft ESM-Treaty (III.)* 3; cf. as well: Ojanen and Salminen, 'Finland: European Integration and International Human Rights Treaties as Sources of Domestic Constitutional Change and Dynamism' 391-392; Leino and Salminen, 'The Euro Crisis and Its Constitutional Consequences for Finland: Is There Room for National Politics in EU Decision-Making?' 464.
164. *Final Assessment Draft ESM-Treaty (III.)* 3; cf. as well: Leino and Salminen, 'The Euro Crisis and Its Constitutional Consequences for Finland: Is There Room for National Politics in EU Decision-Making?' 466.
165. *Final Assessment Draft ESM-Treaty (III.)* 4.
166. *Second Assessment Draft ESM-Treaty (II.)* 2; cf. final assessment: *Final Assessment Draft ESM-Treaty (III.)* 4; cf. as well: Ojanen and Salminen, 'Finland: European Integration and International Human Rights Treaties as Sources of Domestic Constitutional Change and Dynamism' 391-392.

sufficiently confined.[167] In addition, the Committee underscored that Eurocrisis-measures, such as the ESM-Treaty, were necessary steps that had to be taken to guarantee the stability of the Eurozone. The Constitutional Law Committee summarized that Finnish participation in the ESM constituted a joint exercise of national sovereignty of the Eurozone Member States, which enhanced the stability of the single currency.[168] Therefore, the Committee found that neither the parliamentary budgetary prerogatives nor Finnish sovereignty were significantly limited and that the final ESM-Treaty could be adopted by a simple majority.

More recently, the Constitutional Law Committee had to determine the compatibility of the draft NGEU recovery strategy.[169] In its decision, the Committee reiterated its conception of sovereignty established during the Eurocrisis, which emphasizes the importance of budgetary decision-making powers for the Finnish Parliament as part of Finnish sovereignty.[170] Following this conception, the Committee examined the financial responsibilities and limits to budgetary decision-making, which entailed the evaluation of the overall Finnish financial liabilities at EU level, the level of Finnish parliamentary influence as well as the likelihood that liabilities materialize.[171] Regarding NGEU, the Committee raised specific concerns regarding the envisaged funding through EU borrowing, which according to the Committee constituted a crucial modification of EU cooperation, as it seemingly extends the Treaty-mandate given to the EU in Article 310 TFEU and as it can thus not be classified as a 'normal evolution' of EU membership.[172] Overall, the Committee concluded that the envisaged recovery strategy and the underpinning Own Resources Decision constituted a significant interference with Finnish (budgetary) sovereignty that would likely require approval by a two-thirds majority.[173]

When then confronted with the final version of the proposed Own Resources Decision and the connected Own Resources Decision, the Constitutional Law Committee reiterated its initial concerns and further refined its (budgetary) sovereignty

167. *Final Assessment Draft ESM-Treaty (III.)* 3; cf. as well: Leino and Salminen, 'The Euro Crisis and Its Constitutional Consequences for Finland: Is There Room for National Politics in EU Decision-Making?' 464; Ojanen, 'The EU at the Finnish Constitutional Arena' 247.
168. Leino and Salminen, 'The Euro Crisis and Its Constitutional Consequences for Finland: Is There Room for National Politics in EU Decision-Making?' 464.
169. *Commission's Draft EU Recovery Plan and MFF Planning* 10; Leino-Sandberg, 'Who Is Ultra Vires Now? The EU's legal U-Turn in Interpreting Article 310 TFEU'.
170. Which the Committee terms 'budgetary sovereignty', cf. *Commission's Draft EU Recovery Plan and MFF Planning* 11; Anne-Sylvaine Chassany, Guy Chazan and Mehreen Khan, 'Impatient Macron Pushes Merkel Hard on Eurozone Reform' *Financial Times* (London 16 March 2018), https://www.ft.com/content/8c521504-2904-11e8-b27e-cc62a39d57a0, accessed 5 April 2023, 8.
171. *Commission's Draft EU Recovery Plan and MFF Planning* 12; cf. as well: Chassany, Chazan and Khan, 'Impatient Macron Pushes Merkel Hard on Eurozone Reform' 8; *On the Establishment of a European Monetary Fund* 3-4.
172. *Commission's Draft EU Recovery Plan and MFF Planning* 18; cf. as well: Leino-Sandberg, 'Who Is Ultra Vires Now? The EU's Legal U-Turn in Interpreting Article 310 TFEU'.
173. Leino-Sandberg, 'Who Is Ultra Vires Now? The EU's Legal U-Turn in Interpreting Article 310 TFEU'.

doctrine developed during the Eurocrisis.[174] In its final appraisal, the Committee first acknowledged that the decision was based on the pro-rata-principle, thereby restricting Finland's liability, as well as the strict procedural requirements of Article 311 TFEU and the clear objectives of NGEU – which together suggest compliance with Finnish budgetary sovereignty. Nevertheless, and despite these clear safeguards, the Committee subsequently emphasized the long-term implications of the decision for the budget, the still unclear design of the repayment scheme, the fallback-option in case of defaulting Member States and remaining overall uncertainties. The Committee qualified these concerns as significant risks for Finnish budgetary sovereignty and required qualified approval under section 94(2)(2) Finnish Constitution.[175] It should be stressed that the Committee adopted its final opinion by an unusual 8 to 7 majority – thereby breaking with constitutional tradition to aim for unanimous support of opinions.[176] The Finnish Parliament ultimately adopted the Own Resources Decision in a narrow vote.[177] The Committee's decision illustrates a core challenge that the Finnish *ex ante* review poses for EU law more generally. Notably, given its inability to refer preliminary questions to the CJEU, a risk emerges for competing interpretations of EU law – especially in Finland. This not only puts the national legislator in a difficult position but it might also influence the reasoning of other national constitutional actors without enabling the CJEU to establish a coherent and uniform understanding of EU law.

The constitutional appraisal of NGEU and the ESM-Treaty illustrate the advantages of the Finnish constitutional assessment. It allows for an institutionalized and formal dialogue between the Constitutional Law Committee, the Finnish Parliament and the Finnish Government on envisaged EU commitments during negotiations at the national as well as EU level. Therefore, the *ex ante* review exercised by the Constitutional Law Committee may be seen as a constructive and goal-oriented means to design EU integration steps in compliance with the Finnish constitutional requirements. It allows to evaluate the national constitutional implications of debated EU acts before possible conflicts manifest. In that regard, one could even argue that the *negative* opinion of the Constitutional Law Committee on the second draft version of the ESM-Treaty[178] increased the authority of the Finnish position in the supranational negotiations.[179] At the same time, the constitutional appraisal of the Own Resources Decision displays a core risk of *ex ante* review: As Article 267 TFEU is not available for the Constitutional Law Committee, the likelihood of competing understandings of EU law is increased.

174. *Ratification of the Own Resources Decision (II.)*; cf. as well: Leino-Sandberg, 'Between European Commitment and "Taking the Law Seriously"'.
175. *Ratification of the Own Resources Decision (II.)*; cf. as well: Leino-Sandberg and Ruffert, 'Next Generation EU and Its Constitutional Ramifications: A Critical Assessment' 447.
176. Leino-Sandberg, 'Between European Commitment and "Taking the Law Seriously"'; cf. on the previous tradition: De Visser, *Constitutional Review in Europe: A Comparative Analysis* 29.
177. Leino-Sandberg and Ruffert, 'Next Generation EU and Its Constitutional Ramifications: A Critical Assessment' 447.
178. *Second Assessment Draft ESM-Treaty (II.)* 2.
179. Jokela, 'Finland: Towards a More Cautious Europeanization' 49.

Taken together, the assessment illustrates that the Constitutional Law Committee has developed the concept of essential features of the parliament's budgetary competences based on Finnish sovereignty.[180] Notably, the Committee specified in its appraisal of the ESM-Treaty and subsequently of NGEU that an overall assessment of the financial impact of the proposed EU obligations had to be undertaken. In these decisions, the benchmarks for the assessment were the annual Finnish state budget and the overall debt level in order to determine whether the Finnish state would be able to fulfil its constitutional obligations[181] as well as the level of parliamentary control and the likelihood that financial liabilities would manifest.[182] This benchmark is relevant when determining the feasibility of EU fiscal integration steps in Finland. Overall, it can be submitted that the concept of 'budgetary sovereignty' is a relevant benchmark to identify the applicable parliamentary majority requirement, without, however, constituting an absolute or legally insurmountable constitutional *red line* limit.

II Finnish Democracy

The principle of Finnish democracy is enshrined in section 2(1) and (2) Finnish Constitution. Considering its systematic positioning within the Finnish Constitution, democracy occupies a primary position among the 'fundamental principles',[183] which is reflected in the central position that the Finnish Parliament enjoys in the overall constitutional framework.[184] The constitutional importance of the principle of democracy is underscored by section 94(3) Finnish Constitution, which excludes EU cooperation that conflicts with the basic understanding of Finnish democracy.

1 A Normative Core of Finnish Democracy?

In the course of the Finnish constitutional reform, EU matters were assigned to the government under the control of the Finnish Parliament, instead of labelling these as

180. As recently emphasized by the Constitutional Law Committee, cf. *Commission's Draft EU Recovery Plan and MFF Planning* 13; PeVL 12/2020 vp *EIB Proposal for EU Covid-19 Guarantee Fund* (Finnish Constitutional Law Committee) 4; also described as Finnish budgetary autonomy, cf. Tuori and Raitio, 'Finland' 328.
181. Cf. Section 19 in conjunction with section 88 Finnish Constitution; Leino and Salminen, 'The Euro Crisis and Its Constitutional Consequences for Finland: Is There Room for National Politics in EU Decision-Making?' 467; Ojanen, 'The EU at the Finnish Constitutional Arena' 247.
182. *Commission's Draft EU Recovery Plan and MFF Planning* 12; Chassany, Chazan and Khan, 'Impatient Macron Pushes Merkel Hard on Eurozone Reform' 8; *On the Establishment of a European Monetary Fund* 3-4.
183. Mutanen, *Towards a Pluralistic Constitutional Understanding of State Sovereignty in the European Union? The Concept, Regulation and Constitutional Practice of Sovereignty in Finland and Certain other EU Member States* 281-282; Länsineva, 'Fundamental Principles of the Constitution of Finland' 115.
184. Leino and Salminen, 'The Euro Crisis and Its Constitutional Consequences for Finland: Is There Room for National Politics in EU Decision-Making?' 453; Ojanen, 'The EU at the Finnish Constitutional Arena' 248.

foreign affairs under the control of the Finnish President.[185] Given the continuous process of EU integration, this resulted in increasing parliamentary influence. This assignment of institutional responsibilities indicates the evolutionary potential of Finnish democracy, which evolved from being semi-presidential by the end of the twentieth century to being increasingly parliamentarian.

The highlighted evolution equally illustrates that constitutional amendments to the principle of democracy are permissible in Finland. Neither an absolute normative nor systematic limit to protect Finnish democracy against EU fiscal integration is apparent. Taken together, the conception of Finnish democracy seems to focus on the high degree of discretion that the Finnish Parliament enjoys in domestic and EU affairs,[186] as confirmed by the Constitutional Law Committee.[187] This discretion regarding the content of parliamentary decisions seemingly resulted in a focus on procedural elements, notably to ensure that parliamentary decisions are based on the correct procedure, instead of developing substantive requirements or limitations to these decisions. This procedural focus translates into a detailed constitutional framework on parliamentary rights and prerogatives vis-à-vis the EU embedded in Chapter 8 of the Finnish Constitution.

Furthermore, the previous outline of Finnish sovereignty indicates the close interconnection between Finnish sovereignty and democracy. Notably, budgetary prerogatives appear to be institutionally relevant for parliament, as noted in section 3(1) Finnish Constitution. These prerogatives are equally democratically relevant, as section 2(2) Finnish Constitution establishes that individuals have the right to influence societal developments which includes decisions on revenue and expenditure. And finally, these competences are also relevant for Finnish sovereignty, as budgetary competences are characterized as essential sovereign powers to shape the state.

2 *Implications for EU Fiscal Integration Steps*

The consequences for EU fiscal integration proposals appear to be mainly procedural in nature. As concluded, proper parliamentary participation is a key requirement to secure the functioning of Finnish parliamentary democracy. This parliamentary participation in relation to EU integration consists of different layers. First, parliamentary approval is required for the transfer of constitutionally relevant powers to the EU, as established in section 94 Finnish Constitution. Second, the Finnish Parliament can mandate Finnish representatives at EU level following section 96 Finnish Constitution. And finally, parliament enjoys a comprehensive right to receive information on the EU, as laid down in section 97 Finnish Constitution. This suggests that the principle of

185. Mutanen, *Towards a Pluralistic Constitutional Understanding of State Sovereignty in the European Union? The Concept, Regulation and Constitutional Practice of Sovereignty in Finland and Certain Other EU Member States* 285; Ojanen, 'The Europeanization of Finnish Law' 162.
186. Lavapuro, Ojanen and Scheinin, 'Rights-Based Constitutionalism in Finland and the Development of Pluralist Constitutional Review' 509.
187. Jokela, 'Finland: Towards a More Cautious Europeanization' 44.

democracy is operationalized through detailed procedural rules that safeguard parliamentary participation in EU affairs.

A violation of Finnish democracy seems to occur in case the Finnish Parliament is not properly involved in the decision-making. This considerably distinguishes the Finnish approach from, for example, the German conception of democracy, which contains a set of abstract competence areas that are declared democratically sensitive.[188] The *internal* reliance on procedural and participatory safeguards for the Finnish Parliament extends to EU level and it provides a legal framework for the assessment of whether the democratic requirements were respected. Therefore, EU fiscal integration proposals seem to be substantively compatible with the principle of Finnish democracy as long as the outlined procedural framework is followed. Obviously, this might require that EU fiscal integration is designed in light of the Finnish parliamentary participatory requirements.

III Section 94(3) Finnish Constitution: A Finnish *Eternity Clause*?

Finally, section 94(3) Finnish Constitution has to be mentioned, which requires that any form of EU cooperation has to respect the basic democratic fundaments of the Finnish constitutional order:

> An international obligation shall not endanger the democratic foundations of the Constitution.

Until now, this provision did not gain particular prominence in the constitutional debate. The Constitutional Law Committee did not conclusively position itself with regard to the normative content of this restriction.[189] This may either suggest that all forms of EU and international cooperation up to today were clearly in compliance with the democratic foundation. Or it may indicate that the provision is, in fact, not enforceable, thereby merely formulating a constitutional reminder when additional competence conferrals are considered by the Finnish Parliament. In both cases, it seems that section 94(3) Finnish Constitution is not intended to exclude certain state powers from conferral, but it is rather intended as a condition for an envisaged conferral, notably that the EU respects democratic standards and that the Finnish Parliament retains a central role in EU-related decisions.[190]

Section 94(3) Finnish Constitution was introduced into the Finnish constitutional order by the constitutional reform process in 2000. It is thus a relatively new constitutional provision, which might explain the limited constitutional attention.[191]

188. Monica Claes and Jan-Herman Reestman, 'The Protection of National Constitutional Identity and the Limits of European Integration at the Occasion of the *Gauweiler* Case' (2015) 16 German Law Journal 917, 926-927.
189. Leino and Salminen, 'The Euro Crisis and Its Constitutional Consequences for Finland: Is There Room for National Politics in EU Decision-Making?' 463; Husa, *The Constitution of Finland: A Contextual Analysis* 34.
190. Ojanen and Salminen, 'Finland: European Integration and International Human Rights Treaties as Sources of Domestic Constitutional Change and Dynamism' 373.
191. Hautamäki, 'Novel Rules in the Finnish Constitution: The Question of Applicability' 140.

Furthermore, the authoritative preparatory documents drafted during the reform process merely state that the provision was new to the Finnish Constitution, without providing information on the protected content or its function.[192] Generally speaking, one may infer from the introduction of section 94(3) Finnish Constitution an apparent shift in the constitutional focus away from sovereignty to (procedural) democracy.[193] Systematically speaking, it is interesting to observe that section 94(3) Finnish Constitution has no equivalent provision 'internally'. This means that (internal) constitutional amendments or exceptive enactments are not restricted in a comparable manner. Hence, section 94(3) Finnish Constitution is specific to EU and international cooperation. Furthermore, given that the restriction does not apply to constitutional amendments, the constitution-amending legislator could arguably alter section 94(3) Finnish Constitution following section 73 Finnish Constitution.

As it stands, the function of section 94(3) Finnish Constitution is yet to be determined. Given that the Constitutional Law Committee did not provide guidance, it is hardly predicable whether section 94(3) Finnish Constitution will function as an authoritative reminder for preserving democratic standards in supranational cooperation or whether it could develop into a substantive limitation for EU fiscal integration steps. Potentially, section 94(3) Finnish Constitution could provide a degree of rigidity to the otherwise very open and flexible Finnish constitutional approach to supranational cooperation.

IV Conclusive Appraisal: Substantive Flexibility Towards European Fiscal Integration

In conclusion, the assessment of Finnish sovereignty, democracy and section 94(3) Finnish Constitution revealed that the Finnish Parliament appears not to be limited by *substantive* obstacles when deciding on EU cooperation. Instead, the assessment revealed the adaptability and the evolutionary potential of these constitutional principles.

Overall, the connecting element between sovereignty, democracy and section 94(3) Finnish Constitution appears to be the centrality of the Finnish Parliament. In relation to sovereignty, budgetary decisions were considered an important, sovereign competence of the Finnish Parliament. In relation to democracy, the focus on procedural safeguards aims at a comprehensive involvement of the Finnish Parliament in all central budgetary decisions both at the national and EU level. And the additional protection of the Finnish Constitution's democratic fundament laid down in section 94(3) Finnish Constitution appears to underscore the importance of the Finnish

192. Ojanen and Salminen, 'Finland: European Integration and International Human Rights Treaties as Sources of Domestic Constitutional Change and Dynamism' 372-373.
193. Mutanen, *Towards a Pluralistic Constitutional Understanding of State Sovereignty in the European Union? The Concept, Regulation and Constitutional Practice of Sovereignty in Finland and Certain Other EU Member States* 306-307.

Parliament for the democratic decision-making processes. Taken together, this suggests that the effective influence of the Finnish Parliament on decisions taken in a potentially more fiscally integrated EU is of central constitutional importance to attain the required parliamentary support.

E RESULTING CONSTITUTIONAL SPACE: THE FINNISH ROAD TO EU FISCAL INTEGRATION

The Finnish constitutional system vests the Finnish Parliament with far-reaching discretion when deciding on EU cooperation. The assessment revealed that the Finnish constitutional system entails a specific procedure for the conferral of competences to EU level in section 94 Finnish Constitution, which distinguishes between the regular conferral of competences – that are deemed required for EU cooperation – as well as more significant conferrals – that impact the Finnish Constitution or Finnish sovereignty and that can only be adopted by a qualified parliamentary majority. Once competences are conferred, the Finnish Constitution awards parliament with an extensive right to receive information as well as a mandating system through which the Finnish Parliament can shape Finnish EU positions. This comprehensive procedural framework secures the central position of the Finnish Parliament in decision-making processes at both national and EU level. Furthermore, the assessment of the Finnish constitutional appraisal of the various Eurocrisis-measures illustrated the flexible Finnish approach to increased EU cooperation in budgetary and fiscal matters. This *constitutional flexibility* appears to stem from various constitutional elements.

In the first place, it stems from the general design of the Finnish constitutional system which relies heavily on parliamentary sovereignty and which does not entail explicit limits to parliamentary discretion. This wide discretion is illustrated by the 2000 constitutional reform, which altered core features of the Finnish Constitution including the system of governance, judicial review, the framework for EU and international cooperation, as well as essential constitutional principles, such as democracy and sovereignty. In light of the wide constitutional transformation, Finnish *constitutional flexibility* appears to cover all parts of the Finnish constitutional order and it appears to result from the strong reliance on the parliament as the nucleus of constitutional decision-making.

Second, the Finnish mode of constitutional review provides for additional *constitutional flexibility*. This stems from the *ex ante* review that the Committee conducts, which enables the legislator to draft EU integration steps in light of constitutional concerns rather than being *ex post* scrutinized for exceeding constitutional limits. Furthermore, as the Committee is composed of parliamentarians, its institutional approach differs from a traditional constitutional court. Notably, reflecting its institutional position, the Committee refrains from imposing substantive limits to EU integration steps. Instead, it focuses on procedural requirements and adequate involvement of the Finnish Parliament.

Consequently, Finnish *constitutional flexibility* derives from structural, conceptual, and institutional features. Although the resulting flexible constitutional approach seems to allow for EU fiscal integration steps, it should be pointed out that such integration steps could be confronted with high procedural requirements as budgetary and fiscal competences are considered important national powers protected by democracy and sovereignty.

CHAPTER 3

Macro-comparative Assessment of Germany

A GERMANY AND EU INTEGRATION

In contrast to the flexible Finnish constitutional approach, German constitutional law appears to impose strict limitations on EU fiscal integration steps despite the overall importance of EU cooperation for post-war German constitutionalism.[1] However, similar to developments in Finland, the Eurocrisis triggered intense domestic debates on the EU's future. Concerning the various Eurocrisis-measures, the dominant German political view was that financial support had to be tied to strict (austerity) conditionality.[2] This translated into a reluctance to confer additional fiscal competences to the EU. At the same time, the initial political hesitation appears to slowly soften, as demonstrated by the adoption of NGEU.[3]

The political resistance against EU fiscal integration was echoed by the German Federal Constitutional Court,[4] guardian of the German Constitution[5] and the infamous

1. Angelika Scheuer and Hermann Schmitt, 'Sources of EU Support: The Case of Germany' (2009) 18 German Politics 577, 578; Stephen Wood, 'Germany and the Eastern Enlargement of the EU: Political Elites, Public Opinion and Democratic Processes' (2002) 24 Journal of European Integration 23, 29-30.
2. Federico Fabbrini, 'Austerity, the European Council, and the Institutional Future of the European Union: A Proposal to Strengthen the Presidency of the European Council' (2015) 22 Indiana Journal of Global Legal Studies 269, 271, 278-281.
3. Which is based on a Franco-German proposal: Cf. as well: Christina Großner and Sarah Lawton, 'Merkel and Macron Roll Out €500 Billion COVID-19 Recovery Initiative' *EURACTIV* (Schiphol 19 May 2020), https://www.euractiv.com/section/economy-jobs/news/merkel-and-macron-roll-out-e500-billion-covid-19-recovery-initiative/, accessed 5 April 2023; Bojan Pancevski and Laurence Norman, 'France, Germany Propose €500 Billion EU Pandemic Recovery Fund' *The Wall Street Journal* (New York City 18 May 2020), https://www.wsj.com/articles/france-germany-propose-500-billion-eu-pandemic-recovery-fund-11589826351, accessed 5 April 2023.
4. In German: *Bundesverfassungsgericht.*

barking dog that never bites.[6] This metaphor describes the constitutional jurisprudence of the past four decades when the German Court established rigid abstract limits against EU integration without annulling any concrete EU measure.[7] The Court's latest jurisprudence suggests that this barking dog is becoming a biting one as it declared the ECB's PSP-Programme and the *Weiß*-judgment *ultra vires,*[8] the first ever explicit German *ultra vires* finding. Although the German Court equally illustrated how to escape incompatibility with the German Constitution, the PSP-Programme judgment may well signal a judicial readiness to actively challenge EU law. In all cases, it seems likely that the Court will closely scrutinize any future EU fiscal integration steps. While this readiness to enforce existing limits is novel, the constitutional limits themselves are not. The German Constitutional Court clearly displayed its concerns towards EU fiscal and budgetary integration during the Eurocrisis.[9] Although it ultimately accepted all adopted measures, the Court defined substantive, competence-based limits in its *constitutional identity* review. In this case law, the *eternity clause* enshrined in Article 79(3) GG[10] emerged as the pivotal constitutional reference point for EU (fiscal) integration ambitions.[11] The increasing use of the *eternity clause* has significant practical implications, as every element that the Constitutional Court subsumes under Article 79(3) GG is excluded from constitutional amendment[12] and EU fiscal integration reforms might thus be heading into a German constitutional dead-end. In light of these serious German constitutional obstacles, this Chapter investigates the apparent rigidity of the German constitutional approach towards EU fiscal integration proposals. It thereby not only charts existing constitutional limits but also explores whether

5. Mehrdad Payandeh, 'Constitutional Review of EU Law After Honeywell: Contextualizing the Relationship Between the German Constitutional Court and the EU Court of Justice' (2011) 48 Common Market Law Review 9, 15.
6. Joseph H. H. Weiler, 'The "Lisbon Urteil" and the Fast Food Culture' (2009) 20 The European Journal of International Law 505, 505.
7. In chronological order: *Solange I-Decision*; 2 BvR 197/83 *Solange II-Decision* (German Federal Constitutional Court); 2 BvR 2134/92 and 2159/92 *Maastricht-Judgment* (German Federal Constitutional Court); *Lisbon-judgment*; *Honeywell Judgment*; 2 BvR 2728/13, 2 BvR 2729/13, 2 BvR 2730/13, 2 BvR 2731/13, 2 BvE 13/13 *OMT-Reference* (German Federal Constitutional Court); *Final OMT-Judgment*; *Quantitative Easing (PSPP) Reference.*
8. *Quantitative Easing (PSPP) Final Judgment* paras 163, 178.
9. 2 BvR 987/10, 2 BvR 1485/10, 2 BvR 1099/10 *Financial Support for Greece and EFSF* (German Federal Constitutional Court) (issued in September 2011); 2 BvE 8/11 *Participation of Members of German Parliament in the EFSF* (German Federal Constitutional Court) (February 2012); 2 BvE 4/11 *Right to Participation for German Parliament at the Occasion of ESM-Treaty and Euro-Plus-Pact* (German Federal Constitutional Court) (issued in June 2012); 2 BvR 1390, 1421, 1438, 1439, 1440/12, 2 BvE 6/12 *ESM-Treaty and Fiscal Compact (interim relief)* (German Federal Constitutional Court) (issued in July 2012); *OMT-Reference* (issued in January 2014); 2 BvR 1390, 1421, 1438, 1439, 1440/12, 2 BvE 6/12 *ESM-Treaty and Fiscal Compact* (German Federal Constitutional Court) (issued in March 2014); *Final OMT-Judgment* (June 2016); *Quantitative Easing (PSPP) Reference* (issued in July 2017); *Quantitative Easing (PSPP) Final Judgment* (issued in May 2020).
10. The abbreviation GG stands for *Grundgesetz* (Basic Law) and will be used in the following.
11. Christoph Ohler, 'Rechtliche Maßstäbe der Geldpolitik nach dem Gauweiler-Urteil des EuGH' (2015) 34 Neue Zeitschrift für Verwaltungsrecht (NVwZ) 1001, 1002.
12. Jaques Ziller, 'The German Constitutional Court's Friendliness Towards European Law: On the Judgment of *Bundesverfassungsgericht* over the Ratification of the Treaty of Lisbon' (2010) 16 European Public Law 53, 68.

additional flexible constitutional space exists, or may be created, under the current German Constitution.

Following the previous structure, the analysis of the German constitutional approach first outlines the relevant components of the German constitutional system (B). Subsequently, the applicable procedural-institutional framework (C) and the substantive framework for EU fiscal integration are evaluated (D). It is followed by a conclusive overview of the resulting constitutional space under the German Constitution (E). In the final step, the charted constitutional space is deconstructed through *constitutional flexibility* (F).

B SETTING THE STAGE: EU MEMBERSHIP AND THE GERMAN CONSTITUTION

Different to the Finnish constitutional order, which had to incorporate an existing and advanced body of supranational law, German constitutional law evolved alongside the process of EU integration.[13] To understand the impact of EU integration on the German Constitution, the origins of the current constitutional text are outlined (I), before considering the authoritative German Federal Constitutional Court (II).

I Origin of the German Constitution and Its EU Features

The German Constitution was adopted in 1949. Confronted with the horrors of the *Hitler*-dictatorship that emerged under the *Weimar Constitution*, the drafters of the *Grundgesetz* designed a resilient constitutional system based on irreversible constitutional values and devoted to peaceful European cooperation. Hence, the commitment to a unified Europe in the preamble and the initial possibility to confer state powers to the supranational level established in Article 24 GG as well as the prominent commitment to human dignity in Article 1 GG, the following catalogue of fundamental rights in Articles 2-19 GG and the *eternity clause* can be understood as direct reactions to these historic experiences. Specifically, the latter is devised as a constitutional shield against constitutional abuses of the constituted state institutions.[14] This resilient constitutional design is paired with a central constitutional authority that supervises all state action, the German Federal Constitutional Court.[15] The constitutional design and creation of an authoritative constitutional court are historically rooted design choices. Throughout the process of EU integration, both elements became more relevant. For example,

13. For example, with the ratification of the Maastricht Treaty when Article 23 GG was introduced, cf. Claudio Franzius, '70 Jahre Grundgesetz und Europa: Passt das zusammen?' (2019) 54 Europarecht (EuR) 365, 366-367.
14. Ohler, 'Rechtliche Maßstäbe der Geldpolitik nach dem Gauweiler-Urteil des EuGH' 1002.
15. Michaela Hailbronner and Stefan Martini, 'The German Federal Constitutional Court' in András Jakab, Arthur Dyevre and Giulo Itzcovich (eds), *Comparative Constitutional Reasoning* (Cambridge University Press 2017) 356-359.

although the *eternity clause* was originally drafted as an *internal* constitutional safeguard, it is increasingly applied to EU integration.[16]

As EU cooperation intensified, the constitution-amending legislator introduced a specific EU clause when adopting the Maastricht Treaty in Article 23 GG thereby creating a specific framework for EU cooperation. The provision allows for the conferral of competences in Article 23(1)(2) GG,[17] by yet recalling the applicability of the *eternity clause*.[18] Therefore, Article 23 GG functions as the framework for and the limit to German EU membership.[19] The then newly introduced provision complemented the previous constitutional framework, which consisted of a firm commitment to European cooperation in the preamble and Article 24 GG. Today, the Constitutional Court employs all these provisions to construe the general openness of the German Constitution towards EU integration.

II The German Constitutional Court

The constitution establishes the German Constitutional Court as an independent, centralized judicial authority in charge of constitutional review. Its judgments are binding on all state institutions,[20] and through its interpretation of the *eternity clause*, it can identify matters that are located outside the mandate of the constitution-amending legislator.[21] Its authority is historically rooted and unique from a comparative angle.[22] Article 93 GG assigns to the *Bundesverfassungsgericht* the exclusive power to supervise the constitutionality of legislative and other public acts,[23] the competence

16. Rademacher, 'Die "Verfassungsidentität" als Grenze der Kompetenzübertragung auf die Europäische Union?' 147; Franz C. Mayer, 'Rashomon in Karlsruhe: A Reflection on Democracy and Identity in the European Union' (2011) 9 International Journal of Constitutional Law 757, 780-782.
17. Note the explicit wording which indicates a dynamic process, rather than a mere participation in a static supranational organization, cf. 'Art. 23 (1) (1): With a view to establishing a united Europe, the Federal Republic of Germany shall participate in the development of the European Union (...).'
18. In Article 23(1)(3) GG; cf. *OMT-Reference* paras 27-29; Calliess, '70 Jahre Grundgesetz und europäische Integration: "Take Back Control" oder "Mehr Demokratie wagen"?' 685.
19. Thiele, 'Die Integrationsidentität des Art. 23 Abs. 1 GG als (einzige) Grenze des Vorrangs des Europarechts' 371.
20. As stipulated in § 31 BVerfGG, decisions of the Constitutional Court are binding for all state actors and decisions on the constitutionality of legislative acts have the force of law, cf. Klaus Schlaich and Stefan Korioth, *Das Bundesverfassungsgericht – Stellung Verfahren, Entscheidungen* (11th edn, C.H. Beck 2018) paras 495-496; Helmut Philipp Aust and Florian Meinel, 'Entscheidungsmöglichkeiten des BVerfG – Tenor, Systematik und Wirkungen' (2014) 54 Juristische Schulung (JuS) 25, 26.
21. Rademacher, 'Die "Verfassungsidentität" als Grenze der Kompetenzübertragung auf die Europäische Union?' 147; Schwerdtfeger, 'Europäisches Unionsrecht in der Rechtsprechung des Bundesverfassungsgerichts: Grundrechts-, ultra-vires- und Identitätskontrolle im gewaltenteiligen Mehrebenensystem' 293-294, 307.
22. In comparison, the German Federal Constitutional Court is one of the most powerful constitutional courts globally, cf. Georg Vanberg, *The Politics of Constitutional Review in Germany* (Cambridge University Press 2005) 17.
23. As established by the Court based on Article 100 GG, cf. 1 BvL 13/52, 1 BvL 21/53 *Law on Direct (Financial) Support* (German Federal Constitutional Court) para. 33.

to adopt binding decisions on the interpretation of constitutional provisions[24] as well as the power to settle constitutional disputes between institutions.[25]

The 16 judges serving in the Court's two senates are independent.[26] This underscores the judicial nature of the Court, which adjudicates on the basis of constitutional law.[27] The judges are appointed in equal parts by Bundestag and Bundesrat. Candidates have to have the qualification to work as a judge[28] and their appointment has to be confirmed by a two-thirds majority. These requirements ensure that the appointed judges are both qualified and enjoy support beyond a specific political party.[29] Taken together, this illustrates the authoritative and important position the German Constitutional Court occupies under the current constitutional text, which also extends to EU cooperation. Through its constitutional review,[30] the Court determines the relationship between the German and the EU constitutional order, with clear implications for the feasibility of EU fiscal integration.[31]

C PROCEDURAL AND INSTITUTIONAL FRAMEWORK FOR EU COOPERATION

Article 23 GG is the central German provision for EU cooperation, as visualized in Figure 3.1. It prescribes parliamentary approval for the transfer of competences, establishes a right to receive information, and enables both institutions to participate in the exercise of conferred powers. Furthermore, Article 23(3)(3) and (7) GG empower the German legislator to regulate the institutional interaction between parliament and government, now laid down in the Law on the cooperation of the German Government and the German Parliament in matters of the European Union (EUZBBG), as well as the regional and the federal state levels, now laid down in the Law on the cooperation of the federal level and the regional level in matters of the European Union (EUZBLG).[32]

24. As specified in § 31 BVerfGG (Law on the Bundesverfassungsgericht), cf. Rademacher, 'Die "Verfassungsidentität" als Grenze der Kompetenzübertragung auf die Europäische Union?' 144.
25. Cf. the different proceedings listed in Article 93 GG; for an overview, cf. Schlaich and Korioth, *Das Bundesverfassungsgericht – Stellung Verfahren, Entscheidungen* para. 9.
26. Article 97(1) GG and further specified in § 1(1) BVerfGG.
27. The *Bundesverfassungsgericht* pointed out itself that it was not conducting politics, cf. 2 BvF 1/73 *Treaty concerning the Basis of Relations Between the Federal Republic of Germany and the German Democratic Republic* (German Federal Constitutional Court) para. 75; cf. as well: Hailbronner and Martini, 'The German Federal Constitutional Court' 357-358.
28. Following § 2(3) BVerfGG at these courts; additionally, they have to poses the qualification to become a judge under German labour law, following § 3(2) BVerfGG, cf. Schlaich and Korioth, *Das Bundesverfassungsgericht – Stellung Verfahren, Entscheidungen* para. 41.
29. Hailbronner and Martini, 'The German Federal Constitutional Court' 365-366.
30. For an overview: Schwerdtfeger, 'Europäisches Unionsrecht in der Rechtsprechung des Bundesverfassungsgerichts: Grundrechts-, ultra-vires- und Identitätskontrolle im gewaltenteiligen Mehrebenensystem' 292-293.
31. Stefan Pilz, 'Ein Schatzamt für die Eurozone? – Überlegungen zu den Vorschlägen des Europäischen Parlaments und der Kommission zu einer Reform der Wirtschaftsunion' (2017) 28 Europäische Zeitschrift für Wirtschaftsrecht (EuZW) 637, 644.
32. Timm Beichelt, 'Recovering Space Lost? The German Bundestag's New Potential in European Politics' (2012) 21 German Politics 143, 145.

In the subsequent assessment, the constitutional framework for the conferral of competences to the EU (I) and the involvement of the German Parliament (II) as well as the Federal Council (III) in the exercise of conferred competences are analysed. Finally, the procedural requirements for initiating constitutional review are assessed (IV).

Figure 3.1 Different Components of German EU Membership Clause

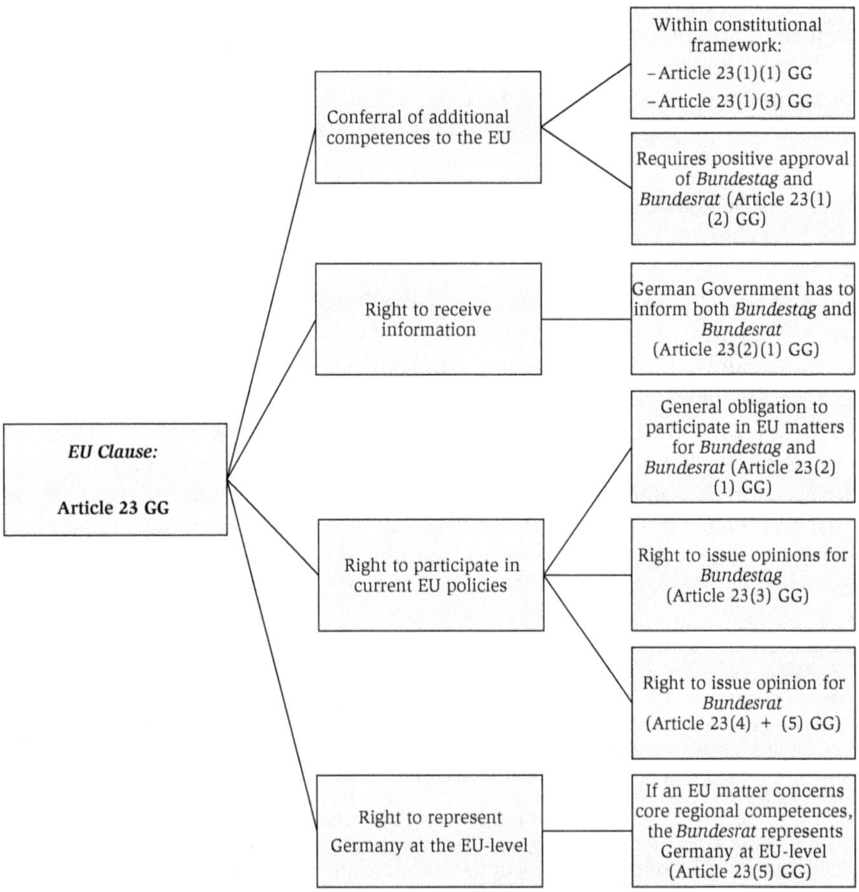

I Conferral of Additional Competences to the EU under Article 23 GG

Article 23(1)(2) GG permits the conferral of competences to the EU.[33] Following the jurisprudence of the Constitutional Court, a conferral of powers is given in case of

33. Wolff Heintschel von Heinegg and Robert Frau, 'Art. 23 GG – Mitwirkung bei Entwicklung der EU' in Volker Epping and Christian Hillgruber (eds), *Beck Online Kommentar zum Grundgesetz*

explicit Treaty amendments,[34] in case EU voting requirements are altered,[35] or in case the EU's flexibility clause in Article 352 TFEU is employed.[36] In all three instances, the German legislator enjoys a so-called *parliamentary reservation*,[37] which prescribes parliamentary approval. This conferral of competences is restricted in two regards.

First, EU cooperation must comply with the requirements established in Article 23(1)(1) GG. Notably, Germany can only participate in supranational cooperation in case the EU complies with core structural requirements, including democracy and the rule of law, which correspond to the EU's foundational values. Hence, the legislator has to establish that the EU conforms to these requirements. However, in contrast to the *eternity clause*, Article 23(1)(1) GG does not formulate absolute limits, but it sketches a general framework for EU cooperation[38] and aims to steer integration towards compliance with core German constitutional values.[39]

Second, Article 23(1)(3) GG clarifies that the internally applicable procedural requirements for constitutional amendments apply to EU integration steps. According to Article 79(2) GG, constitutional amendments require approval by a two-thirds majority in parliament and federal council. Article 79(3) GG precludes amendments to the core constitutional values. By referencing these provisions, Article 23(1)(3) GG clarifies that the internally applicable constitutional framework extends to the EU. Hence, Article 23(1)(3) GG prescribes a two-thirds majority for all EU conferrals that directly or indirectly alter the German Constitution.[40] A constitution-amending majority was, for example, deemed necessary for adopting the ESM and the Fiscal Compact,[41]

(45th edn, C.H. Beck 2020) paras 21-23; Rupert Scholz, 'Art. 23 GG' in Theodor Maunz and Günter Düring (eds), *Grundgesetz-Kommentar* (92nd edn, C.H. Beck 2020) paras 61-64.

34. In the sense of Article 48(1)-(6) TEU; as the Bundesverfassungsgericht clarified, a textual modification of EU primary law always requires approval under Article 23(1)(2) GG, cf. *Lisbon-judgment* para. 243.
35. *Ibid.*, para. 316; cf. as well: Scholz, 'Art. 23 GG' para. 149.
36. *Lisbon-judgment* para. 328.
37. In German: *Parlaments- oder Gesetzesvorbehalt*; then, the approval of the legislator is constitutive, cf. Scholz, 'Art. 23 GG' para. 152.
38. Note the distinction between 'integration goal' in Article 23(1)(1) GG and 'integration limits' in Article 23(1)(3) GG, cf. Calliess, '70 Jahre Grundgesetz und europäische Integration: "Take Back Control" oder "Mehr Demokratie wagen"?' 685-686.
39. Scholz, 'Art. 23 GG' paras 70-71; Calliess, '70 Jahre Grundgesetz und europäische Integration: "Take Back Control" oder "Mehr Demokratie wagen"?' 686.
40. Wissenschaftliche Dienste des Deutschen Bundestages, *Zum Erfordernis eines qualifizierten Mehrheitsbeschlusses des Bundestages hinsichtlich des Zustimmungsgesetzes zum Eigenmittelbeschluss der EU (WD 4 – 3000 – 055/20)* (German Parliament 2020) 5; Ralph Alexander Lorz and Heiko Sauer, 'Verfassungsändernde Mehrheiten für die Stabilisierung des Euro?: Mehrheitserfordernisse bei der Zustimmung zum Fiskalpakt, zum ESM-Vertrag und zur Änderung des AEUV' (2012) 47 Europarecht (EuR) 682, 685.
41. *Right to Participation for German Parliament at the Occasion of ESM-Treaty and Euro-Plus-Pact* paras 135-137; cf. as well: Matthias Ruffert, 'Europarecht für die nächste Generation: Zum Projekt Next Generation EU' (2020) 39 Neue Zeitschrift für Verwaltungsrecht (NVwZ) 1777, 1779; Lena Ketterer, *Zustimmungserfordernis beim Europäischen Stabilitätsmechanismus* (Freiburger Rechtswissenschaftliche Abhandlungen, Mohr Siebeck 2016) 359.

given the instruments' implications on constitutionally enshrined parliamentary prerogatives and their effect on *overall budgetary responsibility*.[42] Less far-reaching EU commitments can be approved by a simple majority.

Overall, Article 23(1)(2) GG empowers the German legislator to confer competences to the EU. This conferral has to comply with the structural requirements in Article 23(1)(1) GG and the procedural requirements in Article 23(1)(3). Therefore, EU fiscal integration steps that involve the conferral of additional competences to the EU will have to be approved by the German legislator. The core question is which parliamentary majority requirements would apply. In light of the constitutional experiences during the Eurocrisis,[43] it seems possible that a qualified two-thirds majority will be required to approve EU fiscal integration steps in particular in light of the implications of EU fiscal integration steps for the budgetary prerogatives of parliament.[44] It should also be highlighted that the German Constitutional Court clarified that the decision on the applicable constitutional majority-requirement can be challenged by individuals.[45] It underscores the constitutional importance of the legislator's decision regarding the applicable majority-threshold for the adoption of EU commitments and makes it nearly certain that any choice for a simple majority would be challenged in front of the German Constitutional Court. Finally, the conferral of competences to the EU presupposes compatibility with the *eternity clause*.

II Participation of Parliament in the Exercise of Conferred Powers

Following Article 23(2)(1) GG, the German *Bundestag* participates in EU matters. This includes a general right to be informed by the government on EU developments, as established in Article 23(2)(2) GG.[46] The information has to be

42. Ariane Richter, *Funktionswandel im Mehrebenensystem? Die Rolle der nationalen Parlamente in der Europäischen Union am Beispiel des Deutschen Bundestags* (Herbert Utz Verlag 2016) 176; Ketterer, *Zustimmungserfordernis beim Europäischen Stabilitätsmechanismus* 6, 277.
43. Ketterer, *Zustimmungserfordernis beim Europäischen Stabilitätsmechanismus* 359; Parliamentary Fraction of CDU/CSU und FDP, *Drucksache 17/9046: Gesetzentwurf der Fraktionen der CDU/CSU und FDP: Entwurf eines Gesetzes zu dem Vertrag vom 2. März 2012 über Stabilität, Koordinierung und Steuerung in der Wirtschafts- und Währungsunion* (German Parliament 2012).
44. Ruffert, 'Europarecht für die nächste Generation: Zum Projekt Next Generation EU' 1779; in particular, in case the proposed act impacts 'democratic self-determination' and entails a high degree of EU-control, cf. Frank Schorkopf, 'Die Europäische Union auf dem Weg zur Fiskalunion – Integrationsfortschritt durch den Rechtsrahmen des Sonderhaushalts "Next Generation EU"' (2020) 73 Neue Juristische Wochenschrift (NJW) 3085, 3089.
45. 2 BvR 739/17 *Decision on the Unified Patent Court* (German Federal Constitutional Court) paras 95-99; cf. as well: Ruffert, 'Europarecht für die nächste Generation: Zum Projekt Next Generation EU' 1779; Schorkopf, 'Die Europäische Union auf dem Weg zur Fiskalunion – Integrationsfortschritt durch den Rechtsrahmen des Sonderhaushalts "Next Generation EU"' 3089.
46. As emphasized by the *Bundesverfassungsgericht* 'matters of the EU' indicate that also decisions with close link to the EU are covered, cf. *ESM-Treaty and Fiscal Compact (interim relief)* para. 182; *Right to Participation for German Parliament at the Occasion of ESM-Treaty and Euro-Plus-Pact* paras 101-104; on the obligation of the German Government to inform parliament, cf. Jörg-Uwe Hahn, 'Die Mitwirkungsrechte von Bundestag und Bundesrat in EU-Angelegenheiten nach dem neuen Integrationsverantwortungsgesetz' (2009) 20 Europäische Zeitschrift für Wirtschaftsrecht (EuZW) 758, 762.

comprehensive[47] and transmitted at the earliest possible moment.[48] Once parliament is informed, an internal parliamentary decision-making process follows, which may result in the issuing of a parliamentary position (Article 23(3) GG). Given the parliamentary workload and the required expertise, decisions are prepared in specialized committees, including the Committee for EU Affairs (hereafter: EU Committee).[49] After an initial screening process supported by a specialized unit of the legal service,[50] the chairman of the EU Committee recommends to the president of the Bundestag the referral to a lead-committee. This committee issues a voting recommendation to the plenary of the Bundestag[51] but it is the plenary that takes the final decision.[52] Although Article 45(2) GG in conjunction with § 93b (2) Rules of Procedure of the German Parliament (GO-BT) allows to delegate power to issue parliamentary positions to the EU Committee, this possibility has never been employed.[53]

Subsequently, the parliamentary view on the envisaged EU legislation is communicated to the government. The wording of Article 23(3) GG reveals that the government is not legally bound by the position,[54] but has to thoroughly consider it.[55] Hence, the position can affect the final governmental view given the political interdependency of government and parliament.

III The Involvement of the German Federal Council

Given Germany's federal structure, the federal *Länder* exercise a central role in constitutional decision-making through the federal council. Article 23 GG extends the federal council's internal prerogatives to EU decisions. It entails a comprehensive right to be informed on EU developments as well as the federal council's participation in EU

47. The Bundesverfassungsgericht adopts a wide definition of the obligation to 'inform', cf. examples provided *Right to Participation for German Parliament at the Occasion of ESM-Treaty and Euro-Plus-Pact* paras 118-124; yet, some executive discretion is preserved, cf. Scholz, 'Art. 23 GG' para. 157.
48. Which is why Article 45(2) and (3) GG allows for a delegation of EU matters to the specialized parliamentary committee, cf. Heintschel von Heinegg and Frau, 'Art. 24 GG – Kollektives Sicherheitssystem' paras 1, 6, 14; Scholz, 'Art. 23 GG' paras 156-157; Scholz, 'Art. 45 GG' para. 8.
49. Article 45 GG was included in the *Grundgesetz* together with the EU enabling clause in Article 23 GG, cf. Heintschel von Heinegg and Frau, 'Art. 24 GG – Kollektives Sicherheitssystem' para. 1; Scholz, 'Art. 45 GG' para. 1.
50. Beichelt, 'Recovering Space Lost? The German Bundestag's New Potential in European Politics' 148.
51. Following Article 93 GO-BT.
52. Conceptually different to the situation in Finland where all matters are decided in specialized committees, cf. Auel and Raunio, 'Debating the State of the Union? Comparing Parliamentary Debates on EU Issues in Finland, France, Germany and the United Kingdom' 19.
53. Against the original intention of the constitution-amending legislator, cf. Heintschel von Heinegg and Frau, 'Art. 24 GG – Kollektives Sicherheitssystem' para. 1; Scholz, 'Art. 45 GG' para. 3.
54. Article 23(3) GG states that the government has to 'take into account' the parliamentary position.
55. Martin Nettesheim, 'Die Integrationsverantwortung: Vorgaben des BVerfG und gesetzgeberische Umsetzung' (2010) 63 Neue Juristische Wochenschrift (NJW) 177, 181.

decisions that would have required its involvement internally.[56] Furthermore, it can issue positions on EU matters that impact its interests, as established in Article 23(5) GG. These positions can be adopted by the Europe-Committee, which is empowered to take decisions on behalf of the entire institution to ensure speedy decision-making.[57] The legal effect of these positions depends on the nature of the affected competences. In case the envisaged EU act alters either exclusive federal competences or concurring federal competences,[58] the federal council's position is non-binding. However, in case the envisaged EU act mainly affects the exclusive competences of the *Länder*, the establishment of *Länder* institutions or their administrative procedures, the forwarded position is generally binding for the German EU vote.[59] Finally, in case EU matters fall within the exclusive competences of the *Länder*, Germany is represented by a member of the *Bundesrat* in the EU Council of Ministers.[60] This central involvement mirrors the internal responsibility for these policy areas and underscores the constitutional importance of federalism.

IV Constitutional Oversight: Proceedings Before the *Bundesverfassungsgericht*

Once competences are conferred, the conferral can be challenged before the *Bundesverfassungsgericht*. Any constitutional challenge has to be admissible, as the German Court cannot proceed *ex officio*.[61] EU acts are mainly challenged by either individuals through constitutional complaints[62] or institutional actors through inter-institutional proceedings.[63]

1 Individuals Initiating Constitutional Proceedings

The constitutional complaint[64] is the most used procedure to challenge EU integration measures before the *Bundesverfassungsgericht*. Its frequent use is encouraged by the

56. For example, the *Länder* enjoy prerogatives in the legislative process, cf. Konrad Hesse, *Grundzüge des Verfassungsrechts der Bundesrepublik Deutschland* (C.F. Müller 1993) paras 510-519.
57. Patrick Melin, 'Die Rolle der deutschen Bundesländer im Europäischen Rechtsetzungsverfahren nach Lissabon' (2011) 46 Europarecht (EuR) 655, 680.
58. Thomas Würtenberger and Eugen Kunz, 'Die Mitwirkung der Bundesländer in Angelegenheiten der Europäischen Union' (2010) 42 Juristische Arbeitsblätter (JA) 406, 408-409.
59. Melin, 'Die Rolle der deutschen Bundesländer im Europäischen Rechtsetzungsverfahren nach Lissabon' 658-659.
60. Wiland Tresselt, *Die Vertreter der Länder im Rat der Europäischen Gemeinschaft* (Books on Demand (BoD) 2006) 205.
61. Following § 23(1) BVerfGG, the *Bundesverfassungsgericht* proceeds upon an application, cf. Schlaich and Korioth, *Das Bundesverfassungsgericht – Stellung Verfahren, Entscheidungen* para. 58.
62. In German: *Verfassungsbeschwerde*.
63. In German: *Organstreitverfahren*.
64. Article 93(1) no. (4a) GG and further specified by ordinary statute in §§ 13 no. (8a), 90 ff. BVerfGG.

Maastricht-judgment, where the Court established that EU measures could be challenged based on the individual's right to vote.[65] The complaint offers legal protection against public acts that infringe on the applicant's individual, fundamental or equivalent rights.[66] Therefore, the Court examines the individual's legal interest in the complaint (*subjective gravamen*),[67] which reflects the legislator's choice not to include a means to proceed in the public interest. Instead, individuals have to demonstrate that their subjective constitutional rights are violated by a public act, as abstract constitutional review is reserved for privileged institutional actors.[68]

a *Possible Violation of Individual Constitutional Rights*

Individuals have to substantiate how the challenged act violates their constitutional rights (subjective gravamen). This requires that applicants demonstrate that the alleged violation personally, immediately and directly affects them in their constitutional rights.[69] Personal concern is given in case the challenged measure is capable of directly affecting the applicants in their constitutional rights.[70] The violation is immediate if it has an on-going effect on the applicants' rights and is therefore not merely hypothetically possible;[71] or, for future violations, in case these seem serious and difficult to reverse.[72] Finally, applicants are directly affected whenever the challenged measure does not require further implementation.[73] As recognized by the *Bundesverfassungsgericht*, these conditions ensure that constitutional complaints can only be initiated in case the applicant has a genuine, subjective legal interest[74] and they prevent the initiation of an *actio popularis*.

65. Alexander Thiele, 'Friendly or Unfriendly Act? The "Historic" Referral of the Constitutional Court to the ECJ Regarding the ECB's OMT Program' (2014) 15 German Law Journal 241, 251-253.
66. Tomuschat, 'Lisbon: Terminal of the European Integration Process? The Judgment of the German Constitutional Court of 30 June 2009' 266.
67. Klaus Ferdinand Gärditz, 'Beyond Symbolism: Towards a Constitutional Actio Popularis in EU Affairs? A Commentary on the OMT Decision of the Federal Constitutional Court' (2014) 15 German Law Journal 183, 186.
68. 1 BvR 213/08 *Copyright-Law Amendment I* (German Federal Constitutional Court) para. 52; cf. as well: Oliver Klein and Christoph Sennekamp, 'Aktuelle Zulässigkeitsprobleme der Verfassungsbeschwerde' (2007) 60 Neue Juristische Wochenschrift (NJW) 945, 949.
69. 1 BvR 1509/91 *Interest-Rate Adjustment for Mortgage Awarded by the GDR* (German Federal Constitutional Court) para. 93; 1 BvR 602/78 *Non-Contributory Health Insurance* (German Federal Constitutional Court) para. 36; 1 BvR 385/77 *Nuclear Plant Mülheim-Kärlich* (German Federal Constitutional Court) para. 35; cf. as well: Schlaich and Korioth, *Das Bundesverfassungsgericht – Stellung Verfahren, Entscheidungen* para. 215.
70. 1 BvR 539/96 *Casino-Regulation of the German Region of Baden-Württemberg* (German Federal Constitutional Court) para. 48; *Non-Contributory Health Insurance* para. 38; cf. as well: Volker Epping, *Grundrechte* (6th edn, Springer Verlag 2015) para. 183.
71. *Casino-Regulation of the German Region of Baden-Württemberg* para. 48; 1 BvR 220/51 *Survivor's Pension I* (German Federal Constitutional Court) paras 27-29.
72. *Casino-Regulation of the German Region of Baden-Württemberg* para. 48; Schlaich and Korioth, *Das Bundesverfassungsgericht – Stellung Verfahren, Entscheidungen* para. 234.
73. 2 BvR 2292/13 *Vereinten Dienstleistungsgewerkschaft (ver.di)* (German Federal Constitutional Court) para. 64; *Casino-Regulation of the German Region of Baden-Württemberg* para. 48.
74. *Survivor's Pension I* paras 26-27; cf. as well: Schlaich and Korioth, *Das Bundesverfassungsgericht – Stellung Verfahren, Entscheidungen* paras 215, 217.

b Application of Subjective Gravamen in EU Matters

The case law reveals that the German Court applies subjective gravamen differently when adjudicating on EU-related matters compared with internal German cases. Notably, individuals can proceed against EU acts based on their right to vote, enshrined in Article 38(1) GG.[75] According to the Court, Article 38(1) GG entails the subjective right to participate in German parliamentary elections.[76] By participating, individuals legitimize the exercise of power by the *Bundestag*. This presupposes that the *Bundestag* is able to take political decisions.[77] Together, this constitutes the core of the right to vote which is protected as part of German democracy, enshrined in Article 20(1) and (2) GG, and rooted in human dignity, enshrined in Article 1(1) GG. According to this jurisprudence, the conferral of competences to the EU could potentially undermine this democratic bond, in case either important political decisions can no longer be taken by the German Parliament or in case EU institutions exercise competences not conferred upon them.[78] In both cases, the individual's right to elect a functioning representation is at risk.[79] The Court initially established in its *Maastricht*-judgment that Article 38(1) GG precluded the conferral of constitutional prerogatives to EU level in conflict with the basic democratic requirements formulated in Article 20(1) and (2) GG, protected by the *eternity clause*.[80] Notably, this entailed the view of the Court that individuals elect a German Parliament that remains in charge of central, substantial policy decisions.[81] This constitutional interpretation was consolidated in the *Lisbon*-judgment[82] and subsequently refined in relation to Eurocrisis-measures, where the Court established that compliance with *overall budgetary responsibility* could be challenged by individuals based on Article 38(1) GG.[83]

75. Schwerdtfeger, 'Europäisches Unionsrecht in der Rechtsprechung des Bundesverfassungsgerichts: Grundrechts-, ultra-vires- und Identitätskontrolle im gewaltenteiligen Mehrebenensystem' 304-305.
76. *Lisbon-judgment* para. 174; *Maastricht-Judgment* para. 61.
77. Martin Nettesheim, 'Verfassungsrecht und Politik in der Staatsschuldenkrise' (2012) 65 Neue Juristische Wochenschrift (NJW) 1409, 1412; Jan-Herman Reestman and Leonard F. M. Besselink, 'Editorial: On the Lissabon-Urteil: Democracy and a Democratic Paradox' (2009) 5 European Constitutional Law Review 341, 341.
78. *Quantitative Easing (PSPP) Final Judgment* para. 113; *OMT-Reference* para. 19; *Maastricht-Judgment* paras 61-62.
79. Which would violate German 'political self-determination', cf. *Final OMT-Judgment* para. 81; *OMT-Reference* para. 52; *Financial Support for Greece and EFSF* para. 98.
80. *Maastricht-Judgment* paras 61-63; cf. as well: Martin Nettesheim, '"Euro-Rettung" und Grundgesetz: Verfassungsgerichtliche Vorgaben für den Umbau der Währungsunion' (2011) 46 Europarecht (EuR) 765, 768-769.
81. Tomuschat, 'Lisbon: Terminal of the European Integration Process? The Judgment of the German Constitutional Court of 30 June 2009' 264.
82. Jürgen Schwarze, 'Die verordnete Demokratie: Zum Urteil des 2. Senats des BVerfG zum Lissabon-Vertrag' (2010) 45 Europarecht (EuR) 108, 114.
83. *Quantitative Easing (PSPP) Final Judgment* paras 102-104; cf. as well: Nettesheim, '"Euro-Rettung" und Grundgesetz: Verfassungsgerichtliche Vorgaben für den Umbau der Währungsunion' 770.

Based on Article 38(1) GG, private applicants can claim that EU integration measures impact parliamentary powers in an unconstitutional way.[84] Applicants then challenge the German act of approval and the accompanying national legislation. In the alternative, applicants may claim that German institutions did not take sufficient steps against alleged EU *ultra vires* acts.[85] In that case, applicants challenge an omission of the competent German institutions.[86] Overall, this enables individuals to challenge EU primary and secondary law based on their right to vote, which would extend to further EU fiscal integration steps as apparent from, *inter alia*, the NGEU-, PSP-Programme- and Outright Monetary Transactions Programme (OMT)-proceedings.

c Emerging Constitutional Double Standard

The following comparison between the internal interpretation and the EU-related interpretation of *subjective gravamen* departs from the assumption that legal systems should apply a consistent interpretation.[87] This generates predictability, minimizes arbitrariness, and contributes to legal certainty. In addition, German participation in the EU entails a responsibility towards the EU and the other 26 EU Member States.[88] This responsibility extends to the Constitutional Court and arguably requires it to adopt a consistent interpretation of German constitutional law. However, in the case law of the Constitutional Court discrepancies can be detected. Notably, the Court *internally* requires individuals to substantiate a violation of their specific subjective right. Although *subjective gravamen* equally applies to constitutional complaints against EU acts, the Court's interpretation of this requirement is less strict in EU-related proceedings. Notably, every individual that is entitled to vote in the sense of Article 38(1) GG can challenge EU-related measures, whereas individuals are unable to challenge the internal allocation of competences between the federal and the regional levels, although this may also affect ones right to vote.

While traditionally limiting the admissibility of constitutional complaints internally by requiring that individuals are personally, immediately and directly affected by their subjective constitutional rights, applicants that initiate constitutional complaints against EU measures can rely on Article 38(1) GG without demonstrating a particular subjective risk for their right to vote. In its jurisprudence, the Constitutional Court seemingly accepts that a general risk for the German constitutional order – namely that

84. This claim can also be put forward in conjunction with another constitutional principle, for example the social state principle enshrined in Article 20(1) GG, cf. *Lisbon-judgment* para. 182.
85. Carl Nägele, 'German Constitutional Law Cases 2012-2015' (2016) 22 European Public Law 439, 442.
86. *Quantitative Easing (PSPP) Final Judgment* paras 105-110; cf. as well: Wolfgang Weiß, 'Die Integrationsverantwortung der Verfassungsorgane' (2018) 58 Juristische Schulung (JuS) 1046, 1047; Nettesheim, 'Die Integrationsverantwortung: Vorgaben des BVerfG und gesetzgeberische Umsetzung' 178-179.
87. Lon L. Fuller, *The Morality of Law* (Revised Edition edn, Yale University Press 1969) 38-40.
88. Particularly visible during the Eurocrisis, cf. Christopher Klotz, 'Die Machtbalance zwischen Politik und verfassungsgerichtlicher Rechtsprechung' (2012) 45 Zeitschrift für Rechtspolitik (ZRP) 5, 5.

either measure taken by EU institutions,[89] or the conferral of additional competences[90] undermine constitutional law – authorizes every individual entitled to vote to proceed against that act.[91] The Court's lenient interpretation of standing in EU-based proceedings may be explained by the reluctance of institutional actors, such as the German Parliament or Government, which largely refrained from challenging EU integration steps, leaving the Court without means to scrutinize EU integration.[92] The now-adopted approach enables the Constitutional Court to adjudicate on the compatibility of EU integration with the German Constitution.

This development raises two major conceptual concerns. First, the constitutional complaint is designed to protect subjective, individual rights. This is obvious from Article 93(1)(4)(a) GG and was continuously advocated by the *Bundesverfassungsgericht* itself.[93] Although it cannot be disputed that EU integration affects the existing German constitutional framework, it is debatable whether such changes indeed directly affect individuals in their subjective rights. It seems that competence conferrals first and foremost affect institutional prerogatives. This conclusion resonates with the traditional internal jurisprudence. Notably, the Court declared, when confronted with a constitutional complaint against the dissolution of the *Bundestag* based on Article 38(1) GG, that the dissolution of parliament affected institutional and not subjective rights as required to establish *subjective gravamen*.[94] More specifically, it concluded that the principle of democracy did not entail the subjective right to constitutionally review the dissolution of parliament.[95] Following this logic, it can be submitted that competence transfers to the EU primarily affect institutional rights. The constitutional system prevents individuals from protecting institutional rights through constitutional complaints. Instead, it is for the empowered institutional actors to apply for constitutional protection.[96]

Second, it should be recalled that the purpose of the constitutional complaint is not to deliver general answers to abstract constitutional questions.[97] This is convincing, as the constitutional complaint is a subjective legal remedy. It entitles individuals

89. Notably against the ECB, cf. *OMT-Reference*; *Quantitative Easing (PSPP) Reference*.
90. Ratification of a new EU Treaty, cf. *Lisbon-judgment*; *Maastricht-Judgment*.
91. Which results in an increasing number of applicants, for example, obvious from the almost 12.000 applications in the *OMT*-case, cf. Nägele, 'German Constitutional Law Cases 2012-2015' 439.
92. Nettesheim, '"Euro-Rettung" und Grundgesetz: Verfassungsgerichtliche Vorgaben für den Umbau der Währungsunion' 768-769.
93. Klein and Sennekamp, 'Aktuelle Zulässigkeitsprobleme der Verfassungsbeschwerde' 949.
94. 2 BvQ 4/82 *Dissolution of the German Parliament* (German Federal Constitutional Court); cf. as well: Franz Reimer, 'Vertrauensfrage und Bundestagsauflösung bei parlamentarischer Anscheinsgefahr' (2005) 45 Juristische Schulung (JuS) 680, 683.
95. BVerfG, 'Kein Rechtsschutz des Bürgers gegen Auflösung des Bundestages' (1983) 36 Neue Juristische Wochenschrift (NJW) 383, 383.
96. By initiating inter-institutional proceedings, cf. Schlaich and Korioth, *Das Bundesverfassungsgericht – Stellung Verfahren, Entscheidungen* para. 79.
97. In contrast to the abstract judicial review of norms, cf. *Copyright-Law Amendment I* para. 52.

to challenge state acts that violate their subjective rights.[98] However, now that every German citizen who enjoys the right to vote can challenge EU measures, the factual outcome seems to suggest the existence of a general constitutional procedure against EU acts. This renders the constitutional complaint a legal remedy that delivers general answers to abstract legal questions, which blurs the distinction between abstract judicial review - reserved to privileged institutional applicants - and subjective constitutional complaints.[99]

The result of this variable interpretation of the *subjective gravamen* requirement is a de facto 'EU constitutional complaint'.[100] *Gärditz* and *Wendel* conclude that this introduces a *popular action* against EU integration into the German constitutional order.[101] Such an *actio popularis* is, however, alien to the German constitutional order.[102] The wide interpretation of *subjective gravamen* in EU matters triggered a major number of applications before the Constitutional Court. For example, more than 190,000 individuals initiated constitutional complaints against the Transatlantic Trade and Investment Partnership (TTIP)-agreement based on their right to vote.[103] Ultimately, this can negatively impact the German Court itself in light of this significant inflow of EU constitutional complaints. Although it is important that EU integration conforms with the German Constitution, it seems equally crucial that the Constitutional Court respects the applicable constitutional framework. If different standing requirements for EU-related proceedings were necessary,[104] it would be for the constitution-amending legislator to alter the current constitutional framework.[105]

98. Which is clear expression of the legislator's choice not to include a *popular* constitutional complaint, cf. Patric Urbaneck, 'Die Zulässigkeitsprüfung im Verfassungsrecht' (2014) 54 Juristische Schulung (JuS) 896, 898; Klein and Sennekamp, 'Aktuelle Zulässigkeitsprobleme der Verfassungsbeschwerde' 949.
99. Namely, the Court allows for abstract constitutional review under the constitutional complaint, cf. Gärditz, 'Beyond Symbolism: Towards a Constitutional Actio Popularis in EU Affairs? A Commentary on the OMT Decision of the Federal Constitutional Court' 192.
100. For example, in relation to the constitutional challenges against the CETA-agreement, cf. 2 BvR 1368/16, 2 BvR 1444/16, 2 BvR 1482/16, 2 BvR 1823/16 and 2 BvE 3/16 *Interim Relief against Comprehensive Economic and Trade Agreement (CETA)* (German Federal Constitutional Court) paras 51, 66.
101. Gärditz, 'Beyond Symbolism: Towards a Constitutional Actio Popularis in EU Affairs? A Commentary on the OMT Decision of the Federal Constitutional Court' 192; Mattias Wendel, 'Kompetenzrechtliche Grenzgänge: Karlsruhes *Ultra-vires*-Vorlage an den EuGH' (2014) 74 Zeitschrift für ausländisches öffentliches Recht und Völkerrecht (ZaöRV) 615, 641-642.
102. Markus Ludwigs, 'Der Ultra-vires-Vorbehalt des BVerfG: Judikative Kompetenzanmaßung oder legitimes Korrektiv' (2015) 34 Neue Zeitschrift für Verwaltungsrecht (NVwZ) 537, 540; Eckhard Pache, 'Das Ende der europäischen Integration? Das Urteil des Bundesverfassungsgerichts zum Vertrag von Lissabon, zur Zukunft Europas und der Demokratie' (2009) 36 Europäische Grundrechte-Zeitschrift (EuGRZ) 285, 287.
103. 2 BvR 1368/16, 2 BvR 1444/16, 2 BvR 1482/16, 2 BvR 1823/16, 2 BvE 3/16 *Transatlantic Trade and Investment Partnership (TTIP)* (German Federal Constitutional Court).
104. Henner Gött, 'Die ultra vires-Rüge nach dem OMT-Vorlagebeschluss des Bundesverfassungsgerichts' (2014) 49 Zeitschrift Europarecht (EuR) 514, 533.
105. Particularly, in light of the Court's own reasoning, cf. *Quantitative Easing (PSPP) Reference* paras 128-129; *Final OMT-Judgment* para. 138; *Lisbon-judgment* para. 250.

2 *Institutional Actors Initiating Constitutional Proceedings*

Furthermore, German institutions can initiate constitutional proceedings.[106] In relation to EU law, inter-institutional proceedings are the most frequently employed proceedings.[107] They are adversarial in nature and occur between two institutions.[108]

a Constitutional Requirements for Initiating Inter-institutional Proceedings

Following Article 93(1) no. (1) GG in conjunction with § 63 BVerfGG, the German President, Parliament, Federal Council, Government as well as parts of these organs that have their own rights under the German Constitution, or the rules of procedure of the Parliament or the Federal Council, can initiate inter-institutional proceedings. For example, parliamentary committees,[109] parliamentary fractions[110] as well as single parliamentarians[111] have such own rights and can thus initiate proceedings. Through these proceedings, the institutions can challenge an act or omission of another institution that allegedly violates their constitutional prerogatives. An example of EU matters is the parliamentary right to receive information on EU policies, following Article 23(2)(2) GG. During the Eurocrisis, the parliamentary fraction 'BÜNDNIS 90/DIE GRÜNEN' initiated inter-institutional proceedings against the government on behalf of the German Parliament claiming a violation of this parliamentary right.[112]

b Application of Adversarial Nature of Proceedings in EU Matters

In EU-related proceedings, the German Constitutional Court adopted a specific interpretation of this requirement and accepted that parliamentary fractions can invoke parliamentary rights against the German Parliament itself.[113] According to this jurisprudence, parliamentary fractions are able to rely on parliamentary prerogatives where they see these prerogatives violated by a parliamentary majority decision. In the *Lisbon*-judgment, for example, the Court declared an application of the fraction DIE

106. Schlaich and Korioth, *Das Bundesverfassungsgericht – Stellung Verfahren, Entscheidungen* paras 77-78.
107. Article 93(1) no. (1) GG and specified in §§ 63 ff. BVerfGG; the Member of the Bundestag of the political party 'DIE LINKE' initiated inter-institutional proceedings against the Lisbon Treaty, the ESM, and the OMT programme, cf. *Lisbon-judgment*; *Right to Participation for German Parliament at the Occasion of ESM-Treaty and Euro-Plus-Pact*; *OMT-Reference*.
108. Schlaich and Korioth, *Das Bundesverfassungsgericht – Stellung Verfahren, Entscheidungen* paras 79, 83.
109. Parliamentary committees may initiate proceedings to warrant their own rights, cf. 2 BvE 11, 15/83 *Committee of Enquiry in the Flick-Matter* (German Federal Constitutional Court).
110. *OMT-Reference* para. 106; *Right to Participation for German Parliament at the Occasion of ESM-Treaty and Euro-Plus-Pact* para. 77; *Lisbon-judgment* para. 202.
111. *Lisbon-judgment* paras 198-199; cf. as well: Christian Walter, 'Art. 93 GG' in Theodor Maunz and Günter Düring (eds), *Grundgesetz-Kommentar* (92nd edn, C.H. Beck 2020) para. 213.
112. *Right to Participation for German Parliament at the Occasion of ESM-Treaty and Euro-Plus-Pact* para. 79.
113. Max-Emanuel Geis and Heidrun Meier, 'Grundfälle zum Organstreitverfahren, Art. 93 I Nr. 1 GG, §§ 13 Nr. 5, 63ff. BVerfGG' (2011) 51 Juristische Schulung (JuS) 699, 703.

LINKE admissible, which claimed that the German act approving the Lisbon Treaty interfered with the parliamentary reservation to deploy the German army.[114] The result is, however, that a parliamentary fraction invoked prerogatives on behalf of the German Parliament against the German Parliament itself.[115] This alters the traditional understanding of the proceedings' adversarial character. Namely, fractions were previously entitled to invoke fraction or minority prerogatives, but not parliamentary prerogatives.[116] Instead, one-fourth of the members of the *Bundestag* were entitled to initiate inter-institutional proceedings against another institution. In comparison, a fraction may only represent 5 % of parliamentarians,[117] thus circumventing the initial procedural threshold. Arguably, this wide interpretation transformed the inter-institutional proceedings into *intra*-institutional proceedings. The apparent transformation was confirmed in the *ESM*-proceedings, where the Court found that fractions could invoke parliamentary budgetary prerogatives on behalf of parliament against the parliamentary approval of the *ESM*.[118] It reiterated this approach in the *OMT*-reference.[119] According to the Court's reasoning, this interpretation secures the rights awarded to parliamentary minorities, as these can judicially challenge governmental policies supported by the coalition majority in parliament.[120]

Although this wide-standing requirement was developed in the context of EU law,[121] the Court highlighted that it applied the same approach internally.[122] The Court's finding suggests that it recognizes the importance of applying the same interpretation of the constitutional standing requirements in internal and in EU-related proceedings. Considering the content of the proceedings that the Court referred to, the fraction *DIE LINKE* challenged the procedural requirements for minority and opposition rights in light of the then vast coalition majority of the German Christian Democratic / Social Union (CDU/CSU) and the German Social Democratic Party (SPD). These two fractions united 503 of the 630 members of Parliament, whereas the opposition of *DIE LINKE* and *BÜNDNIS 90/DIE GRÜNEN* had only 127 seats.[123] Due to

114. As established by the *Bundesverfassungsgericht* based on Article 87a GG, cf. 2 BvE 3/92, 5/93, 7/93, 8/93 *German Participation in NATO Actions* (German Federal Constitutional Court) paras 321-339; cf. as well: Volker Epping, 'Art. 87a GG – Streitkräfte' in Volker Epping and Christian Hillgruber (eds), *Beck Online Kommentar zum Grundgesetz* (45th edn, C.H. Beck 2020) para. 24; Manuel Ladiges, 'Grenzen des wehrverfassungsrechtlichen Parlamentsvorbehalts' (2010) 29 Neue Zeitschrift für Verwaltungsrecht (NVwZ) 1075, 1076.
115. Which is criticized, cf. Schwerdtfeger, 'Europäisches Unionsrecht in der Rechtsprechung des Bundesverfassungsgerichts: Grundrechts-, ultra-vires- und Identitätskontrolle im gewaltenteiligen Mehrebenensystem' 305-306.
116. 2 BvE 1/18 *Constitutional Challenge of German Migration Policy Initiated by the AfD* (German Federal Constitutional Court) para. 18.
117. As enshrined in § 10(1) GO-BT.
118. *ESM-Treaty and Fiscal Compact* para. 125.
119. *Final OMT-Judgment* paras 106-107; *OMT-Reference* para. 54.
120. *Final OMT-Judgment* para. 106.
121. Namely in the Lisbon-judgment for the first time, cf. Franz C. Mayer, 'Der Vertrag von Lissabon im Überblick' (2010) 50 Juristische Schulung (JuS) 189, 194.
122. As the Court references its EU-related jurisprudence in this 'internal' case concerning minority rights of the German Parliament, cf. 2 BvE 4/14 *Opposition Rights in the German Parliament* (German Federal Constitutional Court) para. 67.
123. *Ibid.*, para. 2.

this small number, several constitutional minority rights were unavailable, including, for example, the initiation of a parliamentary 'committee of inquiry'.[124] *DIE LINKE* proposed several constitutional amendments to alter the majority requirements, which were ultimately rejected and triggered the mentioned constitutional proceedings.[125] However, it seems that the opposition in these proceedings was indeed concerned about their minority rights including the possibility to initiate constitutional proceedings, and not about a genuine parliamentary prerogative. This appears to set this *internal* case apart from the highlighted understanding in EU-related proceedings and therefore constitutes a variable interpretation of the standing requirements.

c Possible Constitutional Double Standard

The above suggests that the traditional conception of inter-institutional proceedings as adversarial[126] is altered in EU-related cases. Yet, this adversarial character is essential as inter-institutional proceedings are not devised as an abstract constitutional review of an institutional act, but rather to clarify the extent of institutional powers under the German Constitution.[127] For example, in the outlined *internal* proceedings, the fraction *DIE LINKE* was concerned about the extent of parliamentary minority rights guaranteed by the German Constitution. Thus, the challenge concerned its own rights as parliamentary opposition and not an alleged violation of the general rights of the entire parliament.[128] In contrast to this internal case, the proceedings against EU acts challenged parliamentary decisions, claiming that these would alter general parliamentary prerogatives.[129] Therefore, these institutional challenges were not aimed at defending opposition rights but essentially challenged the material decision made by a parliamentary majority. This leads to the paradoxical situation that the opposition proceeds on the basis of the *Bundestag's* rights against the *Bundestag* itself. The chosen approach, thus, undermines the constitutional framework and the standing requirements to initiate an abstract constitutional review.[130]

Overall, the result is that the standing requirements for institutional actors to initiate constitutional review of legislative acts are lowered in EU-related proceedings.

124. Cf. Article 44(1) GG; 2 BvE 4/14 *Opposition Rights in the German Parliament* (German Federal Constitutional Court) paras 3-17.
125. 2 BvE 4/14 *Opposition Rights in the German Parliament* (German Federal Constitutional Court) paras 66-67.
126. 2 BvE 13/83 *Deployment of Nuclear Weapons* (German Federal Constitutional Court) para. 109.
127. 2 BvE 6/99 *NATO-Concept* (German Federal Constitutional Court) paras 112-114; *Deployment of Nuclear Weapons* para. 109.
128. Here, not the refusal as such was challenged, but rather the underlying question of rights granted to parliamentary minorities and the opposition, cf. *Opposition Rights in the German Parliament* paras 67-69, 76, 80.
129. More precisely, the budgetary prerogatives that the *Bundestag* enjoys following Article 110 GG, cf. Matthias Herdegen, 'Art. 79 GG' in Theodor Maunz and Günter Düring (eds), *Grundgesetz-Kommentar* (92nd edn, C.H. Beck 2020) paras 182-188; Johannes Dietlein, 'Art. 79 GG: Änderungen des Grundgesetzes' in Volker Epping and Christian Hillgruber (eds), *Beck Online Kommentar zum Grundgesetz* (45th edn, C.H. Beck 2020) para. 33.2.
130. As laid down in Article 93(1) no. (2) GG, the status as a fraction is not required, cf. Walter, 'Art. 93 GG' para. 235.

As was obvious during the Eurocrisis,[131] the *Bundesverfassungsgericht* considers applications brought by (small) political groups against erosion of parliamentary prerogatives in the framework of Article 93(1) no. (1) GG admissible.

3 *Apparent Procedural Double Standard*

The *internal-external-comparative* assessment of the standing requirements indicates that the German Constitutional Court applies a divergent interpretation of the established constitutional standing requirements, rendering the initiation of proceedings against EU acts comparably easier for both individuals and institutions. This raises concerns, as the constitutional framework does not distinguish between domestic and EU-related proceedings. Consequently, a consistent standard should be applied. As *traditional* applicants seemingly refrain from proceedings against EU acts, the broad interpretation of the established *standing requirements* ensures that the Court can adjudicate on the compatibility of German constitutional and EU law.[132] Yet, it is for the constitution-amending legislator to address these concerns and possibly modify the standing requirements. Overall, a consistent application would result in higher admissibility hurdles for proceedings against EU acts, which corresponds to the constitution-amending legislator's choice.

V Applicable Procedural and Institutional Framework for EU Fiscal Integration

Article 23 GG comprehensively regulates German EU membership. The assessment illustrated that the provision applies to the conferral of additional competences to the EU. Depending on the impact of the envisaged integration steps on the German Constitution, either a simple or a qualified two-thirds majority applies. Given that EU fiscal integration proposals will likely affect the German Constitution, in particular budgetary prerogatives, such integration steps will likely require support from a qualified majority. This is supported by evidence from the Eurocrisis, where the Fiscal Compact and the ESM-Treaty had to be approved by a two-thirds majority.[133] In addition, Article 23 GG regulates German institutional interaction in EU matters. The enhanced involvement of parliament and federal council in EU affairs reflects the *internal* impact of EU cooperation. Importantly, the participation of both institutions

131. *OMT-Reference* para. 54; the Court also stressed that budgetary responsibility could be invoked by the fraction, cf. *ESM-Treaty and Fiscal Compact* para. 125.
132. Gärditz, 'Beyond Symbolism: Towards a Constitutional Actio Popularis in EU Affairs? A Commentary on the OMT Decision of the Federal Constitutional Court' 198; Matthias Ruffert, 'Europarecht: Vorlagebeschluss des BVerfG zum OMT-Programm – Die Europarechtswidrigkeit des Kaufs von Staatsanleihen durch die EZB im Rahmen des OMT-Programms ist vom EuGH zu prüfen' (2014) 54 Juristische Schulung (JuS) 373, 374.
133. Richter, *Funktionswandel im Mehrebenensystem? Die Rolle der nationalen Parlamente in der Europäischen Union am Beispiel des Deutschen Bundestags* 176; Ketterer, *Zustimmungserfordernis beim Europäischen Stabilitätsmechanismus* 6, 277.

under Article 23 GG is not designed as a right but rather as an obligation, which is emphasized by the Constitutional Court's integration responsibility doctrine.[134]

The German Constitution, hence, contains a detailed procedural and institutional framework to address EU integration. This framework is complemented by the constitutional supervision of the *Bundesverfassungsgericht*, which frequently adjudicates the relationship between German and EU law. However, the identified double standard in the admissibility criteria raises concerns as it renders the initiation of EU-related proceedings comparably easier.

D SUBSTANTIVE FRAMEWORK APPLICABLE TO EU FISCAL INTEGRATION

EU integration has to comply with the German *eternity clause*, as clarified by Article 23(1)(3) GG. However, as the *eternity clause* is framed in an abstract manner, the protected substantive content is determined by the jurisprudence of the German Constitutional Court. The constitutional jurisprudence on the Eurocrisis provides valuable insights into possible conflicts between the *eternity clause* and EU fiscal integration steps. Based on this jurisprudence, the subsequent assessment determines its constitutional content. In the first step the underpinning constitutional mechanisms will be considered (I) before subsequently assessing the protected constitutional principles (II).

I Underpinning Mechanisms

The *eternity clause* provides the basis for protecting core principles against constitutional change (1). To operationalize this constitutional protection against EU cooperation, the Court introduced the fundamental rights, *ultra vires* and *constitutional identity* locks (2) as well as the guiding concepts of EU law friendliness and integration responsibility (3).

1 Eternity Clause

The German *eternity clause* shields a set of constitutional principles against change:

> (3) Amendments to this Basic Law affecting the division of the Federation into Länder, their participation in principle in the legislative process, or the principles laid down in Articles 1 and 20 shall be inadmissible.

Systematically, Article 79(3) GG is an exception to the general rule in Article 79(2) GG, which stipulates that constitutional amendments can be adopted by a two-thirds majority. It limits the power of the constitution-amending legislator by exempting core constitutional principles from the scope of constitutional amendments. Changes to this core require the complete replacement of the German Constitution,

134. Cf. *Quantitative Easing (PSPP) Reference* para. 47; *OMT-Reference* para. 31.

following Article 146 GG.[135] Therefore, the *eternity clause* emerges as a strict limit, which applies to EU fiscal integration steps.[136] Given the limited likelihood of a replacement of the *Grundgesetz*, EU integration has to respect the *eternity clause*.[137] Therefore, the resulting questions relate to the nature of the limit, the covered EU-relevant content and the role of the German Constitutional Court in its interpretation.

When considering the provision its ambiguous design becomes obvious. On the one hand, its wording suggests that Article 79(3) GG constitutes an absolute prohibition. Hence, no balancing of different legal considerations is possible. The mere fact that one of the covered principles is affected suffices to establish a violation of Article 79(3) GG. On the other hand, the protected material content is restricted to the abstract principles enumerated in Article 79(3) as well as Articles 1 and 20 GG. Thus, Articles 1 and 20 GG could be changed, as long as the established principles are not altered.[138] Thus, despite its absolute framing, the *eternity clause*'s substantive reach is limited to essential components of the protected principles.

Article 79(3) GG covers the organization of the federation into *Länder*, the general participation of the *Länder* in the legislative process, as well as the principles laid down in Articles 1 and 20 GG, which include human dignity (Article 1 GG), as well as democracy (Article 20(1) and (2) GG), the social state principle (Article 20(1) GG), federalism (Article 20(1) GG), the rule of law (Article 20(3) GG) and the right to protest against violations of the principles established by Article 20 GG (Article 20(4) GG). Combined, these principles form the unamendable core of the German Constitution also referred to as the German *constitutional identity*.[139] According to the Constitutional Court, this identity differs from the EU protection in Article 4(2) TEU.[140] As the covered principles are framed in an abstract manner it is for the Constitutional Court to specify the protected components,[141] which has immediate implications for the constitution-amending legislator. Whatever the Court identifies as a substantive part of the *eternity clause* is a direct off-limit. Although the Court appears to be aware of its

135. Rademacher, 'Die "Verfassungsidentität" als Grenze der Kompetenzübertragung auf die Europäische Union?' 146; Tobias Herbst, 'Legale Abschaffung des Grundgesetzes nach Art. 146 GG?' (2012) 45 Zeitschrift für Rechtspolitik (ZRP) 33, 33.
136. *Lisbon-judgment* para. 216; cf. as well: Jaggi, 'Revolutionary Constitutional Lawmaking in Germany: Rediscovering the German 1989 Revolution' 619.
137. Rademacher, 'Die "Verfassungsidentität" als Grenze der Kompetenzübertragung auf die Europäische Union?' 150.
138. Cf. for example a 5% threshold for entering parliament is permissible to guarantee the functioning of the German Parliament, cf. Mayer, 'Rashomon in Karlsruhe: A Reflection on Democracy and Identity in the European Union' 760.
139. *Quantitative Easing (PSPP) Reference* para. 54; *Final OMT-Judgment* paras 136-138; interestingly, the concept of *constitutional identity* emerged in relation to EU and international measures, not in internal disputes, cf. Polzin, 'Constitutional Identity, Unconstitutional Amendments and the Idea of Constituent Power: The Development of the Doctrine of Constitutional Identity in German Constitutional Law' 431.
140. *OMT-Reference* para. 29; cf. as well: Rademacher, 'Die "Verfassungsidentität" als Grenze der Kompetenzübertragung auf die Europäische Union?' 145-146.
141. Through its jurisprudence in EU matters, the German Court underscores its constitutional 'referee position', cf. Kottmann and Wohlfahrt, 'Der gespaltene Wächter? Demokratie, Verfassungsidentität und Integrationsverantwortung im Lissabon-Urteil' 461-462.

constitutional responsibility and cautiously applied the *eternity clause*,[142] it seems to follow a more active approach when confronted with EU cooperation.[143]

Historically, the *eternity clause* is a constitutional reaction to the *Hitler* dictatorship.[144] It was designed as a constitutional security mechanism to prevent a new erosion of constitutional values. Recalling this historic origin, one may question whether the *eternity clause* is designed to apply to a potential *external* impact on core constitutional principles triggered by supranational cooperation. In fact, the EU is based on similar values as enshrined in Article 2 TEU.[145] Given this substantive overlap, it appears that EU cooperation offers an external layer of constitutional protection for the principles covered by the *eternity clause*. The immediate benefits of this additional supranational protection can be seen in Poland or Hungary. In both EU Member States, the rule of law is at risk due to national reforms.[146] Seemingly, the available national constitutional safeguards were insufficient to prevent the unfolding erosion and the EU intervened to secure compliance with the common foundational values.[147] Although the effectiveness of the existing EU tools can be questioned,[148] the benefit of securing core constitutional principles at the national *and* supranational levels is evident. Notably, the EU can act as an external mediator that identifies constitutional risks, confronts national governments and ultimately sanctions them in case national safeguards fail. Hence, the diversification of constitutional safeguards offers constitutional benefits. Here, EU cooperation offers an additional layer of protection for (German) constitutional principles and thereby supports the aim of the *eternity clause*.[149]

This shows that the overall function of the *eternity clause* is to establish an outer, absolute limit for state action, which is why Article 79(3) GG is construed as a

142. Christoph Schönberger, 'Die Europäische Union zwischen "Demokratiedefizit" und Bundestaatsverbot – Anmerkungen zum Lissabon-Urteil des Bundesverfassungsgerichts' (2009) 48 Der Staat 535, 553.
143. By defining competence areas that form part of the essence of the principle of democracy, cf. *Lisbon-judgment* paras 251-252; cf. as well: Armin von Bogdandy and Stephan Schill, 'Die Achtung der nationalen Identität unter dem reformierten Unionsvertrag: Zur unionsrechtlichen Rolle nationalen Verfassungsrechts und zur Überwindung des absoluten Vorrangs' (2010) 70 Zeitschrift für ausländisches öffentliches Recht und Völkerrecht (ZaöRV) 701, 723-724.
144. Ulrich Preuss, 'The Implications of "Eternity Clauses": The German Experience' (2012) 44 Israel Law Review 429, 439.
145. Jan Wouters, 'Revisiting Art. 2 TEU: A True Union of Values?' (2020) 5 European Papers 255, 258-260.
146. Poland: Monika Moens De Fernig, 'Factsheet: The Polish Sejm' (*European Parliament: Directorate-General for the Presidency*, 2018), http://www.epgencms.europarl.europa.eu/cmsdata/upload/0398faee-9664-4eb0-8e1b-ac615ab65a49/Factsheet_PL_-_Sejm.pdf, accessed 5 April 2023; Hungary: Corinne Deloy, 'General Elections in Hungary: Viktor Orban Easily Sweeps to Victory for the Third Time Running in the Hungarian Elections' (*Fondation Robert Schuman*, 10 April 2018), https://www.robert-schuman.eu/en/doc/oee/oee-1765-en.pdf, accessed 5 April 2023.
147. For example, through the order of the CJEU that required Poland to undo the retirement of Supreme Court judges, cf. C-619/18 R *Commission v. Poland* (CJEU).
148. Luke Dimitrios Spieker, 'Breathing Life into the Union's Common Values: On the Judicial Application of Article 2 TEU in the EU Value Crisis' (2019) 20 German Law Journal 1182, 1184-1185.
149. Mayer, 'Rashomon in Karlsruhe: A Reflection on Democracy and Identity in the European Union' 763; stressing that the original intention of Article 79(3) GG was to shield the state

constitutional *ultima ratio*.[150] This means, that the *eternity clause* is designed as a mechanism in case traditional means of constitutional dispute resolution fail. Such a case is given when constitutional values are blatantly disregarded.[151] Restricting the application of the eternity clause to such extreme cases corresponds to the original drafting intention. In addition, a restrictive application of the eternity clause strengthens the provision's authority and mitigates the risk of watering down the provision's protective force through excessive use. In internal constitutional jurisprudence, such restricted application can be observed. In contrast, the Court appears to increasingly employ Article 79(3) GG in EU proceedings, at least since its *Lisbon*-judgment.

2 *The Different Limits Employed by the German Constitutional Court*

Furthermore, the Constitutional Court established three locks or reviews, which provide the Court with a framework to substantively assess the German EU commitments.[152] These locks are the *fundamental rights* review, the *ultra vires* and the *constitutional identity* review.

a Fundamental Rights Review

The fundamental rights review constitutes the Court's first lock.[153] Concerned about the lack of fundamental rights protection at EU level, the German Court reserved itself the competence to assess whether EU measures complied with German fundamental rights in its infamous *Solange* I-decision.[154] Once the European Court of Justice established its own fundamental rights regime, the German Court declared that it would refrain from conducting a fundamental rights assessment of EU measures *as*

against drifting into another dictatorship, cf. Schönberger, 'Die Europäische Union zwischen "Demokratiedefizit" und Bundestaatsverbot – Anmerkungen zum Lissabon-Urteil des Bundesverfassungsgerichts' 553.

150. 1 BvR 2378/98 and 1 BvR 1084/99 *Wiretapping II* (German Federal Constitutional Court) paras 108-111; highlighting the exceptional nature of Article 79(3) GG and that it may not be interpreted in a manner that renders fundamental – yet compatible with the overall system – constitutional amendments *impossible*, cf. 2 BvF 1/69, 2 BvR 629/68 und 308/69 *Wiretapping I* (German Federal Constitutional Court) paras 99-100; cf. as well: Mayer, 'Rashomon in Karlsruhe: A Reflection on Democracy and Identity in the European Union' 763; arguing that the Court seems to contradict this *ultima ratio* status in its EU-related jurisprudence, cf. Thomas M.J. Möllers and Katharina Redcay, 'Das Bundesverfassungsgericht als europäischer Gesetzgeber oder als Motor der Union?' (2013) 48 Europarecht (EuR) 409, 425-426.
151. Frank Schorkopf, 'Case Nos. 2 BvE 2/08, 2 BvE 5/08, 2 BvR 1010/08, 2 BvR 1022/08, 2 BvR 1259/08, and 2 BvR 182/09: 123 BVerfGE 267 (2009)' (2010) 104 The American Journal of International Law 259, 263.
152. Schwerdtfeger, 'Europäisches Unionsrecht in der Rechtsprechung des Bundesverfassungsgerichts: Grundrechts-, ultra-vires- und Identitätskontrolle im gewaltenteiligen Mehrebenensystem' 292-294; Erich Vranes, 'German Constitutional Foundations of, and Limitations to, EU Integration: A Systematic Analysis' (2013) 14 German Law Journal 75, 101-110.
153. *Solange II-Decision* para. 132; *Solange I-Decision* para. 43.
154. *Solange I-Decision* para. 56; cf. as well: Polzin, 'Constitutional Identity, Unconstitutional Amendments and the Idea of Constituent Power: The Development of the Doctrine of Constitutional Identity in German Constitutional Law' 426-427.

long as the EU warranted a level of fundamental rights protection similar to the German one.[155]

This illustrates that the fundamental rights limit evolved over time, which could have implications for the *ultra vires* and the *identity* review, too.[156] Notably, it was submitted by *Payandeh* that the German Court seemingly followed a strategic agenda when introducing the fundamental rights review. The Court indirectly invited the EU to improve the EU protection of fundamental rights.[157] Once the EU addressed this concern, the Court relaxed its scrutiny. Although this evolution is specific to the fundamental rights review, a similar pattern could perhaps be envisaged in relation to the other two limits mentioned.[158] Yet, it seems questionable whether the EU would willingly address the concerns underpinning the *ultra vires* and the *constitutional identity* review, as this could limit the effect and reach of EU law.

b Ultra Vires *Review*

In its *Maastricht*-judgment, the Constitutional Court then introduced its *ultra vires* review to determine whether EU institutions acted within their conferred mandate.[159] Hence, the *ultra vires* review constitutes the German supervision of the EU law principle of conferral.[160] In the recent PSP-Programme judgment, the Court for the first time declared EU acts *ultra vires*.[161]

Considering the design of the limit, since its *Honeywell* Judgment,[162] the Court follows a three-stepped approach.[163] First, the Court determines whether the

155. *Solange II-Decision* para. 132; Vranes, 'German Constitutional Foundations of, and Limitations to, EU Integration: A Systematic Analysis' 99-100.
156. Andreas Voßkuhle, 'Der Wandel der Verfassung und seine Grenzen' (2019) 59 Juristische Schulung (JuS) 417, 419.
157. Payandeh, 'Constitutional Review of EU Law after Honeywell: Contextualizing the Relationship Between the German Constitutional Court and the EU Court of Justice' 28; Schwerdtfeger, 'Europäisches Unionsrecht in der Rechtsprechung des Bundesverfassungsgerichts: Grundrechts-, ultra-vires- und Identitätskontrolle im gewaltenteiligen Mehrebenensystem' 308-309.
158. Payandeh, 'Constitutional Review of EU Law after Honeywell: Contextualizing the Relationship Between the German Constitutional Court and the EU Court of Justice' 28.
159. *Maastricht-Judgment* para. 48; cf. as well: Andrej Lang, 'Ultra Vires Review of the ECB's Policy of Quantitative Easing: An Analysis of the German Constitutional Court's Preliminary Reference Order in the PSPP Case' (2018) 55 Common Market Law Review 923, 929.
160. *Maastricht-Judgment*; cf. as well: Wendel, 'Kompetenzrechtliche Grenzgänge: Karlsruhes *Ultra-vires*-Vorlage an den EuGH' 628.
161. *Quantitative Easing (PSPP) Final Judgment* paras 105-111; cf. as well: Calliess, 'Konfrontation statt Kooperation zwischen BVerfG und EuGH? Zu den Folgen des Karlsruher PSPP-Urteils' 900-901.
162. *Honeywell Judgment* para. 56; cf. as well: Payandeh, 'Constitutional Review of EU Law after Honeywell: Contextualizing the Relationship Between the German Constitutional Court and the EU Court of Justice' 22-23.
163. Wendel, 'Exceeding Judicial Competence in the Name of Democracy: The German Federal Constitutional Court's OMT Reference' 273-274.

challenged EU act potentially exceeds the limits of the conferred competences in a manifest way and whether this results in a '[...] structurally significant shift in the division of competences to the detriment of the Member States'.[164,165] Following this jurisprudence, a structurally significant overstepping is, *inter alia*, given in case a Treaty amendment would be required to allocate the disputed competence to the EU[166] or in case the challenged EU act conflicts with the *eternity clause*.[167] Once the German Court identifies an excessive overstepping, it issues in a second step a preliminary reference to the CJEU.[168] Here, the Constitutional Court underscored that it was essential to provide the CJEU with the opportunity to address *ultra vires* concerns in order to preserve the unity of EU law and to respect the CJEU's mandate. At the same time, these considerations can never justify *ultra vires* acts, as the CJEU could otherwise extend the reach of the EU-Treaties beyond the intention of the Member States.[169] Therefore, the German Court will follow the CJEU's guidance on the interpretation of EU law *as long as* this interpretation is based on the traditional European methods of judicial interpretation, coherent and sufficiently motivated.[170]

Until now, the German Court initiated two preliminary references, notably in the OMT[171]- and PSP-Programme proceedings.[172] In the OMT-proceedings, the Court followed the CJEU's guidance. However, in the PSP-Programme proceedings the Court considered the CJEU's interpretation of EU law as 'manifestly incomprehensible' and therefore declared the CJEU's judgment partially *ultra vires* – the third step under the *ultra vires* review before then concluding that the initially challenged PSP-Programme was *ultra vires*.[173] This suggests that the *ultra vires* finding always involves close scrutiny of the CJEU's guiding judgment, and that declaring the initially challenged act *ultra vires* requires declaring the CJEU's judgment *ultra vires*, too.

164. *Quantitative Easing (PSPP) Final Judgment* para. 110.
165. *OMT-Reference* para. 37; cf. as well: Lang, 'Ultra Vires Review of the ECB's Policy of Quantitative Easing: An Analysis of the German Constitutional Court's Preliminary Reference Order in the PSPP Case' 927; Ludwigs, 'Der Ultra-vires-Vorbehalt des BVerfG: Judikative Kompetenzanmaßung oder legitimes Korrektiv' 538.
166. *Quantitative Easing (PSPP) Final Judgment* para. 110.
167. *OMT-Reference* para. 37; *Honeywell Judgment* para. 65.
168. *Quantitative Easing (PSPP) Final Judgment* para. 111; *Honeywell Judgment* paras 60-61; cf. as well: Payandeh, 'Constitutional Review of EU Law after Honeywell: Contextualizing the Relationship Between the German Constitutional Court and the EU Court of Justice' 23-24.
169. *Quantitative Easing (PSPP) Final Judgment* para. 111; cf. as well: Haltern, 'Ultra-vires-Kontrolle im Dienst europäischer Demokratie' 818, 821.
170. *Quantitative Easing (PSPP) Final Judgment* para. 112; cf. as well: Friedemann Kainer, 'Aus der nationalen Brille: Das PSPP-Urteil des BVerfG' (2020) 31 Europäische Zeitschrift für Wirtschaftsrecht (EuZW) 533, 535.
171. *OMT-Reference*.
172. *Quantitative Easing (PSPP) Reference*.
173. Haltern, 'Ultra-vires-Kontrolle im Dienst europäischer Demokratie' 822; Calliess, 'Konfrontation statt Kooperation zwischen BVerfG und EuGH? Zu den Folgen des Karlsruher PSPP-Urteils' 901.

c Constitutional Identity Review

Finally, the German Court introduced the *constitutional identity review*.[174] Based on the *eternity clause*, EU integration cannot undermine core constitutional values protected by Article 79(3) GG.[175] According to the Constitutional Court, the limit requires that certain competence areas remain under the control of the German Parliament and may therefore not be conferred to EU level in order to preserve German democracy protected by Article 20(1) and (2) GG.[176] In case a conflict between EU integration steps and the *eternity clause* occurs, the German legislator is precluded from engaging in these, as it is not competent to overcome Article 79(3) GG.[177] Hence, the identity review enforces the *eternity clause* and protects indispensable constitutional values, which can neither be altered at the German state level nor by engaging in EU integration.[178] In its assessment, the Court takes the German act of approval - and not EU law itself - as a reference point for the constitutional assessment.

d Overlap of Ultra Vires and Identity Review

Ultra vires and *identity* review are independent limits safeguarding different constitutional interests. Notably, under the *ultra vires* review the German Constitutional Court supervises the principle of conferral as to measures adopted based on the EU-Treaties. In contrast, through the *constitutional identity* review the Court determines whether EU integration exceeds the available scope under Article 79(3) GG and it thus primarily applies when additional EU integration steps are considered. Although both limits remain conceptually independent,[179] they can overlap. Since the *ultra vires* limit requires a manifest and structurally significant excess,[180] such overlap can in fact materialize. Notably, an excess of the conferred competences which conflicts with the *eternity clause* is considered structurally significant excess of the conferred powers.[181]

174. *Lisbon-judgment*; cf. as well: Jo Murkens, 'Identity Trumps Integration: The Lisbon Treaty in the German Federal Constitutional Court' (2009) 48 Der Staat 517, 519.
175. *Lisbon-judgment* para. 240; cf. as well: Peter C. Caldwell, *Popular Sovereignty and the Crisis of German Constitutional Law: The Theory and Practice of Weimar Constitutionalism* (Duke University Press 1997) 177.
176. *Final OMT-Judgment* para. 138; *ESM-Treaty and Fiscal Compact* paras 107-109.
177. Cf. distinction between constituted power and constituting power, Rolf Grawert, 'Homogenität, Identität, Souveränität: Positionen jurisdiktioneller Begriffsdogmatik' (2012) 51 Der Staat 189, 197; Bogdandy and Schill, 'Die Achtung der nationalen Identität unter dem reformierten Unionsvertrag: Zur unionsrechtlichen Rolle nationalen Verfassungsrechts und zur Überwindung des absoluten Vorrangs' 715.
178. Andreas Voßkuhle, 'Verfassungsgerichtsbarkeit und europäische Integration' (2013) 32 Neue Zeitschrift für Verwaltungsrecht (NVwZ) 27, 27.
179. Martin Nettesheim, 'Die "haushaltspolitische Gesamtverantwortung" in der Rechtsprechung des BVerfG' in Peter Brandt (ed.), *Verfassung und Krise*, vol. 16 (Berliner Wissenschafts-Verlag (BWV) 2015) 27.
180. *OMT-Reference* para. 37; *Honeywell Judgment* paras 60-61, 71.
181. *Final OMT-Judgment* para. 153.

Consequently, a violation of the German *constitutional identity* by EU institutions is always a structurally significant *ultra vires* act.

3 *Guiding Concepts for Constitutional Jurisprudence on EU Integration*

Finally, the Constitutional Court developed the concepts of EU law friendliness and of integration responsibility that guide its jurisprudence. *Europarechtsfreundlichkeit*[182] implies that the German Constitution is generally open towards EU cooperation[183] and that German constitutional law will be interpreted - as far as possible - in conformity with EU law. It also requires that the Constitutional Court cooperates with the CJEU.[184] Furthermore, it entails that the compatibility assessment of EU law with the German Constitution is centralized with the German Constitutional Court[185] and that the different constitutional limits are applied in a favourable manner towards the EU.[186] Notably, the Court restricts its *ultra vires* review to structurally significant transgressions of the conferred competences and the *constitutional identity* review is exercised in a similarly *EU-friendly manner*.[187]

EU law friendliness is complemented by the concept of *Integrationsverantwortung,*[188] which applies to German institutions when conferring competences to the EU and when supervising the exercise of conferred competences.[189] Its primary aim is to balance the constitutional obligation to participate in EU cooperation with continuous responsibilities under the constitution.[190] The concept is now codified.[191] Integration responsibility requires that the relevant institutional actors determine a specific and

182. In English: *European law friendliness*; based on Article 23 GG and Article 24(1) GG.
183. Voßkuhle, 'Verfassungsgerichtsbarkeit und europäische Integration' 28.
184. *Honeywell Judgment* paras 58-59; cf. as well: Beke Zwingmann, 'The Continuing Myth of Euro-Scepticism? The German Federal Constitutional Court Two Years after *Lisbon*' (2012) 61 International & Comparative Law Quarterly 665. 676-677.
185. Dana Burchardt, 'Die Ausübung der Identitätskontrolle durch das Bundesverfassungsgericht: Zugleich Besprechung des Beschlusses 2 BvR 2735/14 des BVerfG vom 15.12.2015 ("Solange III"/"Europäischer Haftbefehl II")' (2016) 76 Zeitschrift für ausländisches öffentliches Recht und Völkerrecht (ZaöRV) 527, 540.
186. *Lisbon-judgment* para. 240; cf. as well: Zwingmann, 'The Continuing Myth of Euro-Scepticism? The German Federal Constitutional Court Two Years after *Lisbon*' 678-679.
187. *Quantitative Easing (PSPP) Reference* para. 58; *Final OMT-Judgment* paras 121, 154-155; cf. as well: Burchardt, 'Die Ausübung der Identitätskontrolle durch das Bundesverfassungsgericht: Zugleich Besprechung des Beschlusses 2 BvR 2735/14 des BVerfG vom 15.12.2015 ("Solange III"/"Europäischer Haftbefehl II")' 533.
188. In English: *Integration responsibility*.
189. *Quantitative Easing (PSPP) Final Judgment* paras 106-107; cf. as well: Nettesheim, 'Die Integrationsverantwortung: Vorgaben des BVerfG und gesetzgeberische Umsetzung' 178-179.
190. Weiß, 'Die Integrationsverantwortung der Verfassungsorgane' 1046; Andreas Engels, 'Die Integrationsverantwortung des Deutschen Bundestags' (2012) 52 Juristische Schulung (JuS) 210, 210-211.
191. In the direct aftermath of the Lisbon-judgment, the *Bundestag* adopted the integration responsibility law, cf. Nettesheim, 'Die Integrationsverantwortung: Vorgaben des BVerfG und gesetzgeberische Umsetzung' 178.

limited EU integration programme.[192] An increasingly important element deriving from integration responsibility is the continuous supervision of EU action, which gained relevance during the Eurocrisis.[193] Notably, the Constitutional Court requires German institutions to monitor EU action in order to ensure compliance with the determined integration programme.[194] During the Eurocrisis, the German Court continuously employed integration responsibility in conjunction with the *ultra vires* review and the individuals' right to vote enshrined in Article 38(1) GG.[195] Following this constitutional framework, the *Bundestag* has an obligation to shield individuals against potential *ultra vires* acts committed by EU institutions.[196] It suggests that integration responsibility requires German institutions to consider EU integration as a continuous institutional task and that they cannot discharge themselves from their constitutional obligations by adopting an EU integration step.

II Constitutional Principles

Based on this constitutional toolbox, the German Constitutional Court evaluates the effect of EU integration on substantive principles of the German Constitution. In this assessment, one may identify two tendencies that appear to render the application of the *eternity clause* to EU integration highly likely. First, the Court seems to perceive the EU-related transformation of decision-making processes that result in increasing EU control as a potential threat to the state structure. Resulting from this perception is a general tension between the aim of the *eternity clause* – namely the preservation of the German state structure – and the prospect of EU integration – namely the transformation of decision-making processes. And second, given the constitutional indeterminacy of the content protected by the *eternity clause*, EU integration can easily be portrayed as an interference when interpreting the *eternity clause* in light of EU integration.[197] The subsequent assessment focuses on the principle of democracy (1), the concept of *overall budgetary responsibility* (2) as well as German sovereignty (3), the main substantive limits relevant to EU fiscal integration.

192. As the Court emphasized itself, cf. *Quantitative Easing (PSPP) Final Judgment* paras 106-107; *Quantitative Easing (PSPP) Reference* para. 47; *OMT-Reference* para. 31; also highlighted by: Mayer, 'Rashomon in Karlsruhe: A Reflection on Democracy and Identity in the European Union' 761.
193. Weiß, 'Die Integrationsverantwortung der Verfassungsorgane' 1047.
194. *Quantitative Easing (PSPP) Reference* paras 47-49; *Final OMT-Judgment* paras 164-165.
195. *Quantitative Easing (PSPP) Reference* para. 50; *Final OMT-Judgment* para. 166; cf. as well: Engels, 'Die Integrationsverantwortung des Deutschen Bundestags' 213.
196. Weiß, 'Die Integrationsverantwortung der Verfassungsorgane' 1048.
197. For example, from the developed competence catalogue developed by the Court, cf. *Lisbon-judgment* paras 251-252; which was criticized as arbitrary, cf. Schwerdtfeger, 'Europäisches Unionsrecht in der Rechtsprechung des Bundesverfassungsgerichts: Grundrechts-, ultra-vires- und Identitätskontrolle im gewaltenteiligen Mehrebenensystem' 293-294; Bogdandy and Schill, 'Die Achtung der nationalen Identität unter dem reformierten Unionsvertrag: Zur unionsrechtlichen Rolle nationalen Verfassungsrechts und zur Überwindung des absoluten Vorrangs' 723-724.

1 Democracy

The Court's EU-related jurisprudence on democracy reveals three core components that appear vital to guarantee the overarching function of democracy, namely legitimizing the exercise of state powers (d).[198] According to the Constitutional Court, the German people, as legitimizing subjects under the German Constitution (a), have to be able to determine through elections (b), an institutional representation which takes political decisions (c), as visually conceptualized in Figure 3.2. Jointly these elements constitute the core of German democracy in the sense of Article 79(3) GG (e).

Figure 3.2 Core Components of German Democracy

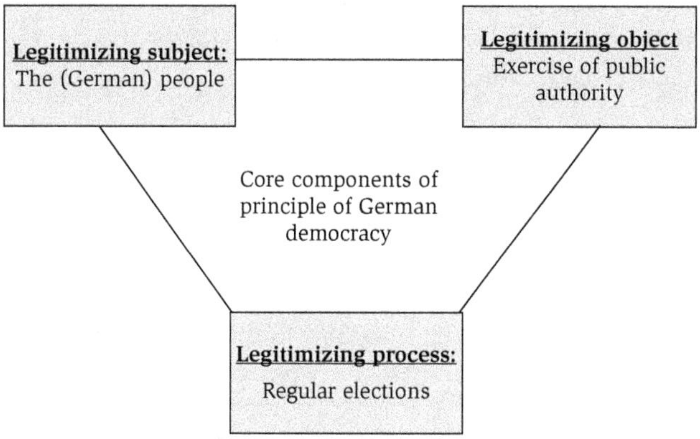

a Legitimizing Subject ('Volkssouveränität')

The first element is the German people as the origin and source of legitimacy for the exercise of (state) authority.[199] The people mandate a representative institution through regular elections to exercise state power and to take political decisions on behalf of them within the available constitutional framework.[200] Given that the people legitimize the exercise of state power, it must be possible to trace back state actions to the people.[201] This is called a *legitimization chain*, which constitutes the backbone of

198. Ulrich Jan Schröder, 'Das Demokratieprinzip des Grundgesetzes' (2017) 49 Juristische Arbeitsblätter (JA) 809, 814; Bodo Pieroth, 'Das Demokratieprinzip des Grundgesetzes' (2010) 50 Juristische Schulung (JuS) 473, 479, 481.
199. Cf. the explicit wording of Article 20(2)(1) GG: 'All state authority derives from the people.'; Lars Vinx, 'The Incoherence of Strong Popular Sovereignty' (2013) 11 International Journal of Constitutional Law 101, 114-115.
200. *Lisbon-judgment* para. 216; cf. as well: Rademacher, 'Die "Verfassungsidentität" als Grenze der Kompetenzübertragung auf die Europäische Union?' 150.
201. 2 BvF 3/89 *Right to Vote for Foreigners II* (German Federal Constitutional Court) para. 39; cf. as well: Jörg Philipp Terhechte, 'Souveränität, Dynamik und Integration – Making Up the Rules as We Go Along? – Anmerkungen zum Lissabon-Urteil des Bundesverfassungsgerichts' (2009) 20 Europäische Zeitschrift für Wirtschaftsrecht (EuZW) 724, 726.

German representative democracy and which illustrates that the people form the conceptual starting point of state authority.[202]

This triggers the question of *who* the people in the sense of Article 20(2)(1) GG are. The Constitutional Court concluded that the term refers to the German people,[203] which corresponds to the scope of the German Constitution.[204] The Court highlighted that Article 20(2)(1) GG refers to the 'people' and *not* to affected individuals, which implies a particular connection to the state. The German people have a particular bond with the German state, which distinguishes them from other individuals.[205] As this special bond is required, only German nationals can participate in the process of legitimizing state action under the German Constitution.[206] According to Article 38(1) GG, only Germans in the sense of Article 116 GG enjoy the right to vote in federal and regional elections.[207] However, the Constitutional Court highlighted that the German Parliament can modify the composition of the people by changing the nationality rules.[208] Nevertheless, it seems unlikely that a European people could emerge under the current German Constitution.[209]

b Elections as a Mechanism to Determine Representation

The mandating of the exercise of public power by the people occurs through elections, which have to comply with the basic requirements established in Article 38(1)(1) GG. These entail that elections are direct, regular, allow for free choice with a secret ballot and that each vote cast has an equal success rate.[210] This has implications for the composition of the German Parliament: the *Bundestag* must represent the vote and views of the people accurately.[211] The equal representation requirement renders degressive proportionality for a directly representative institution incompatible with

202. Andreas Voßkuhle and Anna-Bettina Kaiser, 'Grundwissen: Öffentliches Recht – Demokratische Legitimation' (2009) 49 Juristische Schulung (JuS) 803, 804.
203. *Lisbon-judgment* para. 281; cf. as well: Rademacher, 'Die "Verfassungsidentität" als Grenze der Kompetenzübertragung auf die Europäische Union?' 148.
204. Kottmann and Wohlfahrt, 'Der gespaltene Wächter? Demokratie, Verfassungsidentität und Integrationsverantwortung im Lissabon-Urteil' 446.
205. 2 BvF 2, 6/89 *Right to Vote for Foreigners I* (German Federal Constitutional Court) para. 56; *Right to Vote for Foreigners II* para. 59.
206. Ewgenij Sokolov, 'Wege zur Partizipation für Inländer: Volksbegriff und Einbürgerung im Lichte des Demokratieprinzips' (2016) 35 Neue Zeitschrift für Verwaltungsrecht (NVwZ) 649, 650.
207. *Quantitative Easing (PSPP) Reference* paras 45-46; *Lisbon-judgment* paras 130-133; cf. as well: Terhechte, 'Souveränität, Dynamik und Integration – Making up the Rules As We Go Along? – Anmerkungen zum Lissabon-Urteil des Bundesverfassungsgerichts' 726.
208. Given that Article 116 GG is not covered by the *eternity clause*, as pointed out by the Court, cf. *Right to Vote for Foreigners I* para. 56.
209. Rademacher, 'Die "Verfassungsidentität" als Grenze der Kompetenzübertragung auf die Europäische Union?' 144-145; Schröder, 'Das Demokratieprinzip des Grundgesetzes' 812.
210. As highlighted by the *Bundesverfassungsgericht*, these election principles are rooted in Article 20(2) GG, cf. 2 BvR 1953/95 *Bavarian Municipal Elections* (German Federal Constitutional Court) paras 62-65.
211. Martin Morlok and Hana Kühr, 'Wahlrechtliche Sperrklauseln und die Aufgaben einer Volksvertretung' (2012) 52 Juristische Schulung (JuS) 385, 388.

German democracy.[212] Such degressive representation, for example, employed within the European Parliament, is only permissible for indirectly representative bodies such as the German Federal Council.[213]

The only institution that is directly elected by the entire German people is the German Parliament.[214] It constitutes the primary institutional representation directly accountable to the people and enjoys the highest degree of democratic-political authority.[215] Although the Constitutional Court highlighted that democracy did not shield the existing German institutional set-up, it established that the process of determining a representing institution through free, equal and fair elections constituted a core component of German democracy.[216]

c Legitimizing Object: Components Allowing for a Political Process

The final component of German democracy is state authority. Through elections, the people mandate the exercise of state powers for a determined time. Yet, the exercise of public authority presupposes that state powers exist in the first place[217] and that the German Parliament can take political decisions.[218] Subsequently, representatives have to justify their political decisions in front of the voter in order to secure re-election. During elections, political parties compete with ideas on how to fill the political space available. Two main conclusions result from this. First, the Constitutional Court emphasizes the importance of a plural, party-political environment for the principle of democracy itself. Only if political parties offer alternatives, do voters have a choice. Therefore, the protection of political parties occupies a crucial role under the German Constitution.[219] It is a precondition for the democratic political process. Second, the

212. Kottmann and Wohlfahrt, 'Der gespaltene Wächter? Demokratie, Verfassungsidentität und Integrationsverantwortung im Lissabon-Urteil' 453.
213. *Lisbon-judgment* paras 281-286; cf. as well Matthias Ruffert, Friederike Grischek and Moritz Schramm, 'Europarecht im Examen: Grundfragen und Organisationsstruktur' (2019) 59 Juristische Schulung (JuS) 974, 977.
214. Gött, 'Die ultra vires-Rüge nach dem OMT-Vorlagebeschluss des Bundesverfassungsgerichts' 516, 527.
215. The government is indirectly legitimized through the parliament, cf. Voßkuhle and Kaiser, 'Grundwissen: Öffentliches Recht – Demokratische Legitimation' 804.
216. Rooted in human dignity and non-discrimination, cf. *Final OMT-Judgment* para. 124; 2 BvF 3/11, 2 BvR 2670/11, 2 BvE 9/11 *New Allocation of Seats in the German Parliament* (German Federal Constitutional Court) para. 52.
217. *Lisbon-judgment* para. 250: '[…] Democracy first and foremost lives on, and in, a viable public opinion that concentrates on central acts of determination of political direction and the periodic allocation of highest-ranking political offices in the competition of government and opposition. […]'; cf. as well: Wolfram Cremer, 'Lissabon-Vertrag und Grundgesetz' (2010) 32 JURA – Juristische Ausbildung 296, 299-300.
218. Schröder, 'Das Demokratieprinzip des Grundgesetzes' 814.
219. Article 21 GG constitutionally recognizes political parties, cf. 2 BvB 1/13 *Procedure to Prohibit the Political Party NPD* (German Federal Constitutional Court) paras 516-517; 2 BvF 1/65 *Party-Financing I* (German Federal Constitutional Court) paras 136-139.

Bundesverfassungsgericht established that the elected institution has to preserve central political decision-making powers over time.[220] In other words, German democracy requires that the directly legitimized institution retains the ability to take decisions in core political areas, including citizenship rules, military operations, fiscal and budgetary decisions, criminal law and cultural questions according to the Constitutional Court.[221] This selection of the Court was criticized as arbitrary[222] and the extent of required protection of the enlisted competence areas remains unclear.[223]

Overall, German democracy appears to presuppose a political space in which voters can choose between competing political programmes and in which the elected institution can take its own political decisions. Hence, the principle of democracy contains a temporal dimension that secures decision-making powers at the parliamentary level over time, which limits the political space available to the current representatives.[224]

d Delegation of Public Authority

As illustrated in Figure 3.2, all outlined components are interrelated. The German people determine their representatives through elections which then exercise political authority. The core task of democracy is to secure the delegation of state authority to an institutional representation. Yet, the preservation of political discretion at the level of institutional representation does not prevent the delegation of public authority to the EU.[225]

Article 23(1)(2) GG empowers parliament to engage in EU integration steps without questioning parliamentary powers. EU action is based on parliamentary approval and future parliaments retain the possibility to initiate EU Treaty-change or to withdraw from the EU.[226] Therefore, the German Parliament retains crucial political decision-making abilities, despite continuous EU integration. As it stands, the *Bundestag* represents the primary layer of legitimization and has to remain in charge of central political decisions. The primary aim of the German Court in its conception of democracy seems to be to ensure that the political process remains centrally at the

220. *Final OMT-Judgment* paras 127-128.
221. *Lisbon-judgment* para. 252.
222. Schwerdtfeger, 'Europäisches Unionsrecht in der Rechtsprechung des Bundesverfassungsgerichts: Grundrechts-, ultra-vires- und Identitätskontrolle im gewaltenteiligen Mehrebenensystem' 293-294.
223. Zwingmann, 'The Continuing Myth of Euro-Scepticism? The German Federal Constitutional Court Two Years after *Lisbon*' 690.
224. 2 BvL 1/12 *Relation Between International Law and the German Legal Order* (German Federal Constitutional Court) para. 53; also raised during the Eurocrisis, cf. *Quantitative Easing (PSPP) Reference* para. 56.
225. Calliess, '70 Jahre Grundgesetz und europäische Integration: "Take Back Control" oder "Mehr Demokratie wagen"?' 686.
226. Alexander Thiele, 'Der Austritt aus der EU: Hintergründe und rechtliche Rahmenbedingungen eines "Brexit"' (2016) 51 Europarecht (EuR) 281, 291-292.

national level – insisting that an opening of this process to the EU is impossible, given that no comparable accountability and legitimation exists.[227]

e Resulting Challenge for EU (Fiscal) Integration

The Court's conception of German democracy challenges EU fiscal integration proposals.[228] The first challenge is the conception of the legitimization subject as the 'German people'.[229] The German Court negated that this 'German people' could evolve into a 'European people' based on various constitutional arguments. First, the German Constitution is limited in its scope to Germany.[230] Second, the German Constitution was constituted by the German people and is an expression of their decision to organize the German state in its current manner.[231] Yet, the German Parliament can confer competences to the EU.[232] When transferring such competences, the directly legitimized parliament mandates the EU with the exercise of specific powers. This initial parliamentary approval is the basis for EU action. Therefore, the EU act is based on the German parliamentary mandate, which establishes a link to the German people. Consequently, the 'German people' as core component of German democracy appear to only emerge as a limiting factor for EU fiscal integration that challenges the Member States' (political) existence and that entails the creation of a 'European people' as new – not even partial – legitimizing-subject.[233]

The more immediate limiting factors for less far-reaching fiscal integration steps are the core material competences identified by the Constitutional Court, which are summarized in Figure 3.3.[234] According to the Court, these competences are particularly relevant for the political process and have to remain under the direct control of the German Parliament.[235]

227. Schorkopf, 'Case Nos. 2 BvE 2/08, 2 BvE 5/08, 2 BvR 1010/08, 2 BvR 1022/08, 2 BvR 1259/08, and 2 BvR 182/09: 123 BVerfGE 267 (2009)' 264.
228. Calliess, 'Konfrontation statt Kooperation zwischen BVerfG und EuGH? Zu den Folgen des Karlsruher PSPP-Urteils' 898-899; Nettesheim, 'Verfassungsrecht und Politik in der Staatsschuldenkrise' 1410.
229. Kottmann and Wohlfahrt, 'Der gespaltene Wächter? Demokratie, Verfassungsidentität und Integrationsverantwortung im Lissabon-Urteil' 445.
230. Walther Fürst and Günther Hellmuth, *Grundgesetz – Das Verfassungsrecht der Bundesrepublik Deutschland in den Grundzügen* (Studienbücher Rechtswissenschaft, 3. edn, Verlag W. Kohlhammer 1982) para. 27.
231. Caldwell, *Popular Sovereignty and the Crisis of German Constitutional Law: The Theory and Practice of Weimar Constitutionalism* 177-178.
232. Terhechte, 'Souveränität, Dynamik und Integration – Making up the Rules As We Go Along? – Anmerkungen zum Lissabon-Urteil des Bundesverfassungsgerichts' 727.
233. Kottmann and Wohlfahrt, 'Der gespaltene Wächter? Demokratie, Verfassungsidentität und Integrationsverantwortung im Lissabon-Urteil' 448-449.
234. Möllers and Redcay, 'Das Bundesverfassungsgericht als europäischer Gesetzgeber oder als Motor der Union?' 415-417.
235. *Lisbon-judgment* paras 250-252; cf. as well: Polzin, 'Constitutional Identity, Unconstitutional Amendments and the Idea of Constituent Power: The Development of the Doctrine of Constitutional Identity in German Constitutional Law' 429-431.

Figure 3.3 Democratic Political Space at the Disposition of Bundestag

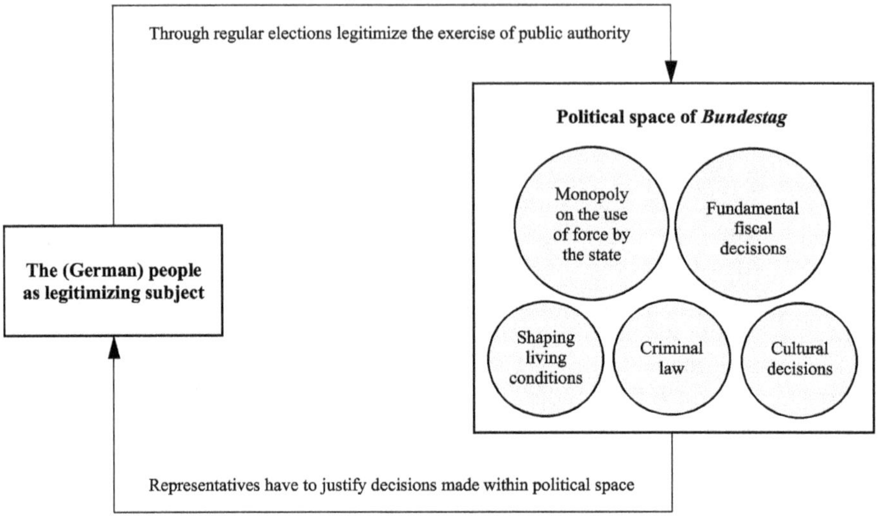

Although the identification of particular material policy areas under Article 79(3) GG is novel and only occurred towards the EU,[236] some similarity with the established internal constitutional jurisprudence can be observed. Notably, the German constitutional order contains so-called legislative[237] and parliamentary reservations.[238] According to these reservations, central political decisions have to be taken by parliament in a legislative act.[239] The German Court applies a *case-to-case* assessment in order to determine whether measures fall under such reservation.[240] This assessment includes the primary question of whether a legislative act is required, but also subsequently how the matter has to be regulated.[241] The Court found, for example, that the peaceful use of nuclear energy,[242] the deployment of chemical weapons,[243] the conditions for the

236. Cf. Schröder, 'Das Demokratieprinzip des Grundgesetzes' 816; Schorkopf, 'Case Nos. 2 BvE 2/08, 2 BvE 5/08, 2 BvR 1010/08, 2 BvR 1022/08, 2 BvR 1259/08, and 2 BvR 182/09: 123 BVerfGE 267 (2009)' 264.
237. In German: *Vorbehalt des Gesetzes*.
238. In German: *Parlamentsvorbehalt*; Wissenschaftlicher Dienst des Deutschen Bundestages, *Reichweite der Wesentlichkeitslehre: Grenzfälle der Wesentlichkeit (WD 3 – 3000 – 043/15)* (Deutscher Bundestag, 2015) 4-5; Voßkuhle and Kaiser, 'Grundwissen: Öffentliches Recht – Demokratische Legitimation' 804.
239. Andreas Voßkuhle, 'Grundwissen: Öffentliches Recht – Der Grundsatz des Vorbehalts des Gesetzes' (2007) 47 Juristische Schulung (JuS) 118, 118.
240. 2 BvL 8/77 *Peaceful Use of Nuclear Energy in Germany* (German Federal Constitutional Court) para. 77; cf. as well: Voßkuhle, 'Grundwissen – Öffentliches Recht: Der Grundsatz des Vorbehalts des Gesetzes' 119.
241. Based on the 'essentiality theory', cf. Pieroth, 'Das Demokratieprinzip des Grundgesetzes' 477-478.
242. *Peaceful Use of Nuclear Energy in Germany*.
243. 2 BvR 624, 1080, 2029/83 *Deployment of Chemical Weapons* (German Federal Constitutional Court).

keeping of laying hens,[244] as well the German spelling reform,[245] fall within the ambit of particularly important decisions that require a legislative act. Furthermore, certain matters are considered to be so essential that only parliament can decide them. A prominent example is the deployment of the German army, which constitutes a historically rooted[246] parliamentary reservation.[247] Overall, the concepts of parliamentary and legislative reservation indicate that specific *internal* decisions require direct involvement of the German Parliament. Interestingly, the Court refrains internally from defining entire competence areas under such reservations. Instead, it requires a *case-to-case* assessment in which the policy area as well as the concrete measures envisaged are evaluated in order to determine whether parliament was (and can be in the future) sufficiently involved.[248] This differs from the Court's EU approach, where entire competence areas were marked as particularly important for parliament. At least two explanations might be relevant here.

First, in contrast to *internal* shifts of competences, the conferral of competences to the EU is more difficult to reverse, simply because other Member States have to jointly agree on possible Treaty-changes or the German Parliament could otherwise only decide to trigger Article 50 TEU.[249] Also, the 'return' of competences from the supranational to the national level is not part of the EU logic that conceptualizes European integration as a process that strives for an 'ever-closer Union'. Thus, even if the Constitutional Court would find that EU actions required additional legitimization by the German Parliament, it is questionable whether such a judicial view could be adequately respected. This risk does not emerge in the same manner internally, given that the German Court is the undisputed final arbiter and other German institutions have to implement its rulings.

Second, the protected areas are connected to competences that are traditionally attributed to a sovereign state.[250] Thus, by identifying these areas as components of the *eternity clause*, the Constitutional Court equally preserves German sovereignty and statehood, which ultimately secures the Court's own powerful position.[251]

Based on these findings it appears that EU fiscal integration steps should award a decisive role to national parliaments in EU level decision-making process. The central involvement of national parliaments could preserve the central position and final authority of Member States in decisions on the identified core state competences – which are closely linked with German democracy according to the jurisprudence of the German Constitutional Court. Taken together, this indicates that EU fiscal integration

244. 2 BvF 3/90 *Conditions for the Keeping of Laying Hens* (German Federal Constitutional Court).
245. 1 BvR 1640/97 *German Spelling Reform* (German Federal Constitutional Court).
246. *German Participation in NATO Actions* para. 330.
247. Mattias G. Fischer and Manuel Ladiges, 'Evakuierungseinsätze der Bundeswehr künftig ohne Parlamentsvorbehalt' (2016) 35 Neue Zeitschrift für Verwaltungsrecht (NVwZ) 32, 32.
248. Given that the Court employs a flexible and open approach, cf. Bundestages, *Reichweite der Wesentlichkeitslehre: Grenzfälle der Wesentlichkeit (WD 3 – 3000 – 043/15)* 6-7.
249. Thomas Groß, 'Erlaubt das Grundgesetz einen Austritt aus der EU?' (2018) 53 Europarecht (EuR) 387, 403-404.
250. Schröder, 'Das Demokratieprinzip des Grundgesetzes' 816.
251. Mayer, 'Rashomon in Karlsruhe: A Reflection on Democracy and Identity in the European Union' 774.

is not necessarily incompatible with German democracy – rather specific forms of EU fiscal integration that merely aim at centralizing powers at the EU level appear incompatible with German democracy.

2 *Overall Budgetary Responsibility*

Based on the competence core of German democracy, the Constitutional Court developed *overall budgetary responsibility*[252] and employed it as the main constitutional vehicle to decide on the compatibility of Eurocrisis-related measures with the German Constitution.[253] The underlying premise of *overall budgetary responsibility* is that central budgetary and fiscal decisions have to be made by the German Parliament.[254] Based on this premise, the Constitutional Court introduced a competence-specific, absolute limit for the conferral of fiscal and budgetary competences to the EU.[255] The subsequent analysis focuses on the underpinning democracy-theoretical considerations (a), before then considering its constitutional conditions (b) as well as their concrete application (c).

a *Underpinning Democracy-Theoretical Considerations*

Overall budgetary responsibility requires that fundamental fiscal and budgetary decisions remain under the direct control of the German Parliament.[256] The concept aims at preserving an open, democratic political process on revenue and expenditure in Germany.[257] Traditionally, budgetary and fiscal competences are characterized as core powers of modern parliaments,[258] given that most political decisions are intertwined

252. Calliess, 'Constitutional Identity in Germany: One for Three or Three in One?' 164-165.
253. Jan-Herman Reestman, 'Legitimacy Through Adjudication: The ESM Treaty and the Fiscal Compact Before the National Courts' in Thomas Beukers, Bruno de Witte and Claire Kilpatrick (eds), *Constitutional Change Through Euro-Crisis Law* (Cambridge University Press 2017) 259; Nettesheim, 'Die "haushaltspolitische Gesamtverantwortung" in der Rechtsprechung des BVerfG' 12.
254. *Quantitative Easing (PSPP) Final Judgment* para. 104; *Lisbon-judgment* paras 252, 256; cf. as well: Mehrdad Payandeh, 'The OMT Judgment of the German Federal Constitutional Court: Repositioning the Court within the European Constitutional Architecture' (2017) 13 European Constitutional Law Review 400, 408.
255. Pilz, 'Ein Schatzamt für die Eurozone? – Überlegungen zu den Vorschlägen des Europäischen Parlaments und der Kommission zu einer Reform der Wirtschaftsunion' 643-644; Franz C. Mayer, 'Rebels Without a Cause? Zur OMT-Vorlage des Bundesverfassungsgerichts' (2014) 49 Europarecht (EuR) 473, 497.
256. *Quantitative Easing (PSPP) Final Judgment* para. 104; *Final OMT-Judgment* para. 212; cf. as well: Herdegen, 'Art. 79 GG' para. 185; Christian Calliess, 'Der Kampf um den Euro: Eine "Angelegenheit der Europäischen Union" zwischen Regierung, Parlament und Volk' (2012) 31 Neue Zeitschrift für Verwaltungsrecht (NVwZ) 1, 6-7.
257. *ESM-Treaty and Fiscal Compact (interim relief)* para. 118; referred to as discretionary decision-making space, cf. Nettesheim, 'Die "haushaltspolitische Gesamtverantwortung" in der Rechtsprechung des BVerfG' 19.
258. Carsten Schneider, 'Exkurs: Die Rolle des Haushaltsausschusses des Bundestages bei Aufstellung und Vollzug des Haushalts: ein Praxisbericht' in Werner Gatzer and Tilmann Schweisfurth (eds), *Öffentliche Finanzwirtschaft in der Staatspraxis* (BWV – Berliner Wissenschafts-Verlag 2015) 295; described as 'crown jewels' of modern parliaments by former German constitutional

with decisions on revenue and expenditure. Political parties campaign based on their budgetary and fiscal planning. These proposals then impact the voter's final vote. Given the importance of these competences for the political sphere, the Court concluded that a sitting parliament must be able to autonomously reverse budgetary and fiscal decisions taken by preceding parliaments.[259] Hence, the underpinning objective of *overall budgetary responsibility* is the protection of the 'democratic self-determination' of the people.[260]

In addition, preserving the democratic decision-making abilities of the German Parliament requires that fiscal and budgetary competences remain permanently within its powers.[261] The so-called future openness of the German budget guarantees that a newly elected *Bundestag* has the ability to take self-responsible budgetary decisions.[262] The general reversibility of fiscal decisions requires political parties to continuously justify their fiscal decisions and budgetary planning before the voters.[263] At the same time, the Court accepted parliamentary discretion to make limited budgetary and fiscal commitments at EU level.

Finally, the German Constitution establishes the German Parliament as the central institutional decision-maker on budgetary matters.[264] Given its institutional position, it carries the overall responsibility for revenue and expenditure as well as for achieving a viable annual state budget.[265] The *Bundestag* is the institution that exercises comprehensive control over all budgetary commitments, which are cumulated in the annual budget. This annual budget serves then as the legal basis for governmental and administrative measures.[266] Moreover, the German Parliament has to include in its appraisal of the annual budget broader constitutional considerations imposed by the German Constitution.[267] Hence, allocating overall responsibility for budgetary planning to the *Bundestag* ensures that the budget is both viable and compatible with wider constitutional requirements.

---

judge Udo di Fabio; cf. Puntscher Riekmann and Wydra, 'Representation in the European State of Emergency: Parliaments Against Governments?' 567; traditionally, also referred to as 'regalian' powers or rights of the crown, cf. Denis Baranger, 'The Apparition of Sovereignty' in Hent Kalmo and Quentin Skinner (eds), *Sovereignty in Fragments: The Past, Present and Future of a Contested Concept* (Cambridge University Press 2010) 61.

259. *Financial Support for Greece and EFSF* para. 124; cf. as well: Nettesheim, '"Euro-Rettung" und Grundgesetz: Verfassungsgerichtliche Vorgaben für den Umbau der Währungsunion' 772.
260. *Quantitative Easing (PSPP) Final Judgment* paras 99-101; cf. as well: De Sadeleer, 'The New Architecture of European Economic Governance' 36.
261. Herrmann, 'Die Bewältigung der Euro-Staatsschulden-Krise an den Grenzen des deutschen und europäischen Währverfassungsrechts' 808.
262. Wendel, 'Exceeding Judicial Competence in the Name of Democracy: The German Federal Constitutional Court's OMT Reference' 285.
263. Cf. *Final OMT-Judgment* para. 130; *ESM-Treaty and Fiscal Compact (interim relief)* para. 122.
264. As established in Article 110(2) Basic Law, the annual budget has to be approved by the parliament through a legislative act, cf. Schneider, 'Exkurs: Die Rolle des Haushaltsausschusses des Bundestages bei Aufstellung und Vollzug des Haushalts: ein Praxisbericht' 295-296.
265. *ESM-Treaty and Fiscal Compact (interim relief)* para. 109; cf. as well: Herrmann, 'Die Bewältigung der Euro-Staatsschulden-Krise an den Grenzen des deutschen und europäischen Währverfassungsrechts' 808.
266. *Financial Support for Greece and EFSF* para. 122; *Lisbon-judgment* para. 256.
267. For example, the social state principle, cf. Nigel Foster and Satish Sule, *German Legal System and Laws* (4th edn, Oxford University Press 2010) 188.

b Requirements of Budgetary Responsibility

Based on these underpinning considerations, the Court identified procedural and institutional characteristics, as well as substantive requirements under *overall budgetary responsibility*:

> On the procedural side, the German Court underscored that the constitutive approval of the German Parliament is compulsory for all budgetary and fiscal commitments that impact the German state budget.[268] Consequently, no financial burden for the German state can arise without prior parliamentary approval. This entails that the German state cannot be liable for budgetary decisions taken by third parties.[269] Instead, the German Parliament has to debate commitments with budgetary implications and evaluate possible financial benefits or risks. Furthermore, large financial commitments might require subsequent constitutive parliamentary approvals on various occasions, in case they are not sufficiently specific and financial risks are not entirely foreseeable.[270] This was relevant for the EFSF and ESM, where the Court concluded that the German Parliament's approval of the general scheme was not sufficient, but instead, constitutive approvals of every country-specific financial support programme drafted under these schemes were required.[271] At the same time, the Court acknowledged and accepted that factual circumstances especially in crisis moments might limit parliamentary choices when approving such budgetary and fiscal commitments.[272]

In order to enable the German Parliament to comprehensively evaluate the commitments, the *Bundestag* has to have all relevant information at its disposal.[273] Based on the received information, parliament can then independently decide whether or not to engage in a proposed supranational financial commitment. Thus, the Court formulated qualitative requirements for the act of approval, which mirror the constitutional requirements imposed for the transfer of competences to the EU: budgetary or fiscal commitments have to be limited in extent and the conferral has to be specific concerning the attached substantive and procedural conditions.[274] Therefore, the German Parliament cannot confer competences which would empower EU institutions to determine autonomously to what extent national budgetary or fiscal powers are to be exercised at the supranational level.[275] Finally, the German Parliament is obliged to

268. Reestman, 'Legitimacy Through Adjudication: The ESM Treaty and the Fiscal Compact Before the National Courts' 259.
269. According to the Court, the Basic Law prohibits such automatic liability, cf. *Quantitative Easing (PSPP) Final Judgment* paras 226-227.
270. Nettesheim, 'Die "haushaltspolitische Gesamtverantwortung" in der Rechtsprechung des BVerfG' 23.
271. Calliess, 'Der Kampf um den Euro: Eine "Angelegenheit der Europäischen Union" zwischen Regierung, Parlament und Volk' 4.
272. Nettesheim, 'Die "haushaltspolitische Gesamtverantwortung" in der Rechtsprechung des BVerfG' 23.
273. *ESM-Treaty and Fiscal Compact (interim relief)* para. 111; cf. as well: Gött, 'Die ultra vires-Rüge nach dem OMT-Vorlagebeschluss des Bundesverfassungsgerichts' 515.
274. *ESM-Treaty and Fiscal Compact (interim relief)* paras 108, 130.
275. Which the Court termed 'blanket empowerments', cf. *ESM-Treaty and Fiscal Compact* para. 160; *Lisbon-judgment* para. 236; cf. as well: Sven Simon, *Grenzen des Bundesverfassungsgerichts im europäischen Integrationsprozess*, vol. 253 (Jus Publicum, Mohr Siebeck 2016) 297.

continuously monitor the exercise of the conferred powers.[276] As a general rule, the Court indicated that the parliamentary intervention and veto possibilities during the monitoring process have to be proportionate to the financial commitment made.[277] Thus, the bigger the financial commitment the more extensive parliamentary intervention possibilities have to be.

On the substantive side, the Court's jurisprudence remains abstract and broad, given that it only conducts a limited constitutional review of the inherently political decisions taken. The Court established that only an 'evident overstepping of the inner boundaries' of the principle of democracy would qualify as a violation of *overall budgetary responsibility* under Article 79(3) Basic Law.[278] It seems that the limited review reflects the constitutionally enshrined political discretion that the German Parliament enjoys when evaluating the impact of financial commitments.[279]

For now, the Court has refrained from defining any fixed sum of money or a specific percentage of the overall budget as an absolute limit for supranational financial commitments.[280] Instead, it conducted the substantive assessment of the parliamentary decision based on broad guiding principles. From this jurisprudence, it can be deduced in the first place, that the Court accepted that financial commitments in the EU-context can be reconciled with the German Constitution.[281] This conclusion is also not altered by the recent decision on the ECB's PSP-Programme. Although the programme was declared *ultra vires*, the constitutional concerns related to a procedural error in the ECB's proportionality assessment and the Court allowed for a three-month transitional period to remedy this error.[282] However, within these various decisions, the Court established that the *Bundestag* may not surrender to:

- either financial obligations as well as liabilities that would factually suspend German budgetary autonomy for a considerable time;[283]

276. Nettesheim, 'Die "haushaltspolitische Gesamtverantwortung" in der Rechtsprechung des BVerfG' 23.
277. *ESM-Treaty and Fiscal Compact (interim relief)* para. 110; cf. as well: Nettesheim, 'Die "haushaltspolitische Gesamtverantwortung" in der Rechtsprechung des BVerfG' 21.
278. Simon, *Grenzen des Bundesverfassungsgerichts im europäischen Integrationsprozess* 188-189.
279. As established in Article 110 Basic Law, cf. Schneider, 'Exkurs: Die Rolle des Haushaltsausschusses des Bundestages bei Aufstellung und Vollzug des Haushalts: ein Praxisbericht' 295-296.
280. *Financial Support for Greece and EFSF* paras 131-135; cf. Payandeh, 'The OMT Judgment of the German Federal Constitutional Court: Repositioning the Court Within the European Constitutional Architecture' 416.
281. Armin Steinbach, 'All's Well That Ends Well? Crisis Policy after the German Constitutional Court's Ruling in Gauweiler' (2017) 24 Maastricht Journal of European and Comparative Law 140, 142.
282. *Quantitative Easing (PSPP) Reference* para. 235.
283. *ESM-Treaty and Fiscal Compact (interim relief)* para. 113; *Financial Support for Greece and EFSF* para. 135; in particular no automatic liability for political decisions made by other actors, cf. *Quantitative Easing (PSPP) Final Judgment* paras 226-227; *Quantitative Easing (PSPP) Reference* para. 129; *Final OMT-Judgment* para. 213.

- or a permanent transfer of essential budgetary powers to EU level, which would enable the EU to determine the type and level of German spending to a considerable degree.[284]

In case one of these two substantive conditions is violated, the German Court would likely conclude that the German Parliament would lose its ability to modify the budgetary planning and make independent fiscal decisions. By imposing these two substantive limits, the Court intends to ensure that the German Parliament remains autonomous in essential budgetary decisions. Ultimately, the German Court saw this requirement sufficiently reflected in the EU-Treaties. Namely, the no-bail-out clause in Article 125 TFEU and the various requirements imposed for sustainable national budgeting and the prohibition of monetary financing presuppose that national parliaments remain responsible for their own national state budgets.[285]

c *Application of These Requirements by the Bundesverfassungsgericht*

In the concrete application of these requirements, the Constitutional Court mainly engaged in a detailed assessment of the procedural elements. Notably, when assessing the different Eurocrisis-related measures, the Court determined whether the supranational financial commitments were limited in volume, sufficiently specific and whether the German Parliament was able to take an informed decision.

In its first comprehensive Eurocrisis-related decision, the Court considered volume, purpose, objective and the specific rules attached to the first Greek loan package as well as the EFSF, in order to determine whether the German commitments complied with the outlined constitutional requirements.[286] In its assessment, the Court distinguished between the Greek loan package, which it considered sufficiently detailed and specific, and the EFSF, which only provided for a general framework for financial stabilization measures. The Court insisted that every specific programme initiated under the EFSF required constitutive approval of the German Parliament. The Court noted that the German act of approval merely stated that the German Government should aim at reaching a common position on specific EFSF-programmes with the

284. *Quantitative Easing (PSPP) Final Judgment* para. 104; *Final OMT-Judgment* para. 210-213; *ESM-Treaty and Fiscal Compact* para. 163; cf. as well: Claes and Reestman, 'The Protection of National Constitutional Identity and the Limits of European Integration at the Occasion of the *Gauweiler* Case' 927.

285. *Quantitative Easing (PSPP) Final Judgment* paras 226-227; *Quantitative Easing (PSPP) Reference* para. 56; *OMT-Reference* para. 28; *ESM-Treaty and Fiscal Compact (interim relief)* para. 110; in his assessment, Nettesheim identifies five core components of the principle of *overall budgetary responsibility*, which correspond in main parts with the previous outline. Namely the concept requires according to his analysis: (1) no external determination of budgetary commitments; (2) the precise determination of any fiscal commitment by the German parliament; (3) the limitation of any such commitment with predictable consequences; (4) the preservation of continuous influence of as well as the reversibility by German actors; and finally (5) the proportionality of the overall amount of the commitments, cf. Nettesheim, '"Euro-Rettung" und Grundgesetz: Verfassungsgerichtliche Vorgaben für den Umbau der Währungsunion' 773-776.

286. *Financial Support for Greece and EFSF* paras 131, 139.

German Parliament, which was deemed insufficient to warrant parliamentary budgetary prerogatives.[287] Thus, the Court strengthened the position of the German Parliament in the EFSF framework and indicated that approving a general scheme, even if including a maximum volume, general conditions and objectives, was not sufficient to comply with *overall budgetary responsibility*. Instead, the German Parliament was required to approve all specific programmes, assess possible financial risks and conduct an overall financial assessment. The Court further clarified that these central decisions could not be delegated to a parliamentary committee but instead, given the right of parliamentarians to equally participate in important parliamentary decisions, these decisions had to be taken in the plenary.[288]

A similar approach was followed in the examination of the ESM-Treaty, where the Court investigated in detail whether the German financial commitment of up to EUR 190 billion could be increased without the *Bundestag's* approval.[289] The Court concluded that in case the ESM-Treaty would be read as allowing the increase of the overall German liability without German parliamentary approval, such reading would violate *overall budgetary responsibility*.[290] It can be deduced from this approach that the German Parliament cannot approve an unspecific entitlement clause, according to which the EU could determine German financial commitments. The requirement that the German legislator has to take all central budgetary decisions itself, implies that no supranational blanket empowerment (*'carte blanche'*) can be issued.[291]

When assessing the substantive components of *overall budgetary responsibility*, the Court restricts its assessment to a limited 'obviousness' review of the taken measures. Namely, only a manifest and evident overstepping of German democracy is scrutinized. In relation to the EFSF and the first Greek loan package, the Court concluded that the combined commitment of up to EUR 170 billion did not pre-empt the budgetary autonomy of the German Parliament for a considerable time, even though this amount was considerably bigger than half of the then enacted annual federal budget.[292] In relation to the ESM-Treaty, the German Court applied a similarly

287. Thomas Beukers, 'The Eurozone Crisis and the Autonomy of Member States in Economic Union: Changes and Challenges' in Panos Koutrakos and Jukka Snell (eds), *Research Handbook on the Law of the EU's Internal Market* (Edward Elgar Publishing Limited 2017) 274; Ketterer, *Zustimmungserfordernis beim Europäischen Stabilitätsmechanismus* 308.

288. *Participation of Members of German Parliament in the EFSF* paras 131, 136; cf. as well: Christian Bumke and Andreas Voßkuhle, *German Constitutional Law: Introduction, Cases, and Principles* (Oxford University Press 2019) paras 1634-1636.

289. Calliess, 'Der Kampf um den Euro: Eine "Angelegenheit der Europäischen Union" zwischen Regierung, Parlament und Volk' 4.

290. Ohler, 'Rechtliche Maßstäbe der Geldpolitik nach dem Gauweiler-Urteil des EuGH' 1005; cf. as well: Wendel, 'Exceeding Judicial Competence in the Name of Democracy: The German Federal Constitutional Court's OMT Reference' 267.

291. *ESM-Treaty and Fiscal Compact* para. 160; *Lisbon-judgment* para. 236; cf. as well: Simon, *Grenzen des Bundesverfassungsgerichts im europäischen Integrationsprozess* 297.

292. The annual federal budget was about EUR 307 billion for the year 2012, cf. German Federal Ministry of Finance, 'Haushaltsrechnung des Bundes für das Haushaltsjahr 2012' (*German Government*, 2013), https://www.bundesfinanzministerium.de/Content/DE/Standardartikel/Themen/Oeffentliche_Finanzen/Bundeshaushalt/Haushalts_und_Vermoegensrechnungen_des_Bundes/2013-06-13-haushaltsrechnung-des-bundes-2012.pdf?__blob=publicationFile&v=1, accessed 5 April 2023.

limited review. It found that the ESM commitment amounting to EUR 190 billion constituted a predictable financial risk compared to the hardly predictable financial consequences for future parliaments in case no supranational steps were taken.[293]

In its more recent jurisprudence, the Constitutional Court established that *overall budgetary responsibility* might also be at risk through commitments made by the ECB and the Eurosystem.[294] The Court identified two particularly contentious constitutional matters. First, the distinction between monetary and economic policies, which according to the Court ultimately concerns a question of competence-conferral.[295] And second, the possible implications of ECB monetary programmes for the German state budget.[296]

Regarding the distinction between monetary and economic policies,[297] suffice it here to point to the possible repercussions of an unclear, unspecific conferral of competences at EU level. Following the German Court, the competence distinction between monetary and economic policies is crucial, given that Member States attached different (procedural) modalities to these competence areas.[298] Thus, the Court invoked the principle of conferral and highlighted that the allocation of competences established in the EU-Treaties had to be respected by EU institutions. Otherwise, the national principles of democracy and sovereignty could be undermined.[299] The *OMT*- and the *PSP-Programme*-proceedings clearly illustrate the importance of a workable and judicially controllable conferral of powers. Given that EU fiscal integration will necessarily affect important national competences, a legally clear-cut, unambiguous conferral seems crucial to reduce the risk of *ultra vires* proceedings in Germany.

In relation to the possible budgetary implications of the ECB's programmes, the German Court argued that due to the participation of the German Central Bank in the implementation of the ECB's monetary policies, the German federal budget might potentially be affected. As the Court highlighted, the German Parliament might be constitutionally obliged to refinance the German Central Bank in case of losses which could result from such ECB programmes.[300] In such a situation a risk to the budgetary autonomy of the German Parliament could materialize, specifically in light of the volume of the PSP-Programme. The Court emphasized that such a programme could

293. *ESM-Treaty and Fiscal Compact (interim relief)* para. 167.
294. Polzin, 'Constitutional Identity, Unconstitutional Amendments and the Idea of Constituent Power: The Development of the Doctrine of Constitutional Identity in German Constitutional Law' 430-431.
295. *Quantitative Easing (PSPP) Final Judgment* paras 138, 159-160; *Final OMT-Judgment* paras 144-145; cf. as well: Steinbach, 'All's Well That Ends Well? Crisis Policy after the German Constitutional Court's Ruling in Gauweiler' 142.
296. Takis Tridimas and Napoleon Xanthoulis, 'A Legal Analysis of the Gauweiler Case: Between Monetary Policy and Constitutional Conflict' (2016) 23 Maastricht Journal of European and Comparative Law 17, 20.
297. An highly debated question, cf. Payandeh, 'The OMT Judgment of the German Federal Constitutional Court: Repositioning the Court Within the European Constitutional Architecture' 410.
298. *Quantitative Easing (PSPP) Final Judgment* para. 142; *Final OMT-Judgment* paras 193-196.
299. *Quantitative Easing (PSPP) Final Judgment* paras 138, 159-160.
300. Based on Article 88GG, cf. *Quantitative Easing (PSPP) Final Judgment* paras 222, 227; *Quantitative Easing (PSPP) Reference* para. 126; *Final OMT-Judgment* paras 216-217.

under no circumstances be employed to 'redistribute sovereign debt' of other Member States and thereby create an automatic liability for budgetary decisions of third parties.[301] It however accepted that the '[...] scheme for the allocation of risk between the national central banks provided for in Art. 6 (3) of Decision 2015/774 [...]' constituted a sufficient safeguard for *overall budgetary responsibility*.[302] On the one hand, this emphasizes the importance of the constitutive, informed approval of the German Parliament regarding budgetary commitments. On the other hand, it indicates that the Court is willing to accept safeguards implemented at EU level to preserve German budgetary autonomy. And finally, the German Court established through its decisions on the *OMT*- and the *PSP*-Programme, that such programmes can be validly initiated on the basis of the ECB's monetary policy prerogative without conflicting with German *overall budgetary responsibility*.

The most recent constitutional decision concerned the 2021 Own Resources Decision and NGEU. In its *interim decision*, the German Constitutional Court established that German *overall budgetary responsibility* could be violated in case EU commitments and liabilities (if materialized) factually suspend German budgetary autonomy for a considerable time.[303] The Court reiterated parliament's wide margin of discretion when evaluating, for example, the likelihood of liability risks, the implications for the national budget including its viability, the economic development and alternative courses of action as well as their consequences. This suggests that German Court will not replace the political assessment made on these points, as long as budgetary autonomy is preserved.[304] In its *interim* appraisal, the German Court highlighted: first, the EU borrowing did not create direct liabilities for the German state budget, but rather for the EU budget and that subsequently a pro-rata liability is foreseen; second, the Own Resources Decision itself formulated an upper limit for the liabilities as well as a specific deadline for the repayment; third, NGEU clearly specified the use of the borrowed funds; and fourth, the obligations under the Own Resources Decision remained temporary and any extension required approval by the German Parliament. The Court concluded that a violation of *overall budgetary responsibility* was unlikely.

In its final judgment, the Court raised concerns regarding the existence of a sufficient legal basis to adopt the recovery strategy and specifically to allow for large-scale EU borrowing under the EU Treaties.[305] It ultimately concluded, however,

301. *Quantitative Easing (PSPP) Final Judgment* paras 222, 227; *Final OMT-Judgment* paras 213-214.
302. *Quantitative Easing (PSPP) Final Judgment* para. 222.
303. 2 BvR 547/21 *Interim Decision on the Ratification of the Own Resources Decision (NGEU)* (German Federal Constitutional Court); on the procedural background, cf. Caroline Heber, 'Europarechtliche Grenzen für den Wiederaufbaufonds' (2021) 56 Europarecht (EuR) 416, 417-418.
304. *Interim Decision on the Ratification of the Own Resources Decision (NGEU)*; Wendel, 'The Fog of Identity and Judicial Contestation: Preventive and Defensive Constitutional Identity Review in Germany' 479.
305. *Final Decision on the Ratification of the Own Resources Decision (NGEU)* paras 148-192; cf. as well: Armin Steinbach and Sebastian Grund, 'Der EU-Corona-Aufbaufonds: nächste Etappe in die Fiskal- und Transferunion?' (2023) 76 Neue Juristische Wochenschrift (NJW) 406, 406;

that the possible overstepping was not sufficiently obvious to declare the Own Resources Decision *ultra vires*. Specifically on *overall budgetary responsibility*, the German Court highlighted that the borrowed funds were strictly tied to a specific purpose, that these were limited in terms of volume and duration, and that the German Parliament had approved them following Article 311(3)(3) TFEU, which guarantees a decisive role for parliament. Based on these considerations, the Court then highlighted that no direct liabilities for the German budget stemmed from the Own Resources Decision, that no permanent mechanism was established through which the German state budget would be liable to finance decisions of third parties, and that the financial burden remained manageable for the German state budget.[306] In this regard, the Court emphasized once again the prerogative of parliament to make the required risk and overall viability evaluation[307] and found no violation of *overall budgetary responsibility*. Although this constitutes a significant constitutional development, it should be highlighted that the German practice of interpreting the EU Treaties (based on the German Constitution) without the involvement of the CJEU threatens the consistency of EU law.[308]

Considering these two decisions, it is obvious that the Court focuses again on its assessment of the *procedural* requirements. The Court has accepted that the EU may borrow funds to finance (emergency) policies, in case these are strictly limited in terms of volume and duration, tied to clearly defined purposes, and based on constitutive approval of the German Parliament (following Article 311(3)(3) TFEU).[309] This clearly broadens the scope for EU fiscal action in the future.[310]

Matthias Ruffert, 'Europarecht und Verfassungsrecht: NextGenerationEU – Der Eigenmittelbeschluss zur Verwirklichung des Programms NextGenerationEU ist nicht offensichtlich unionsrechtswidrig' (2023) 63 Juristische Schulung (JuS) 277, 278-279.

306. *Final Decision on the Ratification of the Own Resources Decision (NGEU)* paras 213, 217, 224, 226; cf. as well: Ruffert, 'Europarecht und Verfassungsrecht: NextGenerationEU – Der Eigenmittelbeschluss zur Verwirklichung des Programms NextGenerationEU ist nicht offensichtlich unionsrechtswidrig' 280; Peter Hilpold, 'Next Generation EU und die "Einnahmensouveränität": Das EU-Eigenmittelsystem vor dem BVerfG – Zugleich Bespr. von BVerfG 6.12.2022: 2 BvR 547/21, 2 BvR 798/21' (2023) 34 Europäische Zeitschrift für Wirtschaftsrecht 169, 174.
307. *Final Decision on the Ratification of the Own Resources Decision (NGEU)* paras 229-230; cf. as well: Ruffert, 'Europarecht und Verfassungsrecht: NextGenerationEU – Der Eigenmittelbeschluss zur Verwirklichung des Programms NextGenerationEU ist nicht offensichtlich unionsrechtswidrig' 280; Hilpold, 'Next Generation EU und die "Einnahmensouveränität": Das EU-Eigenmittelsystem vor dem BVerfG – Zugleich Bespr. von BVerfG 6.12.2022: 2 BvR 547/21, 2 BvR 798/21' 174.
308. Steinbach and Grund, 'Der EU-Corona-Aufbaufonds: nächste Etappe in die Fiskal-und Transferunion?' 409-410; Hilpold, 'Next Generation EU und die "Einnahmensouveränität": Das EU-Eigenmittelsystem vor dem BVerfG – Zugleich Bespr. von BVerfG 6.12.2022: 2 BvR 547/21, 2 BvR 798/21' 170.
309. *Final Decision on the Ratification of the Own Resources Decision (NGEU)* paras 171, 189-192; cf. as well: Steinbach and Grund, 'Der EU-Corona-Aufbaufonds: nächste Etappe in die Fiskal- und Transferunion?' 408; Ruffert, 'Europarecht und Verfassungsrecht: NextGenerationEU – Der Eigenmittelbeschluss zur Verwirklichung des Programms NextGenerationEU ist nicht offensichtlich unionsrechtswidrig' 280.
310. Wendel, 'The Fog of Identity and Judicial Contestation: Preventive and Defensive Constitutional Identity Review in Germany' 479.

d Conclusion on Overall Budgetary Responsibility

Taken together, *overall budgetary responsibility* is a strict substantive limit which could reduce the constitutional space available for EU fiscal integration. Yet, in the concrete application of this limit, the German Constitutional Court confirmed the broad political discretion of the German Parliament when deciding on supranational financial commitments. Notably, as to substantive limits, the Court only conducts a limited review restricted to 'manifest oversteppings' thereby respecting the parliament's discretion.[311]

Furthermore, *overall budgetary responsibility* requires that the German Parliament can take central budgetary decisions autonomously from supranational obligations. Therefore, the parliamentary approval for supranational financial commitments or liabilities has to be constitutive.[312] It also entails that financial commitments remain limited in volume and specific in their objectives. In short, the German Parliament has to remain the central institution that decides whether and how to commit. This can occur by either attaching strict conditions, as the case with the first Greek loan package or under NGEU, or by requiring additional subsequent parliamentary approvals when deciding on the use of the committed funds, as visible in relation to the ESM. Given these requirements, the Constitutional Court continuously emphasized that Germany cannot automatically assume liability for political decisions of other Member States. Such automatism would neither be specific and unlimited nor would it presuppose parliamentary approval. This suggests for EU fiscal integration steps that national parliaments must retain a central role in the administration of fiscal powers and be able to effectively oppose decisions.

e Possible Double Standard in the Conception of Overall Budgetary Responsibility

When comparing the internal and the EU-related constitutional assessment of budgetary decisions or fiscal commitments a divagating appraisal can again be identified. Notably, the exclusive application of *overall budgetary responsibility* to EU matters can be questioned, given that the concept's underlying intention to preserve parliamentary budgetary prerogatives as well as its constitutional basis in Article 20(1) and (2) GG in conjunction with Article 79(3) GG equally apply internally.[313]

311. As highlighted by the Court in the OMT- and the Quantitative Easing-cases, it tries to avoid interfering in the political decision-making process, cf. *Quantitative Easing (PSPP) Reference* paras 53, 58; *Final OMT-Judgment* paras 155-156; it was however question whether the Court achieved this, cf. *OMT-Reference* dissenting opinion Lübbe-Wolff para. 2.

312. *Interim Decision on the Ratification of the Own Resources Decision (NGEU)*; *Quantitative Easing (PSPP) Final Judgment* paras 222, 227.

313. Nettesheim, 'Die "haushaltspolitische Gesamtverantwortung" in der Rechtsprechung des BVerfG' 13-14.

i Constitutional Scrutiny of the German Budget

The German Constitution contains a specific section on public finances in Articles 104a to 115 GG. Despite the interconnection between budgetary and fiscal matters with the principle of democracy, the Constitutional Court refrained from connecting the *eternity clause* to this internal financial constitutional framework. Instead, it relied on the specific constitutional financial framework when assessing *internal* budgetary or fiscal commitments. In addition, the Court emphasized the discretion of the constitution-amending legislator when modifying the constitutional financial framework,[314] without indicating that this discretion could possibly be limited by the *eternity clause*. Given that internal financial and budgetary commitments are only assessed on the basis of this specific framework, the Court, therefore, refrained from identifying potentially absolute constitutional limits to such commitments and focused on procedural constitutional requirements.

Notably, internally the German Constitutional Court established that the principles of completeness and punctuality of the annual German federal state budget are fundamental features of parliamentarian budgetary rights.[315] First, this entails that all federal expenditure and revenue is included in the annual budget to enable parliament to undertake accurate budgetary planning.[316] In essence, the *Bundestag* has to be fully informed by the government on all fiscal and budgetary commitments before approving the annual budgetary planning.[317] Second, parliament has to be informed on planned spending in advance.[318] Here, a temporal dimension is added to the principle of completeness enabling the *Bundestag* in return to predict the development of the German state budget. This ensures the accuracy of the fiscal planning and it is crucial for the democratic process. In EU-related cases, similar procedural guarantees apply. Before engaging in any supranational financial commitment, parliament has to be fully informed and debate the implications of such commitment.[319] Furthermore, *overall budgetary responsibility* establishes that parliament is the 'master of its decisions', which requires that EU fiscal and budgetary commitments are limited and that parliament retains a continuous influence on the decision-making process.[320] Contrasting the internal and the external approach, it is striking that both require parliament to be fully informed, which cements the institutional position of the German Parliament as guardian of the state budget externally and internally. Yet, as the Court relies internally on Article 110 GG and externally on Article 20(1) and (2) GG in conjunction

314. 2 BvF 1/04 *Statute on the Federal Supplementary Budget* (German Federal Constitutional Court) paras 132-133; 2 BvF 1/82 *Public Debt Level* (German Federal Constitutional Court) paras 75, 88.
315. *Statute on the Federal Supplementary Budget* para. 75; as determined in Article 115(1)(1) GG.
316. 2 BvL 1, 4, 6, 16, 18/99, 2 BvL 1/01 *Obligatory Information Concerning Extra Public Charge* (German Federal Constitutional Court) para. 121; 2 BvL 12, 13/88, 2 BvR 1436/87 *Constitutionality of Establishing a Marketing Fund* (German Federal Constitutional Court) para. 83.
317. *Statute on the Federal Supplementary Budget* paras 132-133; *Public Debt Level* paras 75, 88.
318. *Statute on the Federal Supplementary Budget* para. 79.
319. *ESM-Treaty and Fiscal Compact (interim relief)* para. 111.
320. *Ibid.*, para. 170; *Financial Support for Greece and EFSF* para. 120.

with Article 79(3) GG,[321] different constitutional conditions apply. Whereas Article 110 GG may be modified,[322] the external approach is protected against constitutional changes.

Considering public borrowing, the Constitutional Court highlighted *internally* that the rules on borrowing relate to the principle of democracy[323] as they guarantee that future parliaments can decide independently on revenue and expenditure.[324] Therefore, any current decision should take the fiscal choices of future parliaments into due account. *Externally*, the Court established that pre-emption of fiscal competences is not compatible with the German Constitution.[325] In both cases, the principle of democracy contains an obligation to refrain from excessively diminishing future budgetary abilities, either by engaging in too high debts or by transferring too far-reaching fiscal competences to the EU. However, it should be emphasized that neither the Constitutional Court nor the constitution-amending legislator has so far been able to effectively limit an increasing debt burden and guarantee decision-making space for future parliaments.

In fact, most of the German state budget is predetermined by long-term political decisions.[326] Although parliament has to approve the entire budget for a budgetary year, these long-term decisions continue to affect the discretion of the German budgetary legislator.[327] This corresponds to a global trend,[328] for example, visible in the research conducted by *Steuerle* on the US,[329] where the share of discretionary revenue available to US budgetary legislators decreased from about 60% in 1970 to no discretion for the collected revenue in 2009.[330] Considering the research on Germany, the general trend suggests that the German Parliament is increasingly constrained in its budgetary decisions.[331] Although the German Parliament remains formally in

321. *Financial Support for Greece and EFSF* para. 127.
322. As it is not explicitly covered by the *eternity clause*, cf. for example Herdegen, 'Art. 79 GG' para. 14.
323. *Statute on the Federal Supplementary Budget* para. 211; *Public Debt Level* para. 90.
324. *Statute on the Federal Supplementary Budget* para. 211; *Public Debt Level* para. 90.
325. *ESM-Treaty and Fiscal Compact* para. 169.
326. Hanno Kube, 'Art. 110 GG' in Theodor Maunz and Günter Düring (eds), *Grundgesetz-Kommentar* (92nd edn, C.H. Beck 2020) para. 41; Wolfgang Streeck and Daniel Mertens, 'An Index of Fiscal Democracy (2010)' MPIfG Working Paper, https://www.mpifg.de/pu/workpap/wp10-3.pdf, accessed 5 April 2023, 9-12.
327. Streeck and Mertens, 'An Index of Fiscal Democracy (2010)' 8; cf. as well: Lobna Abdellatif et al., 'Transparency of Law Making and Fiscal Democracy in the Middle East' (2019) 43 Public Sector Economics 49, 53.
328. Other examples include, for example, the Czech Republic, where the share of discretionary spending dropped from about 28% in 1995 to about 8% in 2009, cf. Vojtěch Roženský, 'Mandatory Expenditure and the Flexibility of Fiscal Policy in the Czech Republic (in Czech: Mandatorní Výdaje A Flexibilita Fiskální Politiky V Čr)' (2012) 60 Politická ekonomie 40, 47, 57; similar trends were also observed in the Middle East, cf. Abdellatif et al., 'Transparency of Law Making and Fiscal Democracy in the Middle East' 53-54, 71.
329. C. Eugene Steuerle, 'America's Related Fiscal Problems' (2010) 29 Journal of Policy Analysis and Management 876, 878; Streeck and Mertens, 'An Index of Fiscal Democracy (2010)' 6-8; cf. as well: Abdellatif et al., 'Transparency of Law Making and Fiscal Democracy in the Middle East' 52-53.
330. Steuerle, 'America's Related Fiscal Problems' 877.
331. Streeck and Mertens, 'An Index of Fiscal Democracy (2010)' 8-11.

charge,[332] in practice this formal approval does not equal a free decision on budgetary commitments. Consequently, the core premise of *overall budgetary responsibility*, notably that the German Parliament directly controls all central budgetary decisions, can be challenged. As apparent, major parts of the budget are predetermined by long-term policy decisions. Two points should be raised: first, the German Parliament seems factually not to control all central budgetary decisions. Instead, it approves annual financial commitments that largely stem from previous parliamentary decisions.[333] This observation challenges the very conception of *overall budgetary responsibility*. Second, the internal experiences indicate that it might be necessary to make long-term policy decisions, which then necessarily impact the budgetary discretion of future parliaments. One example is pension policy, where long-term commitments are essential to provide individuals with long-term stability. It can be argued that the same logic applies to EU commitments, which require a dedicated (budgetary) commitment to create long-term social, economic and political stability at the supranational level.

Albeit this divagating appraisal might stem from the different nature of the inherent risk of the financial commitment for the German constitutional order, it raises concerns regarding the continuous application of the *eternity clause*. As shown, the *eternity clause* aims to protect democracy regardless of the state level that is affected. However, in its assessment of budgetary and fiscal matters, the Constitutional Court appears to differentiate between *internal* and *EU-related* situations. Notably, in EU-related cases, the Court relies on the *eternity clause* to determine the compatibility of fiscal and budgetary decisions with the German Constitution. Internally the Court relies on the specific framework provided for in Articles 104a to 115 GG. And although the Constitutional Court connected this financial framework to democracy and federalism,[334] both protected by the *eternity clause*, it refrained from pronouncing similarly strict limits for *internal* decisions. Following the Court's conclusion that budgetary matters are central to the democratic process,[335] it would appear imperative to similarly relate the internal financial framework directly to the *eternity clause*.

Overall, the assessment reveals a partially inconsistent assessment of budgetary and fiscal commitments in the jurisprudence of the German Court. Notably, the Court awards a wide discretion in fiscal and budgetary matters *internally* which is apparent in the decreasing discretionary share of the annual German federal state budget.[336] Facing the factual impact of these long-term decisions on the German state budget, the Constitutional Court emphasized that these decisions did not legally limit the discretion of parliament and were therefore permissible.[337] Yet, the factual limitations challenge the underlying claim of *overall budgetary responsibility*. Although one might, thus, claim that parliament is formally taking all these decisions, the political decision-making space is strictly reduced.

332. Kube, 'Art. 110 GG' para. 54.
333. Streeck and Mertens, 'An Index of Fiscal Democracy (2010)' 10-11.
334. Herdegen, 'Art. 79 GG' paras 140-144, 162.
335. *Lisbon-judgment* paras 244, 250.
336. Streeck and Mertens, 'An Index of Fiscal Democracy (2010)' 10-11.
337. *Statute on the Federal Supplementary Budget* para. 144.

3 German Sovereignty

The assessment of democracy and *overall budgetary responsibility* indicates that the Court construes these principles jointly with sovereignty. This is apparent from the concept of *popular sovereignty* and of *budgetary autonomy*. When enacting the *Grundgesetz* in 1949, the Federal Republic of Germany was formally occupied by the Allied Forces.[338] Only the 'Bonn-Paris Conventions' ended the occupation status and recognized Germany's rights as a sovereign state. Therefore, the concept of sovereignty was not included in the original text of the *Grundgesetz* and is until today not explicitly mentioned.[339] Not introducing an explicit provision on sovereignty was a deliberate choice of the constitution-giving committee.[340] Yet, certain constitutional principles imply the existence of sovereignty. For example, the preamble identifies the German people as constituting power which presupposes that the German people can constitute sovereign power. The same logic applies to the *eternity clause*, which distinguishes between the constituting and the constituted powers, as well as Article 20(2)(1) GG which states that all state power derives from the people.[341]

A similar understanding can be observed in constitutional jurisprudence. In a first step, the Court clarified that *Grundgesetz's* conception of sovereignty differed significantly from 'a self-serving and self-glorifying concept of sovereign statehood'.[342] Instead, it subscribed to an open conception of statehood that allowed for supranational and international cooperation, which it derived from the preamble as well as Articles 23 and 24 GG.[343] Based on this conception, the Court underscored that the conferral of sovereign competences to the EU was permissible. Yet, the creation of a European state, and the renouncement of German democracy and state sovereignty, would require a constitutive vote of the German people following the prescribed procedure in Article 146 GG.[344]

Thus, the German Court conceptualizes sovereignty in conjunction with the principle of democracy when considering supranational cooperation.[345] This interrelation was accentuated by the Court in its *Lisbon*-judgment, where it characterizes sovereignty as 'a right of the people to take constitutive decisions concerning fundamental questions' regarding their own identity.[346] This shows the close interrelation of

338. Groß, 'Erlaubt das Grundgesetz einen Austritt aus der EU?' 393-394; Klaus Kröger, 'Die Entstehung des Grundgesetzes' (1989) 42 Neue Juristische Wochenschrift (NJW) 1318, 1319.
339. Mayer, 'Rashomon in Karlsruhe: A Reflection on Democracy and Identity in the European Union' 761.
340. Given that other states, including France and Italy, explicitly referred to sovereignty, cf. Groß, 'Erlaubt das Grundgesetz einen Austritt aus der EU?' 392-393.
341. Paul Konertz, 'Historische und philosophische Grundlagen der Rechtsordnung im Überblick: Am Beispiel von BGB, GG und StGB' (2019) 59 Juristische Schulung (JuS) 201, 203.
342. *Lisbon-judgment* para. 223.
343. Also referred to as 'cooperatives understanding of sovereignty', cf. Daniel Thym, 'Europäische Integration im Schatten souveräner Staatlichkeit: Anmerkungen zum Lissabon-Urteil des Bundesverfassungsgerichts' (2009) 48 Der Staat 559, 560.
344. *Lisbon-judgment* 232; cf. as well: Vinx, 'The Incoherence of Strong Popular Sovereignty' 115.
345. Kottmann and Wohlfahrt, 'Der gespaltene Wächter? Demokratie, Verfassungsidentität und Integrationsverantwortung im Lissabon-Urteil' 445-446.
346. *Lisbon-judgment* para. 340.

democracy and sovereignty, which is further emphasized by the Court when it speaks of the 'safeguarding of sovereignty, demanded by the principle of democracy'.[347] Resulting from the Court's jurisprudence are two fundamental requirements for EU cooperation. First, the EU has to remain a derived legal order and its Member States the Masters of the Treaty.[348] Second, the German legislator cannot confer *Kompetenz-Kompetenz* to the EU.[349] Ultimately, both structural requirements for EU cooperation resonate with the conditions established in relation to the principle of democracy and under *overall budgetary responsibility*. Consequently, *sovereignty* does not emerge as an independent constitutional limit towards EU fiscal integration proposals.

E RESULTING GERMAN CONSTITUTIONAL SPACE FOR EU FISCAL INTEGRATION STEPS

Overall, the assessment illustrates that the German Constitution contains an explicit framework for EU cooperation. This framework establishes the constitutional requirements for the conferral of competences as well as a procedural framework for the engagement of German institutions in the exercise of conferred competences. Following Article 23(1)(2) GG, the German legislator can decide to confer budgetary and fiscal competences to the EU. Depending on the constitutional impact of such conferral, a qualified majority might be required. During the Eurocrisis, the various measures with significant budgetary and financial implications were approved by a two-thirds majority.[350]

In addition, EU integration has to comply with the *eternity clause*, which constitutes the most significant German limitation to EU fiscal integration.[351] Of particular relevance are German democracy and *overall budgetary responsibility*.[352] These require that all central decisions on revenue and expenditure are made by the German Parliament as democratically elected representation of the German people.[353] It presupposes that all budgetary and fiscal commitments at EU level are approved and monitored by the *Bundestag*.[354] During the Eurocrisis, the Constitutional Court accepted that even major financial commitments equalling more than half of the annual

347. Erik Oddvar Eriksen and John Erik Fossum, 'Bringing European Democracy Back In: Or How to Read the German Constitutional Court's Libson Treaty Ruling' (2011) 17 European Law Journal 153, 166.
348. *Lisbon-judgment* para. 231; cf. as well: Thym, 'Europäische Integration im Schatten souveräner Staatlichkeit: Anmerkungen zum Lissabon-Urteil des Bundesverfassungsgerichts' 561.
349. *Lisbon-judgment* para. 231; cf. as well: Cremer, 'Lissabon-Vertrag und Grundgesetz' 303.
350. Ketterer, *Zustimmungserfordernis beim Europäischen Stabilitätsmechanismus* 359.
351. Ohler, 'Rechtliche Maßstäbe der Geldpolitik nach dem Gauweiler-Urteil des EuGH' 1002.
352. Calliess, 'Constitutional Identity in Germany: One for Three or Three in One?' 164-165; Pilz, 'Ein Schatzamt für die Eurozone? – Überlegungen zu den Vorschlägen des Europäischen Parlaments und der Kommission zu einer Reform der Wirtschaftsunion' 643-644.
353. Herrmann, 'Die Bewältigung der Euro-Staatsschulden-Krise an den Grenzen des deutschen und europäischen Währverfassungsrechts' 807-808.
354. *Participation of Members of German Parliament in the EFSF* para. 112; cf. as well: Calliess, 'Der Kampf um den Euro: Eine "Angelegenheit der Europäischen Union" zwischen Regierung, Parlament und Volk' 4.

German federal budget were compatible with German democracy.[355] However, supranational budgetary and fiscal commitments may not put into question the overall budgetary autonomy of parliament. Finally, given that the Court connected this material limit with the *eternity clause*, the outlined limit imposes an absolute restriction to the constitutional space available to parliament when considering EU fiscal integration.[356] At the same time, the concrete application of the limit reveals judicial reluctance and an apparent focus on the procedural components of *overall budgetary responsibility*. For EU fiscal integration proposals this implies that the German Parliament has to be integrated as central decision-maker into the supranational institutional architecture. It should be recalled that in case the Constitutional Court declares EU fiscal integration steps incompatible with Article 79(3) GG, the German legislator is barred from participating.[357]

The assessment also demonstrated that the approach taken in EU matters and the interpretation of constitutional provisions result in a constitutional double standard. It seems that the constitutional requirements for EU integration steps are stricter, compared with the internally applicable requirements. This indicates that additional *constitutional flexibility* for EU fiscal integration can be located and activated by applying a consistent constitutional assessment, as proposed in the following section.

F ADDITIONAL CONSTITUTIONAL SPACE BY APPLYING CONSISTENT CONSTITUTIONAL STANDARD

The German Constitutional Court seems to distinguish EU-related disputes from internal disputes, which the research detected in three different instances. First, the assessment illustrated that it is easier to initiate constitutional proceedings against EU matters, compared to *internal* proceedings. Arguably, this resulted in the introduction of a specific EU *actio popularis* for individuals and in *intra*-institutional proceedings for institutional actors when challenging EU integration. Given that the Constitutional Court relies on the same procedural framework for both *internal* and *external* cases, the varying interpretation of this constitutional framework raises consistency concerns.

Second, it was argued that the *eternity clause* is designed as *ultima ratio*, shielding the German constitutional order against fundamental structural changes.[358] In light of its historic origin, the intentional design as ultimate constitutional protection suggests the restrictive application of Article 79(3) GG, which can be observed in the *internal* case law. However, in EU-related constitutional challenges, the Court consistently applies Article 79(3) GG mainly through its *constitutional identity* review. When considering, for example, the Eurocrisis-related case law, the proceedings involved Article 79(3) GG, without, however, ultimately finding any EU measure in breach of the

355. Nettesheim, 'Die "haushaltspolitische Gesamtverantwortung" in der Rechtsprechung des BVerfG' 19.
356. Preuss, 'The Implications of "Eternity Clauses": The German Experience' 440.
357. Wendel, 'Lisbon Before the Courts: Comparative Perspectives' 125.
358. Mayer, 'Rashomon in Karlsruhe: A Reflection on Democracy and Identity in the European Union' 763.

eternity clause.[359] One consequence of this approach is that the clause's function as ultimate constitutional shield is weakened. After all, German institutions might not perceive the *eternity clause* as a real constitutional obstacle, given that all EU integration steps taken were compatible with the German Constitution. A potential risk is that the *eternity clause* is *watered down*. As highlighted, the *eternity clause* is intended to apply when other constitutional protection mechanisms failed.[360] It seems that the Constitutional Court is not implementing the same range of constitutional mechanisms when confronted with EU integration matters. Applying a modified constitutional approach towards the EU should emphasize the additional benefit that EU integration offers, namely, to shield the structural requirements included in Article 79(3) GG through supranational cooperation.

Finally, the constitutional benchmark applied for the judicial assessment of budgetary and fiscal commitment differs. As indicated, the Court relies *internally* on the financial constitutional framework and the principle of democracy – in conjunction with the *eternity clause* – in EU-related cases. This generates an inconsistent constitutional appraisal of such commitments. As was illustrated, the reluctant and flexible approach *internally* potentially contributed to a factual erosion of parliamentary budgetary prerogatives. Today, the German Parliament is only taking active political decisions in relation to less than 10% of the annual federal budget.[361] Two separate conclusions were drawn on the basis of this development. First, the development of the German state budget suggests that central parts of the German budget are shaped by commitments made by previous parliaments. In its *internal* jurisprudence, the Constitutional Court relied on the fact that parliament was at least theoretically able to modify such commitments. If this reasoning is accepted, one could equally indicate that EU fiscal commitments remain changeable, as the German Parliament can always withdraw from EU cooperation. Second, the *internal* developments challenge the underlying conceptual claim of *overall budgetary responsibility*. In case one accepts, indeed, that factually the German Parliament is not controlling central parts of the German state budget because of the outlined long-term decisions taken by previous parliaments, the question emerges whether the German Parliament can actually violate its budgetary responsibility through the EU budgetary commitments. Thus, in case the German Parliament is factually not controlling all central budgetary commitments *internally* it is questionable whether EU fiscal commitments can actually challenge parliamentary prerogatives in the first place.

The assessment has identified inconsistencies regarding these three points. These double standards suggest that the Constitutional Court has additional constitutional space when adjudicating EU (integration) measures. This additional space is generated

359. For example, in relation to the *OMT-Reference*, cf. Markus Ludwigs, 'Die Krisenpolitik der EZB zwischen Verfassungs- und Unionsrecht' (2017) 70 Neue Juristische Wochenschrift (NJW) 3563, 3563.
360. Schorkopf, 'Case Nos. 2 BvE 2/08, 2 BvE 5/08, 2 BvR 1010/08, 2 BvR 1022/08, 2 BvR 1259/08, and 2 BvR 182/09: 123 BVerfGE 267 (2009)' 263.
361. Streeck and Mertens, 'An Index of Fiscal Democracy (2010)' 7-8.

through a consistent application of the applicable constitutional framework. Concretely, a three-stepped *roadmap* is proposed to address the emerging inconsistency, as visualized in Figure 3.4.

Figure 3.4 Roadmap to Locate Flexible Constitutional Space in Germany

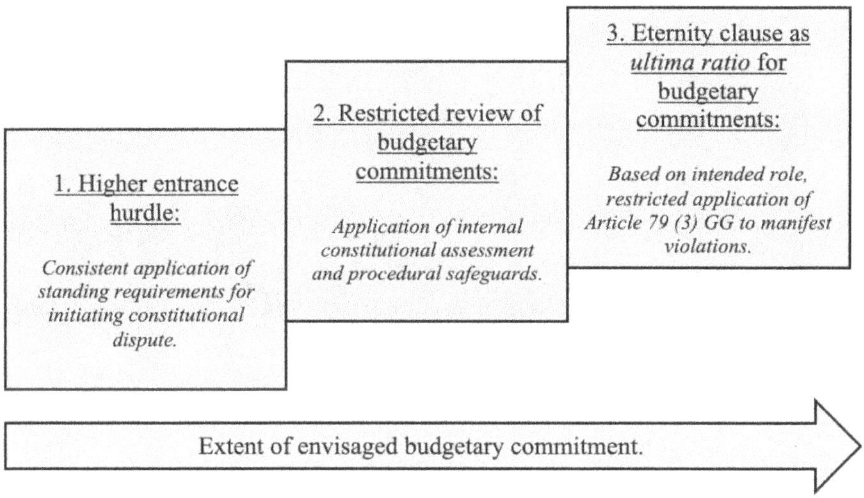

In the first place, the Constitutional Court could apply the constitutional standing requirements consistently. This would entail that individuals had to demonstrate how the challenged EU-related act is affecting them in their subjective constitutional rights. Clearly, the application of this requirement cannot result in a situation where every German individual that enjoys the right to vote following Article 38(1) GG is entitled to initiate a constitutional complaint. Instead, the Court would have to require that a specific subjective risk emerges for the applicant. Furthermore, it implies that the adversarial nature of inter-institutional proceedings is required by the Court in EU matters. In both situations, the consistent application of the constitutional standing requirements would reduce the number of admissible proceedings. Ultimately, the Constitutional Court could avoid addressing complex political questions, which the constitution-amending legislator did not intend the Court to rule on, as reflected in the constitutionally enshrined standing requirements.

Second, the Court could carefully extend the internally applicable financial constitutional framework to EU budgetary and fiscal commitments. This framework mainly relies on procedural safeguards that secure parliament's position as central budgeting authority. Relying on these procedural safeguards provides the Constitutional Court with a comprehensive constitutional framework. It would ensure compliance with the applicable procedural rules that secure parliamentary prerogatives and parliament's general political discretion. Ultimately, this would enable the Constitutional Court to reserve the application of the *eternity clause* to extreme cases. Moreover, the limited application of Article 79(3) GG would avoid an impossible conflict between law and politics as well as strengthen parliament in the exercise of its democratic mandate. Taken together, addressing the identified inconsistencies would generate additional constitutional space for EU fiscal integration by yet fully respecting the German constitutional system and allowing for a more effective defence of German democracy than the current rigid but abstract substantive limits.

CHAPTER 4

Comparative Conclusions on Finland and Germany

A COMPARING FINLAND AND GERMANY

The detailed assessment of the Finnish and the German constitutional approaches to EU integration revealed that EU fiscal integration steps appear generally possible in both systems. This finding is supported by judicial developments during the Eurocrisis and in relation to NGEU, neither the Finnish Constitutional Law Committee nor the German Federal Constitutional Court identified unsurmountable constitutional conflicts. Yet, this jurisprudence equally suggests that EU fiscal integration steps are limited by procedural and substantive requirements. The following assessment compares both national approaches and their implications for EMU-reforms focusing on the national framework for constitutional review (B), the procedural framework for engaging in and administering EU commitments (C) and the substantive benchmarks formulated (D).

B COMPARING THE NATIONAL CONSTITUTIONAL REVIEW

In Finland, constitutional review is conducted by the Constitutional Law Committee.[1] Given that the Committee is part of the Finnish Parliament, its review is integrated into the parliamentary process. It only conducts *ex ante* constitutional review which can be requested by the parliamentary plenary or specialized committees.[2] Therefore, the

1. Ojanen and Salminen, 'Finland: European Integration and International Human Rights Treaties as Sources of Domestic Constitutional Change and Dynamism' 361-362; De Visser, *Constitutional Review in Europe: A Comparative Analysis* 26; Ojanen, 'The EU at the Finnish Constitutional Arena' 252.
2. Leino and Salminen, 'The Euro Crisis and Its Constitutional Consequences for Finland: Is There Room for National Politics in EU Decision-Making?' 459-460.

Constitutional Law Committee's opinions can be directly addressed by the Finnish Parliament before a constitutional conflict manifests. In contrast, the German Constitutional Court as judicial authority is institutionally independent of other German institutions.[3] It conducts *ex post* constitutional review upon request by either institutional or private applicants.[4] Thus, the German constitutional review is separate from the parliamentary process, and it can only be initiated once acts are formally adopted.

The different institutional roles are reflected in the institutions' composition and the legal status of their verdicts. The Finnish Constitutional Law Committee is composed of seventeen parliamentarians. The members of the Committee are not required to have legal qualifications, which is why they are assisted by constitutional law experts.[5] The Committee's final statements or opinions are not legally binding, yet, they are traditionally adhered to in the parliamentary process.[6] In contrast, the sixteen judges on the German Constitutional Court have to be qualified lawyers and its final decisions are legally binding on all other institutions.[7] When comparing the composition and the effect of the final verdicts it becomes obvious that the Finnish and the German constitutional system follow different models. Arguably, these design differences in national constitutional review impact the resulting jurisprudence. The Finnish Committee is required to anticipate constitutional conflicts. Through its opinions, it impacts the parliamentary work that leads to the potential adoption of the act in question. For example, the Committee found that the adoption of a prior version of the ESM-Treaty would have required the support of a two-thirds parliamentary majority, which led the Finnish Government to re-negotiate the Treaty.[8] Hence, the Finnish legislator can react to the Committee's views and alter the reviewed act. One result appears to be that the Constitutional Law Committee focusses mostly on procedural conditions that have to be met instead of imposing strict, substantive limitations. One reason for focusing on procedural requirements is that the Finnish Parliament is still able to comply with these requirements, given that all acts considered by the Finnish Constitutional Law Committee are not yet adopted legislation. Therefore, the Committee exercises both an advisory and supervisory mandate.

This is fundamentally different from the German Federal Constitutional Court, which only considers formally adopted acts. It scrutinizes the work of the German

3. Hailbronner and Martini, 'The German Federal Constitutional Court' 365-366.
4. With the only exception of international agreements, which can be challenged prior to the promulgation of such an agreement following Article 59(1)(1) GG, but after the approval of the legislator following Article 59(2)(1) GG, cf. Hans G. Rupp, 'Judicial Review of International Agreements: Federal Republic of Germany' (1977) 25 The American Journal of Comparative Law 286, 291.
5. Ojanen and Salminen, 'Finland: European Integration and International Human Rights Treaties as Sources of Domestic Constitutional Change and Dynamism' 361-362.
6. Mutanen, *Towards a Pluralistic Constitutional Understanding of State Sovereignty in the European Union? The Concept, Regulation and Constitutional Practice of Sovereignty in Finland and Certain other EU Member States* 325.
7. As stipulated in § 31 BVerfGG, cf. Aust and Meinel, 'Entscheidungsmöglichkeiten des BVerfG – Tenor, Systematik und Wirkungen' 26.
8. Ojanen and Salminen, 'Finland: European Integration and International Human Rights Treaties as Sources of Domestic Constitutional Change and Dynamism' 391-392; Tuori, '§ 98: Verfassungsgerichtsbarkeit in Finnland' 174-175 para. 39.

legislator, instead of instructing it on the applicable procedural requirements. Obviously, this entails that the German Court cannot directly influence the decision-making process that leads to the adoption of a reviewed act. Rather, the Court's jurisprudence has a signalling function for future decisions of the legislator, which could explain the emergence of substantive and material constitutional benchmarks. As the Constitutional Court cannot advise the legislator prior to taking a decision, its *ex post* jurisprudence has a guiding function for future parliamentary decisions.

Overall, this suggests that the moment of constitutional review impacts the resulting jurisprudence. The Finnish Constitutional Law Committee considers acts *ex ante*, which is why its decisions have an advisory function, which is reflected by the fact that only the Finnish Parliament can trigger the review and that decisions are not intended to solve constitutional disputes. In contrast, the German Constitutional Court considers and adjudicates concrete constitutional disputes that are initiated by a wide range of entitled applicants. Therefore, the German jurisprudence does not merely focus on procedural requirements but equally includes substantive considerations in its appraisal, as apparent in relation to EU integration.

C COMPARING THE NATIONAL PROCEDURAL FRAMEWORK FOR EU FISCAL INTEGRATION

When comparing the procedural and institutional constitutional framework, it should be pointed out that both the Finnish Constitution in section 94 as well as the German Constitution in Article 23(1) GG contain specific constitutional bases for the conferral of competences to the EU. In Finland, the conferral of competences has to meet the general framework for supranational cooperation established in section 1(3) Finnish Constitution. Once it is established that EU integration steps contribute to the listed constitutional aims, the transfer of competences can be adopted by a simple parliamentary majority, unless the envisaged conferral affects the national borders, the constitutional text or the principle of sovereignty. In such cases a qualified two-thirds majority requirement is applicable. This suggests that even far-reaching EU integration steps, which conflict with the constitutional text or principles such as Finnish sovereignty, can be adopted by the Finnish Parliament. The determination of the applicable majority requirement is conducted by the Constitutional Law Committee. The Committee clarified that budgetary competences are important parliamentary prerogatives,[9] therefore it is likely that EU fiscal integration steps, which impact national budgetary decisions, will require the support of a qualified parliamentary majority.

Similarly, the German Constitution formulates structural requirements for EU cooperation laid down in Article 23(1)(1) GG. Once these are met, the German Constitution imposes different majority requirements depending on the extent of the envisaged conferral. Notably, Article 23(1)(3) GG clarifies that the internally applicable procedural framework for constitutional amendments applies to EU cooperation. EU

9. Leino and Salminen, 'The Euro Crisis and Its Constitutional Consequences for Finland: Is There Room for National Politics in EU Decision-Making?' 463; Ojanen, 'The EU at the Finnish Constitutional Arena' 247.

fiscal integration proposals that alter the German Constitution, for example, by transferring budgetary competences to EU level, will likely require the support of a qualified two-thirds majority,[10] provided that the conferral complies with the *eternity clause*.[11]

When comparing the framework for competence conferrals, it appears that in both countries integration steps that impact parliament's fiscal and budgetary prerogatives have to be adopted by a two-thirds majority, given the importance of these prerogatives for parliament, the democratic process and sovereignty. Hence, both constitutional systems consider budgetary and fiscal competences as highly important constitutional prerogatives of the national parliament and therefore impose a qualified majority threshold for the conferral of such powers. Although the constitutional implications differ, the underpinning constitutional consideration is highly similar. One major difference appears to be that the German Court defined the content of the *eternity clause* in its jurisprudence thereby restricting the substantive scope for EU integration, whereas the Finnish Constitutional Law Committee refrained from employing the mentioned Finnish *eternity-clause-like* provision in section 94(3) Finnish Constitution. One explanation for this difference may lie in the national constitutional conception of parliamentary prerogatives. The Finnish constitutional system appears to establish the Finnish Parliament as a strong institutional actor, which is able to overcome constitutional conflicts by amending the constitutional text. The primary focus rests on the procedural involvement of parliament, which is then competent to engage in any commitment, provided the required parliamentary majority is attained.[12] In contrast, the drafters of the German Constitution deliberately decided to limit the powers of the constituted institutions. This restriction is laid down in the *eternity clause*, which exempts core constitutional principles from change. The constitutional text thus distinguishes between the constituting powers which only provided a limited mandate to the constituted institutions.[13] This limited mandate extends to EU cooperation and therefore limits the constitutional space for EU integration steps.

Once competences are conferred to the EU, both constitutional systems ensure parliamentary participation in the national preparation of EU secondary acts. Notably, in Finland, this involvement is regulated in detail in the constitutional text itself. According to this framework, the parliamentary opinion is prepared by various parliamentary committees including, if necessary, the Constitutional Law Committee.

10. Cf. in general on Artikel 23 GG: Heintschel von Heinegg and Frau, 'Art. 23 GG – Mitwirkung bei Entwicklung der EU' paras 24-27; Scholz, 'Art. 23 GG' para. 118; Hans D. Jarass, 'Art. 23 GG – Europäische Union' in Hans D. Jarass and Bodo Pieroth (eds), *Grundgesetz für die Bundesrepublik Deutschland – Kommentar* (9th edn, C.H. Beck 2007).
11. Through its identity review, cf. *Quantitative Easing (PSPP) Final Judgment* paras 114-115; cf. as well: Voßkuhle, 'Verfassungsgerichtsbarkeit und europäische Integration' 27.
12. Ojanen and Salminen, 'Finland: European Integration and International Human Rights Treaties as Sources of Domestic Constitutional Change and Dynamism' 373, 391-392; Leino and Salminen, 'The Euro Crisis and Its Constitutional Consequences for Finland: Is There Room for National Politics in EU Decision-Making?' 458-459.
13. Grawert, 'Homogenität, Identität, Souveränität: Positionen jurisdiktioneller Begriffsdogmatik' 197.

In this opinion, parliament can formulate a political mandate to the Finnish Government for EU negotiations.[14] Consequently, parliament is actively involved in the national preparation of EU decisions, which is firmly secured by the Finnish Constitution. Similarly, the German Constitution translates the internal framework for the legislator's involvement to the domestic preparation of EU law. Depending on which state level is competent, either the German Parliament or the Federal Council can issue a position to the government, which is required to carefully consider the communicated views. However, many details of the concrete institutional interaction between German institutions are laid down in secondary provisions, which contrasts with the approach in Finland. Obviously, this more comprehensive constitutional basis available under the Finnish Constitution strengthens the position of the Finnish Parliament. As highlighted in the previous assessment, this comprehensive constitutional basis and, more importantly, the political culture surrounding the inclusion of the Finnish Parliament into the EU decision-making process could serve as a *best practice* example that could potentially soften German constitutional concerns apparent under the procedural dimension of *overall budgetary responsibility.*

Specifically, the exemplary Finnish system allows for the issuing of parliamentary positions through a parliamentary Committee, traditionally the Grand Committee.[15] This delegation of responsibilities ensures a quicker engagement of specialized parliamentarians and it can thereby ensure a thorough involvement of the Finnish Parliament in EU decision-making prior to reaching an agreement on the matter among governmental representatives at EU level. Here, the German Constitutional Court could relax the outlined reservations[16] and re-consider the possibility to delegate limited decision-making powers to the German EU Committee following Article 45(2) GG in conjunction with § 93b (2) GO-BT, which would ensure quicker parliamentary decisions and ultimately guarantee that the German Parliament is not merely approving already taken EU decisions but that it can actively impact the content of such decisions.

Overall, the national constitutional framework suggests that the conferral of budgetary and fiscal competences is permissible both in Finland and in Germany. This was illustrated during the Eurocrisis, where EU-related measures such as the Fiscal Compact or the ESM were held to be compatible with national constitutional law. However, in both Member States budgetary and fiscal competences are considered particularly important prerogatives of the national parliament. In Finland, this was underscored by the Constitutional Law Committee when considering a draft version of the ESM-Treaty. Following the Committee, in case the financial commitment of Finland could be increased against the will of the Finnish Parliament, this would have required the support of a constitution-amending majority.[17] Similarly, the German

14. Raunio and Tiilikainen, *Finland in the European Union* 86.
15. Miller, 'Finnish Judges and the European Union: An American Perspective' 503.
16. *Participation of Members of German Parliament in the EFSF* paras 131, 136; cf. as well: Bumke and Voßkuhle, *German Constitutional Law: Introduction, Cases, and Principles* paras 1634-1636.
17. Ojanen and Salminen, 'Finland: European Integration and International Human Rights Treaties as Sources of Domestic Constitutional Change and Dynamism' 391-392; Leino and Salminen,

Constitutional Court has constantly underscored the importance of budgetary competences for the German Parliament and with it German democracy through its *overall budgetary responsibility* doctrine.[18] Hence, EU fiscal integration proposals will likely require the support of a qualified parliamentary majority in both Finland and Germany, given the potential implications for parliamentary budgetary prerogatives. This qualified parliamentary majority might be challenging to attain in Finland, given an increasing Euroscepticism which impacts parliamentary work.[19] As a result, EU fiscal integration proposals might be constitutionally attainable in Finland, but they are confronted with an uncertain political context which could ultimately limit them. In contrast, in Germany, too far-reaching EU fiscal integration steps might result in an unsurmountable conflict with the *eternity clause*.

D COMPARING THE NATIONAL SUBSTANTIVE BENCHMARK FOR EU FISCAL INTEGRATION

The analysis revealed that the German Constitutional Court increasingly relies on substantive limitations when confronted with EU integration proposals. In its jurisprudence, the Court identified particularly important competences under German democracy. Following its *Lisbon*-judgment, these protected competences include, *inter alia*, decisions on revenue and expenditure, which are characterized as core powers of the German Parliament essential for the democratic process.[20] A conferral of these competences to EU level could significantly alter German democracy, which is built on an accountability and legitimacy relation between parliament and the people.[21] As emphasized by the Court, in case the German Parliament is stripped of its core competences, the people legitimize a parliament without the ability to take political decisions.[22] Given that budgetary and fiscal powers are considered particularly important domestic competences, the Constitutional Court raised serious constitutional concerns regarding the compatibility of increasing budgetary constraints with the

'The Euro Crisis and Its Constitutional Consequences for Finland: Is There Room for National Politics in EU Decision-Making?' 464; Ojanen, 'The EU at the Finnish Constitutional Arena' 247.

18. *Quantitative Easing (PSPP) Final Judgment* paras 103-104; *Lisbon-judgment* paras 252, 256; cf. as well: Calliess, 'Constitutional Identity in Germany: One for Three or Three in One?' 164-165.
19. Iso-Markku, 'Finland: Pro-European Arguments Prevail Despite the Rise of Euroscepticism' 65, 73; Leino and Salminen, 'The Euro Crisis and Its Constitutional Consequences for Finland: Is There Room for National Politics in EU Decision-Making?' 455.
20. *Lisbon-judgment* paras 252, 256; cf. as well: Christian Calliess, 'Bausteine einer erneuerten Europäischen Union: Auf der Suche nach dem europäischen Weg: Überlegungen im Lichte des Weißbuchs der Europäischen Kommission zur Zukunft Europas' (2018) 37 Neue Zeitschrift für Verwaltungsrecht (NVwZ) 1, 3; Ludwigs, 'Die Krisenpolitik der EZB zwischen Verfassungs- und Unionsrecht' 3565.
21. *Quantitative Easing (PSPP) Final Judgment* paras 99-101; cf. as well: De Sadeleer, 'The New Architecture of European Economic Governance' 36.
22. Gött, 'Die ultra vires-Rüge nach dem OMT-Vorlagebeschluss des Bundesverfassungsgerichts' 516, 527; Kottmann and Wohlfahrt, 'Der gespaltene Wächter? Demokratie, Verfassungsidentität und Integrationsverantwortung im Lissabon-Urteil' 447-448.

principle of democracy and *overall budgetary responsibility*.[23] Notably, the Court introduced *overall budgetary responsibility* as a specific constitutional concept to address an increasing supranationalization of budgetary and fiscal competences. Similarly, the Finnish Constitutional Law Committee is concerned that EU budgetary and fiscal integration could undermine constitutional concepts such as Finnish sovereignty or parliamentary prerogatives in budgetary matters.[24] However, until now, these concerns only translated into procedural requirements, notably the adoption by the qualified parliamentary majority.

When considering the German constitutional opposition to budgetary and fiscal integration in greater detail, it should be emphasized that the relevant concept of *overall budgetary responsibility* has a procedural dimension and a substantive dimension. It suggests that the German Parliament can engage in budgetary and fiscal commitments at EU level, as long as these commitments remain reversible and as long as the central and major part of budgetary decisions is taken by the German Parliament itself. At the same time, national budgets are increasingly constrained by long-term political decisions, such as pension schemes, social policy or public health policy decisions, which limit the discretion of future parliaments.[25] Nevertheless, the jurisprudence implies that EU fiscal integration is restricted both in procedural terms, meaning how powers are conferred and what role the national parliament plays, as well as in substantive terms. Although the Constitutional Court did not yet define a specific percentage of the German federal state budget that has to remain under the control of the domestic level, the recent PSP-Programme-judgment illustrates that the Court is carefully monitoring fiscal integration steps.[26] In contrast, the Finnish Constitutional Law Committee focused on procedural safeguards for parliamentary involvement in budgetary decisions.

According to the German Constitutional Court, the substantive dimension of *overall budgetary responsibility* protects the unamendable constitutional core of the *Grundgesetz* protected by Article 79(3) GG.[27] Therefore, *overall budgetary responsibility* constitutes an absolute limitation for EU fiscal integration steps which cannot be overcome by the German constitution-amending legislator. As highlighted, these material or substantive reservations are framed as *national constitutional identity*

23. Payandeh, 'The OMT Judgment of the German Federal Constitutional Court: Repositioning the Court Within the European Constitutional Architecture' 408; Wendel, 'Exceeding Judicial Competence in the Name of Democracy: The German Federal Constitutional Court's OMT Reference' 285.
24. Tomuschat, 'Lisbon: Terminal of the European Integration Process? The Judgment of the German Constitutional Court of 30 June 2009' 4-5; cf. as well: Ojanen and Salminen, 'Finland: European Integration and International Human Rights Treaties as Sources of Domestic Constitutional Change and Dynamism' 391-392.
25. Abdellatif et al., 'Transparency of Law Making and Fiscal Democracy in the Middle East' 53; Streeck and Mertens, 'An Index of Fiscal Democracy (2010)' 8.
26. *Quantitative Easing (PSPP) Final Judgment* paras 103-104; cf. as well: Calliess, 'Konfrontation statt Kooperation zwischen BVerfG und EuGH? Zu den Folgen des Karlsruher PSPP-Urteils' 902.
27. Herbst, 'Legale Abschaffung des Grundgesetzes nach Art. 146 GG?' 33.

concerns by the German Constitutional Court.[28] Given the absolute nature of these substantive identity concerns, they constitute a direct and serious limitation to the prospect of EU fiscal integration. Overall, such *national constitutional identity* concerns that protect budgetary and fiscal prerogatives constitute the most immediate and serious restrictions for EU fiscal integration proposals. Yet, as the term 'identity concern' already suggests, these are specific to the national constitutional order and vary in their design across Member States. Therefore, the subsequent Section assesses different national *constitutional identity* concerns raised in the context of EU cooperation to identify conceptual overlap and determine their potential limiting impact on EU fiscal integration ambitions.

In addition, in both Member States, the principle of sovereignty is invoked when evaluating supranational budgetary and fiscal commitments. In Finland, the principle of sovereignty occupies a historically important position and is enshrined in section 1(1) Finnish Constitution.[29] As outlined, the initial absolute conception of Finnish sovereignty was altered by the constitution-amending legislator.[30] Therefore, not every conferral of powers to the EU is construed as a conflict with Finnish sovereignty. In Germany, the Constitutional Court employs the principle of sovereignty in conjunction with democracy. Given its historic origin, the German Constitution does not mention sovereignty explicitly but instead implies it.[31] Taken together, this illustrates that both national authorities employ national sovereignty when considering EU integration steps. The German Court seemingly addressed these concerns by emphasizing the derived status of the EU as well as by underscoring that *Kompetenz-Kompetenz* cannot be conferred to EU level. Similarly, the Finnish Constitutional Law Committee was concerned when evaluating the draft ESM-Treaty that the Finnish financial commitment could be increased without prior Finnish parliamentary approval, which would have equipped the EU with the power to overrule the Finnish Parliament and which would have resulted in some sort of EU *Kompetenz-Kompetenz*.[32] Furthermore, the Finnish Constitutional Law Committee started to equally consider the factual benefits that stem from EU cooperation for national sovereignty. According to the Committee, EU commitments are not primarily limiting Finnish sovereignty, but instead increasing the Finnish impact in a globalized world. For example, negotiating a trade agreement as a Union of almost 450 million inhabitants enhances the final agreement for Finland

28. Schwerdtfeger, 'Europäisches Unionsrecht in der Rechtsprechung des Bundesverfassungsgerichts: Grundrechts-, ultra-vires- und Identitätskontrolle im gewaltenteiligen Mehrebenensystem' 293-294.
29. Mutanen, *Towards a Pluralistic Constitutional Understanding of State Sovereignty in the European Union? The Concept, Regulation and Constitutional Practice of Sovereignty in Finland and Certain Other EU Member States* 331-332.
30. Notably, Finnish sovereignty has to be balanced against the principle of internationality, cf. Ojanen and Salminen, 'Finland: European Integration and International Human Rights Treaties as Sources of Domestic Constitutional Change and Dynamism' 366.
31. Cf. the German Court speaks of the sovereignty of the people, cf. Konertz, 'Historische und philosophische Grundlagen der Rechtsordnung im Überblick: Am Beispiel von BGB, GG und StGB' 203.
32. Leino and Salminen, 'The Euro Crisis and Its Constitutional Consequences for Finland: Is There Room for National Politics in EU Decision-Making?' 464; Ojanen, 'The EU at the Finnish Constitutional Arena' 247.

– as a less populated Member State – too.[33] Therefore, the Committee argues that EU cooperation can in fact increase sovereign powers, which is factored into the constitutional assessment and illustrates a flexible conception of substantive constitutional principles to EU integration steps.

E OVERALL COMPARATIVE CONCLUSION

Overall, EU fiscal integration steps seem possible in Finland and Germany. However, given that budgetary and fiscal competences are considered particularly important prerogatives for national parliaments, additional procedural and substantive requirements apply to future EU fiscal integration steps. In addition, the German *constitutional identity limit*, specifically *overall budgetary responsibility*, restricts the available constitutional space for such integration. Notably, EU fiscal integration steps cannot restrict the German Parliament's ability to take all central budgetary decisions. In contrast, the Finnish Constitutional Law Committee did not develop such substantive limitations, but instead relied on effective parliamentary involvement and underscored the overall discretion of the Finnish Parliament when deciding on EU integration. Therefore, the Finnish constitutional system appears more flexible towards EU integration compared to the German constitutional order. Given that Finland has no domestic constitutional court, which could scrutinize *ex post* parliamentary work and given the traditionally wide discretion that the Finnish Parliament enjoys, no substantive limitation to EU (fiscal) integration emerged. In contrast, the German constitutional order can be characterized as more rigid in light of its constitutional features, the institutional framework and the analysed constitutional jurisprudence.

Despite all major differences, the comparison revealed that the Finnish Constitutional Law Committee and the German Federal Constitutional Court base their constitutional assessment on comparable principles, notably national sovereignty and democracy, and that their appraisal is framed by the domestic enabling clause. Therefore, considerable conceptual overlap exists, and the constitutional departure point appears similar. However, given the identified differences in the overall constitutional and institutional design of both systems, both authorities reach different final conclusions on the relationship between the respective national constitution and the EU legal order.

In light of the identified conceptual overlap, the comparative exchange of constitutional interpretation and arguments appears generally possible. Although, of course, the respective domestic interpretation of, for example, democracy is a prerogative of the national authority, the conceptual overlap may be employed as input to reconsider the national interpretation of certain principles. For example, the Finnish Constitutional Law Committee includes the factual benefits of EU cooperation in its evaluation of Finnish sovereignty. Similarly, one could consider the factual benefits stemming from EU budgetary and fiscal integration when constitutionally assessing the

33. Mutanen, *Towards a Pluralistic Constitutional Understanding of State Sovereignty in the European Union? The Concept, Regulation and Constitutional Practice of Sovereignty in Finland and Certain Other EU Member States* 334.

impact of such integration steps on the principle of democracy in Germany. An additional means to achieving this *constitutional flexibility* is the application of a consistent constitutional standard and thus not distinguishing between internal cases and cases with an EU dimension, as currently apparent in the German constitutional practice. Hence, even the rigid German constitutional order appears to offer additional constitutional space for EU integration steps in budgetary and fiscal matters, which is explored in PART II.

Section II

Micro-comparative Assessment of Selected National Material Limits to EU Fiscal Integration

Introducing the **micro-comparative** *assessment*

Based on a thorough assessment of the German constitutional approach, the *macro-comparison* reveals that the feasibility of EU fiscal integration steps can be significantly constrained in such rigid constitutional systems. These constraints stem from substantive limits that rigid systems formulate against increasing EU cooperation.[1] As substantiated in the previous analysis, the German *constitutional identity limit* does set absolute restrictions to possible EU integration ambitions.[2] Not even the constitution-amending legislator is competent to overcome this absolute restriction, which reduces the German Parliament's discretion for engaging in EU fiscal integration steps. In case EU fiscal integration measures are found to be incompatible with German *constitutional identity,* these measures are unattainable under the German Constitution.[3] The German example illustrates that EU fiscal integration does not only depend on national political-parliamentary support but equally on compatibility with domestic constitutional limits.[4]

National *constitutional identity limits* emerge as the most likely constitutional obstacles for EU fiscal integration steps. As demonstrated within the *macro-comparison,* EU fiscal integration steps affect national fiscal and budgetary powers,

1. Claes, 'National Idenity: Trump Card or up for Negotiation?' 116; Wendel, 'Lisbon Before the Courts: Comparative Perspectives' 131.
2. Calliess, 'Constitutional Identity in Germany: One for Three or Three in One?' 161-162.
3. Rademacher, 'Die "Verfassungsidentität" als Grenze der Kompetenzübertragung auf die Europäische Union?' 146.
4. Saiz Arnaiz and Alcoberro Llivina, 'Why Constitutional Identity Suddently Matters: A Tale of Brave States, a Mighty Union and the Decline of Sovereignty' 14-15.

which are core state competences and important parliamentary prerogatives.[5] EU fiscal integration could require the transfer of these important budgetary prerogatives to create fiscal capacities at the supranational level, to guide national fiscal policies or to possibly introduce joint guarantees of all Eurozone Member States building on the NGEU example. These integration steps seem difficult to attain as budgetary and fiscal competences are characterized as essential for the national democratic-political process protected by national *constitutional identity limits*.[6]

Given the severity of these constitutional limits, the book examines *constitutional identity limits* which will likely apply to EU fiscal integration steps. Based on political, geographical and overall constitutional relevance, this comparative assessment focusses on a sample of four *constitutional identity limits*, namely the German, French, Spanish and Polish limits. In order to allow for this comparison, the four national *constitutional identity limits* will be analysed first separately (Chapter V). And in the second step, the findings per constitutional system are compared and contrasted (Chapter VI).

5. Puntscher Riekmann and Wydra, 'Representation in the European State of Emergency: Parliaments Against Governments?' 567; Baranger, 'The Apparition of Sovereignty' 61.
6. Schyff, 'Exploring Member State and European Union Constitutional Identity' 228.

CHAPTER 5

Micro-comparative Assessment of French, German, Polish and Spanish Limit to EU Fiscal Integration

A INTRODUCTION

To structure the assessment and to facilitate the comparison, the assessment is structured based on the *Constitutional Identity Classification Board* displayed in Table 5.1. The assessment first considers the French *constitutional identity limit* (B), before then considering the Spanish (C) and the Polish one (D). Subsequently, the findings on the German *constitutional identity limit* are reiterated (E).

Table 5.1 Design of the Constitutional Identity Classification Board

Components of the Constitutional Identity Classification Board
1. Which institutional actor enforces the constitutional limit?
2. How can the *constitutional identity limit* be triggered?
3. What is the constitutional basis of the *constitutional identity limit*?
4. What constitutional principles and substantive content are covered?
5. How - if at all - can the *constitutional identity limit* be overcome (longevity/absoluteness of the limit)?

B THE FRENCH CONSTITUTIONAL APPROACH TO EU FISCAL INTEGRATION

France occupies an influential position within the Eurozone. Politically, France is the crucial driving force behind integration dynamics within the Eurozone next to Germany.[1] Economically, France is the second biggest Eurozone-economy, which translates, for example, into the ESM-funding guarantee that France represents. Jointly, France and Germany represent almost 50% of the ESM funding guarantees.[2] This illustrates the economic, political and relative power of France both individually and jointly with Germany. Arguably any EMU-reform will require the support of the French-German axis. Furthermore, the current French President Macron continuously advocated an ambitious fiscally more integrated single currency.[3] Yet, these far-reaching political ambitions must be separated from possible legal obstacles towards EU fiscal integration that might exist under the French Constitution.

When considering the French constitutional approach to EU integration, certain features of a rigid constitutional system become apparent. In the first place, the French constitutional approach is shaped by an influential constitutional authority, the *Conseil Constitutionnel*.[4] The *Conseil* has the prerogative to conduct *ex ante* constitutional review – including the review of new EU commitments.[5] Thus, the compatibility of EU commitments with the French Constitution is determined prior to their ratification.[6] In addition, the *Conseil* conducts a limited review of the national implementation of EU-related obligations.[7] All its decisions are legally binding[8] and overall the *Conseil* can

1. Amandine Crespy and Vivien Schmidt, 'The Clash of Titans: France, Germany and the Discursive Double Game of EMU Reform' (2014) 21 Journal of European Public Policy 1085, 1085-1086.
2. Federico Fabbrini, *Economic Governance in Europe: Comparative Paradoxes and Constitutional Challenges* (Oxford University Press 2016) Chapter 2.3.B (Difference in Power); Carri Ginter and Raul Narits, 'The Perspective of a Small Member State to the Democratic Deficiency of the ESM' (2013) 38 Review of Central and East European Law 54, 65.
3. Tony Barber, 'Eurozone Reform Deadlock Reflects Deep Malaise Over Integration: The Fiscal Stalemate Derives in Part from the Frictions in Franco-German Relations' *Financial Times* (London 26 December 2019), https://www.ft.com/content/8ffa04c6-1815-11ea-8d73-6303645ac406, accessed 5 April 2023.
4. In English: Constitutional Council.
5. As enshrined in Articles 54 and 61 French Constitution, cf. Ziller, 'European Union Law in the Jurisprudence of French Supreme Courts: Europe-Friendliness with a French Touch' 769-770.
6. Millet, 'Constitutional Identity in France: Vices and – Above All – Virtues' 139; De Visser, *Constitutional Review in Europe: A Comparative Analysis* 102.
7. Chloé Charpy, 'Droit constitutionnel et droit communautaire: Le statut constitutionnel du droit communautaire dans la jurisprudence (récente) du Conseil constitutionnel et du Conseil d'État' (2009) 80 Revue Française de Droit Constitutionnel 795, 801-802; Thomas M. Pfeiffer, 'Zur Verfassungsmäßigkeit des Gemeinschaftsrechts in der aktuellen Rechtsprechung des französischen Conseil constitutionnel' (2007) 67 Zeitschrift für ausländisches öffentliches Recht und Völkerrecht (ZaöRV) 469, 475.
8. Cf. Article 62 French Constitution: Arthur Dyevre, 'The *Melki* Way: The *Melki* Case and Everything You Always Wanted to Know about French Judicial Politics (But Were Afraid to Ask)' in Monica Claes and others (eds), *Constitutional Conversations in Europe* (Intersentia 2012) 319.

be described as the central adjudicator for constitutional questions in France.[9] Considering its institutional prerogatives and the effect of its decisions, the *Conseil* can thus be compared to traditional constitutional courts such as the German *Bundesverfassungsgericht*. At the same time, the *Conseil* is mainly composed of (former) politicians, including former French Presidents.[10] Its composition and the *ex ante* involvement resemble thus more that of a constitutional advisory body, comparable to the Finnish Constitutional Law Committee. Hence, the *sui generis* institutional nature of the *Conseil Constitutionnel*, which reflects both flexible and rigid constitutional features, offers an interesting addition to complement the *macro-comparison*.

Moreover, the French Constitution formulates different limits toward EU cooperation. Prominently, Article 89(5) French Constitution excludes constitutional amendments that alter the republican status of France, which could possibly restrict EU fiscal integration.[11] In addition, the *Conseil Constitutionnel* has established a French sovereignty limit[12] and an explicit *constitutional identity limit*[13] which both define the constitutional space available for EU fiscal integration steps under the French Constitution.

The subsequent analysis is structured in four parts. In the first step, the relevant constitutional framework for EU fiscal integration steps is identified and the ambiguity of the constitutional terminology in relation to '*constitutional identity*' is discussed (I). Second, the French sovereignty limit, as the most immediate constitutional restriction for the conferral of additional competences to the EU is evaluated (II). Third, the particularities of the French *constitutional identity limit* are outlined (III). Finally, the resulting French constitutional space for EU fiscal integration is determined (IV).

I Identifying the Relevant French Constitutional Limits

Three French *final* judicial authorities adjudicate on the interaction between French and EU law based on their field of judicial responsibility.[14] Notably, the *Conseil Constitutionnel* adjudicates on constitutional law questions, the *Conseil d'État* (Council of State) in last instance on administrative law, and the *Cour de Cassation* (Supreme Court) in last instance on civil as well as criminal law.[15] The focus of the subsequent

9. Marie-Luce Paris, 'France: The French System of Rights-Based Review: From Exceptionalism to Parochial Constitutionalism' in John Bell and Marie-Luce Paris (eds), *Rights-Based Constitutional Review: Constitutional Courts in a Changing Landscape* (Edward Elgar Publishing Limited 2016) 328-329.
10. Eva Steiner, *French Law: A Comparative Approach* (Oxford University Press 2018) 68.
11. Wendel, 'Lisbon Before the Courts: Comparative Perspectives' 124.
12. Millet, 'Constitutional Identity in France: Vices and – Above All – Virtues' 138.
13. Vranes, 'Constitutional Foundation of, and Limitations to, EU Integration in France' 548; Germany and France are driving actors on *constitutional identity* discours, cf. Saiz Arnaiz and Alcoberro Llivina, 'Why Constitutional Identity Suddently Matters: A Tale of Brave States, a Mighty Union and the Decline of Sovereignty' 7-8.
14. Dyevre, 'The *Melki* Way: The *Melki* Case and Everything You Always Wanted to Know about French Judicial Politics (But Were Afraid to Ask)' 313.
15. Ziller, 'European Union Law in the Jurisprudence of French Supreme Courts: Europe-Friendliness with a French Touch' 766-767; De Visser, *Constitutional Review in Europe: A Comparative Analysis* 137.

analysis rests specifically on constitutional law questions. Therefore, the analysis is limited to the jurisprudence of the *Conseil Constitutionnel*, given its central position as constitutional adjudicator.[16] This position was strengthened by the 2008 French constitutional reform, which introduced a referral system for constitutional law questions.[17] By initiating a so-called *Question Prioritaire de Constitutionalité* (*QPC*), lower courts can refer questions on the constitutionality of a French legislative act to the *Conseil Constitutionnel*. This referral mechanism integrates the different branches of the judiciary and reinforces the position of the *Conseil Constitutionnel* as the most authoritative adjudicator on constitutional law questions in France.[18]

The *Conseil Constitutionnel* conducts a constitutional review, *inter alia*, on the compatibility of EU law with the French Constitution. This review can either be initiated against the conferral of additional powers to the EU[19] or against the national implementation of EU secondary law.[20] The intensity of the review and the employed constitutional concepts depend on the challenged act. Notably, when assessing new EU primary commitments, the *Conseil* conducts a full *ex ante* constitutional review.[21] In contrast, when confronted with EU secondary law, the *Conseil* conducts a limited review, as the secondary act benefits from the presumption of constitutionality of ratified international agreements.[22] This is now specifically acknowledged for EU law obligations in Article 88-1(2) French Constitution: '[France] shall participate in the European Union in the conditions provided for by the Treaty of Lisbon [...]'.[23] Furthermore, the *Conseil's* jurisdiction is limited to French law, which restricts the review of EU secondary law to the French implementation act.[24] One consequence is that no direct conflict between secondary EU law and French constitutional law can

16. Arthur Dyevre, 'The French Constitutional Council' in András Jakab, Arthur Dyevre and Giulio Itzcovich (eds), *Comparative Constitutional Reasoning* (Cambridge University Press 2017) 328.
17. Enshrined in Article 61-1 French Constitution and entered into force on 1 March 2010, cf. Otto Pfersmann, 'Concrete Review As Indirect Constitutional Complaint in French Constitutional Law: A Comparative Perspective' (2010) 6 European Constitutional Law Review 223, 227.
18. Paris, 'France: The French System of Rights-Based Review: From Exceptionalism to Parochial Constitutionalism' 328-329.
19. Following Article 54 French Constitution, cf. Claes, 'National Idenity: Trump Card or up for Negotiation?' 126-127; Vranes, 'Constitutional Foundation of, and Limitations to, EU Integration in France' 540.
20. Following Article 61 (2) French Constitution, cf. Jan-Herman Reestman, 'The Franco-German Constitutional Divide: Reflections on National and Constitutional Identity' (2009) 5 European Constitutional Law Review 374, 386.
21. Any competence conferral to the EU has to be compatible with the French Constitution, potentially requiring constitutional amendment, cf. Millet, 'Constitutional Identity in France: Vices and – Above All – Virtues' 138.
22. Federico Fabbrini, 'The Euro-Crisis and the Courts: Judicial Review and the Political Process in Comparative Perspective' (2014) 32 Berkeley Journal of International Law 101, 121.
23. Vranes, 'Constitutional Foundation of, and Limitations to, EU Integration in France' 533; Jan-Herman Reestman, 'France: *Conseil Constitutionnel* on the Status of (Secondary) Community Law in the French Internal Order – Decision of 10 June 2004, 2004-496 DC' (2005) 1 European Constitutional Law Review 302, 303.
24. Chloé Charpy, 'The Status of (Secondary) Community Law in the French Internal Order: the Recent Case-Law of the *Conseil Constitutionnel* and the *Conseil d'Etat*' (2007) 3 European Constitutional Law Review 436, 442; Jacqueline Dutheil de la Rochère, 'Conseil constitutionnel (French Constitutional Court), Decision No. 2004-496 of 10 June 2004, Loi Pour La Confiance Dans L'Économie Numérique (Ecommerce)' (2005) 42 Common Market Law Review 859, 861.

emerge in front of the *Conseil*, which showcases the *Conseil's* respect for the prerogatives of the CJEU.[25] Nevertheless, the *Conseil Constitutionnel* developed a *constitutional identity limit* applicable to the French implementation of EU secondary law.[26]

1 *Relevant Constitutional Limits for EU Primary Law*

When adjudicating on the compatibility of an anticipated conferral of competences to the EU, the *Conseil* applies a threefold constitutional scrutiny.[27] This scrutiny consists of both formal and material elements that restrict the constitutional space. The *Conseil* established:

> Considering however that where the commitments signed to this effect or which are closely related to this goal contain a clause which *is unconstitutional, call into question the rights and freedoms guaranteed by the Constitution or run contrary to the essential conditions for the exercise of national sovereignty* [emphasis added], [authorization] to ratify them may only be granted after the Constitution has been amended.[28]

According to this constitutional benchmark, envisaged new EU obligations may not explicitly contradict the French Constitution, as this would result in a direct, formal conflict with French constitutional law. This formal requirement is complemented by substantive restrictions which exclude competence conferrals that either conflict with constitutional rights or with the French sovereignty doctrine.[29] Considering the first, the conferral may not challenge 'rights and freedoms guaranteed by the Constitution', which constitutes a safeguard for the protection of fundamental and other subjective rights recognized by the French Constitution.[30] Concerning the latter, the conferral may not violate 'the essential conditions for the exercise of national sovereignty'. Whereas

25. Millet, 'Constitutional Identity in France: Vices and – Above All – Virtues' 142.
26. Joris Larik, 'Prêt-à-Ratifier: The CETA Decision of the French *Conseil constitutionnel* of 31 July 2017' (2017) 13 European Constitutional Law Review 759, 764; Claes, 'National Idenity: Trump Card or up for Negotiation?' 127.
27. Decision 2007-560 DC *Lisbon Treaty* (French Conseil Constitutionnel) para. 9; *Entwurf eines Gesetzes zu dem Beschluss des Europäischen Rates vom 25. März 2011 zur Änderung des Artikels 136 des Vertrags über die Arbeitsweise der Europäischen Union hinsichtlich eines Stabilitätsmechanismus für die Mitgliedstaaten, deren Währung der Euro ist (Drucksache 17/9047)* (German Parliament 2012) para. 10; cf. as well: Ziller, 'European Union Law in the Jurisprudence of French Supreme Courts: Europe-Friendliness with a French Touch' 772.
28. *Entwurf eines Gesetzes zu dem Beschluss des Europäischen Rates vom 25. März 2011 zur Änderung des Artikels 136 des Vertrags über die Arbeitsweise der Europäischen Union hinsichtlich eines Stabilitätsmechanismus für die Mitgliedstaaten, deren Währung der Euro ist (Drucksache 17/9047)* para. 10; cf. as well: Millet, 'Constitutional Identity in France: Vices and – Above All – Virtues' 138; Vranes, 'Constitutional Foundation of, and Limitations to, EU Integration in France' 541.
29. Although one might actually identify three separate limits in this, the academic writing emphasized that a 'simple' textual/formal contradiction is not sufficient for identifying a conflict, cf. Millet, 'Constitutional Identity in France: Vices and – Above All – Virtues' 138; Ziller, 'European Union Law in the Jurisprudence of French Supreme Courts: Europe-Friendliness with a French Touch' 771-772; Vranes, 'Constitutional Foundation of, and Limitations to, EU Integration in France' 539.
30. Millet, 'Constitutional Identity in France: Vices and – Above All – Virtues' 138.

the prior substantive limit protects individual, subjective rights, this second substantive limit is more structural as it protects sovereignty and the democratic decision-making process in France.[31]

In case the *Conseil Constitutionnel* identifies a conflict between envisaged EU commitments and a constitutional limit, the French legislator can either modify the EU commitment or amend the French Constitution.[32] Since the Maastricht Treaty, the constitution-amending legislator opted for the latter and modified the French Constitution whenever the *Conseil Constitutionnel* identified an incompatibility. The French Constitution, therefore, contains several explicit acknowledgements of competence transfers to the EU in its Title XV.[33] When confronted with EU fiscal integration proposals, the sovereignty limit appears to be the most relevant obstacle, as can be deduced from the *Conseil's* decisions in which it labelled monetary, economic and fiscal competences as closely related to national sovereignty.[34]

2 Relevant Constitutional Limits for EU Secondary Law

In light of the *internal* constitutional obligations that apply to ratified international and EU commitments,[35] the *Conseil Constitutionnel* conducts a less comprehensive constitutional review of EU secondary acts. The previously outlined material limits are not applicable. Instead, the *Conseil* developed the concept of French '*constitutional identity*':[36]

---

31. Ziller, 'European Union Law in the Jurisprudence of French Supreme Courts: Europe-Friendliness with a French Touch' 772; Vranes, 'Constitutional Foundation of, and Limitations to, EU Integration in France' 539-541; Loïc Azoulai and Felix Ronkes Agerbeek, '*Conseil constitutionnel* (French Constitutional Court), Decision No. 2004-505 DC of 19 November 2004, on the Treaty establishing a Constitution for Europe' (2005) 42 Common Market Law Review 871, 884.
32. Following Article 89 French Constitution, as emphasized by the *Conseil*, cf. *Review of Maastricht Treaty (Maastricht I)* para. 14; *Treaty Establishing a Constitution for Europe* para. 7; *Lisbon Treaty* para. 9; cf. as well Millet, 'Constitutional Identity in France: Vices and – Above All – Virtues' 138; Wendel, 'Lisbon Before the Courts: Comparative Perspectives' 123.
33. Introduced with the Maastricht Treaty, cf. Peter Oliver, 'The French Constitution and the Treaty of Maastricht' (1994) 43 International & Comparative Law Quarterly 1, 16.
34. *See* for example the constitutional assessment of EMU, which was deemed to affect essential sovereign competences, cf. *Review of Maastricht Treaty (Maastricht I)* para. 43; or the assessment of the Fiscal Compact under the sovereignty limit, cf. *Entwurf eines Gesetzes zu dem Beschluss des Europäischen Rates vom 25. März 2011 zur Änderung des Artikels 136 des Vertrags über die Arbeitsweise der Europäischen Union hinsichtlich eines Stabilitätsmechanismus für die Mitgliedstaaten, deren Währung der Euro ist (Drucksache 17/9047)* paras 16, 30; cf. as well: Reestman, 'Legitimacy Through Adjudication: The ESM Treaty and the Fiscal Compact Before the National Courts' 265.
35. Namely, the combined reading of the concept 'immunité des conventions ratifiées' and the principle of 'pacta sunt servanda' that apply to international commitments according to the *Conseil Constitutionnel*, cf. Reestman, 'France: *Conseil Constitutionnel* on the Status of (Secondary) Community Law in the French Internal Order – Decision of 10 June 2004, 2004-496 DC' 303.
36. Decision 2017-749 DC *Comprehensive Economic and Trade Agreement (CETA)* (French Conseil Constitutionnel) para. 14; Decision 2010-605 DC *Act Pertaining to the Opening Up to Competition and the Regulation of Online Betting and Gambling* (French Conseil Constitutionnel) para. 18; Decision 2008-564 DC *French Law on Genetically Modified Organisms* (French Conseil Constitutionnel) para. 44; Decision 2006-540 DC *Copyright and Related Rights in the Information*

> Firstly, the transposition of a Directive cannot run counter to *a rule or principle inherent to the constitutional identity of France* [emphasis added], except when the constituting power consents thereto [...].[37]

Based on this concept, it assesses whether the French implementation of EU secondary law commitments, initially EU Directives, conflicts with core constitutional values.[38] The *Conseil* extended the scope of this *constitutional identity* review to the implementation of obligations stemming from EU regulations[39] and to international agreements that are based on exclusive EU competences,[40] yet it did never apply it to EU primary law obligations.

Although the primary focus of the comparison rests on the available constitutional space for EU fiscal integration steps, and thus material limits that apply to the conferral of additional competences, the French *constitutional identity* doctrine is equally assessed. One reason for this is that the French conception of *constitutional identity* differs from other Member States, which established *constitutional identity limits* as strict restrictions for the conferral of powers. The French limit constitutes a *best practice* example for a different design of *national constitutional identity* concerns. Moreover, EU fiscal integration ambitions likely require the enactment of EU secondary law, which would be confronted with the French *constitutional identity limit*.[41]

II Essential Conditions for the Exercise of National Sovereignty

Based on the jurisprudence of the *Conseil Constitutionnel*, the *essential conditions for the exercising of national sovereignty ('conditions essentielles d'exercice de la souveraineté nationale')*[42] constitute the most immediate constitutional obstacle to EU fiscal integration.[43] Based on this concept, the *Conseil* determines whether an envisaged transfer of competences (limitation of sovereignty due to substantive changes) or

Society (French Conseil Constitutionnel) para. 19; cf. as well Édouard Dubout, '"Les règles ou principes inhérents à l'identité constitutionelle de la France": une supra-constitutionalité?' (2010) 83 Revue francaise de Droit constitutionnel 451, 452.

37. *Copyright and Related Rights in the Information Society* para. 19.
38. Vranes, 'Constitutional Foundation of, and Limitations to, EU Integration in France' 548.
39. Decision 2018-765 DC *National Law Related to the Protection of Personal Data under the GDPR* (French Conseil Constitutionnel) paras 3, 26; cf. as well: Millet, 'Constitutional Identity in France: Vices and - Above All - Virtues' 143.
40. *Comprehensive Economic and Trade Agreement (CETA)* para. 14; cf. as well: Larik, 'Prêt-à-Ratifier: The CETA Decision of the French *Conseil constitutionnel* of 31 July 2017' 764.
41. Millet, 'Constitutional Identity in France: Vices and - Above All - Virtues' 148.
42. Consistently employed by the *Conseil Constitutionnel* in relation to EU commitments since the Maastricht Treaty, cf., *Entwurf eines Gesetzes zu dem Beschluss des Europäischen Rates vom 25. März 2011 zur Änderung des Artikels 136 des Vertrags über die Arbeitsweise der Europäischen Union hinsichtlich eines Stabilitätsmechanismus für die Mitgliedstaaten, deren Währung der Euro ist (Drucksache 17/9047)* para. 10; *Lisbon Treaty* para. 9; *Treaty Establishing a Constitution for Europe* para. 7; Decision 97-394 DC *Revision of Amsterdam Treaty* (French Conseil Constitutionnel) para. 7; *Review of Maastricht Treaty (Maastricht I)* para. 14.
43. Reestman, 'Legitimacy Through Adjudication: The ESM Treaty and the Fiscal Compact Before the National Courts' 265; Fabbrini, 'The Euro-Crisis and the Courts: Judicial Review and the Political Process in Comparative Perspective' 122-123; Claes, 'National Idenity: Trump Card or up for Negotiation?' 126.

whether a modification of the conditions for the exercise of already conferred competences to the EU (limitation of sovereignty due to procedural changes) affect French sovereignty.[44]

1 *Institutional Actor Enforcing the Limit*

The French sovereignty limit was developed by the *Conseil Constitutionnel*.[45] The constitutional drafters envisaged the *Conseil* as an independent supervisor of the French separation of power.[46] Thus, the *Conseil* was created to monitor the political process and the new division of competences between the executive and the legislative powers under the 1958 Constitution.[47] The established institution resembled in its structure, an organization as well as its initial tasks a constitutional advisory body, which is also reflected in its name: a 'constitutional *council*' rather than a 'constitutional *court*'.[48]

The conception as 'advisory body' is reflected in its composition and the appointment of its members. The nine members of the *Conseil Constitutionnel* are appointed in equal parts by the French President, the President of the *Assemblée Nationale* and the President of the *Sénat* for a term of nine years. The appointed members are not required to have a legal background. [49] Furthermore, former French Presidents have the right to sit on the *Conseil Constitutionnel* as *members by law*.[50] Hence, the *Conseil's* members are not trained lawyers and have clear political affiliations. These affiliations seem to impact its final verdict. As research by *Brouard* shows, in case a majority of the members share the same political affiliation as the government, the *Conseil* is more likely to rule in favour of the government.[51] This suggests that political considerations when appointing new members permeate into the judgments.[52] From the initial design as an 'advisory body', the *Conseil Constitutionnel* developed into an increasingly *judicial* institution. It conducts constitutional review[53]

44. *Lisbon Treaty* para. 20; *Revision of Amsterdam Treaty* paras 27-28; cf. as well: Anne Bonnie, 'The Constitutionality of Transfers of Sovereignty: The French Approach' (1998) 4 European Public Law 517, 526.
45. Paris, 'France: The French System of Rights-Based Review: From Exceptionalism to Parochial Constitutionalism' 306.
46. David Pollard, 'France's Conseil Constitutionnel: Not Yet a Constitutional Court?' (1988) 23 Irish Jurist 2, 7.
47. Susan Wright, 'The French *Conseil Constitutionnel* under an Evolving Constitution' (2017) 23 European Public Law 245, 251; Paris, 'France: The French System of Rights-Based Review: From Exceptionalism to Parochial Constitutionalism' 306.
48. Pollard, 'France's Conseil Constitutionnel: Not Yet a Constitutional Court?' 7.
49. Sophie Boyron, 'Constitutional Law' in John Bell, Sophie Boyron and Simon Whittaker (eds), *Principles of French Law* (2nd edn, Oxford University Press 2008) 156; John Bell, *French Legal Culture* (Butterworths 2001) 42.
50. As established in Article 56 French Constitution.
51. Sylvain Brouard, 'The Politics of Constitutional Veto in France: Constitutional Council, Legislative Majority and Electoral Competition' (2009) 32 West European Politics 384, 394.
52. Paris, 'France: The French System of Rights-Based Review: From Exceptionalism to Parochial Constitutionalism' 302.
53. Pfersmann, 'Concrete Review As Indirect Constitutional Complaint in French Constitutional Law: A Comparative Perspective' 223.

and its decisions are final and binding on all French state authorities.[54] Clearly, the highlighted new referral mechanism for constitutional questions (*QPC*) integrates the *Conseil Constitutionnel* into the judicial branch of state power and thereby supports the on-going transformation.[55] The mechanism requires the *Conseil Constitutionnel* to address concrete private disputes and adjudicate on subjective constitutional rights, which constitutes a core task of constitutional courts.[56]

Overall, the *Conseil Constitutionnel* adjudicates centrally on the constitutionality of EU primary law. In case the *Conseil* identifies a conflict between the sovereignty limit and a conferral of competences such conferral requires a prior amendment of the constitutional text.[57] Through its review, the *Conseil* traditionally functions as a constitutional '*pointsman*'[58] that identifies constitutional conflicts, which can then be overcome by the French legislator.[59]

2 *Procedural Framework: Or How to Trigger the Limit*

The *Conseil Constitutionnel* applies the sovereignty limit in its abstract *ex ante* constitutional review of EU competence conferrals. Article 54 French Constitution empowers the French President, the French Prime Minister, the President of the *Assemblée Nationale*, the President of the *Senat*, 60 members of the *Assemblée Nationale* or 60 senators, to initiate this abstract *ex ante* review of the EU agreement itself prior to its ratification. It should be highlighted that all EU-Treaties since Maastricht were reviewed following Article 54 French Constitution, with the exception of the Nice Treaty.[60] The same would likely apply to future EU Treaty reforms, including possible conferrals required to accommodate EU fiscal integration. In case the new EU commitment is not directly challenged, the conferral of powers can also be

54. Cf. Article 62 French Constitution, Steiner, *French Law: A Comparative Approach* 68; Dyevre, 'The *Melki* Way: The *Melki* Case and Everything You Always Wanted to Know About French Judicial Politics (But Were Afraid to Ask)' 319.
55. De Visser, *Constitutional Review in Europe: A Comparative Analysis* 137.
56. Wright, 'The French *Conseil Constitutionnel* under an Evolving Constitution' 250-251.
57. Paris, 'France: The French System of Rights-Based Review: From Exceptionalism to Parochial Constitutionalism' 306; Franz C. Mayer, Edgar Lenski and Mattias Wendel, 'Der Vorrang des Europarechts in Frankreich: zugleich Anmerkungen zur Entscheidung des französischen Conseil d'Etat vom 8. Februar 2007 (Arcelor u.a.)' (2008) 43 Europarecht (EuR) 63, 69.
58. Ziller, 'European Union Law in the Jurisprudence of French Supreme Courts: Europe-Friendliness with a French Touch' 771.
59. *Entwurf eines Gesetzes zu dem Beschluss des Europäischen Rates vom 25. März 2011 zur Änderung des Artikels 136 des Vertrags über die Arbeitsweise der Europäischen Union hinsichtlich eines Stabilitätsmechanismus für die Mitgliedstaaten, deren Währung der Euro ist (Drucksache 17/9047)* para. 10; *Lisbon Treaty* para. 9; *Treaty Establishing a Constitution for Europe* para. 7; cf. as well: Millet, 'Constitutional Identity in France: Vices and – Above All – Virtues' 138; Claes, 'National Idenity: Trump Card or up for Negotiation?' 127.
60. Azoulai and Ronkes Agerbeek, '*Conseil constitutionnel* (French Constitutional Court), Decision No. 2004-505 DC of 19 November 2004, on the Treaty Establishing a Constitution for Europe' 871.

indirectly disputed by proceeding *ex ante* against the French legislative act that ratifies the EU Treaty following Article 61(2) French Constitution.[61]

Furthermore, it might be possible that a *concrete ex post* review is initiated following the *QPC*-mechanism.[62] Based on this procedure, private applicants can challenge the validity of a French statue claiming that their constitutionally guaranteed rights and freedoms are violated. The matter is then submitted to either *Conseil d'État* or the *Cour de Cassation*, which filters the references based on constitutional importance.[63] Considering the potential implications of this mechanism for challenges against EU primary law, three observations can be submitted. First, the *Conseil Constitutionnel* has refused to review statutes against international agreements, including EU law, given the special status to duly ratified international law following Article 55 French Constitution.[64] Second, an evaluation of the EU-Treaties or a Treaty-provision through the *QPC*-mechanism is conceptually excluded as the *Conseil Constitutionnel* is not re-considering matters it already ruled on.[65] Given that most EU-related competence conferrals were reviewed under Article 54 French Constitution, an additional consideration of the constitutionality of EU-Treaties through Article 61-1 French Constitution appears pre-empted.[66] And finally, it is questionable whether EU fiscal integration steps would directly violate subjective constitutional rights, which constitute the basis of this *concrete constitutional review*.

Consequently, it seems that EU fiscal integration measures will likely be challengeable *ex ante* by privileged applicants following Article 54 or 61(2) French Constitution. These procedures impose tight deadlines as the Conseil is required to deliver its ruling within one month from receipt of the application. The government may even request an expedited eight-day procedure.[67] Particularly in light of the complexity of EU-Treaties, these deadlines seem very tight. Yet, they ensure that the ratification of international commitments is not delayed in France because of constitutional proceedings. Taken together, the conducted *ex ante* review underscores the *Conseil Constitutionnel's* function as *'pointsman'*,[68] given that the *Conseil* identifies constitutional conflicts before they actually materialize.

61. Vranes, 'Constitutional Foundation of, and Limitations to, EU Integration in France' 529; Christine Maugüé, 'Le Conseil Constitutionnel et le droit supranational' (2003) 2 Le Seuil 53, 53.
62. Pfersmann, 'Concrete Review As Indirect Constitutional Complaint in French Constitutional Law: A Comparative Perspective' 231-232.
63. *Ibid.*, 238-239.
64. , 'An Index of Fiscal Democracy (2010)' paras 11, 16; cf. as well: Ziller, 'European Union Law in the Jurisprudence of French Supreme Courts: Europe-Friendliness with a French Touch' 778-779; Alina Berger, *Anwendungsvorrang und nationale Verfassungsgericht*, vol. 113 (Jus Internationale et Europaeum, Mohr Siebeck 2015) 230.
65. Decision 2010-14/22 QPC *Mr Daniel W and Others* (French Conseil Constitutionnel) paras 12-13; *Revision of Amsterdam Treaty* para. 27.
66. As outlined, it is a political convention to challenge EU-Treaties *ex ante*, cf. Millet, 'Constitutional Identity in France: Vices and – Above All – Virtues' 139; subsequently, principle of res judicata prevents *Conseil* to reconsider the matter, cf. *Mr Daniel W and Others* paras 12-13.
67. As stipulated in Article 61(3) French Constitution, cf. Vranes, 'German Constitutional Foundations of, and Limitations to, EU Integration: A Systematic Analysis' 530-531.
68. Ziller, 'European Union Law in the Jurisprudence of French Supreme Courts: Europe-Friendliness with a French Touch' 771.

3 *Constitutional Basis of the Employed Limit*

The French '*essential conditions for the exercising of national sovereignty*'[69] limit was established by the *Conseil Constitutionnel* and is based on French sovereignty. It derives from a combined reading of several provisions of the French *bloc de constitutionnalité*, namely Article 3 *Declaration* of 1789, Articles 3 and 53 French Constitution (of 1958), as well as § 15 Preamble of the French Constitution of 1946.[70] Since its decision on the EU Constitutional Treaty, the *Conseil* also refers to the EU enabling clause in Article 88-1 French Constitution.[71] Hence, the French sovereignty doctrine is enshrined in different constitutional provisions, which jointly constitute the textual and conceptual basis of the sovereignty limit.

The enumerated provisions serve different constitutional functions. Article 3 *Declaration* of 1789 and Article 3 French Constitution (1958) are primarily concerned with establishing the principle of sovereignty as such. To that end, Article 3 *Declaration* of 1789 establishes that sovereignty lies in the Nation, whereas Article 3 French Constitution (1958) establishes that sovereignty is vested in the people. One may identify here a combination of conceptual elements relating to national sovereignty and elements of popular sovereignty, as *Ziller* observes.[72] In addition, Article 3 French Constitution (1958) establishes the principle of democracy, including the right to vote and the electoral principles, and thus the form of exercising French sovereignty.[73] Subsequently, Article 53 French Constitution (1958) determines that the conclusion of international agreements requires parliamentary approval. § 15 Preamble of the French Constitution of 1946 clarifies that French sovereignty can be limited for the sake of international cooperation, however requiring that such limitation of sovereignty is

69. *Entwurf eines Gesetzes zu dem Beschluss des Europäischen Rates vom 25. März 2011 zur Änderung des Artikels 136 des Vertrags über die Arbeitsweise der Europäischen Union hinsichtlich eines Stabilitätsmechanismus für die Mitgliedstaaten, deren Währung der Euro ist (Drucksache 17/9047)* para. 10; *Lisbon Treaty* para. 9; *Treaty Establishing a Constitution for Europe* para. 7; *Revision of Amsterdam Treaty* para. 7; *Review of Maastricht Treaty (Maastricht I)* para. 14; cf. as well: Millet, 'Constitutional Identity in France: Vices and - Above All - Virtues' 138; Ziller, 'European Union Law in the Jurisprudence of French Supreme Courts: Europe-Friendliness with a French Touch' 772; Claes, 'National Idenity: Trump Card or up for Negotiation?' 126; Vranes, 'Constitutional Foundation of, and Limitations to, EU Integration in France' 541.
70. *Lisbon Treaty* paras 3-5; *Entwurf eines Gesetzes zu dem Beschluss des Europäischen Rates vom 25. März 2011 zur Änderung des Artikels 136 des Vertrags über die Arbeitsweise der Europäischen Union hinsichtlich eines Stabilitätsmechanismus für die Mitgliedstaaten, deren Währung der Euro ist (Drucksache 17/9047)* paras 4-6; for historic reasons, the 1958 French Constitution incorporates parts of previous French constitutional documents, which together form the so-called *bloc de constitutionnalité*, cf. Ziller, 'European Union Law in the Jurisprudence of French Supreme Courts: Europe-Friendliness with a French Touch' 773; Vranes, 'Constitutional Foundation of, and Limitations to, EU Integration in France' 538; Pfeiffer, 'Zur Verfassungsmäßigkeit des Gemeinschaftsrechts in der aktuellen Rechtsprechung des französischen Conseil constitutionnel' 491.
71. Vranes, 'Constitutional Foundation of, and Limitations to, EU Integration in France' 538.
72. Jaques Ziller, 'Sovereignty in France: Getting Rid of the Mal de Bodin' in Neil Walker (ed.), *Sovereignty in Transition* (Hart Publishing 2003) 267.
73. Bonnie, 'The Constitutionality of Transfers of Sovereignty: The French Approach' 520.

based on reciprocity.[74] And finally, Article 88-1 French Constitution (1958) reiterates these conditions for EU cooperation, thereby clarifying that it entails a common exercise of the conferred powers, and importantly not the conferral of sovereignty as such.[75]

These five constitutional provisions cover the conceptual origin of French sovereignty as well as conditions and requirements for the exercise of sovereign powers. This underlying intention is equally reflected in the name of the constitutional limit '*essential conditions for the exercising of national sovereignty*', which suggests that the limit is focused on the use or the exercise of sovereign powers, rather than merely preserving sovereignty as such. In addition, given the reference to Article 88-1 French Constitution, the conception of the sovereignty limit is specific to the conferral of competences to the EU.[76]

4 Substantive Core Protected by the Limit

The resulting French sovereignty limit is a judicial creation of the *Conseil Constitutionnel* defined on a case-to-case basis.[77] The subsequent analysis will determine the substantive content of this constitutional limit vis-à-vis EU fiscal integration based on the underpinning French sovereignty doctrine (a) and subsequently the relevant case law (b).

a The Conception of the French Sovereignty Doctrine

The principle of sovereignty serves as a basis for limiting the conferral of competences to the EU. Obviously, this constitutional principle predates EU integration. The principle of sovereignty is of historical importance, as can be deduced from the *Conseil's* reference to Article 3 *Declaration* of 1789, and it has been subject to intense academic and political debate.[78] An important element of this historically rooted debate is the distinction between sovereignty of the nation and sovereignty of the people.[79] Despite the historic importance of sovereignty in the French constitutional culture, it should be emphasized that the references to Article 3 *Declaration* of 1789 and to § 15

74. Andrea Hamann, 'Sur un "sentiment" de souveraineté' (2018) 20-21 Jus Politicum - Revue de droit politique 187, 188; Vranes, 'Constitutional Foundation of, and Limitations to, EU Integration in France' 538.
75. Azoulai and Ronkes Agerbeek, '*Conseil constitutionnel* (French Constitutional Court), Decision No. 2004-505 DC of 19 November 2004, on the Treaty Establishing a Constitution for Europe' 884.
76. Vranes, 'Constitutional Foundation of, and Limitations to, EU Integration in France' 533-535; Rochère, 'Conseil constitutionnel (French Constitutional Court), Decision No. 2004-496 of 10 June 2004, Loi Pour La Confiance Dans L'Économie Numérique (Ecommerce)' 861-862.
77. As the *Conseil* limits its assessment to what is strictly required to deliver a decision, cf. Ziller, 'European Union Law in the Jurisprudence of French Supreme Courts: Europe-Friendliness with a French Touch' 773.
78. Ziller, 'Sovereignty in France: Getting Rid of the Mal de Bodin' 264; Bonnie, 'The Constitutionality of Transfers of Sovereignty: The French Approach' 519-520.
79. Olivier Beaud, 'Le Conseil constitutionnel sur la souveraineté et ses approximations' (2018) 20-21, Jus Politicum - Revue de droit politique 143, 147.

Preamble of the French Constitution of 1946 are a judicial creation of the *Conseil Constitutionnel*.[80] The Preamble of the current French Constitution merely acknowledges an 'attachment' of the French people to the principle of sovereignty as established in the *Declaration* of 1789 and complemented by the Preamble of the French Constitution of 1946.[81] This historic origin of the French principle of sovereignty continues to impact the *Conseil's* jurisprudence, as competence transfers of *traditionally* important competences are generally deemed incompatible with French sovereignty.[82]

In addition, the constitutional significance of the principle of sovereignty can be deduced from the systematic position of the principle within the French Constitution. As already mentioned, the Preamble refers to the principle of sovereignty in its first phrase, together with fundamental rights and the protection of the environment. Furthermore, the first title of the French Constitution, which covers Articles 2 to 4, is entitled 'On Sovereignty'. The principle is further specified in Articles 3(1) and 4(1)(3) French Constitution, which link sovereignty to the people and the principle of democracy. Given the prominent position within the constitutional text, one can deduce that sovereignty is a core constitutional principle with a close link to the principle of democracy. Based on this constitutional framework, the *Conseil* draws several conclusions which are summarized in its sovereignty limit.[83]

First, the *Conseil Constitutionnel* infers from the conception of sovereignty in the French Constitution, that the French legislator may limit sovereignty by participating at the international or EU level. Here, the *Conseil Constitutionnel* refers to Articles 53 and 88-1 French Constitution to point out that the constitutional text allows explicitly for a limitation of national sovereignty.[84] As a result, not every transfer of competences to the EU conflicts in an unconstitutional manner with the principle of sovereignty, but rather transfers of competences which affect the *essential conditions of the exercising of national sovereignty*.[85]

80. Pfeiffer, 'Zur Verfassungsmäßigkeit des Gemeinschaftsrechts in der aktuellen Rechtsprechung des französischen Conseil constitutionnel' 491-492.
81. Reflecting the highlighted 'bloc de constitutionnalité', cf. Bonnie, 'The Constitutionality of Transfers of Sovereignty: The French Approach' 518; Oliver, 'The French Constitution and the Treaty of Maastricht' 2.
82. Hamann, 'Sur un "sentiment" de souveraineté' 188; Bonnie, 'The Constitutionality of Transfers of Sovereignty: The French Approach' 520.
83. Azoulai and Ronkes Agerbeek, '*Conseil constitutionnel* (French Constitutional Court), Decision No. 2004-505 DC of 19 November 2004, on the Treaty Establishing a Constitution for Europe' 873; Bonnie, 'The Constitutionality of Transfers of Sovereignty: The French Approach' 520.
84. *Lisbon Treaty* para. 7; *Entwurf eines Gesetzes zu dem Beschluss des Europäischen Rates vom 25. März 2011 zur Änderung des Artikels 136 des Vertrags über die Arbeitsweise der Europäischen Union hinsichtlich eines Stabilitätsmechanismus für die Mitgliedstaaten, deren Währung der Euro ist (Drucksache 17/9047)* para. 8; cf. as well: Wendel, 'Lisbon Before the Courts: Comparative Perspectives' 132.
85. *Entwurf eines Gesetzes zu dem Beschluss des Europäischen Rates vom 25. März 2011 zur Änderung des Artikels 136 des Vertrags über die Arbeitsweise der Europäischen Union hinsichtlich eines Stabilitätsmechanismus für die Mitgliedstaaten, deren Währung der Euro ist (Drucksache 17/9047)* para. 10; *Lisbon Treaty* para. 9; *Review of Maastricht Treaty (Maastricht I)* para. 14; cf. as well: Millet, 'Constitutional Identity in France: Vices and – Above All – Virtues' 138-139; Sophie Boyron, 'The French Constitution and the Treaty of Amsterdam: A Lesson in European Integration' (1999) 6 Maastricht Journal of European and Comparative Law 169, 175-176.

Second, the *Conseil Constitutionnel* changed its rhetoric in the course of EU integration. Originally, it argued that the French Constitution allowed for a limitation but not a transfer of sovereignty to the supranational level. In its first EU-related decision on the direct election of the European Parliament, the *Conseil* established:

> [...] France may consent to such limitations of sovereignty that are necessary for the establishment and preservation of peace, *no provision of the French Constitution authorizes transfers of the entire or parts of national sovereignty* [emphasis added] to any international organization whatsoever.[86]

Hence, initially, the *Conseil* apparently distinguished between the limitation of sovereignty, which was permissible, and the impermissible transfer of sovereignty.[87] This constitutional benchmark proved difficult to apply, given that a limitation of sovereignty conceptually entails the partial shared exercise of sovereign decision-making at supranational level.[88] Subsequently, the *Conseil* altered its approach in the Maastricht Treaty decision:

> It follows from these various institutional provisions that respect for national sovereignty does not preclude France, acting in accordance with the Preamble to the 1946 Constitution, from concluding international agreements relating to participation in the establishment or development of a permanent international [organization] enjoying legal personality and decision-making powers on the basis of *transfers of powers decided on by the Member States* [emphasis added], subject to reciprocity.[89]

Thus, the *Conseil Constitutionnel* clarified that the French sovereignty doctrine allowed for a transfer of (sovereign) powers.[90] The previously established prohibition of a transfer of sovereignty was lifted by the *Conseil*, as has become obvious from subsequent decisions.[91] According to the new conception, powers and competences can be conferred to the European level, which is in fact the exercise of national sovereignty by the legislator, without putting French sovereignty directly into question. This indicates an evolution of the principle of sovereignty from being absolute, and indivisible to a more open conception, which allows for the conferral of competences

86. Decision 76-71 DC *Direct Election of the European Parliament* (French Conseil Constitutionnel) para. 2.
87. Ziller, 'Sovereignty in France: Getting Rid of the Mal de Bodin' 274-275.
88. Jörg Gundel, *Die Einordnung des Gemeinschaftsrechts in die französische Rechtsordnung*, vol. 42 (Schriften zum Europäischen Recht, Duncker & Humblot 1997) 119; Oliver, 'The French Constitution and the Treaty of Maastricht' 8.
89. *Review of Maastricht Treaty (Maastricht I)* para. 13.
90. Bonnie, 'The Constitutionality of Transfers of Sovereignty: The French Approach' 523.
91. *Entwurf eines Gesetzes zu dem Beschluss des Europäischen Rates vom 25. März 2011 zur Änderung des Artikels 136 des Vertrags über die Arbeitsweise der Europäischen Union hinsichtlich eines Stabilitätsmechanismus für die Mitgliedstaaten, deren Währung der Euro ist (Drucksache 17/9047)* para. 9 (although speaking of "transfer of competences" in this decision); *Lisbon Treaty* para. 8; *Treaty Establishing a Constitution for Europe* para. 6; *Revision of Amsterdam Treaty* para. 6; cf. as well: Azoulai and Ronkes Agerbeek, '*Conseil constitutionnel* (French Constitutional Court), Decision No. 2004-505 DC of 19 November 2004, on the Treaty Establishing a Constitution for Europe' 884.

to the supranational level without eroding French sovereignty.[92] The apparent openness of French sovereignty towards the conferral of competences to EU level is, however, confined by the *essential conditions limit*.[93]

Finally, the altered conception of the French sovereignty doctrine indicates that the judicial review of sovereignty conducted by the *Conseil Constitutionnel* focuses on the transfer of powers and competences to the EU. The emerging question becomes whether the EU commitment under consideration entails a shift of powers to the EU which is relevant for the exercise of national sovereignty.[94] Based on this conception, it seems likely that EU fiscal integration steps could conflict with French sovereignty as these integration steps would entail the conferral of important national competences, which is substantiated in the following.

b Sovereignty as a Limit to EU Integration: A Competence-Based Approach

The established case law illustrates that Union citizenship, cooperation in Area of Freedom, Security and Justice (AFSJ) matters and the free movement of persons (i) as well as second, the EMU and the single currency (ii) were particularly contentious under the French sovereignty limit.

i Union Citizenship, AFJS and Free Movement

In its *Maastricht*-judgment, the *Conseil Constitutionnel* identified two envisaged competence transfers in this area as constitutionally problematic. The first one concerned the right of EU citizens to vote and stand as candidates in French municipal elections.[95] In its appraisal, the *Conseil* pointed out that the proposed rights conflicted with the French Constitution, given that Article 3 French Constitution limited the right to vote and stand in French municipal elections to French citizens. In contrast, the right to vote and stand in the French elections to the European Parliament for EU citizens was deemed unproblematic, for two reasons. First, according to the Conseil, Article 3 French Constitution only applied to elections provided by the French Constitution and

92. Pfeiffer, 'Zur Verfassungsmäßigkeit des Gemeinschaftsrechts in der aktuellen Rechtsprechung des französischen Conseil constitutionnel' 492.
93. Millet, 'Constitutional Identity in France: Vices and – Above All – Virtues' 138-139; Claes, 'National Idenity: Trump Card or up for Negotiation?' 126.
94. *Entwurf eines Gesetzes zu dem Beschluss des Europäischen Rates vom 25. März 2011 zur Änderung des Artikels 136 des Vertrags über die Arbeitsweise der Europäischen Union hinsichtlich eines Stabilitätsmechanismus für die Mitgliedstaaten, deren Währung der Euro ist (Drucksache 17/9047)* para. 10; *Lisbon Treaty* para. 9; *Treaty Establishing a Constitution for Europe* para. 7; *Revision of Amsterdam Treaty* para. 7; *Review of Maastricht Treaty (Maastricht I)* para. 14; cf. as well: Ziller, 'European Union Law in the Jurisprudence of French Supreme Courts: Europe-Friendliness with a French Touch' 772; Claes, 'National Idenity: Trump Card or up for Negotiation?' 126.
95. *Review of Maastricht Treaty (Maastricht I)* paras 26-27; cf. as well: Gerald L. Neuman, 'The Brakes That Failed: Constitutional Restriction of International Agreements in France' (2012) 45 Cornell International Law Journal 257, 297.

the European Parliament is an institution based on the EU-Treaties.[96] Second, the *Conseil* emphasized that the European Parliament was not 'a sovereign assembly with general lawmaking power'.[97] In a legislative follow-up, the constitution-amending legislator addressed these concerns and introduced Article 88-3 French Constitution.

The second concern was related to the common EU visa system. Initially, all decisions were to be taken unanimously by the EU Council. The *Conseil Constitutionnel* clarified that under these procedural rules, no conflict with the French sovereignty limit arose.[98] However, given that the procedural rules would change to a qualified majority vote by 1 January 1996, the *Conseil* identified a constitutional conflict with the French Constitution.[99] In the subsequent proceedings on the Amsterdam Treaty, the *Conseil Constitutionnel* was again confronted with the common EU visa system. In its decision, the *Conseil* clarified that it would not consider the general conferral of competences, as the 'status of res judicata of the Constitutional Council's decision preclude[d]'[100] to re-consider this conferral. However, it highlighted that the procedural conditions for the exercise of the conferred powers changed, given that following the proposed rule the co-decision procedure would apply after five years.[101] Hence, the changes to the procedural framework required an additional amendment to the French Constitution.

In its subsequent case law, the *Conseil* identified a sovereignty conflict between the new competences under the title 'Asylum, immigration and crossing of internal borders', which was introduced by the Amsterdam Treaty. Interestingly, coordinating the decision-making process at EU level was not deemed problematic under the sovereignty limit, as long as decisions were taken in the Council by unanimity.[102] However, the Treaty provisions allowed for a modification of the procedural requirements from a unanimous vote in the EU Council to the co-decision procedure after five years.[103] The *Conseil* pointed out that such a change of the procedural requirement would not require national ratification[104] and therefore a constitutional amendment was required.[105] It becomes obvious that not only the nature of the conferred competences is closely reviewed by the *Conseil* but also the conditions attached to the

96. *Review of Maastricht Treaty (Maastricht I)* paras 32-35; cf. as well: Oliver, 'The French Constitution and the Treaty of Maastricht' 13.
97. *Review of Maastricht Treaty (Maastricht I)* para. 34.
98. *Ibid.*, para. 49; cf. as well: Oliver, 'The French Constitution and the Treaty of Maastricht' 15.
99. *Review of Maastricht Treaty (Maastricht I)* para. 49; cf. as well: Neuman, 'The Brakes That Failed: Constitutional Restriction of International Agreements in France' 296.
100. *Revision of Amsterdam Treaty* para. 27; as the Conseil confirmed the original conferral, cf. Decision 92-312 DC *Compatibility of the Maastricht Treaty with the French Constitution after Constitutinal Amendments ('Maastricht II')* (French Conseil Constitutionnel) paras 37-40.
101. *Revision of Amsterdam Treaty* para. 28.
102. *Ibid.*, para. 23.
103. Andoni Perez Ayala, 'La Unión Europea y el Proceso de Revisión Constitucional en Francia (1992-2008)' (2009) 75-76 Revista de Derecho Político 409, 427; Boyron, 'The French Constitution and the Treaty of Amsterdam: A Lesson in European Integration' 177.
104. *Revision of Amsterdam Treaty* para. 24.
105. Marie-Luce Paris, 'Europeanization and Constitutionalization: The Challenging Impact of a Double Transformative Process on French Law' (2010) 29 Yearbook of European Law 21, 28; Ingolf Pernice, 'Multilevel Constitutionalism and the Treaty of Amsterdam: European Constitution-Making Revisited?' (1999) 36 Common Market Law Review 703, 717.

exercise of this competence – and therefore the remaining control of national parliaments over the decision taken – at the supranational level. Hence, the *essential conditions* limit has both a substantive as well as a procedural or *institutional* dimension to it.[106] From the previous outline, it appears that common decision-making at EU level in important sovereign matters is permissible, as long as decisions are taken by unanimity. In case decisions on these matters are taken by a qualified majority vote, a conflict with the French sovereignty limit will emerge. Therefore, it seems that both the substantive dimension, namely, to identify an *essential* sovereign competence, and the procedural dimension, namely, to consider the procedural modalities attached to them, are cumulative.[107]

This finding is confirmed by the *Conseil's Lisbon*-judgment. In this judgment, the *Conseil* identified additional conflicting competence transfers in relation to AFSJ-matters enshrined in Title V of the TFEU.[108] Regarding these transfers, the *Conseil* paid particular attention to the attached procedural framework. The *Conseil* noted:

> The provisions of the Treaty of Lisbon which transfer to the European Union under the *'ordinary legislative procedure'* [emphasis added] powers inherent in the exercising of national sovereignty require a revision of the Constitution.[109]

Hence, the modalities attached to the conferral are as important for the *Conseil's* assessment as the concerned competence area. Overall, the outline reveals that citizenship rights, the control of national borders, including immigration and asylum, cooperation in security matters, for example, by police forces, and judicial cooperation are competence areas that are 'inherent to the exercising of national sovereignty'.[110] As previously outlined, limiting sovereign powers to exercise them jointly at EU level is perceived as an exercise of French sovereignty and is therefore, as such, not incompatible with the French Constitution. Yet, in case the legislator transfers these important competences to the supranational level without retaining a constitutive say, a conflict with the sovereignty limit can emerge.

ii EMU and Single Currency

The *Conseil Constitutionnel* also identified decision-making powers on EMU policies as important for the exercising of national sovereignty. In the *Maastricht*-decision, the

106. Azoulai and Ronkes Agerbeek, '*Conseil constitutionnel* (French Constitutional Court), Decision No. 2004-505 DC of 19 November 2004, on the Treaty Establishing a Constitution for Europe' 884-885.
107. Boyron, 'The French Constitution and the Treaty of Amsterdam: A Lesson in European Integration' 176.
108. Notably, Articles 75, 77, 79 (2) lit. d, 81, 82, 83, and 86 TFEU, cf. *Lisbon Treaty* paras 18, 19; cf. as well: Paris, 'Europeanization and Constitutionalization: The Challenging Impact of a Double Transformative Process on French Law' 56.
109. *Lisbon Treaty* para. 18.
110. Vranes, 'Constitutional Foundation of, and Limitations to, EU Integration in France' 541; Boyron, 'The French Constitution and the Treaty of Amsterdam: A Lesson in European Integration' 176.

Conseil found the Treaty provisions on the creation of the EMU, and more specifically the creation of the Euro, to be in conflict with national sovereignty:

> The effect of the provisions applicable from the beginning of the third stage of economic and monetary union is that such an objective will result in the conduct of *single monetary and exchange-rate policies* according to arrangements which deprive the Member States of their own powers in a matter which is *vital to the exercise of national sovereignty.*[111]

Thus, the *Conseil* characterized monetary policy, including specifically exchange-rate policy, as a core competence area of the sovereign state.[112] Consequently, the French constitution-amending legislator was required to amend the French Constitution, and introduced Article 88-2(1), which enshrined French participation in the EMU into the constitutional text.[113] The *Conseil* confirmed this constitutional assessment in relation to the Fiscal Compact during the Eurocrisis, where it determined that economic and fiscal policies are competences that are closely related to the core of national sovereignty.[114] Following the *Conseil's* reasoning, economic and fiscal decisions are crucial elements of the annual budgetary planning which is conducted by the French Parliament and which relates to the individual's right to democracy.[115] Specifically, the *Conseil* recalls that the democratic parliamentary control of the budget stems from Article 14 *Declaration* of 1789.[116] As outlined in the decision, the importance of democratic parliamentary control of the budget translates into parliamentary prerogatives constitutionally enshrined in Articles 24, 34, 47 and 47-1 French Constitution.[117]

When assessing the Fiscal Compact, the *Conseil* concluded that it did not establish any new constraints on national sovereignty, as it was merely reiterating the already existing EU-balanced budget rules.[118] The *Conseil* conducted a more nuanced assessment of the requirement to implement the balanced budget rule into constitutional – or similarly binding national – law. Following the *Conseil's* assessment, two different readings of this obligation may be adopted: either, a directly binding rule would have to be enacted which would alter parliamentary and governmental

111. *Review of Maastricht Treaty (Maastricht I)* para. 43; cf. as well: Neuman, 'The Brakes That Failed: Constitutional Restriction of International Agreements in France' 296.
112. *Review of Maastricht Treaty (Maastricht I)* para. 45; cf. as well Vranes, 'Constitutional Foundation of, and Limitations to, EU Integration in France' 540.
113. *Compatibility of the Maastricht Treaty with the French Constitution after Constitutinal Amendments ('Maastricht II')* para. 3.
114. *Entwurf eines Gesetzes zu dem Beschluss des Europäischen Rates vom 25. März 2011 zur Änderung des Artikels 136 des Vertrags über die Arbeitsweise der Europäischen Union hinsichtlich eines Stabilitätsmechanismus für die Mitgliedstaaten, deren Währung der Euro ist (Drucksache 17/9047)* para. 16.
115. *Ibid.*, para. 13.
116. *Ibid.*
117. *Ibid.*
118. *Ibid.*, paras 14, 16; cf. as well: Reestman, 'Legitimacy Through Adjudication: The ESM Treaty and the Fiscal Compact Before the National Courts' 265.

budgetary prerogatives, enshrined in Articles 34 and 47 French Constitution.[119] Such a binding rule would then require a constitutional amendment.[120] Or, in the alternative, if only an institutional act – which sits in the hierarchy of norms below the constitution and which could determine multiannual guidelines for public finances – would have to be adopted, no constitutional amendment would be required.[121] Such an institutional act would only establish a (temporary) framework for the exercise of these prerogatives, which would furthermore be reviewed by the *Conseil Constitutionnel* according to Article 61(1) French Constitution.[122] The *Conseil* left the decision concerning the applicable interpretation to the legislator,[123] which opted for the second interpretation and did not amend the French Constitution. This appears paradoxical, as it undermines the objective of the Fiscal Compact to ensure the permanent national implementation of the balanced budget rule.[124]

Based on this jurisprudence, it can be concluded that economic and fiscal policies are considered essential for the exercising of national sovereignty. This equally covers the process of determining the national budget, without being legally restricted by international or EU commitments. Any such binding commitment would conflict with the parliamentary and governmental budgetary prerogatives enshrined in Articles 34 and 47 French Constitution. Both provisions constitutionally secure the democratic control of the people over budgetary decisions covered as an important element by the French sovereignty limit,[125] which has major implications for EU fiscal integration proposals.

119. *Entwurf eines Gesetzes zu dem Beschluss des Europäischen Rates vom 25. März 2011 zur Änderung des Artikels 136 des Vertrags über die Arbeitsweise der Europäischen Union hinsichtlich eines Stabilitätsmechanismus für die Mitgliedstaaten, deren Währung der Euro ist (Drucksache 17/9047)* para. 21; cf. as well: Reestman, 'Legitimacy Through Adjudication: The ESM Treaty and the Fiscal Compact Before the National Courts' 265.

120. *Entwurf eines Gesetzes zu dem Beschluss des Europäischen Rates vom 25. März 2011 zur Änderung des Artikels 136 des Vertrags über die Arbeitsweise der Europäischen Union hinsichtlich eines Stabilitätsmechanismus für die Mitgliedstaaten, deren Währung der Euro ist (Drucksache 17/9047)* para. 21; cf. as well: Fabbrini, 'The Euro-Crisis and the Courts: Judicial Review and the Political Process in Comparative Perspective' 120.

121. *Entwurf eines Gesetzes zu dem Beschluss des Europäischen Rates vom 25. März 2011 zur Änderung des Artikels 136 des Vertrags über die Arbeitsweise der Europäischen Union hinsichtlich eines Stabilitätsmechanismus für die Mitgliedstaaten, deren Währung der Euro ist (Drucksache 17/9047)* paras 23-24; cf. as well: Reestman, 'Legitimacy Through Adjudication: The ESM Treaty and the Fiscal Compact Before the National Courts' 265;

122. *Entwurf eines Gesetzes zu dem Beschluss des Europäischen Rates vom 25. März 2011 zur Änderung des Artikels 136 des Vertrags über die Arbeitsweise der Europäischen Union hinsichtlich eines Stabilitätsmechanismus für die Mitgliedstaaten, deren Währung der Euro ist (Drucksache 17/9047)* para. 27; cf. as well: Fabbrini, 'The Euro-Crisis and the Courts: Judicial Review and the Political Process in Comparative Perspective' 122.

123. Pietro Faraguna, 'Taking Constitutional Identities Away from the Courts' (2016) 42 Brooklyn Journal of International Law 491, 508.

124. Reestman, 'Legitimacy Through Adjudication: The ESM Treaty and the Fiscal Compact Before the National Courts' 266.

125. *Entwurf eines Gesetzes zu dem Beschluss des Europäischen Rates vom 25. März 2011 zur Änderung des Artikels 136 des Vertrags über die Arbeitsweise der Europäischen Union hinsichtlich eines Stabilitätsmechanismus für die Mitgliedstaaten, deren Währung der Euro ist (Drucksache 17/9047)* para. 13.

c Interim Conclusion: A Substantive Limit to EU Fiscal Integration?

The assessment reveals that the sovereignty limit is mainly construed as a competence-based restriction to EU integration. The *Conseil* identified two broad competence areas that are important for the exercise of national sovereignty.[126] These are, first, citizenship rights, the control of national borders, the judiciary and security matters, as well as second, budgetary, economic, financial, fiscal and monetary policies. In particular, the parliamentary and governmental fiscal, budgetary prerogatives enshrined in Articles 24, 34, 47 and 47-1 French Constitution as well as the individual's right to democratically control fiscal decisions, enshrined in Article 14 *Declaration* of 1789, might conflict with EU fiscal integration proposals.[127] The assessment further revealed that the modalities attached to the conferred competences significantly affect the appraisal. Hence, mere coordination of decisions appears less problematic, even in important competence areas. However, in case France is no longer able to take its own decisions or veto decisions at EU level, the exercising of national sovereignty is affected. Therefore, the procedural framework attached to EU fiscal integration steps is important to determine whether a conflict with French sovereignty exists.

5 Longevity and Absoluteness of the Constitutional Limit

The subsequent question is whether a possible conflict between EU fiscal integration and the French sovereignty limit could be overcome. Considering its constitutional mandate, it can be established that *Conseil Constitutionnel* is not competent to review constitutional amendments. Through its decisions, the *Conseil Constitutionnel* identifies conflicts, which can then be overcome by amending the constitution following Article 89 French Constitution.[128] Subsequently, however, these constitutional amendments cannot be reviewed by the *Conseil Constitutionnel.* Put differently, in case the French legislator amends the constitution, which requires broad political[129] or popular support,[130] the *Conseil* cannot scrutinize such

126. Corresponding to the outlined 'regalian' competences, cf. Bonnie, 'The Constitutionality of Transfers of Sovereignty: The French Approach' 527.
127. *Entwurf eines Gesetzes zu dem Beschluss des Europäischen Rates vom 25. März 2011 zur Änderung des Artikels 136 des Vertrags über die Arbeitsweise der Europäischen Union hinsichtlich eines Stabilitätsmechanismus für die Mitgliedstaaten, deren Währung der Euro ist (Drucksache 17/9047)* para. 13.
128. *Review of Maastricht Treaty (Maastricht I)* paras 36-44; cf. as well: Steiner, *French Law: A Comparative Approach* 7; Vranes, 'Constitutional Foundation of, and Limitations to, EU Integration in France' 535.
129. As outlined in Article 89(3) French Constitution, requiring a three-fifth-majority of the votes casted in Congress (the joined assembly of the Assemblée Nationale and the Sénat), cf. Maria Cahill, 'Ever Closer Remoteness of the Peoples of Europe? Limits on the Power of Amendment and National Constituent Power' (2016) 75 Cambridge Law Journal 245, 266-267.
130. As established in Article 89(2) in conjunction with Article 11 French Constitution; for example, employed in relation to the Maastricht Treaty and the Constitutional Treaty, cf. Thomas König and Simon Hug, 'Ratifying Maastricht: Parliamentary Votes on International Treaties and Theoretical Solution Concepts' (2000) 1 European Union Politics 93, 99-100.

amendments.[131] Therefore, the constitution-amending legislator can overcome a constitutional conflict with the sovereignty limit by amending the French Constitution, even though the amendment may not fully cover or address the obstacles identified by the *Conseil*.

Second, the French Constitution does not contain 'supra-constitutional' principles.[132] Although Article 89(5) French Constitution stipulates a limit to the powers of the constitution-amending legislator, this provision seemingly only has a symbolic function, as apparent from the intention of the drafters of the 1958 French Constitution, who did not intend to establish an absolute material limit to the powers of the constitution-amending legislator.[133] Furthermore, the previous outline indicates that the *Conseil Constitutionnel* as 'pointsman' would not be in an institutional position to enforce such supra-constitutional provision.[134] The result is that the constitution-amending legislator is competent to modify the constitutional text as it sees fit to accommodate EU integration.

Therefore, the *essential conditions of the exercising of national sovereignty* limit do not impose absolute restrictions on EU fiscal integration proposals. A potential conflict between such integration proposals and the French Constitution can be overcome by amending the constitutional text. This ultimately transforms substantive limits into procedural limits – as the main legal hurdle is to attain the required constitution-amending majority.

III Particularity of the French Constitutional Identity Limit

Furthermore, the *Conseil Constitutionnel* developed an explicit *constitutional identity limit* (*'identité constitutionnel de la France'*).[135] The subsequent assessment focuses on the scope of application (1) and the substantive content of the French *constitutional identity limit* (2) in order to allow for a comparison with the other national *constitutional identity limits*.

131. Denis Baranger, 'The Language of Eternity: Judicial Review of the Amending Power in France (Or the Absence Thereof)' (2011) 41 Israel Law Review 389, 413.
132. *Compatibility of the Maastricht Treaty with the French Constitution after Constitutinal Amendments ('Maastricht II')* para. 19; cf. as well: Baranger, 'The Language of Eternity: Judicial Review of the Amending Power in France (Or the Absence Thereof)' 402-403.
133. Baranger, 'The Language of Eternity: Judicial Review of the Amending Power in France (Or the Absence Thereof)' 402-403; Ziller, 'Sovereignty in France: Getting Rid of the Mal de Bodin' 271.
134. Ziller, 'European Union Law in the Jurisprudence of French Supreme Courts: Europe-Friendliness with a French Touch' 771; Ziller, 'Sovereignty in France: Getting Rid of the Mal de Bodin' 271.
135. *National Law Related to the Protection of Personal Data under the GDPR* paras 2-3; *Comprehensive Economic and Trade Agreement (CETA)* paras 13-14; *Act Pertaining to the Opening Up to Competition and the Regulation of Online Betting and Gambling* para. 18; *French Law on Genetically Modified Organisms* para. 44; Decision 2006-543 DC *French Act Pertaining to the Energy Sector* (French Conseil Constitutionnel) para. 6; *Copyright and Related Rights in the Information Society* para. 19; cf. as well: Vranes, 'Constitutional Foundation of, and Limitations to, EU Integration in France' 546-547; Claes, 'National Idenity: Trump Card or up for Negotiation?' 127.

1 *Scope of Application of the Constitutional Identity Limit*

Generally, the *Conseil Constitutionnel* does not review EU secondary law, as Article 55 French Constitution stipulates that duly ratified international law prevails over acts of parliament.[136] In addition, Article 88-1 French Constitution formulates the commitment to participate in the EU and to commonly exercise conferred competences, which entails the constitutional obligation to implement EU law.[137] As a result, EU law has a special status under French constitutional law and is generally not reviewed by the *Conseil*.[138]

Nevertheless, the *Conseil Constitutionnel* started to review French legislative acts, which implement EU law obligations, under Article 61(2) French Constitution, which results in an indirect review of EU secondary law.[139] Initially, the *Conseil* established that the constitutional obligation of the French legislator to implement EU law could not violate an 'express contrary provision of the [French] Constitution'.[140] The concept of *explicit contrary provision* was criticized as unspecific, and replayed by the concept of '*identité constitutionnel de la France*'.[141] Following this new concept, the implementation of EU Directives may not conflict with 'a rule or principle inherent to the *constitutional identity* of France, except when the constituting power consents thereto'.[142] The *Conseil* requires, however, that the French implementation is manifestly incompatible with the respective EU Directive, before declaring a conflict with the French *constitutional identity* doctrine. On the one hand, this pays tribute to the outlined special status of EU law. On the other hand, given that the *Conseil Constitutionnel* operates under strict procedural deadlines, it is unable to refer preliminary questions to the CJEU.[143] The reluctant application of the *constitutional identity limit* acknowledges this procedural constraint. Nevertheless, the *Conseil Constitutionnel*

136. Vranes, 'Constitutional Foundation of, and Limitations to, EU Integration in France' 531.
137. Reestman, 'France: *Conseil Constitutionnel* on the Status of (Secondary) Community Law in the French Internal Order – Decision of 10 June 2004, 2004-496 DC' 305-307.
138. Philippe Blachèr and Guillaume Protière, 'Le Conseil Constitutionnel, Gardien de la Constitution Face aux Directives Communautaires' (2007) 69 Revue francaise de Droit constitutionnel 123, 126.
139. Cf. Charpy, 'The Status of (Secondary) Community Law in the French Internal Order: The Recent Case-Law of the *Conseil Constitutionnel* and the *Conseil d'Etat*' 442-443.
140. Decision 2004-496 DC *Digital Economy* (French Conseil Constitutionnel) para. 7; cf. as well: Vranes, 'Constitutional Foundation of, and Limitations to, EU Integration in France' 533; Dubout, '"Les règles ou principes inhérents à l'identité constitutionelle de la France": une supra-constitutionalité?' 452; Rochère, 'Conseil constitutionnel (French Constitutional Court), Decision No. 2004-496 of 10 June 2004, Loi Pour La Confiance Dans L'Économie Numérique (Ecommerce)' 862.
141. Vranes, 'Constitutional Foundation of, and Limitations to, EU Integration in France' 546-547.
142. *Copyright and Related Rights in the Information Society* para. 19; *French Act Pertaining to the Energy Sector* para. 6; cf. as well: Vranes, 'Constitutional Foundation of, and Limitations to, EU Integration in France' 547-548; Mayer, Lenski and Wendel, 'Der Vorrang des Europarechts in Frankreich: zugleich Anmerkungen zur Entscheidung des französischen Conseil d'Etat vom 8. Februar 2007 (Arcelor u.a.)' 71.
143. *Copyright and Related Rights in the Information Society* para. 20; *French Act Pertaining to the Energy Sector* para. 7; cf. as well: Vranes, 'Constitutional Foundation of, and Limitations to, EU Integration in France' 548.

expanded the scope of application in its jurisprudence to the transposition of obligations stemming from EU regulations[144] and international (trade) agreements based on exclusive EU competences.[145]

The *constitutional identity limit* can be triggered by privileged applicants based on Article 61(2) French Constitution. The *Conseil* will then assess whether the French implementing law conflicts with French *constitutional identity* and whether the French implementation manifestly conflicts with EU secondary law, or whether the French legislator enjoyed discretion when implementing it.[146] In contrast, individuals are generally barred from challenging French implementing acts based on the *constitutional identity limit*, as the identity limit is based on Article 88-1 French Constitution and concerns the constitutional duty to implement EU law.[147] This constitutional duty is, however, no subjective right or freedom in the sense of Article 61-1 French Constitution and it can therefore not serve as a basis for concrete constitutional review following the *QPC*-mechanism.[148] The limited procedural means to enforce the *constitutional identity limit* correspond with the importance that the French constitutional system assigns to adhering to EU law obligations and the special status of EU law under the French Constitution.[149]

2 *Substantive Content Covered by the French Constitutional Identity Limit*

The concept of *constitutional identity* is based on the case law of the *Conseil Constitutionnel* and it is defined on a case-to-case basis. In the first place, the *Conseil*

144. Millet, 'Constitutional Identity in France: Vices and – Above All – Virtues' 143.
145. The power to conclude such agreements in areas of exclusive competences was explicitly conferred upon the EU, which is why the *Conseil Constitutionnel* does not see itself competent conduct a full constitutional review, cf. *Comprehensive Economic and Trade Agreement (CETA)* paras 13-14; cf. as well: Xavier Magnon, 'Commentaire de Décisions: Décision n° 2017-749 DC du 31 juillet 2017, Accord économique et commercial global entre le Canada, d'une part, et l'Union européenne et ses États membres, d'autre part' (2018) 113 Revue française de droit constitutionnel 173, 176-177.
146. *Copyright and Related Rights in the Information Society* paras 19-20; cf. as well: Ziller, 'European Union Law in the Jurisprudence of French Supreme Courts: Europe-Friendliness with a French Touch' 776; Vranes, 'Constitutional Foundation of, and Limitations to, EU Integration in France' 548.
147. Mayer, Lenski and Wendel, 'Der Vorrang des Europarechts in Frankreich: zugleich Anmerkungen zur Entscheidung des französischen Conseil d'Etat vom 8. Februar 2007 (Arcelor u.a.)' 70-71.
148. Decision 2010-79 QPC *Mr Kamel D.* (French Conseil Constitutionnel) para. 3; which could amount to an indirect review that is excluded by Article 55 French Constitution, cf. Paris, 'France: The French System of Rights-Based Review: From Exceptionalism to Parochial Constitutionalism' 321.
149. Namely, the outlined concept of 'immunité des conventions ratifiées', cf. Pfeiffer, 'Zur Verfassungsmäßigkeit des Gemeinschaftsrechts in der aktuellen Rechtsprechung des französischen Conseil constitutionnel' 478-479.
Reestman, 'France: *Conseil Constitutionnel* on the Status of (Secondary) Community Law in the French Internal Order – Decision of 10 June 2004, 2004-496 DC' 303.

appears to aim at protecting French constitutional particularities with this limit, including for example the principle of secularism ('laïcité'), the principle of equality and the indivisibility of the nation,[150] the 'French' separation of powers enshrined, *inter alia*, in Articles 34, 37 French Constitution and the republican status enshrined in Article 89(5) French Constitution.[151] It seems that the *Conseil Constitutionnel* mainly conducts an equivalence assessment to determine whether the EU legal order protects the respective French constitutional principle at stake in an equivalent manner.[152] In case such protection is warranted or in case the constitution-amending legislator consented to a limitation of the French constitutional particularity,[153] the *Conseil Constitutionnel* will not find a conflict with the French *constitutional identity limit*. Obviously, this implies that the *Conseil* accepts that the EU legal order is capable of protecting core French constitutional values and a conceptual overlap with the *Solange*-jurisprudence can be identified, as the French *constitutional identity limit* is only applied in case the EU is not offering an equivalent level of protection.[154]

Furthermore, the *Conseil Constitutionnel* employs an evolutionary conception of French *constitutional identity*. Namely, as the *Conseil* emphasized both in relation to EU primary law and also EU secondary law obligations, the constitution-amending legislator is able to modify the constitutional text and thereby overcome constitutional conflicts including conflicts with French *constitutional identity*. Given that such amendments are common practice in France, the constitutional framework regularly changes.[155]

For EU fiscal integration proposals, it seems that the division of powers between French institutions as enshrined in Articles 34 and 37 French Constitution, the indivisibility of the nation as well as the republican status are particularly relevant. All three aspects are concerned with the state and the institutional structure of France. In case EU fiscal integration proposals interfere with these areas through discretionary EU secondary law obligations, which are then implemented into French law, the French *constitutional identity* is possibly triggered. In addition, the French *constitutional identity limit* is not absolute in nature but can be overcome by the French constitution-amending legislator.[156]

150. Millet, 'Constitutional Identity in France: Vices and – Above All – Virtues' 148.
151. Dubout, '"Les règles ou principes inhérents à l'identité constitutionelle de la France": une supra-constitutionalité?' 474-475; Blachèr and Protière, 'Le Conseil Constitutionnel, Gardien de la Constitution Face aux Directives Communautaires' 135.
152. Dubout, '"Les règles ou principes inhérents à l'identité constitutionelle de la France": une supra-constitutionalité?' 454; Reestman, 'The Franco-German Constitutional Divide: Reflections on National and Constitutional Identity' 387-388.
153. Claes, 'National Idenity: Trump Card or up for Negotiation?' 127; Wendel, 'Lisbon Before the Courts: Comparative Perspectives' 133.
154. Vranes, 'Constitutional Foundation of, and Limitations to, EU Integration in France' 547.
155. Paris, 'France: The French System of Rights-Based Review: From Exceptionalism to Parochial Constitutionalism' 306; Bonnie, 'The Constitutionality of Transfers of Sovereignty: The French Approach' 530.
156. Claes, 'National Idenity: Trump Card or up for Negotiation?' 127.

3 *Interim Conclusion: No Immediate Limit for EU Fiscal Integration*

The *Conseil Constitutionnel* applies French *constitutional identity* in a very limited manner. In the first place, the application is limited to the French implementation of EU law obligations. Second, the *Conseil Constitutionnel* will only declare a French implementing law invalid based on this limit, in case the implementing law manifestly conflicts with the EU act. The Conseil emphasized that it is not able to refer preliminary questions to the CJEU, which is why it refused to strike down French implementing acts which are merely transposing unconditional EU law obligations.[157] Moreover, the substantive content of the *constitutional identity concept* only covers French particularities that are not protected at EU level in an equivalent manner, and it is open to modification by the French constitution-amending legislator.

Consequently, the French *constitutional identity* seems to be only of indirect importance for EU fiscal integration proposals. Given the very narrow scope of application and the confined instances in which the *Conseil Constitutionnel* will strike down a French law based on the *constitutional identity limit*, it seems unlikely that the limit has an immediate limiting effect on EU fiscal integration.

IV Conclusion on the French Constitutional Identity Limit(s)

EU fiscal integration proposals will very likely trigger a conflict with the French sovereignty limit. In case the privileged applicants request the *Conseil* to assess EU fiscal integration steps, a full constitutional assessment will be conducted. As part of this scrutiny, the *Conseil* assesses whether the new EU commitments entail a transfer of competences that could affect the *essential conditions of the exercising of national sovereignty*.[158] The *Conseil* developed a two-stepped approach under its sovereignty limit. It first assesses whether the conferral occurs in an important competence area. In its jurisprudence, the *Conseil* identified economic, financial, fiscal and monetary policies as such particularly important competence areas.[159] In a second step, the *Conseil* reviews the modalities that are attached to the conferral of such important competences. Based on case law, it seems that a conflict with the sovereignty limit will arise if the conferred important competences are to be exercised under the ordinary legislative procedure, by a qualified majority vote or if France loses its ability to initiate legislation.[160] The *Conseil Constitutionnel* applies this limit to new EU commitments prior to their adoption, following the procedure established in Article 54 French

157. Ziller, 'European Union Law in the Jurisprudence of French Supreme Courts: Europe-Friendliness with a French Touch' 776; Vranes, 'Constitutional Foundation of, and Limitations to, EU Integration in France' 548.
158. Ziller, 'European Union Law in the Jurisprudence of French Supreme Courts: Europe-Friendliness with a French Touch' 771-772; Claes, 'Luxembourg, Here We Come? Constitutional Courts and the Preliminary Reference Procedure' 126.
159. Millet, 'Constitutional Identity in France: Vices and – Above All – Virtues' 139; Vranes, 'Constitutional Foundation of, and Limitations to, EU Integration in France' 540.
160. Perez Ayala, 'La Unión Europea y el Proceso de Revisión Constitucional en Francia (1992-2008)' 427.

Constitution. In case the *Conseil* identifies a constitutional conflict, the constitution-amending legislator can modify the French Constitution to explicitly accommodate the conflicting EU obligations.[161]

Once EU law obligations are ratified by the French legislator, the *Conseil Constitutionnel* can review them upon referral. EU law, including EU secondary law, benefits from the special status the French constitutional order awards to ratified international law more generally.[162] Nevertheless, the *Conseil* developed a French *constitutional identity limit*, which applies to the French implementation of EU-law-related obligations.[163] However, the *Conseil Constitutionnel* only applies the *constitutional identity limit* in case the French legislator enjoyed discretion in the implementation of EU law.[164] Therefore, French *constitutional identity* embraces the assumption that EU law is in accordance with the French Constitution.[165]

In addition, the *Conseil Constitutionnel* consistently held that the EU legal order is a derived legal order and is thus based on the French Constitution.[166] Yet, the French Constitution provides a high degree of flexibility, as the constitution-amending legislator can alter the constitutional text to accommodate EU law obligations. It seems therefore that EU fiscal integration proposals are mainly confronted with procedural-political obstacles in France.

Table 5.2 Constitutional Identity Classification Board for France

Constitutional Identity Classification Board for France
1. Which institutional actor enforces the constitutional limit?
The *Conseil Constitutionnel* applies the *national sovereignty limit*. The *Conseil* issues binding decisions on the compatibility of acts – including EU law – with the French Constitution. It acts as 'pointsman' that identifies constitutional conflicts.
2. How can the constitutional identity limit be triggered?
The *national sovereignty limit* is employed by the *Conseil Constitutionnel* in the *ex ante* constitutional review of EU primary law commitments following Article 54 or Article 61(2) French Constitution. The review can only be initiated by privileged actors.

161. Ziller, 'Sovereignty in France: Getting Rid of the Mal de Bodin' 272.
162. Berger, *Anwendungsvorrang und nationale Verfassungsgericht* 247.
163. With potentially indirect consequences for EU law, cf. Millet, 'Constitutional Identity in France: Vices and – Above All – Virtues' 142-143; Wendel, 'Lisbon Before the Courts: Comparative Perspectives' 132-133.
164. Ziller, 'European Union Law in the Jurisprudence of French Supreme Courts: Europe-Friendliness with a French Touch' 776.
165. Reestman, 'The Franco-German Constitutional Divide: Reflections on National and Constitutional Identity' 388.
166. Vranes, 'Constitutional Foundation of, and Limitations to, EU Integration in France' 539.

3. What is the constitutional basis of the constitutional identity limit?

The concept of 'fundamental conditions of the exercising of national sovereignty', is based on a combined reading of Articles 3, 53 and 88-1 French Constitution of 1958, Article 3 Declaration of 1789 and § 15 Preamble of the French Constitution of 1946, which protect national sovereignty and which allow at the same time for international cooperation.

4. What constitutional principles and substantive content are covered?

The limit is based on the principle of French sovereignty. It is conceptualized by the *Conseil* as a competence-based limit. Hence, it verifies whether the envisaged conferral concerns an important sovereign area as well as the final modalities attached to the exercise of the considered conferral of competences at EU level. The *Conseil* identified budgetary, economic, fiscal and monetary matters as particularly important competences, which suggests that EU fiscal integration proposals will likely conflict with French sovereignty.

5. How – if at all – can the constitutional identity limit be overcome (longevity/ absoluteness of the limit)?

The national sovereignty limit may be overcome by the French constitution-amending legislator by modifying the French Constitution. Subsequently, the *Conseil Constitutionnel* has no jurisdiction to review such constitutional amendments. Hence, French sovereignty does not impose absolute limits on EU fiscal integration proposals.

C THE SPANISH CONSTITUTIONAL PERSPECTIVE: AN EMERGING *CONSTITUTIONAL IDENTITY*?

An emerging constitutional opposition to EU (fiscal) integration can also be observed in Spain. The Spanish Constitutional Tribunal has established a material constitutional limit that restricts the available constitutional space for the conferral of competences to the EU. This Spanish *constitutional identity limit* was first established in the Tribunal's opinion on the EU Constitutional Treaty.[167] Since then, however, the Tribunal only referred once to this limit in its well-known *Melloni*-judgment on the European Arrest Warrant.[168] The highly restricted judicial use of the *identity limit* might be surprising in light of the major impact that the Eurocrisis had on Spain. Spain was among the Eurozone Member States worst hit by the Eurocrisis. In fact, it had to request a bailout programme for its banks, with considerable (internal) political and legal implications: the EU financial support for the Spanish banking sector was tied to strict bailout conditions.[169] Given this impact and the constitutional debate triggered elsewhere in

167. *Treaty Establishing a Constitution for Europe* sections II.2. and II.3.; cf. in particular: Fernando Castillo de la Torre, '*Tribunal Constitucional* (Spanish Constitutional Court), Opinion 1/2004 of 13 December 2004, on the Treaty Establishing a Constitution for Europe' (2005) 42 Common Market Law Review 1169, 1185-1186.
168. Aida Torres Pérez, 'Constitutional Dialogue on the European Arrest Warrent: The Spanish Constitutional Court Knocking on Luxembourg's Door; Spanish Constitutional Court, Order of 9 June 2011, ATC 86/2011' (2012) 8 European Constitutional Law Review 105.
169. Sebastián Royo and Federico Steinberg, 'Using a Sectoral Bailout to Make Wide Reforms: the Case of Spain' in Michele Chang, Federico Steinberg and Francisco Torres (eds), *The Political Economy of Adjustment Throughout and Beyond the Eurozone Crisis: What Have We Learned?*

light of all the Eurocrisis-related measures,[170] it seems remarkable that the Spanish Constitutional Tribunal did not test the *constitutional identity limit* against these measures. The subsequent assessment analyses whether the *identity limit* has the potential to develop into a constitutional obstacle for EU fiscal integration proposals – or whether it constitutes an example of a more *flexible* application of the *constitutional identity limit*.

The *constitutional identity limit* was established by the Spanish Constitutional Tribunal, which functions as a strong and independent institutional guardian of the constitutional order. Its institutional design was modelled on the German Constitutional Court.[171] Thus, the institutional competences and prerogatives as well as the procedural framework for the work of the Spanish Constitutional Tribunal all bear similarities with its German counterpart. Given this similarity, the assessment of the Spanish *constitutional identity limit* offers an alternative perspective on how a similarly authoritative constitutional actor can devise its constitutional role towards the EU in a potentially less confrontational manner.

One unique Spanish aspect of potential constitutional turmoil is the relationship between the regional (Autonomous Communities) and the federal level, which created continuous constitutional conflicts. Despite the primarily internal tension, particularly regarding Spanish unity and indivisibility in the sense of Article 2 Spanish Constitution,[172] these conflicts have an obvious EU dimension. In fact, considering the constitutional challenges initiated during the Eurocrisis, it becomes clear that most challenges against EU-related decisions were initiated as constitutional review of the internal allocation of competences between Autonomous Communities and the Spanish Federation.[173] Although the Constitutional Tribunal did not review national laws against EU law, given that the Tribunal can only review Spanish legislation against constitutional law,[174] a possible judgment of unconstitutionality of an EU-related Spanish measure could have had major consequences for the underlying EU law, too.

(Routledge 2019) 164-166; Franz-Josef Meiers, *Germany's Role in the Euro Crisis: Berlin's Quest for a More Perfect Monetary Union* (Springer 2015) 91, 116-117.

170. Cf. Germany, where the Constitutional Court developed *overall budgetary responsibility*: Reestman, 'Legitimacy Through Adjudication: The ESM Treaty and the Fiscal Compact Before the National Courts' 259.
171. Joan Solanes Mullor and Aida Torres Pérez, 'The Constitution of Spain: The Challenges for the Constitutional Order under European and Global Governance' in Anneli Albi and Samo Bardutzky (eds), *National Constitutions in European and Global Governance: Democracy, Rights, the Rule of Law* (Asser Press 2019) 544; De Visser, *Constitutional Review in Europe: A Comparative Analysis* 68.
172. Enric Martínez-Herrera and Thomas Jeffrey Miley, 'The Constitution and the Politics of National Identity in Spain' (2010) 16 Nations and Nationalism 6, 17.
173. Cristina Fasone, 'Constitutional Courts Facing the Euro Crisis: Italy, Portugal, and Spain in a Comparative Perspective (2014)' EUI Working Papers (Max Weber Programme), https://cadmus.eui.eu/bitstream/handle/1814/33859/MWP_WP_2014_25.pdf?sequence=1&isAllowed=y, accessed 5 April 2023, 36.
174. Solanes Mullor and Torres Pérez, 'The Constitution of Spain: The Challenges for the Constitutional Order under European and Global Governance' 567-568; Benito Alaez Corral and Abel Arias Castaño, 'The Role of the Spanish Constitutional Court in the Judicial Review of Parliamentary Legislation' (2009) 15 European Public Law 597, 604.

All four points, namely the existence of a *constitutional identity limit*, the practical experiences during the Eurocrisis, the centralized constitutional review with a strong constitutional authority as well as the federal tensions, are compelling reasons for including Spain in this comparative exercise. The subsequent assessment will first provide a brief outline of the Spanish constitutional approach to EU cooperation (I), before subsequently analysing the *constitutional identity limit* in detail (II).

I Identifying the Core Constitutional Limit to EU Fiscal Integration in Spain

Spanish EU membership coincided with a domestic constitutional transformation, which was successfully initiated with the adoption of the new Spanish Constitution in 1978, and it equally falls into the period of returning to a democratic state structure after the end of the *Franco*-dictatorship.[175] In light of the (constitutional) experiences during the dictatorship, the drafters of the 1978 Spanish Constitution awarded special protection to fundamental rights and the basic democratic structure of Spain.[176] Furthermore, the drafters anticipated Spanish accession to the European Communities and included Article 93 in the new constitutional text, which allowed for the conferral of competences to the international and supranational levels.[177] The broad political support for EU cooperation resulted in Spanish EU accession in 1986.[178]

The current Spanish constitutional approach to EU integration is influenced by a political and a legal-constitutional layer. Among Spanish political institutions support for EU integration is traditionally high. It is, for example, visible in the design of the Spanish EU enabling clause in Article 93 Spanish Constitution, which allows for the conferral of competences to the EU by an absolute majority after the constitutional legislator explicitly rejected the introduction of a qualified majority requirement.[179] Hence, political openness is reflected in the constitutional framework for EU cooperation. It is subsequently reflected in the broad support across political parties for Spanish EU membership.[180] And it can be deduced from the fact that the only two constitutional amendments successfully enacted in Spain related to EU integration steps. The first amendment in 1992 introduced the right for EU citizens to vote and stand as candidates

175. Juan Luis Requejo Pagés, 'The Spanish Constitutional Tribunal' in Armin von Bogdandy, Peter Michael Huber and Christoph Grabenwarter (eds), *Constitutional Adjudication: Institutions*, vol. III (The Max Planck Handbook in European Public Law, Oxford University Press 2020) 723-724.
176. Obvious from the extremely high threshold for amending these parts of the Spanish Constitution, as enshrined in Article 168 Spanish Constitution, cf. Ascensión Elvira, 'Spain' in Carlo Fusaro and Dawn Oliver (eds), *How Constitutions Change: A Comparative Study* (Hart Publishing 2011) 282-283.
177. Carmen Plaza, 'The Constitution for Europe and the Spanish Constitutional Court' (2006) 12 European Public Law 353, 354.
178. David Ramiro Troitino, *European Integration: Building Europe* (Nova Publishers 2013) 76; Juan Díez-Nicolás, 'Spaniards' Long March Towards Europe' in Sebastián Royo and Paul Christopher Manuel (eds), *Spain and Portugal in the European Union: The First Fifteen Years* (Frank Cass and Company Limited 2003) 100.
179. Antonio Estella de Noriega, 'A Dissident Voice: The Spanish Constitutional Court Case Law on European Integration' (1999) 5 European Public Law 269, 273.
180. *Ibid.*, 273-274.

in municipal elections.[181] The second amendment was adopted in 2011 and implemented the EU balanced budget rule into Article 135 Spanish Constitution.[182]

The legal-constitutional dimension is shaped by the Spanish Constitutional Tribunal, which was partly described as 'hostile'[183] or 'unreceptive'[184] regarding EU law. One example is the Tribunal's refusal to adjudicate on conflicts between EU law and Spanish law.[185] Although this initial resistance changed more recently,[186] the Tribunal maintains constitutional reservations that reduce the available constitutional space for EU integration and that limit the effect of EU law in Spain. The initial Spanish constitutional reservation to EU law, the so-called Spanish constitutional nucleus, covered Spanish sovereignty and the protection of fundamental rights.[187] Subsequently, this constitutional nucleus transformed into the *national constitutional identity limit*, a substantive limit that the legislator has to respect when conferring powers to the EU.[188] Although this *constitutional identity* remains abstract, the Tribunal might further refine this limit in relation to EU fiscal integration. Here, the Tribunal might also draw further inspiration from the constitutional developments in other Member States, given the importance of comparative reasoning in the Spanish constitutional jurisprudence.[189]

Bringing both dimensions together, a nuanced picture emerges. On the one hand, Spain is politically receptive to EU integration. On the other hand, the Spanish Constitutional Tribunal adopts a more reluctant approach towards EU law and developed substantive limits to further EU cooperation, with implications for EU fiscal integration.

181. José Martín Y Pérez de Nanclares, 'Constitutional Identity in Spain: Commitment to European Integration Without Giving up the Essence of the Constitution' in Christian Calliess and Gerhard van der Schyff (eds), *Constitutional Identity in a Europe of Multilevel Constitutionalism* (Cambridge University Press 2019) 270; Victor Ferreres Comella, 'The Spanish Constitutional Court: Time for Reforms' (2008) 3 Journal of Comparative Law 22, 27.
182. Bustos Gisbert, 'National Constitutional Identity in European Constitutionalism: Revisiting the Tale of the Emperor's New Clothes in Spain?' 85-86.
183. Estella de Noriega, 'A Dissident Voice: The Spanish Constitutional Court Case Law on European Integration' 275.
184. Requejo Pagés, 'The Spanish Constitutional Tribunal' 773-774.
185. Estella de Noriega, 'A Dissident Voice: The Spanish Constitutional Court Case Law on European Integration' 277.
186. The Tribunal initiated, for example, its first preliminary reference, cf. AUTO 86/2011 *Preliminary Reference Concerning EAW (Melloni)* (Spanish Constitutional Tribunal); cf. as well: Torres Pérez, 'Constitutional Dialogue on the European Arrest Warrent: The Spanish Constitutional Court Knocking on Luxembourg's Door; Spanish Constitutional Court, Order of 9 June 2011, ATC 86/2011'.
187. Castillo de la Torre, '*Tribunal Constitucional* (Spanish Constitutional Court), Opinion 1/2004 of 13 December 2004, on the Treaty Establishing a Constitution for Europe' 1185.
188. Martín Y Pérez de Nanclares, 'Constitutional Identity in Spain: Commitment to European Integration Without Giving up the Essence of the Constitution' 279; Pierre Bon, 'La Identidad Nacional o Constitucional, una Nueva Noción Jurídica' (2014) 100 Revista Española de Derecho Constitucional 167, 172-173.
189. Martín Y Pérez de Nanclares, 'Constitutional Identity in Spain: Commitment to European Integration Without Giving up the Essence of the Constitution' 269; Marian Ahumada Ruiz, 'The Spanish Constitutional Court' in András Jakab, Arthur Dyevre and Giulio Itzcovich (eds), *Comparative Constitutional Reasoning* (Cambridge University Press 2017) 629.

II Spanish Constitutional Identity Limit

The Tribunal established the Spanish *constitutional identity limit* in its Declaration 1/2004,[190] where it suggested that EU integration is confronted with a material limit deriving from Article 93 Spanish Constitution.

1 Institutional Actor Enforcing the Limit

The Tribunal is a judicial institution, separate from the other judicial branches in the Spanish legal system. It is in charge of supervising that Spanish state institutions comply with the obligations and rights laid down in the Spanish Constitution. To that extent, the Tribunal has the monopoly to conduct constitutional review.[191] In its constitutional assessment, the Constitutional Tribunal is bound by the constitutional questions raised by the applicants.[192] All its judgments are final, binding decisions with *erga omnes* effect.[193] Thus, the Tribunal is an authoritative institutional actor that can restrict the political decision-making space based on the Spanish Constitution.[194]

The Tribunal consists of 12 constitutional judges. Four judges are elected by the Spanish Congress of Deputies and an additional four by the Spanish Senate – confirmed respectively by a three-fifths majority. Two judges are nominated by the Government and an additional two by the Council for the Judiciary.[195] The Spanish Constitution requires that the appointed candidates are qualified jurists with legal working experience of at least 15 years.[196] Constitutional judges are appointed for a not directly

190. *Treaty Establishing a Constitution for Europe* section II. 3.; cf. as well: Bon, 'La Identidad Nacional o Constitucional, una Nueva Noción Jurídica' 172-173; Bustos Gisbert, 'National Constitutional Identity in European Constitutionalism: Revisiting the Tale of the Emperor's New Clothes in Spain?' 77; Pablo Pérez Tremps, 'National Idenity in Spanish Constitutional Court Case-Law' in Alejandro Saiz Arnaiz and Carina Alcoberro Llivina (eds), *National Constitutional Idenity and European Integration* (Intersentia Ltd 2013) 270.
191. Nuno Garoupa, Fernando Gomez-Pomar and Veronica Grembi, 'Judging under Political Pressure: An Empirical Analysis of Constitutional Review Voting in the Spanish Constitutional Court' (2011) 29 The Journal of Law, Economics, and Organization 513, 517; Alaez Corral and Arias Castaño, 'The Role of the Spanish Constitutional Court in the Judicial Review of Parliamentary Legislation' 598.
192. The Constitutional Tribunal is not competent to investigate a matter 'ex officio', cf. Pérez Tremps, 'National Idenity in Spanish Constitutional Court Case-Law' 270.
193. According to Article 164(1) Spanish Constitution as well as Articles 38 and 39 Constitutional Court Act (Organic Law 2/1979); cf. Ahumada Ruiz, 'The Spanish Constitutional Court' 611; Alaez Corral and Arias Castaño, 'The Role of the Spanish Constitutional Court in the Judicial Review of Parliamentary Legislation' 599.
194. Ferreres Comella, 'The Spanish Constitutional Court: Time for Reforms' 27.
195. As established in Article 159(1) Spanish Constitution, cf. Ahumada Ruiz, 'The Spanish Constitutional Court' 616; Garoupa, Gomez-Pomar and Grembi, 'Judging under Political Pressure: An Empirical Analysis of Constitutional Review Voting in the Spanish Constitutional Court' 517; Michael T. Newton and Peter J. Donaghy, *Institutions of Modern Spain: A Political and Economic Guide* (Cambridge University Press 1997) 26; James Casey, 'The Spanish Constitutional Court' (1990) 25 Irish Jurist 26, 33.
196. According to Article 159(2) Spanish Constitution, cf. Requejo Pagés, 'The Spanish Constitutional Tribunal' 729; Ahumada Ruiz, 'The Spanish Constitutional Court' 616; Alaez Corral and Arias Castaño, 'The Role of the Spanish Constitutional Court in the Judicial Review of Parliamentary Legislation' 599.

renewable mandate of nine years with an alternated replacement every three years.[197] Overall, this makes the Tribunal less vulnerable to political interference. First, the appointed judges have to be trained jurists with considerable working experience, which ensures that candidates are professionally fit for the office. Second, constitutional judges that are elected by Congress or the Senate require support by a broad three-fifths majority, which ensures that the nominated candidates are respected across political parties.[198] Third, the replacement of judges on the bench of the Constitutional Tribunal is not aligned with the legislative term.[199]

2 *Procedural Framework: Or How to Trigger the Limit*

The Spanish *constitutional identity limit* can be triggered through different constitutional procedures.[200] Prior to the ratification of new EU commitments, the Spanish Government, the Congress, or the Senate may initiate an abstract *ex ante* constitutional review based on Article 95(2) Spanish Constitution. Following this procedure, privileged applicants can request the Tribunal to assess whether an envisaged international or EU agreement conflicts with the Spanish Constitution. Subsequently, the Constitutional Tribunal issues a binding 'declaration', which determines the compatibility of this envisaged commitment with the Spanish Constitution. Similar to Finland and France, this *ex ante* review enables the legislator to tackle potential constitutional conflicts prior to the enactment of the EU agreement. Until today, the procedure has been employed twice, in relation to the Maastricht Treaty and the EU Constitutional Treaty.[201]

However, the possibility to initiate an *ex ante* review does not preclude an *ex post* constitutional review of commitments.[202] After ratification of EU commitments, the Prime Minister, 50 deputies from the Congress, 50 Senators, the Ombudsperson, the government of any Autonomous Community or their legislative assemblies are able to

197. De Visser, *Constitutional Review in Europe: A Comparative Analysis* 219-220; Garoupa, Gomez-Pomar and Grembi, 'Judging under Political Pressure: An Empirical Analysis of Constitutional Review Voting in the Spanish Constitutional Court' 517; Ferreres Comella, 'The Spanish Constitutional Court: Time for Reforms' 24; Casey, 'The Spanish Constitutional Court' 33.
198. Which requires governing majority and opposition to work together, cf. Nuno Garoupa, Joan Solanes Mullor and Teresa Violante, 'Constitutional Courts and National Parliaments in Spain and Portugal' in Jorge M. Fernandes and Cristina Leston-Bandeira (eds), *The Iberian Legislatures in Comparative Perspective* (Routledge 2019) 242; De Visser, *Constitutional Review in Europe: A Comparative Analysis* 209.
199. Garoupa, Gomez-Pomar and Grembi, 'Judging under Political Pressure: An Empirical Analysis of Constitutional Review Voting in the Spanish Constitutional Court' 517.
200. Alaez Corral and Arias Castaño, 'The Role of the Spanish Constitutional Court in the Judicial Review of Parliamentary Legislation' 600, 603; Ferreres Comella, 'The Spanish Constitutional Court: Time for Reforms' 27; Casey, 'The Spanish Constitutional Court' 35.
201. Declaration 1/1992 *Constitutional Review of the Maastricht Treaty* (Spanish Constitutional Tribunal); *Treaty Establishing a Constitution for Europe*; cf. as well: Solanes Mullor and Torres Pérez, 'The Constitution of Spain: The Challenges for the Constitutional Order under European and Global Governance' 546.
202. Ferreres Comella, 'The Spanish Constitutional Court: Time for Reforms' 27; Estella de Noriega, 'A Dissident Voice: The Spanish Constitutional Court Case Law on European Integration' 294.

initiate an abstract *ex post*-constitutional review based on Article 162(1) lit. a Spanish Constitution.[203] It seems that this provides an important procedural tool for political minorities and opposition parties to challenge legislative decisions.[204] In addition, regional governments and legislative assemblies employ the proceedings in order to defend their respective regional prerogatives against the federal level.[205] Particularly, the interpretation of Articles 147-150 Spanish Constitution on the federal division of competences triggers judicial challenges, which could be observed during the Eurocrisis. Notably, Autonomous Communities proceeded to defend their budgetary and fiscal prerogatives against federal intervention before the Constitutional Tribunal.[206]

In addition, the Spanish Constitution allows for concrete constitutional review, which can be initiated by a reference from an ordinary court.[207] However, it seems less likely that EU fiscal integration measures will be challenged following this procedure. Ordinary courts are required to interpret the challenged law in conformity with the Spanish Constitution,[208] and they have to establish that the law in question is crucial for deciding the case,[209] prior to referring the matter to the Tribunal. Furthermore, the Constitutional Tribunal only considers the compatibility of the challenged act with the Spanish Constitution.[210] Various challenges were brought by Spanish trade unions against EU-related measures based on the outlined procedure, which were however found to not affect the underlying EU law obligation itself.[211]

Finally, the Constitutional Tribunal also hears individual constitutional complaints against alleged fundamental rights violations.[212] Such individual complaints are, however, restricted to violations of fundamental rights enshrined in Chapter II section 1 (Articles 15-29) of the Spanish Constitution, the non-discrimination principle in Article 14 Spanish Constitution, or the objection against military duties enshrined in Article 30(2) Spanish Constitution.[213] Furthermore, the complaint can only be brought

203. Ahumada Ruiz, 'The Spanish Constitutional Court' 612; Garoupa, Gomez-Pomar and Grembi, 'Judging under Political Pressure: An Empirical Analysis of Constitutional Review Voting in the Spanish Constitutional Court' 517.
204. Alaez Corral and Arias Castaño, 'The Role of the Spanish Constitutional Court in the Judicial Review of Parliamentary Legislation' 601; Ferreres Comella, 'The Spanish Constitutional Court: Time for Reforms' 34.
205. As laid down in Article 32(2) Constitutional Court Act, cf. Garoupa, Gomez-Pomar and Grembi, 'Judging under Political Pressure: An Empirical Analysis of Constitutional Review Voting in the Spanish Constitutional Court' 518.
206. Fasone, 'Constitutional Courts Facing the Euro Crisis: Italy, Portugal, and Spain in a Comparative Perspective (2014)' 36.
207. Alaez Corral and Arias Castaño, 'The Role of the Spanish Constitutional Court in the Judicial Review of Parliamentary Legislation' 607.
208. Ferreres Comella, 'The Spanish Constitutional Court: Time for Reforms' 26-27.
209. Alaez Corral and Arias Castaño, 'The Role of the Spanish Constitutional Court in the Judicial Review of Parliamentary Legislation' 607; Casey, 'The Spanish Constitutional Court' 40.
210. Solanes Mullor and Torres Pérez, 'The Constitution of Spain: The Challenges for the Constitutional Order under European and Global Governance' 567-568.
211. María Luz Rodríguez, 'Labour Rights in Crisis in the Eurozone: The Spanish Case' in Claire Kilpatrick and Bruno De Witte (eds), *Social Rights in Times of Crisis in the Eurozone: The Role of Fundamental Rights' Challenges*, vol. 2014/05 (EUI Working Paper LAW, EUI 2014) 106.
212. De Visser, *Constitutional Review in Europe: A Comparative Analysis* 146-147.
213. Ferreres Comella, 'The Spanish Constitutional Court: Time for Reforms' 28; Casey, 'The Spanish Constitutional Court' 28-29.

against an administrative or judicial decision, and not against legislative acts.[214] Given both restrictions, it is unlikely that individuals would be able to challenge EU fiscal integration measures. This conclusion corresponds with observations made during the Eurocrisis.[215]

Taken together, the Spanish procedural framework entrusts privileged applicants to initiate a constitutional review either in an abstract *ex ante* manner following Article 95(2) Spanish Constitution or in an abstract *ex post* manner according to Article 162(1) lit. a Spanish Constitution. The judicial experiences during the Eurocrisis reveal that most constitutional challenges were initiated by Autonomous Communities and concerned the compliance with the internal competence allocation between Autonomous Communities and the Spanish federal government.[216] Despite the fact that these challenges centred around a primarily internal constitutional conflict, the constitutional decisions issued on these matters might ultimately have consequences for the related EU law as well.

3 Constitutional Basis of the Employed Limit

The *Constitutional Tribunal* developed its *constitutional identity limit* on the basis of Article 93 Spanish Constitution,[217] which states:

> Authorization may be granted by an organic act for concluding treaties by which powers derived from the Constitution shall be transferred to an international organization or institution.

Based on the wording, the Tribunal traditionally conceptualized Article 93 Spanish Constitution as a mere procedural provision that proclaimed the constitutional requirements for empowering an international or EU institution to exercise a specific competence.[218] However, since its findings in Declaration 1/2004,[219] the Constitutional Tribunal recognizes that Article 93 Spanish Constitution also contains a material or

214. Ahumada Ruiz, 'The Spanish Constitutional Court' 613; De Visser, *Constitutional Review in Europe: A Comparative Analysis* 146-147.
215. Fasone, 'Constitutional Courts Facing the Euro Crisis: Italy, Portugal, and Spain in a Comparative Perspective (2014)' 8; Maribel González Pascual, 'Welfare Rights and Euro Crisis: The Spanish Case' in Claire Kilpatrick and Bruno De Witte (eds), *Social Rights in Times of Crisis in the Eurozone: The Role of Fundamental Rights' Challenges*, vol. 2014/05 (EUI Working Paper LAW, EUI 2014) 98.
216. Fasone, 'Constitutional Courts Facing the Euro Crisis: Italy, Portugal, and Spain in a Comparative Perspective (2014)' 36.
217. Martín Y Pérez de Nanclares, 'Constitutional Identity in Spain: Commitment to European Integration Without Giving up the Essence of the Constitution' 270.
218. Castillo de la Torre, '*Tribunal Constitucional* (Spanish Constitutional Court), Opinion 1/2004 of 13 December 2004, on the Treaty Establishing a Constitution for Europe' 1182-1183; Estella de Noriega, 'A Dissident Voice: The Spanish Constitutional Court Case Law on European Integration' 295.
219. Pérez Tremps, 'National Idenity in Spanish Constitutional Court Case-Law' 269-270.

substantive dimension, which shields core constitutional matters from being conferred to the international or EU level.[220] Notably, the Tribunal stipulated in this decision:

> Therefore, the constitutional transfer which is made possible by Article 93 Spanish Constitution *has material limits, which apply to the transfer of powers itself* [emphasis added]. These material limits, which are not expressly set out in the constitutional text, but which are implicitly derived from the Spanish Constitution and its essential meaning, translate into respect for the sovereignty of the Spanish state, for our basic constitutional structures and for the system of values and principles enshrined in our Constitution, in which fundamental rights acquire their own substantive effect (Article 10.1 EC) [...].[221]

As noted by the Constitutional Tribunal, the material content covered by Article 93 Spanish Constitution is not linked to specific constitutional provisions but rather to general constitutional concepts, including sovereignty, the structural organization of the state including democracy and the protection of fundamental rights. This rather general framing might result from the broad questions referred to the Tribunal within these proceedings by the Spanish Government.[222] Overall, this suggests that the *constitutional identity limit* derives essentially from the jurisprudence of the Spanish Constitutional Tribunal: The Tribunal proclaimed that Article 93 Spanish Constitution entailed a material core which protects a set of constitutional principles and restricts Spanish participation in the EU integration process.

4 *Substantive Core Protected by the Limit*

Based on the Tribunal's Declaration 1/2004, three substantive constitutional aspects that fall under the material dimension of Article 93(1) Spanish Constitution can be identified: first, Spanish sovereignty; second, the constitutional structure of the state; and third, the protection of fundamental rights, which are seen as an expression of Spanish constitutional values.[223] Together, these three aspects form the implicit material core that the Spanish legislator has to respect when conferring competences to the international or the supranational level. Yet, the Tribunal formulates these aspects

220. The Spanish Constitutional Tribunal confirmed this jurisprudence in: Sentencia 26/2014 *Constitutional Complaint Melloni* (Spanish Constitutional Tribunal) section II. 3.; cf. as well: Bustos Gisbert, 'National Constitutional Identity in European Constitutionalism: Revisiting the Tale of the Emperor's New Clothes in Spain?' 77; Plaza, 'The Constitution for Europe and the Spanish Constitutional Court' 361.
221. *Treaty Establishing a Constitution for Europe* section II.2.; cf. as well: Martín Y Pérez de Nanclares, 'Constitutional Identity in Spain: Commitment to European Integration Without Giving up the Essence of the Constitution' 279.
222. Pérez Tremps, 'National Idenity in Spanish Constitutional Court Case-Law' 270; Plaza, 'The Constitution for Europe and the Spanish Constitutional Court' 356-357.
223. Martín Y Pérez de Nanclares, 'Constitutional Identity in Spain: Commitment to European Integration Without Giving up the Essence of the Constitution' 279; Victor Ferreres Comella, 'La Constitución española ante la cláusula de primacía del Derecho de la Unión Europea – Un comentario a la Declaración 1/2004 del Tribunal Constitucional' in Carlos Closa Montero (ed.), *Constitución Española y Constitución Europea – Análisis de la Declaración del Tribunal Constitucional (DTC 1/2004, de 13 de Diciembre)* (Centro de Estudios Políticos y Constitucionales 2015) 82.

in an abstract, general manner, without further defining the specific material conditions attached to them.[224] Given this vagueness, the subsequent analysis considers the Spanish *constitutional identity limit* from three different dimensions, namely the Tribunal's explicit intention to protect Spanish sovereignty and with it Spanish statehood (a), the underlying intention to shield the Spanish Constitution as such (b), and finally the Tribunal's concrete application of this vague constitutional benchmark (c).[225]

a Protecting Spanish Sovereignty and Its Statehood

The constitutionally most authoritative substantive element that the Tribunal enumerates under its *constitutional identity limit* is the principle of Spanish sovereignty. Sovereignty was previously employed by the Constitutional Tribunal as a constitutional benchmark for the assessment of EU integration steps.[226] Therefore, this prior jurisprudence can be considered when determining the protective scope of Spanish sovereignty. Although it appears that the Tribunal did not (yet) provide a conclusive definition of sovereignty,[227] its case law reveals several characteristics that seem particularly important in the interpretation:

First, the Spanish Constitution establishes in Article 1(2) that 'National sovereignty is vested in the Spanish people, from whom emanate the powers of the State.' Hence, the constitutional text identifies the Spanish people as the origin of sovereign power, which establishes a close link between sovereignty and democracy.[228] Article 1(3) Spanish Constitution clarifies that this sovereign power is framed in a parliamentary monarchy. Hence, the people confer the sovereign power to representative state institutions, which creates a bond between the Spanish people and these institutions as recognized by the Constitutional Tribunal. Notably, when asked whether extending the right to vote in Spanish municipal elections to EU citizens interfered with Spanish sovereignty the Tribunal concluded:

> Without entering into other considerations, it is sufficient to note [...] that the attribution to non-nationals of the right to vote in elections to representative bodies could only be constitutionally contentious [...] if such bodies were those that hold powers directly attributed by the Constitution and the Statutes of Autonomy and therefore linked to the ownership of sovereignty by the Spanish people.[229]

224. Martín Y Pérez de Nanclares, 'Constitutional Identity in Spain: Commitment to European Integration Without Giving up the Essence of the Constitution' 279.
225. Inspired by the distinction made here: Pérez Tremps, 'National Idenity in Spanish Constitutional Court Case-Law' 270-271.
226. *Constitutional Review of the Maastricht Treaty* section II.3.C.; namely, under the theory of the constitutional nucleus, cf. Estella de Noriega, 'A Dissident Voice: The Spanish Constitutional Court Case Law on European Integration' 276, 297.
227. Luis I. Gordillo, *Interlocking Constitutions: Towards an Interordinal Theory of National, European and UN Law* (Hart Publishing 2012) 37 para. 30.
228. *Treaty Establishing a Constitution for Europe* section II.4.; *Constitutional Review of the Maastricht Treaty* section II.3.C.
229. *Constitutional Review of the Maastricht Treaty* section II.3.C.

The Tribunal found that this was not the case for municipal institutions, which do not hold powers that are directly attributed to them by the Constitution. Consequently, entitling EU foreigners to vote in municipal elections was not in contradiction with Spanish democracy or sovereignty.[230] Based on this decision, it is apparent that the Tribunal is mainly concerned about the exercise of constitutionally assigned powers (or competences) by state institutions, which are in turn representing the Spanish people. Hence, the Spanish Tribunal seems to construe sovereignty as a competence-based limitation for the EU integration process. The consequence is that a set of core competences has to remain at the national level under the control of Spanish institutions.[231]

Moreover, the Tribunal emphasized that the introduction of Article 93 Spanish Constitution constituted 'an unmistakable act of exercise of the sovereignty of Spain'.[232] One consequence is, that the conferral of powers by the Spanish legislator according to Article 93 Spanish Constitution is perceived as an exercise of sovereign powers.[233] At the same time, the Tribunal underscored that Article 93 Spanish Constitution did not automatically entail a constitutional amendment, but instead, in case of conflicts between Spanish constitutional law and supranational cooperation, the constitutional text would have to be amended following the framework established in Articles 167 and 168 Spanish Constitution.[234] Therefore, compliance with the principle of sovereignty requires that the constitutional procedures are complied with.

In addition, Article 93 Spanish Constitution does not transfer the actual competence to the supranational level, but merely mandates the exercise of this competence. The sovereign competence remains at the national level.[235] This implies, in the first place, that the EU legal order is derived from and depends on the Spanish Constitution. It furthermore suggests that the sovereign powers remain at the national level, and supranational cooperation constitutes only a shared exercise of certain powers. This shared exercise is, in itself, an expression of Spanish sovereignty, given that the Spanish legislator decided to enable supranational cooperation through Article 93 Spanish Constitution and subsequently to transfer certain powers by adopting the EU-Treaties.[236] An additional indication for the preservation of Spanish sovereignty is,

230. Castillo de la Torre, '*Tribunal Constitucional* (Spanish Constitutional Court), Opinion 1/2004 of 13 December 2004, on the Treaty Establishing a Constitution for Europe' 1185.
231. Pérez Tremps, 'National Idenity in Spanish Constitutional Court Case-Law' 271.
232. *Treaty Establishing a Constitution for Europe* section II.2.
233. *Ibid.*, section II.2.; cf. as well: Castillo de la Torre, '*Tribunal Constitucional* (Spanish Constitutional Court), Opinion 1/2004 of 13 December 2004, on the Treaty Establishing a Constitution for Europe' 1175.
234. *Constitutional Review of the Maastricht Treaty* section II.3.C.; cf. as well: Berger, *Anwendungsvorrang und nationale Verfassungsgericht* 283-284.
235. Castillo de la Torre, '*Tribunal Constitucional* (Spanish Constitutional Court), Opinion 1/2004 of 13 December 2004, on the Treaty Establishing a Constitution for Europe' 1182.
236. *Treaty Establishing a Constitution for Europe* section II.2.; cf. as well: Castillo de la Torre, '*Tribunal Constitucional* (Spanish Constitutional Court), Opinion 1/2004 of 13 December 2004, on the Treaty establishing a Constitution for Europe' 1175.

according to the Tribunal, the explicit possibility to withdraw from EU cooperation following Article 50 TEU.[237] The Tribunal concluded on this point:

> Therefore, the primacy operates with regard to the competences transferred to the Union by the sovereign will of the State and also sovereignly recoverable by means of the procedure of 'voluntary withdrawal' as set forth in Article I-60 of the Treaty.[238]

Finally, the Tribunal connected the principle of sovereignty with the overall constitutional framework, which is an expression of the sovereign decision of how to organize the functioning of the state. The Tribunal ruled:

> [The] transfer of the exercise of competences to the European Union and the consequent integration of Community legislation into our own [legislation] impose[s] *unavoidable limits to the sovereign faculties of the State* [emphasis added], acceptable only when European legislation is compatible with *the fundamental principles of the social and democratic State of Law* [emphasis added] established by the national Constitution.[239]

This confirms the observation that the Tribunal is not merely shielding the principle of sovereignty in isolation. Instead, it relates sovereignty to the ability of the state to take core structural and organizational decisions, which clearly connects sovereignty with the principle of democracy. At the same time, the Tribunal seems to strengthen the hierarchical position of the Spanish Constitution. Notably, the Tribunal requires that supranational cooperation complies with the core constitutional principles protected by the Spanish Constitution. This suggests in the first place that the Spanish legislator can only transfer powers to the extent that this is compatible with the Spanish Constitution – or it would have to otherwise modify the constitutional text. But it also reinforces the position of the Spanish Constitution as the most authoritative legal document in the hierarchy of legal norms in Spain. At the same time, one could see in this passage a request of the Constitutional Tribunal to the Spanish constitution-legislator to establish clear structural requirements for the EU within the constitutional text.[240]

b *Protecting the Hierarchical Position of the Spanish Constitution*

The analysed jurisprudence suggests that the Spanish Constitutional Tribunal protects sovereignty together with the overarching constitutional framework. Notably, the Spanish Constitution is understood as a formal expression of sovereignty.[241] As

237. *Treaty Establishing a Constitution for Europe* section II.4.; cf. as well: Berger, *Anwendungsvorrang und nationale Verfassungsgericht* 286-287.
238. *Treaty Establishing a Constitution for Europe* section II.3.
239. *Ibid.*, section II.2.
240. Martín Y Pérez de Nanclares, 'Constitutional Identity in Spain: Commitment to European Integration Without Giving up the Essence of the Constitution'.
241. Sentencia 28/1991 *Spanish Rules on the Elections to the European Parliament* (Spanish Constitutional Tribunal) section II.4.; cf. as well: Pérez Tremps, 'National Idenity in Spanish Constitutional Court Case-Law' 270.

expressed through Article 93, the Spanish Constitution forms the basis for the Spanish EU membership, as competences have to be conferred following the requirements established by the Spanish constitutional text.[242] Therefore, the Tribunal emphasized in its assessment that the Spanish Constitution had to remain the basis for Spanish participation in EU cooperation, and with it the constitutionally prescribed procedure in Article 93 Spanish Constitution, which includes the mentioned material *constitutional identity* dimension.[243] As noted by the Tribunal:

> By virtue of Article 93, the Cortes Generales can [...] attribute the exercise of 'powers derived from the Constitution', but not disposing of the Constitution itself [...].[244]

This implies that the Spanish Constitution forms the basis for and sits hierarchically on top of EU law. Therefore, EU law may not challenge the integrity of Spanish constitutional law. Any direct (textual) conflict between the Spanish Constitution and EU law has to be resolved in favour of the constitution. The Tribunal established a reserve competence to give preference to the Spanish Constitution in case of conflict between the Spanish Constitution and EU law in case the EU itself did not resolve the Spanish concerns against the EU legal provision in question. The Spanish legislator cannot confer powers to the EU which contradicts the Spanish Constitution. Hence, in case such a conflict would be identified a sort of EU *ultra vires* act would be given, which the Tribunal considers unconstitutional in Spain.[245] However, this review is very unlikely to occur and the Tribunal itself considers it only a hypothetical option at this point.[246] In addition, the Tribunal would allow the EU to address the matter in the first place. This corresponds with the Tribunal's conception of the EU and Spanish legal order as separate systems, that have their respective tools and mechanisms to address legal questions.[247] Finally, the Tribunal appears rather reluctant in its scrutiny of EU law, which suggests that an open conflict between EU and Spanish law is unlikely to emerge.[248]

Furthermore, the three aspects that the Tribunal identified as material dimensions of Article 93 Spanish Constitution, namely sovereignty, state structure, and constitutional rights are covered by Article 168 Spanish Constitution.[249] This provision imposes additional procedural requirements for constitutional amendments that concern particularly important constitutional matters, notably amendments to the Preliminary Part (Articles 1 to 9 Spanish Constitution), Part 1 Chapter II Division 1 (Articles 15

242. Pérez Tremps, 'National Idenity in Spanish Constitutional Court Case-Law' 271.
243. Martín Y Pérez de Nanclares, 'Constitutional Identity in Spain: Commitment to European Integration Without Giving up the Essence of the Constitution' 273.
244. *Constitutional Review of the Maastricht Treaty* section II.4 (own translation).
245. *Treaty Establishing a Constitution for Europe* section II.4.; cf. as well: Pérez Tremps, 'National Idenity in Spanish Constitutional Court Case-Law' 271.
246. *Treaty Establishing a Constitution for Europe* section II.4.
247. Ferreres Comella, 'The Spanish Constitutional Court: Time for Reforms' 36; Estella de Noriega, 'A Dissident Voice: The Spanish Constitutional Court Case Law on European Integration' 293.
248. In contrast to the German Constitutional Court, which frequently employed the *ultra vires* review as a means to adjudicate on German and EU law questions, cf. *Quantitative Easing (PSPP) Final Judgment.*
249. Bon, 'La Identidad Nacional o Constitucional, una Nueva Noción Jurídica' 183.

to 29 Spanish Constitution), as well as Part II (Articles 56 to 65 Spanish Constitution). Therefore, it seems that the Constitutional Tribunal extends the special constitutional protection awarded to a particularly important provision of the Spanish Constitution – which can only be amended under the strict amendment-procedure in Article 168 Spanish Constitution – to EU integration.

c The Tribunal's Concrete Assessment

When considering the concrete application of the *constitutional identity limit*, it can be observed that the Tribunal frames the Spanish limit in its jurisprudence in vague and broad terms.[250] One consequence of this abstract wording is that no actual, concrete conflict with the constitutional text was identified until now. This might suggest that the Tribunal does not have the intention to impose strict constitutional limits to EU integration steps. Instead, it could be argued that the Tribunal aims to recall core constitutional principles and values vis-à-vis the Spanish legislator, which decides on EU integration steps. Put differently, through the *constitutional identity limit* the Tribunal illustrates the transformative constitutional impact that EU integration has and thereby requires the legislator to consider this specific impact when debating EU integration steps. The Tribunal's limit counterbalances the open wording of Article 93 Spanish Constitution.[251] At the same time, the Constitutional Tribunal clarified its own role in the constitutional appraisal of EU integration steps. Although the Tribunal remains largely in the background, it confirmed its competence to adjudicate on conflicts between Spanish and EU law if required.[252]

In the concrete application of the *constitutional identity limit* against the EU Constitutional Treaty, the Tribunal found that the EU commitments replicated the Spanish constitutional core. Namely, the proposed Treaty included the protection of national constitutional identities, the protection of core constitutional values, and the protection of EU fundamental rights.[253] This suggests that the Constitutional Tribunal is receptive to accepting EU-law-based protection of material constitutional concerns.[254]

250. Martín Y Pérez de Nanclares, 'Constitutional Identity in Spain: Commitment to European Integration Without Giving up the Essence of the Constitution' 279.
251. *Ibid.*, 277.
252. Pérez Tremps, 'National Idenity in Spanish Constitutional Court Case-Law' 271; José M. De Areilza Carvajal, 'La Inserción de España en la Nueva Unión Europea: La Relación entre la Constitución Española y el Trato Constitucional (Comentario a la DTC 1/2004, de 13 de diciembre de 2004)' (2005) 73 Revista Española de Derecho Constitucional 365, 368.
253. Ferreres Comella, 'La Constitución española ante la cláusula de primacía del Derecho de la Unión Europea – Un comentario a la Declaración 1/2004 del Tribunal Constitucional' 83; Plaza, 'The Constitution for Europe and the Spanish Constitutional Court' 359.
254. Pérez Tremps, 'National Idenity in Spanish Constitutional Court Case-Law' 263; Castillo de la Torre, '*Tribunal Constitucional* (Spanish Constitutional Court), Opinion 1/2004 of 13 December 2004, on the Treaty Establishing a Constitution for Europe' 1185-1186.

Finally, once EU-Treaties are adopted, EU law is seen as 'infra-constitutional', which implies that it lacks constitutional status.[255] Therefore, the Constitutional Tribunal refused to review national law against EU law, which it considered instead a matter for the other Spanish courts.[256] During the Eurocrisis, one could observe the consequences stemming from this approach. Notably, in constitutional challenges brought by the Spanish Autonomous Community of Catalonia against the federal balanced budget rules, which translated EU requirements into Spanish law. In its decision, the Tribunal confirmed that the Spanish law was closely interrelated with EU law, however, it subsequently assessed whether the federal law was compatible with the Spanish Constitution.[257]

d Interim Conclusion on the Spanish Substantive Core

The substantive core protected by the Spanish *constitutional identity limit* remains vague. The vagueness stems from the open constitutional framework for conferring competences to the EU enshrined in Article 93 Spanish Constitution. The absence of further detail explains the Tribunal's intention to compensate for a lacking material constitutional guidance for this conferral.[258]

The Constitutional Tribunal identified Spanish sovereignty, basic constitutional principles, and the protection of fundamental rights as the core material concerns that EU integration is confronted with.[259] When considering EU fiscal integration proposals, the prior two are of immediate constitutional relevance. The Tribunal seems to construe Spanish sovereignty as a competence-based constitutional limit which secures that core powers remain under the democratic control of the Spanish people. Although the Tribunal did not yet specify which powers fall into this category, it seems very likely that fiscal, budgetary and financial matters could be conceived as such important powers. First, the competences are traditionally characterized as particularly

255. De Visser, *Constitutional Review in Europe: A Comparative Analysis* 263; Berger, *Anwendungsvorrang und nationale Verfassungsgericht* 292.
256. De Visser, *Constitutional Review in Europe: A Comparative Analysis* 263.
257. Giacomo Delledonne, 'A Legalization of Financial Constitutions in the EU? Reflections on the German, Spanish, Italian and French Experiences' in Maurice Adams, Federico Fabbrini and Pierre Larouche (eds), *The Constitutionalization of European Budgetary Constraints* (Hart Publishing 2014) 188.
258. A constitutional reform was discussed at the time when Declaration 1/2004 was issued, cf. Martín Y Pérez de Nanclares, 'Constitutional Identity in Spain: Commitment to European Integration Without Giving up the Essence of the Constitution' 280; Antonio López Castillo, 'La Unión Europea "en constitución" y la Constitución estatal en (espera de) reformas – A propósito de la DTC 1/2004 de 13 de diciembre' in Carlos Closa Montero (ed.), *Constitución Española y Constitución Europea – Análisis de la Declaración del Tribunal Constitucional (DTC 1/2004, de 13 de Diciembre)* (Centro de Estudios Políticos y Constitucionales 2015) 49.
259. Ferreres Comella, 'La Constitución española ante la cláusula de primacía del Derecho de la Unión Europea – Un comentario a la Declaración 1/2004 del Tribunal Constitucional' 82; Bustos Gisbert, 'National Constitutional Identity in European Constitutionalism: Revisiting the Tale of the Emperor's New Clothes in Spain?' 77.

important powers of a sovereign state.[260] And second, the Constitutional Tribunal incorporates comparative constitutional considerations into its constitutional jurisprudence. It seems that particularly the German and the French constitutional debates are influential in that regard.[261] Given that both constitutional systems identified fiscal, budgetary and financial powers as relevant under the principles of sovereignty and democracy,[262] it seems possible that the Spanish Constitutional Tribunal follows.

Moreover, the *constitutional identity limit* aims at securing the hierarchical position of the Spanish Constitution. As pointed out, the Tribunal determined that Article 93 Spanish Constitution formed the basis for EU cooperation in Spain, that the legislator was not entitled to confer constitution-amending powers to EU level, and that Spain retained the possibility to withdraw from the supranational cooperation.[263] By conceptualizing the EU legal order as derived from the Spanish Constitution, the Tribunal clearly limits the available constitutional space for EU (fiscal) integration steps.[264] Although the Tribunal indicated readiness to accept possible EU safeguards as well as showed reluctance in the concrete application of this limit, it might ultimately use its competences in the future to formulate more detailed substantive requirements for EU cooperation.[265] At the same time, the Tribunal refrained from refining the *constitutional identity limit* when confronted with Eurocrisis-measures, which could indicate a general reluctance to apply the limit to (EU) budgetary and fiscal policy decisions.

5 *Longevity and Absoluteness of the Constitutional Limit*

Finally, the question is whether this *constitutional identity limit* constitutes an absolute limit to EU fiscal integration proposals. When considering the constitutional framework, it is first apparent that Articles 167 and 168 Spanish Constitution do not contain

260. Schneider, 'Exkurs: Die Rolle des Haushaltsausschusses des Bundestages bei Aufstellung und Vollzug des Haushalts: ein Praxisbericht' 295; Puntscher Riekmann and Wydra, 'Representation in the European State of Emergency: Parliaments Against Governments?' 567; Baranger, 'The Apparition of Sovereignty' 61.
261. Martín Y Pérez de Nanclares, 'Constitutional Identity in Spain: Commitment to European Integration Without Giving up the Essence of the Constitution' 279; Ahumada Ruiz, 'The Spanish Constitutional Court' 629.
262. *For Germany: Lisbon-judgment* paras 252, 256; cf. as well: Calliess, 'Constitutional Identity in Germany: One for Three or Three in One?' 164-165; *And for France: Entwurf eines Gesetzes zu dem Beschluss des Europäischen Rates vom 25. März 2011 zur Änderung des Artikels 136 des Vertrags über die Arbeitsweise der Europäischen Union hinsichtlich eines Stabilitätsmechanismus für die Mitgliedstaaten, deren Währung der Euro ist (Drucksache 17/9047)* para. 13; cf. as well Neuman, 'The Brakes That Failed: Constitutional Restriction of International Agreements in France' 296.
263. Pérez Tremps, 'National Idenity in Spanish Constitutional Court Case-Law' 271; De Areilza Carvajal, 'La Inserción de España en la Nueva Unión Europea: La Relación entre la Constitución Española y el Trato Constitucional (Comentario a la DTC 1/2004, de 13 de diciembre de 2004)' 373-374.
264. Martín Y Pérez de Nanclares, 'Constitutional Identity in Spain: Commitment to European Integration Without Giving up the Essence of the Constitution' 279.
265. Pérez Tremps, 'National Idenity in Spanish Constitutional Court Case-Law' 270; Castillo de la Torre, '*Tribunal Constitucional* (Spanish Constitutional Court), Opinion 1/2004 of 13 December 2004, on the Treaty Establishing a Constitution for Europe' 1186.

any restriction for the scope of constitutional amendments. Conversely, this implies that the Spanish Constitution can be amended in all parts.[266] Therefore, one may conclude that possible conflicts between EU fiscal integration proposals and the *constitutional identity limit* can be overcome in principle.

Furthermore, it seems that the Tribunal has no competence to review constitutional amendments. According to Article 161(1) lit. a Spanish Constitution and Article 27 Constitutional Court Act, which together define the Tribunal's jurisdictional competences, the Tribunal can review the constitutionality of 'laws and regulations having the force of law'.[267] A constitutional amendment is neither a law nor a regulation having the force of law, as becomes obvious from the wording in Articles 167 and 168 Spanish Constitution. This suggests that Article 161(1) lit. a Spanish Constitution confers upon the Tribunal 'merely' the power to review parliamentary and governmental acts but not constitutional law as such.[268] Thus, the constitution-amending legislator could overcome the *constitutional identity limit* by amending the Spanish Constitution in order to accommodate conflicting EU fiscal integration steps.

As a result, EU fiscal integration proposals are confronted with the procedural requirements enshrined in Article 167 Spanish Constitution or with the stricter requirements enshrined in Article 168 Spanish Constitution, in case important areas are modified.[269] Following the ordinary procedure, the constitutional amendment can be adopted by a three-fifths majority in Congress and Senate.[270] According to Article 168 Spanish Constitution, stricter procedural requirements apply to any constitutional reform which affects (fully or in parts)[271] the Preliminary Part (Articles 1 to 9 Spanish Constitution), Part 1 Chapter II Division 1 (Articles 15 to 29 Spanish Constitution), or Part II (Articles 56 to 65 Spanish Constitution) of the Spanish Constitution. Under the strict constitutional amendment procedure Congress and Senate have to be dissolved by the approval of a two-thirds majority as a first step. Subsequently, the newly elected assemblies have to confirm the constitutional amendments with a two-thirds majority. Finally, the approved constitutional amendment will have to be confirmed by public referendum.[272] When applying this framework to the EU fiscal integration steps, it seems that the stricter amendment procedure is applicable in case such integration steps conflict with the *constitutional identity limit* and thus with core constitutional

266. Ahumada Ruiz, 'The Spanish Constitutional Court' 636; Leonardo Álvarez, 'Die spanische Dogmatik der Verfassungstreue – Geschichte einer fehlgeschlagenen Rezeption des deutschen Verfassungsdenkens' (2010) 70 Zeitschrift für ausländisches öffentliches Recht und Völkerrecht (ZaöRV) 433, 442.
267. De Visser, *Constitutional Review in Europe: A Comparative Analysis* 119.
268. Alaez Corral and Arias Castaño, 'The Role of the Spanish Constitutional Court in the Judicial Review of Parliamentary Legislation' 603.
269. Martín Y Pérez de Nanclares, 'Constitutional Identity in Spain: Commitment to European Integration Without Giving up the Essence of the Constitution' 282.
270. Elvira, 'Spain' 282.
271. Given the broad wording, any textual change of the covered constitutional provision has to comply with the strict procedural requirements, cf. Richard Albert, *Constitutional Amendments: Making, Breaking, and Changing Constitutions* (Oxford University Press 2019) 192; Victor Ferreres Comella, *The Constitution of Spain: A Contextual Analysis* (Hart Publishing 2013) 57.
272. Elvira, 'Spain' 282-283.

principles of the Spanish Constitution. Nevertheless, the Tribunal continuously emphasized that the Spanish Constitution is open for a full revision,[273] which suggests that the *constitutional identity limit* constitutes ultimately a high procedural hurdle for the constitution-amending legislator.

III Conclusion

The assessment revealed that the Constitutional Tribunal established the *constitutional identity limit* to protect a material constitutional core of the Spanish Constitution against EU integration. The limit protects Spanish sovereignty, the basic constitutional structure as well as fundamental rights against constitutional erosion.[274] It was pointed out that the precise substantive content of the *constitutional identity limit* remains vague, given its sporadic application by the Tribunal. Yet, by taking previous decisions into account, it was shown that the Tribunal's main intention appears to be the protection of Spanish statehood as well as sovereign and democratic decision-making.[275] The latter seems to imply that core competences have to remain at the national level under the democratic control of the Spanish Congress, the democratic representation of the Spanish people.

These core competences likely include budgetary, financial and fiscal decisions, which impact the proposed EU fiscal integration ambitions. However, the Tribunal did not yet provide specific guidance on the competence areas covered by the *constitutional identity limit*. At the same time, the Tribunal accepted in its appraisal that the EU legal order might offer adequate protection for the outlined constitutional concerns.[276] When applying this abstract constitutional benchmark to EU fiscal integration proposals, it seems that these proposals could be considered to affect important sovereign competences which might require confirmation under the strict constitutional amendment procedure.[277]

Overall, this suggests that the Tribunal has no intention to employ the *constitutional identity limit* as an absolute constitutional restriction to EU fiscal integration proposals. Over the past decades, the Tribunal remained constructive and open towards EU law and further integration steps. One example in that regard is the refusal

273. Sentencia 259/2015 *Catalan Independence Declaration* (Spanish Constitutional Tribunal) section II. 7.; cf. as well: Martín Y Pérez de Nanclares, 'Constitutional Identity in Spain: Commitment to European Integration Without Giving up the Essence of the Constitution' 167-168; Pérez Tremps, 'National Idenity in Spanish Constitutional Court Case-Law' 272.
274. Martín Y Pérez de Nanclares, 'Constitutional Identity in Spain: Commitment to European Integration Without Giving up the Essence of the Constitution' 279; Ferreres Comella, 'La Constitución española ante la cláusula de primacía del Derecho de la Unión Europea - Un comentario a la Declaración 1/2004 del Tribunal Constitucional' 82.
275. Pérez Tremps, 'National Idenity in Spanish Constitutional Court Case-Law' 270-271; Castillo de la Torre, '*Tribunal Constitucional* (Spanish Constitutional Court), Opinion 1/2004 of 13 December 2004, on the Treaty Establishing a Constitution for Europe' 1183.
276. Plaza, 'The Constitution for Europe and the Spanish Constitutional Court' 359.
277. As Article 168 Spanish Constitution allows for a 'total revision', cf. *Catalan Independence Declaration* section II. 7.; cf. as well: Martín Y Pérez de Nanclares, 'Constitutional Identity in Spain: Commitment to European Integration Without Giving up the Essence of the Constitution' 281.

of the Constitutional Tribunal to generally review EU law but instead restrict itself to matters that are close to the Spanish constitutional core.[278] Obviously, this approach reduces the risk of direct conflicts between Spanish (constitutional) and EU law. As it stands, the Spanish *constitutional identity limit* is an abstract constitutional warning towards the political institutions of Spain to preserve Spanish statehood, the basic constitutional structures, and the protection of fundamental rights.[279]

Table 5.3 Constitutional Identity Classification Board for Spain

Constitutional Identity Classification Board for Spain
1. Which institutional actor enforces the constitutional limit?
The Spanish *constitutional identity limit* was developed by the Spanish Constitutional Tribunal, which is in charge of constitutional review. Its decisions are final and binding.
2. How can the constitutional identity limit be triggered?
Most commonly, EU (integration) measures are challenged through abstract ex ante (Article 95(2) Spanish Constitution) or ex post review (Article 161(1) lit. a Spanish Constitution). The Eurocrisis-measures triggered internal conflicts on the allocation of competences.
3. What is the constitutional basis of the constitutional identity limit?
Article 93 Spanish Constitution is the basis on which the Constitutional Tribunal grounds its *constitutional identity limit*. In Declaration 1/2004, it identified that this provision has a material dimension which shields core constitutional principles and values.
4. What constitutional principles and substantive content are covered?
The material core identified by the Constitutional Tribunal covers Spanish sovereignty; basic constitutional structures; the system of constitutional values and principles; as well as fundamental rights. The jurisprudence on the *constitutional identity limit* is brief and its content remains abstract and vague. In light of EU fiscal integration proposals, the Tribunal seems mainly concerned about preserving core decision-making abilities in central sovereign competence areas within the Spanish constitutional order.
5. How – if at all – can the constitutional identity limit be overcome (longevity/absoluteness of the limit)?
The Spanish Constitution does not restrict the scope for constitutional amendments. Given that EU fiscal integration steps might impact core constitutional principles, the strict constitutional amendment procedure in Article 168 Spanish Constitution appears to apply.

D THE POLISH PERSPECTIVE ON EU FISCAL INTEGRATION

Finally, the comparison considers the material limits that the Polish constitutional order formulates against EU fiscal integration proposals. In light of the comparative setting, Poland provides for an interesting addition for at least four related reasons.

278. Castillo de la Torre, '*Tribunal Constitucional* (Spanish Constitutional Court), Opinion 1/2004 of 13 December 2004, on the Treaty establishing a Constitution for Europe' 1200.
279. Bustos Gisbert, 'National Constitutional Identity in European Constitutionalism: Revisiting the Tale of the Emperor's New Clothes in Spain?' 77.

First, Poland is not (yet) a member of the Eurozone, which distinguishes it from the previously analysed Member States. However, the EU's *acquis communautaire*, to which Poland subscribed in 2004, establishes a legal obligation for the country to accede to the single currency once it meets the prescribed convergence criteria.[280] Therefore, Poland currently has the perspective of a Euro-candidate country and not that of a Eurozone member. Nevertheless, the currently debated EU fiscal integration steps are equally relevant for Euro-candidate countries, as they might render Eurozone membership harder to achieve, leading to a clash between the EU obligation to join and possible constitutional obstacles to the level of fiscal integration required for joining. This seems likely as several constitutional limits have already been established by the Polish Constitutional Tribunal[281] against too far-reaching competence conferrals to the EU.[282] A more integrated Eurozone could trigger these limits and render Polish accession to the Euro constitutionally impossible. Therefore, it seems crucial to include the constitutional perspective of Euro-candidate Member States in the assessment in order to balance the required reform steps with, on the one hand, the political ambitions of the current 20 Eurozone countries, and, on the other hand, the ambition to extend the Eurozone. Hence, EU fiscal integration should take the available constitutional space in Euro-candidate countries into account to keep full Eurozone-membership constitutionally attainable for these countries.[283]

Second, Poland is historically shaped by its communist past under the influence of the Soviet Union. The Polish Constitution of 1997 was drafted in light of these experiences and it entails strong fundamental rights protection as well as constitutional safeguards against the (institutional) abuse of public power.[284] These constitutional characteristics equally developed in other Central and Eastern European states.[285] The Polish constitutional order can therefore be seen as a representative example of a wider group of Member States that joined the European Union since 2004. Consequently, the conclusions drawn on the Polish material limits to EU fiscal integration proposals might be equally relevant for these other constitutional systems.

280. Jeno Czuczai, 'Accession to the EU, But to Which EU? The Legal Impact of the Constantly Evolving EMU Acquis on the EU Enlargement Process' in Stanislas Adam and others (eds), *The European Union in the World: Essays in Honour of Professor Marc Maresceau* (Martinus Nijhoff Publishers 2014) 595; Lastra and Louis, 'European Economic and Monetary Union: History, Trends, and Prospects' 72-73; Jean-Victor Louis, 'The Economic and Monetary Union: Law and Institutions' (2004) 41 Common Market Law Review 575, 605.

281. In Polish: *Trybunał Konstytucyjny.*

282. K 18/04 *Poland's EU Membership* (Polish Constitutional Tribunal) Point 18.7; cf. as well: Adam Łazowski, 'Case Note: Accession Treaty – Polish Constitutional Tribunal: Conformity of the Accession Treaty with the Polish Contitution: Decision of 11 May 2005' (2007) 3 European Constitutional Law Review 148, 161.

283. Jan Barcz, 'Polish Policy in the Context of the Euro Area Reform' (2013) 16 Yearbook of Polish European Studies 69, 71.

284. Czaputowicz, 'Sovereignty in Theories of European Integration and the Perspective of the Polish Constitutional Tribunal' 31.

285. Stanislaw Biernat and Monika Kawczyńska, 'The Role of the Polish Constitution (Pre-2016): Development of a Liberal Democracy in the European and International Context' in Anneli Albi and Samo Bardutzky (eds), *National Constitutions in European and Global Governance: Democracy, Rights, the Rule of Law* (T.M.C. Asser Press 2019) 748.

Third, the Polish constitutional approach to EU integration is shaped by an authoritative constitutional court. The Constitutional Tribunal established the Polish *constitutional identity limit*, through which it protects core constitutional principles against EU integration.[286] Hence, the institutional design and the existence of substantive constitutional limits characterize the Polish constitutional order as relatively rigid towards EU integration, which squarely fits within the employed comparative framework. In addition, the Polish Constitutional Tribunal itself draws inspiration from the constitutional jurisprudence of other EU constitutional courts.[287] This comparative approach is especially noticeable in relation to the *constitutional identity limit*, which was strongly influenced by German jurisprudence.[288]

Lastly, the Polish constitutional system is undergoing a process of constitutional decay, which is scrutinized at the supranational level with limited success.[289] This decay concerns in particular the rule of law since the election of the PiS[290]-party into governmental power in 2015. The contested measures taken by the government were, *inter alia*, targeting the Polish Constitutional Tribunal.[291] Naturally, these developments put constitutional precedent and the Tribunal's established approach to EU matters into question.[292] This constitutes a challenge for the subsequent analysis, as the future Polish constitutional jurisprudence might be more difficult to predict due to the on-going constitutional transformation. Assuming that the current political interferences remain temporary, the relevant constitutional jurisprudence established prior to 2015 will likely regain significance – or otherwise serve as a basis for an even more protectionist and nationalist constitutional approach. Consequently, the focus on the established approach seems justified. In addition, analysing the Polish case also offers the possibility to reflect on the potential stabilizing function of national constitutional values through supranational cooperation. Furthermore, it will allow for a reflection on the importance of the rule of law – possibly even a necessary precondition – for the stability of the Euro.

The following assessment first outlines the applicable constitutional framework (I), before subsequently evaluating the *constitutional identity limit* (II) as well as substantiating the rule of law concerns and its implications for EU fiscal integration (III).

286. *Treaty of Lisbon* section III.2.1; cf. as well Śledzińska-Simon and Ziółkowski, 'Constitutional Identity in Poland: Is the Emperor Putting on the Old Clothes of Sovereignty' 243.
287. Magdalena Bainczyk, 'Die erste Vorabentscheidungsfrage des polnischen Verfassungsgerichtshofs an den EuGH' (2017) 52 Europarecht (EuR) 121, 123.
288. *Treaty of Lisbon* section III.3.3.; cf. as well: Wendel, 'Lisbon Before the Courts: Comparative Perspectives' 130-131.
289. Walter Rech, 'Some Remarks on the EU's Action on the Erosion of the Rule of Law in Poland and Hungary' (2018) 26 Journal of Contemporary European Studies 334, 335-336, 343; Tomasz Tadeusz Koncewicz, 'The Capture of the Polish Constitutional Tribunal and Beyond: Of Institution(s), Fidelities and the Rule of Law in Flux' (2018) 43 Review of Central and East European Law 116, 134-136.
290. Referring to Poland's Law and Justice political party (in Polish: *Prawo i Sprawiedliwość*).
291. Wojciech Sadurski, 'Constitutional Crisis in Poland' in Mark A. Graber, Sanford Levinson and Mark Tushnet (eds), *Constitutional Democracy in Crisis?* (Oxford University Press 2018) 262.
292. Martin Krygier, 'The Challenge of Institutionalisation: Post-Communist "Transitions", Populism, and the Rule of Law' (2019) 15 European Constitutional Law Review 544, 547, 572-573.

I Identifying the Core Constitutional Limits to EU Fiscal Integration in Poland

Since Polish accession to the EU in 2004, the Constitutional Tribunal developed a detailed constitutional approach to EU integration and its effect in Poland. This constitutional approach includes an *ultra vires limit* as well as a *constitutional identity limit*, which were both inspired by German jurisprudence.[293] Both limits are rooted in the principle of Polish sovereignty – which entails that core decisions have to be taken by Polish institutions and which protects the supreme status of the Polish Constitution.[294] Through its *ultra vires* review, the Tribunal scrutinizes competence excesses of EU institutions not covered by the mandate awarded by the Polish legislator through Article 90 Polish Constitution.[295] It is thus primarily applied to the exercise of conferred competences. In contrast, the *constitutional identity limit* restricts the available material constitutional scope for the conferral of competences.[296] Under the *identity limit* the Tribunal reviews whether EU integration steps sufficiently respect Polish democracy, the rule of law, fundamental rights, as well as Polish sovereignty and statehood.[297] When considering EU fiscal integration proposals, the *constitutional identity limit* seems particularly relevant, as it formulates restrictions to the material scope available for such integration steps under the Polish Constitution.

In addition to constitutional limits, the Polish Constitutional Tribunal also established more receptive approaches towards EU law. One example in this regard is its so-called *multi-centric* approach according to which legal norms enacted by different authorities can coexist in Poland.[298] The most prominent example is the coexistence of Polish and EU law. Corresponding to the idea of the EU as a pluralistic constitutional legal order, the Constitutional Tribunal aims at avoiding conflicts between legal instruments stemming from the different orders. This multi-centric approach also entails that the Tribunal adopts a *European-law-friendly* interpretation of the Polish

293. *Treaty of Lisbon* section III.3.; cf. as well: Śledzińska-Simon and Ziółkowski, 'Constitutional Identity in Poland: Is the Emperor Putting on the Old Clothes of Sovereignty' 243.
294. As enshrined in Article 8(1) Polish Constitution, cf. Czaputowicz, 'Sovereignty in Theories of European Integration and the Perspective of the Polish Constitutional Tribunal' 32.
295. Wendel, 'Lisbon Before the Courts: Comparative Perspectives' 130-131; Sven Höbel, 'Polish and German Constitutional Jurisprudence on Matters of European Community Law: A Comparison of the Constitutional Courts' (2007) 3 Croation Yearbook of European Law and Policy 515, 525-526.
296. Rideau, 'The Case-Law of the Polish, Hungarian and Czech Constitutional Courts on National Idenity and the "German Model"' 252; Wróbel, 'Die Grenzen der europäischen Integration im Lichte jüngerer Entscheidungen des polnischen Verfassungsgerichts' 501.
297. *Treaty of Lisbon* section III.2.1.; cf. as well: Władysław Czapliński, 'Recent Constitutional Jurisprudence Concerning the European Union: Some Remarks on 2010 Judgments of the Polish Constitutional Court' (2011) 12 ERA Forum 197, 201.
298. Marcin Górski, 'European Union Law Before National Judges: The Polish Experience – Adept Multicentric Vision or Creeping Hierarchical Practice' in Bruno de Witte et al. (eds), *Judicial Review and Cooperation Series, National Courts and EU Law: New Issues, Theories and Method* (Edward Elgar Publishing Limited 2016) 132; Krystyna Kowalik-Bańczyk, 'Should We Polish It Up? The Polish Constitutional Tribunal and the Idea of Supremacy of EU Law' (2005) 6 German Law Journal 1355, 1363-1364.

Constitution and that it presumes the constitutionality of newly enacted EU obligations.[299] Taken together, the multi-centric approach enables the Tribunal to reduce hierarchical disputes between Polish and EU law. Obviously, this would equally extend to EU fiscal integration measures. In the first place, such integration steps would benefit from the rebuttable presumption of constitutionality. And subsequently, once the measures are duly ratified, the Tribunal would likely adopt a European-law-friendly reading of the Polish Constitution in light of possible new obligations although only if the *constitutional identity limit* is respected. Therefore, the subsequent assessment will focus on the possible substantive restrictions of this limit for EU fiscal integration steps.

II The Polish *Constitutional Identity* Limit: Protecting a *Sovereign* Poland?

The Polish *constitutional identity limit* imposes substantive restrictions on the conferral of powers to the EU.[300] Comparable to the function of these *limits* in other EU Member States, the Polish limit shields core constitutional principles against external intervention.[301]

1 *Institutional Actor Enforcing the Limit*

The Polish *constitutional identity limit* was established by the Polish Constitutional Tribunal. The Tribunal was initially created on a provisional basis under Communist rule in 1982 with only a limited set of responsibilities.[302] The apparent underlying aim of its creation was to convey the impression that Poland was a constitutional system under the supervision of an 'independent' *constitutional court*.[303] Its institutional position as guardian of the Polish Constitution was cemented under the new 1997 Polish Constitution, with widely extended competences.[304] It is established as an independent judicial actor, as explicitly established in Article 173 Polish Constitution, and entitled to conduct a constitutional review of acts of parliaments and normative

299. Wendel, 'Lisbon Before the Courts: Comparative Perspectives' 107.
300. Claes, 'National Idenity: Trump Card or up for Negotiation?' 129.
301. *Treaty of Lisbon* section III.2.1. and section III.3.; cf. as well: Śledzińska-Simon and Ziółkowski, 'Constitutional Identity in Poland: Is the Emperor Putting on the Old Clothes of Sovereignty' 253.
302. Including a mechanism according to which decisions by the Tribunal on the compatibility of legislative acts with the constitutional text were referred to the Polish Parliament, which could then confirm the constitutionality by overruling the constitutional decision, cf. De Visser, *Constitutional Review in Europe: A Comparative Analysis* 71-72.
303. Csilla Kiss, *Constitutional Democracy in Eastern Europe: The Role of Constitutional Courts in Democratic Consolidation in Post-Communist Hungary and Poland* (ProQuest Dissertations Publishing 2005) 56.
304. De Visser, *Constitutional Review in Europe: A Comparative Analysis* 72-73.

acts including governmental decrees as well as international agreements.[305] Furthermore, its judgments are binding for all Polish state institutions.[306] In its function as guardian of the Polish Constitution, it furthermore delivered crucial judgments on the relationship between Polish constitutional law and EU law.

The Constitutional Tribunal is composed of 15 constitutional judges, which are appointed for nine-year terms by the Polish Parliament (Sejm). The Sejm votes on proposals that are either submitted by the *Presidium of the Sejm* or by at least 50 members of the Sejm. A proposed candidate requires the support of a simple majority, with at least half of the parliamentarians participating in the vote.[307] Both the Tribunal's President and the Vice-President are appointed by the Polish President upon the proposal of the Assembly of all 15 constitutional judges.[308] In order to be nominated as a constitutional judge, candidates need to be qualified to become a judge at either the Polish Supreme Court or the Highest Administrative Court, which requires, *inter alia*, 10 years of working experience in the legal profession.[309] As can be witnessed since the eruption of the rule of law crisis, particularly the low majority requirement for the appointment of constitutional judges (simple majority in parliament) allows for the appointment of controversial, highly political candidates.

2 *Procedural Framework: Or How to Trigger the Limit*

The main procedure to trigger the *constitutional identity limit* is the initiation of constitutional review of an international or EU agreement following Article 188 No. 1 Polish Constitution. This review can be either initiated *ex ante* by the Polish President following Article 133(2) Polish Constitution[310] or *ex post* by various privileged applicants enumerated in Article 191(1) No. 1 Polish Constitution. These privileged applicants are, *inter alia*, the Polish President, the Marshal of the Sejm and of the Senate, the Prime Minister, and 50 members of the Sejm or 30 Senators.[311] Both the *ex ante* and the *ex post* constitutional review are conducted *in abstracto*. Interestingly, the Constitutional Tribunal requires that the applicable standing requirements are met

305. As established in Article 188 Polish Constitution, cf. Kowalik-Bańczyk, 'Should We Polish It Up? The Polish Constitutional Tribunal and the Idea of Supremacy of EU Law' 1361.
306. Established in Article 190(1) Polish Constitution.
307. Established in Article 5(4) Act on the Polish Constitutional Tribunal, cf. De Visser, *Constitutional Review in Europe: A Comparative Analysis* 207.
308. As laid down in Article 194(2) Polish Constitution as well as Article 15(1) and (2) Act on the Polish Constitutional Tribunal.
309. De Visser, *Constitutional Review in Europe: A Comparative Analysis* 212.
310. Magdalena Bainczyk, 'Folgen einer mangelnden Anpassung der polnischen Verfassung nach dem Vertrag von Lissabon im Lichte des Urteils des polnischen Verfassungsgerichtshofes zum Beschluss des Europäischen Rates zur Änderung von Art. 136 AEUV' (2017) 52 Europarecht (EuR) 306, 319; Nina Półtorak and Sławomir Dudzik, '"The Court of the Last Word": Competences of the Polish Constitutional Tribunal in the Review of European Union Law' (2012) 15 Yearbook of Polish European Studies 225, 227.
311. Anna Wyrozumska, 'Poland' in Dinah Shelton (ed.), *International Law and Domestic Legal Systems: Incorporation, Transformation, and Persuasion* (Oxford University Press 2011) 471.

throughout the entire proceedings. An application against the Fiscal Compact was declared inadmissible after two of the thirty senators that initiated the challenge in March 2013 transferred to the European Parliament in 2014.[312] Similarly, applications initiated by the Sejm have to be confirmed after general elections by the newly elected Sejm to determine whether the proceedings still enjoy parliamentary support.[313] Hence, the Constitutional Tribunal assesses the admissibility of the application throughout the entire proceedings, and not only at the moment of submission of the application.[314]

Moreover, the *constitutional identity limit* could also be triggered by individuals initiating a constitutional complaint. However, the constitutional framework establishes that individuals may only challenge a 'statute or *another normative act*' that violates their constitutional rights.[315] The Constitutional Tribunal specified, in this regard, that the term 'normative act' covers EU law acts, both primary and secondary law, as they have direct implications for the constitutional rights of individuals and therefore qualify as normative acts.[316] Yet, for a constitutional complaint to be admissible individuals have to substantiate that the protection of constitutional rights at EU level is considerably lower than the protection awarded by the Polish Constitution. This suggests that the presumption exists that the EU fundamental rights protection corresponds to national protection. Overall, it shifts the burden of proof to the applicants who have to substantiate a lower fundamental rights protection at EU level, which makes the admissibility of such complaints, particularly against EU fiscal integration steps, relatively unlikely.[317] It further suggests that individual constitutional complaints against future EU fiscal integration will likely be considered inadmissible by the Tribunal.

Overall, this indicates that constitutional review can be triggered by both privileged and non-privileged applicants at different stages. The review can take the form of an abstract *ex ante* or *ex post* constitutional review as well as a concrete *ex post*

312. Bainczyk, 'Folgen einer mangelnden Anpassung der polnischen Verfassung nach dem Vertrag von Lissabon im Lichte des Urteils des polnischen Verfassungsgerichtshofes zum Beschluss des Europäischen Rates zur Änderung von Art. 136 AEUV' 319.
313. K 11/13 *Challenge Against the Fiscal Compact* (Polish Constitutional Tribunal); cf. as well: Biernat and Kawczyńska, 'The Role of the Polish Constitution (Pre-2016): Development of a Liberal Democracy in the European and International Context' 774; Alicia Hinarejos Parga, *The Euro Area Crisis in Constitutional Perspective* (Oxford University Press 2015) 148.
314. Difficult political questions might thus be avoided by the Tribunal, cf. Bainczyk, 'Folgen einer mangelnden Anpassung der polnischen Verfassung nach dem Vertrag von Lissabon im Lichte des Urteils des polnischen Verfassungsgerichtshofes zum Beschluss des Europäischen Rates zur Änderung von Art. 136 AEUV' 320.
315. Cf. wording in Article 79(1) Polish Constitution; cf. as well De Visser, *Constitutional Review in Europe: A Comparative Analysis* 151.
316. SK 54/05 *Constitutional Complaint Against Protocol No. 4 to the European Agreement* (Polish Constitutional Tribunal); cf. as well: Wyrozumska, 'Poland' 471; regarding EU secondary law: Katarzyna Granat, 'Kontrolle des EU-Sekundärrechts durch den polnischen Verfassungsgerichtshof: Anmerkung zum Beschluss des polnischen Verfassungsgerichtshofs vom 16. November 2011, SK 45/09' (2013) 48 Europarecht (EuR) 205, 208.
317. Bainczyk, 'Folgen einer mangelnden Anpassung der polnischen Verfassung nach dem Vertrag von Lissabon im Lichte des Urteils des polnischen Verfassungsgerichtshofes zum Beschluss des Europäischen Rates zur Änderung von Art. 136 AEUV' 310.

review. In relation to specifically EU primary law, constitutional review is most commonly initiated by privileged applicants in an abstract *ex post*-manner. Although the Polish Constitution also provides for an *ex ante* assessment, the Polish President did not yet employ this prerogative in relation to EU integration steps.[318]

3 Constitutional Basis of the Employed Limit

The Polish *constitutional identity limit* is a judicial concept established by the Polish Constitutional Tribunal. Its conceptual basis is the Polish sovereignty doctrine and the Tribunal established that the concept of *constitutional identity* corresponds to the normative, substantive manifestation of sovereignty, which is specified in different provisions of the Polish Constitution.[319] Namely, it covers important sovereign competences that have to remain under the control of Polish institutions laid down in the Preamble as well as Articles 2, 4, 5, 8, 90, 104(2) and 126(1) Polish Constitution.[320] These provisions protect core constitutional principles, such as sovereignty, (representative) democracy, the rule of law, Polish statehood, the supreme status of the Polish Constitution, the protection of fundamental rights, and national security, as well as the constitutional basis for the conferral of competences to the EU. Article 90 Polish Constitution can be identified as the main constitutional vehicle for the operationalization of the *constitutional identity limit*. The provision states:

> The Republic of Poland may, by virtue of international agreements, delegate to an international organization or international institution the competence of organs of State authority in relation to certain matters.

Thus, the Polish legislator can confer powers to the EU as long as the conferral remains limited 'to certain matters'. The Tribunal interpreted this restriction as a direct acknowledgement of the Polish *constitutional identity* doctrine, as it only allows for conferral of a limited set of competences.[321] In the reading of the Constitutional Tribunal, this implies, on the one hand, that the conferral to the EU has to be specific and limited in scope,[322] and, on the other hand, that the conferral of powers may not occur in competence areas that are covered by Polish *constitutional identity*, as these are not included in the term 'certain matters'.[323] According to the Tribunal the wording 'certain matters' indicates that the Polish constitutional legislator wanted to exclude

318. Wendel, 'Lisbon Before the Courts: Comparative Perspectives' 107.
319. *Treaty of Lisbon* section III.2.1; cf. as well: Śledzińska-Simon and Ziółkowski, 'Constitutional Identity in Poland: Is the Emperor Putting on the Old Clothes of Sovereignty' 248.
320. Rideau, 'The Case-Law of the Polish, Hungarian and Czech Constitutional Courts on National Idenity and the "German Model"' 525.
321. *Treaty of Lisbon* section III.2.1.; cf. as well: Rideau, 'The Case-Law of the Polish, Hungarian and Czech Constitutional Courts on National Idenity and the "German Model"' 252.
322. Kowalik-Bańczyk, 'Should We Polish It Up? The Polish Constitutional Tribunal and the Idea of Supremacy of EU Law' 1364.
323. *Treaty of Lisbon* section III.2.1.; cf. as well: Rideau, 'The Case-Law of the Polish, Hungarian and Czech Constitutional Courts on National Idenity and the "German Model"' 525.

competence areas from the possibility of conferral. It should be added that although Article 90(1) Polish Constitution limits the scope for EU cooperation, the provision has to be distinguished from the German *eternity clause*, which entails a scope restriction for constitutional amendments in general.[324]

4 *Substantive Core Protected by the Limit*

As concluded, the *constitutional identity limit* imposes substantive restrictions for the conferral of competences. Conceptually, the Constitutional Tribunal derives the limit from the material manifestation of Polish sovereignty, which it bases on Article 90 Polish Constitution.[325] These substantive restrictions are defined in the Tribunal's jurisprudence on a case-to-case basis and mainly depend on the questions raised by the applicants.[326] Here, the fact that Poland is not yet a member of the Eurozone becomes relevant. Up to this point, the Tribunal did not conduct an elaborate assessment of the constitutional implications of Polish Eurozone-membership or of the Eurocrisis-measures taken by the Eurozone. It considered these questions as hypothetical and thus inadmissible. As established in Article 90(1) Polish Constitution, the Polish legislator has to *confer the competence* to enact legally binding measures.[327] However, given that Poland is currently only a Euro-candidate country, no legally binding obligations can directly derive for Poland. The Tribunal emphasized in this regard that Poland is currently merely bound by the EU convergence rules.[328] The Tribunal nevertheless noted that accession to the Euro might require an amendment of Article 227 Polish Constitution.[329]

Despite the absence of specific Euro-related jurisprudence, the Tribunal identified a set of constitutional principles that are particularly important for the Polish constitutional system. These principles are covered by the *constitutional identity limit* (a), and they are subsequently evaluated in light of EU fiscal integration proposals (b).

324. Śledzińska-Simon and Ziółkowski, 'Constitutional Identity in Poland: Is the Emperor Putting on the Old Clothes of Sovereignty' 246; Magdalena Bainczyk, 'Die praktische Anwendung des Unionsrechts in Polen: Anmerkung zum Urteil des EuGH v. 7.3.2017, Rs. C-390/15 (RPO), und zum Beschluss des polnischen Verfassungsgerichtshofes v. 17.5.2017, Akz. K 61/13' (2017) 52 Europarecht (EuR) 725, 742.
325. *Treaty of Lisbon* section 2.1.; K 33/12 *Challenges Against Article 136 (3) TFEU and ESM-Treaty* (Polish Constitutional Tribunal) section 6.4.1.; cf. as well: Adam Łazowski, 'Half Full and Half Empty Glass: The Application of EU Law in Poland (2004-2010)' (2011) 48 Common Market Law Review 503, 510-511.
326. The Tribunal is bound by the application brought, cf. Bainczyk, 'Die praktische Anwendung des Unionsrechts in Polen: Anmerkung zum Urteil des EuGH v. 7.3.2017, Rs. C-390/15 (RPO), und zum Beschluss des polnischen Verfassungsgerichtshofes v. 17.5.2017, Akz. K 61/13' 740-741.
327. Reestman, 'Legitimacy Through Adjudication: The ESM Treaty and the Fiscal Compact Before the National Courts' 249.
328. *Challenges Against Article 136 (3) TFEU and ESM-Treaty* section 7.6.1.
329. *Poland's EU Membership* Point 33; cf. as well: Łazowski, 'Half Full and Half Empty Glass: The Application of EU Law in Poland (2004-2010)' 509.

a Constitutional Identity Limit: General Characteristics

In its *Lisbon*-judgment the Constitutional Tribunal established that Polish *constitutional identity* covers the inalienable institutional prerogatives which are the 'normative manifestation' of the principle of sovereignty.[330] Although the Tribunal explicitly highlighted that it was difficult to provide a detailed list of inalienable competences, it provided a non-exhaustive overview of 'matters' that fall under a 'complete prohibition of conferral' under Article 90 Polish Constitution.[331] According to the Tribunal, these matters are:

> [...] decisions specifying the fundamental principles of the Constitution and decisions concerning the rights of the individual which determine the identity of the state, including, *in particular* [emphasis added], the requirement of protection of human dignity and constitutional rights, the principle of statehood, the principle of democratic governance, the principle of a state ruled by law, the principle of social justice, the principle of subsidiarity, as well as the requirement of ensuring better implementation of constitutional values and the prohibition to confer the power to amend the Constitution and the competence to determine competences [...].[332]

Considering this list, one can identify four broad constitutional areas covered, namely the protection of fundamental rights, the preservation of the Polish state, the protection of the state structure as well as retaining *Kompetenz-Kompetenz*.[333] Obviously, this list is formulated in an abstract manner and only covers broad constitutional considerations, without identifying more specific underlying constitutional provisions or competences connected to them. Moreover, some of the identified matters are already affected by EU law. For example, the protection of fundamental rights is largely regulated at EU level based on the Charter of Fundamental Rights[334] and General Principles of EU law. The Polish Tribunal explicitly acknowledged the equivalent degree of fundamental rights protection awarded by both legal orders.[335] Therefore, the enlisted constitutional areas are not entirely banned from supranational cooperation, which is why the Tribunal's wording referring to a 'complete prohibition' is misleading. Instead, the Tribunal seems to suggest that the ultimate control or the 'heart of the

330. *Treaty of Lisbon* section III.2.1.
331. *Ibid.*, section III.2.1.; the non-exhaustive character stems from the Tribunal's wording 'in particular', cf. Czapliński, 'Recent Constitutional Jurisprudence Concerning the European Union: Some Remarks on 2010 Judgments of the Polish Constitutional Court' 201.
332. *Treaty of Lisbon* section III.2.1.
333. Śledzińska-Simon and Ziółkowski, 'Constitutional Identity in Poland: Is the Emperor Putting on the Old Clothes of Sovereignty' 253; Magdalena Bainczyk, 'Das Ratifizierungsverfahren des Vertrages von Lissabon in Polen' (2009) 44 Europarecht (EuR) 145, 157-158.
334. To which Poland negotiated Protocol 30, however, the CJEU clarified that the Protocol did not alter the obligation of Poland to comply with the Charter, cf. Joined Cases C-411/10 and C-493/10 *N.S. and M.E. et al. v. Minister for Justice, Equality and Law Reform* (CJEU) para. 120.
335. Granat, 'Kontrolle des EU-Sekundärrechts durch den polnischen Verfassungsgerichtshof: Anmerkung zum Beschluss des polnischen Verfassungsgerichtshofs vom 16. November 2011, SK 45/09' 213.

matter'[336] remains at the Polish constitutional level. This can be observed in relation to fundamental rights protection, where the Tribunal employs the presumption that the EU protection corresponds to the Polish Constitution.[337] This is equally visible in relation to the *constitutional identity* doctrine, where the Tribunal identified the EU protection of national (constitutional) identities in Article 4(2) TEU as an 'equivalent' concept.[338] Nevertheless, both *identity* concepts remain independent from each other and the Constitutional Tribunal retains the ability to employ the *constitutional identity limit* in case the EU protection is no longer considered as equivalent.[339]

Considering the matters covered by the *constitutional identity limit*, it can be observed that the major concern relates to the preservation of the Polish state, including its sovereign decision-making abilities based on a democratic structure and guided by the protection of subjective constitutional rights.[340] This corresponds to the Tribunal's conclusions on Polish EU membership where it established that Article 90(1) Polish Constitution did '[...] not [authorize] the delegation of competences to such an extent that it would signify the inability of the Republic of Poland *to continue functioning as a sovereign and democratic state* [emphasis added]'.[341] Hence, the Tribunal clarified that the existing constitutional framework in Article 90 Polish Constitution, which forms the basis for the *constitutional identity limit*, restricts the scope of EU integration. Notably, the EU may not develop into its own state, thereby transforming Poland into a (federal) state entity and depriving it of its statehood.[342]

This confirms that the Tribunal mainly shields Polish statehood through the *constitutional identity limit*. To that end, it identified a list of core competences that may not be transferred to the EU. The Tribunal infers this restriction from the wording in Article 90 Polish Constitution, which limits the conferral to 'certain matters'.[343] However, these specific constitutional matters remain abstract and they entail only limited guidance for EU fiscal integration proposals. The subsequent analysis, therefore, focuses on the principle of sovereignty, which is the conceptual-normative basis of the Polish *constitutional identity limit*.

336. *Treaty of Lisbon* section III.2.1.
337. SK 45/09 *Constitutional Complaint Against Brussels I Regulation* (Polish Constitutional Tribunal) section III.2.2.; *Poland's EU Membership* Point 23; cf. as well: Granat, 'Kontrolle des EU-Sekundärrechts durch den polnischen Verfassungsgerichtshof: Anmerkung zum Beschluss des polnischen Verfassungsgerichtshofs vom 16. November 2011, SK 45/09' 213.
338. *Treaty of Lisbon* section III.2.1.; cf. as well: Elke Cloots, *National Identity in EU Law* (Oxford University Press 2015) 170.
339. Śledzińska-Simon and Ziółkowski, 'Constitutional Identity in Poland: Is the Emperor Putting on the Old Clothes of Sovereignty' 254-255.
340. *Treaty of Lisbon* section III.2.5.; cf. as well: Rideau, 'The Case-Law of the Polish, Hungarian and Czech Constitutional Courts on National Idenity and the "German Model"' 252-253.
341. *Poland's EU Membership* Point 8.
342. Śledzińska-Simon and Ziółkowski, 'Constitutional Identity in Poland: Is the Emperor Putting on the Old Clothes of Sovereignty' 251-253; Rideau, 'The Case-Law of the Polish, Hungarian and Czech Constitutional Courts on National Idenity and the "German Model"' 252-253.
343. *Treaty of Lisbon* section III.2.5.; cf. as well: Łazowski, 'Half Full and Half Empty Glass: The Application of EU Law in Poland (2004-2010)' 510.

b Polish Sovereignty

The assessment of the Polish sovereignty doctrine is divided into a general outline of the principle (i) and a following assessment of the material competences covered by it (ii).

i General Conception of Polish Sovereignty

The concept of sovereignty is of particular historic importance for the Polish constitutional order. Poland was only able to claim political autonomy and sovereignty over its own national decisions in the aftermath of the Communist past and after the breakdown of the Iron Curtain.[344] This historic consideration might explain the restrictive framework for the conferral of powers to the supranational level laid down in Article 90 Polish Constitution. As highlighted, Article 90 Polish Constitution is restricted to 'certain matters' and the procedural requirements for the conferral of competences under Article 90(1) Polish Constitution are stricter than for constitutional amendments.[345] At the same time, Article 90 Polish Constitution is an expression of the sovereign decision to open the Polish Constitution and to allow for supranational cooperation.[346] Both, the historic importance of sovereignty and the constitutional decision to allow for supranational cooperation under strict conditions are reflected in the jurisprudence of the Polish Constitutional Tribunal.

Notably, the Tribunal concluded that the conferral of competences to EU level following Article 90 Polish Constitution constituted in itself an exercise of sovereign powers.[347] It furthermore stressed that the conferral of competences did not entail a transfer of sovereignty, but that it rather constituted a revocable and democratic

344. Christoph Grabenwarter, 'National Constitutional Law Relating to the European Union' in Armin von Bogdandy and Jürgen Bast (eds), *Principles of European Constitutional Law* (2nd edn, Hart Publishing and C.H. Beck 2009) 98; Cezary Mik, 'State Sovereignty and European Integration: Public International Law, EU Law and Constitutional Law in the Polish Context' in Neil Walker (ed.), *Sovereignty in Transition* (Hart Publishing 2003) 393.
345. As laid down in Article 235 Polish Constitution; cf. Śledzińska-Simon and Ziółkowski, 'Constitutional Identity in Poland: Is the Emperor Putting on the Old Clothes of Sovereignty' 249-250; Wendel, 'Lisbon Before the Courts: Comparative Perspectives' 107.
346. Magdalena Bainczyk and Ulrich Ernst, 'Urteil des polnischen Verfassungsgerichtshofs vom 11. 05. 2005 AZ.K 18/04' (2006) 41 Europarecht (EuR) 236, 241.
347. Miroslaw Granat and Katarzyna Granat, *The Constitution of Poland: A Contextual Analysis* (Hart Publishing 2019) 27; Czaputowicz, 'Sovereignty in Theories of European Integration and the Perspective of the Polish Constitutional Tribunal' 33; Wróbel, 'Die Grenzen der europäischen Integration im Lichte jüngerer Entscheidungen des polnischen Verfassungsgerichts' 499; Łazowski, 'Half Full and Half Empty Glass: The Application of EU Law in Poland (2004-2010)' 510-511; Łazowski, 'Case Note: Accession Treaty – Polish Constitutional Tribunal: Conformity of the Accession Treaty with the Polish Contitution – Decision of 11 May 2005' 157; Bainczyk and Ernst, 'Urteil des polnischen Verfassungsgerichtshofs vom 11. 05. 2005 AZ.K 18/04' 241; Mik, 'State Sovereignty and European Integration: Public International Law, EU Law and Constitutional Law in the Polish Context' 398.

restriction of Poland's ability to take unilateral decisions on the conferred matters.[348] Hence, the conferral only entails a substantive limitation of national sovereign competences to allow for joint action at the supranational level. It, however, does not constitute a loss of these competences to the EU or a challenge to the supreme status of the Polish Constitution, which is further clarified in Article 8(1) Polish Constitution.[349] Therefore, the principle of sovereignty imposes at least two requirements for EU integration steps:

First, the Polish legislator's decision is constitutive for the conferral, as enshrined in Article 90(1) Polish Constitution. Hence, the EU can only exercise competences that were attributed to it by the Polish legislator. Obviously, the EU's principle of conferral mirrors this Polish constitutional requirement.[350] As a conceptual opposite, the Tribunal further requires that Poland can terminate supranational cooperation, as enshrined in Article 50 TEU.[351] This implies that Poland retains the final say over the extent of EU commitments.

Second, the conferral only entails the exercise of the conferred sovereign competences and not the loss of the competence itself. Therefore, the conferral is only a restriction on the exercise of sovereign powers by Polish institutions for the benefit of joint EU action. Conceptually, this can be secured by characterizing the EU as a derived legal order, which is based on the Polish Constitution.[352] For EU fiscal integration proposals, this implies that the approval of the Polish legislator for the conferral of powers following Article 90(1) Polish Constitution is constitutive. Furthermore, the derived status of the EU legal order and the Member States' status as 'Masters of the Treaties' may not be altered by such integration steps.

At the same time, the Constitutional Tribunal established in its jurisprudence the dynamic and evolutionary character of the principle of sovereignty.[353] This evolutionary potential can be triggered by EU cooperation, which is introduced into the Polish

348. Śledzińska-Simon and Ziółkowski, 'Constitutional Identity in Poland: Is the Emperor Putting on the Old Clothes of Sovereignty' 250; Czaputowicz, 'Sovereignty in Theories of European Integration and the Perspective of the Polish Constitutional Tribunal' 32, 34.
349. Śledzińska-Simon and Ziółkowski, 'Constitutional Identity in Poland: Is the Emperor Putting on the Old Clothes of Sovereignty' 250-251; as the Tribunal already pointed out in its judgment on Polish EU accession, cf. Łazowski, 'Half Full and Half Empty Glass: The Application of EU Law in Poland (2004-2010)' 509.
350. *Treaty of Lisbon* section III.2.2.; cf. as well: Wróbel, 'Die Grenzen der europäischen Integration im Lichte jüngerer Entscheidungen des polnischen Verfassungsgerichts' 500.
351. *Treaty of Lisbon* section III.2.1.; cf. as well: Bainczyk, 'Das Ratifizierungsverfahren des Vertrages von Lissabon in Polen' 156; Article 90 Polish Constitution is seemingly based on the assumption that the conferral is revocable, cf. Mik, 'State Sovereignty and European Integration: Public International Law, EU Law and Constitutional Law in the Polish Context' 398.
352. *Treaty of Lisbon* section III.2.1.
353. *Challenges Against Article 136 (3) TFEU and ESM-Treaty* section 6.4.2.; cf. as well: *Treaty of Lisbon* section III.2.1.; Granat and Granat, *The Constitution of Poland: A Contextual Analysis* 26.

constitutional order by a sovereign Polish decision.[354] Obviously, if the Polish Constitution allows for an opening of the Polish constitutional order the principle of sovereignty is required to evolve, for example, by accepting the exercise of sovereign competence at the supranational level.[355] The Tribunal even highlighted that the 'modern' interpretation of the principle of sovereignty requires international cooperation in order to achieve constitutional commitments laid down in the Polish Constitution.[356] Here, once again the protection of fundamental rights is a good example, which in a globalized world requires, according to the Tribunal, the opening of the domestic order to EU and international commitments in order effectively protect fundamental rights.[357] Given the evolutionary potential of Polish sovereignty, and given that sovereignty constitutes the basis of Polish *constitutional identity*, it seems convincing to argue that the *constitutional identity limit* is – just as the underlying principle of sovereignty – able to evolve. From that perspective, the Polish *constitutional identity limit* is not a fixed, inflexible substantive core of constitutional principles, but rather a concept open to future developments.

Furthermore, the Tribunal explicitly recognized that a 'modern' interpretation of sovereignty requires international and supranational cooperation in order to comply with national constitutional duties. One might apply the same logic to *national constitutional identity* and submit that the protection of core constitutional values is no longer only a domestic matter but instead requires supranational cooperation. The potential stabilizing benefits of EU safeguards for national constitutional values can be seen with regard to the current rule-of-law-crisis in Poland. Here the EU carefully monitors and tries to prevent the deterioration of this core constitutional value, which is equally protected by the Polish *constitutional identity limit*.

The principle of sovereignty is thus a historically important constitutional concept reflected in the constitutional basis for supranational cooperation in Article 90 Polish Constitution. This provision allows for a limited transfer of the exercise of sovereign power. According to the Constitutional Tribunal, the fact that supranational cooperation is based on the sovereign Polish decision to transfer competences and that Poland retains the possibility to withdraw suggests that full sovereignty is preserved. At the same time, the Tribunal recognized that the understanding of sovereignty must evolve, which indicted that also the *constitutional identity limit* is receptive to such evolution.

354. Bainczyk and Ernst, 'Urteil des polnischen Verfassungsgerichtshofs vom 11. 05. 2005 AZ.K 18/04' 241.
355. Czaputowicz, 'Sovereignty in Theories of European Integration and the Perspective of the Polish Constitutional Tribunal' 34; Wróbel, 'Die Grenzen der europäischen Integration im Lichte jüngerer Entscheidungen des polnischen Verfassungsgerichts' 498-499.
356. *Challenges Against Article 136 (3) TFEU and ESM-Treaty* section 6.4.2.; *Treaty of Lisbon* section III.2.1.; cf. as well: Czapliński, 'Recent Constitutional Jurisprudence Concerning the European Union: Some Remarks on 2010 Judgments of the Polish Constitutional Court' 200.
357. Reestman, 'Legitimacy Through Adjudication: The ESM Treaty and the Fiscal Compact Before the National Courts' 271-272.

ii Specific Material Dimension of Sovereignty Covered by Constitutional Identity Limit

The Constitutional Tribunal developed a material, competence-based conception of the principle of sovereignty.[358] Notably, in its *Lisbon*-judgment the Tribunal established the subsequent list of particularly important domestic competences:

> having the exclusive power of jurisdiction as regards the territory of a given state and its citizens, conducting foreign policy, deciding about war and peace, freedom as to [recognizing] other states and governments, maintaining diplomatic relations, deciding about military alliances and membership in international political [organizations], conducting an independent financial, budget and fiscal policies [...].[359]

Thus, the Constitutional Tribunal identified a wide field of important competences of Polish institutions that are the expression of Polish sovereignty and that constitute the Polish *constitutional identity*.[360] As previously already submitted in relation to the matters listed under the *constitutional identity limit*, this material dimension of sovereignty can hardly be seen as completely off-limit. Clearly, EU integration already triggered constitutional transformation in these areas, without putting Polish sovereignty and *constitutional identity* into question. This is equally recognized by the Tribunal, which subsequently referred to the previously outlined evolution of sovereignty that moved away from absolute and strict sovereignty claims to a more modern, contemporary understanding of this doctrine.[361] Therefore, not every conferral of competences, which affects these competence areas, is seen as a violation of Polish sovereignty but they serve rather as constitutional guidance.[362]

Considering the prospect of EU fiscal integration proposals, the mentioned 'conducting an independent financial, budget and fiscal policies'[363] as a protected competence area seems particularly relevant. A more integrated Eurozone would most likely require a conferral of competences in these areas. However, the Tribunal identified all three areas as particularly important competences under the Polish sovereignty doctrine.[364] Based on this finding, one may conclude that EU fiscal

358. Śledzińska-Simon and Ziółkowski, 'Constitutional Identity in Poland: Is the Emperor Putting on the Old Clothes of Sovereignty' 253; Wróbel, 'Die Grenzen der europäischen Integration im Lichte jüngerer Entscheidungen des polnischen Verfassungsgerichts' 499.
359. *Treaty of Lisbon* section III.2.1.
360. *Challenges Against Article 136 (3) TFEU and ESM-Treaty* section 6.4.1.; *Treaty of Lisbon* section III.2.1.; cf. as well: Śledzińska-Simon and Ziółkowski, 'Constitutional Identity in Poland: Is the Emperor Putting on the Old Clothes of Sovereignty' 253.
361. As recognized by the Tribunal: *Challenges Against Article 136 (3) TFEU and ESM-Treaty* section 6.4.2.; *Treaty of Lisbon* section III.2.1.; and as highlighted in the academic writing, cf. Granat and Granat, *The Constitution of Poland: A Contextual Analysis* 26; Wróbel, 'Die Grenzen der europäischen Integration im Lichte jüngerer Entscheidungen des polnischen Verfassungsgerichts' 498.
362. Reestman, 'Legitimacy Through Adjudication: The ESM Treaty and the Fiscal Compact Before the National Courts' 271-272.
363. Cf. wording of the Tribunal: *Treaty of Lisbon* section III.2.1.
364. *Ibid.*, section III.2.1.; the Constitutional Tribunal was confronted with the question whether the Fiscal Compact eroded fiscal and economic competences in a manner incompatible with the

integration proposals could potentially conflict with the competence-based material conception of Polish sovereignty. Yet, given the evolutionary nature of the sovereignty doctrine, and given that supranational cooperation in the identified three areas might be deemed necessary, the Tribunal could consider the conferral of these competences to be less problematic by invoking the modern interpretation of national sovereignty.[365] Furthermore, the Tribunal already indicated that Polish Eurozone-membership might require internal constitutional amendments,[366] which implies that the conferral required for such membership is generally attainable.

When considering the overall Polish constitutional framework, the Tribunal's concern for financial, budget and fiscal policies seems to correspond with the institutional prerogatives enshrined in Articles 146 and 219 Polish Constitution.[367] Article 146 Polish Constitution establishes, *inter alia*, the competence of the Polish Ministerial Council to implement the domestic economic policy. Article 219 Polish Constitution establishes the prerogative of the Sejm to adopt the annual budget as well as the different budgetary commitments under this state budget. In proceedings against the ESM-Treaty and the amendment of Article 136(3) TFEU, the applicants submitted that European Council Decision 2011/199/EU violated these two constitutional provisions. However, the Tribunal did not rule on the substance of these claims, given that the applicants did not further elaborate on the possible constitutional conflict that could arise.[368] Nevertheless, it seems that these institutional prerogatives could be seen as specific constitutional concretizations and thus fall under the essential competences covered by Polish sovereignty.

At the same time, this remains indicative. For now, the Polish Constitutional Tribunal did not mention these two provisions when enumerating the constitutional core protected by the *constitutional identity limit* – which might stem from the fact that Poland is not yet a Eurozone member and therefore the Tribunal never had to consider the implications of a transfer of competences in financial, fiscal, and budgetary matters in detail. In all cases, it seems likely that a conferral in these areas will undergo close constitutional scrutiny.

Polish Constitution, which was clearly inspired by this benchmark, however, the Tribunal did not have to answer the question due to the inadmissibility of the action, cf. *Challenge Against the Fiscal Compact*; cf. as well: Bainczyk, 'Folgen einer mangelnden Anpassung der polnischen Verfassung nach dem Vertrag von Lissabon im Lichte des Urteils des polnischen Verfassungsgerichtshofes zum Beschluss des Europäischen Rates zur Änderung von Art. 136 AEUV' 314-315.

365. Wróbel, 'Die Grenzen der europäischen Integration im Lichte jüngerer Entscheidungen des polnischen Verfassungsgerichts' 498; Czapliński, 'Recent Constitutional Jurisprudence Concerning the European Union: Some Remarks on 2010 Judgments of the Polish Constitutional Court' 200.
366. Specifically, the amendment of Article 227 Polish Constitution on the National Central Bank, cf. *Poland's EU Membership* Point 33; cf. as well: Łazowski, 'Half Full and Half Empty Glass: The Application of EU Law in Poland (2004-2010)' 509.
367. Which were raised in constitutional proceedings on the ESM, cf. *Challenges Against Article 136 (3) TFEU and ESM-Treaty* section 7.7.
368. *Ibid.*, section 7.7.; cf. as well: Bainczyk, 'Folgen einer mangelnden Anpassung der polnischen Verfassung nach dem Vertrag von Lissabon im Lichte des Urteils des polnischen Verfassungsgerichtshofes zum Beschluss des Europäischen Rates zur Änderung von Art. 136 AEUV' 314.

c Interim Conclusion

The *constitutional identity limit* shields core national competences, that are crucial for the sovereign Polish political democratic process, against the transfer to EU level. To that end, the Tribunal identified four core constitutional matters, which are described as inalienable institutional competences. These matters cover the protection of fundamental rights, the preservation of Polish statehood, the defending of the constitutional structure of the state as well as the continuous existence of the Polish Constitution itself.[369] However, the Tribunal did not point out specific constitutional or institutional features that had to be preserved in the process of conferring competences to the EU.

Further guidance on the substantive content of the *constitutional identity limit* may be derived from the sovereignty doctrine, which constitutes the conceptual basis of this limit.[370] Here, the assessment revealed that the doctrine protects the initial decision to confer competences to the EU and the conception of the EU as derived legal order. Furthermore, the Tribunal adopted a modern interpretation of sovereignty, which allowed for the evolution of the doctrine from an absolute, strict reading to a more open, EU-friendly understanding.[371] Given the intrinsic interconnection between sovereignty and *constitutional identity*, this evolutionary potential will likely apply to the *constitutional identity limit*.

Finally, it was illustrated that budgetary, financial, and fiscal competences are characterized by the Tribunal as traditionally important sovereign competence areas,[372] which is of particular relevance for EU fiscal integration steps. Yet, the Tribunal did not specify any institutional prerogatives that fall under the *constitutional identity limit*. Until now, the Tribunal has refused to engage with the compatibility of Eurozone-obligations with the Polish constitutional order, given their now only hypothetical nature.

5 *Longevity and Absoluteness of the Constitutional Limit*

Ultimately, the question emerges whether the substantive content protected by the Polish *constitutional identity limit* can be amended. Considering the constitutional framework, Article 90(1) Polish Constitution explicitly limits competence conferrals to 'certain matters'.[373] Furthermore, the Polish Constitution treats the conferral of competences to the international or EU level as a particularly important and yet highly

369. Górski, 'European Union Law Before National Judges: The Polish Experience – Adept Multicentric Vision or Creeping Hierarchical Practice' 129.
370. Claes, 'National Idenity: Trump Card or up for Negotiation?' 128.
371. Czaputowicz, 'Sovereignty in Theories of European Integration and the Perspective of the Polish Constitutional Tribunal' 32.
372. Wróbel, 'Die Grenzen der europäischen Integration im Lichte jüngerer Entscheidungen des polnischen Verfassungsgerichts' 499.
373. *Treaty of Lisbon* section III.2.1.; cf. as well: Śledzińska-Simon and Ziółkowski, 'Constitutional Identity in Poland: Is the Emperor Putting on the Old Clothes of Sovereignty' 251; Rideau, 'The Case-Law of the Polish, Hungarian and Czech Constitutional Courts on National Idenity and the "German Model"' 252; Łazowski, 'Half Full and Half Empty Glass: The Application of EU Law in Poland (2004-2010)' 510.

restricted matter.[374] This is visible from the procedural requirements that Article 90 Polish Constitution establishes for this conferral. Conferring competences to the EU requires the support of a two-thirds majority in the Polish Sejm and Senate or approval by referendum. These are the highest procedural thresholds that the Polish Constitution imposes. Even the requirements for amending the Polish Constitution itself are less strict.[375] At the same time, although the procedural requirements for the conferral of competences are stricter than the requirements for constitutional amendments, a conferral of powers may not violate the constitutional text itself. Thus, competence conferrals might require a constitutional amendment.[376] The emerging question is therefore whether Article 90(1) Polish Constitution may be amended by the constitution-amending legislator to possibly overcome the *constitutional identity limit*.

Until now, the Polish Constitutional Tribunal did not have to rule on this question.[377] Nonetheless, certain conclusions may be drawn from the Tribunal's established jurisprudence. In the first place, the Constitutional Tribunal underscored that the constitution-amending legislator had three alternatives when confronted with a conflict between national constitutional law and new EU obligations. First, the legislator could change the Polish Constitution. Second, the legislator could aim at changing the EU commitment. Or third, the legislator could decide to withdraw from the EU.[378] In fact, underscoring these three possibilities emphasizes the sovereign abilities of the Polish legislator.[379] Put differently, excluding certain competence areas from the constitution-amending legislator's powers might result in a limitation of the sovereign decision-making process in Poland. Therefore, it seems convincing to argue that the Polish constitution-amending legislator can overcome the *constitutional identity limit* by changing the Polish Constitution. Such changes might entail a modification of the Polish sovereignty doctrine, the framework for conferring powers and most notably Article 90 Polish Constitution. The Constitutional Tribunal already indicated that a future Eurozone membership might require a constitutional amendment to Article 227 Polish Constitution,[380] which suggests that this constitutional amendment is constitutionally feasible.

The absence of explicit mentioning suggests that the Polish limit is not absolute and may in fact be overcome following the prescribed framework. Particularly in light of the political divide in the Polish party system, the required support seems, however,

374. Śledzińska-Simon and Ziółkowski, 'Constitutional Identity in Poland: Is the Emperor Putting on the Old Clothes of Sovereignty' 249-250.
375. Cf. Article 235 Polish Constitution: Wendel, 'Lisbon Before the Courts: Comparative Perspectives' 107.
376. Łazowski, 'Case Note: Accession Treaty – Polish Constitutional Tribunal: Conformity of the Accession Treaty with the Polish Contitution – Decision of 11 May 2005' 155.
377. Śledzińska-Simon and Ziółkowski, 'Constitutional Identity in Poland: Is the Emperor Putting on the Old Clothes of Sovereignty' 244.
378. Wioleta Brandt, 'Verfassungsrecht in Polen: Verfassungsbeschwerde und Rechtsprechung des polnischen Verfassungsgerichtshofes zu Fragen der EU-Mitgliedschaft' (2009) 44 Europarecht (EuR) 131, 139.
379. Czaputowicz, 'Sovereignty in Theories of European Integration and the Perspective of the Polish Constitutional Tribunal' 33.
380. Łazowski, 'Case Note: Accession Treaty – Polish Constitutional Tribunal: Conformity of the Accession Treaty with the Polish Contitution – Decision of 11 May 2005' 161.

hardly achievable. Furthermore, constitutional amendments are very rare in Poland. Between 1997 and 2019 only two constitutional amendments were enacted on less far-reaching matters.[381] Although the constitution-amending legislator is competent to overcome the *constitutional identity limit*, the required constitutional amendment seems challenging.

III Rule of Law at Risk in Poland: The Independence of the Constitutional Tribunal

After having analysed the established Polish constitutional approach to possible EU fiscal integration steps, the subsequent outline constitutes a conceptual caveat. Namely, the Polish rule-of-law-crisis erupted in the aftermath of the parliamentary elections in late 2015 during which the PiS-party obtained an absolute majority in the Sejm (235 out of 460 seats) and the Polish Senate (61 out of 100 seats).[382] Since 2016, this process is critically monitored by the EU as well as by the Venice Commission of the Council of Europe.[383] The political crisis also received great academic attention.[384] The following analysis does not claim to be comprehensive but will instead focus on the impact of this crisis on the Polish Constitutional Tribunal. In particular, three significant actions taken by the Polish Parliament and Government are outlined to assess their impact on the discussed Polish constitutional approach.[385]

First, the appointment of several constitutional judges raises serious concerns. In 2015, the Sejm of the seventh legislative term elected five new constitutional judges, shortly before the 2015 parliamentary elections. However, at that moment only three constitutional seats were vacant, the two additional seats were only becoming vacant during the next legislative term. In response, the newly elected Sejm controlled by new political majorities annulled the nomination of all five constitutional judges and elected instead five new judges. These newly elected five judges were subsequently appointed by the Polish President.[386] In a judgment delivered by the Constitutional Tribunal on the matter, the constitutional bench found that the original nomination of the three

381. Granat and Granat, *The Constitution of Poland: A Contextual Analysis* 42.
382. Tomasz Tadeusz Koncewicz, 'Of Institutions, Democracy, Constitutional Self-Defence and the Rule of Law: The Judgments of the Polish Constitutional Tribunal in Cases K 34/15, K 35/15 and Beyond' (2016) 53 Common Market Law Review 1753, 1754.
383. Sadurski, 'Constitutional Crisis in Poland' 262; Sava Jankovic, 'Polish Democracy under Threat? An Issue of Mere Politics or a Real Danger?' (2016) 9 Baltic Journal of Law & Politics 49, 51.
384. Cf. Wojciech Sadurski, *Poland's Constitutional Breakdown* (Oxford University Press 2019); Miroslaw Wyrzykowski, 'Experiencing the Unimaginable: The Collapse of the Rule of Law in Poland' (2019) 11 Hague Journal on the Rule of Law 417; Marcin Matczak, 'Poland's Rule of Law Crisis: Some Thoughts' (2019) 11 Hague Journal on the Rule of Law 407.
385. Pablo Castillo-Ortiz, 'The Illiberal Abuse of Constitutional Courts in Europe' (2019) 15 European Constitutional Law Review 48, 57-58; Krygier, 'The Challenge of Institutionalisation: Post-Communist "Transitions", Populism, and the Rule of Law' 547-548.
386. Wojciech Sadurski, 'Polish Constitutional Tribunal under PiS: From an Activist Court, to a Paralysed Tribunal, to a Governmental Enabler' (2019) 11 Hague Journal on the Rule of Law 63, 65-66; Koncewicz, 'Of Institutions, Democracy, Constitutional Self-Defence and the Rule of Law: The Judgments of the Polish Constitutional Tribunal in Cases K 34/15, K 35/15 and Beyond' 1755-1757.

judges, who were filling the seats that became vacant during the seventh legislative term, was constitutional. However, the nomination of the two additional judges, whose seats became vacant during the eighth legislative term, was unconstitutional.[387] Despite a clear verdict from the Constitutional Tribunal, the judgment was never implemented by the government. Later, after the composition of the constitutional bench shifted in favour of the PiS-party, the Tribunal even reverted its initial judgment and confirmed the appointment of all five constitutional judges appointed by the Sejm of the eighth legislative term.[388] Regarding this second judgment, two points may be raised. First, the shift in the political affiliation of the constitutional judges obviously affected the final verdict. In its decision, the Constitutional Tribunal altered established, long-standing constitutional jurisprudence in relation to Article 194(1) Polish Constitution,[389] which illustrates a severe risk, namely that constitutional jurisprudence is disrupted by political actors in Poland. Second, the latter case concerned *indirectly* the nomination of the controversial three constitutional judges from 2015. The judgment validated their appointment, however, two of these *controversial* judges were part of the deliberations and ruled therefore on their own case.[390] Overall, this instance demonstrates the risk that constitutional courts are confronted with, namely the political interference in their independent work through the composition of the constitutional bench.

The second instance concerns the appointment of Judge *Julia Przyłębska* as President of the Constitutional Tribunal. Judge *Przyłębska* was appointed as President of the Constitutional Tribunal by the Polish President, without having been properly elected by the Assembly of constitutional judges, as required by both Article 194(2) Polish Constitution and Articles 15(1) and 14(1) No. 3 Act on the Polish Constitutional Tribunal.[391] Notably, the General Assembly of constitutional judges did not have a quorum to issue a formal nomination.[392] Nevertheless, the Polish President appointed *Przyłębska* as president, only one day after receiving a letter informing him about her

387. K 34/15 *Appointment of Constitutional Judges* (Polish Constitutional Tribunal); cf. as well Sadurski, 'Polish Constitutional Tribunal under PiS: From an Activist Court, to a Paralysed Tribunal, to a Governmental Enabler' 66; Piotr Czarny, 'Der Streit um den Verfassungsgerichtshof in Polen 2015-2016' (2018) 64 Osteuropa Recht (OER) 5, 6.
388. Namely, in the decision K 1/17 *Constitutionality of Introductory Provisions to the Act on the Organisation of the Constitutional Tribunal and the Mode of Proceedings Before the Constitutional Tribunal* (Polish Constitutional Tribunal); as pointed out by, Sadurski, 'Polish Constitutional Tribunal under PiS: From an Activist Court, to a Paralysed Tribunal, to a Governmental Enabler' 67; cf. as well: Śledzińska-Simon and Ziółkowski, 'Constitutional Identity in Poland: Is the Emperor Putting on the Old Clothes of Sovereignty' 264.
389. Sadurski, 'Polish Constitutional Tribunal under PiS: From an Activist Court, to a Paralysed Tribunal, to a Governmental Enabler' 67.
390. *Ibid.*, 67; Sadurski, *Poland's Constitutional Breakdown* 63-64.
391. Czarny, 'Der Streit um den Verfassungsgerichtshof in Polen 2015-2016' 17.
392. Jens Brauneck, 'Rettet die EU den Rechtsstaat in Polen?' (2018) 37 Neue Zeitschrift für Verwaltungsrecht (NVwZ) 1423, 1424; Czarny, 'Der Streit um den Verfassungsgerichtshof in Polen 2015-2016' 17; Tina de Vries, 'Bedrohungen für die Unabhängigkeit der Justiz in Polen: Teil 1' (2018) 27 Wirtschaft und Recht in Osteuropa (WiRO) 105, 106.

apparent election.[393] This instance illustrates again the emerging political interference in the established work of the Constitutional Tribunal as well as the limited means of the Tribunal to resist such political interference. The Polish President and the Government deliberately disregarded the applicable rules to foster a favourable outcome for the PiS-governmental majority.[394]

The third instance concerns the refusal of the Polish government to publish the judgments of the Constitutional Tribunal. The Polish Constitution prescribes that constitutional judgments must be published in order to acquire binding legal effect, as enshrined in Article 190(2) and (3) Polish Constitution.[395] The refusal to publish certain judgments in the official journal, therefore, implied that these judgments could not acquire binding force. It is sufficient here to point out that the refusal to publish a selection of judgments indicates that the government conducted a political 'quality control' - thereby deciding which judgments should be binding. Obviously, this significantly hinders the work of the Constitutional Tribunal and entails a challenge to the constitutionally enshrined balance of powers.[396] One result was that the Tribunal could no longer perform its core task, namely to supervise the constitutionality of parliamentary and governmental actions.

These three instances illustrate clear political interference with the Polish Constitutional Tribunal. Given that the constitutional judges are appointed by the Sejm in Poland and given the absolute majority that the PiS-party commands in the Sejm, candidates with clear political affiliations have been elected. These politically motivated appointments affect the work of the Tribunal considerably, by questioning established precedent and by siding increasingly with the governing party, which, according to *Sadurski*, transformed the Tribunal into a 'government's ally'.[397] Obviously, this has implications for EU law, too. On the one hand, the current governing party has been critical towards the EU,[398] which is increasingly reflected in the jurisprudence of the Tribunal. On the other hand, the established constitutional

393. Sadurski, 'Polish Constitutional Tribunal under PiS: From an Activist Court, to a Paralysed Tribunal, to a Governmental Enabler' 69; Czarny, 'Der Streit um den Verfassungsgerichtshof in Polen 2015-2016' 17-18.

394. Namely, that the Tribunal seemingly rules increasingly in line with the governmental positions, cf. Sadurski, *Poland's Constitutional Breakdown* 84-86; Krygier, 'The Challenge of Institutionalisation: Post-Communist "Transitions", Populism, and the Rule of Law' 547.

395. Sadurski, 'Polish Constitutional Tribunal under PiS: From an Activist Court, to a Paralysed Tribunal, to a Governmental Enabler' 74; Czarny, 'Der Streit um den Verfassungsgerichtshof in Polen 2015-2016' 13.

396. Sadurski, 'Polish Constitutional Tribunal under PiS: From an Activist Court, to a Paralysed Tribunal, to a Governmental Enabler' 74; Krygier, 'The Challenge of Institutionalisation: Post-Communist "Transitions", Populism, and the Rule of Law' 547.

397. Sadurski, *Poland's Constitutional Breakdown* 85; Śledzińska-Simon and Ziółkowski, 'Constitutional Identity in Poland: Is the Emperor Putting on the Old Clothes of Sovereignty' 264; thereby, the Tribunal lost its core function as guardian of the Polish Constitution, cf. Wyrzykowski, 'Experiencing the Unimaginable: The Collapse of the Rule of Law in Poland' 417; the Constitutional Tribunal is employed as a 'tool for constitutional mutation', cf. Castillo-Ortiz, 'The Illiberal Abuse of Constitutional Courts in Europe' 69.

398. Śledzińska-Simon and Ziółkowski, 'Constitutional Identity in Poland: Is the Emperor Putting on the Old Clothes of Sovereignty' 246.

approach towards the EU might shift, as the Tribunal could decide to alter its constitutional appraisal of EU integration steps significantly.

Considering the content covered by the *constitutional identity limit*, it could be argued that the current internal political interferences with the judiciary - which is established as an independent institutional branch of the state according to Articles 45(1), 173, 178(1), 195(1) and 199(3) Polish Constitution - undermine core constitutional principles, namely the rule of law, democracy and the separation of powers.[399] As indicated, the EU can offer an external safeguard and become a supplementary guarantor of such constitutional principles. These foundational principles are mainly enshrined in Article 2 TEU and largely correspond with the principles covered by the Polish *constitutional identity limit*.[400] This illustrates that the EU legal order has an additional protective value for core constitutional principles and can thereby function as an external stabilizer for national *constitutional identity*.

Furthermore, considering the analysis of the Polish *constitutional identity limit* it seems that adverse constitutional developments within one Member State have not only internal consequences but also impact the EU and its Member States. Obviously, these negative external impacts are equally applicable to EU fiscal integration proposals. Given the dismantling of the Polish Constitutional Tribunal, it is hardly predictable what substantive limits EU fiscal integration proposals are confronted with in the future. Hence, these interferences reduce the reliability and predictability of the Polish constitutional stance on EU matters.

IV Conclusion

The Polish *constitutional identity limit* was established by the Constitutional Tribunal. The limit is rooted in the Polish provision for the conferral of competences to the EU as well as the Polish sovereignty doctrine. More specifically, the Tribunal established in its *Lisbon*-judgment that the *constitutional identity limit* covers the inalienable institutional competences that constitute the 'normative manifestation' of the principle of sovereignty.[401] Thus, *constitutional identity* and the principle of sovereignty are closely interconnected in Polish constitutional jurisprudence. Furthermore, the Tribunal identified budgetary, financial and fiscal policy decisions as particularly important sovereign competences.[402] It, however, equally indicated that the interpretation of sovereignty evolves, particularly in light of increasing international and supranational

399. Wyrzykowski, 'Experiencing the Unimaginable: The Collapse of the Rule of Law in Poland' 418.

400. *Treaty of Lisbon* section III.2.2.; cf. as well Śledzińska-Simon and Ziółkowski, 'Constitutional Identity in Poland: Is the Emperor Putting on the Old Clothes of Sovereignty' 255-256.

401. *Treaty of Lisbon* section III.2.1.

402. *Ibid.*, section III.2.1.; *Challenges Against Article 136 (3) TFEU and ESM-Treaty* section 6.4.1.; cf. as well: Śledzińska-Simon and Ziółkowski, 'Constitutional Identity in Poland: Is the Emperor Putting on the Old Clothes of Sovereignty' 253.

cooperation in a globalizing world.[403] This might indicate a general openness towards more integrated supranational cooperation.

When applying this *constitutional identity limit* to EU fiscal integration proposals, the conclusions are only indicative: First, EU fiscal integration proposals affect competence areas that are particularly important under the principle of sovereignty.[404] Second, the conception of the EU as a derived legal order, the required constitutive approval of the Polish Parliament for the conferral of powers to EU level, the preservation of *Kompetenz-Kompetenz* and the ability of Poland to withdraw from EU cooperation jointly guarantee according to the Tribunal that Poland retains its statehood and that EU cooperation is not challenging the Member States as sovereign entities.[405] Given that the material content of sovereignty is currently evolving, it is possible that the required conferral of competences in budgetary, financial and fiscal matters is finally deemed permissible under the *constitutional identity doctrine*.[406] This illustrates that the *constitutional identity limit* is flexible, and the protected content crucially depends on the findings of the Constitutional Tribunal.

Regardless of whether the Tribunal identifies a conflict between EU fiscal integration steps and the *constitutional identity limit*, it is to be expected that the Tribunal will find a conflict between such EU integration and the text of the Polish Constitution which would require a constitutional amendment. In particular, Articles 146, 219 and 227 Polish Constitution were previously identified as potentially conflicting with Eurozone-membership.[407] It was emphasized that such constitutional amendments are practically rare and the conferral of powers will depend on both the procedural requirements in Articles 90 and 235 Polish Constitution. At the same time, given that the procedural hurdles for the conferral of powers in Article 90 Polish Constitution are higher compared to the procedural requirements in Article 235 Polish Constitution, it seems likely that a constitutional amendment can be adopted in case the conferral of power is supported by the required majority.

Therefore, even a conflict between the Polish *constitutional identity limit* with EU fiscal integration proposals might be overcome by amending the Polish Constitution. This corresponds in the first place with the Tribunal's established jurisprudence.[408] What is more, the combined effort of amending the Polish Constitution following Article 235 and subsequently the conferral of competences following Article 90 Polish Constitution would require compliance with high constitutional procedural hurdles

403. *Challenges Against Article 136 (3) TFEU and ESM-Treaty* section 6.4.2.; *Treaty of Lisbon* section III.2.1.; cf. as well: Granat and Granat, *The Constitution of Poland: A Contextual Analysis* 26.
404. *Treaty of Lisbon* section III.2.1.; cf. as well: Śledzińska-Simon and Ziółkowski, 'Constitutional Identity in Poland: Is the Emperor Putting on the Old Clothes of Sovereignty' 253.
405. Łazowski, 'Half Full and Half Empty Glass: The Application of EU Law in Poland (2004-2010)' 509.
406. *Treaty of Lisbon* section III.2.1.; *Challenges Against Article 136 (3) TFEU and ESM-Treaty* section 6.4.1.; cf. as well: Rideau, 'The Case-Law of the Polish, Hungarian and Czech Constitutional Courts on National Idenity and the "German Model"' 252.
407. *Poland's EU Membership* Point 33; *Challenge Against the Fiscal Compact* section 7.7.; cf. as well: Łazowski, 'Case Note: Accession Treaty – Polish Constitutional Tribunal: Conformity of the Accession Treaty with the Polish Contitution – Decision of 11 May 2005' 161.
408. *Poland's EU Membership* Point 13; cf. as well: Kowalik-Bańczyk, 'Should We Polish It Up? The Polish Constitutional Tribunal and the Idea of Supremacy of EU Law' 1364.

and therefore vest this undertaking with significant democratic legitimacy.[409] Thus, it seems that the *constitutional identity limit* does not impose absolute limits on Polish participation in EU fiscal integration.[410] Instead, such integration steps mainly face a political-procedural hurdle, as attaining the required majorities might prove challenging. All these conclusions ultimately depend on the future course of the Constitutional Tribunal. This showcases an immanent risk when relying on strong (independent) constitutional courts for determining the constitutional feasibility of EU fiscal integration.

Table 5.4 Constitutional Identity Classification Board for Poland

1. Which institutional actor enforces the constitutional limit?
The Polish Constitutional Tribunal established the *constitutional identity limit* in Poland. The Tribunal takes binding decisions on the compatibility of international agreements with the Polish Constitution (Articles 188(1) and 190(1) Polish Constitution).
2. How can the constitutional identity limit be triggered?
The *constitutional identity limit* can be triggered either *ex ante* by the Polish President, or *ex post* by a set of privileged applicants enlisted in Article 190(1) Polish Constitution, including Members of the Sejm or the Senate.
3. What is the constitutional basis of the constitutional identity limit?
The Polish Constitutional Tribunal developed the *constitutional identity limit* on the basis of the normative manifestation of the Polish sovereignty doctrine, which is specified in the Preamble as well as Articles 2, 4, 5, 8, 90, 104(2), 126(1) of the Polish Constitution. Besides, the Tribunal employs Article 90(1) Polish Constitution as a constitutional basis for the limit.
4. What constitutional principles and substantive content are covered?
The Polish *constitutional identity limit* protects, *inter alia*, Polish statehood, the state structure, the status of the constitution and fundamental rights. This protection mainly translates into formal safeguards, including the principle of conferral, the preservation of *Kompetenz-Kompetenz*, the derived status of the EU and the withdrawal possibility. In addition, the Tribunal emphasized the evolutionary potential of the principle of sovereignty.
5. How – if at all – can the constitutional identity limit be overcome (longevity/ absoluteness of the limit)?
As it stands, the Polish Constitutional Tribunal did not establish the absoluteness of the *constitutional identity limit* which suggests that the constitution-amending legislator is able to overcome any conflict with EU fiscal integration proposals.

409. Bainczyk, 'Das Ratifizierungsverfahren des Vertrages von Lissabon in Polen' 150.
410. Rideau, 'The Case-Law of the Polish, Hungarian and Czech Constitutional Courts on National Idenity and the "German Model"' 253.

E RESEARCH FINDINGS ON GERMAN CONSTITUTIONAL IDENTITY LIMIT

The German *constitutional identity limit* is based on the German *eternity clause* enshrined in Article 79(3) Basic Law, which applies to EU integration steps following Article 23(1)(3) Basic Law. From this, the German Constitutional Court, as the most authoritative interpreter of the German constitutional text, developed an absolute substantive limit for EU integration. When considering EU fiscal integration proposals, the most apparent conflict arises from *overall budgetary responsibility*, which the Court developed during the Eurocrisis.[411]

This limit can be triggered by both private individuals and privileged institutional applicants. The assessment revealed that the constitutional standing requirements are, however, applied differently when deciding on EU-related matters. It was outlined that the Court is inclined to find EU-related proceedings more readily admissible.[412] The result is that a wide range of institutional and private actors could proceed against EU fiscal integration proposals and thereby trigger the *constitutional identity limit*.[413]

Overall budgetary responsibility shields central fiscal and budgetary decisions against too far-reaching supranationalization in order to preserve the democratic decision-making process on these political matters within Germany. The underlying aim of this judicial concept is to ensure that the German Parliament, as the directly democratically legitimized institution, retains the necessary space to make politically important decisions, which include fiscal and budgetary matters. Therefore, the Court required that supranational fiscal and budgetary commitments remain sufficiently limited in volume, connected to strict conditions as well as clear objectives, and finally, no automatic liability may arise.[414] The parliament has to remain the central institution evaluating fiscal and budgetary commitments that impact the German state budget.

Finally, given that the German Constitutional Court connects its limit to the *eternity clause*, the limit imposes an absolute restriction on the constitutional space available for EU fiscal integration proposals.[415] At the same time, the concrete application of the limit reveals a degree of judicial reluctance. Consequently, one can conclude that the Court focusses on the procedural requirements of *overall budgetary responsibility*, which ensure that the key political decisions are taken by the German Parliament, within predictable, reasonable limits. For EU fiscal integration proposals

---

411. Reestman, 'Legitimacy Through Adjudication: The ESM Treaty and the Fiscal Compact Before the National Courts' 259; Wendel, 'Exceeding Judicial Competence in the Name of Democracy: The German Federal Constitutional Court's OMT Reference' 285.
412. Calliess, 'Constitutional Identity in Germany: One for Three or Three in One?' 172; Schwerdtfeger, 'Europäisches Unionsrecht in der Rechtsprechung des Bundesverfassungsgerichts: Grundrechts-, ultra-vires- und Identitätskontrolle im gewaltenteiligen Mehrebenensystem' 305.
413. Gärditz, 'Beyond Symbolism: Towards a Constitutional Actio Popularis in EU Affairs? A Commentary on the OMT Decision of the Federal Constitutional Court' 192.
414. *ESM-Treaty and Fiscal Compact (interim relief)* para. 124; cf. as well: Nettesheim, '"Euro-Rettung" und Grundgesetz: Verfassungsgerichtliche Vorgaben für den Umbau der Währungsunion' 772.
415. *OMT-Reference* para. 29; *Lisbon-judgment* para. 216; cf. as well: Rademacher, 'Die "Verfassungsidentität" als Grenze der Kompetenzübertragung auf die Europäische Union?' 150.

this implies that the German Parliament has to be integrated as a central decision-maker into the supranational institutional architecture.

Table 5.5 Constitutional Identity Classification Board for Germany

1. Which institutional actor enforces the constitutional limit?

The German *constitutional identity limit* is developed by the German Constitutional Court. The Court takes authoritative and binding decisions on the compatibility of the German Constitution with EU integration steps.

2. How can the constitutional identity limit be triggered?

The experiences during the Eurocrisis show that individual constitutional complaints (Article 93(1) no. (4a) Basic Law) and institutional proceedings (Article 93(1) no. (1) Basic Law) are the most relevant proceedings to challenge Euro-related measures.

3. What is the constitutional basis of the constitutional identity limit?

Article 79(3) Basic Law is the constitutional basis for the German *constitutional identity limit*, which shields core constitutional values against constitutional amendments, and against EU integration, as specified in Article 23(1)(3) Basic Law. The content includes the principle of democracy, which is the conceptual basis for *overall budgetary responsibility*.

4. What constitutional principles and substantive content are covered?

When considering EU fiscal integration, the concept of *overall budgetary responsibility* seems most relevant. According to this concept, core budgetary decisions have to remain at the domestic level. This requires that fiscal commitments remain limited in volume, restricted to specific objectives, attached to clear conditions and that the German parliamentary approval has to remain constitutive for any German participation. Furthermore, the Court established an abstract material benchmark, according to which the budgetary decision-making ability of the German Parliament may not be suspended for a considerable time.

5. How – if at all – can the constitutional identity limit be overcome (longevity/absoluteness of the limit)?

Article 79(3) Basic Law formulates an absolute limit to the powers of the constitution-amending legislator, which can only be overcome by adopting a new constitution.

CHAPTER 6

Comparing the Different National *Constitutional Identity Limits* and Their Implications for EU Fiscal Integration Proposals

A INTRODUCING THE COMPARATIVE EVALUATION

The observations made in relation to the German, French, Spanish and Polish *constitutional identity limits* indicate a degree of conceptual, substantive and institutional convergence, despite the limits' intention to protect core national constitution particularities as can be deduced from the combined national *constitutional identity* classification board in Table 6.1.

The subsequent comparison of these limits first considers the substantive dimension, which includes the determination of the constitutional space for EU fiscal integration (B). Then the institutional and procedural sides of the analysed limits are compared in order to evaluate the likelihood of *constitutional identity* challenges against EU fiscal integration (C) before concluding on the combined limiting effect that the assessed *constitutional identity limits* have on the proposed EU fiscal integration ambitions (D).

Table 6.1 Combined Constitutional Identity Classification Board

	Germany	***France***	***Spain***	***Poland***
1. Which institutional actor enforces the constitutional limit?	Constitutional Court (judicial)	Constitutional Council (quasi-judicial, advisory body)	Constitutional Court (judicial)	Constitutional Court (judicial)
2. How is the *constitutional identity limit* triggered?	*Ex post* Privileged and non-privileged applicants	*Ex ante* Privileged applicants	*Ex ante + ex post* Privileged applicants	*Ex ante + ex post* Privileged and non-privileged applicants
3. What is the basis of the *constitutional identity limit*?	EU enabling clause + *eternity clause*	EU enabling clause + core constitutional provisions	EU enabling clause	EU enabling clause + core constitutional provisions
4. What constitutional principles and substantive content are covered?	Democracy (competence-centric, including budgetary and fiscal competences)	Sovereignty (competence-centric, including budgetary, fiscal and monetary matters)	Sovereignty + democratic decision-making	Sovereignty (competence-centric, financial, budget and fiscal policy)
5. How – if at all – can the *constitutional identity limit* be overcome (longevity/absoluteness of the limit)?	Absolute limitations (replacement by the new constitution)	Amendable (normal constitutional amendment procedure)	Amendable (strict constitutional amendment procedure)	Amendable (strict constitutional amendment procedure)

B WHAT NATIONAL CONSTITUTIONAL SPACE FOR EU FISCAL INTEGRATION?

Although national constitutional systems and their constitutional actors employ their own distinctive terminology and constitutional mechanisms,[1] the assessment of the four *national constitutional identity limits* uncovered clear similarities in their underlying objectives, their constitutional basis and the protected core principles and material content. A key aim of the limits is to protect sufficient space for national democratic decision-making, whether this is seen as part of the right to vote, democracy more generally, or more abstract notions such as sovereignty or statehood. The significant substantive overlap is further demonstrated by the fact that all the compared systems identify very similar substantive domains as the most *contentious* and *threatening* aspects of EU (fiscal) integration.

Such overlap is visible with regard to the constitutional basis of the *constitutional identity limits*. The Spanish Constitutional Tribunal, the Polish Constitutional Tribunal and the French *Conseil Constitutionnel* all base their limits, at least partly, on the domestic clause that regulates the conferral of competences to the EU. The Spanish Constitutional Tribunal derives its *constitutional identity limit* from Article 93 Spanish Constitution, which allows for the conferral of powers to the supranational or international level.[2] The Polish Constitutional Tribunal employs Article 90 Polish Constitution as the legal basis for its limit, which allows for the transfer of 'certain powers' to an international organization.[3] Finally, the French *Conseil Constitutionnel* lists Article 88 French Constitution as one of the constitutional bases for its essential conditions limit.[4] One can equally argue that even the *Bundesverfassungsgericht* bases its identity review (partly) on the German EU clause. Although the underpinning constitutional mechanism found in Article 79(3) as well as Article 20(2) and (3) Basic Law is not specific to EU cooperation, the German Court mentioned the German enabling clause in Article 23(1)(3) Basic Law in its EU-related review.[5]

Thus, all four *constitutional identity limits* are (at least partly) based on the national provisions that allow for participation in EU and international cooperation. The resulting constitutional review is consequently rooted in constitutional provisions that are specifically designed for EU cooperation. These provisions depart from the perspective that the national constitution is the basis and also limit for any EU collaboration, and they traditionally aim to balance the possibility to participate in EU

1. Azoulai and Ronkes Agerbeek, '*Conseil constitutionnel* (French Constitutional Court), Decision No. 2004-505 DC of 19 November 2004, on the Treaty Establishing a Constitution for Europe' 878.
2. *Treaty Establishing a Constitution for Europe* section II.2.; cf. as well: Martín Y Pérez de Nanclares, 'Constitutional Identity in Spain: Commitment to European Integration Without Giving up the Essence of the Constitution' 270.
3. Śledzińska-Simon and Ziółkowski, 'Constitutional Identity in Poland: Is the Emperor Putting on the Old Clothes of Sovereignty' 251; Rideau, 'The Case-Law of the Polish, Hungarian and Czech Constitutional Courts on National Idenity and the "German Model"' 252.
4. In addition to other provisions of the '*bloc de constitutionnalité*', cf. Ziller, 'European Union Law in the Jurisprudence of French Supreme Courts: Europe-Friendliness with a French Touch' 773.
5. Mayer, 'Rashomon in Karlsruhe: A Reflection on Democracy and Identity in the European Union' 763.

integration with the preservation of national constitutional principles. Notably, EU cooperation requires a modified constitutional approach in the national constitutional systems. An illustrative example is the protection of fundamental rights, which constitutes a pivotal part of all considered national constitutional orders and their *constitutional identity limits*.[6] Given that fundamental rights are extensively protected at EU level, the German Constitutional Court developed its *Solange*-approach, which was followed by other constitutional courts.[7] The Polish Constitutional Tribunal even established that an effective protection of fundamental rights, as warranted under the Polish Constitution, requires international cooperation.[8] This indicates that national constitutional systems are able to consider and take into account the constitutional value of supranational cooperation when determining the overall balance between integration and protecting the national constitution and space for domestic (political) decision-making.

When considering the relevant substantive issues protected under the *constitutional identity limits* clear conceptual similarities can be identified, too. Notably, the four assessed *limits* protect – to a varying degree – national sovereignty, the democratic decision-making process, and the hierarchical position of their national constitution.

Regarding the principle of sovereignty, all four national constitutional actors refer directly to this concept. The German Constitutional Court established that EU integration had to respect the sovereignty of the German people to take autonomous decisions in a list of core competence areas.[9] Similarly, the French *Conseil Constitutionnel* found that a transfer of competences may not affect the essential conditions for the exercise

6. *Germany: Solange II-Decision* para. 132; *Solange I-Decision* para. 56; cf. as well: Schwerdtfeger, 'Europäisches Unionsrecht in der Rechtsprechung des Bundesverfassungsgerichts: Grundrechts-, ultra-vires- und Identitätskontrolle im gewaltenteiligen Mehrebenensystem' 292; *France: Entwurf eines Gesetzes zu dem Beschluss des Europäischen Rates vom 25. März 2011 zur Änderung des Artikels 136 des Vertrags über die Arbeitsweise der Europäischen Union hinsichtlich eines Stabilitätsmechanismus für die Mitgliedstaaten, deren Währung der Euro ist (Drucksache 17/9047)* para. 10; *Lisbon Treaty* para. 9; cf. as well: Millet, 'Constitutional Identity in France: Vices and – Above All – Virtues' 138; *Spain: Treaty Establishing a Constitution for Europe* section II.2.; cf. as well: Pérez Tremps, 'National Idenity in Spanish Constitutional Court Case-Law' 270; *Poland: Treaty of Lisbon* section III.2.1.; cf. as well: Górski, 'European Union Law Before National Judges: The Polish Experience – Adept Multicentric Vision or Creeping Hierarchical Practice' 129.
7. The Spanish Constitutional Tribunal only scrutinizes Spanish implementing acts that violate the core of a fundamental right, cf. Torres Pérez, 'Constitutional Dialogue on the European Arrest Warrent: The Spanish Constitutional Court Knocking on Luxembourg's Door; Spanish Constitutional Court, Order of 9 June 2011, ATC 86/2011' 108; the *Conseil Constitutionnel* conducts an equivalence assessment under its *constitutional identity limit*, cf. Vranes, 'Constitutional Foundation of, and Limitations to, EU Integration in France' 547.
8. Reestman, 'Legitimacy Through Adjudication: The ESM Treaty and the Fiscal Compact Before the National Courts' 271-272; one motivation for Central and Eastern European Member States to join the EU was in fact the stabilization of core constitutional values, cf. Paul Craig and Gráinne de Búrca, *EU Law Text, Cases, and Materials* (6th edn, Oxford University Press 2015) 304.
9. *Quantitative Easing (PSPP) Final Judgment* para. 104; cf. as well: Pilz, 'Ein Schatzamt für die Eurozone? – Überlegungen zu den Vorschlägen des Europäischen Parlaments und der Kommission zu einer Reform der Wirtschaftsunion' 644.

of national sovereignty.[10] The Spanish Constitutional Tribunal concluded that certain constitutional competences were closely linked to Spanish sovereignty as well as the Spanish people as sovereign.[11] Finally, the Polish Tribunal held that supranational cooperation cannot alter the substantive manifestation of Polish sovereignty.[12] Hence, all four *constitutional identity limits* identify sovereignty as a core principle, which they aim to protect through their review. Put differently, one of the core functions of the four *constitutional identity limits* is to shield national sovereignty against EU integration steps. In parts, this relates to the protection of statehood in a process of ever-closer supranational cooperation.[13] At the same time, the assessment revealed that sovereignty is mostly construed in conjunction with the principle of national democracy. Therefore, a major aim of the analysed limits is to prevent a too closely integrated EU cooperation - that could otherwise replace national constitutional systems - to guarantee democratic decision-making in the Member States, while the protection of statehood appears to mostly function as a conceptual means to attain this objective.

In addition, national constitutional actors characterize EU integration as a reversible transfer of competences. Here, the derived legal status of the EU legal order can be identified as the core similarity across all systems, which entails that the national constitution remains the highest legal authority.[14] Also, the reversibility of the transfer of competences was emphasized as an important conceptual element, which is now explicitly enshrined in Article 50 TEU. In the context of Brexit, the CJEU explicitly acknowledged that triggering Article 50 TEU constituted a sovereign decision of the Member State.[15] In the national constitutional conception, the possibility to withdraw is, on the one hand, an expression of the derived status of EU cooperation - which implies that the EU is not replacing the national constitutional system.[16] On the other

10. *Entwurf eines Gesetzes zu dem Beschluss des Europäischen Rates vom 25. März 2011 zur Änderung des Artikels 136 des Vertrags über die Arbeitsweise der Europäischen Union hinsichtlich eines Stabilitätsmechanismus für die Mitgliedstaaten, deren Währung der Euro ist (Drucksache 17/9047)* para. 10; cf. as well: Millet, 'Constitutional Identity in France: Vices and - Above All - Virtues' 138-139.
11. *Constitutional Review of the Maastricht Treaty* section II.3.C.; cf. as well: Castillo de la Torre, '*Tribunal Constitucional* (Spanish Constitutional Court), Opinion 1/2004 of 13 December 2004, on the Treaty establishing a Constitution for Europe' 1185.
12. *Treaty of Lisbon* section III.2.1.
13. For example, the perception in Poland, cf. Rideau, 'The Case-Law of the Polish, Hungarian and Czech Constitutional Courts on National Idenity and the "German Model"' 252-253.
14. *Germany: Quantitative Easing (PSPP) Final Judgment* para. 102; cf. as well: Wendel, 'Exceeding Judicial Competence in the Name of Democracy: The German Federal Constitutional Court's OMT Reference' 273-274; *France: Lisbon Treaty* para. 8; cf. as well: Azoulai and Ronkes Agerbeek, '*Conseil constitutionnel* (French Constitutional Court), Decision No. 2004-505 DC of 19 November 2004, on the Treaty Establishing a Constitution for Europe' 877; *Spain: Treaty Establishing a Constitution for Europe* section II.2.; cf. as well: Castillo de la Torre, '*Tribunal Constitucional* (Spanish Constitutional Court), Opinion 1/2004 of 13 December 2004, on the Treaty Establishing a Constitution for Europe' 1175; *Poland: Treaty of Lisbon* sections III.2.2. and III.2.3.; cf. as well: Wróbel, 'Die Grenzen der europäischen Integration im Lichte jüngerer Entscheidungen des polnischen Verfassungsgerichts' 500.
15. C-621/18 *Wightman* (CJEU) para. 50.
16. As apparent in *Spain: Treaty Establishing a Constitution for Europe* section II.4.; cf. as well: Berger, *Anwendungsvorrang und nationale Verfassungsgericht* 286-287; or *Poland: Treaty of Lisbon* section III.2.1.; cf. as well: Bainczyk, 'Das Ratifizierungsverfahren des Vertrages von Lissabon in Polen' 156.

hand, it indicates that Member States can take the decision to terminate the limitation to their sovereign powers and exercise them independently from EU coordination, after withdrawal.[17] Obviously, allocating the highest legal importance to the national constitution equally safeguards the position of the constitutional authorities that established the national *constitutional identity limits*.

Regarding the substantive dimension of national sovereignty and democracy, all four constitutional actors operationalized the principle of sovereignty by identifying a core of substantive competence areas – which arguably relates back to the principle of democracy. The most detailed 'competence-catalogue' was developed by the German Constitutional Court, which established that revenue and expenditure had to remain under the (sovereign) national democratic control of the German Parliament following the *overall budgetary responsibility* limit.[18] This limit excludes that parliamentary budgetary prerogatives are transferred to such an extent that the German Parliament can no longer determine revenue and spending autonomously to a sufficiently significant degree.[19] The French *Conseil Constitutionnel* identified monetary, economic, fiscal and budgetary policies as 'vital for the exercise of national sovereignty'.[20] Therefore, the introduction of the Euro was found to conflict with the French sovereignty doctrine, and the adoption of the Maastricht Treaty required thus a constitutional amendment in France.[21] The Spanish Constitutional Tribunal appears to adopt a similar competence-based conception of Spanish sovereignty when assessing EU integration steps, albeit being less detailed.[22] And finally, the Polish Constitutional Tribunal also established a list of core competences that have to remain at the national level, which seem to include financial, budget and fiscal policy decisions.[23]

Consequently, all four national constitutional limits protect core sovereign competences against EU integration steps. In Germany, France and Poland, the constitutional authorities explicitly identified budgetary-related competences, including economic, financial and fiscal competences as particularly important national

17. As established by the Spanish Constitutional Tribunal, cf. *Treaty Establishing a Constitution for Europe* section II.4.; cf. as well: Berger, *Anwendungsvorrang und nationale Verfassungsgericht* 286-287.
18. *Quantitative Easing (PSPP) Final Judgment* paras 102-104; *Financial Support for Greece and EFSF* para. 120; *Lisbon-judgment* paras 250-252; cf. as well: Zwingmann, 'The Continuing Myth of Euro-Scepticism? The German Federal Constitutional Court Two Years after *Lisbon*' 682-683.
19. Summarized under the concept 'budgetary autonomy', cf. *Quantitative Easing (PSPP) Final Judgment* para. 104; cf. as well: Simon, *Grenzen des Bundesverfassungsgerichts im europäischen Integrationsprozess* 70.
20. *Entwurf eines Gesetzes zu dem Beschluss des Europäischen Rates vom 25. März 2011 zur Änderung des Artikels 136 des Vertrags über die Arbeitsweise der Europäischen Union hinsichtlich eines Stabilitätsmechanismus für die Mitgliedstaaten, deren Währung der Euro ist (Drucksache 17/9047)* para. 16; *Review of Maastricht Treaty (Maastricht I)* para. 43; cf. as well Neuman, 'The Brakes That Failed: Constitutional Restriction of International Agreements in France' 296.
21. *Review of Maastricht Treaty (Maastricht I)* para. 35; cf. as well: Neuman, 'The Brakes That Failed: Constitutional Restriction of International Agreements in France' 302.
22. Pérez Tremps, 'National Idenity in Spanish Constitutional Court Case-Law' 271; Castillo de la Torre, '*Tribunal Constitucional* (Spanish Constitutional Court), Opinion 1/2004 of 13 December 2004, on the Treaty Establishing a Constitution for Europe' 1183-1184.
23. For the competences, cf. *Treaty of Lisbon* section III.2.1.; for the general conception, cf. *ibid.*, section III.2.5.; cf. as well: Łazowski, 'Half Full and Half Empty Glass: The Application of EU Law in Poland (2004-2010)' 510.

competences, that enjoy the protection of the national *constitutional identity limits*. Although the Spanish Constitutional Tribunal did not yet identify these competence areas explicitly under the *constitutional identity limit*, it seems likely that it would consider these matters as particularly important, too.[24] Considering the concrete application of these limits, it was observed that Eurozone-membership required an amendment of the French Constitution, given that it was found incompatible with the French sovereignty doctrine.[25] The Polish Constitutional Tribunal indicated that Eurozone-membership will likely trigger constitutional conflicts.[26] In Spain and Germany, such constitutional conflicts between Euro-related integration steps and the principle of sovereignty (in conjunction with democracy) did not yet materialize. Regarding the German approach, it can be noted that the German Constitutional Court has so far appeared rather reluctant, as it has merely defined certain procedural safeguards, given that any conflict between *overall budgetary responsibility* and EU integration steps could be overcome.[27] Based on the constitutional precedent in all four Member States, it can be argued that future EU fiscal integration steps will be considered constitutionally contentious conferrals. This corresponds with the traditional characterization of budgetary and fiscal competences as core, sovereign state powers.[28] Hence, a conferral of decision-making powers in these competence areas opens the 'material scope of application' attached to the national *constitutional identity limits*.

However, it appears that even if this *material scope of application* is triggered no immediate outright prohibition is resulting. Instead, the assessment revealed that the German Constitutional Court and the French *Conseil Constitutionnel* equally consider the modalities attached to the conferral of these important competences. Notably, the German Court emphasized the importance of German parliamentary approval for budgetary commitments and underscored that any conferral of such competences to the supranational level had to be specific and limited.[29] According to the German case

24. Particularly, given that comparative constitutional reasoning is employed by the Spanish Constitutional Tribunal, cf. Martín Y Pérez de Nanclares, 'Constitutional Identity in Spain: Commitment to European Integration Without Giving up the Essence of the Constitution' 279; Pérez Tremps, 'National Idenity in Spanish Constitutional Court Case-Law' 270.
25. *Entwurf eines Gesetzes zu dem Beschluss des Europäischen Rates vom 25. März 2011 zur Änderung des Artikels 136 des Vertrags über die Arbeitsweise der Europäischen Union hinsichtlich eines Stabilitätsmechanismus für die Mitgliedstaaten, deren Währung der Euro ist (Drucksache 17/9047)* para. 16; *Review of Maastricht Treaty (Maastricht I)* para. 43; cf. as well Neuman, 'The Brakes That Failed: Constitutional Restriction of International Agreements in France' 296.
26. Notably Article 227 Polish Constitution, cf. Łazowski, 'Case Note: Accession Treaty - Polish Constitutional Tribunal: Conformity of the Accession Treaty with the Polish Contitution - Decision of 11 May 2005' 161.
27. Rademacher, 'Die "Verfassungsidentität" als Grenze der Kompetenzübertragung auf die Europäische Union?' 146; Bogdandy and Schill, 'Die Achtung der nationalen Identität unter dem reformierten Unionsvertrag: Zur unionsrechtlichen Rolle nationalen Verfassungsrechts und zur Überwindung des absoluten Vorrangs' 715.
28. Puntscher Riekmann and Wydra, 'Representation in the European State of Emergency: Parliaments Against Governments?' 567; Bonnie, 'The Constitutionality of Transfers of Sovereignty: The French Approach' 527.
29. As highlighted, no 'blanket empowerment' can be given to the EU, cf. *ESM-Treaty and Fiscal Compact* para. 160; *Lisbon-judgment* para. 236; cf. as well: Simon, *Grenzen des Bundesverfassungsgerichts im europäischen Integrationsprozess* 297.

law, these safeguards are intended to ensure that the '[…] the type and level of public spending are [not], to a significant extent, determined at the supranational level, [which would otherwise deprive] the Bundestag of its decision-making prerogative […].'[30] Thus, the German Constitutional Court not only developed a substantive dimension but also a procedural dimension under its *constitutional identity* review.

Notably, the German Constitutional Court assesses the procedural arrangements connected to the conferral of competences to determine the institutional and general impact on the national constitutional framework. A similar observation was made in relation to the French approach, where the *Conseil Constitutionnel* established that the modalities attached to the conferred competences were equally important to determine the impact on the competence area affected. Namely, the principle of sovereignty would only be violated in case the exercise of the conferred competences is supranationalized and France is prevented from acting autonomously.[31] It appears that the Spanish and the Polish Constitutional Tribunal do not employ a separate assessment of these procedural modalities, however, it seems that the degree of supranational influence when exercising the competence is equally important for their constitutional assessment. Consequently, the procedural requirements attached to the conferral of fiscal competences to the EU are highly relevant. In particular, the nature of the competence (i.e., exclusive, shared, or coordinating competence), the legislative procedure attached to it (i.e., ordinary or special legislative procedure), the veto possibilities, the degree of harmonization, and the extent of the competence (i.e., fixed volume, temporary financial framework, conditions for increase), all have to be taken into consideration in order to determine their compatibility with the national *constitutional identity limits*. In other words, when designing EU fiscal integration, the question is not only how far the EU can go substantively but also how all these national procedural requirements, including especially the required sufficient influence of national parliaments, can be met, without making the resulting system unworkable.

In addition, the assessment reveals that national systems are not concerned about the principle of sovereignty in isolation, but rather about the principle in conjunction with other constitutional principles, including, in particular, the principle of democracy. In Germany, the Constitutional Court established the importance of budgetary and fiscal decisions for the democratic process and the self-determination of the German people.[32] In France, the *Conseil Constitutionnel* reviews whether the essential conditions for the exercising of sovereignty are affected,[33] which clearly focusses on the

30. *Quantitative Easing (PSPP) Final Judgment* para. 104.
31. *Lisbon Treaty* para. 18; cf. as well: Boyron, 'The French Constitution and the Treaty of Amsterdam: A Lesson in European Integration' 176.
32. De Sadeleer, 'The New Architecture of European Economic Governance' 36.
33. Millet, 'Constitutional Identity in France: Vices and – Above All – Virtues' 138; Ziller, 'European Union Law in the Jurisprudence of French Supreme Courts: Europe-Friendliness with a French Touch' 771.

ability and process of employing national sovereignty. Similarly, the Spanish Constitutional Tribunal connects the preservation of sovereignty with structural and organizational characteristics of the state, including democracy,[34] just as the Polish Constitutional Tribunal.[35] Consequently, the protection of sovereignty occurs jointly with the protection of national democracy, as the four analysed national constitutional actors are concerned about the exercise of the important sovereign competences by the democratically legitimized domestic state institutions. Obviously, this interconnection between sovereignty and democracy is equally reflected in the detailed assessment of the modalities attached to the conferred competences – including the remaining influence of national parliaments – that national constitutional actors conduct. Thus, the crucial question is not only at what level a competence is located (i.e., national or supranational level) but also who is essentially controlling this competence and how this control is framed.

Finally, the comparison revealed that only the German Constitutional Court established the *constitutional identity limit* as an absolute limit to the powers of the constitution-amending legislator. Based on Article 79(3) Basic Law, the German Court concluded that the *constitutional identity limit* can only be overcome by replacing the German Constitution altogether.[36] The power to amend the German Constitution on matters covered by Article 79(3) Basic Law is not vested in the German legislator. Hence, any conflict between EU fiscal integration proposals and the German *constitutional identity limit* could only be overcome by following the replacement of the German Constitution. In contrast, the constitutional authorities in France, Spain and Poland have highlighted the possibility to amend the constitutional framework in order to accommodate EU integration.[37] None of the three national constitutions seems to contain a restriction for constitutional amendments comparable to the German *eternity clause*, and hence the respective domestic *constitutional identity limits* appear not to set absolute restrictions to the process of EU (fiscal) integration in these Member States.

34. Ferreres Comella, 'La Constitución española ante la cláusula de primacía del Derecho de la Unión Europea – Un comentario a la Declaración 1/2004 del Tribunal Constitucional' 82; Castillo de la Torre, '*Tribunal Constitucional* (Spanish Constitutional Court), Opinion 1/2004 of 13 December 2004, on the Treaty Establishing a Constitution for Europe' 1176.
35. Górski, 'European Union Law Before National Judges: The Polish Experience – Adept Multicentric Vision or Creeping Hierarchical Practice' 129; Czapliński, 'Recent Constitutional Jurisprudence Concerning the European Union: Some Remarks on 2010 Judgments of the Polish Constitutional Court' 201.
36. Calliess, 'Constitutional Identity in Germany: One for Three or Three in One?' 164-165; Christian Calliess, 'The Future of the Eurozone and the Role of the German Federal Constitutional Court' (2012) 31 Yearbook of European Law 402, 407.
37. *France: Compatibility of the Maastricht Treaty with the French Constitution after Constitutinal Amendments ('Maastricht II')* para. 19; cf. as well: Baranger, 'The Language of Eternity: Judicial Review of the Amending Power in France (Or the Absence Thereof)' 402-403; *Spain: Catalan Independence Declaration* section II.7.; cf. as well: Martín Y Pérez de Nanclares, 'Constitutional Identity in Spain: Commitment to European Integration Without Giving up the Essence of the Constitution' 281; Álvarez, 'Die spanische Dogmatik der Verfassungstreue – Geschichte einer fehlgeschlagenen Rezeption des deutschen Verfassungsdenkens' 442; *And Poland:* Brandt, 'Verfassungsrecht in Polen: Verfassungsbeschwerde und Rechtsprechung des polnischen Verfassungsgerichtshofes zu Fragen der EU-Mitgliedschaft' 139.

Even though the respective national constitutional authorities emphasize the significance of a constitutional conflict by framing it through the *constitutional identity review,* the constitution-amending legislator may overcome these constitutional concerns by following the prescribed procedure. Consequently, EU fiscal integration proposals could be overcome in France, Spain and Poland by amending the constitutional text, which requires, however, compliance with the strict procedural requirements that appear particularly difficult to attain in Spain and Poland. As highlighted, it seems likely that Article 168 Spanish Constitution would apply to accommodate far-reaching EU fiscal integration in Spain, which requires the dissolution of Congress and Senate, supported by two-thirds majorities, the confirmation of the constitutional amendment within the newly elected Congress and Senate, again supported by two-thirds majorities, and finally approval by public referendum.[38] Although in Poland the procedural requirements for a constitutional amendment under Article 235 Polish Constitution are 'lighter' compared with the requirements that apply to the conferral of competences to EU level,[39] constitutional practice illustrates that constitutional amendments are only rarely considered a (political) possibility.[40]

Taken together, it should be pointed out that none of the examined constitutional limits has so far proven to be an insurmountable legal barrier to further EU integration. All identified constitutional obstacles in relation to the Treaty of Maastricht in France and Spain as well as in relation to the EU Constitutional Treaty in France were overcome by amending the constitutional text. The same holds true for the German constitutional order, which imposes seemingly the strictest limit to EU integration steps. Although the *eternity clause* could theoretically result in an unsolvable constitutional conflict, the German Constitutional Court did (until now) conclude that all EU integration steps were compatible with the German Constitution. What is more, the emergence of the *constitutional identity limit* discourse is arguably only re-framing previously articulated national constitutional concerns. When considering EU fiscal integration steps, the most relevant constitutional concerns are national sovereignty and democratic decision-making. In order to render such EU fiscal integration steps constitutionally attainable, it therefore seems required to design EMU-reforms in light of the identified constitutional concerns. A particular focus thereby rests on the procedural and institutional framework envisaged for EU fiscal competences. As highlighted, the weaker the role of the democratically legitimized national parliaments in the exercise of supranationally coordinated EU fiscal competences, the more likely a conflict with national sovereignty and national democracy becomes. Ultimately, such conflict can result in the unattainability of EU fiscal integration, either because of absolute constitutional hurdles, as the case in Germany, or because of the parliamentary majorities required to first amend the constitutional text and subsequently confer the powers to the EU, as the case in France, Spain and Poland.

38. Elvira, 'Spain' 282-283.
39. Wendel, 'Lisbon Before the Courts: Comparative Perspectives' 107.
40. Granat and Granat, *The Constitution of Poland: A Contextual Analysis* 42.

C INSTITUTIONAL AND PROCEDURAL FRAMEWORK OF NATIONAL *CONSTITUTIONAL IDENTITY* LIMITS

As with the substantive limits, the institutional and procedural framework underpinning the four assessed *constitutional identity limits* entails clear overlap. In all four Member States the *constitutional identity limit* is established by an independent constitutional court – or quasi-court in the case of France.[41] Importantly, the respective national constitutional framework guarantees their institutional independence and entitles them to conduct a constitutional review.[42] The judgments of all four constitutional actors are binding on the state institutions and can therefore limit the constitutional space available for political action.[43] One could argue that the competence of the German Constitutional Court is even more far-reaching, as its findings on the *eternity clause* are outside the reach of the constitution-amending legislator.

The institutional independence is reflected in the composition of the German Court and the Spanish Tribunal, which consist of qualified lawyers appointed by different institutional actors. In Germany, constitutional judges are appointed to equal parts by *Bundestag* and *Bundesrat* by a two-thirds majority.[44] Given the qualified majority threshold, constitutional judges have to enjoy cross-party support, which renders political appointments less likely.[45] A similar constitutional decision in favour of a more 'unpolitical' constitutional bench can be observed in Spain, where respectively four judges are appointed by the Spanish Congress and the Senate by a three-fifths majority and respectively an additional two judges are appointed by the government and the Council for the Judiciary.[46] Hence, the Spanish nomination procedure combines high majority thresholds with diversification across different institutional actors. The French Constitution also diversifies the appointment prerogatives. In equal parts, the French President, the President of the Parliament and the

41. Cf. on the specific institutional design and the position of the *Conseil Constitutionnel*, Ziller, 'Sovereignty in France: Getting Rid of the Mal de Bodin' 267.
42. *Germany:* Florian Meinel, 'The Constitutional Miracle on the Rhine: Towards a History of West German Constitutionalism and the Federal Constitutional Court' (2016) 14 International Journal of Constitutional Law 277, 283; Ewald Wiederin, 'Die Gesetzeskraft der Entscheidungen des Bundesverfassungsgerichts' in Michael Brenner, Peter M. Huber and Markus Möstl (eds), *Der Staat des Grundgesetzes – Kontinuität und Wandel: Festschrift für Peter Badura zum siebzigsten Geburtstag* (Mohr Siebeck 2004) 605-608; *France:* Steiner, *French Law: A Comparative Approach* 68; Vranes, 'Constitutional Foundation of, and Limitations to, EU Integration in France' 539; *Spain:* Ahumada Ruiz, 'The Spanish Constitutional Court' 611; Alaez Corral and Arias Castaño, 'The Role of the Spanish Constitutional Court in the Judicial Review of Parliamentary Legislation' 599; *And Poland:* De Visser, *Constitutional Review in Europe: A Comparative Analysis* 260; Kowalik-Bańczyk, 'Should We Polish It Up? The Polish Constitutional Tribunal and the Idea of Supremacy of EU Law' 1361.
43. Claes, 'National Idenity: Trump Card or up for Negotiation?' 116; Wendel, 'Lisbon Before the Courts: Comparative Perspectives' 131.
44. De Visser, *Constitutional Review in Europe: A Comparative Analysis* 214.
45. Hailbronner and Martini, 'The German Federal Constitutional Court' 366.
46. Ahumada Ruiz, 'The Spanish Constitutional Court' 616; Garoupa, Gomez-Pomar and Grembi, 'Judging under Political Pressure: An Empirical Analysis of Constitutional Review Voting in the Spanish Constitutional Court' 517.

President of the French Senate appoint the nine members of the *Conseil Constitutionnel*.[47] However, judges do not have to be qualified lawyers, which reflects the institution's original advisory role.[48] Finally, Polish constitutional judges are elected by a simple majority in the Polish Sejm and subsequently appointed by the Polish President.[49] The judges have to be legally qualified with a considerable working experience in the legal profession.[50] The lower majority requirement as well as the lacking institutional diversification therefore concentrate the prerogative to nominate constitutional judges in the parliamentary governing majority. Although the strong role of the Sejm in the appointment of constitutional judges is counterbalanced by the mentioned qualification requirement, the Polish developments since 2015 illustrate the central importance of institutional diversification, higher majority thresholds, but also a cross-party dialogue on the nomination of constitutional judges. Otherwise, constitutional courts risk being captured between opposing political interests, as visible in Poland.[51]

Clearly, the internal constitutional problems in Poland have implications for the EU. On the one hand, the jurisprudence of constitutional judges impacts EU law and EU integration. Through their jurisprudence, national constitutional courts ensure that EU law enjoys constitutional authority, which complements the political authority that national parliaments vest in EU law by ratifying the EU-Treaties. In case national constitutional courts cannot exercise constitutional review independently, EU law can arguably not acquire full constitutional authority. On the other hand, the interferences with the composition of the national constitutional court reflect a broader rule-of-law problem. However, EU law in general and Eurozone cooperation, in particular, are based on *legal* safeguards. This is apparent for example in the EU balanced budget rules, as the Fiscal Compact specifically requires Member States to implement them into constitutional law - or a source equally effective - in order to create legal safeguards against the violation of Eurozone rules.[52] Consequently, such a potential rule-of-law crisis in a Eurozone Member State could cast doubts regarding the credibility of the Eurozone and negatively affect all other Member States.

Considering the constitutional review of EU law, it was outlined that such national constitutional review will be, most likely, initiated by privileged applicants and will either take the form of an abstract *ex ante* review (mostly the case in France and Spain) or an abstract *ex post* review (mostly the case in Germany and Poland). Suffice it here to point out that the advantages of an *ex ante* review are most visible in France - and the flexible Finnish system - where the constitution-amending legislator overcame the incompatibility between envisaged EU commitments and the French

47. John Bell, 'Court Institutions' in John Bell, Sophie Boyron and Simon Whittaker (eds), *Principles of French Law* (2nd edn, Oxford University Press 2008) 42.
48. *Ibid.*, 42.
49. De Visser, *Constitutional Review in Europe: A Comparative Analysis* 207.
50. *Ibid.*, 212.
51. Sadurski, 'Polish Constitutional Tribunal under PiS: From an Activist Court, to a Paralysed Tribunal, to a Governmental Enabler' 65-66; Castillo-Ortiz, 'The Illiberal Abuse of Constitutional Courts in Europe' 57.
52. Tuori and Tuori, *The Eurozone Crisis: A Constitutional Analysis* 241-243.

Constitution by modifying the constitutional text so that a conflict would not materialize in the first place.[53] The possible problems that could emerge from an *ex post* unconstitutional verdict against EU law are well visible in Germany, where such a decision from the Court in Karlsruhe risks destabilizing the Euro.[54] In addition, the criticized double standard employed by the German Constitutional Court in EU matters renders proceedings against EU law more likely.[55] For EU fiscal integration measures, this entails that the constitutional status and the ability to challenge such measures depend on the national system.

D IMPLICATIONS OF THE COMPARATIVE FINDINGS FOR EU FISCAL INTEGRATION

The comparison demonstrates that EU fiscal integration steps are not per definition unconstitutional. All four national constitutional actors recognize fiscal competences as important domestic sovereign powers, which require a high degree of democratic control. Therefore, the modalities and specific design of EU fiscal integration steps are crucial for the constitutional assessment. Particularly the German and the French jurisprudence place great importance on sufficient national parliamentary (or presidential) control of fiscal decisions, which suggests that conferring upon the EU an exclusive competence in fiscal matters would likely be declared incompatible with the national constitution. As highlighted on different occasions, this would prevent German participation in such far-reaching fiscal integration steps, in light of the *eternity clause*. Instead, coordination of this policy field seems more realistically achievable, whereby particular attention has to be paid to preserve the *right kind* and *right amount* of national decision-making capacity without rendering the coordination and collaboration ineffective. As long as national consent remains constitutive for any additional financial commitment, for example, and as long as the German Parliament is not liable for budgetary decisions taken by other EU Member States, such supranational cooperation seems also achievable under the rigid German Basic Law.

Given the importance of the concrete design of EU fiscal integration measures to determine their compatibility with the available national constitutional space, the subsequent PART II uses the framework developed so far and in particular the *charted* national constitutional space to assess several concrete proposals for deeper EU fiscal integration. Through this application the outlined comparative conclusions are further sharpened and the limiting potential of the respective national *constitutional identity limit* – but also more generally of more flexible and more rigid constitutional systems – in relation to EU fiscal integration steps is determined in broader detail.

53. Millet, 'Constitutional Identity in France: Vices and – Above All – Virtues' 139; Paris, 'France: The French System of Rights-Based Review – From Exceptionalism to Parochial Constitutionalism' 306.
54. Lang, 'Ultra Vires Review of the ECB's Policy of Quantitative Easing: An Analysis of the German Constitutional Court's Preliminary Reference Order in the PSPP Case' 936.
55. Calliess, 'Constitutional Identity in Germany: One for Three or Three in One?' 172; Gärditz, 'Beyond Symbolism: Towards a Constitutional Actio Popularis in EU Affairs? A Commentary on the OMT Decision of the Federal Constitutional Court' 192.

Part II
Testing the Charted National Constitutional Space

Introduction: The Constitutional Feasibility of EU Fiscal Integration Proposals

The Eurocrisis exposed the structural shortcomings in the design of the Euro. Although the precise root causes of this crisis remain disputed,[1] it is widely acknowledged that fundamental reforms are required in order to stabilize the Euro in the long run.[2] To that end, many proposals have already been submitted at the EU, national, academic and civil-societal levels since the beginning of the crisis. These proposals suggest a variety of EU reform steps, including further completing the Banking Union,[3] the establishment of a Capitals Market Union,[4] the initiation of a European Monetary Fund,[5] or even

1. Notably, the close relationship between public finances and the banking sector, cf. Lionello, *The Pursuit of Stability of the Euro Area as a Whole: The Reform of the European Economic Union and Perspectives of Fiscal Integration* 162; or, the lacking fiscal discipline and the weakened EU rules in that regard, cf. Craig and Markakis, 'EMU Reform' 1401; Lionello, *The Pursuit of Stability of the Euro Area as a Whole: The Reform of the European Economic Union and Perspectives of Fiscal Integration* 162; Ruffert, 'The Future of the European Economic and Monetary Union: Issues of Constitutional Law' 36; or, three economic trends identified as cause of the Eurocrisis, cf. Tuori and Tuori, *The Eurozone Crisis: A Constitutional Analysis* 61; or finally, the asymmetric Treaty design of the EMU, cf. Fabbrini, 'Fiscal Capacity' 107.
2. Craig and Markakis, 'EMU Reform' 1404; Ruffert, 'The Future of the European Economic and Monetary Union: Issues of Constitutional Law' 34; Dawson, Enderlein and Joerges, 'Introduction: The Governance of the Transformation of Europe's Economic, Political, and Constitutional Constellation Since the Euro-Crisis' 3.
3. Commission, *Reflection Paper on the Deepening of the Economic and Monetary Union* 19-20; Juncker et al., *The Five Presidents' Report: Completing Europe's Economic and Monetary Union* 4; European Commission, *Communication from the Commission to the European Parliament and the Council: A Roadmap Towards a Banking Union (COM (2012) 510)* (European Commission 2012).
4. Craig and Markakis, 'EMU Reform' 1434.
5. The initial proposals of the Commission: Commission Proposal for a Regulation of the European Parliament and of the Council on the establishment of a European Monetary Fund (COM (2017) 827); Commission, *Reflection Paper on the Deepening of the Economic and Monetary Union* 28; cf. as well: Craig and Markakis, 'EMU Reform' 1407; Editorial Comments, 'Editorial Comments: Tinkering with Economic and Monetary Union' (2018) 55 Common Market Law Review 1, 3-4.

the creation of a Political Union.[6] As substantiated, another widely discussed reform ambition is further EU fiscal integration.[7] Although these EU fiscal integration steps appear to be a vital reform component to build a stable, resilient single currency, their design and the required degree of integration remain politically contested.[8]

The political controversy around EU fiscal integration coincides with extensive legal-constitutional opposition. As revealed in PART I, national constitutional authorities appear to increasingly scrutinize EU measures that are linked to budgetary or fiscal policies,[9] which could seriously restrict the constitutional feasibility of the proposed fiscal integration steps. It results in a dilemma: EU fiscal integration is necessary to stabilize the Euro and yet constitutionally impossible to attain. Confronting this apparent dilemma, the following assessment determines the compatibility of a broad selection of EU fiscal integration proposals with the previously charted national constitutional space.

To facilitate this compatibility assessment, the subsequent section first maps the most authoritative and representative fiscal integration proposals to provide a nuanced outline of possible design options. The book determines the 'authority' of the proposals based on the actor that submitted them as well as their reception within the political and academic debate. In light of this litmus test, the analysis includes the various proposals submitted by the European Commission. This covers the 2015 EU Five Presidents' Report, the follow-up to the White Paper on the future of Europe as well as the Reflection Paper on the deepening of the EMU both published in 2017, the Budgetary Instrument for Convergence and Competitiveness (BICC) circulated in 2019,[10] the most recently adopted

6. As proposed by the Five Presidents' Report, cf. Juncker et al., *The Five Presidents' Report: Completing Europe's Economic and Monetary Union* 4, 17; cf. as well: Lionello, *The Pursuit of Stability of the Euro Area as a Whole: The Reform of the European Economic Union and Perspectives of Fiscal Integration* 226-227.
7. Commission, *Reflection Paper on the Deepening of the Economic and Monetary Union* 23-26; Juncker et al., *The Five Presidents' Report: Completing Europe's Economic and Monetary Union* 14-15; cf. as well: Fabbrini, 'Fiscal Capacity' 114-115, 125; Stefaan Van den Bogaert and Armin Cuyvers, 'Of Carrots and Sticks: What Direction to Take for Economic and Monetary Union?' in Bernard Steunenberg, Wim Voermans and Stefaan Van den Bogaert (eds), *Fit for the Future? Reflections From Leiden on the Functioning of the EU* (Eleven International Publishing 2016) 133; Miguel Poiares Maduro, 'Foreword: Fiscal Capacity and Constitutional Reform in the EMU' in Maurice Adams, Federico Fabbrini and Pierre Larouche (eds), *The Constitutionalization of European Budgetary Constraints* (Hart Publishing 2014) vi; Tuori and Tuori, *The Eurozone Crisis: A Constitutional Analysis* 255-256; Hinarejos, 'The Euro Area Crisis and Constitutional Limits to Fiscal Integration' 14.
8. Ruffert, 'The Future of the European Economic and Monetary Union: Issues of Constitutional Law' 65.
9. Claes, 'National Idenity: Trump Card or Up for Negotiation?' 110; Wendel, 'Lisbon Before the Courts: Comparative Perspectives' 125-128.
10. *See* the original proposal by the Commission: Commission Proposal for a Regulation of the European Parliament and of the Council on the Governance Framework for the Budgetary Instrument for Convergence and Competitiveness for the Euro Area (COM(2019) 354); which was encouraged and supported by Council and European Council, cf. Eurogroup, *Term Sheet on the Budgetary Instrument for Convergence and Competitiveness* (Eurogroup 2019); Euro Summit, *Statement of the Euro Summit, 14 December 2018 (EURO 503/18)* (General Secretariat of the Council 2018); cf. as well: Lionello, *The Pursuit of Stability of the Euro Area as a Whole: The Reform of the European Economic Union and Perspectives of Fiscal Integration* 185-186; Paul

NGEU,[11] as well as an early proposal on Eurobonds from 2011.[12] It should be recalled that NGEU does not qualify as a reform of the single currency. Nevertheless, the design choices made in this proposal illustrate how a feasible Eurozone financial capacity might be devised. Taken together, these proposals constitute a comprehensive and authoritative reform package for EU fiscal integration steps.

In addition to these Commission proposals, the assessment covers the Franco-German proposal on establishing a Eurozone-budget,[13] as well as the proposal of France and Germany that led to the adoption of NGEU.[14] Moreover, various proposals on Eurobonds, the proposal on establishing an 'automatic' investment budget for the Euroarea[15] and an early *Bruegel* proposal on the creation of a full-fledged Fiscal Union are included in the assessment.[16] Finally, several academic publications that evaluate these proposals and introduce their own ideas are incorporated to complement the assessment.[17] Combined, the various proposals, displayed in chronological order in Figure 1, offer a comprehensive overview of authoritative and innovative design options available for deeper EU fiscal integration.

Dermine, 'The Commission's December Package 18 Months Later' (2019) Maastricht Law – Faculty of Law Working Paper Series 7, 11-12.

11. As concluded by the European Council, cf. Council, *Conclusions Special Meeting of the European Council (17, 18, 19, 20 and 21 July 2020) – EUCO 10/20.*
12. European Commission, *Green Paper on the Feasibility of Introducing Stability Bonds (COM (2011) 818)* (European Commission 2011); subsequently considered in several publications, cf. Hans-Bernd Schäfer and Jochen Bigus, 'Consequences of Different Eurobonds Proposals' (2016) 12 Review of Law & Economics 523, 553; Alexandra Hild, Bernhard Herz and Christian Bauer, 'Structured Eurobonds: Limiting Liability and Distributing Profits' (2014) 52 Journal of Common Market Studies 250, 251.
13. Meeting, *Erklärung von Meseberg: Das Versprechen Europas für Sicherheit und Wohlstand erneuern*; cf. as well: Fabbrini, 'Fiscal Capacity' 122.
14. Bundeskanzlerin, *Press Release 173/20: A French-German Initiative for the European Recovery from the Coronavirus Crisis* (Presse- und Informationsamt der Bundesregierung 18 May 2020).
15. Jörg Bibow, 'Making the Euro Viable: The Euro Treasury Plan' (2015) Levy Economics Institute Working Paper Collection 2-4.
16. Benedicta Marzinotto, André Sapir and Guntram B. Wolff, 'What Kind of Fiscal Union? (2011)' Bruegel Policy Brief, https://www.bruegel.org/2011/11/what-kind-of-fiscal-union/, accessed 5 April 2023.
17. Lionello, *The Pursuit of Stability of the Euro Area as a Whole: The Reform of the European Economic Union and Perspectives of Fiscal Integration*; Craig and Markakis, 'EMU Reform'; Ruffert, 'The Future of the European Economic and Monetary Union: Issues of Constitutional Law'; Fabbrini, 'Fiscal Capacity'; Tuori and Tuori, *The Eurozone Crisis: A Constitutional Analysis*.

Figure 1 Chronological Overview of Assessed EU Fiscal Integration Proposals

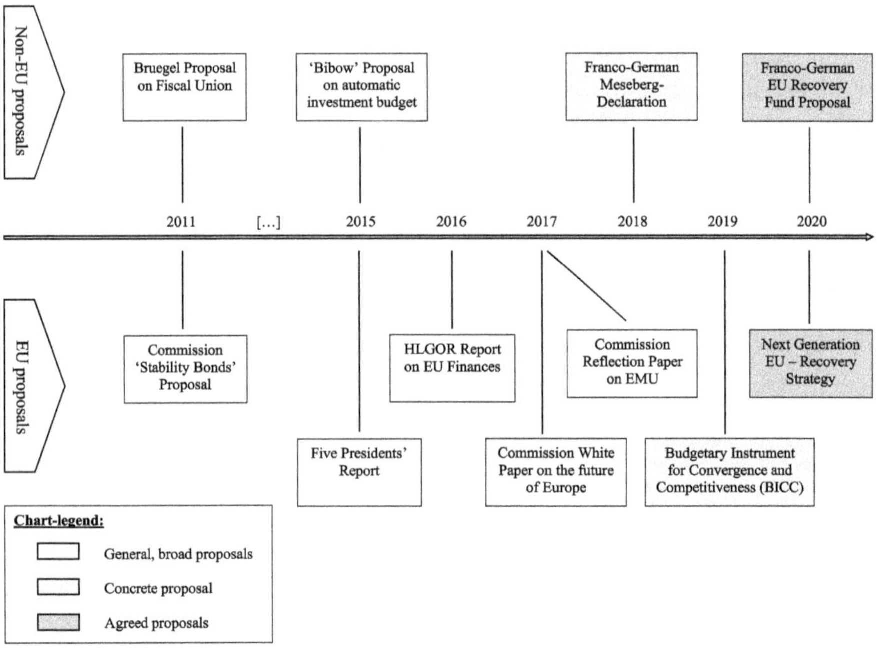

Given that a separate compatibility assessment of each proposal with the charted national constitutional space is not feasible, the book adopts an expedient two-fold functional approach. In the first step, all proposals are dismantled and organized into four substantive *reform elements*.[18] These four elements are the creation of a Eurozone fiscal capacity,[19] the financing options of potential additional EU expenditure,[20] the establishment of institutional capacities, most prominently a Eurozone Minister of Finance,[21] and the strengthened EU supervision over national budgeting.[22]

18. Building on a distinction employed here: Ruffert, 'The Future of the European Economic and Monetary Union: Issues of Constitutional Law' 48.
19. Commission, *Reflection Paper on the Deepening of the Economic and Monetary Union* 25-26; Juncker et al., *The Five Presidents' Report: Completing Europe's Economic and Monetary Union* 15; cf. as well: Fabbrini, 'Fiscal Capacity' 125; Tuori and Tuori, *The Eurozone Crisis: A Constitutional Analysis* 254.
20. To generate up to 3% of national GDP in EU revenue cf. Lionello, *The Pursuit of Stability of the Euro Area as a Whole: The Reform of the European Economic Union and Perspectives of Fiscal Integration* 182; Yves-Emmanuel Bara et al., 'A Contribution to the Work on the Strengthening of the Euro Area' (2017) Trésor-Economics 8.
21. Commission, *Reflection Paper on the Deepening of the Economic and Monetary Union* 23-26; European Commission, *Completing Europe's Economic and Monetary Union: A European Minister of Economy and Finance* (European Commission 2017); Juncker et al., *The Five Presidents' Report: Completing Europe's Economic and Monetary Union* 18.
22. Commission, *Reflection Paper on the Deepening of the Economic and Monetary Union* 23-26; Juncker et al., *The Five Presidents' Report: Completing Europe's Economic and Monetary Union* 9.

In the second step, the deconstructed proposals are subsequently differentiated based on the degree of *EU influence* or the intensity of *EU integration* they envisage. The apparent differences in the proposed intensity of supranational cooperation reflect the academic distinction between 'decentralized' and 'centralized' approaches to EMU-reforms. Following the strictest 'decentralized approach'[23] or the '*surveillance model*',[24] Member States retain control over fiscal decisions, no additional competences are conferred to EU level and the supranational level only has indirect influence by coordinating policy decisions. Based on these concepts, proposals that aim to retain responsibility for budgetary and fiscal decisions at the national level, and thereby largely preserve the current distribution of competences, are conceptualized as *coordination approaches* in the following. In contrast, proposals that follow a strict 'centralized approach'[25] or the '*classic fiscal federalism model*'[26] aim to assign core budgetary and fiscal competences to EU level. This implies greater administrative powers for EU institutions. These proposals entail the conferral of a considerable extent of competences to the EU and are labelled *integration approaches* subsequently.

Following the outlined two-fold functional approach, the identified EU fiscal integration proposals are deconstructed into the four core substantive elements as well as the degree of cooperation envisaged (Chapter VII), as visualized in Figure 2. The adopted distinction allows to then determine *what form* of EU fiscal integration is achievable within the previously charted national constitutional space – even beyond the directly assessed proposals (Chapter VIII). The assessment also explores whether the developed concept of *constitutional flexibility* could create additional constitutional space for EU fiscal integration in the analysed Member States as well as whether fiscal integration proposals could be re-conceptualized to better fit national constitutional concerns.

23. Lionello, *The Pursuit of Stability of the Euro Area as a Whole: The Reform of the European Economic Union and Perspectives of Fiscal Integration* 164.
24. Alicia Hinarejos, 'Fiscal Federalism in the European Union: Evolution and Future Choices for EMU' (2013) 50 Common Market Law Review 1621, 1634-1635; cf. as well: Armin Steinbach, 'Insurance-Type Cooperation Mechanisms under EU Law' (2017) 27 Swiss Review of International and European Law 19, 20.
25. Lionello, *The Pursuit of Stability of the Euro Area as a Whole: The Reform of the European Economic Union and Perspectives of Fiscal Integration* 164.
26. Steinbach, 'Insurance-Type Cooperation Mechanisms under EU Law' 20; Hinarejos, 'Fiscal Federalism in the European Union: Evolution and Future Choices for EMU' 1635-1636.

Figure 2 Visualization of the Two-Fold Functional Approach Employed to Organize Proposals

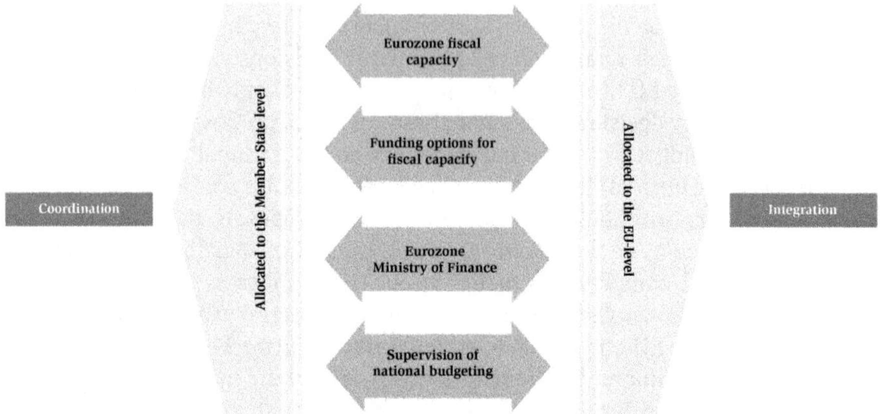

Chapter 7

Deconstructing EU Fiscal Integration Proposals

A INTRODUCTION

The subsequent section organizes the identified EU fiscal integration proposals into the four core substantive elements, which serve as the framework to structure and conduct the detailed comparative compatibility assessment subsequently. These are the creation of a Eurozone budgetary capacity (B), the introduction of new EU revenue sources (C), the establishment of an 'EU Ministry of Finance' – or more generally additional administrative or executive capacities at EU level (D) – as well as finally enhanced EU supervision over national fiscal decision-making (E). Within each substantive element, the proposed concrete ideas will be tentatively organized based on the envisaged extent of EU fiscal integration following the established linear distinction between 'cooperation' and 'integration' approaches.

B CREATING A EUROZONE FISCAL CAPACITY

The creation of a Eurozone fiscal capacity – which covers a range of design options varying from the creation of new EU fiscal emergency funds to the initiation of a full-fledged EMU budget to conduct fiscal and economic policy[1] – appears to constitute the most comprehensively discussed reform component of EU fiscal integration. The centrality of this component in the assessed proposals can be explained by two interrelated considerations. First, it appears that the design of the fiscal capacity necessarily determines the overall nature of EMU cooperation. Notably, the more fiscal powers Member States decide to attribute to the EU, the more the EU is replacing

1. Alessandro D'Alfonso and Andrej Stuchlik, *A Fiscal Capacity for the Euro Area?* (European Parliament 2016) 9-10.

national fiscal decisions with supranational political decision-making. Thus, additional Eurozone fiscal capacities could equip the EU with the power to determine fiscal policy-decisions, thereby directing national policy decisions in this area. Given the close link between the budget and national democracy as well as policy-making, the allocation of such fiscal capacities would shift the current power balance between both levels towards greater EU influence and in doing so modify the nature of EMU cooperation – and even EU integration as a whole. And second, the design of the fiscal capacity impacts all other substantive elements, too – including the required amount of revenue to finance it or the necessary EU institutional framework to administer it. Taken together, this suggests that the design of the fiscal capacity is not only a reform question of structural importance but it is also of central interest to the political and the national constitutional discourse given its possible implications for the future of EU cooperation altogether.

As to the specific design of a possible Eurozone fiscal capacity, the various proposals distinguish between two general options. The first option is to equip the Eurozone with an additional – possibly large – budget that could operate as a preventive tool to strive for economic cohesion across the Euroarea (I).[2] In the alternative, Member States could decide to establish additional emergency instruments in order to better support Member States impacted by asymmetric economic shocks (II).[3]

I Eurozone-Budget

Following the *integration approach* various reform proposals envisage the creation of a genuine Eurozone-budget.[4] Such a budget would operate on a continuous basis in parallel with or integrated into[5] the regular EU budget. According to most proposals, this budget would function as a tool geared towards stabilizing the Euro by fostering economic convergence and competitiveness across Member States.[6] This function corresponds to the fundamental requirements for optimum currency areas under

2. Lionello, *The Pursuit of Stability of the Euro Area as a Whole: The Reform of the European Economic Union and Perspectives of Fiscal Integration* 172.
3. Craig and Markakis, 'EMU Reform' 1420.
4. As envisaged by the EU Five Presidents' Report, the Meseberg Declaration, and the BICC, cf. Juncker et al., *The Five Presidents' Report: Completing Europe's Economic and Monetary Union* 15; Meeting, *Erklärung von Meseberg: Das Versprechen Europas für Sicherheit und Wohlstand erneuern*; Commission Proposal for a Regulation of the European Parliament and of the Council on the Governance Framework for the Budgetary Instrument for Convergence and Competitiveness for the Euro Area (COM(2019) 354); Eurogroup, *Term Sheet on the Budgetary Instrument for Convergence and Competitiveness*; Summit, *Statement of the Euro Summit, 14 December 2018 (EURO 503/18)*; as well as the Bruegel-proposal, cf. Marzinotto, Sapir and Wolff, 'What Kind of Fiscal Union? (2011)' 5, 7.
5. Schoeller, 'Preventing the Eurozone Budget: Issue Replacement and Small State Influence in EMU' 9-11; Dermine, 'The Commission's December Package 18 Months Later' 11-12.
6. Lionello, *The Pursuit of Stability of the Euro Area as a Whole: The Reform of the European Economic Union and Perspectives of Fiscal Integration* 184-185.

Mundell's economic theory.[7] The main objectives of the budget are to foster the economic and structural development of the Eurozone as well as social cohesion.

The Commission's BICC would, for example, fund 'reforms in product and labour markets, education, tax reforms, the development of capital markets, reforms to improve the business environment as well as investment in human capital and public administration reforms'.[8] According to the Commission's evaluation, these national reforms are likely to foster economic convergence by equally targeting broader EU objectives.[9] Similarly, the European Parliament advocated that a fiscal capacity should 'support growth and social cohesion addressing imbalances, structural divergences and financial emergencies which are directly connected to the monetary union'.[10] Thus, the envisaged Eurozone-budget would pursue both economic as well as social objectives by allocating funds across Member States guided by the general objective to achieve convergence within the Eurozone.[11]

The Commission substantiated that such a Eurozone-budget would target in particular national reforms that increase the competitiveness of the national economy and that equally have a positive 'spill-over effect' for other Eurozone economies.[12] When considering the required size of the Eurozone-budget, the different proposals suggest a minimum budget of around 1%-3% of the Eurozone-GDP to be fully effective.[13] In light of this considerable financial volume and the potentially wide discretion enjoyed by the EU when allocating the available funds, various proposals envision enhanced democratic legitimacy at the supranational level by, for example, including national parliaments in the decision-making.[14]

Finally, the proposals consider different legal bases to establish the budget. Based on previous instruments, a Eurozone-budget intended to fund structural reforms could

---

7. Jager and Hafner, 'The Optimum Currency Area Theory and the EMU: An Assessment in the Context of the Eurozone Crisis' 316; Eichengreen, *European Monetary Unification: Theory, Practice, and Analysis* 51-52.
8. European Commission, *Communication from the Commission to the European Parliament, the European Council, the Council, the European Economic and Social Committee and the Committee of the Regions: A Modern Budget for a Union That Protects, Empowers and Defends the Multiannual Financial Framework for 2021-2027 (COM (2018) 321)* (European Commission 2018) 10.
9. Lionello, *The Pursuit of Stability of the Euro Area as a Whole: The Reform of the European Economic Union and Perspectives of Fiscal Integration* 180-181.
10. European Parliament Resolution of 20 November 2012 with Recommendations to the Commission on the Report of the Presidents of the European Council, the European Commission, the European Central Bank and the Eurogroup 'Towards a Genuine Economic and Monetary Union' (2012/2151(INI)) (2012) para. 11.
11. Craig and Markakis, 'EMU Reform' 1415, 1418; Lionello, *The Pursuit of Stability of the Euro Area as a Whole: The Reform of the European Economic Union and Perspectives of Fiscal Integration* 182.
12. Commission, *Communication from the Commission to the European Parliament, the European Council, the Council, the European Economic and Social Committee and the Committee of the Regions: A Modern Budget for a Union That Protects, Empowers and Defends the Multiannual Financial Framework for 2021-2027 (COM (2018) 321)* 10.
13. Lionello, *The Pursuit of Stability of the Euro Area as a Whole: The Reform of the European Economic Union and Perspectives of Fiscal Integration* 182; Craig and Markakis, 'EMU Reform' 1423; Bara et al., 'A Contribution to the Work on the Strengthening of the Euro Area' 8.
14. Puntscher Riekmann and Wydra, 'Representation in the European State of Emergency: Parliaments Against Governments?' 567.

possibly be based on Article 175(3) TFEU.[15] Other proposals suggest the possible use of Article 136(1) TFEU,[16] the initiation of a budgetary capacity following enhanced cooperation[17] or even an intergovernmental solution. In addition, Treaty-based solutions would likely be tied to the EU's own resources decision in the sense of Article 311 TFEU to generate the required revenue. In the alternative, Member States could equally decide to allocate additional competences to EU level and establish a specific framework including the creation of new legal bases for a Eurozone-budget, which would, however, require Treaty amendment.

II Emergency Budgetary Instruments

An additional idea is the introduction of a temporary budgetary instrument connected to a specific purpose, such as to stabilize public investments in times of asymmetric shocks[18] or to support Member States in the payment of unemployment benefits in economic downturns to free fiscal space for investments.[19] The latter could replace the recently enacted Support to mitigate Unemployment Risks in an Emergency (SURE) scheme, under which the EU issues on a temporary basis loans to the Member States.[20] These temporary instruments are envisaged as emergency mechanisms and follow a more *coordination approach*, given that EU intervention remains only secondary to the primary competence of the Member States.[21]

The underlying idea of such emergency instruments is that Member States tend to cut public investment in case of economic shocks, which renders the domestic recovery process lengthy, and which has adverse consequences for the Eurozone. Hence, financing public investments at a fixed level in case of an economic downturn could speed up national – and EU – recovery efforts.[22] Similarly, exploding unemployment costs during economic shocks puts pressure on public finances. Through temporary support in the financing of unemployment costs important national fiscal space could be freed to guarantee that public investments are maintained despite the economic downturn.[23] Hence, both proposed instruments would operate on a demand-basis

15. The legal basis for Regulation 2015/1072, under which, *inter alia*, strategic investments are financed.
16. Lionello, *The Pursuit of Stability of the Euro Area as a Whole: The Reform of the European Economic Union and Perspectives of Fiscal Integration* 205-206.
17. Fabbrini, *Economic Governance in Europe: Comparative Paradoxes and Constitutional Challenges* 169.
18. Juncker et al., *The Five Presidents' Report: Completing Europe's Economic and Monetary Union* 15; cf. as well: Comments, 'Editorial Comments: Tinkering with Economic and Monetary Union' 6.
19. Commission, *Reflection Paper on the Deepening of the Economic and Monetary Union* 26.
20. László Andor, 'SURE: EU Capacity for Stabilising Employment and Incomes in the Pandemic' (2020) 55 Intereconomics – Review of European Economic Policy 139, 139.
21. Lionello, *The Pursuit of Stability of the Euro Area as a Whole: The Reform of the European Economic Union and Perspectives of Fiscal Integration* 164.
22. Commission, *Reflection Paper on the Deepening of the Economic and Monetary Union* 25; cf. as well: Fabbrini, 'Fiscal Capacity' 118.
23. Commission, *Reflection Paper on the Deepening of the Economic and Monetary Union* 25; cf. as well: Craig and Markakis, 'EMU Reform' 1426.

mainly intended to smoothen the consequences of an economic shock, thereby preventing economic distress in the Eurozone. Contrary to a Eurozone-budget, such emergency instruments would neither have the intention nor the ability to finance national structural reforms. Instead, they support a speedier recovery after asymmetric shocks within the Eurozone and address potential contagious effects.

According to the considered proposals, the possible legal bases for establishing temporary budgetary instruments are Article 175(3) TFEU, which is employed for the Recovery and Resilience Facility under NGEU.[24] Similarly, more limited budgetary instruments, such as the proposed Investment Stabilization Fund, could be based on Article 175(3) TFEU,[25] or Article 122(2) TFEU.[26] In both cases, the precise modalities, the funding eligibility and the procedural steps would be established within a secondary act, which has to be adopted following the ordinary legislative procedure.

An additional, intermediate proposal that combines the idea of a Eurozone-budget and emergency instruments was submitted by Jörg Bibow. Bibow proposed the introduction of an automatic investment budget to stabilize Eurozone investments in the long run. According to this proposal, Member States would initially agree on the annual volume of Eurozone investments and a desired growth rate. Subsequently, the investment budget runs 'automatically' without being subject to political discussions.[27] The required budget would be funded by common debt, which is invested in a shared EU future. The fund would thus operate on a permanent basis and require the pre-determination of major political decisions by national parliaments to guarantee the 'automatic' functioning of the budget subsequently as well as the commitment of considerable funds to finance Member States' public investment through such EU-based scheme.[28] Obviously, this would result in greater supranational powers albeit in a very limited framework, as the proposal would deliberately not involve the conferral of political discretion on spending to EU level. Bibow pointed out that such an automatized investment stabilization budget would ensure that structural investments are secured over time, which could enhance economic performance and convergence. Automatized investments would similarly escape the debate on democratic legitimacy, as such a budget would run on 'auto-pilot'.[29] Yet, it can be submitted that this 'auto-pilot' would ultimately not render its function less democratically contentious, as national parliaments would effectively be stripped of their prerogatives to determine how national funds are allocated.

24. Commission Proposal for a Regulation of the European Parliament and of the Council establishing a Recovery and Resilience Facility (COM(2020) 408).
25. Which was, for example, also employed as legal basis to adopt Regulation 2015/1072 on the European Fund for Strategic Investments, the European Investment Advisory Hub and the European Investment Project Portal and amending Regulations (EU) No 1291/2013 and (EU) No. 1316/2013, cf. Fabbrini, 'Fiscal Capacity' 126-127.
26. Which constitutes the legal basis for the EFSM, cf. Council Regulation 407/2010 establishing a EFSM.
27. Bibow, 'Making the Euro Viable: The Euro Treasury Plan' 4.
28. *Ibid.*, 4.
29. *Ibid.*

C FUNDING OPTIONS FOR FISCAL INTEGRATION

The design of any EU fiscal capacity determines the EU's financial needs. Notably, a permanent Eurozone-budget through which the EU allocates grants would require a stable, reliable revenue stream. In contrast, the proposed emergency instruments would depend to a lesser extent on continuous revenue and could operate under, for example, the ESM financing structure which combines a small amount of paid-in capital with a larger amount of callable capital.[30] Hence, in order to determine possible funding sources (II), it appears essential to tentatively establish the financing need of a Eurozone-budget or an emergency instrument (I).

I The Required Funding

It was already pointed out that the proposals aiming at creating a permanent Eurozone-budget envisage a minimum size of 1 %-3 % of the Eurozone-GDP to be fully effective.[31] Based on data from 2019, prior to COVID-19, this commitment would translate into an annual Eurozone budget of around EUR 115 to 343 billion.[32] This would constitute a significant increase of the EU's fiscal capacities as can be seen in comparison to the EU's regular budget. Notably, the MFF for the period of 2021 to 2027 has a volume of EUR 1,074 billion[33] whereas the envisaged Eurozone-budget would amount to an additional EUR 805 billion to up to EUR 2,401 billion in the same timeframe. Comparing these absolute numbers, it suggests a major increase in the EU's financial capacity would be required and it remains questionable whether Member States would agree to allocate these additional financial means to the EU. This reluctance was reflected in the BICC which was projected to have a size of EUR 25 billion for the period of 2021 to 2027.[34] Obviously, this constitutes only a fraction of the required financial firepower and indicates the limited political willingness across the Eurozone to establish a significant EU budget. Although one could submit that establishing such a budget with limited financial means, could be a stepping stone towards a more substantial

30. On the ESM financing structure, cf. Tuori and Tuori, *The Eurozone Crisis: A Constitutional Analysis* 95; Lastra and Louis, 'European Economic and Monetary Union: History, Trends, and Prospects' 104.
31. Lionello, *The Pursuit of Stability of the Euro Area as a Whole: The Reform of the European Economic Union and Perspectives of Fiscal Integration* 182; Craig and Markakis, 'EMU Reform' 1423; Bara et al., 'A Contribution to the Work on the Strengthening of the Euro Area' 8.
32. According to The World Bank, 'GDP (Current US$): Euro Area' (*The World Bank,* 2020), https://data.worldbank.org/indicator/NY.GDP.MKTP.CD?end = 2019&locations = XC&start = 2006&view = chart, accessed 5 April 2023; other proposals envisaged an annual budget of EUR 90 billion based on data from 2011, cf. Marzinotto, Sapir and Wolff, 'What Kind of Fiscal Union? (2011)' 7.
33. Council, *Conclusions Special Meeting of the European Council (17, 18, 19, 20 and 21 July 2020): EUCO 10/20* 7.
34. Cf. the European Commission's proposal on the MFF: Commission, *Communication from the Commission to the European Parliament, the European Council, the Council, the European Economic and Social Committee and the Committee of the Regions: A Modern Budget for a Union That Protects, Empowers and Defends the Multiannual Financial Framework for 2021-2027 (COM (2018) 321)* 10; cf. Fabbrini, 'Fiscal Capacity' 118.

Eurozone-budget,[35] it remains questionable whether the apparent political deadlock towards establishing more substantial financial EU means can be overcome.[36]

Different to a permanently operating Eurozone-budget, the proposed specialized temporary budgetary instruments would only be triggered in case of asymmetric economic shocks.[37] Therefore, their financing needs and funding structures are different to the ones of a permanent budget. Concretely, the Commission proposed that the envisaged European Investment Stabilization Function could operate through back-to-back loans guaranteed by the EU budget.[38] According to the Commission, such European Investment Stabilization Function could provide loans of up to EUR 30 billion between 2021 and 2027.[39] Given that these EUR 30 billion would be guaranteed through the existing EU budget no direct additional financial commitments would arise for the Member States. However, it seems questionable whether the Function is equipped to support larger Member States. The German share of public investments in the federal budget in 2019, for example, by itself already amounted to almost EUR 39 billion in a single year,[40] which would clearly overburden the envisaged scheme. Therefore, it has to be questioned whether the proposed funding is sufficient to stabilize the Euro.[41] In addition, the Commission also proposed to support Member States through an interest rate subsidy in order to free fiscal space in the national budget, which could be financed by contributions of all Eurozone Member States.[42]

Taken together, this illustrates that the initiation of a Eurozone-budget would require a considerable financial commitment from the Member States. A budget of up to 3% of GDP for the Eurozone alone triples the budgetary capacities available at EU level and presupposes a stable revenue stream. In contrast, the proposed emergency tools would largely operate on a loan-basis, which implies that the EU financial commitment is paid back by the recipient Member State. The other Member States

35. Lionello, *The Pursuit of Stability of the Euro Area as a Whole: The Reform of the European Economic Union and Perspectives of Fiscal Integration* 182.
36. Schoeller, 'Preventing the Eurozone Budget: Issue Replacement and Small State Influence in EMU' 11-12.
37. Fabbrini, 'Fiscal Capacity' 115; Comments, 'Editorial Comments: Tinkering with Economic and Monetary Union' 6.
38. Commission, *Communication from the Commission to the European Parliament, the European Council, the Council, the European Economic and Social Committee and the Committee of the Regions: A Modern Budget for a Union That Protects, Empowers and Defends the Multiannual Financial Framework for 2021-2027 (COM (2018) 321)* 11; cf. as well: Craig and Markakis, 'EMU Reform' 1426.
39. Commission, *Communication from the Commission to the European Parliament, the European Council, the Council, the European Economic and Social Committee and the Committee of the Regions: A Modern Budget for a Union That Protects, Empowers and Defends the Multiannual Financial Framework for 2021-2027 (COM (2018) 321)* 11; cf. as well: Fabbrini, 'Fiscal Capacity' 118.
40. German Federal Ministry of Finance, *Bundeshaushalt 2019* (German Government 2019) 18.
41. Lionello, *The Pursuit of Stability of the Euro Area as a Whole: The Reform of the European Economic Union and Perspectives of Fiscal Integration* 217.
42. Commission, *Communication from the Commission to the European Parliament, the European Council, the Council, the European Economic and Social Committee and the Committee of the Regions: A Modern Budget for a Union That Protects, Empowers and Defends the Multiannual Financial Framework for 2021-2027 (COM (2018) 321)* 11; cf. as well: Craig and Markakis, 'EMU Reform' 1426.

would then mostly guarantee the loans, for example, by increased own resources ceilings, and therefore carry the risk of default.

II Funding Sources

If a budgetary capacity is created, the question of funding emerges. To that end, several options are discussed, which include the establishment of new EU own resources, the possibility of introducing genuine EU taxation, increased contributions by the Member States, the allocation of additional funds by the Member States as externally assigned revenues, as well as EU debts or joint liabilities.[43] These options will be considered below both as to their legal design and their potential maximum financing ability, distinguishing between Treaty-based solutions (1) and options beyond the current Treaty-framework (2).

1 Treaty-Based Funding Sources

According to various proposals, the first possibility is to increase the EU's own resources in order to finance a budgetary capacity for the Eurozone. This could be achieved by increasing the own resources ceilings established by the Council Decision on the system of own resources[44] established under Article 311(3) TFEU and the corresponding outline of the use of the additional funding through a Council regulation based on Article 312(2) TFEU.[45] In light of the current composition of the EU's own resources, such an increase would presumably lead to higher contributions from the Member States in order to 'top up' the difference between the own resource ceiling and the resources generated from other sources, including the traditional own resources and the VAT-based component.[46]

When negotiating a new Council Decision on the system of the EU's own resources, the higher national contributions could be limited to Eurozone Member States by either setting two sets of own resource ceilings distinguishing between Eurozone and non-Eurozone Member States or by otherwise allocating specific rebates to the non-Eurozone Member States in order to secure the required unanimous support. Yet, such higher national contributions would reinforce the political debate on 'just return' for the Member States.[47] In the alternative, Member States could establish a new source of traditional own resources, for example, by introducing a financial

43. Ruffert, 'The Future of the European Economic and Monetary Union: Issues of Constitutional Law' 49-51.
44. Cf. Council Decision 2014/335; cf. as well: *ibid.*, 51.
45. Richard Crowe, 'The European Budgetary Galaxy' (2017) 13 European Constitutional Law Review 428, 437.
46. Identified as less favourable option given the political tensions that might arise, as national contributions are seen as a 'zero-sum game', cf. Monti et al., *Future Financing of the EU: Final Report and Recommendations of the High Level Group on Own Resources December 2016* 68.
47. Ruffert, 'The Future of the European Economic and Monetary Union: Issues of Constitutional Law' 50; Alcidi and Gros, 'Next Generation EU: A Large Common Response to the COVID-19 Crisis' 203.

transaction tax and allocating the revenue to the scheme of own resources.[48] Hence, the Member States would establish the tax at the national level, levy it and then attribute it to the EU based on Article 311 TFEU. Following the model of the traditional own resources, such revenue is not introduced into the national budgetary process but instead transferred to the EU, which limits the involvement of national parliaments.[49]

An alternative, which would also be based on the current framework, could be to agree on additional national contributions that are not directly injected into the EU's budget as own resources but rather as targeted externally assigned revenue in the sense of Article 21 Financial Regulation (EU, Euratom) 1046/2018.[50] Such externally assigned revenues are independent of the EU budget adopted according to Article 314 TFEU and constitute a commitment of the Member State to fund specific EU activities.[51] Given their voluntary character, Member States could commit in an intergovernmental agreement to the payment of externally assigned revenue and thereby render the inflow of financial resources more predictable.[52]

Further options are EU borrowing and EU debts as recently exemplified by NGEU. Following the European Council's conclusions, the Commission would borrow money on the financial markets and issue EU debts on behalf of the EU, which are subsequently serviced by either the re-payment of the loans by the recipient Member States, possible interest rate gains or, as a final option, through increased contributions by the Member States under the own-resources system guaranteed by higher national ceilings.[53] However, the EU's borrowing power is strictly confined by the mandate spelt out in both the European Council Conclusions and subsequently in the amended Own Resources Decision, which both require unanimous support and even national approval.[54] This implies that the EU cannot engage autonomously in such borrowing activities, as the principle of equilibrium of budgeting requires that any possible EU liability is guaranteed, for example, by increased own resources ceilings.[55]

All three funding options have in common that they crucially and continuously depend on national (parliamentary) approval. Notably, the own resources decision is traditionally amended with the MFF Regulation every seven years. Hence, Member States can alter their financial commitments, which renders the revenue inflow uncertain in the longer run. This is particularly the case in case the budgetary capacity requires direct contributions of Member States, as these are financed through the general budget of the Member States. At the same time, given the flexible character of these Treaty-based funding options, their funding potential is relatively big as long as

48. Lionello, *The Pursuit of Stability of the Euro Area as a Whole: The Reform of the European Economic Union and Perspectives of Fiscal Integration* 205.
49. Crowe, 'The European Budgetary Galaxy' 431.
50. Fabbrini, 'Fiscal Capacity' 127-128.
51. Crowe, 'The European Budgetary Galaxy' 441.
52. Fabbrini, 'Fiscal Capacity' 127-128.
53. Council, *Conclusions Special Meeting of the European Council (17, 18, 19, 20 and 21 July 2020): EUCO 10/20* 2-3.
54. Lionello, *The Pursuit of Stability of the Euro Area as a Whole: The Reform of the European Economic Union and Perspectives of Fiscal Integration* 205; European Union, *European Union Public Finance* (Publications Office of the European Union 2014) 131-132.
55. Union, *European Union Public Finance* 159-160, 282.

the Member States reach a (political) agreement on committing a sizeable amount of money.

2 *Extending the Current Treaty-Framework*

In addition, the proposals also suggest the creation of more autonomous revenue streams for the EU which would extend the currently available Treaty-framework. One suggestion is to equip the EU directly with a (limited) taxation competence.[56] Accordingly, the EU would be able to determine the level of taxation in a specific area, possibly in relation to the activities of the EU. Different to proposals building on the existing own resources framework, for example, put forward by the Monti-Report, following which Member States would be in charge of enacting a tax and would then transfer the revenue generated from that tax to EU level,[57] equipping the EU with a genuine taxation power would entail that the tax and the modalities attached to it are determined by the EU autonomously. In the first place, this would, however, require EU Treaty-change, as the current Treaties do not grant the EU the power to tax and it would subsequently trigger serious democratic concerns, as the power to tax traditionally presupposes a high degree of democratic legitimacy.[58] As long as the EU lacks the required democratic capacity, allocating genuine taxation power to EU level might trigger considerable national constitutional concerns, as will be assessed.[59] Practically speaking, a genuine EU taxation power would make the revenue of the EU less dependent on the Member States.

In addition, some proposals submit that the fiscal capacity could be financed through shared liabilities or EU debts, possibly in the shape of Eurobonds.[60] The underpinning idea is that the Member States would either directly or through the EU issue EU bonds which could partially finance the EU financial deficit. Given the beneficial credit rating of the EU, Member States would likely have to reserve less money for servicing the debts thereby freeing up fiscal space. This would entail that Member States jointly guarantee the entire or at least parts of the national debt, which

56. Monti et al., *Future Financing of the EU: Final Report and Recommendations of the High Level Group on Own Resources December 2016* 68; Marzinotto, Sapir and Wolff, 'What Kind of Fiscal Union? (2011)' 5.
57. Monti et al., *Future Financing of the EU: Final Report and Recommendations of the High Level Group on Own Resources December 2016* 68.
58. Jussi Jaakkola, 'A Democratic Dilemma of European Power to Tax: Reconstructing the Symbiosis Between Taxation and Democracy Beyond the State?' (2019) 20 German Law Journal 660, 663; Fabbrini, 'Fiscal Capacity' 131; under the current Treaties, the EU has no 'fiscal rights', cf. Lionello, *The Pursuit of Stability of the Euro Area as a Whole: The Reform of the European Economic Union and Perspectives of Fiscal Integration* 202-203.
59. Lionello, *The Pursuit of Stability of the Euro Area as a Whole: The Reform of the European Economic Union and Perspectives of Fiscal Integration* 204.
60. Commission, *Green Paper on the Feasibility of Introducing Stability Bonds (COM (2011) 818)*; cf. as well: Hild, Herz and Bauer, 'Structured Eurobonds: Limiting Liability and Distributing Profits' 252; Franz C. Mayer and Christian Heidfeld, 'Verfassungs- und europarechtliche Aspekte der Einführung von Eurobonds' (2012) 65 Neue Juristische Wochenschrift (NJW) 422, 422-423; Hanno Beck and Dirk Wentzel, 'Eurobonds: Wunderwaffe oder Sprengsatz für die Europäische Union?' (2011) 91 Wirtschaftsdienst – Zeitschrift für Wirtschaftspolitik 717, 720-721.

arguably involves a liability risk for national budgets. Hence, Eurobonds would primarily facilitate access to the financial markets for the Member States, without however generating direct revenue for the EU itself. Yet, the EU could also be empowered to issue Eurobonds to finance an EU budgetary capacity, ultimately resulting in EU debts. Regarding the issuing of EU debts, the current Treaties establish the principle of equilibrium or the principle of balance of payments in Article 310(1)(3) TFEU, which requires that the revenue and expenditure of the EU are balanced.[61] Although this suggests the potential incompatibility of EU debts with EU law, the EU developed a system under which the Commission can borrow money on the financial markets and subsequently lend it to other countries in order to achieve wider Union objectives. Examples are the Balance of Payments Facility, which grants financial assistance to Member States outside the Eurozone that experience difficulties in the balance of their current payments,[62] and the European Financial Stabilization Mechanism (EFSM), which grants loans under strict conditions to Member States that are affected by extraordinary circumstances in order to enhance their fiscal position,[63] or by providing budgetary guarantees to the European Investment Bank.[64] Hence, it illustrates that the EU is generally able to borrow money in order to loan it to different actors, including the Member States of the Eurozone. However, the current Treaty-framework requires that the EU finances remain balanced in the long run, which suggests that EU debts would have to be adequately secured by corresponding guarantees.

3 *Interim Conclusion on Possible Funding Sources*

Comparing the different funding options, the most far-reaching proposals envisage a genuine EU taxation competence independent from direct Member States' control, which would require Treaty-change and trigger major democratic concerns. On the other end of the spectrum, the proposed emergency instruments could operate based on EU borrowing which is guaranteed by the Member States, following the existing ESM-example. Given that these emergency instruments work on a loan-basis, the resulting debts would be re-paid. The collective of all Member States would, however, be liable in case of default. Other financing proposals are designed based on the existing EU framework surrounding the EU's own resources system. Taken together, the proposals identify a range of different financing schemes and funding options that could underpin the envisaged budgetary capacity or instruments. These raise a variety of constitutional concerns and face domestic legal hurdles as will be analysed.

61. Union, *European Union Public Finance* 159-160, 282.
62. *Ibid.*, 292-293.
63. *Ibid.*, 293-294.
64. *Ibid.*, 285.

D EU MINISTRY OF FINANCE: CREATING ADMINISTRATIVE-EXECUTIVE CAPACITY

The third substantive idea is the creation of an EU Minister of Finance or EU Treasury to better coordinate the existing powers in a single institution.[65] The core idea is an alteration of the current institutional framework in order to establish a central EU authority in charge of fiscal decision-making. Despite the fact that the envisaged institutional modifications could increase the EU-impact in these areas as a result of centralizing them in a single actor, these reform plans are comparably less controversial as they focus on institutional reforms and a re-shuffling of already conferred responsibilities without necessarily requiring the transfer of additional substantive competences. Nevertheless, the proposed introduction of such EU Treasury and the required institutional alterations are likely to trigger national constitutional concerns albeit depending on the precise institutional role assigned to it.

Considering the concrete proposals, the EU Five Presidents' Report encouraged the creation of a Euroarea Treasury which is projected to facilitate joint fiscal decision-making among Eurozone Member States, without however altering the existing division of competences between the national and EU level.[66] This suggests that the Treasury would mainly perform a coordinating function. The initial proposal was further fleshed out in the Commission's Reflection Paper on the EMU, which confirmed the idea to bundle the existing EU budgetary, economic and fiscal competences within the proposed Euroarea- Treasury.[67] In a subsequent Communication,[68] the Commission specified that an EU Minister of Finance could be appointed as Vice-President of the Commission, as President of the Eurogroup and as chair of the envisaged European Monetary Fund.[69] According to the Commission, such a Minister could enhance economic policy coordination, more effectively supervise the compliance with budgetary and fiscal benchmarks, overview the implementation of EU

65. Commission, *Completing Europe's Economic and Monetary Union: A European Minister of Economy and Finance*; Commission, *Reflection Paper on the Deepening of the Economic and Monetary Union* 27; Juncker et al., *The Five Presidents' Report: Completing Europe's Economic and Monetary Union* 14, 18; Marzinotto, Sapir and Wolff, 'What Kind of Fiscal Union? (2011)' 5; Ruffert, 'The Future of the European Economic and Monetary Union: Issues of Constitutional Law' 59-61.
66. Juncker et al., *The Five Presidents' Report: Completing Europe's Economic and Monetary Union* 14, 18; cf. as well: Lionello, *The Pursuit of Stability of the Euro Area as a Whole: The Reform of the European Economic Union and Perspectives of Fiscal Integration* 188; Ruffert, 'The Future of the European Economic and Monetary Union: Issues of Constitutional Law' 59-61.
67. Commission, *Reflection Paper on the Deepening of the Economic and Monetary Union* 28; cf. as well: Comments, 'Editorial Comments: Tinkering with Economic and Monetary Union' 8; Pilz, 'Ein Schatzamt für die Eurozone? – Überlegungen zu den Vorschlägen des Europäischen Parlaments und der Kommission zu einer Reform der Wirtschaftsunion' 638.
68. Commission, *Completing Europe's Economic and Monetary Union: A European Minister of Economy and Finance*.
69. Commission, *Reflection Paper on the Deepening of the Economic and Monetary Union* 27; cf. as well: Ruffert, 'The Future of the European Economic and Monetary Union: Issues of Constitutional Law' 61; Comments, 'Editorial Comments: Tinkering with Economic and Monetary Union' 8.

funding,[70] ensure global representation, as well as draft future fiscal policies for the Euroarea given the envisaged triple hatted institutional position.[71]

The Bruegel-proposal on reforming the EMU envisages an even stronger position for the EU Ministry of Finance, which should be elected by the European Parliament and the Council in Eurogroup formation.[72] To that end, it was even proposed to create a Eurozone Assembly, which could, for example, consist of four-fifths of national parliamentarians of Eurozone Member States and one-fifths of members of the European Parliament,[73] and which would continuously monitor EMU decision-making. The Bruegel-proposal furthermore envisaged that the Ministry could operate as a lender of last resort to illiquid but otherwise solvent Member States.[74] This presupposes a high degree of political authority and adequate fiscal abilities, which could be generated by the Ministry itself through an independent revenue power.[75] The authors submit that the Ministry would need emergency taxing competences of about 2% of GDP to cover potential losses resulting from loans granted to illiquid Eurozone Member States.[76] The proposal further advocates for a permanent, annual revenue of about 1% of Eurozone-GDP, which could be employed to create sufficient borrowing capacities at EU level to assist bigger Eurozone Member States.[77] And finally, the Ministry would be granted the power to veto national budget plans that are in conflict with EU fiscal rules.[78]

Nevertheless, the submitted ideas on creating a Eurozone Ministry of Finance remain relatively vague, which could stem from the highlighted central importance of the fiscal capacity's design, which will determine the required institutional capacities as well. From that perspective, the design and the institutional role of the Ministry inherently depend on the characteristics of the fiscal capacity. Nevertheless, two central design elements for the EU Ministry are discussed in the various proposals. Notably, the institutional position the Ministry would occupy within the EU institutional framework and the institutional powers that could be assigned to it, both trigger questions of EU law.

---

70. Pilz, 'Ein Schatzamt für die Eurozone? – Überlegungen zu den Vorschlägen des Europäischen Parlaments und der Kommission zu einer Reform der Wirtschaftsunion' 638.
71. Commission, *Reflection Paper on the Deepening of the Economic and Monetary Union* 27; cf. as well: Lionello, *The Pursuit of Stability of the Euro Area as a Whole: The Reform of the European Economic Union and Perspectives of Fiscal Integration* 189-190; Comments, 'Editorial Comments: Tinkering with Economic and Monetary Union' 8-9.
72. Marzinotto, Sapir and Wolff, 'What Kind of Fiscal Union? (2011)' 7; echoed by other proposals that intend to enhance legitimacy of the final decisions, cf. Ruffert, 'The Future of the European Economic and Monetary Union: Issues of Constitutional Law' 59-60.
73. Ruffert, 'The Future of the European Economic and Monetary Union: Issues of Constitutional Law' 59-60; Manifesto for the Democratization of Europe, *Draft Treaty on the Democratization of the Governance of the Euro Area ('T-Dem')* (2020) Article 4 (1); which might, however, require Treaty-change, cf. Lionello, *The Pursuit of Stability of the Euro Area as a Whole: The Reform of the European Economic Union and Perspectives of Fiscal Integration* 226.
74. Marzinotto, Sapir and Wolff, 'What Kind of Fiscal Union? (2011)' 5.
75. *Ibid.*, 5.
76. *Ibid.*, 7.
77. *Ibid.*, 7.
78. *Ibid.*, 6.

First, re-shuffling and re-organizing the existing institutional responsibilities to pool them in a central institutional actor arguably challenges the existing institutional balance established by the EU-Treaties. The envisaged EU Ministry could be entitled to exercise economic policies, supervise national budgeting, undertake fiscal decisions, chair decisions on financial assistance in the ESM[79] and potentially even administer its own budgetary capacity.[80] This illustrates that the EU Ministry would be a highly powerful institutional actor, which triggers legal concerns. In the first place, the current EU-Treaties do not establish a central institution such as the EU Ministry in charge of the Eurozone policies. Quite the contrary: even the existing, less far-reaching powers are distributed across different actors.[81] A re-shuffling of the existing allocation of responsibilities would inevitably affect the institutional balance established by the EU-Treaties, which could only be altered by explicit Treaty-change. This conclusion is confirmed by a systematic reading of the Treaties, as the office of the High Representative, which also wears a 'double hat' and has various institutional responsibilities and loyalties, is explicitly established.[82] When now creating a comparable double- or even triple-hatted position in EMU matters[83] it seems convincing to require an explicit recognition of the particular institutional position that the Minister would occupy.[84]

Second, the question of whether additional competences would be assigned to the envisaged Minister or the Ministry of Finance. It has been proposed to transfer additional competences, for example regarding the administration of the previously outlined budgetary capacity to the Minister, which could improve accountability and transparency, in light of the currently existing overlapping and unclear responsibilities.[85] The Minister could be, for example, accountable to either the European Parliament or a special chamber consisting of national and EU parliamentarians,[86] which would, however, equally require explicit Treaty recognition. If no such Treaty-change is initiated, a possible EU Minister of Finance would mainly facilitate the existing processes without however being conferred real decision-making powers. This would essentially continue the status quo, without altering the ultimate institutional responsibilities.

79. Commission, *Reflection Paper on the Deepening of the Economic and Monetary Union* 28; cf. as well: Comments, 'Editorial Comments: Tinkering with Economic and Monetary Union' 8.
80. Lionello, *The Pursuit of Stability of the Euro Area as a Whole: The Reform of the European Economic Union and Perspectives of Fiscal Integration* 189.
81. Pilz, 'Ein Schatzamt für die Eurozone? – Überlegungen zu den Vorschlägen des Europäischen Parlaments und der Kommission zu einer Reform der Wirtschaftsunion' 641.
82. Cf. Article 18 TEU; Ruffert, 'The Future of the European Economic and Monetary Union: Issues of Constitutional Law' 61.
83. Commission, *Reflection Paper on the Deepening of the Economic and Monetary Union* 27; Commission, *Completing Europe's Economic and Monetary Union: A European Minister of Economy and Finance*; cf. as well: Ruffert, 'The Future of the European Economic and Monetary Union: Issues of Constitutional Law' 61; Comments, 'Editorial Comments: Tinkering with Economic and Monetary Union' 8.
84. Comments, 'Editorial Comments: Tinkering with Economic and Monetary Union' 9.
85. Lionello, *The Pursuit of Stability of the Euro Area as a Whole: The Reform of the European Economic Union and Perspectives of Fiscal Integration* 190; Craig and Markakis, 'EMU Reform' 1441.
86. Ruffert, 'The Future of the European Economic and Monetary Union: Issues of Constitutional Law' 61, 64.

Overall, in case the Minister would be accorded additional (discretionary) competences, additional means of (national) control and supervision might be required. For example, by establishing a link with a parliamentary body, which could be either the European Parliament, a newly created chamber of national and EU parliamentarians, or directly with the national parliaments. Obviously, this would impact the entire institutional design of the EU and would therefore require a comprehensive Treaty-reform.[87] In addition, given that the Ministry would be located between the institutions, questions regarding the Minister's loyalty to other EU institutions as well as towards the Member States might be triggered, which should be explicitly clarified within the EU-Treaties.[88] Taken together this illustrates that the creation of this new institutional actor is of major relevance for the national constitutional debate, given that the Ministry might ultimately be empowered to take centralized fiscal decisions that impact national budgets, at least under the more ambitious integration proposals.

E ENHANCED SUPERVISION OF NATIONAL BUDGETING

Finally, various proposals envisage enhanced supervision of national budgeting to improve compliance with the existing EU fiscal rules, an area that became particularly relevant during the Eurocrisis which triggered the enactment of various measures. The introduced measures include the European Semester, which streamlines budgetary processes across the Eurozone,[89] the Macroeconomic Imbalance Procedure, which functions as an early-warning system for emerging economic problems,[90] as well as the Fiscal Compact, which requires Member States to implement the balanced budget rule into their constitutional order.[91] The main goal of this tightened fiscal supervision was to restore fiscal discipline across the Member States, as the previous approach based on market control and ineffective political supervision under the Stability and Growth Pact could not prevent excessive national public debts.[92] Consequently, the EU increased its supervision to complement the insufficient control exercised by the financial markets. As these measures were adopted at the height of the Eurocrisis, many rules create overlapping responsibilities and duties.[93] Therefore, various reform proposals advanced ideas on how to make the existing framework more coherent and how to enhance effective EU supervision over national budgeting.

To that end, the Five Presidents' Report proposed an enhanced supervision of national budgeting in order to render the European Semester more effective and to

87. Craig and Markakis, 'EMU Reform' 1441.
88. Comments, 'Editorial Comments: Tinkering with Economic and Monetary Union' 9.
89. Lastra and Louis, 'European Economic and Monetary Union: History, Trends, and Prospects' 121-122.
90. Fabbrini, 'Fiscal Capacity' 111; Tuori and Tuori, *The Eurozone Crisis: A Constitutional Analysis* 106-107; Marzinotto, Sapir and Wolff, 'What Kind of Fiscal Union? (2011)' 3.
91. Tuori and Tuori, *The Eurozone Crisis: A Constitutional Analysis* 109-110; Lastra and Louis, 'European Economic and Monetary Union: History, Trends, and Prospects' 124.
92. Lionello, *The Pursuit of Stability of the Euro Area as a Whole: The Reform of the European Economic Union and Perspectives of Fiscal Integration* 162-163.
93. Craig and Markakis, 'EMU Reform' 1441; Marzinotto, Sapir and Wolff, 'What Kind of Fiscal Union? (2011)' 3.

guarantee fiscal discipline in the Euroarea.[94] Concretely, the Report envisaged the creation of domestic 'Competitiveness Authorities' that evaluate the national economic development, which is then incorporated in the Commission's assessment in the framework of the European Semester.[95] In addition, the Report called for a more vigorous Macroeconomic Imbalance Procedure to target adverse national developments that could endanger the stability of the Euroarea at an early stage as well as for a stronger focus on the domestic labour market and social performance across the Member States.[96] More specifically, building upon the already existing enhanced supervision of national budgeting in the European Semester, the Report proposed the creation of an advisory European Fiscal Board which could stimulate a wider public debate and improve the coordination of budgeting across the Member States.[97]

An additional idea introduced by the Commission was that available EU funds should be increasingly linked with the country-specific recommendations of the European Semester,[98] an approach that was subsequently adopted in parts of the MFF 2014-2020. Hence, in order to maximize the benefits of EU supervision over national budgeting, a more integrated approach towards EU funding and the European Semester could be followed. This suggests that the Commission aims to make the existing framework more coherent and ensure that national parliaments have clear incentives to comply with existing EU fiscal rules.

The previously mentioned Bruegel-proposal even went one step further and proposed to give the EU a genuine veto power against unsustainable budgetary planning in the Member States and against budgets that are in conflict with the commonly agreed fiscal rules.[99] At the same time, it was submitted that the combination of market pressure exercised through the no-bailout clause and the requirements for national budgeting established in the Stability and Growth Pact should be paired with greater national responsibility to create ownership for the decisions within the Member States, following the approach of the Fiscal Compact.[100]

94. Juncker et al., *The Five Presidents' Report: Completing Europe's Economic and Monetary Union* 8; and reiterated, cf. Commission, *Reflection Paper on the Deepening of the Economic and Monetary Union* 24; cf. as well: Ruffert, 'The Future of the European Economic and Monetary Union: Issues of Constitutional Law' 55.
95. Juncker et al., *The Five Presidents' Report: Completing Europe's Economic and Monetary Union* 8; cf. as well: Lionello, *The Pursuit of Stability of the Euro Area as a Whole: The Reform of the European Economic Union and Perspectives of Fiscal Integration* 169-170.
96. Juncker et al., *The Five Presidents' Report: Completing Europe's Economic and Monetary Union* 8.
97. The European Fiscal Board was created in 2015 by a decision of the European Commission, cf. Commission Decision on Establishing an Independent Advisory European Fiscal Board (COM 2015/1937); cf. as well: Frédéric Allemand, 'European Economic Constitution: From Soft to Hard Policy Coordination?' in Herwig C.H. Hofmann, Katerina Pantazatou and Giovanni Zaccaroni (eds), *The Metamorphosis of the European Economic Constitution* (Edward Elgar Publishing Limited 2019) 100.
98. Commission, *Reflection Paper on the Deepening of the Economic and Monetary Union* 24-25; Marzinotto, Sapir and Wolff, 'What Kind of Fiscal Union? (2011)' 6.
99. Marzinotto, Sapir and Wolff, 'What Kind of Fiscal Union? (2011)' 6; c. as well: Lionello, *The Pursuit of Stability of the Euro Area as a Whole: The Reform of the European Economic Union and Perspectives of Fiscal Integration* 170.
100. Ruffert, 'The Future of the European Economic and Monetary Union: Issues of Constitutional Law' 55.

Taken together, the most far-reaching *integration* proposal envisages the allocation of a real EU blocking power to oppose national budgeting – as proposed by the Bruegel-proposal.[101] This would alter the existing framework and is different to initiating, for example, an Excessive Deficit Procedure, as the EU could effectively block national fiscal decisions.[102] Obviously, this has implications for national budgetary prerogatives, which are vested in the national parliaments and would require EU Treaty amendment. On a general level, it should be emphasized that increasing EU supervision over national budgeting, even without veto power, limits national constitutional principles such as parliamentary responsibility for the state budget or democratic control over fiscal policy decisions.[103] Here, proposals that aim to increase national ownership of the EU fiscal rules and thereby internalize the applicable framework into the national constitutional thinking, appear less invasive. These proposals follow a *coordination approach*, which aims to preserve national decision-making power by emphasizing the national commitment to EU fiscal rules and including these rules better into the national political process.

F CONCLUSION: THE ENVISAGED EU FISCAL INTEGRATION

These four aspects constitute the core substantive points of discussion when it comes to EU fiscal integration proposals. As becomes obvious, particularly the introduction of a new fiscal capacity is widely and controversially debated. Overall, the proposed ideas for designing a budgetary tool, its funding sources, but also on the introduction of a Ministry of Finance and the enhanced supervision of national budgeting can be distinguished regarding the envisaged intensity of EU integration steps as well as the proposed degree of EU influence. These variations in the design of the substantive elements of EU fiscal integration can be organized based on the adopted linear distinction between *integration* and *coordination approaches*.

The assessment revealed, in the first place, that a variety of different ideas are circulated, which provide a diverse framework for drafting EU fiscal integration steps in light of national constitutional concerns. This overview equally suggests that many of the proposals might not only run into national constitutional concerns but equally EU law challenges, as EU Treaty amendments appear to be required particularly for the implementation of ideas that follow an *integration approach*.

101. Marzinotto, Sapir and Wolff, 'What Kind of Fiscal Union? (2011)' 6.
102. Lionello, *The Pursuit of Stability of the Euro Area as a Whole: The Reform of the European Economic Union and Perspectives of Fiscal Integration* 170; Marzinotto, Sapir and Wolff, 'What Kind of Fiscal Union? (2011)' 6.
103. Lionello, *The Pursuit of Stability of the Euro Area as a Whole: The Reform of the European Economic Union and Perspectives of Fiscal Integration* 200.

CHAPTER 8

The Compatibility of EU Fiscal Integration Proposals with National Constitutional Concerns

A INTRODUCTION

The comparative assessment of the national constitutional framework for EU fiscal integration illustrates how constitutional systems in the Member States address, regulate and conceptualize EU integration. The comparison illustrates that while most national constitutional approaches are rooted in the same or similar constitutional principles, including national sovereignty and democracy, they have taken different shapes and can be distinguished based on their intensity. The book has conceptualized this variety of approaches based on the flexible-rigid linear spectrum. These varying approaches result from differences in the domestic design of the institutional framework, the constitutional text itself and the overall constitutional framework. Despite this variation, it appears that fiscal integration proposals are confronted *primarily* with (strict) procedural requirements imposed by the domestic constitutional framework. In addition, the *rigid* German Constitution contains the *eternity clause* which sets abstract absolute limits to the process of EU integration. In Finland, a comparable substantive limitation to EU cooperation does not exist. The subsequent *micro-comparative* assessment of a selection of strict national *constitutional identity limits* provides a detailed insight into the variety of substantive constitutional concerns that are formulated against EU fiscal integration steps.

The following compatibility assessment employs this broadly charted constitutional space to test the deconstructed elements of EU fiscal integration proposals. Based on the findings, fiscal integration proposals are confronted with four general types of constitutional hurdles ranging from simple procedural requirements as the 'lightest obstacle' to absolute limitations, as depicted in Figure 8.1. The coding that is introduced in the figure is subsequently used to illustrate the results of the compatibility assessment in a graphic overview per substantive element of EU fiscal integration proposals.

Figure 8.1 Categorization of National Constitutional Hurdles to EU Fiscal Integration

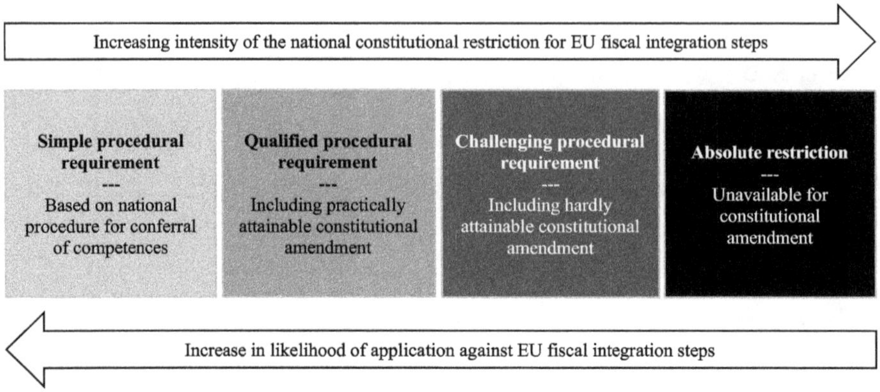

The compatibility assessment determines which EU fiscal integration ideas are achievable within the existing national constitutional framework and which proposals might be confronted with severe national constitutional obstacles (B). In a separate sub-section (C), the assessment employs the research findings concerning the possibility to induce additional *constitutional flexibility* in the strict constitutional limits. This assesses if more EU fiscal integration becomes legally feasible if one applies the different flexibility tools to national constitutional limits. Moreover, this assessment allows to determine to what extent national constitutional concerns can be accommodated by EU fiscal integration steps in order to soften the apparent opposition emerging in some Member States.

B COMPATIBILITY OF FISCAL INTEGRATION WITH CURRENT NATIONAL CONSTITUTIONAL SPACE

I Compatibility of an EU Fiscal Capacity with National Constitutional Space

When considering the compatibility of an EU budgetary capacity or instrument with the charted national constitutional requirements, two separate legal situations can be distinguished. A first set of ideas is achievable within the existing EU Treaty-framework (1), without requiring the conferral of additional competences from the national to EU level, as is the case, for example, with NGEU, BICC or the European Investment Protection Schemes. A second set of ideas requires amendments to the EU Treaty-framework (2).

1 *A Fiscal Capacity or Instrument Based on the Existing Treaty-Framework*

The proposed Eurozone-budget could be devised under the EU-Treaties as a limited support fund that is financed through the MFF. For example, Articles 175(3) and 197(2) TFEU served as the legal bases to establish Regulation 2017/825, which created the Structural Reform Support Programme for the period of 2017 to 2020 with a total volume of EUR 142.8 million in funding to support structural reforms in the Member States.[1] This combined legal basis was equally envisaged for the Reform Support Programme Regulation, the underpinning regulation for the BICC.[2] In contrast, under NGEU the Recovery Instrument was based on Article 122 TFEU, which allows for solidarity support in case of *asymmetric* economic shocks, and the specific Recovery and Resilience Facility Regulation was then based (again) on Article 175(3) TFEU.[3]

The proposed more limited emergency instruments, including the proposed European Investment Protection Scheme[4] as well as the European Unemployment Reinsurance Fund,[5] would operate as so-called insurance-type mechanisms.[6] These schemes could be based on Article 122(2) TFEU, too, if established as emergency instruments that only operate in times of economic downturn.[7] The EU-Treaties thus contain various legal bases to accommodate a Eurozone budgetary capacity, which might however trigger national constitutional resistance.

a *Compatibility with the Charted Macro-comparative Constitutional Space*

In Finland, the creation of a Treaty-based fiscal capacity could either require parliamentary approval following section 94 Finnish Constitution in case Finnish financial

1. Cf. Article 4 Regulation 2017/825; which was subsequently increased by EUR 80 million by Regulation 2018/1671; c. as well: Menelaos Markakis, *Accountability in the Economic and Monetary Union: Foundations, Policy, and Governance* (Oxford Studies in European Law, Oxford University Press 2020) 310-311.
2. Jointly with the proposed Regulation (COM(2019) 354) for the governing framework of the BICC, which was based on Articles 136(1)(b) and 121(6) TFEU.
3. Bruno De Witte, 'The European Union's COVID-19 Recovery Plan: The Legal Engineering of an Economic Policy Shift' (2021) 58 Common Market Law Review 635, 655, 658.
4. Commission, *Reflection Paper on the Deepening of the Economic and Monetary Union* 26; Juncker et al., *The Five Presidents' Report: Completing Europe's Economic and Monetary Union* 15; cf. as well: Craig and Markakis, 'EMU Reform' 1426; Fabbrini, 'Fiscal Capacity' 115.
5. Commission, *Reflection Paper on the Deepening of the Economic and Monetary Union* 26; cf. as well: Craig and Markakis, 'EMU Reform' 1426; Steinbach, 'Insurance-Type Cooperation Mechanisms under EU Law' 22.
6. Comments, 'Editorial Comments: Tinkering with Economic and Monetary Union' 6-7; Steinbach, 'Insurance-Type Cooperation Mechanisms under EU Law' 22.
7. As the case for the agreed SURE-scheme, cf. European Commission, 'SURE: Supporting Member States to Help Protect People in Work and Jobs' (*European Commission*, 2020), https://ec.europa.eu/info/sites/info/files/economy-finance/sure_factsheet.pdf, accessed 5 April 2023 Recitals 1-2; for a general analysis on the legal bases for such schemes, cf. Steinbach, 'Insurance-Type Cooperation Mechanisms under EU Law' 24-29.

commitments are increased[8] or trigger the internal monitoring system enshrined in section 96 Finnish Constitution.[9] The proposed establishment of a Eurozone-budget or the envisaged emergency instruments would establish financial obligations for the Member States. It thus concerns the allocation of financial resources and has implications for the EU's financial planning itself, which affects the Member State's own finances. According to section 3(1) Finnish Constitution, the Finnish Parliament determines the State Finances, which covers the adoption of the state budget, according to section 83(1) Finnish Constitution, including all revenue and expenditure, as established in section 84(1) Finnish Constitution.[10]

In light of these constitutional considerations, and building upon the experiences during the Eurocrisis, it appears that the Finnish constitutional appraisal differs for the different Eurozone-budget and the emergency instruments proposed. Regarding the allocation of funds under the proposed Eurozone-budget based on the current EU Treaty-framework, the monitoring procedure in section 96 Finnish Constitution seems to apply, given that the envisaged secondary law-based budget concerns fiscal decisions, which are assigned to the Finnish Parliament. Therefore, the Finnish Parliament must engage in an ex ante assessment upon referral, which involves all relevant specialized parliamentary committees, including the Constitutional Law Committee. Finally, the Grand Committee will have to communicate the final parliamentary position to the Finnish representative in the EU Council of Ministers. Although the position is not legally binding, it has high political authority given the strong institutional position of the Finnish Parliament within the Finnish constitutional system as well as the governmental dependence on continuous parliamentary support.[11] The parliamentary position will hence likely be followed by the Finnish representative, thereby securing an authoritative involvement of the Finnish Parliament in the adoption of any EU secondary act that would underpin an EU budgetary capacity.

Furthermore, any underlying core financial commitment to fund the Eurozone-budget – which would certainly increase Finnish financial responsibilities towards the EU – would likely be based on Article 311 TFEU and would thus require Finnish parliamentary approval under section 94 Finnish Constitution as will be established subsequently in more detail. Suffice it here to highlight that the allocation of additional financial capacities to EU level requires parliamentary authorization following section 94 Finnish Constitution, given that the exercise of (financial) powers is conferred from the national to EU level.[12] In contrast, the subsequent use of these additional financial powers, based on the highlighted legal bases included in the EU-Treaties, would *only*

8. Leino and Salminen, 'The Euro Crisis and Its Constitutional Consequences for Finland: Is There Room for National Politics in EU Decision-Making?' 452.
9. Ojanen, 'The EU at the Finnish Constitutional Arena' 247.
10. Leino and Salminen, 'The Euro Crisis and Its Constitutional Consequences for Finland: Is There Room for National Politics in EU Decision-Making?' 457.
11. Ojanen, 'The Europeanization of Finnish Law' 170; Ojanen, 'The Impact of EU Membership on Finnish Constitutional Law' 556; Raunio and Tiilikainen, *Finland in the European Union* 86.
12. *Commission's Draft EU Recovery Plan and MFF Planning* 10; Leino-Sandberg, 'Who Is Ultra Vires Now? The EU's Legal U-Turn in Interpreting Article 310 TFEU'.

have to be monitored by the Finnish Parliament following section 96 Finnish Constitution.

Considering the adoption of an emergency instrument, similar constitutional considerations apply. Notably, as such an EU instrument would depend on additional national contributions and liabilities, which would increase the Finnish financial EU commitment, parliamentary approval following section 94 Finnish Constitution seems required, as already established by the Constitutional Law Committee in its appraisal of the EFSF- and the ESM-Treaty.[13] Depending on the precise modalities of the emergency instrument, the Finnish Parliament will likely have to approve these additional financial commitments by a simple majority, unless the EU would be empowered to increase the Finnish commitment or liability autonomously without parliamentary approval which would require the support of a two-thirds parliamentary majority, as exemplified in relation to the draft ESM-Treaty.[14]

This suggests that the Finnish constitutional appraisal focuses on whether the proposed fiscal integration steps actually increase the national financial commitment. If this is the case, the procedure in section 94 Finnish Constitution seems applicable. Otherwise, the Finnish Parliament can mandate the Finnish representative at EU level to vote for the adoption of secondary law solutions pursuant to section 96 Finnish Constitution.

Similarly, under the more rigid German constitutional system, the provision for the conferral of competences enshrined in Article 23(1)(2) GG seems not applicable to the allocation of the funds available under the proposed Eurozone-budget. This is because no additional competences are allocated to EU level but rather the existing EU Treaty-framework is employed.[15] Instead, the German Government would have to inform the German Parliament about the intention to adopt an EU budgetary capacity or instrument as required by Article 23(2) GG. Given that the allocation of the Eurozone-budget would likely be established as an EU legislative act, and given that the identified possible legal bases in Articles 122, 175(3), 197(2) TFEU prescribe the adoption of an act following a legislative procedure, the German Parliament would be required to issue a parliamentary position following Article 23(3) GG, which the Government has to take into account.[16] Therefore, comparable to the Finnish Parliament, the Bundestag is centrally involved in the domestic ex ante assessment of the relevant EU secondary act.

13. *First Assessment Draft ESM-Treaty (I.)*; *Second Assessment Draft ESM-Treaty (II.)*; *Final Assessment Draft ESM-Treaty (III.)*; cf. as well: Leino and Salminen, *Constitutional Change Through Euro Crisis Law: 'Finland'* VIII.1; Ojanen, 'The EU at the Finnish Constitutional Arena' 247.
14. *Second Assessment Draft ESM-Treaty (II.)* 2; cf. as well: Ojanen and Salminen, 'Finland: European Integration and International Human Rights Treaties as Sources of Domestic Constitutional Change and Dynamism' 391-392; Tuori and Raitio, 'Finland' 328; Leino and Salminen, 'The Euro Crisis and Its Constitutional Consequences for Finland: Is There Room for National Politics in EU Decision-Making?' 464.
15. *See* reasoning of the German Court regarding the ORD, cf. *Interim Decision on the Ratification of the Own Resources Decision (NGEU)* para. 79; cf. as well: *Lisbon-judgment* para. 243.
16. Nettesheim, 'Die Integrationsverantwortung: Vorgaben des BVerfG und gesetzgeberische Umsetzung' 181.

Furthermore, the allocation of additional funds for this Eurozone-budget, which could be financed through the own resources system under the current EU-Treaties, would require German parliamentary approval under Article 23(1)(2) GG - as substantiated subsequently. Hence, the applicable constitutional procedures in Germany bear obvious similarities with those in Finland. Notably, the allocation of additional financial means to the EU level requires constitutive approval by the German Parliament given that the EU powers are extended - and hence Article 23(1)(2) GG applies. In contrast, the allocation of the available funds is a matter of EU law and can be implemented based on a legal basis under the EU-Treaties. Given that the Treaty-framework itself was already ratified by national parliaments, the allocation of EU funds as a matter of EU secondary law is only monitored by the national parliament.

Considering now the adoption of the proposed emergency instruments, it appears that such instrument would likely require parliamentary approval following Article 23(1)(3) in conjunction with Article 79(2) GG - as displayed in relation to the adoption of the ESM-Treaty - given the possible considerable impact on German parliamentary budgetary prerogatives.[17] As highlighted in relation to the Eurozone-budget, the fact that additional financial means seem to be required to establish such EU instruments indicates that a conferral of (financial) competences from the national to the EU level is necessary. This conferral can only be adopted through constitutive approval by the German Parliament.

In addition to the national *ex ante* parliamentary involvement in the preparation of the adoption of such a Eurozone-budget and the parliamentary approval of the proposed emergency instruments, it seems, moreover, almost certain that constitutional review will be initiated against the envisaged measures. In contrast to the Finnish constitutional system, which limits the constitutional assessment to the *ex ante* involvement of the Constitutional Law Committee, an *ex post* constitutional review seems highly likely in Germany in light of the identified lowered standing requirements in EU-related proceedings.[18] Notably, it is likely that individuals would challenge such EU secondary law through a constitutional complaint claiming that the legislative act exceeds the competences conferred upon the EU or that the resulting fiscal capacity violates the German *constitutional identity*.[19] Similar concerns could be raised by, for example, a political fraction through inter-institutional proceedings.[20] The German

17. Ruffert, 'Europarecht für die nächste Generation: Zum Projekt Next Generation EU' 1779; Ketterer, *Zustimmungserfordernis beim Europäischen Stabilitätsmechanismus* 359.
18. Gärditz, 'Beyond Symbolism: Towards a Constitutional Actio Popularis in EU Affairs? A Commentary on the OMT Decision of the Federal Constitutional Court' 192; Wendel, 'Kompetenzrechtliche Grenzgänge: Karlsruhes *Ultra-vires*-Vorlage an den EuGH' 641-642.
19. *Interim Decision on the Ratification of the Own Resources Decision (NGEU)* para. 81; *Quantitative Easing (PSPP) Final Judgment* para. 113; cf. as well: Thiele, 'Friendly or Unfriendly Act? The "Historic" Referral of the Constitutional Court to the ECJ Regarding the ECB's OMT Program' 251-253; Vranes, 'German Constitutional Foundations of, and Limitations to, EU Integration: A Systematic Analysis' 108-109; Tomuschat, 'Lisbon: Terminal of the European Integration Process? The Judgment of the German Constitutional Court of 30 June 2009' 266.
20. *Lisbon-judgment* paras 204-206; cf. as well: Schwerdtfeger, 'Europäisches Unionsrecht in der Rechtsprechung des Bundesverfassungsgerichts: Grundrechts-, ultra-vires-und Identitätskontrolle im gewaltenteiligen Mehrebenensystem' 305-306; Mayer, 'Der Vertrag von Lissabon im Überblick' 194.

Constitutional Court would then assess whether the German Parliament, the German Federal Council or the German Government violated their integration responsibility, which imposes a constitutional obligation to continuously review that the EU adheres to its mandate, that EU action does not violate the German *constitutional identity* and that, if they do, German institutions take appropriate steps to remedy such a violation.[21] In light of the established jurisprudence of the Court, it is likely that such constitutional review would be admissible.

The subsequent question is whether such applications are also likely to succeed. Regarding the assessment under the *ultra vires* review, the German Constitutional Court requires in a first step that the EU act in question constitutes a manifest overstepping of the conferred powers which results in a structurally significant shift of powers to the disadvantage of the Member State.[22] A major determining factor for this assessment will be the actual size, the remaining control of the *Bundestag* as well as the source of funding for such a fiscal capacity, which will be addressed in the subsequent section.

When considering the substantive question of conferral, focusing on the broad idea of initiating a Eurozone-budget to support structural reforms, this appears generally compatible with the legal bases in Articles 175(3) and 197(2) TFEU, as already illustrated by Regulations 2017/825 and 2018/1671.[23] These established the Structural Reform Support Programme between 2017 and 2020 and did not trigger German constitutional concerns. Article 175(3) TFEU empowers the European Parliament and the Council to adopt 'specific actions' to complement the Structural Funds established under Article 175(1) TFEU in order to attain the objective of an economically, socially and territorially more cohesive EU.[24] Arguably, a Eurozone-budget could complement the general scheme of Structural Funds by specifically targeting economic and social cohesion in the Euroarea, as also explicitly envisaged by the European Commission.[25] Hence, it seems convincing to argue that a Eurozone-budget could be generally based on Articles 175(3) and 197(2) TFEU in case it is geared towards economic as well as social cohesion and in case it remains limited in size, given the

21. *Quantitative Easing (PSPP) Final Judgment* paras 106-107; cf. as well: Weiß, 'Die Integrationsverantwortung der Verfassungsorgane' 1047; Engels, 'Die Integrationsverantwortung des Deutschen Bundestags' 212-213.
22. *Quantitative Easing (PSPP) Final Judgment* para. 110; cf. as well: Lang, 'Ultra Vires Review of the ECB's Policy of Quantitative Easing: An Analysis of the German Constitutional Court's Preliminary Reference Order in the PSPP Case' 927.
23. Markakis, *Accountability in the Economic and Monetary Union: Foundations, Policy, and Governance* 310-311.
24. As determined by Article 174(1) TFEU; cf. as well: Bastian Kern and Christoph Eggers, 'Art. 174 AEUV – Ziele, Regionen und benachteiligte Gebiete' in Eberhard Grabitz, Meinhard Hilf and Martin Nettesheim (eds), *Das Recht der Europäischen Union – Kommentar* (70th edn, C.H. Beck 2020) paras 22-26.
25. Notably in relation to the proposed European Investment Stabilization Function, cf. European Commission, *Commission Staff Working Document: Impact Assessment – Accompanying the Document for Proposal for a Regulation of the European Parliament and of the Council on the Establishment of a European Investment Stabilisation Function (COM (2018) 297)* (European Commission 2018); cf. as well: Fabbrini, 'Fiscal Capacity' 127.

only supplementary function that Article 175(3) TFEU seems to have. In the alternative, Article 136(1)(b) in conjunction with Article 121(6) TFEU could constitute a possible legal basis as suggested by the Commission in its BICC proposal.[26] However, these legal bases only enable the EU to establish a framework for the governance of economic policy coordination, whereas the financial capacity would have to be established on a different legal basis. Regarding these different legal bases, the German Constitutional Court is not likely to find an excess of the conferred mandate, which depends, however, on the precise design of the EU acts. Similarly, the creation of the proposed emergency instruments based on Article 122 TFEU appears compatible with the EU-Treaties, as long as they remain indeed emergency tools.[27] Therefore, the establishment of such instruments would likely not be considered *ultra vires* by the German Court, presupposing that the respective schemes remain limited in scope and size.

A subsequent question in the constitutional evaluation is whether a Eurozone-budget or an EU emergency instrument would be compatible with German *overall budgetary responsibility*.[28] As established, the concept has a procedural and a substantive dimension. At a procedural level, *overall budgetary responsibility* requires that German parliamentary approval remains constitutive for any budgetary commitment with an impact on the German budget, that parliament is fully informed about the commitment as well as potential financial risks and that the commitment remains limited.[29] Applying this benchmark to the envisaged Eurozone-budget, the German Parliament was and will be involved in several stages of the adoption process. In the first place, the budget proposed here would be based on the EU-Treaties, which were ratified by the German Parliament. Thus, the parliament explicitly approved the legal bases in Articles 175(3) and 197(2) TFEU or Article 136(1)(b) in conjunction with Article 121(6) TFEU. In addition, the previously outlined institutional *ex ante* involvement of the German Parliament secures parliamentary participation in the drafting of the secondary law details. Although this involvement does not include a constitutive approval of the German Parliament, given that the German Government is not legally mandated by the parliamentary position and given that the vote in the Council is taken by a qualified majority if the act is adopted based on the mentioned provisions, the German Parliament can nevertheless impact the EU decision.

Moreover, the envisaged BICC as an example of a secondary-law-based budgetary capacity would be financed through the MFF, which in return is funded through the EU's own resources that are approved by the Member States according to national

26. Commission Proposal for a Regulation of the European Parliament and of the Council on the Governance Framework for the Budgetary Instrument for Convergence and Competitiveness for the Euro Area (COM(2019) 354); cf. as well: Lionello, *The Pursuit of Stability of the Euro Area as a Whole: The Reform of the European Economic Union and Perspectives of Fiscal Integration* 185-186.
27. Steinbach, 'Insurance-Type Cooperation Mechanisms under EU Law' 24-29.
28. *Quantitative Easing (PSPP) Final Judgment* para. 104; *Final OMT-Judgment* para. 212; cf. as well: Herdegen, 'Art. 79 GG' paras 177-179; Reestman, 'Legitimacy Through Adjudication: The ESM Treaty and the Fiscal Compact Before the National Courts' 259.
29. *Quantitative Easing (PSPP) Reference* para. 48; cf. as well: Calliess, '70 Jahre Grundgesetz und europäische Integration: "Take Back Control" oder "Mehr Demokratie wagen"?' 688.

constitutional requirements as established in Article 311(3) TFEU. In Germany, this national adoption includes approval by the German Parliament. Hence, even in case the general scheme for a Eurozone-budget is based on Articles 175(3) and 197(2) TFEU or governed by Articles 136(1)(b) and 121(6) TFEU, the budget itself would be financed through the general EU budget which is funded by the EU's resources determined based on Article 311(3) TFEU and thus secures the constitutive German parliamentary approval. Overall, the outlined framework thus comprehensively involves the German Parliament, secures the constitutive approval for additional financial commitments and specifies the use of the attributed financial means through the EU Treaty-framework. Therefore, it seems that the procedural requirements of *overall budgetary responsibility* would be complied with.

Regarding the establishment of an emergency instrument under Article 122 TFEU the constitutional conclusions drawn by the German Constitutional Court in relation to the ESM-Treaty and more recently NGEU appear applicable. Concerning the ESM, the Court established that the German Parliament could adopt the general scheme but it required that the concrete financial assistance programmes receive prior approval by the German Parliament in order to provide parliament with the possibility to evaluate the inherent risk of the granted assistance.[30] Regarding NGEU, the Court highlighted that the provision enables Member States to establish a recovery strategy to overcome severe difficulties, including the economic disruption caused by COVID-19. However, the funding under NGEU via borrow funds was not based on Article 122 TFEU but rather the Own Resources Decision adopted under Article 311(3) TFEU.[31] Thus, considering the proposed emergency instruments which target asymmetric economic shocks, a similar design to the ESM, following which Member States retain an impact on the financial assistance offered, or a similar design to NGEU, where Member States confirmed their financial commitment pursuant to Article 311(3) TFEU, could be employed. In both cases, the constitutive German parliamentary approval of financial commitments required under *overall budgetary responsibility* as established by the German Constitutional Court would be preserved. Taken together, this suggests that the envisaged emergency instruments could be drafted in conformity with the procedural requirements under *overall budgetary responsibility* – which was displayed by the EFSF- and ESM-Treaty as well as NGEU which were found to be in conformity with the German Constitution.

Regarding the substantive requirements of *overall budgetary responsibility*, the Court established that the German Parliament could neither surrender budgetary autonomy for a considerable time nor transfer essential budgetary powers that would enable EU institutions to independently determine German spending.[32] Moreover, it

30. *Participation of Members of German Parliament in the EFSF* para. 112; cf. as well: Nettesheim, 'Die "haushaltspolitische Gesamtverantwortung" in der Rechtsprechung des BVerfG' 23; Calliess, 'Der Kampf um den Euro: Eine "Angelegenheit der Europäischen Union" zwischen Regierung, Parlament und Volk' 4.
31. *Final Decision on the Ratification of the Own Resources Decision (NGEU)* paras 171-172.
32. Claes and Reestman, 'The Protection of National Constitutional Identity and the Limits of European Integration at the Occasion of the *Gauweiler* Case' 927.

was established that the German Constitutional Court seems reluctant in the application of this substantive benchmark, which acknowledges the parliament's wide discretion and showcases the inherent difficulty of defining an enforceable substantive reference value.[33]

When applying this substantive framework to the proposed Eurozone-budget it seems that the financial impact of the proposed budget would be limited given its insignificant size. For example, the reform programme initiated under Articles 175(3) and 197(2) TFEU for the timeframe between 2017 and 2020 included financial commitments of EUR 222.8 million.[34] The proposed BICC was envisaged to 'only' have a financial volume of EUR 25-55 billion for the timeframe between 2021 and 2027.[35] Given that the financing under the scheme would be guaranteed through the EU budget, Germany would only partially contribute to such a Eurozone-budget. Therefore, the financial and budgetary impact of the suggested Eurozone-budget remains limited and is not likely to suspend German budgetary autonomy. This conclusion seems particularly convincing when considering the significantly higher German commitments during the Eurocrisis and under NGEU. The ESM, for example, amounted to total potential commitments of up to EUR 190 billion for Germany yet was deemed compatible with *overall budgetary responsibility*.[36] This is also confirmed by the German Constitutional Court's appraisal of NGEU, which was found compatible with *overall budgetary responsibility* specifically because of its temporary, limited nature as well as its connection to the Own Resources Decision.[37] It appears, therefore, that a similar conclusion can be drawn in relation to any future emergency instruments, which would provide financial assistance to Member States in strictly limited circumstances, and which would be limited in size.

Overall, this suggests that both an additional EU budgetary capacity as well as possible emergency instruments can be conceived in compliance with the German concept of *overall budgetary responsibility*. However, this presupposes that financial commitments remain limited in scope, that they are strictly confined in their overall size and that they remain under the final control of the German Parliament. Furthermore, it requires that the maximum financial liability for Germany is strictly determined to avoid German budgetary autonomy being suspended for a considerable time. Given that most proposals remain inherently vague on the specific details until their final adoption, it is only possible to indicate the general compatibility of such proposals with the German Constitution at this point.

33. Cf. the assessment and the conclusions drawn in Chapter 3 section D.II.2.c.
34. Cf. amendments to Article 10(1) Regulation 2017/825 introduced by Regulation 2018/1671; cf. as well: Markakis, *Accountability in the Economic and Monetary Union: Foundations, Policy, and Governance* 310-311.
35. Lionello, *The Pursuit of Stability of the Euro Area as a Whole: The Reform of the European Economic Union and Perspectives of Fiscal Integration* 217.
36. *ESM-Treaty and Fiscal Compact (interim relief)* para. 167; Claes and Reestman, 'The Protection of National Constitutional Identity and the Limits of European Integration at the Occasion of the *Gauweiler* Case' 928.
37. *Final Decision on the Ratification of the Own Resources Decision (NGEU)* para. 213.

b Compatibility with the Charted Micro-comparative Constitutional Space

How would the other constitutional authorities compared apply their respective national *constitutional identity limit* to a potential Eurozone-budget or an emergency instrument based on EU secondary law? When considering the compatibility of such a Eurozone-budget with the French *constitutional identity limit*, it seems that the '*essential conditions for the exercise of national sovereignty*'-limit is not applicable, as this only applies to new EU primary law commitments.[38] Instead, the *constitutional identity limit*, which the *Conseil Constitutionnel* introduced for the French implementation of EU secondary law obligations, applies.[39] Following this limit, an EU secondary law obligation may not violate a 'principle inherent to the *constitutional identity* of France'[40], in particular the institutional balance enshrined in the French Constitution, the indivisibility of the French nation and France's republican status, without explicit confirmation of the constitution-amending legislator.[41] However, it seems that this constitutional benchmark is not applicable to the proposed Eurozone-budget or emergency instruments, as these constitute EU secondary acts that do not require implementation into French law. Given that the Conseil does not generally review EU law but merely the implementation thereof into French law, no direct limit emerges.

When considering the Spanish *constitutional identity limit*, the Constitutional Tribunal developed this limit specifically in the context of conferring additional powers to EU level by ratifying a new EU Treaty or amending the existing framework. This is apparent from the limit's underpinning constitutional basis in Article 93 Spanish Constitution that regulates the conclusion of supranational agreements.[42] In addition, the Tribunal emphasized that EU secondary law is based on ratified primary law and that it would generally not scrutinize secondary law, as the EU-Treaties provide procedures to remedy excessive EU legislation and as EU primary law must comply with the Spanish *constitutional identity limit* in order to be validly adopted.[43] Consequently, given that the Eurozone-budget considered here would be adopted based on EU primary law, the Spanish *constitutional identity limit* would only be applied by the Constitutional Tribunal in case of manifest violations by the EU act in question.[44] Given that establishing the Eurozone-budget as well as the emergency instruments in the proposed way appears generally compatible with the EU Treaty-framework, it is

38. Fabbrini, 'The Euro-Crisis and the Courts: Judicial Review and the Political Process in Comparative Perspective' 122-123; Pfeiffer, 'Zur Verfassungsmäßigkeit des Gemeinschaftsrechts in der aktuellen Rechtsprechung des französischen Conseil constitutionnel' 491.
39. Dubout, '"Les règles ou principes inhérents à l'identité constitutionelle de la France": une supra-constitutionalité?' 452.
40. Vranes, 'Constitutional Foundation of, and Limitations to, EU Integration in France' 547-548.
41. Millet, 'Constitutional Identity in France: Vices and – Above All – Virtues' 148; Reestman, 'The Franco-German Constitutional Divide: Reflections on National and Constitutional Identity' 388.
42. Martín Y Pérez de Nanclares, 'Constitutional Identity in Spain: Commitment to European Integration Without Giving up the Essence of the Constitution' 270.
43. Bustos Gisbert, 'National Constitutional Identity in European Constitutionalism: Revisiting the Tale of the Emperor's New Clothes in Spain?' 77.
44. De Visser, *Constitutional Review in Europe: A Comparative Analysis* 263; Berger, *Anwendungsvorrang und nationale Verfassungsgericht* 292; Estella de Noriega, 'A Dissident Voice: The Spanish Constitutional Court Case Law on European Integration' 277.

unlikely that a conflict between the Spanish *constitutional identity limit* and the respective EU secondary legislation emerges. Furthermore, it seems particularly important for the Spanish Constitutional Tribunal that EU cooperation retains its derived status and that the Spanish legislator retains control within the process of EU cooperation.[45] This control is given in relation to the own resources decision, which would likely constitute the underlying funding mechanism for the proposed Eurozone-budget.[46] In the alternative, and in particular, in relation to the proposed emergency instruments, the Member States' financial commitments might be determined by an intergovernmental agreement comparable to, for example, the ESM-Treaty, which equally requires national parliamentary approval. The Spanish Parliament thus retains the required fundamental involvement when determining financial commitments.

When evaluating the compatibility of the proposed reforms with the Polish *constitutional identity limit*, it seems that no constitutional conflict emerges either. In the first place, Poland is not yet a Member State of the Eurozone,[47] therefore, a constitutional conflict remains hypothetical at this point. Yet, these reform steps could impact the Polish ability to join the Eurozone in case EU fiscal integration would be subsequently deemed constitutionally unattainable. Furthermore, given that the envisaged Eurozone-budget could be financed by the EU's own resources, Polish approval is required according to Article 311(3) TFEU. Given that Article 311(3) TFEU prescribes unanimity in the Council as well as national approval, Poland could potentially block the adoption of the own resources decision, as recently illustrated in relation to NGEU and the MFF for 2021-2027. This could render the attainability of the Eurozone-budget difficult and even expose the Eurozone to demands from non-Euro Member States in return for their approval.

Considering the Polish *constitutional identity limit*, which could be invoked against a Eurozone-budget or an emergency instrument after Polish accession to the Eurozone, no immediate conflict emerges. Notably, the Polish *constitutional identity limit* protects Polish statehood, the structure of the state with its institutions, the hierarchical position of the Polish Constitution as well as fundamental rights.[48] An additional budgetary capacity or instrument based on EU secondary law requires a primary law basis, which must be ratified by the Polish legislator according to Article 90 Polish Constitution.[49] Therefore, in case any budgetary solution is validly enacted based on EU secondary law, it presupposes prior Polish approval of the general commitment. At the same time, given the current developments in Poland, new constitutional hurdles might emerge in the future.[50]

45. Pérez Tremps, 'National Idenity in Spanish Constitutional Court Case-Law' 271.
46. Margit Schratzenstaller and Alexander Krenek, 'Tax-Based Own Resources to Finance the EU Budget' (2019) 54 Intereconomics – Review of European Economic Policy 171, 174.
47. Czuczai, 'Accession to the EU, but to Which EU? The Legal Impact of the Constantly Evolving EMU Acquis on the EU Enlargement Process' 595.
48. Śledzińska-Simon and Ziółkowski, 'Constitutional Identity in Poland: Is the Emperor Putting on the Old Clothes of Sovereignty' 253.
49. Rideau, 'The Case-Law of the Polish, Hungarian and Czech Constitutional Courts on National Idenity and the "German Model"' 252-253.
50. Sadurski, *Poland's Constitutional Breakdown* 85.

c Interim Conclusion

Overall, this suggests that the initiation of a Eurozone-budget and limited emergency instruments based on EU secondary law are generally compatible with the assessed national *constitutional identity limits* as well as with the overarching constitutional framework in Finland and Germany. The assessment indicates that a secondary law solution is confronted with only limited constitutional concerns in the Member States, as even in more rigid systems the assumption prevails that the underpinning EU primary law basis was validly ratified by national parliaments. The assessment revealed that according to national constitutional logic the adoption of the general scheme – which allocates EU funds – has to be distinguished from the prior allocation of additional funds to EU level. The latter triggers additional constitutional concerns given that the EU would be equipped with additional (financial) competences.

When considering the EU secondary law solution in isolation, momentarily dis-regarding the legal details concerning possible funding, national constitutional courts appear to only adopt a subsidiary constitutional control. What is more, given that the most likely options concerning the funding of any of the proposed fiscal integration steps would either be integrated into the EU budget, and thus based on the own resources decision which has to be adopted by national parliaments, or on an intergovernmental solution, which equally requires national parliamentary approval, the respective national parliaments retain a major say on how extensive the domestic financial commitment would be. Arguably, this secures national control over the own national state budget and it thereby confines the discretion on the side of the EU.

2 *A Budgetary Capacity or Instrument Introduced by EU Treaty Amendment*

A future Eurozone-budget or emergency instrument could also be established by amending the EU-Treaties. Accordingly, a new legal basis or framework for EU budgeting could be introduced into the EU-Treaties. Arguably, Treaty-reform appears ambitious in the current political context, but it could provide an explicit basis for the envisaged Eurozone-budget or emergency instruments. A clarification of the Treaty-framework, comparable to the amendment of Article 136 TFEU, could be attainable under Article 48(6) TFEU by a simple parliamentary majority in Finland and Germany.[51] However, more fundamental changes to the EMU structure as envisaged by the proposed fiscal capacity would likely require a comprehensive Treaty amendment under Article 48(1)(1) TFEU.

51. *Finland:* Leino and Salminen, 'The Euro Crisis and Its Constitutional Consequences for Finland: Is There Room for National Politics in EU Decision-Making?' 469; *And Germany:* Birgit Daiber, 'Das Integrationsverantwortungsgesetz in der Praxis des Deutschen Bundestages' (2012) 43 Zeitschrift für Parlamentsfragen 293, 296-298.

a Compatibility with the Charted Macro-comparative Constitutional Space

When testing the charted *macro-comparative* constitutional framework against the creation of budgetary tools through EU Treaty amendment, particularly those proposals that aim to alter core constitutional features of the EMU-framework, including national responsibility for economic and fiscal policies as well as the no-bailout commitment, could be seen as transforming the nature of E(M)U-cooperation. Notably, the proposed changes could empower the EU to establish financial commitments that impact or reduce national budgetary prerogatives. As a result, a qualified parliamentary majority might be necessary to ratify such Treaty-changes in Finland[52] and Germany,[53] as will be analysed in detail in the subsequent section on funding sources.

In addition, it is questionable whether the initiation of a far-reaching Eurozone-budget or additional emergency instruments are compatible with German *overall budgetary responsibility*. Given the lowered standing requirements in EU-related proceedings, the initiation of admissible constitutional proceedings challenging the required conferral of competences is certain.[54] As determined, *overall budgetary responsibility* imposes procedural and substantive requirements, which are violated in case core budgetary competences are conferred to EU level outside German parliamentary control.[55] Specifically, the idea to create a Eurozone-budget of up to 3% Eurozone GDP[56] appears problematic as it would entail a permanent re-allocation of national revenue through the EU and require the EU to conduct fiscal policy. In the alternative, the envisaged emergency mechanisms[57] could result in large financial risks for all Eurozone Member States in case provided loans are defaulting. In both situations, the German budget is impacted either directly by transferring revenue to EU level[58] or indirectly by guaranteeing financial risks. In light of the potential wide transformative impact on national budgetary and fiscal decision-making, it is imperative that the established requirements under *overall budgetary responsibility* are adhered to.

On the procedural level, the requirements prescribe that major financial commitments with implications for the German budget have to be confirmed by the *Bundestag*

52. *Ratification of the Own Resources Decision (II.)*; cf. as well: Leino-Sandberg, 'Who Is Ultra Vires Now? The EU's Legal U-Turn in Interpreting Article 310 TFEU'.
53. As highlighted by the Legal Service of the German Parliament, cf. Bundestages, *Zum Erfordernis eines qualifizierten Mehrheitsbeschlusses des Bundestages hinsichtlich des Zustimmungsgesetzes zum Eigenmittelbeschluss der EU (WD 4 – 3000 – 055/20)* 5.
54. Gärditz, 'Beyond Symbolism: Towards a Constitutional Actio Popularis in EU Affairs? A Commentary on the OMT Decision of the Federal Constitutional Court' 192.
55. Calliess, 'Constitutional Identity in Germany: One for Three or Three in One?' 164-165; Payandeh, 'The OMT Judgment of the German Federal Constitutional Court: Repositioning the Court Within the European Constitutional Architecture' 408.
56. Lionello, *The Pursuit of Stability of the Euro Area as a Whole: The Reform of the European Economic Union and Perspectives of Fiscal Integration* 182.
57. Comments, 'Editorial Comments: Tinkering with Economic and Monetary Union' 6.
58. Note that even in case new taxes or levies are introduced to fund the additional EU budgetary capacity, these revenue sources are no longer available for the German Parliament and the budgetary space is thus curtate, cf. Lionello, *The Pursuit of Stability of the Euro Area as a Whole: The Reform of the European Economic Union and Perspectives of Fiscal Integration* 208.

and that these commitments remain limited in size and scope.[59] This indicates that the German Parliament has to retain a central role in the approval and administration of larger financial commitments. The constitutional jurisprudence suggests that for larger commitments with uncertain financial risks parliamentary approval is required at various stages.[60] It seems that a core constitutional element apparent in this jurisprudence is the concept of financial risk, which the parliament must be able to assess. Under the ESM, the German Parliament had to be involved in the adoption of country-specific programmes to fully evaluate the immanent financial risk for the German state budget. Under NGEU, the German Court highlighted the clearly defined objectives and the limited scope of the financial commitment both in size and duration.

For Germany, the maximum ESM-guarantees amount to EUR 190 billion, which is however only activated in case of defaulting loans.[61] Obviously, the probability of defaulting loans granted through the ESM's financial assistance programmes depends on the specific Member State in question and the agreed conditions for receiving such assistance are crucial to determine the long-term impact of the financial support. These are essential considerations when determining the financial risk inherent in the commitment that the German Parliament has to approve. In case the decision on financial assistance would be exclusively exercised at ESM or EU level, the German Parliament would be unable to assess the projected concrete financial risk which would undermine parliamentary responsibility for national budgeting as protected by Article 79(3) GG and more specifically the principle of democracy. For the envisaged EU budgetary capacity or instrument this suggests that the German financial commitments require that parliament is able to project the inherent financial risks. Hence, in case the EU Treaty amendment would introduce a legal basis to establish a Eurozone-budget or an emergency instrument, it seems constitutionally required to enable national parliaments to continuously evaluate the financial risks attached to the national financial commitment – and it would thus correspond to wider domestic constitutional calls for comprehensive involvement of national parliaments in budgetary and fiscal decisions.[62]

Next to the solution in the ESM-Treaty, Article 311(3) TFEU illustrates how national parliamentary confirmation of financial commitments at EU level can be soundly implemented as illustrated under NGEU. Notably, Article 311(3) TFEU requires the approval of the EU's own resources decision, which determines the EU's revenue and the Member States' maximum financial commitment to finance this revenue, in accordance with the national constitutional requirements applicable in the

59. Reestman, 'Legitimacy Through Adjudication: The ESM Treaty and the Fiscal Compact Before the National Courts' 259.
60. Calliess, 'Der Kampf um den Euro: Eine "Angelegenheit der Europäischen Union" zwischen Regierung, Parlament und Volk' 4.
61. Beukers, 'The Eurozone Crisis and the Autonomy of Member States in Economic Union: Changes and Challenges' 274.
62. Nettesheim, 'Die "haushaltspolitische Gesamtverantwortung" in der Rechtsprechung des BVerfG' 23.

Member States.[63] This enables national parliaments to continuously assess the financial risk attached to the national financial commitment. Subsequently, these resources are broadly allocated to the different EU policy fields in the MFF-regulation which requires unanimous approval by the Council according to Article 312(2)(2) TFEU,[64] and which thus again involves national parliaments through the outlined procedures applicable to the domestic *ex ante* control over EU decision-making.[65] Put differently, national parliaments have constitutive control over the maximum domestic commitments to the EU as well as decisive control over the allocation of funds according to policy fields under the current Treaty-framework.

In practice, the MFF-ceilings are agreed upon by the European Council in a unanimous decision as established by Article 15(4) TEU, which was illustrated in relation to the 2021-2027 MFF-framework.[66] The chancellor, accountable to the German Parliament, represents Germany in the European Council.[67] Institutionally speaking, this guarantees a limited degree of parliamentary control also in relation to the initial European Council decision on the allocation of the EU's own resources. Finally, the current framework consisting of the EU's own resources decision as well as the MFF-regulation is limited in time,[68] which ensures that the German financial obligations towards the EU are regularly re-negotiated. The outlined framework appears exemplary regarding national parliamentary involvement, which is comprehensive, compulsory regarding maximum financial liabilities, as well as temporary and thereby it appears to comply with the procedural requirements formulated under *overall budgetary responsibility*. When designing EU Treaty amendments to introduce either a comprehensive Eurozone-budget or an emergency instrument to tackle asymmetric economic shocks, the submitted observations have to be taken into consideration.

On the substantive level, *overall budgetary responsibility* requires that Germany is not establishing automatic liabilities for political decisions taken by third parties, in order to preserve budgetary autonomy, and that essential budgetary competences remain at the national level.[69] It was established that the German Constitutional Court adopts a reluctant stance when applying these substantive requirements and that until now all EU-related financial commitments were deemed compatible with *overall budgetary responsibility*. However, this conclusion might be different in the case of

63. Lionello, *The Pursuit of Stability of the Euro Area as a Whole: The Reform of the European Economic Union and Perspectives of Fiscal Integration* 205; Union, *European Union Public Finance* 131-132.
64. Crowe, 'The European Budgetary Galaxy' 437.
65. In Finland section 96 Finnish Constitution, Ojanen, 'The Impact of EU Membership on Finnish Constitutional Law' 556; in Germany Article 23(3)-(6) GG, *Right to Participation for German Parliament at the Occasion of ESM-Treaty and Euro-Plus-Pact* paras 127-131.
66. Notably, the conclusions of the European Council contain a detailed outline of the MFF-ceilings per policy field, cf. Council, *Conclusions Special Meeting of the European Council (17, 18, 19, 20 and 21 July 2020) – EUCO 10/20* 17-65.
67. As established in Article 67(1) GG, cf. as well: Jens Kersten, 'Parlamentarismus und Populismus' (2018) 58 Juristische Schulung (JuS) 929, 930.
68. Crowe, 'The European Budgetary Galaxy' 437.
69. Claes and Reestman, 'The Protection of National Constitutional Identity and the Limits of European Integration at the Occasion of the *Gauweiler* Case' 927.

larger, permanent contributions to the EU budget as would be required by some of the more far-reaching proposals that advocate an annual Eurozone-budget of up to 3% Eurozone GDP,[70] which would amount to EUR 343 billion annually based on the available 2019 data.[71] In case the financing structure for the proposed Eurozone budget would follow a comparable approach to the current one, the annual German contribution could amount to around 27%[72] which would translate into up to EUR 92.6 billion annually. In absolute numbers and percentages, the German EU financial commitment could then be classified as substantial as under the current calculation about 25% of the German federal budget[73] would be effectively transferred to EU level. In light of the current conception of *overall budgetary responsibility*, the German Court might consider this as too extensive given that the German Parliament would be prevented from exercising its budgetary prerogatives in relation to one-quarters of the annual German budget.

The presented arguments suggest that the German Constitutional Court could consider the creation of the most far-reaching Eurozone-budget in conflict with *overall budgetary responsibility* given that it limits *permanently* direct German parliamentary control over a significant part of the German budget. This would seriously undermine the prospect of EU fiscal integration. Therefore, the book evaluates in a separate section below (C) whether the charted *constitutional flexibility* in the German constitutional approach could be employed to ease the apparent constitutional conflict.

b Compatibility with the Charted Micro-comparative Constitutional Space

As previously established, national constitutional limits protect similar constitutional principles, in particular national sovereignty, democracy and parliamentary control over budgeting. In light of this material overlap and given the previously established potential conflicts with German democracy, it appears likely that the French, Spanish and Polish *constitutional identity limits* equally conflict with the prospect of introducing a sizeable Eurozone-budget or an emergency instrument. Yet, given that constitutional systems adopt specific strategies on how to address conflicts with these core national principles, it has to be determined whether the respective *constitutional identity limit* imposes concrete limitations towards the attainment of these integration steps.

70. Craig and Markakis, 'EMU Reform' 1423.
71. As determined previously, the Euroarea GDP amounted to around EUR 11,430 billion according to the World Bank, cf. Bank, 'GDP (Current US$): Euro Area'.
72. Based on EU data considering overall revenue from national contributions among Eurozone Member States (amounting to EUR 94,245.5 million in 2019; EUR 93,445.4 million in 2018; EUR 72,720 million in 2017) and the German share of national contributions (amounting to EUR 25,820 million in 2019; EUR 25,266.7 million in 2018; EUR 19,587 million in 2017) the share was 27.4% in 2019, 27% in 2018 and 26.9% in 2017, cf. the data: European Commission, *EU Expenditure and Revenue 2014-2020 (Dataset)* (DG Budget data 2020).
73. Based on the previous calculation and data; EUR 72 billion constitute 20.2% of the 2019 federal budget which amounted to EUR 356 billion in 2019.

In France, the *Conseil Constitutionnel* could be requested to rule on the compatibility of such a Treaty amendment with the French Constitution.[74] As established, the required conferral of competences to the EU can be challenged by a set of privileged applicants based on Article 54 or Article 61(2) French Constitution.[75] In light of the previous constitutional practice,[76] it seems highly likely that such a review will be initiated in light of the constitutional importance of the matter.[77] The *Conseil* would then mainly determine whether the envisaged conferral of power is compatible with the French sovereignty doctrine. In that regard, the *Conseil* established that not every conferral of competences to EU level is automatically in conflict with French sovereignty but only such conferrals that affect the 'essential conditions for the exercise of national sovereignty'.[78]

It appears that the *Conseil* construed these *essential conditions* mainly on a competence-centric basis. For example, the initiation of EMU and the required conferral of monetary competences to the EU required a constitutional amendment given that monetary competence was deemed an important competence area under French sovereignty and given that these competences were shifted to EU level.[79] In contrast, in its evaluation of the Fiscal Compact the *Conseil Constitutionnel* established that the intergovernmental instrument largely reiterated already conferred competences, which did not require anew confirmation through an explicit constitutional amendment.[80]

Therefore, the central point of the *Conseil's* scrutiny when assessing the fiscal integration steps appears to be whether the proposed EU Treaty amendment would alter the original EMU commitment introduced by the Maastricht Treaty and whether in that regard additional competences are conferred to EU level. The constitutional assessment will depend on the concrete design of the Treaty amendment and the envisaged conferral of national powers. However, particularly the introduction of a bigger Eurozone- budget could impact French fiscal competences in the view of the *Conseil Constitutionnel*. At the same time, the *Conseil* was until now very reluctant to identify a conflict with the sovereignty limit in relation to EMU integration steps taken during the Eurocrisis,[81] which were, however, largely introduced as EU secondary law measures. Overall, it appears at least possible that the *Conseil* would find the proposed

74. Azoulai and Ronkes Agerbeek, '*Conseil constitutionnel* (French Constitutional Court), Decision No. 2004-505 DC of 19 November 2004, on the Treaty Establishing a Constitution for Europe' 884.
75. Millet, 'Constitutional Identity in France: Vices and – Above All – Virtues' 139.
76. Vranes, 'Constitutional Foundation of, and Limitations to, EU Integration in France' 539.
77. Neuman, 'The Brakes That Failed: Constitutional Restriction of International Agreements in France' 296.
78. Claes, 'National Idenity: Trump Card or up for Negotiation?' 126; Oliver, 'The French Constitution and the Treaty of Maastricht' 12.
79. Bonnie, 'The Constitutionality of Transfers of Sovereignty: The French Approach' 527; Gundel, *Die Einordnung des Gemeinschaftsrechts in die französische Rechtsordnung* 133.
80. Fabbrini, 'The Euro-Crisis and the Courts: Judicial Review and the Political Process in Comparative Perspective' 120.
81. Vranes, 'Constitutional Foundation of, and Limitations to, EU Integration in France' 540; Neuman, 'The Brakes That Failed: Constitutional Restriction of International Agreements in France' 296; Bonnie, 'The Constitutionality of Transfers of Sovereignty: The French Approach' 527.

establishment of a bigger Eurozone-budget or the introduction of emergency instruments accompanied by EU Treaty amendment to be in conflict with the French sovereignty limit. Especially more far-reaching proposals would significantly alter the original conception of EMU-cooperation and therefore exceed the initial conferral.

In case the *Conseil Constitutionnel* would conclude that the proposed Treaty amendment conflicts with French sovereignty, a constitutional amendment would be required in France to ratify the new EU obligations.[82] Such constitutional amendments can be enacted following Article 89 French Constitution, which requires the support of a three-fifths majority in Congress.[83] These constitutional amendments are not uncommon in France prior to the ratification of new EU-Treaties and the *Conseil* will not check if the adopted amendments themselves violate French *constitutional identity*.[84] Overall, the *Conseil Constitutionnel* occupies in this process its institutional role as 'pointsman' that identifies constitutional conflicts with EU integration steps but that refrains from imposing absolute limitations to the powers of the constitution-amending legislator.[85]

Similarly, in Spain, the Constitutional Tribunal established that EU cooperation is limited by the Spanish *constitutional identity* doctrine. The *constitutional identity* doctrine protects, *inter alia*, Spanish sovereignty in conjunction with democracy as well as the fundamental constitutional structure established by the Spanish Constitution.[86] From its jurisprudence, it can be deduced that the Tribunal construes Spanish sovereignty as an exercise of constitutional powers and thus as a competence-based restriction to EU integration.[87] Furthermore, the Tribunal emphasized the constitutional importance of preserving *Kompetenz-Kompetenz* and, more generally, the hierarchical position of the Spanish Constitution.[88] Based on this broad conceptual framework, it appears that budgetary and fiscal prerogatives are likely covered by the Spanish *constitutional identity limit*. Notably, the Spanish Constitution assigns the constitutional responsibility for the state budget in Article 66(2) to the *Cortes Generales* – the joint assembly of the Spanish Parliament and Spanish Senate. In addition, Article 75(3) Spanish Constitution clarifies that these budgetary prerogatives cannot be delegated to a standing legislative committee, but that they have to be exercised by the plenary. The constitutional consideration apparent in this constitutional provision suggests that the decision-making on the Spanish state budget is of high democratic importance as it requires approval by the entire *Cortes Generales*.

82. Baranger, 'The Language of Eternity: Judicial Review of the Amending Power in France (Or the Absence Thereof)' 402-403.
83. Cahill, 'Ever Closer Remoteness of the Peoples of Europe? Limits on the Power of Amendment and National Constituent Power' 266-267.
84. Ziller, 'European Union Law in the Jurisprudence of French Supreme Courts: Europe-Friendliness with a French Touch' 772.
85. Millet, 'Constitutional Identity in France: Vices and – Above All – Virtues' 150-151.
86. Martín Y Pérez de Nanclares, 'Constitutional Identity in Spain: Commitment to European Integration Without Giving up the Essence of the Constitution' 279.
87. Pérez Tremps, 'National Idenity in Spanish Constitutional Court Case-Law' 271.
88. Castillo de la Torre, '*Tribunal Constitucional* (Spanish Constitutional Court), Opinion 1/2004 of 13 December 2004, on the Treaty Establishing a Constitution for Europe' 1193-1194.

Any EU Treaty amendments, which would introduce a genuine Eurozone-budget or an emergency instrument to tackle asymmetric economic shocks, would likely alter these central constitutional prerogatives of the Spanish *Cortes Generales*, and thus affect Spanish democracy and sovereignty. Through such EU Treaty amendment, the EU could be entitled to take its own, independent budgetary and fiscal decisions as well as potentially generate its own revenue, which could interfere with the constitutional task to control the state budget assigned to the *Cortes Generales*. Notably, the possible additional national expenditure or potential financial liabilities could affect the principle of the completeness of budgetary planning and the currently required parliamentary approval for budgetary, financial as well as fiscal decisions. As a result, a constitutional amendment might likely be required to prepare the conferral of the required budgetary and fiscal competences from the national to EU level.

Such constitutional amendments are governed by Articles 167 and 168 Spanish Constitution.[89] The likely affected constitutional provisions in Articles 66(2), 75(3), and 134 Spanish Constitution, are not situated within the sections of the constitution enumerated in Article 168 Spanish Constitution. Amendments to these provisions would therefore not be considered 'essential reforms' of the constitutional text and the stricter procedural framework is not applicable.[90] Hence, amendments to these provisions can be approved by a three-fifths majority in the Spanish Parliament and Senate.[91] Yet, the identified possible conflict with the Spanish *constitutional identity limit*, and more specifically with the principle of democracy and sovereignty alters this conclusion. Notably, budgetary and fiscal competences are not merely parliamentary prerogatives protected by the Spanish Constitution, but they have a particular constitutional link to these two principles. Consequently, the envisaged EU Treaty-changes might not only alter the specifically identified constitutional provisions, but these amendments appear to equally affect core constitutional principles enlisted in the Preliminary Part of the Spanish Constitution which compromises Articles 1 to 9. Concretely, Article 1(1) and (2) Spanish Constitution establish the principle of democracy and sovereignty respectively. Consequently, the envisaged EU Treaty amendments could be characterized as amendments to these principles, which would result in an 'essential reform' in the sense of Article 168 Spanish Constitution.[92] Such essential reform has to be approved by a two-thirds majority of the Spanish Parliament and Senate. Both houses then have to be immediately dissolved and after new elections are concluded, the newly elected houses have to confirm the reform again by a two-thirds majority followed by a public referendum.[93] This constitutes a high constitutional hurdle that was never taken until now.

Taken together, this indicates that the Constitutional Tribunal might identify a conflict between the proposed EU Treaty amendments and the Spanish *constitutional identity limit*. The precise evaluation remains anticipatory, as the Tribunal did only

89. Martín Y Pérez de Nanclares, 'Constitutional Identity in Spain: Commitment to European Integration Without Giving up the Essence of the Constitution' 282.
90. Albert, *Constitutional Amendments: Making, Breaking, and Changing Constitutions* 192.
91. Elvira, 'Spain' 282.
92. Ferreres Comella, *The Constitution of Spain: A Contextual Analysis* 57.
93. Elvira, 'Spain' 282-283.

define its *constitutional identity limit* on two occasions in a very abstract manner. However, given the projected major impact on core Spanish constitutional responsibilities and the general receptiveness to comparative reasoning,[94] the emergence of such conflict is conceivable. In case this conflict emerges, the Spanish constitution-amending legislator is empowered to overcome it by amending the constitutional text under the strict revision procedure following Article 168 Spanish Constitution. Given that the Spanish Constitutional Tribunal is not competent to review constitutional amendments, such amendments could not be challenged themselves.[95] Yet, the strict constitutional amendment procedure and the highly exceptional status of constitutional amendments in Spain[96] both render its attainability uncertain.

Finally, the application of the Polish *constitutional identity limit* to the proposed EU Treaty amendment appears to result in comparable constitutional concerns, albeit this conflict remains hypothetical for now as Poland is not yet a member of the Eurozone.[97] As established in the *micro-comparative* assessment, the Polish Constitutional Tribunal identified the ability to design financial, budgetary and fiscal policies as a central component of Polish sovereignty.[98] Article 219 Polish Constitution assigns the prerogative to adopt the state budget to the Sejm and the constitutional text empowers the Polish Council of Ministers to draft internal policies, including economic and fiscal policies, following Article 146 Polish Constitution.[99] Obviously, the amendments to the EU-Treaties could result in shifts of responsibilities in economic and fiscal matters to EU level. These modifications would then challenge the outlined constitutional responsibilities and prerogatives in financial, budgetary as well as fiscal competences of the Polish Parliament and the Polish Council of Ministers, which were identified as core components of Polish sovereignty. Therefore, it seems that the Polish Constitutional Tribunal will likely conclude that any proposed Treaty-changes on these matters alter constitutional provisions in Poland and will thus require explicit confirmation by the Polish legislator following Article 90(1) and (2) Polish Constitution.[100]

The subsequent question is whether the proposed EU Treaty amendment and the identified constitutional challenges would also be found to impact the material core of the Polish Constitution as protected by the *constitutional identity limit*. Although the Polish Constitutional Tribunal identified fiscal competences as particularly important

94. Martín Y Pérez de Nanclares, 'Constitutional Identity in Spain: Commitment to European Integration Without Giving up the Essence of the Constitution' 269.
95. De Visser, *Constitutional Review in Europe: A Comparative Analysis* 119.
96. Solanes Mullor and Torres Pérez, 'The Constitution of Spain: The Challenges for the Constitutional Order under European and Global Governance' 545-548.
97. Reestman, 'Legitimacy Through Adjudication: The ESM Treaty and the Fiscal Compact Before the National Courts' 249.
98. Bainczyk, 'Folgen einer mangelnden Anpassung der polnischen Verfassung nach dem Vertrag von Lissabon im Lichte des Urteils des polnischen Verfassungsgerichtshofes zum Beschluss des Europäischen Rates zur Änderung von Art. 136 AEUV' 314-315.
99. *Challenges Against Article 136 (3) TFEU and ESM-Treaty* section 7.7.; cf. as well: Bainczyk, 'Folgen einer mangelnden Anpassung der polnischen Verfassung nach dem Vertrag von Lissabon im Lichte des Urteils des polnischen Verfassungsgerichtshofes zum Beschluss des Europäischen Rates zur Änderung von Art. 136 AEUV' 314.
100. Granat and Granat, *The Constitution of Poland: A Contextual Analysis* 27.

under Polish sovereignty, the Tribunal equally acknowledged the evolutionary potential of Polish sovereignty.[101] The evolutionary conception of sovereignty might ultimately even allow for the conferral of competences to the EU which were traditionally perceived as core powers of the sovereign state.[102] Furthermore, the Tribunal construed EU cooperation as an exercise of sovereign powers and argued that the respective competences remained at the national level, merely their exercise is transferred to the supranational level.[103] In addition, the conception of EU cooperation as a shared exercise of competences attached to the national level is reflected in the derived status of the EU and the prohibition to confer *Kompetenz-Kompetenz* to EU level.[104] To that end, the Tribunal underscored that the conferral of competences is restricted to 'certain matters', which presupposes that the Polish legislator clearly outlines the extent of the conferred competences.[105]

When applying this constitutional benchmark to the envisaged EU Treaty amendment it is conceivable that the Polish Constitutional Tribunal would identify a major conflict with Polish *constitutional identity*, given that financial, budgetary and fiscal competences are core powers under Polish sovereignty. In case major parts of these competences are conferred to EU level, the Tribunal might find a violation of the constitutional framework for the conferral of competences established in Article 90 Polish Constitution and in particular the requirement that the transfer of competences has to be limited to 'certain matters'.

In case the outlined EU fiscal integration steps would be deemed incompatible with Polish *constitutional identity* and the EU enabling clause in Article 90 Polish Constitution, it appears that the Polish constitution-amending legislator is competent to overcome the resulting constitutional conflict. Although the Polish Constitutional Tribunal did never explicitly affirm this,[106] it continuously indicated that the Polish legislator could overcome a conflict between the Polish Constitution and envisaged EU commitments by either amending the constitutional text, modifying the EU commitment, or by withdrawing from the EU following Article 50 TEU.[107] This can be seen as a confirmation of the wide discretion of the Polish legislator.[108] Moreover, it can be submitted that a possible absolute character of the Polish *constitutional identity limit*

101. Czapliński, 'Recent Constitutional Jurisprudence Concerning the European Union: Some Remarks on 2010 Judgments of the Polish Constitutional Court' 200.
102. Wróbel, 'Die Grenzen der europäischen Integration im Lichte jüngerer Entscheidungen des polnischen Verfassungsgerichts' 498.
103. Mik, 'State Sovereignty and European Integration: Public International Law, EU Law and Constitutional Law in the Polish Context' 398.
104. Śledzińska-Simon and Ziółkowski, 'Constitutional Identity in Poland: Is the Emperor Putting on the Old Clothes of Sovereignty' 251; Łazowski, 'Half Full and Half Empty Glass: The Application of EU Law in Poland (2004-2010)' 510.
105. Rideau, 'The Case-Law of the Polish, Hungarian and Czech Constitutional Courts on National Idenity and the "German Model"' 252.
106. Śledzińska-Simon and Ziółkowski, 'Constitutional Identity in Poland: Is the Emperor Putting on the Old Clothes of Sovereignty' 244.
107. Łazowski, 'Case Note: Accession Treaty – Polish Constitutional Tribunal: Conformity of the Accession Treaty with the Polish Contitution – Decision of 11 May 2005' 157.
108. Czaputowicz, 'Sovereignty in Theories of European Integration and the Perspective of the Polish Constitutional Tribunal' 33.

would have already been emphasized by the Polish Constitutional Tribunal. Therefore, the Polish constitution-amending legislator would likely be able to overcome a conflict between the Polish *constitutional identity limit*, specifically Polish sovereignty, and the envisaged EU Treaty amendment. However, the possibly required modifications in relation to core constitutional principles included in Chapter I of the Polish Constitution – in particular the conception of Polish sovereignty enshrined in Article 4 Polish Constitution – would have to be confirmed by public referendum as established in Article 235(6) Polish Constitution. Hence, the required constitutional amendment to accommodate fiscal integration seems to entail major procedural hurdles.

c Interim Conclusion

The creation of an EU budgetary capacity or the introduction of emergency instruments through EU Treaty amendment is possible in Finland, France, Spain and Poland. Only the German *constitutional identity limit* appears to impose an absolute restriction on its attainment. However, it was established that attaining the required two-thirds majority threshold in Finland could be politically challenging and similarly the feasibility of constitutional amendments in Spain remains questionable in light of the high procedural threshold as well as the generally rare use of the amendment procedure. The latter corresponds to the situation in Poland where possible constitutional conflicts can be overcome, however, the attainability of the required majority to enact both a constitutional amendment including possibly a public referendum and subsequently to approve the conferral of competences under Article 90 Polish Constitution seems highly questionable, particularly in light of the current political situation.

Hence, the most far-reaching integration proposals concerning the creation of an additional EU fiscal capacity are confronted with significant national constitutional opposition that ranges from requiring support by a qualified majority in Finland, requiring constitutional amendments in France, Spain and Poland to being seemingly incompatible with the German *eternity clause*. Thus, the most central question when designing the envisaged fiscal capacity appears to be to what extent the resulting budgetary tools are specific, limited in size and scope, what sort of control national parliaments can exercise as well as how they are financed. In case the introduction of the envisaged tools follows the existing framework of EU budgeting, it appears that no incompatible constitutional conflicts emerge, given that the central position of national parliaments in the control of fiscal and budgetary decisions would be warranted. In case, however, the Treaty amendment would confer discretionary decision-making in relation to these instruments for example regarding their size, national parliamentary prerogatives would be clearly impacted, and the outlined constitutional concerns would be triggered.

3 Conclusion on the Feasibility of EU Budgetary Capacity or Instrument

The assessment reveals that the envisaged EU Treaty amendment to introduce a budgetary capacity for the Euroarea or an emergency instrument to address asymmetric economic shocks affects important constitutional principles within the Member States. These constitutional principles are national democracy in combination with national sovereignty as well as the institutional prerogatives of the national parliaments. Given the importance of these principles for the respective national constitutional systems, the constitutional text as well as the constitutional authorities appear to impose additional hurdles to confirm the required conferral of competences to engage in the suggested EU Treaty amendments. However, in Finland, France, Poland and Spain it appears that constitutional concerns can be addressed by the constitution-amending legislator by explicitly confirming the conferral of competences through a constitutional amendment - with partly high procedural hurdles. Only in Germany, the constitutional concerns might partly not be overcome by amending the constitutional text itself. Overall, the assessment thus reveals that the emerging constitutional concerns are rooted in a similar conception of national democracy and national sovereignty, according to which budgetary and fiscal competences are essential powers of the national parliaments protected by both mentioned principles.

Furthermore, the compatibility assessment revealed that the German *overall budgetary responsibility* limit provides a constitutional litmus test for the drafting of EU fiscal integration steps more generally, as it covers most constitutional concerns identified in other Member States given its comprehensive and far-reaching conception. As highlighted, the limit distinguishes between procedural and substantive requirements.[109] On the procedural level, the German Constitutional Court requires that financial commitments remain limited in scope as well as overall size and that the German Parliament retains a central position in the approval as well as administration of EU fiscal decision-making.[110] For the design of the EU Treaty amendments, several design requirements appear to emerge. These design requirements include a compulsory involvement of the German Parliament in all major budgetary and fiscal decisions at EU level. For a Eurozone-budget, this would imply developing a structure comparable to the current EU budgetary framework, which makes national parliamentary approval obligatory for determining EU revenue according to Article 311(3) TFEU and which subsequently allows national parliaments to advice their respective national Council and European Council representatives according to the internally applicable procedures. In that regard, given that the fiscal decision-making space would be significantly increased under the envisaged scheme, additional national parliamentary involvement could be envisaged to tackle possible further constitutional concerns. In addition, the conferral of powers has to be limited in size and scope, which requires that national parliaments clearly define their financial commitments and that this commitment cannot be increased against the will of the respective national parliament.

Through these procedural requirements, the German Court aims to preserve the constitutionally enshrined control of the German Parliament over budgetary and fiscal

109. Claes and Reestman, 'The Protection of National Constitutional Identity and the Limits of European Integration at the Occasion of the *Gauweiler* Case' 927.
110. Reestman, 'Legitimacy Through Adjudication: The ESM Treaty and the Fiscal Compact Before the National Courts' 259; Nettesheim, 'Die "haushaltspolitische Gesamtverantwortung" in der Rechtsprechung des BVerfG' 23.

decisions, which are essential competence areas under German democracy.[111] The result of these procedural requirements is ultimately that fiscal integration steps seemingly have to take a hybrid character, which allows for EU decision-making under strict German parliamentary control. The resulting hybrid character of fiscal decision-making in the specific areas identified is neither exclusively confined to the national level nor is it independently administered by the EU. Instead, the institutional requirements appear to balance decisive control of national parliaments with allocating fiscal decision-making space to EU level. The existing model under Article 311 (3) TFEU might serve as an example in that regard, although increased fiscal decision-making space in case of a larger Eurozone-budget appears to require an even more comprehensive involvement of national parliaments.

Adhering to the German procedural requirements under *overall budgetary responsibility* and pursuing a hybrid model for fiscal integration appear to not merely address the constitutional concerns of the German Constitutional Court. They appear to equally address potential constitutional concerns in the other evaluated Member States in relation to their national *constitutional identity limits*. Arguably, the central involvement of national parliaments in the fiscal decision-making of a more integrated EU might more generally address sovereignty or democracy concerns. Notably, in France and Spain the constitutional authorities appear to restrict the conferral of particularly important competences to EU level, but they seem not to necessarily oppose the shared exercise of core sovereign competences.[112] It can be submitted that respecting the German procedural requirements under *overall budgetary responsibility* ensures that democratically relevant constitutional budgetary and fiscal powers are not fully conferred to EU level but are instead only jointly exercised. The result might be that no constitutional amendment would be required in these Member States as the constitutional prerogatives are ultimately preserved. The German procedural requirements under *overall budgetary responsibility* could thus function as an indicatory constitutional benchmark for EU fiscal integration proposals in other EU Member States.

In addition, the resulting overview indicates that only the German *constitutional identity limit* imposes an irreconcilable limitation to the conferral of powers at EU level. Notably, in case the envisaged EU Treaty amendment conflicts with the substantive dimension of *overall budgetary responsibility* and therefore violates the core of German democracy, the German legislator may not ratify the required conferral of powers.[113]

111. Calliess, 'Constitutional Identity in Germany: One for Three or Three in One?' 164-165.
112. On the Finnish conception of sovereignty, which allows to filter in the factual benefits that stem from supranational cooperation, cf. Mutanen, *Towards a Pluralistic Constitutional Understanding of State Sovereignty in the European Union? The Concept, Regulation and Constitutional Practice of Sovereignty in Finland and Certain Other EU Member States* 334; on the conception of French sovereignty, cf. Vranes, 'Constitutional Foundation of, and Limitations to, EU Integration in France' 532; on the conception of Spanish sovereignty, cf. Castillo de la Torre, '*Tribunal Constitucional* (Spanish Constitutional Court), Opinion 1/2004 of 13 December 2004, on the Treaty establishing a Constitution for Europe' 1175; as well as on the Polish conception of sovereignty, which emphasizes the only temporary limitation of sovereignty through EU cooperation, cf. Bainczyk, 'Das Ratifizierungsverfahren des Vertrages von Lissabon in Polen' 156.
113. Rademacher, 'Die "Verfassungsidentität" als Grenze der Kompetenzübertragung auf die Europäische Union?' 144.

Consequently, *overall budgetary responsibility* can be identified as the strictest constitutional hurdle for introducing the envisaged EU Treaty amendment to establish a discretionary Eurozone-budget and the proposed large financial instruments envisaged against asymmetric shocks in order to stabilize the Euro both in a preventive manner as well as in emergency situations. In contrast to the assessed *constitutional identity limits* in France, Poland and Spain, which could all be overcome by the constitution-amending legislator, the German Constitution does not allow constitutional modifications that affect the *eternity clause* in Article 79(3) GG. Changes to this provision require the enactment of a new constitutional text following Article 146 GG confirmed by the constituting power in Germany.[114] It was already highlighted that such a thorough constitutional reform process is currently unlikely in Germany, which is why EU fiscal integration has to address the German constitutional demands. Yet, it was submitted that different constitutional arguments could be included in order to deconstruct the substantive dimension of *overall budgetary responsibility* and thereby generate additional constitutional flexibility, as will be further elaborated below (C). As it stands, the most ambitious EU fiscal integration steps will be likely considered incompatible with the German *constitutional identity limit*. The overall research findings on the creation of a Eurozone fiscal capacity are summarized in Table 8.1.

114. Herbst, 'Legale Abschaffung des Grundgesetzes nach Art. 146 GG?' 33.

Table 8.1 Compatibility of Charted Constitutional Space with Proposals on Fiscal Capacity

Member State	***Emergency Instrument (ESM-Design)***	***Discretionary Emergency Instrument (Treaty-Change)***	***Budgetary Capacity Based on Article 311 TFEU***	***Discretionary Budgetary Capacity (Treaty-Change)***
Finland	Parliamentary approval by a simple majority (section 94(2)(1) Finnish Constitution (FC)).	Qualified parliamentary approval (section 94(2)(2) FC).	*Ex ante* parliamentary monitoring (section 96 FC). Own resources decision possibly by qualified parliamentary majority (section 94(2)(2) FC).	Qualified parliamentary approval (section 94(2)(2) FC).
Germany (including constitutional identity limit)	Parliamentary approval by a two-thirds majority (Article 23(1)(3) in conjunction with Article 79(2) GG).	Apparent conflict with the German *eternity clause* (size of commitment and suspension of nat. parliamentary control). Partly flexibilization of conflict is possible through: - EU benefits. - Net. calculation. - Consistent standard.	*Ex ante* parliamentary involvement (Article 23(3) GG). Parliamentary approval of own resources decision by a two-thirds majority (Article 23(1)(3) in conjunction with Article 79(2) GG).	Apparent conflict with the German *eternity clause* (size of commitment and suspension of nat. parliamentary control). Partly flexibilization of conflict is possible through: - EU benefits. - Net. calculation. - Consistent standard.

Member State	***Emergency Instrument (ESM-Design)***	***Discretionary Emergency Instrument (Treaty-Change)***	***Budgetary Capacity Based on Article 311 TFEU***	***Discretionary Budgetary Capacity (Treaty-Change)***
French sovereignty limit	No apparent conflict with the *sovereignty limit.*	Apparent conflict, can be overcome by const. amendment (Article 89 French Constitution (FC)), which is common practice in France.	Not applicable to EU secondary law.	Apparent conflict, can be overcome by const. amendment (Article 89 FC), which is common practice in France.
Polish constitutional identity limit	No apparent conflict with the *constitutional identity limit.*	Possible conflict which might require const. amendment (Article 236 Polish Constitution (PC)), including possibly referendum.	Not applicable to EU secondary law.	Possible conflict which might require const. amendment (Article 236 PC), including possibly referendum.
		Apparent conflict, can be possibly overcome through 'modern' interpretation of Polish sovereignty.		Apparent conflict, can be possibly overcome through 'modern' interpretation of Polish sovereignty.
Spanish constitutional identity limit	No apparent conflict with the *constitutional identity limit.*	Apparent conflict, can be overcome under strict const. amendment procedure in Article 168 Spanish Constitution (SC) which imposes a high threshold and is practically difficult to attain.	Generally not applicable to EU secondary law.	Apparent conflict, can be overcome under strict const. amendment procedure in Article 168 SC which imposes a high threshold and is practically difficult to attain.

II Compatibility of Funding Options with National Constitutional Space

The current EU-Treaties enable Member States to fund shared projects, policy goals or objectives, without putting the national constitutional order into question. As established, the current budgeting practice at EU level relies on the Member States. Notably, and in addition to the fact that the EU budget is adopted following the special legislative procedure according to Article 314(1) TFEU requiring approval of both the European Parliament and the Council,[115] the underpinning revenue has to be approved by the Member States as laid down in Article 311(3) TFEU.[116] Therefore, Member States retain control over their budgetary commitments under the Treaty structure, which warrants domestic parliamentary control over financial involvement at EU level, deemed a core procedural component of *overall budgetary responsibility* by the German Constitutional Court.[117]

Different ideas were presented to make EU revenue less dependent on the national budgets. These proposals include the introduction of new EU own resources possibly generated through jointly introduced taxes (1), more far-reaching proposals suggesting the introduction of a genuine EU taxation power (2) or the initiation of EU debts and shared liabilities (3).

1 Introducing New Tax-Based Own Resources for the EU

One possibility to generate additional EU revenue is to reform the existing EU own resources system. As mentioned before, currently almost three-quarters of the EU's own resources are financed through the direct contributions of the Member States.[118] These funds are thus an expenditure for the Member States, which triggers particular domestic interests regarding the use of these funds, also referred to as 'just return' discussion.[119] To overcome this rhetoric, the *Monti*-Report proposed the introduction of new sources of genuine EU own resources, which could be based on a levy or tax imposed upon EU-related improvements or achievements.[120] The idea of introducing new genuine own resources, which would be levied by the Member States but directly transferred to the EU without entering the national budgetary process,[121] was equally

115. Cf. for example: Crowe, 'The European Budgetary Galaxy' 440-441.
116. Lionello, *The Pursuit of Stability of the Euro Area as a Whole: The Reform of the European Economic Union and Perspectives of Fiscal Integration* 205.
117. *Quantitative Easing (PSPP) Reference* para. 48; Reestman, 'Legitimacy Through Adjudication: The ESM Treaty and the Fiscal Compact Before the National Courts' 259.
118. Fabbrini, 'Fiscal Capacity' 128-129.
119. Monti et al., *Future Financing of the EU: Final Report and Recommendations of the High Level Group on Own Resources December 2016* 68; cf. as well: Alcidi and Gros, 'Next Generation EU: A Large Common Response to the COVID-19 Crisis' 203.
120. Monti et al., *Future Financing of the EU: Final Report and Recommendations of the High Level Group on Own Resources December 2016* 68, 41-56.
121. Crowe, 'The European Budgetary Galaxy' 431; similar to the current system according to which genuine own resources do not enter the budgetary process in the Member States, cf. Lionello, *The Pursuit of Stability of the Euro Area as a Whole: The Reform of the European Economic Union and Perspectives of Fiscal Integration* 203.

submitted by the European Council conclusions on NGEU.[122] These new own resources would be largely tax-based and could include, for example, a carbon-emission tax on flight tickets, a general carbon tax, a nuclear power tax, a national surcharge on fuel tax, a financial transaction tax, or even a wealth tax.[123] Such tax-based own resources could be established based on the tax approximation clauses in Articles 113 and 115 TFEU or designed as fiscal measures to pursue the environmental and energy-related objectives established in the Treaties based on Articles 192 and 194 TFEU.[124] Subsequently, Member States would have to agree to purpose the revenues from these harmonized or environmental taxes as own resources of the EU under Article 311 TFEU.[125]

When applying the national constitutional framework to the adoption of such EU secondary law, it appears that national parliaments would retain considerable influence given the unanimity requirement for the Council voting in case national constitutions prescribe parliamentary *ex ante* participation comparable to the Finnish or German system. In addition, Article 311(3) TFEU prescribes adoption by special legislative procedure following a unanimous vote in the Council after consultation of the European Parliament as well as the subsequent approval by all EU Member States following their constitutional procedures.[126]

In Finland, this national implementation would require parliamentary approval according to section 94 Finnish Constitution, as budgetary powers of the Finnish Parliament are affected by the envisaged commitment.[127] The required parliamentary majority to approve these financial commitments depends on the impact of the envisaged own resources decision on the Finnish Constitution. The Constitutional Law Committee has pointed out that a Council Decision based on Article 311(3) TFEU can be generally approved by a simple majority and that it is compatible with the Finnish sovereignty doctrine, as long as the general nature of EU cooperation is not altered by it.[128] Following the Committee, this requires in particular that the upper limits of the Finnish liabilities are determined in order to secure Finnish parliamentary budgetary

122. Which include, for example, a revenue generated from non-recycled plastic waste, a carbon border adjustment mechanism, a digital levy, cf. Council, *Conclusions Special Meeting of the European Council (17, 18, 19, 20 and 21 July 2020): EUCO 10/20* 8 (A 29).
123. Cf. for example the various proposals submitted by the *Monti*-Report, Monti et al., *Future Financing of the EU: Final Report and Recommendations of the High Level Group on Own Resources December 2016* 41-56; for a full overview, cf. Margit Schratzenstaller, 'The EU Own Resources System: Reform Needs and Options' (2013) 48 Intereconomics – Review of European Economic Policy 303, 311-312.
124. Schratzenstaller and Krenek, 'Tax-Based Own Resources to Finance the EU Budget' 174-175.
125. *Ibid.*, 175.
126. Lionello, *The Pursuit of Stability of the Euro Area as a Whole: The Reform of the European Economic Union and Perspectives of Fiscal Integration* 205; Union, *European Union Public Finance* 131-132.
127. As for example visible in relation to Council Decision 2014/355, which required approval under section 94(1) Finnish Constitution, cf. Finnish Parliament, 'HE 248/2014 on the Government Proposal to Parliament on the Adoption of the Council Decision on the System of the European Union's Own Resources (2014/335 / EU, Euratom)' (*Finnish Parliament*, 2014), https://www.finlex.fi/fi/esitykset/he/2014/20140248#idp446520544, accessed 5 April 2023 point 7.1.
128. *Commission's Draft EU Recovery Plan and MFF Planning* 17.

sovereignty.[129] In that regard, it appears that the proposed tax-based own revenues would be clearly limited within the EU own resources decision both in relation to the taxes that are covered (scope restriction) as well as the maximum Finnish liabilities (size restriction).

Under the German constitutional framework, the Council Decision on the EU's own resources system has to be approved by the German legislator following Article 23(1)(3) GG, as it supplements the EU-Treaties.[130] Accordingly, Article 23(1)(3) and Article 79(2)(3) GG applies to the adoption of the envisaged decision, which suggests that it would have to be adopted by a constitution-amending majority in case it alters the German Constitution.[131] Considering that the allocation of tax-based revenues has considerable consequences for national budgetary prerogatives, notably the German Parliament could not freely decide on the future use of the transferred revenue, it appears likely that a constitution amending two-thirds majority would be deemed applicable. This conclusion is supported by the outlined German constitutional jurisprudence, which during the Eurocrisis continuously emphasized the importance of (free) parliamentary control over revenue and expenditure decisions – as summarized under *overall budgetary responsibility*.

Taken together, this suggests that in both EU Member States, the proposed tax-based own resources could be adopted based on the domestic EU clause, possibly by a qualified parliamentary majority. The national approval is constitutive for the adoption of the EU own resources decision, as specified in Article 311(3) TFEU. Furthermore, national parliaments can influence the subsequent allocation of the new EU revenue through the analysed domestic *ex ante* preparatory procedures applicable to EU secondary law. Finally, the scheme is negotiated for a limited period of time which ensures continuous parliamentary involvement. This comprehensive involvement of national parliaments appears to satisfy the German constitutional requirements under *overall budgetary responsibility*.[132]

Furthermore, given that the proposed tax-based own resources would be entirely based on existing EU law and would be implemented based on EU secondary law, Member States retain the possibility to alter their financial commitments. Notably, the own resources decision is re-considered jointly with the EU's MFF every seven years.[133] Therefore, the national commitment appears more easily reversible compared to, for example, an explicit primary law commitment. If indeed enshrined in EU secondary

129. *Ratification of the Own Resources Decision (II.)*; cf. as well: Ojanen and Salminen, 'Finland: European Integration and International Human Rights Treaties as Sources of Domestic Constitutional Change and Dynamism' 391-392.
130. As established by the German Constitutional Court, cf. *Lisbon-judgment* paras 313-314; cf. as well: Henning Tappe and Rainer Wernsmann, *Öffentliches Finanzrecht* (2nd edn, C.F. Müller 2019) 196 (Recitals 809-810).
131. Bundestages, *Zum Erfordernis eines qualifizierten Mehrheitsbeschlusses des Bundestages hinsichtlich des Zustimmungsgesetzes zum Eigenmittelbeschluss der EU (WD 4 – 3000 – 055/20)* 4-5.
132. Financial commitments have to be reversible, cf. *ESM-Treaty and Fiscal Compact* para. 244; cf. as well: Simon, *Grenzen des Bundesverfassungsgerichts im europäischen Integrationsprozess* 188-189.
133. Union, *European Union Public Finance* 130-132.

law and if the outlined procedure continues to apply, national parliaments can regularly alter the financial commitments enshrined within the EU own resources decision. In addition, as a secondary law solution, the proposed tax-based own resources would not alter the EU and EMU constitutional framework, including core pillars such as economic policy coordination (Article 121(1) TFEU) and the no-bailout clause (Article 125(1) TFEU).[134]

Therefore, the constitutional impact of the proposed tax-based own resources appears limited. It further suggests that no constitutional conflict with the charted national constitutional limit is likely to emerge. As illustrated, neither the French nor the Spanish constitutional court engages in a thorough assessment of EU secondary law with national constitutional law.[135] Although one could consider the EU own resources decision as a legal act that resembles EU primary law given its procedural requirements,[136] the adopted own resources decision is nevertheless embedded in the previously ratified EU-Treaties. The adoption of this decision can therefore be seen as an exercise of the adopted Treaty-framework rather than as a substantial alteration of the EU-Treaties which warrants anew constitutional review in these Member States. In Poland, despite the apparent hypothetical nature of the conflict,[137] it appears questionable whether the *constitutional identity limit* applies, given the multi-centric conception of EU membership according to which both the Polish and the EU legal order co-exist[138] as well as the focus of the limit on scrutinizing the conferral of powers.[139] In the present case, the initial conferral is already confirmed by the Polish Constitutional Tribunal and introducing tax-based own resources does not alter this conferral.

Taken together, this suggests that the introduction of the proposed EU tax-based own resources would amend but not fundamentally change the existing own resources system. Member States have established constitutional approaches to confirm their maximum financial commitments to the EU following Article 311(3) TFEU. It was illustrated that in Finland and Germany, additional procedures secure the *ex ante* involvement of national parliaments in the designing of the EU's budget. Both instances of national parliamentary involvement secure the decisive control of the national parliaments over the national budgetary and fiscal decision-making space. Through this involvement, parliaments specify their commitments for a limited time in terms of size as well as scope, which appears to meet German procedural requirements under *overall budgetary responsibility*. Furthermore, given that the proposed reform is based on the existing EU Treaty-framework and given the decisive role national

134. Lastra and Louis, 'European Economic and Monetary Union: History, Trends, and Prospects' 91, 98.
135. In France: Millet, 'Constitutional Identity in France: Vices and – Above All – Virtues' 139; and in Spain: De Visser, *Constitutional Review in Europe: A Comparative Analysis* 263; Berger, *Anwendungsvorrang und nationale Verfassungsgericht* 292.
136. Tappe and Wernsmann, *Öffentliches Finanzrecht* 196 (Recital 810).
137. Reestman, 'Legitimacy Through Adjudication: The ESM Treaty and the Fiscal Compact Before the National Courts' 249.
138. Górski, 'European Union Law Before National Judges: the Polish Experience – Adept Multicentric Vision or Creeping Hierarchical Practice' 132.
139. Rideau, 'The Case-Law of the Polish, Hungarian and Czech Constitutional Courts on National Idenity and the "German Model"' 252.

parliaments retain, no immediate conflict with the analysed national *constitutional identity limits* emerges.

2 Genuine EU Taxation Competence

A different, more far-reaching possibility is to confer upon the EU a genuine taxation competence, which would empower it to levy taxes in a pre-defined area.[140] As a result, the EU would no longer depend on the Member States' decision regarding the EU's funding, but instead, it could unilaterally determine its own revenues.[141] This would obviously require an amendment to the EU-Treaties and the explicit conferral of such taxation power to EU level, as the current Treaty-framework does not enable the EU to exercise genuine taxation competences itself.[142] At the same time, such taxation powers would alter the mode of cooperation when determining the EU's revenue. In contrast, such taxation competence would allocate additional discretion in fiscal matters to the EU,[143] it would limit the national control over taxation, which is already indirectly affected by EU policies and taxation approximation,[144] and challenge core national constitutional principles, such as democracy as well as (budgetary) sovereignty.

a Compatibility with the Charted Macro-comparative Constitutional Space

When testing the charted constitutional space against this far-reaching integration idea, a major difference to the previously analysed tax-based own resources proposal is that an explicit EU Treaty amendment would be required to award such taxation power directly to the EU. As established, section 94 Finnish Constitution regulates the conferral of additional powers to the EU in Finland. The provision prescribes different parliamentary majority requirements depending on the intensity and extent of the envisaged conferral.[145] The Constitutional Law Committee identified budgetary and fiscal competence as core parliamentary prerogatives, which are essential for Finnish sovereignty and the related principle of democracy.[146] The proposed EU taxation power would limit national budgetary sovereignty, as the EU would be empowered to

140. Fabio Wasserfallen, 'Political and Economic Integration in the EU: The Case of Failed Tax Harmonization' (2014) 52 Journal of Common Market Studies 420, 424-425.
141. Lionello, *The Pursuit of Stability of the Euro Area as a Whole: The Reform of the European Economic Union and Perspectives of Fiscal Integration* 183-184.
142. *Ibid.*, 202-203; Walter Deffaa, 'New Impetus for EU Taxation Policy' (2011) 46 Intereconomics - Review of European Economic Policy 287, 287.
143. Lionello, *The Pursuit of Stability of the Euro Area as a Whole: The Reform of the European Economic Union and Perspectives of Fiscal Integration* 184.
144. Wasserfallen, 'Political and Economic Integration in the EU: The Case of Failed Tax Harmonization' 425.
145. Leino and Salminen, 'The Euro Crisis and Its Constitutional Consequences for Finland: Is There Room for National Politics in EU Decision-Making?' 458.
146. Mutanen, *Towards a Pluralistic Constitutional Understanding of State Sovereignty in the European Union? The Concept, Regulation and Constitutional Practice of Sovereignty in Finland and Certain Other EU Member States* 306-307.

determine its tax revenue independently from the Finnish Parliament, which limits parliamentary authority over taxation.[147] Although the Constitutional Law Committee adopted a highly flexible understanding of Finnish sovereignty, it underscored that fundamental changes to the functioning of the EU with relevance to the Finnish Constitution had to be approved by a constitution-amending parliamentary majority.[148] This approach was developed during the Eurocrisis and subsequently applied to NGEU, where the Committee established that the Own Resources Decision entailed serious interference with budgetary sovereignty and therefore had to be approved by a constitution-amending majority.[149]

When applying this jurisprudence to the introduction of an EU taxation competence, it can be first established that such a competence alters the current mode of EU cooperation given that the EU would be able to determine its own revenue independent from national control and thereby different to the current model established by Article 311(3) TFEU.[150] Second, the proposed EU taxation competence would impact parliament's authority over budgeting and more specifically its own prerogative to determine taxation in Finland, as proclaimed in sections 3(1) and 81(1) Finnish Constitution.[151] Both observations indicate that any Treaty amendment to introduce an EU taxation competence would require the support of a qualified two-thirds majority, given its implications for Finnish sovereignty and parliamentary budgetary prerogatives. Despite potentially serious political difficulties to attain this majority, the introduction of EU taxation powers is, however, constitutionally possible in Finland.

In Germany, the envisaged conferral requires parliamentary approval under Article 23(1) GG, most likely by a qualified majority in the sense of Article 23(1)(3) GG in conjunction with Article 79(2) GG. Notably, Article 23(1)(3) GG specifies that EU Treaty-changes which amend the material content of the German Constitution have to be approved by a constitution-amending two-thirds majority according to Article 79(2) GG.[152] Article 105 GG grants the power to introduce taxation to the federal as well as the regional German state level. Allocating a genuine taxation power, defined as the power to introduce a financial contribution that is not attached to a direct return service and that is imposed by the state or public authority to generate revenue,[153] to a different

147. *Commission's Draft EU Recovery Plan and MFF Planning* 12; *On the Establishment of a European Monetary Fund* 3-4; *Second Assessment Draft ESM-Treaty (II.)* 2.
148. *Commission's Draft EU Recovery Plan and MFF Planning* 18; cf. as well: Leino-Sandberg, 'Who Is Ultra Vires Now? The EU's Legal U-Turn in Interpreting Article 310 TFEU'.
149. *Ratification of the Own Resources Decision (II.)*; cf. as well: Leino-Sandberg and Ruffert, 'Next Generation EU and Its Constitutional Ramifications: A Critical Assessment' 447.
150. As pointed out, such a taxation competence is not included in the current Treaty, cf. Lionello, *The Pursuit of Stability of the Euro Area as a Whole: The Reform of the European Economic Union and Perspectives of Fiscal Integration* 202-203.
151. Leino and Salminen, 'The Euro Crisis and Its Constitutional Consequences for Finland: Is There Room for National Politics in EU Decision-Making?' 457-458.
152. Lorz and Sauer, 'Verfassungsändernde Mehrheiten für die Stabilisierung des Euro?: Mehrheitserfordernisse bei der Zustimmung zum Fiskalpakt, zum ESM-Vertrag und zur Änderung des AEUV' 685.
153. *See* for the definition of 'taxation' in the sense of Article 105 GG: Hanno Kube, 'Art. 105 GG – Steuergesetzgebungskompetenz' in Volker Epping and Christian Hillgruber (eds), *Beck Online Kommentar zum Grundgesetz* (45th edn, C.H. Beck 2020) paras 3-4.

organizational level would alter this German constitutional framework. Consequently, and in light of the general importance of democratic control over taxation,[154] it seems that the conferral of taxation competences to EU level has to be approved by constitution-amending two-thirds majority. Even this, of course, is only possible if the conferral of budgetary and fiscal competences is compatible with *overall budgetary responsibility*.[155]

As indicated, the Constitutional Court requires under *overall budgetary responsibility* that the German Parliament retains full control over all central budgetary and fiscal decisions.[156] On a procedural level, the Court requires that parliamentary approval remains constitutive for financial commitments and that these commitments remain limited as well as specific.[157] On a substantive level, the Court demands that German budgetary autonomy is not suspended for a considerable period of time and that central competences remain at the national level, including explicitly the competence to determine the type, level and size of German revenue and expenditure.[158] When applying this constitutional benchmark to the proposed EU taxation competences, which would necessarily confer a degree of political discretion to EU level, two major constitutional concerns emerge.

In the first place, taxation is intrinsically linked to the principle of democracy.[159] As highlighted before, the decision of how, at what level and whom to tax constitutes an essential political prerogative at the core of the decision-making space that democratically legitimized institutions enjoy, and which is controlled by the voters through regular elections.[160] In case these core political decisions are conferred to EU level, the people would only have an indirect impact on the content of the taken decisions. This is democratically problematic in light of the centrality of revenue decisions for political decision-making. The power to tax thus concerns a competence associated with the nucleus of German democracy.[161]

Second, the conferral of tax powers might deprive the German Parliament of one source of public revenue. Notably, empowering the EU to tax a specific field or a

154. Fabbrini, 'Fiscal Capacity' 131.
155. *Interim Decision on the Ratification of the Own Resources Decision (NGEU)* paras 98-102; cf. as well: Ohler, 'Rechtliche Maßstäbe der Geldpolitik nach dem Gauweiler-Urteil des EuGH' 1002.
156. Reestman, 'Legitimacy Through Adjudication: The ESM Treaty and the Fiscal Compact Before the National Courts' 259; Nettesheim, 'Die "haushaltspolitische Gesamtverantwortung" in der Rechtsprechung des BVerfG' 12.
157. Calliess, '70 Jahre Grundgesetz und europäische Integration: "Take Back Control" oder "Mehr Demokratie wagen"?' 688; Simon, *Grenzen des Bundesverfassungsgerichts im europäischen Integrationsprozess* 297.
158. Claes and Reestman, 'The Protection of National Constitutional Identity and the Limits of European Integration at the Occasion of the *Gauweiler* Case' 927.
159. Jaakkola, 'A Democratic Dilemma of European Power to Tax: Reconstructing the Symbiosis Between Taxation and Democracy Beyond the State?' 662; Fabbrini, 'Fiscal Capacity' 131.
160. Cremer, 'Lissabon-Vertrag und Grundgesetz' 299-300; Kottmann and Wohlfahrt, 'Der gespaltene Wächter? Demokratie, Verfassungsidentität und Integrationsverantwortung im Lissabon-Urteil' 447-448.
161. Particularly in light of the apparent lacking democratic safeguards at EU level, cf. Marija Bartl, 'The Way We Do Europe: Subsidiarity and the Substantive Democratic Deficit' (2015) 21 European Law Journal 23, 24.

specific service deprives the Member State from generating the same revenue.[162] Therefore, it appears that German budgetary autonomy would be impacted for a considerable time due to a restriction of potential revenue sources and ultimately an associated decrease in national revenue. This could expose the German state budget to political decisions taken by a third party, notably the EU, including hardly predictable financial risks, which was deemed incompatible with *overall budgetary responsibility* by the German Constitutional Court.[163] The specific assessment depends on the scope and size of the EU taxation power - including possible limitations that could be attached to the conferral of such competences to EU level.

Nevertheless, as it stands, any proposed EU taxation competence would trigger serious constitutional concerns in both Finland and Germany given its discretionary character and its inherently political nature which involve hardly predictable financial risks for the national state budget. This appears to translate into a conflict with the German concept of *overall budgetary responsibility* which could result in the constitutional unattainability of such reform ambitions under the current German Constitution. Precisely the independent, discretionary character of the proposed EU taxation competence, which could secure an autonomous means to generate EU revenue, conflicts with the outlined national constitutional framework.

b *Compatibility with the Charted Micro-comparative Constitutional Space*

When evaluating the compatibility of the outlined EU taxation power with the assessed national *constitutional identity limits*, it appears that the constitutional concerns are largely comparable to the German concerns. Notably, in France, the sovereignty limit would be applicable to any conferral of tax powers to the EU, which would be governed by Article 88-1 French Constitution.[164] The *Conseil Constitutionnel* would have to determine, upon referral of a privileged institutional applicant, whether the introduction of EU taxation competences entails a significant shift of powers in domestic budgetary and fiscal prerogatives as laid down in Articles 34 and 47 French Constitution.[165] Article 34 French Constitution stipulates that taxation has to be based on a statute, which according to Article 24(1) French Constitution can only be adopted by the French Parliament. Consequently, the French Constitution assigns the power to tax exclusively to the French Parliament.[166] Hence, awarding this prerogative to the EU, even partially, would alter the current constitutional *status quo*. Furthermore, given the

162. Lionello, *The Pursuit of Stability of the Euro Area as a Whole: The Reform of the European Economic Union and Perspectives of Fiscal Integration* 208.
163. As established by the German Constitutional Court, cf. *Quantitative Easing (PSPP) Final Judgment* paras 226-227; *Final OMT-Judgment* para. 213.
164. Vranes, 'Constitutional Foundation of, and Limitations to, EU Integration in France' 538.
165. Fabbrini, 'The Euro-Crisis and the Courts: Judicial Review and the Political Process in Comparative Perspective' 119-120.
166. *Entwurf eines Gesetzes zu dem Beschluss des Europäischen Rates vom 25. März 2011 zur Änderung des Artikels 136 des Vertrags über die Arbeitsweise der Europäischen Union hinsichtlich eines Stabilitätsmechanismus für die Mitgliedstaaten, deren Währung der Euro ist (Drucksache 17/9047)* paras 13, 21; cf. as well: Reestman, 'Legitimacy Through Adjudication: The ESM Treaty and the Fiscal Compact Before the National Courts' 265.

constitutionally enshrined importance of taxation powers to the French Parliament, a conferral of such competences to EU level would likely be seen as a significant interference with the French sovereignty limit. The resulting anticipated constitutional conflict could be overcome by the French constitution-amending legislator following Article 89 French Constitution, which prescribes the adoption by a three-fifths majority in the *Congrès*.[167] Given that the *Conseil Constitutionnel* is not empowered to review constitutional amendments,[168] these amendments would subsequently not be scrutinized. Moreover, enacting such constitutional reforms to accommodate EU integration steps is a common practice in France.[169] Consequently, the proposed EU taxation power will likely trigger a conflict with the French sovereignty limit, which can be overcome by the French legislator.

In Spain, the conferral of competences to EU level requires parliamentary approval following Article 93 Spanish Constitution. This conferral must respect the *constitutional identity limit*. As previously established, the Spanish constitutional order stresses the particular bond between the parliament and budgetary as well as fiscal decision-making, apparent in Articles 66(2), 75(3) and 134 Spanish Constitution. It is furthermore reflected in the fact that the general power to tax is assigned to the Spanish legislator according to Article 133(1) Spanish Constitution. Although the Constitutional Tribunal did not yet conclude that taxation prerogatives are covered by the Spanish *constitutional identity limit*, it established that sovereignty, democracy and the overall constitutional structure are covered by this limit.[170] Given the crucial link between the power to tax and the principle of democracy,[171] which is recognized in other Member States too,[172] and given that the Spanish Constitution explicitly recognizes this important relationship in Article 133(1) Spanish Constitution, it seems likely that taxation prerogatives are covered by the Spanish *constitutional identity limit*. Therefore, the proposed discretionary EU taxation competence would indeed conflict with the Spanish *constitutional identity* given its implications for budgetary sovereignty as well as the parliamentary, democratically legitimized control over taxation. Yet, in case such a conflict with the Spanish *constitutional identity limit* is found by the Spanish

167. Cahill, 'Ever Closer Remoteness of the Peoples of Europe? Limits on the Power of Amendment and National Constituent Power' 266-267.
168. Ziller, 'Sovereignty in France: Getting Rid of the Mal de Bodin' 271.
169. Steiner, *French Law: A Comparative Approach* 7; Ziller, 'European Union Law in the Jurisprudence of French Supreme Courts: Europe-Friendliness with a French Touch' 772.
170. Martín Y Pérez de Nanclares, 'Constitutional Identity in Spain: Commitment to European Integration Without Giving up the Essence of the Constitution' 279; Bustos Gisbert, 'National Constitutional Identity in European Constitutionalism: Revisiting the Tale of the Emperor's New Clothes in Spain?' 77.
171. On the traditional relationship between taxation and democracy, cf. Jaakkola, 'A Democratic Dilemma of European Power to Tax: Reconstructing the Symbiosis Between Taxation and Democracy Beyond the State?' 662; as well as on the traditional link of fiscal powers with democracy and sovereignty, cf. Puntscher Riekmann and Wydra, 'Representation in the European State of Emergency: Parliaments Against Governments?' 567.
172. Reestman, 'Legitimacy Through Adjudication: The ESM Treaty and the Fiscal Compact Before the National Courts' 265.

Constitutional Tribunal, the constitution-amending legislator can overcome the resulting conflict by altering the constitutional text.[173] Given the outlined link of a possible EU taxation competence with Spanish sovereignty, democracy and the general state structure, it seems that the reform would be considered essential and thus Article 168(1) Spanish Constitution is applicable, which imposes the previously mentioned strict procedural requirements.[174] Furthermore, the exceptional nature of constitutional amendments in Spain should be recalled. Therefore, although allocating the proposed taxation power to the EU would be theoretically attainable – as the constitution assigns a clear procedural avenue to implement the required constitutional changes, the practical feasibility remains questionable.

In Poland, the conferral of the required competences to introduce an EU taxation power will likely require parliamentary confirmation following Article 90 Polish Constitution. The core constitutional question is whether EU taxation powers are compatible with the Polish *constitutional identity limit*. It was already established that the Constitutional Tribunal would consider constitutional challenges against Eurozone-measures as being merely hypothetical at this point.[175] Nevertheless, given the Polish obligation to accede to the Eurozone, an anticipatory analysis of the compatibility of an EU taxation competence with the Polish Constitution seems possible. As established, the Polish *constitutional identity limit* protects the power to conduct financial, budgetary and fiscal policies.[176] This power includes the power of the Polish Sejm to adopt the budget as established in Article 219(1) Polish Constitution, that the Polish Council of Ministers devises economic internal policies as established in Article 146(1) Polish Constitution, but also that taxes can only be introduced by means of a statute by the Polish legislator, as established in Article 217 in conjunction with Articles 95(1), 120 and 121 Polish Constitution.[177] Conferring the power to tax to the EU would alter the outlined constitutional prerogatives, which are equally covered by the competence-centric conception of Polish sovereignty. Therefore, it appears likely that a constitutional amendment would be required, either to overcome the explicit conflict with the Polish Constitution or to address the anticipated conflict with the Polish *constitutional identity limit*, as prescribed by Article 235 Polish Constitution. Yet, the attainability of such constitutional amendment remains questionable given the high procedural hurdles and the current political circumstances.

173. Pérez Tremps, 'National Idenity in Spanish Constitutional Court Case-Law' 272.

174. Martín Y Pérez de Nanclares, 'Constitutional Identity in Spain: Commitment to European Integration Without Giving up the Essence of the Constitution' 282; Ferreres Comella, *The Constitution of Spain: A Contextual Analysis* 57.

175. Reestman, 'Legitimacy Through Adjudication: The ESM Treaty and the Fiscal Compact Before the National Courts' 249.

176. Rideau, 'The Case-Law of the Polish, Hungarian and Czech Constitutional Courts on National Idenity and the "German Model"' 252; Czapliński, 'Recent Constitutional Jurisprudence Concerning the European Union: Some Remarks on 2010 Judgments of the Polish Constitutional Court' 200.

177. Bainczyk, 'Folgen einer mangelnden Anpassung der polnischen Verfassung nach dem Vertrag von Lissabon im Lichte des Urteils des polnischen Verfassungsgerichtshofes zum Beschluss des Europäischen Rates zur Änderung von Art. 136 AEUV' 314.

c Interim Conclusion

Taken together, major national constitutional concerns appear to exist against the prospect of conferring a discretionary taxation competence to EU level. In all charted Member States, taxation is a constitutionally assigned parliamentary prerogative which is deeply rooted in the national conception of democracy and protected by *constitutional identity limits*.[178] This suggests that the emerging constitutional conflict with national democracy and (budgetary) sovereignty can only be overcome by constitutional amendment. The assessment equally revealed that the German *constitutional identity limit* appears to fully exclude the conferral of far-reaching tax competences to EU level as this might qualify as a violation of German democracy as well as permanent interference with budgetary autonomy.

3 EU Debts and Shared Liabilities

A final possibility to fund an EU budget or an emergency instrument is issuing either EU debt, as for example envisaged by NGEU,[179] or shared liabilities.[180] To that end, NGEU sparked considerable national constitutional discussion. Notably, the national reactions to the envisaged EU recovery strategy revealed general concerns as to whether the extent of EU debts to fund the Recovery Facility is compatible with EU primary law, most notably Article 310(1)(3) TFEU, as well as national constitutional law.

a Compatibility with the Charted Macro-comparative Constitutional Space

These requirements are apparent in the jurisprudence of the Finnish Constitutional Law Committee. The Committee established that significant changes to the working of the EU would be considered a major encroachment of Finnish sovereignty which could only be approved by a two-thirds parliamentary majority.[181] Two examples of significant changes are the Own Resources Decision and the increase of Finnish financial commitments under the ESM-level, both were seen as significant alterations of Finnish

178. Notably the important link between taxation and democracy, cf. Fabbrini, 'Fiscal Capacity' 131.
179. Alcidi and Gros, 'Next Generation EU: A Large Common Response to the COVID-19 Crisis' 203.
180. As envisaged by the Commission, cf. Commission, *Green Paper on the Feasibility of Introducing Stability Bonds (COM (2011) 818)*; cf. as well: Schäfer and Bigus, 'Consequences of Different Eurobonds Proposals' 553; Hild, Herz and Bauer, 'Structured Eurobonds: Limiting Liability and Distributing Profits' 251; Franz C. Mayer and Christian Heidfeld, 'Eurobonds, Schuldentilgungsfonds und Projektbonds: Eine dunkle Bedrohung?' (2012) 45 Zeitschrift für Rechtspolitik 129, 129; Mayer and Heidfeld, 'Verfassungs- und europarechtliche Aspekte der Einführung von Eurobonds' 422.
181. *Commission's Draft EU Recovery Plan and MFF Planning* 18; *Adoption of the Lisbon Treaty* 5; cf. as well: Leino-Sandberg, 'Who Is Ultra Vires Now? The EU's Legal U-Turn in Interpreting Article 310 TFEU'.

budgetary sovereignty.[182] Specifically building on the conclusions of the *ESM*, the Finnish Constitutional Law Committee submitted in relation to NGEU that the proposed financing structure through EU debts could significantly alter the mode of EU cooperation, as under the current Treaty-framework the EU finances its expenditure through own resources assigned by the Member States in order to achieve a balanced budget in accordance with Article 310 TFEU.[183] Furthermore, NGEU appears to increase Finnish liabilities to a not fully predictable degree and the Finnish Parliament retains only very limited control over the subsequent spending of the newly available EU funds, which is considered by the Committee as a major interference with Finnish budgetary sovereignty.[184] Additionally, section 82(2) Finnish Constitution requires parliamentary approval for the issuing of state guarantees, which might be relevant to secure the proposed EU borrowing.[185] In light of these considerations, the Constitutional Law Committee concluded that NGEU had a significant impact on Finnish sovereignty and that the adoption of the EU own resources decision required the approval by a qualified two-thirds majority following section 94(2)(2) Finnish Constitution.[186]

When applying the outlined Finnish constitutional benchmark to the suggested EU debt through Eurobonds, it seems that the Constitutional Law Committee would equally consider Eurobonds as a considerable modification of the current EU-Treaties as well. More specifically, the Committee emphasized that Article 125 TFEU allowed for financial assistance among Member States as long as the Member States remained liable for their own obligations.[187] Arguably, Eurobonds would introduce shared liabilities and thereby alter the current conception of the EMU. Furthermore, given the possible overall size of the issued Eurobonds, it can be argued that considerable liabilities might arise and that these entail hardly predictable financial risks for the national budget. Notably, in case a Member State experiences difficulties and is unable to service its debts, the other Member States might be required to guarantee the financial obligations. This could have significant implications for Finnish budgetary sovereignty and affect the ability of Finnish state authorities to comply with their

182. *Ratification of the Own Resources Decision (II.)*; *Second Assessment Draft ESM-Treaty (II.)* 2; cf. as well: Leino-Sandberg and Ruffert, 'Next Generation EU and Its Constitutional Ramifications: A Critical Assessment' 447.
183. *Ratification of the Own Resources Decision (II.)*; *Commission's Draft EU Recovery Plan and MFF Planning* 17-18; cf. as well: Leino-Sandberg and Ruffert, 'Next Generation EU and its Constitutional Ramifications: A Critical Assessment' 447; Leino-Sandberg, 'Who Is Ultra Vires Now? The EU's Legal U-Turn in Interpreting Article 310 TFEU'.
184. *Ratification of the Own Resources Decision (II.)*; *Commission's Draft EU Recovery Plan and MFF Planning* 13.
185. *Ratification of the Own Resources Decision (II.)*; *Commission's Draft EU Recovery Plan and MFF Planning* 12; *EIB Proposal for EU Covid-19 Guarantee Fund* 5.
186. *Ratification of the Own Resources Decision (II.)*; *Commission's Draft EU Recovery Plan and MFF Planning* 17; cf. as well: Leino-Sandberg and Ruffert, 'Next Generation EU and Its Constitutional Ramifications: A Critical Assessment' 447.
187. *Ratification of the Own Resources Decision (II.)*; *Commission's Draft EU Recovery Plan and MFF Planning* 13; PeVP 34/2020 vp *Protocol Concerning Possible EU COVID-19 Rescue Measures* (Finnish Constitutional Law Committee) 3.

constitutional obligations.[188] Therefore, the Constitutional Law Committee would likely require a two-thirds majority in the sense of section 94(2)(2) Finnish Constitution to confer any competences to EU level to issue Eurobonds. In addition, subsequent parliamentary approval might be required to approve any connected Finnish state guarantee in the sense of section 82(2) Finnish Constitution in order to provide a sound constitutional basis.

Comparable constitutional concerns arise in Germany. Considering the national adoption of NGEU and the issuing of EU debts, German parliamentary approval in the sense of Article 23(1) GG is required to adopt the EU decision in compliance with Article 311(3) TFEU.[189] Given the extent of the proposed programme and the considerable increase in national financial commitments, it has to be determined whether the qualified majority threshold applies in the sense of Article 23(1)(3) in conjunction with Article 79(2) GG or whether the German legislator might be barred to approve the proposed recovery scheme due to a potential conflict with the *eternity clause*. Article 23(1)(3) GG is applicable in case an amendment to EU primary law or a comparable measure alters the substantive content of the German Constitution.[190] The own resources decision is characterized as a measure *comparable* to an EU Treaty amendment, given the unanimity requirement and the national constitutional confirmation prescribed by Article 311(3) TFEU.[191] The resulting question was whether this decision and NGEU result in an amendment to the content of the German Constitution. This is the case if competences are conferred, which would enable the EU to deviate from the German Constitution or in case a comparable domestic act would have required a constitutional amendment.[192] Considering the German constitutional framework, it appears that the German Constitution prescribes the approval of state borrowing through an act of parliament that determines the actual size of the intended borrowing according to Article 115(1) GG.[193] However, the envisaged borrowing to finance NGEU is not financed through borrowing on behalf of the Member States but through borrowing on behalf of the EU, which is why Article 115 GG cannot be directly applicable.[194]

188. *Ratification of the Own Resources Decision (II.)*; *Commission's Draft EU Recovery Plan and MFF Planning* 13.
189. Bundestages, *Zum Erfordernis eines qualifizierten Mehrheitsbeschlusses des Bundestages hinsichtlich des Zustimmungsgesetzes zum Eigenmittelbeschluss der EU (WD 4 – 3000 – 055/20)* 4-5.
190. Schorkopf, 'Die Europäische Union auf dem Weg zur Fiskalunion – Integrationsfortschritt durch den Rechtsrahmen des Sonderhaushalts "Next Generation EU"' 3089.
191. Bundestages, *Zum Erfordernis eines qualifizierten Mehrheitsbeschlusses des Bundestages hinsichtlich des Zustimmungsgesetzes zum Eigenmittelbeschluss der EU (WD 4 – 3000 – 055/20)* 5; as also highlighted by the German Constitutional Court, cf. *Lisbon-judgment* paras 313-314.
192. Bundestages, *Zum Erfordernis eines qualifizierten Mehrheitsbeschlusses des Bundestages hinsichtlich des Zustimmungsgesetzes zum Eigenmittelbeschluss der EU (WD 4 – 3000 – 055/20)* 5-6.
193. *Ibid.*, 6.
194. *Interim Decision on the Ratification of the Own Resources Decision (NGEU)* para. 99; partly seen differently, cf. Schorkopf, 'Die Europäische Union auf dem Weg zur Fiskalunion – Integrationsfortschritt durch den Rechtsrahmen des Sonderhaushalts "Next Generation EU"' 3090.

Yet, the proposed increase of the own resources ceiling to finance the envisaged EU debts could entail a material amendment to the constitution. Here, the concept of *overall budgetary responsibility* was particularly relevant. Following the jurisprudence of the German Constitutional Court, the German Parliament has to remain in charge of all central budgetary decisions and must retain budgetary autonomy. Any suspension of *overall budgetary responsibility* is incompatible with the *eternity clause* and therefore constitutionally unachievable in Germany.[195] To that end, strictly limited budgetary commitments can be adopted by a simple parliamentary majority following Article 23(1)(2) GG.[196] Financial commitments that are significant given their overall size as well as the attached modalities, but that do not suspend *overall budgetary responsibility* for a considerable time, have to be adopted by a constitution-amending majority, as they alter the constitutionally enshrined parliamentary responsibility for budgetary decisions.[197]

Considering the own resources decision, the German Constitutional Court has clarified that neither the Own Resources Decision nor NGEU entailed a competence conferral – rather these were devised based on and within the current EU Treaty framework and consequently, the qualified majority requirement in Article 23(1)(3) was not applicable.[198] Nevertheless, the Court reviewed compliance with the *eternity clause*. Considering the substance of the financial commitment, the envisaged maximum commitment under the NGEU would amount to a maximum annual financial commitment of up to 1.4% of the Gross National Income (GNI) plus an additional 0.6% of the GNI until 2058 to fund the emergency schemes to tackle the economic impact of COVID-19.[199] This would entail an increase of the national commitment from previously 1.23% to now up to 2% of the GNI.[200] In absolute numbers, this would translate into annual financial commitments of up to EUR 70.7 billion based on the GNI of 2019.[201] This in itself constitutes a considerable amount in comparison to the overall German federal expenditure for 2019 which amounted to EUR 356.4 billion.[202]

At the same time, the factual development of German contributions to the EU budget reveals that the own resources ceiling is traditionally not fully exhausted. For example, in 2019 the overall German contributions to the EU's own resources

195. Mayer, 'Rebels Without a Cause? Zur OMT-Vorlage des Bundesverfassungsgerichts' 497; Calliess, 'The Future of the Eurozone and the Role of the German Federal Constitutional Court' 407.
196. Schorkopf, 'Die Europäische Union auf dem Weg zur Fiskalunion – Integrationsfortschritt durch den Rechtsrahmen des Sonderhaushalts "Next Generation EU"' 3089.
197. Bundestages, *Zum Erfordernis eines qualifizierten Mehrheitsbeschlusses des Bundestages hinsichtlich des Zustimmungsgesetzes zum Eigenmittelbeschluss der EU (WD 4 – 3000 – 055/20)* 7.
198. *Interim Decision on the Ratification of the Own Resources Decision (NGEU)* para. 79.
199. Council, *Conclusions Special Meeting of the European Council (17, 18, 19, 20 and 21 July 2020) – EUCO 10/20* 3 (point A9).
200. Cf. the scheme established for the period from 2014 to 2020 by Article 3(1) Council Decision 2014/335/EU on the system of own resources of the European Union; as well as the new own resources ceiling: *ibid.*, 3 (point A9); cf. as well: Schorkopf, 'Die Europäische Union auf dem Weg zur Fiskalunion – Integrationsfortschritt durch den Rechtsrahmen des Sonderhaushalts "Next Generation EU"' 3087.
201. Commission, *EU expenditure and revenue 2014-2020 (dataset)*.
202. German Government, *Unterrichtung durch die Bundesregierung: Finanzplan des Bundes 2018 bis 2022 (Drucksache 19/3401)* (German Government 2018).

amounted to 0.846%, in 2018 to 0.847% and in 2017 to 0.713% of GNI.[203] This underscores that the own resources decision merely prescribes an upper limit of German commitments. Furthermore, although the supplementary increase of up to 0.6% of GNI applies until 2058, the core commitment of up to 1.4% of GNI is linked to the MFF which applies from 2021 to 2027.[204] Moreover, the supplementary increase may only be triggered in case other means to service the EU debts are exhausted, as clarified by the European Council.[205] And in addition, this supplementary charge is designated to fund NGEU, which although amounting to EUR 750 billion has to be further distinguished into grants, which amount to EUR 390 billion, and into favourable loans, which amount to EUR 360 billion, that have to be paid back by the Member States benefiting from them. Consequently, the supplementary own resources are mainly designated to finance the share of grants under NGEU.

When projecting the possible financial implications for the German budget based on the calculations of the 2019 EU budget, where Germany contributed EUR 29.91 billion to the overall EU own resources of EUR 163.92 billion which equals 18.2%, the German commitment could amount to around EUR 71.2 billion until 2058. This would amount to around EUR 2 billion projected over a 36-year framework, which in comparison to the overall German budget is an arguably limited commitment. Despite the long-term implications of the additional commitment and the considerable increase in the own resources ceiling from 1.23% of GNI to 2% of GNI, the financial commitments remain limited. This suggests that *overall budgetary responsibility* and budgetary autonomy are sufficiently safeguarded.

In its final judgment, the Court raised concerns regarding the existence of a sufficient legal basis to adopt the recovery but concluded the Own Resources Decision was not *ultra vires*. Specifically on *overall budgetary responsibility*, the German Court highlighted that the borrowed funds were tied to a specific purpose, that these were limited in volume and duration, and that the German Parliament had approved them following Article 311(3)(3) TFEU. Based on these considerations, the Court then highlighted that no direct liabilities for the German budget stemmed from the Own Resources Decision, that no permanent mechanism was established through which the German state budget would be liable to finance decisions of third parties, and that the financial burden remained manageable for the German state budget.[206] Here, the Court reiterated the parliamentary prerogative to make the required risk and overall viability

203. Based on data from Commission, *EU expenditure and revenue 2014-2020 (dataset)*.
204. Council, *Conclusions Special Meeting of the European Council (17, 18, 19, 20 and 21 July 2020): EUCO 10/20* 8 (point A28).
205. *Ibid.*, 4 (point A10).
206. *Final Decision on the Ratification of the Own Resources Decision (NGEU)* paras 213, 217, 224, 226; cf. as well: Ruffert, 'Europarecht und Verfassungsrecht: NextGenerationEU – Der Eigenmittelbeschluss zur Verwirklichung des Programms NextGenerationEU ist nicht offensichtlich unionsrechtswidrig' 280; Hilpold, 'Next Generation EU und die "Einnahmensouveränität": Das EU-Eigenmittelsystem vor dem BVerfG – Zugleich Bespr. von BVerfG 6.12.202: 2 BvR 547/21, 2 BvR 798/21' 174.

evaluation.[207] Hence, even significant EU borrowing as conducted under NGEU was deemed compatible with *overall budgetary responsibility*.

The assessment suggests that even more far-reaching forms of EU debts or shared liabilities are constitutionally feasible in Germany. As apparent in relation to NGEU, which limits the maximum national financial liabilities, and as equally apparent in relation to the ESM, which similarly determines a maximum commitment, any such scheme has to be capped to prevent unpredictable financial risks for the national budget. This was continuously emphasized by the German Constitutional Court under its *overall budgetary responsibility* doctrine.[208] Hence, any form of EU debts or shared liabilities would have to be limited in their overall size, for example, through the maximum ceilings established by the EU own resources decision. Hence, under the current German Constitution, the EU could not be empowered to autonomously engage in its own borrowing or introduce shared liabilities without acquiring prior confirmation from the German Parliament. When subsequently considering the substantive dimension of the German *overall budgetary responsibility* doctrine it is hard to anticipate when this abstractly defined benchmark established by the Constitutional Court is violated. In all cases, far-reaching proposals that envisage a wide-scale supranationalization of national debts through shared guarantees, for example apparent in the blue-and red-bond proposal,[209] seem incompatible with *overall budgetary responsibility* given the hardly predictable financial impact on the German state budget.

Hence, EU debts, borrowing or shared liabilities appear to be compatible with the German Constitution in case they are based on limited financial commitments confirmed by the German Parliament, thereby preserving central parliamentary control over budgetary and fiscal decision-making. An apparent example that complies with these requirements is NGEU. In contrast, proposals such as the envisaged blue and red-bonds would likely be considered to entail unpredictable financial commitments that could undermine *overall budgetary responsibility* and would therefore be incompatible with the German *eternity clause*.

b *Compatibility with the Charted Micro-comparative Constitutional Space*

When considering the compatibility of EU debts, shared liabilities and in particular NGEU with the different national *constitutional identity limits*, certain similarities with

207. *Final Decision on the Ratification of the Own Resources Decision (NGEU)* paras 229-230; cf. as well: Ruffert, 'Europarecht und Verfassungsrecht: NextGenerationEU – Der Eigenmittelbeschluss zur Verwirklichung des Programms NextGenerationEU ist nicht offensichtlich unionsrechtswidrig' 280; Hilpold, 'Next Generation EU und die "Einnahmensouveränität": Das EU-Eigenmittelsystem vor dem BVerfG – Zugleich Bespr. von BVerfG 6.12.2022: 2 BvR 547/21, 2 BvR 798/21' 174.
208. *Interim Decision on the Ratification of the Own Resources Decision (NGEU)* paras 98-102; cf. as well: Simon, *Grenzen des Bundesverfassungsgerichts im europäischen Integrationsprozess* 297.
209. Commission, *Green Paper on the Feasibility of Introducing Stability Bonds (COM (2011) 818)* 14; Jacques Delpla and Jakob von Weizsäcker, 'The Blue Bond Proposal (2010)' Bruegel Policy Brief, https://www.bruegel.org/wp-content/uploads/imported/publications/1005-PB-Blue_Bonds.pdf, accessed 5 April 2023, 1-3.

the assessment of the proposed EU taxation power can be identified. Despite differences in the legal design, both the power to tax as well as the ability to engage in public borrowing have considerable implications for the budgetary prerogatives of national parliaments. In both situations, the domestic fiscal discretionary decision-making space is limited, either due to reduced tax revenue or given that the respective debt might have to be serviced. Therefore, the previously drawn constitutional conclusions apply accordingly.

In France, NGEU including the intended financing through debts had to be approved by the French legislator according to Article 53(1) French Constitution, given the decision's impact on the finances of the French state.[210] Yet, as the decision is based on an existing EU Treaty provision, notably Article 311 TFEU, it does not entail the conferral of additional competences in the sense of Article 88-1 French Constitution and consequently, the sovereignty limit appears not to be applicable.[211] This conclusion is in conformity with early decisions of the *Conseil Constitutionnel* concerning the EU's own resources system, where the *Conseil* highlighted that the decision was based on ratified international obligations that enjoyed primacy according to Article 55 French Constitution and that the decision had to be approved by the French legislator according to Article 53 French Constitution.[212] Therefore, the sovereignty limit is not applicable.[213]

Instead, the *Conseil Constitutionnel* would evaluate whether the proposed own resources decision as EU secondary law violates the French *constitutional identity limit* that applies to EU secondary acts.[214] It protects the division of competences as established in Articles 34 and 37 French Constitution, including parliamentary responsibility to determine state revenue and expenditure in a Finance Act.[215] It appears that this constitutional benchmark is largely respected by the own resources decision, which prescribes national approval and which complies with Article 53(1) French Constitution. In that regard, it seems that Article 53(1) French Constitution extends the internally applicable responsibility for budgetary decisions enshrined in Article 34(4) French Constitution to supranational cooperation. Given that EU law allows for this national framework to apply, it can be submitted that the final own resources decision does not alter the established constitutional division of powers. This conclusion is also

210. *Conseil des Ministres* submitted to the French legislator in the so-called Jaune Budgétaire, French Conseil des Ministres, 'Annex au Project de Loi de Finances pour 2021 (Jaune Budgétaire): Relations Financières avec l'Union Européenne' (*French Conseil des Ministres*, 2020), https://www.budget.gouv.fr/documentation/file-download/6871, accessed 5 April 2023, 15.
211. *Ibid.*, 15.
212. Decision 70-39 DC *Introduction of the EU's System of Own Resources* (French Conseil Constitutionnel) paras 5-6; cf. as well the subsequent findings of the *Conseil Constitutionnel*: Decision 77-90 DC *Concerning the Introduction of an Isoglucose Levy* (French Conseil Constitutionnel) para. 4.
213. *Introduction of the EU's System of Own Resources* para. 9.
214. Millet, 'Constitutional Identity in France: Vices and – Above All – Virtues' 141; Dubout, '"Les règles ou principes inhérents à l'identité constitutionelle de la France": une supra-constitutionalité?' 452.
215. Fabbrini, 'The Euro-Crisis and the Courts: Judicial Review and the Political Process in Comparative Perspective' 120.

not put into question by the fact that NGEU is largely financed through EU debts, as the underpinning funding mechanism established by the own resources system remains unchanged in its core function. Member States guarantee funds up to the own resources ceilings, which are then allocated through the EU budget and the recovery and resilience fund. As a result, no constitutional conflict arises between the own resources decision or the proposed EU debts and the French Constitution as long as the French Parliament approves the decision following Article 53(1) French Constitution by an act of parliament.

This assessment would differ in case additional competences are conferred to the EU, for example, in order to introduce an independent EU power to engage in public borrowing or to establish shared liabilities. In such cases, the French sovereignty limit becomes applicable.[216] As highlighted, budgetary and fiscal prerogatives are constitutionally assigned to the French legislator, as laid down in Article 34(4) French Constitution.[217] In case the EU would be entitled to engage in larger borrowing following a mechanism that differs from the own resources framework or by establishing shared liabilities following the Eurobond proposals, new challenges to these parliamentary prerogatives would emerge. Notably, Member States might be required to guarantee financial commitments made through the EU, which alters the current framework that builds on national parliamentary approval for the determination of maximum financial commitments. Member States would guarantee larger borrowing jointly, with hardly predictable financial risks that could negatively impact national budgetary sovereignty as well as the parliamentary prerogatives to establish the state budget. The resulting interference with French sovereignty, democracy and parliamentary prerogatives[218] would likely be deemed incompatible with the French sovereignty limit. Therefore, it appears likely that a constitutional amendment would be required to adopt the proposed EU borrowing competence or the envisaged Eurobonds.[219] As previously emphasized, enacting constitutional amendments constitutes a common practice and a prerogative of the legislature, which is not scrutinized by the *Conseil Constitutionnel*.[220]

---

216. *Entwurf eines Gesetzes zu dem Beschluss des Europäischen Rates vom 25. März 2011 zur Änderung des Artikels 136 des Vertrags über die Arbeitsweise der Europäischen Union hinsichtlich eines Stabilitätsmechanismus für die Mitgliedstaaten, deren Währung der Euro ist (Drucksache 17/9047)* para. 10; *Lisbon Treaty* para. 9; cf. as well: Wendel, 'Lisbon Before the Courts: Comparative Perspectives' 123-124.
217. Reestman, 'Legitimacy Through Adjudication: The ESM Treaty and the Fiscal Compact Before the National Courts' 265.
218. *Entwurf eines Gesetzes zu dem Beschluss des Europäischen Rates vom 25. März 2011 zur Änderung des Artikels 136 des Vertrags über die Arbeitsweise der Europäischen Union hinsichtlich eines Stabilitätsmechanismus für die Mitgliedstaaten, deren Währung der Euro ist (Drucksache 17/9047)* para. 10; *Lisbon Treaty* para. 9; cf. as well: Claes, 'National Idenity: Trump Card or up for Negotiation?' 126; Bonnie, 'The Constitutionality of Transfers of Sovereignty: The French Approach' 526-529.
219. Ziller, 'European Union Law in the Jurisprudence of French Supreme Courts: Europe-Friendliness with a French Touch' 772; Vranes, 'Constitutional Foundation of, and Limitations to, EU Integration in France' 535.
220. As emphasized by the *Conseil Constitutionnel*, cf. *Lisbon Treaty* paras 9, 34; cf. as well: Millet, 'Constitutional Identity in France: Vices and – Above All – Virtues' 150-151; Ziller, 'Sovereignty in France: Getting Rid of the Mal de Bodin' 271.

In Spain, NGEU, and more specifically the underpinning own resources decision, required national approval following Article 94(1)(d) as an international agreement 'which [implies] financial liabilities for the Public Treasury [...]'.[221] As the own resources decision is based on the existing EU Treaty-framework, no constitutional amendment is required to approve this decision in Spain. Arguably, the general system underpinning the EU's own resources was already ratified by the Spanish legislator when adopting the Lisbon Treaty, and therefore the own resources decision can be seen as a concretization of this initial commitment. What is more, the Spanish Constitutional Tribunal is generally not assessing the compatibility of EU secondary law with the Spanish Constitution.[222]

Regarding the more far-reaching proposals concerning EU borrowing competences or the introduction of shared liabilities, the Spanish *constitutional identity limit* seems applicable. As clarified, the Spanish *constitutional identity limit* remains abstract and the Constitutional Tribunal did not yet define budgetary and fiscal competences as part of this limit. However, given that Spanish sovereignty and democracy are covered by it,[223] given that budgetary decisions have particular importance for the electorate,[224] and given that the Spanish Constitution protects, in several places, the parliamentary control over state budgeting, it appears convincing to argue that budgetary and fiscal prerogatives are covered by the Spanish *constitutional identity limit*.[225] As an extension of this parliamentary responsibility for the state budget, Article 135(3) Spanish Constitution moreover prescribes a legislative act to approve public borrowing.

When applying this constitutional benchmark to wider EU borrowing competence or shared liabilities through Eurobonds, several constitutional concerns arise. Notably, these new competences could result in considerable, hardly predictable financial risks for the Spanish state budget. Specifically, in case the borrowing or the shared liabilities are guaranteed by the Member States, given that the EU currently has

221. As for example pointed out by the Spanish Parliament in its assessment of Council Decision 2014/335, cf. Spanish Congreso de los Diputados, *Dictamen de la Comisión de Asuntos Exteriores (110/000176): Decisión del Consejo de 26 de mayo de 2014 sobre el sistema de recursos propios de la Unión Europea (2014/335/UE, EURATOM), adoptada en Bruselas el 26 de mayo de 2014.* (Boletín Oficial de las Cortes Generales 2015).
222. Estella de Noriega, 'A Dissident Voice: The Spanish Constitutional Court Case Law on European Integration' 277.
223. Pérez Tremps, 'National Idenity in Spanish Constitutional Court Case-Law' 270.
224. Lionello, *The Pursuit of Stability of the Euro Area as a Whole: The Reform of the European Economic Union and Perspectives of Fiscal Integration* 222; Bonnie, 'The Constitutionality of Transfers of Sovereignty: The French Approach' 527.
225. Pérez Tremps, 'National Idenity in Spanish Constitutional Court Case-Law' 271; Castillo de la Torre, '*Tribunal Constitucional* (Spanish Constitutional Court), Opinion 1/2004 of 13 December 2004, on the Treaty Establishing a Constitution for Europe' 1183-1184; this conclusion can also be substantiated from a comparative perspective, for example visible from the German *overall budgetary responsibility* concept, cf. *Quantitative Easing (PSPP) Final Judgment* paras 226-227; *Lisbon-judgment* paras 252, 256; cf. as well: Payandeh, 'The OMT Judgment of the German Federal Constitutional Court: Repositioning the Court Within the European Constitutional Architecture' 408; or from the French jurisprudence, cf. *Review of Maastricht Treaty (Maastricht I)* para. 45; cf. as well Vranes, 'Constitutional Foundation of, and Limitations to, EU Integration in France' 540.

no major revenue stream that is independent of the Member States, the factual decisions on Spanish revenue and expenditure might be taken at EU level. Such a system would challenge the currently established constitutional design which allocates budgetary and fiscal decision-making to the Spanish legislator. The apparently resulting conflict with the Spanish *constitutional identity limit* would require a constitutional amendment following Article 168 Spanish Constitution,[226] which might be practically difficult to attain.

And finally, the compatibility of the various proposals with the Polish *constitutional identity limit* is considered. Regarding NGEU and the underlying EU own resources decision, national approval following Article 89(1)(4) Polish Constitution was required, which prescribes that the Polish Parliament confirms agreements with 'considerable financial responsibilities imposed on the State'. Different to the conferral of competences according to Article 90(1) Polish Constitution, which has to be approved by a two-thirds majority in the Polish Sejm,[227] Article 89 Polish Constitution does not impose a qualified majority requirement. However, Article 311 TFEU was ratified as part of the Lisbon Treaty by the Sejm based on Article 90 Polish Constitution. Given the resulting dual parliamentary confirmation and the general constitutional respect for EU law obligations,[228] the own resources decision is vested with high democratic legitimacy and the financing through EU borrowing does not alter that conclusion, as the mechanism in Article 311 TFEU allows for a continuous modification of the national financial commitment towards the EU.[229]

Regarding the more far-reaching proposal concerning EU borrowing competences or the introduction of shared liabilities, the Polish *constitutional identity limit* appears applicable. As established, the Polish Constitutional Tribunal identified the competence to conduct independent budgetary, financial and fiscal policies as a particularly important power under the Polish principle of sovereignty.[230] This includes the parliamentary responsibility for adopting the state budget enshrined in Article 219 Polish Constitution and the Sejm's responsibility to determine the conditions for state borrowing according to Article 216(4) Polish Constitution.[231] The proposed conferral of competences to the EU would increase Polish liabilities and alter the current constitutional conception according to which state borrowing and state guarantees have to be approved by the Sejm. In addition, the budgetary discretion available to parliament would be reduced in case financial risks manifest at EU level, which could impact national budgeting. As a result, the Constitutional Tribunal might consider the envisaged EU cooperation in conflict with the Polish *constitutional identity limit*. Such conflict can be overcome by amending the constitutional text as previously established.

226. Ferreres Comella, *The Constitution of Spain: A Contextual Analysis* 57.
227. Bainczyk, 'Folgen einer mangelnden Anpassung der polnischen Verfassung nach dem Vertrag von Lissabon im Lichte des Urteils des polnischen Verfassungsgerichtshofes zum Beschluss des Europäischen Rates zur Änderung von Art. 136 AEUV' 321.
228. Wendel, 'Lisbon Before the Courts: Comparative Perspectives' 107.
229. Bainczyk, 'Das Ratifizierungsverfahren des Vertrages von Lissabon in Polen' 148.
230. *Treaty of Lisbon* section III.2.1.; cf. as well: Wróbel, 'Die Grenzen der europäischen Integration im Lichte jüngerer Entscheidungen des polnischen Verfassungsgerichts' 499.
231. Cf. the constitutional arguments submitted in the inadmissible ESM-proceedings: *Challenges Against Article 136 (3) TFEU and ESM-Treaty* section 7.7.

Although a constitutional amendment might be practically difficult to achieve, the *constitutional identity limit* does not impose an absolute limitation on the constitution-amending legislator.[232]

c Interim Conclusion

Overall, the compatibility assessment revealed that NGEU was deemed largely compatible with the national constitutional frameworks, even if financed through EU borrowing. It was highlighted that the Finnish Constitutional Law Committee raised concerns, as it characterized the proposed scheme as a departure from the current practice of EU budgeting under the EU-Treaties.[233] Therefore, the Committee required a two-thirds parliamentary majority for the adoption of NGEU. In contrast, the German Constitutional Court found that neither the Own Resources Decision nor NGEU entailed a transfer of additional powers to the EU, hence, a qualified majority for its adoption in the sense of Article 23(1)(3) GG was not required.[234]

Furthermore, no additional substantive constitutional concerns appear to emerge under the national *constitutional identity limits* across the assessed Member States. This appears to result from the fact that NGEU is built on the existing EU Treaty-framework, which was already ratified by national legislators. The fact that the EU finances parts of its activities through borrowing appears not to alter the general financing structure of the EU's budget and it in fact appears to be caused by the aim to kick-start the EU recovery strategy in the aftermath of the COVID-19, which requires a major financial impulse in a short period of time. The envisaged financing structure through EU borrowing guaranteed by the Member States based on the EU own resources ceilings ensures that national budgets are not immediately overwhelmed by the required large financial investments. Given its design is based on the existing EU budgeting framework and given that Member States retain a constitutive say under Article 311(3) TFEU, NGEU appears not to limit parliamentary budgetary prerogatives in an unconstitutional manner – and thus be seen as a *constructive* example of how to devise EU fiscal integration steps in a legal-constitutionally sound manner.

Regarding a wider EU borrowing competence or the introduction of shared EU liabilities through Eurobonds, serious constitutional concerns appear to emerge. These concerns relate, on the one hand, to the potential impact of such EU discretionary competences on the national state budget and, on the other hand, to the difficulty of determining the potential financial risk inherent in the required national financial commitment. Here, a conceptual similarity with the constitutional concerns against a possible EU taxation competence can be identified. In fact, the discretionary competences to tax and issue debts appear to constitute the metaphorical two sides of the same coin. Notably, by conferring taxation competences to the EU, Member States

232. Śledzińska-Simon and Ziółkowski, 'Constitutional Identity in Poland: Is the Emperor Putting on the Old Clothes of Sovereignty' 244.
233. *Commission's Draft EU Recovery Plan and MFF Planning* 17; cf. as well: Leino-Sandberg, 'Who Is Ultra Vires Now? The EU's Legal U-Turn in Interpreting Article 310 TFEU'.
234. *Interim Decision on the Ratification of the Own Resources Decision (NGEU)* para. 79.

reduce their own prerogatives on generating state revenue which limits their fiscal decision-making space. Similarly, EU debts and liabilities could trigger financial obligations for the Member States, which restricts future domestic fiscal discretion.[235] Consequently, both types of proposals trigger similar national constitutional concerns.

As it stands, the constitutional concerns in Finland as well as the possible *constitutional identity* conflicts in France, Poland and Spain can be overcome based on the support of a qualified parliamentary majority that either confirms the EU commitment or that enacts the required national constitutional amendments in order to allow for the conferral of powers to EU level. Yet, the practical-political feasibility of the required majority requirements seems questionable. Furthermore, only in Germany, an absolute obstacle seems to exist, given the identified procedural and substantive conflicts with *overall budgetary responsibility*. Thereby, some of these concerns might be smoothened by deconstructing the conception of *overall budgetary responsibility*, addressing the apparent constitutional double standard and including the direct as well as indirect benefits from EU financial commitments in the constitutional appraisal, which is assessed in detail below (C).

4 Conclusion: Altering Constitutional Appraisal of Eurozone Budgetary Tool

The constitutional compatibility assessment of the possible funding options for the Eurozone revealed that the current EU Treaty-framework provides space to generate additional EU revenue in compliance with national constitutional law. Under the existing framework in Article 311 TFEU, national parliaments retain a final vote on the maximum financial commitments as well as influence on the administration of the conferred funds. Given that Article 311 TFEU is not limited in scope, Member States are able to assign new revenues to EU level. They can do so either by raising the national own resources ceiling and thereby increasing the direct national contributions, or, in the alternative, by introducing new tax-based EU resources that are collected at the national level and then assigned to the EU through the own resources decision, comparable to other traditional own resources.[236] The second option appears particularly interesting, given that it provides the EU with a more stable source of revenue different independent of 'just return' debates.[237] Moreover, Member States and in particular national parliaments retain ultimate control over the content of the own resources decision, which enables them to re-direct the proposed new traditional revenues if desired.

235. Violeta Ruiz Almendral, 'The European Fiscal Consolidation Legal Framework: Its Impact on National Fiscal Constitutions and Parliamentary Democracy' in Thomas Beukers, Bruno De Witte and Claire Kilpatrick (eds), *Constitutional Change Through Euro Crisis Law* (Cambridge University Press 2017) 29.

236. Such as sugar levies, for example, cf. Crowe, 'The European Budgetary Galaxy' 431.

237. Ruffert, 'The Future of the European Economic and Monetary Union: Issues of Constitutional Law' 50; Alcidi and Gros, 'Next Generation EU: A Large Common Response to the COVID-19 Crisis' 203.

In contrast, allocating discretionary power in order to either introduce taxation or engage in larger EU borrowing appears to interfere with national constitutional law. Inherent in such discretionary power is a degree of political decision-making power and flexibility which sits uneasily with national democratic concerns as well as (sovereign) budgetary planning, which involves the evaluation of financial risks. Therefore, the introduction of the discretionary funding option seems constitutionally contested in Finland, France, Poland and Spain as well as prevented by the absolute German *constitutional identity limit*. Hence, these funding options seem hardly attainable within the currently available national constitutional space. The overall compatibility findings on the various EU funding options are summarized in Table 8.2.

Table 8.2 Compatibility of Charted Constitutional Space with Proposed EU Funding Options

Member State	***New Own resources***	***Discretionary EU Taxation Competence***	***EU Debts/Borrowing***	***NGEU***
Finland	Parliamentary approval by a simple majority (section 94(2)(1) FC).	Qualified parliamentary approval (section 94(2)(2) FC).	Qualified parliamentary approval (section 94(2)(2) FC).	Qualified parliamentary approval (section 94(2)(2) FC) for the adoption of the underlying own resources decision.
Germany (including constitutional identity limit)	Parliamentary approval by a two-thirds majority (Article 23(1)(3) in conjunction with Article 79(2) GG).	Apparent conflict with the German *eternity clause* (given the discretionary nature, hardly predictable financial risks and the close link of taxation power with political decision-making which requires democratic control in Germany).	If the design corresponds to NGEU: Parliamentary approval by a two-thirds majority (Article 23(1)(3) in conjunction with Article 79(2) GG). If unlimited shared liability or discretionary EU competence to engage in borrowing without prior nat. approval of the resulting financial commitments: Apparent conflict with the German *eternity clause.*	Parliamentary approval by a two-thirds majority (Article 23(1)(3) in conjunction with Article 79(2) GG) for the adoption of the underlying own resources decision.

Member State	*New Own resources*	*Discretionary EU Taxation Competence*	*EU Debts/Borrowing*	*NGEU*
French sovereignty limit	Limit not applicable to EU secondary law.	Apparent conflict, can be overcome by const. amendment (Article 89 FC), which is common practice in France.	Apparent conflict, can be overcome by const. amendment (Article 89 FC), which is common practice in France.	Limit not applicable to EU secondary law. Parliamentary approval of the underpinning own resources decision (Article 53(1) FC).
Polish constitutional identity limit	Limit not applicable to EU secondary law.	Apparent conflict which might require const. amendment (Article 236 PC), including a possible referendum.	Apparent conflict which might require const. amendment (Article 236 PC), including a possible referendum.	Limit not applicable to EU secondary law. Parliamentary approval of the underpinning own resources decision (Article 89(1)(4) PC).
Spanish constitutional identity limit	Limit not applicable to EU secondary law.	Apparent conflict which might require const. amendment (Article 168 SC).	Apparent conflict which might require const. amendment (Article 168 SC).	Limit not applicable to EU secondary law. Parliamentary approval of the underpinning own resources decision (Article 94(1)(d) SC).

III Compatibility of Proposals Envisaging an EU Ministry of Finance with National Constitutional Space

Considering the various proposals for creating a Eurozone Ministry of Finance, it was established that two particularly relevant elements for the national constitutional appraisal can be distinguished. In the first place, a structural-institutional dimension, which includes the general idea to pool existing EMU-related competences in one central EU institution[238] as well as the proposal to establish a Euroarea parliamentary assembly to supervise the Ministry (1).[239] Second, a more substantive-institutional dimension which includes reform ideas to allocate new competences, such as a discretionary taxation competence or an EU veto power for national budgets, to this Eurozone Ministry (2).[240]

1 *Structural-Institutional Dimension of the Proposed Eurozone Ministry*

The different proposals advocate for the creation of the Eurozone Ministry of Finance in charge of the pooled existing EMU-powers as such[241] and the establishment of a Eurozone parliamentary assembly that could supervise and administer the actions of this Ministry.[242]

a *Compatibility with the Charted Macro-comparative Constitutional Space*

When assessing the compatibility of these institutional reform steps with the charted *macro-comparative* space, constitutional concerns arise in Finland concerning the implementation of the structural-institutional reforms at EU level as well as the potentially required conferral of additional competences to attain the proposed

238. Commission, *Reflection Paper on the Deepening of the Economic and Monetary Union* 28; Juncker et al., *The Five Presidents' Report: Completing Europe's Economic and Monetary Union* 14, 18; cf. as well: Lionello, *The Pursuit of Stability of the Euro Area as a Whole: The Reform of the European Economic Union and Perspectives of Fiscal Integration* 188; Ruffert, 'The Future of the European Economic and Monetary Union: Issues of Constitutional Law' 59-61.
239. Ruffert, 'The Future of the European Economic and Monetary Union: Issues of Constitutional Law' 59-60; Lionello, *The Pursuit of Stability of the Euro Area as a Whole: The Reform of the European Economic Union and Perspectives of Fiscal Integration* 226.
240. Marzinotto, Sapir and Wolff, 'What Kind of Fiscal Union? (2011)' 6-7.
241. Commission, *Completing Europe's Economic and Monetary Union: A European Minister of Economy and Finance*; Commission, *Reflection Paper on the Deepening of the Economic and Monetary Union* 27; Juncker et al., *The Five Presidents' Report: Completing Europe's Economic and Monetary Union* 14, 18; cf. as well: Ruffert, 'The Future of the European Economic and Monetary Union: Issues of Constitutional Law' 59-61; Fabbrini, 'Fiscal Capacity' 131.
242. Cf. for example: Craig and Markakis, 'EMU Reform' 1441; the proposed Ministry could at least render the decision-making more transparent, cf. Lionello, *The Pursuit of Stability of the Euro Area as a Whole: The Reform of the European Economic Union and Perspectives of Fiscal Integration* 188-189.

structural-institutional modifications. The Finnish Constitutional Law Committee established that changes to the EU institutional framework could constitute a modification of the initial parliamentary approval given to ratify the EU-Treaties.[243] Furthermore, the Committee established that budgetary and fiscal competences are considered particularly important competences of the Finnish Parliament according to section 3(1) and Chapter 7 Finnish Constitution.[244] Therefore, any institutional modification on the administration and modalities of EMU-related competences may be seen as particularly relevant to the Finnish Parliament and more specifically the Finnish sovereignty doctrine.[245] Finally, the Committee established that fundamental changes to the *modes* of EU cooperation could constitute a significant interference with Finnish sovereignty and thus require approval by a two-thirds majority.[246]

In light of this constitutional benchmark, it appears that the creation of a new institutional actor in charge of the coordination of EMU-related competences would require parliamentary approval following section 94(1) Finnish Constitution, as the initial parliamentary EU commitment is amended. Notably, the current EU-Treaties did not envisage the creation of a Ministry of Finance and the introduction of such a new institution, even if based on EU secondary law, would likely be seen as an amendment to the institutional balance currently enshrined in the EU-Treaties.

Furthermore, the proposed institutional reform step could alter Finnish parliamentary control over EMU decision-making. Notably, the Finnish Parliament participates in the national *ex ante* preparation of EMU decisions that are of parliamentary relevance.[247] Thereby the Finnish mandating practice only extends to the Finnish representative in the Council and European Council. Moreover, the parliamentary right to be informed about EU developments only obliges the Finnish Government following section 97 Finnish Constitution.[248] Any changes to the existing EU institutional framework could also impact this constitutionally secured parliamentary oversight, as decisions might be centrally prepared by an EU Ministry – instead of the Council. What is more, relevant information might be accumulated outside the direct reach of the Finnish Government, and hence the Finnish Parliament. Consequently, the envisaged creation of an EU Ministry of Finance would not only alter the initial parliamentary approval of the EU-Treaties but it could equally have significant implications for the national parliamentary knowledge of and involvement in the EU decision-making

243. Leino and Salminen, 'The Euro Crisis and Its Constitutional Consequences for Finland: Is There Room for National Politics in EU Decision-Making?' 472.
244. Mutanen, *Towards a Pluralistic Constitutional Understanding of State Sovereignty in the European Union? The Concept, Regulation and Constitutional Practice of Sovereignty in Finland and Certain Other EU Member States* 306-307.
245. Ojanen and Salminen, 'Finland: European Integration and International Human Rights Treaties as Sources of Domestic Constitutional Change and Dynamism' 391-392.
246. *Ratification of the Own Resources Decision (II.)*; *Second Assessment Draft ESM-Treaty (II.)* 2; cf. as well: Leino-Sandberg and Ruffert, 'Next Generation EU and Its Constitutional Ramifications: A Critical Assessment' 447; Leino-Sandberg, 'Who Is Ultra Vires Now? The EU's Legal U-Turn in Interpreting Article 310 TFEU'.
247. As established in section 96 Finnish Constitution; cf. as well: Ojanen, 'The Impact of EU Membership on Finnish Constitutional Law' 556.
248. Leino and Salminen, 'The Euro Crisis and Its Constitutional Consequences for Finland: Is There Room for National Politics in EU Decision-Making?' 459.

process. These constitutional concerns are reinforced since the competence areas involved are particularly important parliamentary prerogatives protected by Finnish sovereignty. To a similar extent, the initiation of a Eurozone assembly would alter the initial parliamentary approval and with it the institutional framework, as such chamber would unite democratic structures of the national and EU level. These combined parliamentary structures are not anticipated by the current EU-Treaties and would thus alter the Finnish parliamentary EU-mandate. A new approval under section 94(1) Finnish Constitution therefore appears required to confirm these institutional modifications.

The subsequent question is whether real decision-making responsibilities would be assigned to such an assembly. In case such powers would be indeed allocated to the Eurozone assembly, this would constitute a shift of responsibilities from the exclusively national constitutional level to a combined national-EU decision-making space, which clearly impacts the outlined important budgetary prerogatives constitutionally protected in section 3(1) and Chapter 7 Finnish Constitution. Although the new Eurozone assembly would include Finnish parliamentarians, it would operate in a constitutional *in-between* space between the EU and the national level, in which neither of the established parliamentary tools appears to apply. In addition, the current functioning of the EU does not include such *sui generis* Eurozone parliamentary assembly, which may be thus classified as a major institutional transformation that alters the current *mode* of EU-cooperation.

Taken together, this suggests that both institutional reform steps could have a major impact on the exercise of budgetary prerogatives, which are particularly important Finnish parliamentary competences. As a result, it seems that the required Treaty recognition and institutional transformation would likely necessitate confirmation by a qualified two-thirds parliamentary majority, as established in section 94(2)(2) Finnish Parliament.

In Germany, the established constitutional jurisprudence – similar to the Finnish one – underscores the importance of explicitly recognizing institutional alterations such as the proposed structural-institutional modifications through a Treaty amendment. Otherwise, the Constitutional Court could be inclined to consider such modifications enacted on the basis of EU secondary law as *ultra vires*.[249] As illustrated, the fact that constitutional proceedings are highly likely given the lowered standing requirements[250] might incentivize the German legislator to be diligent in its supervision of EU action under *integration responsibility* doctrine.[251] Considering that the EU-Treaties do neither establish an EU Ministry of Finance nor a Eurozone assembly to supervise such Ministry and in light of the considerable authority that the different proposals aim to delegate and pool within this envisaged institutional actor, it seems

249. Haltern, 'Ultra-vires-Kontrolle im Dienst europäischer Demokratie' 818.
250. Gärditz, 'Beyond Symbolism: Towards a Constitutional Actio Popularis in EU Affairs? A Commentary on the OMT Decision of the Federal Constitutional Court' 192.
251. Weiß, 'Die Integrationsverantwortung der Verfassungsorgane' 1047.

likely that a Treaty amendment would be deemed necessary from a German constitutional perspective. This conferral might then require approval by a qualified majority under Article 23(1)(3) in conjunction with Article 79(2) GG.

As previously clarified, Article 23(1)(3) GG prescribes a constitution-amending two-thirds majority for EU integration steps that amend the material content of the German Constitution.[252] This qualified majority was, for example, required to adopt the ESM-Treaty as well as the Fiscal Compact,[253] given the instruments' implications for parliament's budgetary prerogatives.[254] Considering the reform proposals, it appears that the establishment of a Eurozone Ministry of Finance and a Eurozone assembly controlling EMU-related decisions would alter the currently applicable institutional framework, including the German constitutional framework that guarantees parliamentary involvement in the preparation of EU decisions with parliamentary relevance. Comparable to the framework in Finland, the German Constitution establishes the parliamentary obligation to issue a statement to the German Government on EU secondary law decisions that concern its constitutional prerogatives according to Article 23(3) GG.[255]

In addition, given that budgetary and fiscal prerogatives are assigned to the German Parliament and protected under *overall budgetary responsibility*[256] as well as recalling that the German Constitutional Court clarified that central budgetary decisions may not be delegated to a parliamentary committee but have to be taken by the entire *Bundestag*,[257] it seems incompatible with the German Constitution to confer the parliamentary responsibilities to the proposed Eurozone assembly. Instead, all central decisions have to be determined by the German Parliament, as for example the case under Article 311(3) TFEU. The proposed Eurozone assembly cannot replace the confirmation of financial commitments by the democratically elected German Parliament.

Furthermore, establishing a state-like institutional structure consisting of an EU Ministry and the corresponding parliamentary assembly might have a centralizing effect, which could result in a situation where the EU gains increasing control over budgetary and fiscal decisions in the long run. Given the possible implications for these competences, which are particularly protected under Articles 104a to 115 GG, as well as a potential decrease in German parliamentary oversight over EU decision-making as Article 23(3) GG does not cover decisions by the EU Minister or the proposed Eurozone

252. Lorz and Sauer, 'Verfassungsändernde Mehrheiten für die Stabilisierung des Euro?: Mehrheitserfordernisse bei der Zustimmung zum Fiskalpakt, zum ESM-Vertrag und zur Änderung des AEUV' 685.
253. Ketterer, *Zustimmungserfordernis beim Europäischen Stabilitätsmechanismus* 359.
254. Richter, *Funktionswandel im Mehrebenensystem? Die Rolle der nationalen Parlamente in der Europäischen Union am Beispiel des Deutschen Bundestags* 176.
255. Nettesheim, 'Die Integrationsverantwortung: Vorgaben des BVerfG und gesetzgeberische Umsetzung' 181.
256. *Interim Decision on the Ratification of the Own Resources Decision (NGEU)*; *Quantitative Easing (PSPP) Final Judgment* para. 104; cf. as well: Reestman, 'Legitimacy Through Adjudication: The ESM Treaty and the Fiscal Compact Before the National Courts' 259.
257. Bumke and Voßkuhle, *German Constitutional Law: Introduction, Cases, and Principles* paras 1634-1636.

assembly, it seems likely that a constitution-amending majority in the sense of Article 23(1)(3) in conjunction with Article 79(2) GG will be deemed necessary to confirm the proposed institutional reform steps.

These institutional reforms remain restricted by *overall budgetary responsibility*.[258] Regarding the concept's constitutional requirements, it appears that the institutional reform steps themselves do not contain an incompatible conferral of competences, given that the proposals only create an institutional framework or infrastructure for the administration of existing EMU competences. These competences are already conferred at EU level without resulting in a conflict with the *eternity clause* and the proposed modifications do not alter the current ultimate control over budgetary decisions. Consequently, the proposed institutional modifications appear not to result in incompatibility with *overall budgetary responsibility*.

b Compatibility with the Charted Micro-comparative Constitutional Space

However, it is possible that substantive constitutional concerns emerge under the other charted national *constitutional identity limits*. In France, the proposed institutional reform steps could trigger a conflict with the sovereignty limit[259] which protects budgetary and fiscal competences.[260] Therefore, the central question is whether the envisaged EU integration steps would confer additional competences to EU level, and would thus require an explicit constitutional amendment.[261] As previously highlighted, the proposed institutional reform steps appear to reallocate existing EU responsibilities. The proposed reform steps therefore do not appear to entail an additional conferral of competences from the national to EU level but rather a re-shuffling of already conferred powers. Consequently, national budgetary and fiscal prerogatives appear not to be modified by these structural-institutional steps. Rather, the steps intend to render EU decision-making in these areas more transparent and more effective, which appears beneficial for the functioning of the single currency. At the same time, the *Conseil* continuously underscored in its constitutional decisions that the modalities attached to the conferred competences are similarly important for the conducted review.[262] However, it appears that the proposed initiation of the Ministry of Finance does not alter the final decision-making modalities itself but it would rather impact the preparation of such decisions. This seems not to conflict with the French sovereignty limit. Taken together, it appears that the *Conseil Constitutionnel* is unlikely to detect a conflict with the sovereignty limit given that the existing division of competences

258. Calliess, '70 Jahre Grundgesetz und europäische Integration: "Take Back Control" oder "Mehr Demokratie wagen"?' 688.
259. Vranes, 'Constitutional Foundation of, and Limitations to, EU Integration in France' 540.
260. Reestman, 'Legitimacy Through Adjudication: The ESM Treaty and the Fiscal Compact Before the National Courts' 265; Gundel, *Die Einordnung des Gemeinschaftsrechts in die französische Rechtsordnung* 133; Oliver, 'The French Constitution and the Treaty of Maastricht' 13, 15.
261. Fabbrini, 'The Euro-Crisis and the Courts: Judicial Review and the Political Process in Comparative Perspective' 120.
262. Boyron, 'The French Constitution and the Treaty of Amsterdam: A Lesson in European Integration' 176.

between the EU and the Member States appears not to be impacted by the proposed institutional modifications.

In Spain, the Constitutional Tribunal similarly established that EU integration steps have to respect Spanish *constitutional identity*, which protects sovereignty, democracy and the constitutional structure.[263] From the Tribunal's jurisprudence, it can be deduced that the concept is conceptualized as a competence-based limitation to the process of EU integration.[264] Consequently, the Tribunal is mainly concerned with the conferral of competences to EU level, which could alter the Spanish constitutional order in a manner that is incompatible with the identity of the Spanish Constitution for example by conferring *Kompetenz-Kompetenz* to EU level.[265] As illustrated, the structural-institutional reform steps appear to focus on modifications to the EU's institutional framework, which has implications for the mandate that the Member States conferred upon the EU. Notably, the modalities and conditions attached to the exercise of transferred competences are equally important for the constitutional conferral. However, given that the envisaged institutional reform steps do not entail an additional change of competences from the national to EU level or alter the final decision-making responsibility these modifications seem not contentious under the Spanish *constitutional identity limit*.

When now considering the Polish *constitutional identity limit*, it appears questionable whether a conflict would be triggered by the proposed institutional modifications. As highlighted, the Polish Constitutional Tribunal established that the conferral of powers to the EU is limited by the principle of sovereignty, which requires that important competence areas remain at the national level, including economic, financial and fiscal competences.[266] As established in relation to France, Germany, and Spain, the here envisaged institutional modifications do not concern the conferral of competences, but rather an alteration of the modalities of already conferred competences. These modifications do, however, not change the final decision-making authority. Therefore, it appears that the equally competence-centric *constitutional identity* concerns do not apply to the proposed reform steps, as the division of competences between the EU and the Member States as well as the ultimate responsibility for the decisions taken on these competences would remain unchanged by these proposals.

263. Bustos Gisbert, 'National Constitutional Identity in European Constitutionalism: Revisiting the Tale of the Emperor's New Clothes in Spain?' 77.
264. Castillo de la Torre, '*Tribunal Constitucional* (Spanish Constitutional Court), Opinion 1/2004 of 13 December 2004, on the Treaty Establishing a Constitution for Europe' 1183-1184.
265. *Constitutional Review of the Maastricht Treaty* section II.4.; cf. as well: Pérez Tremps, 'National Idenity in Spanish Constitutional Court Case-Law' 271.
266. *Treaty of Lisbon* section III.2.1.; cf. as well: Bainczyk, 'Folgen einer mangelnden Anpassung der polnischen Verfassung nach dem Vertrag von Lissabon im Lichte des Urteils des polnischen Verfassungsgerichtshofes zum Beschluss des Europäischen Rates zur Änderung von Art. 136 AEUV' 314-315.

c Interim Conclusion

Overall, it seems that the introduction of an EU Minister or Ministry of Finance might require additional national constitutional approval in Finland and Germany. Notably, the creation of such an institutional actor would alter the currently existing EU institutional balance as enshrined in the EU-Treaties. Furthermore, the envisaged alterations to the EU institutional framework could impact national procedures that ensure parliamentary participation in EU decision-making. The result could be that national parliaments would not be as comprehensively involved in the adoption of EMU-policies, which modify the initial conferral of competences as well as the modalities attached to it. Therefore, these alterations could require a new confirmation by national parliaments – possibly even by a qualified majority in case these institutional changes are deemed to modify the current mode of cooperation within the EMU. In addition, the compatibility assessment illustrated that no conflict under the French, German, Polish or Spanish *constitutional identity limit* seems to emerge, given that the proposed institutional reform steps mainly concern the modalities attached to the exercise of already conferred competences and given that the ultimate decision-making responsibility appears not to be altered by these structural proposals. Therefore, these institutional modifications do not directly confer additional competences to EU level, which appears to be the most relevant requirement for triggering the national *constitutional identity limits*.

2 Conferring New Competences to the Eurozone Ministry

A second set of ideas relates to the allocation of additional competences to the proposed EU Ministry of Finance. These competences include, for example, a discretionary taxation competence to empower the EU to autonomously raise revenue if required[267] or the power to veto national budgeting.[268] Allocating these competences to EU level would require Treaty-recognition.

a Compatibility with the Charted Macro-comparative Constitutional Space

In Finland, the conferral of additional, far-reaching institutional responsibilities to an EU Ministry of Finance could conflict with Finnish sovereignty, which would require approval by a qualified parliamentary majority following Article 94(2)(2) Finnish Constitution. As previously established in relation to the introduction of a discretionary EU taxation competence, the Constitutional Law Committee considers budgetary and

267. Cf. the Bruegel-proposal: Marzinotto, Sapir and Wolff, 'What Kind of Fiscal Union? (2011)' 7.
268. Lionello, *The Pursuit of Stability of the Euro Area as a Whole: The Reform of the European Economic Union and Perspectives of Fiscal Integration* 169; Tuori and Tuori, *The Eurozone Crisis: A Constitutional Analysis* 255; Marzinotto, Sapir and Wolff, 'What Kind of Fiscal Union? (2011)' 6.

fiscal competences particularly important parliamentary prerogatives.[269] Following its decisions, these prerogatives cover the introduction of new taxation under sections 3(1) and 81(1) Finnish Constitution, the general adoption of the state budget, as clarified in section 83(1) Finnish Constitution, including all revenue and expenditure, as well as finally the issuing of state guarantees, as clarified in section 82(3) Finnish Constitution.[270]

In light of this constitutional benchmark, it appears that a discretionary taxation competence for the envisaged Eurozone Ministry of Finance would challenge precisely these parliamentary prerogatives established under section 3(1) Finnish Constitution. In addition, a veto possibility regarding the national budget after the approval of the Finnish Parliament alters the constitutional framework for national budgeting established under section 83(1) Finnish Constitution. Given that budgetary and fiscal prerogatives are essential competences under the sovereignty doctrine, and given that the EU influence would be considerable, it appears that the envisaged powers could only be conferred by a qualified parliamentary majority in the sense of section 94(2)(2) Finnish Parliament. This conclusion is supported by the fact that the proposed reform steps would likely alter the general mode of EU cooperation which conflicts with Finnish sovereignty. Notably, core decision-making abilities would be shifted from the national to the EU level thereby reducing the powers of the Finnish Parliament.[271] Hence, it seems likely that a qualified two-thirds majority would be required in Finland in order to equip the proposed EU Ministry of Finance with the envisaged substantive competences.

In Germany, the allocation of a discretionary taxation competence and an EU veto power regarding the national state budget to the proposed Eurozone Ministry of Finance would also likely result in a major constitutional conflict. In the first place, both envisaged EU competences alter the German Constitution. Article 105 GG allocates the power to tax to the federal as well as the regional state level.[272] In addition, Article 110 GG assigns the independent responsibility to establish the German federal budget to the German Parliament.[273] Both parliamentary prerogatives would be modified by the proposed substantive reform steps and would therefore require approval by a constitution-amending two-thirds majority following Article 23(1)(3) GG.

However, these reform steps could also conflict with *overall budgetary responsibility* given their impact on budgetary and fiscal parliamentary prerogatives. As stated,

269. *Ratification of the Own Resources Decision (II.)*; *Second Assessment Draft ESM-Treaty (II.)* 2; cf. as well: Mutanen, *Towards a Pluralistic Constitutional Understanding of State Sovereignty in the European Union? The Concept, Regulation and Constitutional Practice of Sovereignty in Finland and Certain Other EU Member States* 306-307; Ojanen, 'The Impact of EU Membership on Finnish Constitutional Law' 541.
270. Leino and Salminen, 'The Euro Crisis and Its Constitutional Consequences for Finland: Is There Room for National Politics in EU Decision-Making?' 457-458.
271. Leino-Sandberg, 'Who Is Ultra Vires Now? The EU's Legal U-Turn in Interpreting Article 310 TFEU'.
272. Kube, 'Art. 105 GG – Steuergesetzgebungskompetenz' paras 1-2.
273. Schneider, 'Exkurs: Die Rolle des Haushaltsausschusses des Bundestages bei Aufstellung und Vollzug des Haushalts: ein Praxisbericht' 295-296.

the German Constitutional Court requires that budgetary and financial commitments remain specific, limited and under the control of the German Parliament[274] as well as that German budgetary autonomy is not suspended.[275] When applying this benchmark to the prospect of a discretionary taxation competence for the EU Ministry of Finance, the previously established conclusions in relation to the allocation of discretionary revenue powers to the EU apply. Notably, a discretionary EU taxation competence reduces the national fiscal decision-making space in Germany, and it would shift political decision-making outside the reach of democratic control through the German people.[276]

Furthermore, the proposed EU veto power for national budgets would establish the EU as the final authorizer of national budgeting and thereby alter the current conception, which establishes national parliaments as the highest budgetary authority. Such veto power would significantly alter the current framework, according to which Member States have to comply with the established fiscal rules as they could be otherwise sanctioned. Yet, this gives national parliaments a genuine political choice to either modify the national budgetary planning or to risk EU sanctions. This genuine political choice would be challenged in case an EU institution could simply block the adoption of a domestic state budget. Therefore, it appears that the proposed increase in EU powers for the envisaged EU Ministry of Finance could be considered incompatible with *overall budgetary responsibility*. The proposed substantive reform steps appear thus constitutionally impossible in Germany in light of the current jurisprudence of the Constitutional Court and particularly its interpretation of Article 79(3) GG.[277]

b Compatibility with the Charted Micro-comparative Constitutional Space

The outlined apparent conflict between the proposed discretionary decision-making abilities and the German *constitutional identity limit* indicates that these reform ambitions might be more generally constitutionally contentious on other Member States with a *constitutional identity limit* as well. The outlined German constitutional concerns appear to be echoed in France, where the *Conseil Constitutionnel* focuses within its sovereignty limit, particularly on protecting domestic budgetary and fiscal prerogatives as laid down in Articles 34 and 47 French Constitution.[278] Both provisions establish the French legislator's responsibility to determine the broader budgeting

274. *Interim Decision on the Ratification of the Own Resources Decision (NGEU)* paras 84-85; *Quantitative Easing (PSPP) Reference* para. 48; cf. as well: Nettesheim, 'Die "haushaltspolitische Gesamtverantwortung" in der Rechtsprechung des BVerfG' 23.
275. *Interim Decision on the Ratification of the Own Resources Decision (NGEU)* para. 85; *Quantitative Easing (PSPP) Final Judgment* paras 226-227; *Final OMT-Judgment* para. 213; cf. as well: Claes and Reestman, 'The Protection of National Constitutional Identity and the Limits of European Integration at the Occasion of the *Gauweiler* Case' 927.
276. Schröder, 'Das Demokratieprinzip des Grundgesetzes' 814.
277. Rademacher, 'Die "Verfassungsidentität" als Grenze der Kompetenzübertragung auf die Europäische Union?' 144; Ohler, 'Rechtliche Maßstäbe der Geldpolitik nach dem Gauweiler-Urteil des EuGH' 1002.
278. Fabbrini, 'The Euro-Crisis and the Courts: Judicial Review and the Political Process in Comparative Perspective' 119-120.

framework, the sources of revenue and planned expenditure as well as the requirement that the French state budget has to be adopted by a legislative act. Clearly, the introduction of a discretionary taxation competence administered by the proposed EU Ministry of Finance would limit the constitutionally secured parliamentary taxation prerogatives of the French legislator. And the proposed EU veto power over national budgeting would challenge the parliamentary responsibility for establishing the state budget. Notably, the current French Constitution does not provide for the possibility that an EU institution can effectively block the adoption of the French state budget. As a result, the French legislator would be significantly restricted in its constitutionally assigned budgetary and fiscal prerogatives. Therefore, the proposed discretionary powers appear to require a constitutional amendment in France prior to confirming the required conferral of competences to the EU. Such amendments are possible in all parts of the constitutional text and in fact common practice in France.[279]

In Spain, the *constitutional identity limit* protects national sovereignty and democracy,[280] which seemingly includes the parliamentary prerogative to enact taxation[281] as well as to establish the state budget.[282] The proposed discretionary EU taxation competences would challenge this taxation authority of the Spanish legislator. It could furthermore impact national budgeting more, in case the resources generated by the EU are no longer available for the national budgetary process. In addition, Article 134(1) Spanish Constitution establishes, in an exhaustive manner, that the *Cortes Generales* is responsible for examining, amending and approving the Spanish state budget. The provision does not qualify this prerogative by, for example, a veto option for the EU. Hence, a veto possibility for the proposed Eurozone Ministry of Finance would clearly alter these exclusive Spanish parliamentary prerogatives with potential implications for Spanish democracy. Notably, the Spanish legislator would no longer be the final arbiter in the adoption process of the state budget. Given these major implications, the proposed substantive reform steps appear to require confirmation through constitutional amendment following Article 168 Spanish Constitution.[283] This suggests that the conferral of the required competences is constitutionally possible, but might prove highly challenging to attain.

In Poland, following an anticipatory constitutional analysis,[284] it appears that similar constitutional conflicts with the Polish *constitutional identity limit* could emerge. Notably, the Polish Constitutional Tribunal established that economic, financial and fiscal decision-making competences were particularly important under Polish

279. Steiner, *French Law: A Comparative Approach* 7; Ziller, 'European Union Law in the Jurisprudence of French Supreme Courts: Europe-Friendliness with a French Touch' 772.
280. Martín Y Pérez de Nanclares, 'Constitutional Identity in Spain: Commitment to European Integration Without Giving up the Essence of the Constitution' 279; De Areilza Carvajal, 'La Inserción de España en la Nueva Unión Europea: La Relación entre la Constitución Española y el Trato Constitucional (Comentario a la DTC 1/2004, de 13 de diciembre de 2004)' 370-371.
281. Established in Article 133(1) Spanish Constitution.
282. Established in Article 134(1) Spanish Constitution.
283. Albert, *Constitutional Amendments: Making, Breaking, and Changing Constitutions* 192; Ferreres Comella, *The Constitution of Spain: A Contextual Analysis* 57.
284. Reestman, 'Legitimacy Through Adjudication: The ESM Treaty and the Fiscal Compact Before the National Courts' 249.

sovereignty.[285] This is explicitly confirmed by the Polish Constitution itself, which assigns these competences to the Polish Council of Ministers and the Polish Parliament as established in Articles 146 and 219 Polish Constitution.[286] Any discretionary decision-making powers on taxation at EU level or the EU's ability to veto national budgeting would challenge the established constitutional framework for budgeting in Poland. It is likely that the Tribunal would see in this a serious limit to the ability of the legislator to independently design budgetary and fiscal decisions, which was characterized as an essential component under Polish sovereignty. Therefore, the proposed substantive reform steps and the required conferral of competences to EU level appear to result in a conflict with the Polish *constitutional identity limit*. However, the resulting conflict can be accommodated by amending the constitutional text following Article 235 Polish Constitution.[287] The political feasibility of such constitutional reform remains questionable.

c Interim Conclusion

Overall, this suggests that the proposed substantive reform steps, which are intended to equip the envisaged EU Ministry of Finance as well as the composed Eurozone assembly with discretionary decision-making possibilities, are confronted with serious constitutional obstacles. Both in Finland and Germany, these concerns would likely trigger the qualified majority threshold for confirming the conferral of powers to the EU.

In addition, these constitutional concerns could potentially result in a conflict with German *overall budgetary responsibility*. Arguably, awarding discretionary taxation powers or a veto over national budgeting to the EU challenges German budgetary autonomy and amends the responsibility of the German Parliament for the German state budget. Comparable constitutional concerns can be identified in France, Poland and Spain, where the proposed substantive reform steps appear to result in conflicts with the respective national *constitutional identity limit*. However, only the German *constitutional identity limit* imposes an absolute limitation to the process of EU integration, which might consequently translate into an irreconcilable conflict with the German *eternity clause* in Article 79(3) GG.

3 Conclusion on the Creation of an EU Ministry of Finance

National constitutional concerns primarily emerge in relation to the proposed conferral of substantive decision-making competences to EU level and to a lesser extent in

285. *Treaty of Lisbon* section III.2.1.
286. Bainczyk, 'Folgen einer mangelnden Anpassung der polnischen Verfassung nach dem Vertrag von Lissabon im Lichte des Urteils des polnischen Verfassungsgerichtshofes zum Beschluss des Europäischen Rates zur Änderung von Art. 136 AEUV' 314.
287. Śledzińska-Simon and Ziółkowski, 'Constitutional Identity in Poland: Is the Emperor Putting on the Old Clothes of Sovereignty' 244; Brandt, 'Verfassungsrecht in Polen: Verfassungsbeschwerde und Rechtsprechung des polnischen Verfassungsgerichtshofes zu Fragen der EU-Mitgliedschaft' 139.

relation to the mere modification of the existing EU structural-institutional framework. This observation appears to confirm that national *constitutional identity limits* are mainly construed in light of competence areas and competence conferrals. As illustrated within the *macro-* and *micro-comparative* constitutional assessment, national constitutional authorities seem to conceptualize national sovereignty or national democracy, which constitute central principles under the various national *constitutional identity limits*, by identifying particularly important national competence areas and powers within the protected scope under these limits. Based on this competence-centric conception of national *constitutional identity limits*, the required conferral of competences to allocate the outlined substantive powers to EU level would likely trigger the outlined major conflicts with national sovereignty and democracy.

In contrast, the envisaged structural-institutional modifications – that would result in the creation of the envisaged EU Ministry of Finance – seem to trigger fewer constitutional concerns under the national *constitutional identity limits*. However, these reform ambitions appear to require additional parliamentary support in Finland and Germany given that they alter the currently existing institutional framework. Depending on the resulting impact on the constitutionally secured involvement of national parliaments in EU decision-making as well as the potential implications for the *modus operandi* of the EMU – notably, by moving away from mere coordination of fiscal decision-making towards taking these decisions at EU level – it is even conceivable that these structural-institutional reform ambitions would require qualified parliamentary support. The overall compatibility findings on the establishment of a Eurozone Ministry of Finance are summarized in Table 8.3.

Table 8.3 Compatibility of Charted Constitutional Space with Proposed Eurozone Ministry of Finance

Member State	***Institutional Dimension of Establishing Eurozone Ministry***	***Substantive Dimension of Establishing Eurozone Ministry***
Finland	Qualified parliamentary approval (section 94(2)(2) FC).	Qualified parliamentary approval (section 94(2)(2) FC).
Germany (including constitutional identity limit)	Parliamentary approval by a two-thirds majority (Article 23(1)(3) in conjunction with Article 79(2) GG).	Apparent conflict with the German *eternity clause* (size of commitment and suspension of nat. parliamentary control). Partly flexibilization of absolute conflict possible through: - EU benefits. - Consistent standard.
French sovereignty limit	No apparent conflict with the sovereignty limit.	Apparent conflict, can be overcome by const. amendment (Article 89 FC), which is common practice in France.

Member State	*Institutional Dimension of Establishing Eurozone Ministry*	*Substantive Dimension of Establishing Eurozone Ministry*
Polish constitutional identity limit	No apparent conflict with the *constitutional identity limit.*	Possible conflict which might require const. amendment (Article 236 PC), including a possible referendum.
		Apparent conflict, can be possibly overcome through 'modern' interpretation of Polish sovereignty.
Spanish constitutional identity limit	No apparent conflict with the *constitutional identity limit.*	Apparent conflict, can be overcome under strict const. amendments procedure in Article 168 SC which imposes a high threshold and is practically difficult to attain.

IV Compatibility of Tightened EU Supervision with National Constitutional Space

A final set of ideas relates to the enhanced EU supervision over national budgeting. To that end, it was established that the proposals mainly aim at better integrating the existing supervisory tools into the national and the EU budgetary process.[288] The Commission proposed the establishment of independent domestic 'Competitiveness Authorities' that evaluate the national economic development[289] as well as the comprehensive use of the national recommendations issued under the European Semester for the allocation of EU funds.[290] The most far-reaching proposal suggested the allocation of the discussed EU veto power over national budgeting.[291]

Obviously, the increased EU supervision of national budgetary and fiscal decision-making has implications for the Member States as these rules limit national discretion. At the same time, EU fiscal rules were consistently identified as an important tool to ensure compliance with national responsibility towards the Eurozone to avoid moral hazard.[292]

288. Craig and Markakis, 'EMU Reform' 1441; Marzinotto, Sapir and Wolff, 'What Kind of Fiscal Union? (2011)' 3.
289. Juncker et al., *The Five Presidents' Report: Completing Europe's Economic and Monetary Union* 8.
290. Commission, *Reflection Paper on the Deepening of the Economic and Monetary Union* 24-25.
291. Lionello, *The Pursuit of Stability of the Euro Area as a Whole: The Reform of the European Economic Union and Perspectives of Fiscal Integration* 170.
292. Ruffert, 'The Future of the European Economic and Monetary Union: Issues of Constitutional Law' 55.

1 Compatibility with the Charted Macro-comparative Constitutional Space

In relation to Finland, it was established that parliamentary budgetary prerogatives are considered central sovereign competences that enjoy enhanced constitutional protection.[293] Furthermore, EU integration steps are generally compatible with the Finnish sovereignty limit unless they impact essential features of parliamentary budgetary prerogatives or in case the general *modus operandi* of EU cooperation is altered. In light of these constitutional concerns, it seems that the proposed more integrated European Semester and the establishment of the national 'Competitiveness Authority' do not entail a significant shift of powers to EU level. Rather, they build on the currently existing framework established for EU fiscal supervision. To that end, the Constitutional Law Committee even emphasized the benefits that stem from a stable Euro for Finland,[294] which may be attained through the envisaged increased fiscal supervision. Consequently, a better integrated European Semester with data provided by an independent domestic authority and a possible connection of EU funds to the recommendations issued under the European Semester strengthen the effectiveness of the existing framework. Therefore, these ideas can be confirmed by a simple parliamentary majority. The assessment would differ in case the EU obtained veto power over national parliaments. Taken together, this suggests that additional EU supervision and EU-based incentives to comply with EU recommendations are compatible with the Finnish Constitution as long as they remain *voluntary*.

In Germany, the proposed enhanced enforcement of the existing framework as well as the creation of a new domestic authority appears not to entail additional challenges for *overall budgetary responsibility*. Hence, the proposed alterations would largely preserve the decision-making responsibility within the Member States – and the EU would thus mainly incentivize national parliaments to prioritize certain political decisions. This implies that Member States retain the final decision-making power and that compliance would thus remain *voluntary*. As a result, the proposed improvements of the European Semester and the increased incentives to comply with the EU rules appear compatible with the German Constitution, as no additional powers or competences are conferred to EU level.

In contrast, awarding EU level with genuine veto power over national budgeting would seriously interfere with the national constitutional framework and would challenge the German Parliament's position as the final arbiter in budgetary matters.[295] Hence, similar to Finland, the German constitutional framework appears to allow for the conferral of additional supervisory competence to the EU as long as Member States

293. Ojanen, 'The Europeanization of Finnish Law: Observations on the Transformations of the Finnish Scene of Constitutionalism' 101.

294. Leino and Salminen, 'The Euro Crisis and Its Constitutional Consequences for Finland: Is There Room for National Politics in EU Decision-Making?' 464.

295. *Interim Decision on the Ratification of the Own Resources Decision (NGEU)* paras 84-85; cf. as well: Claes and Reestman, 'The Protection of National Constitutional Identity and the Limits of European Integration at the Occasion of the *Gauweiler* Case' 927.

retain the autonomous decision-making power to comply or disregard the recommended EU action. In case the EU can overrule a national decision or take decisions on behalf of the Member State a conflict with German *overall budgetary responsibility* arises.

2 *Compatibility with the Charted Micro-comparative Constitutional Space*

The reform proposals might equally trigger other *constitutional identity* concerns. In France, the *constitutional identity limit* covers the parliamentary competence to establish budgetary planning and adopt the state budget, as established in Article 34 French Constitution.[296] This corresponds to the parliamentary budgeting powers established in Article 134(1) Spanish Constitution[297] as well as in Article 219 Polish Constitution.[298] In light of these prerogatives, and considering the current framework according to which Member States are incentivized to comply with various EU fiscal rules as well as increased EU monitoring, EU restrictions for national budgeting seem generally compatible with national *constitutional identity limits*.

Importantly, however, the existing rules entail in the first place a political dimension, which is visible under the Excessive Deficit Procedure that has to be confirmed by a vote in the Council of Ministers according to Article 126(6) TFEU.[299] And second, these procedures can *strongly incentivize* Member States to comply with the agreed EU fiscal rules, with the possible imposition of penalties following Article 126(11) TFEU. Conceptually, the EU rules build on the *voluntary compliance* of the Member States, with the possibility to fine any violation. Yet, Member States and more specifically national parliaments retain the possibility to make an autonomous decision, which preserves political discretion at the national level. The proposed enhanced operation of the European Semester and possible amendments to fiscal supervision in the Member States both appear not to alter this cornerstone of the EMU-architecture. Therefore, it appears that no conflict with the charted national *constitutional identity limits* arises in relation to these reform ambitions.

In contrast, the introduction of EU discretionary fiscal instruments, such as the veto power for national budgets, appears to conflict with the fundamental underlying notion that compliance with EU fiscal rules is incentivized but remains a political responsibility of the Member States' parliaments. Therefore, the introduction of *mandatory* or *non-discretionary* elements appears to conflict with these *constitutional*

296. Fabbrini, 'The Euro-Crisis and the Courts: Judicial Review and the Political Process in Comparative Perspective' 119-120.
297. Bustos Gisbert, 'National Constitutional Identity in European Constitutionalism: Revisiting the Tale of the Emperor's New Clothes in Spain?' 77.
298. Bainczyk, 'Folgen einer mangelnden Anpassung der polnischen Verfassung nach dem Vertrag von Lissabon im Lichte des Urteils des polnischen Verfassungsgerichtshofes zum Beschluss des Europäischen Rates zur Änderung von Art. 136 AEUV' 314.
299. Lastra and Louis, 'European Economic and Monetary Union: History, Trends, and Prospects' 109-110.

identity limits in all three Member States, and the adoption of such steps would thus require constitutional amendments.

3 *Conclusion on Tightened EU Fiscal Supervision*

Overall, this suggests that the tightened EU supervision over budgetary and fiscal decisions in the Member States is generally compatible with the national constitutional framework, as long as those decisions follow the current mode of cooperation which allocates the final decision-making power to the Member State. As highlighted, the current system identifies unsustainable national budgeting, confronts Member States with the EU concerns and might result in a penalty. The system builds on the *voluntary* cooperation of the Member States, without awarding the EU with autonomous decision-making power over domestic decision-making. Hence, the Commission can identify unsustainable fiscal policies, it might engage with Member States on the matter and even suggest financial penalties, it can, however, not change the contested domestic policy decision. Therefore, the political responsibility for budgetary and fiscal decisions is preserved at the national level.

It was substantiated that the allocation of an EU enforcement or veto power for common fiscal rules would challenge this traditional conception and result in substantive conflicts with the charted national *constitutional identity limits*. Notably, national parliaments would no longer be able to adopt autonomously their respective state budget but instead, the EU could block their adoption. Ultimately, this would undermine the position of national parliaments as final arbiters of budgetary decision-making which appears to conflict with the national conception of sovereignty and democracy in Finland, France, Germany, Poland and Spain. This seems to suggest that the bigger EU discretion in budgetary and fiscal matters is, the more limited the national decision-making powers are respectively – which is constitutionally contentious. The findings of the compatibility assessment concerning an enhanced EU supervision of national budgeting are summarized in Table 8.4.

Finally, EU fiscal rules provide an important stability factor in the Eurozone as they discipline national fiscal decision-making and thereby confine the possible emergence of moral hazard.[300] From that perspective, these *soft* EU fiscal limits to national budgeting provide a major stabilization advantage for the Eurozone as a whole. Therefore, enhancing the operation of the European Semester, a better interconnection of EU funding with EU fiscal rules as well as more effective supervisory instruments appear constitutionally beneficial, as pointed out in the Finnish constitutional debate.

300. Lionello, *The Pursuit of Stability of the Euro Area as a Whole: The Reform of the European Economic Union and Perspectives of Fiscal Integration* 218; Craig and Markakis, 'EMU Reform' 1421.

Table 8.4 Compatibility of Charted Constitutional Space with Enhanced EU Supervision

Member State	*Enhanced EU Supervision Based on Voluntary Tools*	*Enhanced EU Supervision Based on Compulsory Tools*
Finland	Parliamentary approval by a simple majority (section 94(2)(1) FC).	Qualified parliamentary approval (section 94(2)(2) FC).
Germany (including constitutional identity limit)	Parliamentary approval by a simple majority (Article 23(1)(2) GG).	Apparent conflict with the German *eternity clause* (suspension of nat. parliamentary control). Partly flexibilization of absolute conflict possible through: - EU benefits.
French sovereignty limit	No apparent conflict with the sovereignty limit.	Apparent conflict, can be overcome by const. amendment (Article 89 FC), which is common practice in France.
Polish constitutional identity limit	No apparent conflict with the *constitutional identity limit.*	Possible conflict which might require const. amendment (Article 236 PC), including a possible referendum. Apparent conflict, can be possibly overcome through 'modern' interpretation of Polish sovereignty.
Spanish constitutional identity limit	No apparent conflict with the *constitutional identity limit.*	Apparent conflict, can be overcome under strict const. amendments procedure in Article 168 SC which imposes a high threshold and is practically difficult to attain.

V Interim Conclusion: Compatibility of Fiscal Integration with Current Constitutional Space

The compatibility assessment demonstrated that while further EU fiscal integration within the current EU Treaty-logic appears largely feasible, more far-reaching integration proposals that envisage the conferral of discretionary, political competences to EU level seem to alter core national constitutional principles. In particular, the establishment of a discretionary budgetary capacity, the discretion to engage in EU borrowing, a discretionary tax competence, a veto power for the envisaged Ministry of Finance as well as the enhanced supervision conferring direct enforcement powers for EU level appear to conflict with the current conception of national democracy, sovereignty and parliamentary fiscal prerogatives.

The chapter demonstrates that the implementation of these proposals would likely require confirmation of the competence conferral by a qualified parliamentary majority and, regarding national *constitutional identity limits*, most likely constitutional amendments in order to overcome the emerging conflicts. Notably, in Finland and Germany the required conferral of competences would likely have to be adopted by a qualified two-thirds majority following section 94(2)(2) Finnish Constitution or Article 23(1)(3) in conjunction with Article 79(2) GG respectively - and in France, Poland as well as Spain the apparent conflict with the *constitutional identity limit* could only be overcome by constitutional amendment. Although such constitutional amendments are common practice in France, their attainability remains questionable in Poland in light of the political circumstances and in Spain given the high majority requirements. Finally, the apparent conflict with German democracy and *overall budgetary responsibility* could violate the *eternity clause*.[301] Taken together, these constitutional obstacles seriously impact the feasibility of far-reaching EU fiscal integration.

Comparing the resulting constitutional conflict per assessed Member State, it is apparent that while being confronted with strict procedural requirements in Finland, France, Poland and Spain, only the German Constitution imposes absolute limitations on the prospect of EU fiscal integration. In anticipation of this conflict with German *red-lines*, the research employed the concept of *constitutional flexibility* in the *micro-comparative* assessment. It thereby revealed that the seemingly rigid German constitutional limitations entail constitutional flexibility that could ease the deadlock between EU fiscal integration steps and the German *constitutional identity limit*.

C COMPATIBILITY THROUGH *CONSTITUTIONAL FLEXIBILITY*

The following assessment outlines how the different methods employed to locate *constitutional flexibility* in the German constitutional approach can help to overcome the apparent deadlock. The first part of the assessment focuses on the application of the previous conclusions on the apparent German constitutional double standard (I) as well as the application of *best practice* examples to the strict German constitutional limit (II), which has obvious implications for the other restrictive national constitutional approaches as well. In the second part, the research considers the possibility to re-conceptualize the competence-centric national *constitutional identity limits* more generally in order to better reflect the constitutional advantages stemming from EU cooperation within the national evaluation of EU (fiscal) integration steps (III).

I Consistent Constitutional Standards in Germany

The first method to locate and activate *constitutional flexibility* under the seemingly rigid German constitutional approach is through the application of a constitutional consistency assessment. The conducted evaluation of the German constitutional

301. *Quantitative Easing (PSPP) Final Judgment* paras 114-115; *Lisbon-judgment* para. 230; cf. as well: Rademacher, 'Die "Verfassungsidentität" als Grenze der Kompetenzübertragung auf die Europäische Union?' 144.

jurisprudence revealed that the Constitutional Court applies a constitutional double standard in the interpretation of constitutional concepts and provisions to the disadvantage of EU cooperation. Therefore, the application of a consistent interpretation is proposed, which could have the net effect of flexibilising some of the currently more rigid constitutional limits to EU integration more generally, thereby potentially creating additional constitutional space for the adoption of EU fiscal integration proposals.

Following the conclusions in Chapter III, for Germany this consistent application would first entail a stricter application of the constitutionally enshrined standing requirements for the initiation of constitutional proceedings. The result would be fewer admissible constitutional proceedings. In turn, this corresponds to the German constitutional framework which excludes procedures in the general interest, and restricts access to the Court for privileged applicants. The Court would thereby apply its established *internal* jurisprudence on the admissibility of constitutional proceedings towards EU-related applications. Although this would certainly reduce the likelihood of admissible constitutional proceedings against the identified EU integration steps, the underlying substantive constitutional question remains in place and in fact other traditional privileged applicants might be inclined to challenge these EU fiscal integration steps given their apparent impact on core German constitutional principles. Second, as previously established, the consistent application of the constitutional framework would entail a more reluctant application of the substantive dimension of constitutional principles as well as the *eternity clause*, as practised *internally*. Notably, the Court seems very cautious in the scrutiny of internal budgetary and fiscal decisions in order to respect the political discretion that the German Parliament enjoys constitutionally. Furthermore, it was substantiated that the underlying assumption of *overall budgetary responsibility*, which suggests that the German Parliament controls all central budgetary and fiscal decisions, can be challenged, as the national budgetary decision-making space is increasingly limited by *internal* long-term policy decisions. And finally, the Court refrained from applying the *eternity clause* to internal budgetary commitments, which contrasts with its EU-related approach where the *eternity clause* is continuously applied with the ultimate consequence that constitutional conflicts cannot be overcome by the German legislator.

The latter two points demonstrate that the Constitutional Court adopts a more reluctant stance towards *internal* budgetary commitments of the German Parliament, which could potentially be extended to EU fiscal integration steps. The following evaluation explores four considerations that could be employed by the German Court to conceptualize and apply *overall budgetary responsibility* – together with the *eternity clause* – in a more flexible, consistent and effective way. Notably, additional German flexibility towards EU fiscal integration could be achieved by carefully assessing the *actual* financial commitment at EU level (1), by focusing on the *operating budgetary balance* (2), by including *wider EU advantages* as well as the German economic dependency on a functioning Eurozone into the constitutional appraisal (3) and finally by focusing on the procedural dimension of *overall budgetary responsibility* (4). All four considerations are presented as brief constitutional arguments that could be adopted by the Constitutional Court when applying *overall budgetary responsibility*.

1 *Actual German Contributions to the EU Budget*

A first consideration that could be incorporated into the German constitutional assessment of parliamentary decisions with budgetary or fiscal implications is the actual German contribution to the EU budget, which differs from the agreed maximum contribution established by the own resources ceilings. Considering previous commitments, under the 2014 EU Own Resources Decision (Council Decision 2014/335/EU) the own resources ceilings were determined at 1.23% of GNI. These own resources ceilings establish the upper limit for national contributions. The actual national contributions are, however, calculated by the Commission based on the EU's financial needs. For Germany, these actual contributions amounted in 2019 to 0.846% of GNI, in 2018 to 0.847% of GNI and in 2017 to 0.713% of GNI.[302] Hence, the actual German contributions were significantly lower than the maximum target values determined by the 2014 EU Own Resources Decision.

This suggests that the own resources ceilings are generally not fully exhausted by the EU. Instead, these ceilings can be conceptualized as maximum, upper national financial commitments. These upper commitments are generally not fully employed as apparent from the outlined actual German contributions between 2017 and 2019 – which amounted to around two-thirds of the maximum target value determined by the own resources ceiling. Hence, when constitutionally assessing new national financial commitments towards EU level the discrepancy between maximum and anticipated actual national contribution could be more thoroughly examined and taken into account in order to determine the national contributions that can be realistically expected.

2 *Net Contribution of Germany*

A subsequent consideration is the direct, immediate financial 'return' from the German contribution to the EU budget through the allocation of EU funds to Germany. To conceptualize this 'return', the Commission determines the so-called operating budgetary balance, which indicates the balance between the EU funds allocated to the respective Member State minus the Member State's actual contribution to the EU budget.[303] The underlying argument is that the national contribution of funds to EU level is not a one-directional effort for the Member State, but it in fact entails direct financial benefits for the respective Member State – thereby making it a two-directional transaction; i.e., Germany does not only pay money but it also receives money from the EU budget, which should be taken into account.

For Germany, the operating budgetary balance amounted to EUR -14.323 billion or -0.41% of GNI in 2019. This suggests that the German contributions were in fact higher than the immediate financial 'return' allocated to Germany through the various

302. Based on data from Commission, *EU expenditure and revenue 2014-2020 (dataset)*.
303. For an explanation of the concept, cf. Zsolt Darvas, 'A New Look at Net Balances in the European Union's Next Multiannual Budget' (2019) Bruegel Working Paper 3.

EU policies.[304] Nevertheless, by contrasting the EU funds allocated to Germany, which amounted to EUR 12.214 billion in 2019, with the total German own resources contribution, which amounted to EUR 25.820 billion in the same year, it becomes obvious that almost half of the German contribution directly returned to Germany through, for example, agricultural subsidies or cohesion funds.

Thus, the German contributions to the EU budget result in direct financial 'returns' that could be incorporated into the constitutional appraisal of any new German financial commitments to the EU. Although these 'returning' funds are administered under EU law – yet within the Treaty-framework approved by the German Parliament – the operating budgetary balance illustrates that national financial contributions are in fact two-directional and result in direct financial benefits in the Member States, in addition to generating wider domestic benefits such as access to the internal market.

3 Wider EU Advantages and German Interest in a Functioning Euro

In addition to these direct 'returns', reforming the Eurozone in order to stabilize the Euro could result in broader economic advantages for Germany. For example, German exports to the Eurozone accounted for 37.5% of all German exports in 2018.[305] The German economy is thus closely intertwined with the Eurozone economy, and it has a genuine economic interest in the overall well-being of the Euroarea.

Moreover, studies estimate that the German GDP growth could be at least 0.5% lower without German membership within the single currency.[306] Therefore, German Eurozone membership translates into a higher GDP and additional economic prosperity, which underscores the German interest in a functioning single currency.

Furthermore, the discussed fiscal integration reforms could render the EMU more potent in the long run, particularly in case an increased budgetary capacity is created or in case new, bigger emergency instruments against macroeconomic shocks are initiated. Two immediate benefits appear to emerge from these reforms for Germany. In the first place, increasing particularly the firepower of the emergency instruments could guarantee that the Eurozone is equipped to financially assist Germany in the future as well if needed. Hence, the envisaged reforms could provide a supranational safety net in case Germany experiences economic hardship. And second, the proposed comprehensive reforms of the Euro intend to make the single currency crisis-resistant for the future, which would make *ad-hoc* crisis solutions – as were required during the Eurocrisis or as apparent now in relation to the recovery from COVID-19 and the economic implications of the Russian war of aggression against Ukraine – with high immediate costs less likely.

304. For the data, cf. Commission, *EU expenditure and revenue 2014-2020 (dataset)*.
305. Federal Ministry for Economic Affairs and Energy (BMWi), *Facts about German Foreign Trade* (German Government 2019) 1.
306. Thieß Petersen, Michael Böhmer and Henning vom Stein, 'How Germany Benefits from the Euro in Economic Terms (Policy Brief # 2013/01)' (*Bertelsmann Stiftung*, 2013), https://www.bertelsmann-stiftung.de/fileadmin/files/BSt/Presse/imported/downloads/xcms_bst_dms_37730_37731_2.pdf, accessed 5 April 2023, 6.

These considerations illustrate that the envisaged EU fiscal integration steps are in fact in the genuine interest of Germany, given the economic interconnection within the Eurozone, the possible safety net stemming from the envisaged EU instruments as well as to prevent a new crisis situation. The constitutional appraisal of possible EU fiscal integration steps could thus more thoroughly rely on the added benefits that stem from such integration measures for the German constitutional order, thereby relaxing the outlined constitutional resistance expressed through *overall budgetary responsibility*.

4 *Focus on the Procedural Dimension of Overall Budgetary Responsibility*

A final example of a more consistent and thus more flexible German constitutional approach towards the proposed EU fiscal integration steps is to re-evaluate the creation of the substantive requirement under *overall budgetary responsibility* which appears to constitute a major potential hurdle for more far-reaching integration.

Notably, the basic assumption underlying this substantive requirement is that the German Parliament actually controls all central budgetary decisions. However, the research established that in reality, the German Parliament has only limited discretion in budgetary and fiscal decisions *internally* given the impact of long-term political commitments on the state budget.[307] In case parliament is not actively determining the majority of budgetary and fiscal decisions given that these are pre-determined by previous parliaments, it is questionable whether EU fiscal integration steps can undermine an internally non-existent independent fiscal decision-making space of the German Parliament.

Therefore, the research submitted that instead of introducing an upper limit of financial commitments as a substantive requirement under *overall budgetary responsibility*, which can be challenged in light of the apparent reduction in discretionary fiscal decision-making space, the concept could be limited to procedural requirements. These procedural requirements ensure that the German Parliament retains final control over budgetary commitments – as long as Article 50 TEU allows for the unilateral withdrawal from EU cooperation. Arguably, this provision allows to retrieve any transferred fiscal competences – and hence a newly elected German Parliament could ultimately reverse EU budgetary commitments if desired.

Thus, it can be argued that the German Parliament retains ultimate control over fiscal decisions as long as it can reverse such commitment. This reversibility opens a political decision-making space that a newly elected parliament can explore if so desired. It furthermore underscores the final decision-making responsibility of the German Parliament and protects cornerstones of the German constitutional approach to EU cooperation, namely the derived status of the EU as well as *Kompetenz-Kompetenz*. The research furthermore substantiated that the availability of only future, medium-term reversibility corresponds to the *internal* budgetary and fiscal planning

307. Streeck and Mertens, 'An Index of Fiscal Democracy (2010)' 8-11.

process which is increasingly dominated by long-term political decisions, and which appears to comply with constitutional requirements under German democracy.

Adopting the suggested approach - apparent in the *internal* constitutional appraisal of fiscal decisions - to EU-related proceedings would offer additional flexibility for German participation in the proposed EU fiscal integration steps. Within this assessment, the focus would then rest on the procedural involvement of the German Parliament and the underscored cornerstones of the German perspective on EU cooperation. These requirements correspond with the procedural requirements formulated under *overall budgetary responsibility*.

5 *Interim Conclusion on the German Constitutional Approach*

Jointly, these considerations could be employed to devise the German constitutional assessment of EU fiscal integration steps and in particular the concept of *overall budgetary responsibility* in a more flexible manner. As established, this additional *constitutional flexibility* could result from a stronger focus on the political discretion that the German Parliament enjoys when devising EU integration steps within the constitutional appraisal of the German Constitutional Court. Notably, it would enable the Court to be more receptive towards the economic, political and societal advantages stemming from EU cooperation. Moreover, these advantages correspond to German constitutional goals. Namely, the EU offers an additional supranational layer of protection for core constitutional principles such as democracy, the rule of law or fundamental rights. Other constitutional authorities even highlighted that the attainment of some of these principles required supranational cooperation.[308] Thus, the proposed more flexible conception of German constitutional limits contributes to a more effective protection of German constitutional principles.

This constitutional flexibility can derive from a stronger focus on the procedural requirements under *overall budgetary responsibility*, an explicit acknowledgement that Article 50 TEU secures ultimate control of the German Parliament over EU-centred budgetary prerogatives as well as from an abstention to enforce an abstract substantive dimension of *overall budgetary responsibility*. Ultimately, this modified constitutional approach would acknowledge the necessity for national parliaments to make long-term, major budgetary commitments which are binding upon successive parliaments – which is accepted within the *internal* jurisprudence of the German Constitutional Court.

Overall, this suggests that the German Constitutional Court could generate additional constitutional space for the outlined EU fiscal integration steps that appear to currently conflict with *overall budgetary responsibility*. In addition, the proposed more flexible approach to EU fiscal integration would enable the German Court to

308. Granat and Granat, *The Constitution of Poland: A Contextual Analysis* 26; Czaputowicz, 'Sovereignty in Theories of European Integration and the Perspective of the Polish Constitutional Tribunal' 32.

effectively protect the core constitutional values that are at the centre of its constitutional jurisprudence. However, the potential success of the proposed approach depends on the receptiveness of the German Court which must balance national constitutional considerations protected by the absolute *eternity clause* with continuous EU integration.

II Best Practice Examples

An additional method to generate *constitutional flexibility* is the exchange of *best practices* across constitutional systems. Through a transnational exchange of constitutional reasoning and arguments,[309] seemingly strict national constitutional limitations can be redesigned. The exchange of constitutional reasoning is facilitated due to the identified overlap of constitutional principles - notably democracy, sovereignty and parliamentary prerogatives - employed by national constitutional authorities when reviewing the compatibility of EU fiscal integration proposals with the domestic constitution.

In particular, the conception of EU cooperation in both Finland and Poland offers a constructive perspective on how to balance the principles of national sovereignty with EU integration ambitions. Notably, it was established that the Finnish Constitutional Law Committee emphasized in its decisions the wider benefits that EU cooperation entails for Finland. Specifically, the Committee highlighted in its interpretation of Finnish sovereignty that EU cooperation constitutes an exercise of sovereign powers and that it increases the reach of national powers through the pooling of competences at the supranational level.[310] Similarly, the Polish Constitutional Tribunal highlighted that the 'modern' interpretation of Polish sovereignty presupposed international cooperation in order to achieve wider constitutional commitments established within the Polish Constitution.[311] Both examples illustrate that the national constitutional authorities conceptualize EU integration not exclusively as a decrease in national, sovereign decision-making competences but instead as a potential increase in the reach or impact of sovereign powers. Hence, through EU cooperation the Member States can attain wider national constitutional objectives, for example, the protection of fundamental rights, environmental objectives or the supranational stabilization of core national values, but also to compete in a globalized world, for example by negotiating trade agreements as Union of 27 Member States instead of negotiating as an individual country.

309. Ginsburg and Dixon, 'Introduction' 4.
310. Mutanen, *Towards a Pluralistic Constitutional Understanding of State Sovereignty in the European Union? The Concept, Regulation and Constitutional Practice of Sovereignty in Finland and Certain Other EU Member States* 334.
311. *Challenges Against Article 136 (3) TFEU and ESM-Treaty* section 6.4.2.; *Treaty of Lisbon* section III.2.1.; cf. as well: Czaputowicz, 'Sovereignty in Theories of European Integration and the Perspective of the Polish Constitutional Tribunal' 32; Czapliński, 'Recent Constitutional Jurisprudence Concerning the European Union: Some Remarks on 2010 Judgments of the Polish Constitutional Court' 200.

Taken together, this suggests that traditional constitutional principles, such as national sovereignty, can be construed in a more EU-friendly but equally effective manner in case national constitutional authorities are willing to consider the resulting national benefits stemming from EU cooperation in their appraisal of EU integration. As highlighted, through an exchange of constitutional reasoning, other national constitutional authorities could implement similar interpretations which would render the highlighted EU integration more attainable. At the same time, the compatibility assessment illustrated that even these flexible *best practices* could potentially reach a limit when confronted with more far-reaching integration steps that would alter the general *modus operandi* of the EU. Therefore, the potential constitutional flexibilization through these *best practices* remains ultimately limited.

These *best practices* could mark the starting point of a more receptive national constitutional approach towards EU fiscal integration steps and trigger a necessary engagement with the question of how to adapt existing internal national constitutional doctrines to a global reality. When applying these *best practices* to the most rigid limit apparent in Germany, it seems that the previously outlined flexibilization of *overall budgetary responsibility* through consistent application could be supplemented by a 'modern' or receptive interpretation of German democracy. Notably, the German Constitutional Court could include the direct and indirect benefits of EU cooperation for national democracy - outlined before - into the constitutional appraisal. Ultimately, this would contribute to a more flexible interpretation of German democracy vis-à-vis EU fiscal integration steps.

III Re-conception of National Approach and EU Benefits

A final proposition relates to the re-conception of the assessed national *constitutional identity limits*. Notably, the compatibility assessment revealed that these *constitutional identity limits* appear to be devised and designed as *competence-centric* limitations against EU integration steps. National constitutional authorities in all assessed Member States identified a list of national competences as particularly important for national sovereignty or democracy under their *constitutional identity* doctrines.[312] According to

312. *On France: Entwurf eines Gesetzes zu dem Beschluss des Europäischen Rates vom 25. März 2011 zur Änderung des Artikels 136 des Vertrags über die Arbeitsweise der Europäischen Union hinsichtlich eines Stabilitätsmechanismus für die Mitgliedstaaten, deren Währung der Euro ist (Drucksache 17/9047)* para. 21; cf. as well: Reestman, 'Legitimacy Through Adjudication: The ESM Treaty and the Fiscal Compact Before the National Courts' 265; *On Germany: Quantitative Easing (PSPP) Final Judgment* para. 104; cf. as well: Calliess, '70 Jahre Grundgesetz und europäische Integration: "Take Back Control" oder "Mehr Demokratie wagen"?' 688; Pilz, 'Ein Schatzamt für die Eurozone? – Überlegungen zu den Vorschlägen des Europäischen Parlaments und der Kommission zu einer Reform der Wirtschaftsunion' 644; *On Poland: Challenges Against Article 136 (3) TFEU and ESM-Treaty* section 7.7.; cf. as well: Bainczyk, 'Folgen einer mangelnden Anpassung der polnischen Verfassung nach dem Vertrag von Lissabon im Lichte des Urteils des polnischen Verfassungsgerichtshofes zum Beschluss des Europäischen Rates zur Änderung von Art. 136 AEUV' 314; *On Spain:* Martín Y Pérez de Nanclares, 'Constitutional Identity in Spain: Commitment to European Integration Without Giving up the Essence of the Constitution' 279; Bustos Gisbert, 'National Constitutional Identity in European Constitutionalism: Revisiting the Tale of the Emperor's New Clothes in Spain?' 77.

this conception, the conferral of such important competences to EU level triggers the *constitutional identity limit* by default. This was illustrated within the previous compatibility assessment which demonstrated that the conferral of budgetary and fiscal competences, which qualify as particularly important competence areas under the national sovereignty and democracy throughout all assessed Member States, is in itself sufficient to trigger the *constitutional identity limit*.

For example, the German Constitutional Court focusses on the impact of an envisaged financial commitment on the German budget to determine whether increased German EU contributions or additional liabilities reduce German budgetary autonomy.[313] Through this conception, the German Constitutional Court emphasizes the direct impact of EU financial commitments for the German state budget without, however, thoroughly considering the added benefit that might stem from the conferral of these competences to EU level. Hence, the apparent competence-centric conception of *constitutional identity limits* seems to render national constitutional systems partially un-receptive to benefits that might arise for national budgetary and fiscal prerogatives through supranational cooperation. A more flexible approach, which acknowledges the benefits that supranational cooperation might entail, and which thereby is not only focused on preserving a set of core competences at the national level, could reduce the identified constitutional conflicts.

The proposed constructive conception of *national constitutional identity limits* could be further stimulated by EU fiscal integration proposals by connecting fiscal integration steps to actual EU achievements. For example, an EU taxation power or new EU levy could be devised in a substantive area that is a direct consequence of EU cooperation and thus a revenue stream that the national budgetary legislator would not have at its disposition without supranational cooperation.[314] The EU would then generate its revenue through its own activities or advantages directly generated from EU cooperation, which has to be conceptually differentiated from the traditional budgetary decision-making potential available within a Member State under the control of the national legislator. Here, the proposed conception could be considered less contentious under the domestic principle of democracy as the budgetary powers traditionally enjoyed by national parliaments would not be curtailed. Conceptually, the EU would only occupy the budgetary space that it created itself, which should render such integration steps less contentious under the competence-centric conception of national *constitutional identity limits*.

313. *Interim Decision on the Ratification of the Own Resources Decision (NGEU)* paras 84-85; *Quantitative Easing (PSPP) Final Judgment* para. 104; cf. as well: Claes and Reestman, 'The Protection of National Constitutional Identity and the Limits of European Integration at the Occasion of the *Gauweiler* Case' 927.

314. As proposed by the *Monti*-Report, cf. Monti et al., *Future Financing of the EU: Final Report and Recommendations of the High Level Group on Own Resources December 2016* 68, 41-56; cf. as well: Lionello, *The Pursuit of Stability of the Euro Area as a Whole: The Reform of the European Economic Union and Perspectives of Fiscal Integration* 183; Fabbrini, 'Fiscal Capacity' 129.

IV Interim Conclusion: EU Integration as a Two-Way Street

Additional *constitutional flexibility* can be generated within even seemingly strict national constitutional limitations. This *flexibility* can be activated through the conducted constitutional consistency assessment, which albeit being limited to the German constitutional approach here can be extended to other Member States. Furthermore, national *best practices* can stimulate constitutional re-configurations across the EU. Here, the Finnish and Polish examples illustrate how traditional national constitutional concepts can be interpreted in a 'modern', receptive way. And finally, the research identified that *national constitutional identity limits* appear to be devised in a competence-centric manner through which national constitutional authorities consider conferrals of budgetary and fiscal decision-making powers to the EU as a de facto conflict with these limits. To that end, the research proposed a more comprehensive constitutional appraisal that allows filtering EU benefits into the constitutional assessment. Furthermore, considering these EU benefits, it was proposed to devise EU fiscal integration proposals based on EU achievements. Overall, these steps could ease the partially detected national constitutional opposition against EU fiscal integration steps by at the same time offering national constitutional systems an apparently more efficient and effective manner to protect the underlying constitutional values in a changing, globalized world.

D FINAL CONCLUSIONS ON THE CONSTITUTIONAL FEASIBILITY OF EU FISCAL INTEGRATION

All these observations on the various components of EU fiscal integration proposals and their compatibility with the charter national constitutional space result in a complex, multi-layered picture. Notably, core structural proposals such as the initiation of an additional Eurozone budget or an emergency instrument with an underlying funding structure that corresponds to the current Treaty-logic as well as the establishment of an EU Ministry of Finance and enhanced supervision of national fiscal decision-making appear feasible within the existing constitutional framework. However, the evaluation equally demonstrated that several core components of the various 'integration' reform proposals, notably the allocation of discretionary powers to the EU, are constitutionally contested in all assessed Member States.

Concretely, the comparative assessment suggests that the creation of a secondary-law-based emergency instrument – comparable to the ESM-design – to stabilize public investments or to support Member States in the payment of unemployment benefits during asymmetric shocks, as proposed by the European Commission,[315] is compatible with national constitutional law. Similarly, the creation of a (limited) Eurozone budget, as proposed by the EU Five Presidents' Report, the BICC, and as

315. Commission, *Reflection Paper on the Deepening of the Economic and Monetary Union* 26; Juncker et al., *The Five Presidents' Report: Completing Europe's Economic and Monetary Union* 15; cf. as well: Fabbrini, 'Fiscal Capacity' 115; Comments, 'Editorial Comments: Tinkering with Economic and Monetary Union' 6.

implemented under NGEU to foster economic recovery after COVID-19,[316] is attainable under national constitutional law if based on the existing EU Treaty-framework, and specifically Article 311 TFEU. It was established within the assessment that the required national budgetary commitments will likely require confirmation by a simple parliamentary majority in Finland and by a two-thirds majority in Germany. As the proposed emergency instruments and the budget would be devised within the EU Treaties, the central and constitutive involvement of national parliaments in the creation of a Eurozone fiscal capacity is secured which pre-empts national constitutional democracy and sovereignty concerns. Furthermore, the assessment illustrated that the required additional funds to sustain the fiscal capacity could be devised under the existing EU Treaty framework, either by increasing the own resources ceilings, as the case with NGEU or as put forward by the BICC proposal,[317] or by introducing new own resources, as proposed by the HLGOR Report.[318] These funding options will likely require confirmation by a qualified majority in the Finnish Parliament - although the size of the funding potential is essential and might alter this assessment - and in Germany, a two-thirds majority will likely be applicable. Again, the *constitutional identity limits* seem not to conflict with the proposed funding options, as they are devised under the current EU Treaties and thus preserve central control of national parliaments. In addition, the comparative assessment revealed that pooling existing EMU competences in a 'Eurozone Ministry' - as proposed by the Five Presidents' Report - is generally attainable if the final decision-making modalities remain unchanged. Finally, no constitutional concerns emerge against additional EU supervision of national budgetary processes as long as this remains *voluntary* and Member States cannot be legally forced to modify their budgetary planning.

In contrast, the implementation of larger, long-term-oriented budgetary commitments, as for example proposed by *Bibow*,[319] or the allocation of discretionary fiscal powers to the Eurozone, which would empower the EU to take and implement independent fiscal decisions, as envisioned by the *Bruegel*-proposal,[320] appear more difficult to achieve within the charted national constitutional space. Notably, the comparative assessment revealed that a two-thirds majority would likely be required to adopt the necessary EU Treaty changes in Finland. In Germany, a conflict with *overall budgetary responsibility* appears to emerge as the central oversight of the German

316. In chronological order: Juncker et al., *The Five Presidents' Report: Completing Europe's Economic and Monetary Union* 15; Summit, *Statement of the Euro Summit, 14 December 2018 (EURO 503/18)*; Commission Proposal for a Regulation of the European Parliament and of the Council on the Governance Framework for the Budgetary Instrument for Convergence and Competitiveness for the Euro Area (COM(2019) 354); Council, *Conclusions Special Meeting of the European Council (17, 18, 19, 20 and 21 July 2020): EUCO 10/20* 2-3.
317. Commission Proposal for a Regulation of the European Parliament and of the Council on the Governance Framework for the Budgetary Instrument for Convergence and Competitiveness for the Euro Area (COM(2019) 354); Eurogroup, *Term Sheet on the Budgetary Instrument for Convergence and Competitiveness*; Summit, *Statement of the Euro Summit, 14 December 2018 (EURO 503/18)*.
318. Monti et al., *Future Financing of the EU: Final Report and Recommendations of the High Level Group on Own Resources December 2016* 68.
319. Bibow, 'Making the Euro Viable: The Euro Treasury Plan' 4.
320. Marzinotto, Sapir and Wolff, 'What Kind of Fiscal Union? (2011)' 5, 7.

Parliament over budgetary and fiscal decisions would be challenged by discretionary EU decisions on these matters. Comparable conflicts with the *constitutional identity limits* in France, Poland and Spain appear to emerge – as will be further explained below. While overcoming the resulting constitutional conflict by constitutional amendment seems practically achievable in France, the high majority thresholds in Poland and Spain for confirming constitutional amendments put the feasibility of these more ambitious EU integration steps into question. These constitutional concerns equally apply to the proposed discretionary funding options, including the introduction of a genuine EU taxation power, as proposed by the Bruegel-proposal,[321] or the discretionary issuing of Eurobonds, as initially suggested by the European Commission.[322] Notably, the comparative assessment illustrated that any funding solution, which would offer the Eurozone discretionary funding powers independent from Member States' approval, would likely have to be adopted by a two-thirds majority in the Finnish Parliament. In Germany, such discretionary funding powers could even be characterized as a conflict with *overall budgetary responsibility* and therefore be constitutionally unattainable. Similar constitutional concerns appear to emerge in France, Poland and Spain, which suggests that constitutional amendments are required in order to overcome the conflicts with national *constitutional identity limits*. Finally, these concerns equally apply to conferring the power to veto national budgeting to a Eurozone Ministry.[323]

When considering the substance of the applicable national constitutional limits, the assessment revealed that the identified concerns against the most ambitious EU fiscal integration steps are based on national sovereignty, national democracy and the parliamentary prerogatives in fiscal competences or a combination of these. Therefore, even in the highly flexible Finnish constitutional system, a qualified parliamentary majority appears mandatory to confirm the required conferral of competences to EU level. In France, Poland and Spain the anticipated conflict with the *constitutional identity limits* seems to require constitutional amendments and in Germany, the reform ambitions appear to collide with the *eternity clause* which constitutes an almost unsurmountable hurdle for EU integration.[324] Therefore, while the constitutional conflicts in France, Poland and Spain, could be overcome by amending the constitutional text with all related practical and procedural difficulties, the German Constitution appears to impose an absolute limit to these integration ambitions.

Although, this suggests that the German *overall budgetary responsibility* limit imposes the most rigid substantive hurdle for EU fiscal integration steps, the strict national procedural requirements apparent in the other Member States seem equally challenging. Therefore, the research identified the proposals which envisage the establishment of a discretionary budgetary capacity, the discretion to engage in EU

321. *Ibid.*, 5, 7.
322. Commission, *Green Paper on the Feasibility of Introducing Stability Bonds (COM (2011) 818)*; cf. as well: Hild, Herz and Bauer, 'Structured Eurobonds: Limiting Liability and Distributing Profits' 252.
323. Marzinotto, Sapir and Wolff, 'What Kind of Fiscal Union? (2011)' 6.
324. Rademacher, 'Die "Verfassungsidentität" als Grenze der Kompetenzübertragung auf die Europäische Union?' 144.

borrowing, a discretionary tax competence, a veto power for the envisaged Ministry of Finance as well as the enhanced supervision conferring direct enforcement powers for EU level as hardly feasible under the current national constitutional space given the apparent conflict with national democracy, national sovereignty and the parliamentary prerogatives in fiscal matters.

Obviously, this conclusion significantly limits the fiscal reform possibilities for the EU, which is why the research employed the concept of *constitutional flexibility* in order to soften the rigid constitutional opposition in Germany, which proves to be the key bottleneck. Furthermore, to ease the apparent constitutional deadlock between EU fiscal integration ambitions and national constitutional concerns the research proposed modifications to the conception of national *constitutional identity limits* as well as the design of EU fiscal integration proposals.

Considering national *constitutional identity limits*, it was established that the assessed national constitutional authorities appear to mainly devise these essential restrictions as competence-centric limitations to EU integration ambitions. As established, the French, German, Polish and Spanish constitutional authorities identified a set of core competences that are particularly important for national sovereignty or democracy and that are thus covered by the respective *constitutional identity limit*.[325] The result is that these limits are focused on a shift of competences or decision-making powers from the national to EU level. This is particularly apparent in relation to budgetary and fiscal competences, which are traditionally important constitutional prerogatives of national parliaments.[326] Given that these competences are identified as core sovereign and democratic powers protected by *constitutional identity limits*, EU fiscal integration steps are almost automatically considered as interference with these limits. Here, the research proposed an alternative design or conception of *constitutional identity limits* in order to allow for the holistic appraisal of added values and advantages that stem from EU cooperation in these competence areas, which was conceptualized within the *constitutional flexibility* assessment.

As pointed out within the national *best practices*, the consideration of factual benefits stemming from EU cooperation is already conducted by the Finnish Constitutional Law Committee[327] and it appears to offer the opportunity to include the constitutional advantages of EU integration steps into the constitutional appraisal. Ultimately, this could result in a flexibilization of national *constitutional identity*

325. *On France:* Fabbrini, 'The Euro-Crisis and the Courts: Judicial Review and the Political Process in Comparative Perspective' 119-120; *On Germany:* Calliess, '70 Jahre Grundgesetz und europäische Integration: "Take Back Control" oder "Mehr Demokratie wagen"?' 688; *On Poland:* Bainczyk, 'Folgen einer mangelnden Anpassung der polnischen Verfassung nach dem Vertrag von Lissabon im Lichte des Urteils des polnischen Verfassungsgerichtshofes zum Beschluss des Europäischen Rates zur Änderung von Art. 136 AEUV' 314; *On Spain:* Pérez Tremps, 'National Idenity in Spanish Constitutional Court Case-Law' 270.
326. Dawson and De Witte, 'Constitutional Balance in the EU after the Euro-Crisis' 827.
327. Mutanen, *Towards a Pluralistic Constitutional Understanding of State Sovereignty in the European Union? The Concept, Regulation and Constitutional Practice of Sovereignty in Finland and Certain Other EU Member States* 334.

concerns without compromising on the effective protection of the underlying constitutional core, which could allow for the implementation of more far-reaching EU fiscal integration steps.

Considering the general conception of EU fiscal integration, it was highlighted that current reform plans focus on the conferral of competences from the national to EU level, which sparks the outlined conflict with the competence-centric national *constitutional identity limits*. This focus on 'competence-shifts' is problematic and the research, therefore, suggested modifying the conception of EU fiscal integration proposals. Notably, EU fiscal integration proposals could be designed based on the advantages and benefits directly resulting from EU cooperation. The underlying argument is that EU integration creates or enables Member States to tap additional fiscal space that would otherwise not be available to the Member States. Hence, EU cooperation results in direct or indirect financial benefits – for example through access to the internal market – which the Member States could not have created independently. By devising EU fiscal integration steps within this EU-generated fiscal space, the EU would arguably not undermine traditional national fiscal competences controlled by national parliaments which would remain unaffected. In addition, it could be submitted that as long as the financial benefits outweigh the financial costs and Member States are thus able to partially exploit the EU-generated fiscal space, supranational cooperation as well as possible EU fiscal integration steps can be characterized as beneficial for the budgetary, financial and fiscal decision-making powers of Member States.

More generally, the identified potential to locate and activate *constitutional flexibility* within (rigid) national constitutional limits, but also the proposed reflection on how to best design EU fiscal integration in light of national constitutional concerns, both are relevant beyond EMU. Arguably, national constitutional law and EU law concepts must understand and regulate our current (global) reality in which supranational cooperation entails benefits for national constitutional law. National policy objectives in environmental, health, digital, or defence matters – which are often reflected in constitutional guarantees – can often better and even sometimes only be achieved at the supranational level. The employed *constitutional flexibility* provides national constitutional actors with a tool to comprehensively include the benefits that supranational cooperation entails for national constitutional objectives.

Overall, this indicates that more far-reaching EU fiscal integration steps could be possible in case the national constitutional space would more thoroughly incorporate EU benefits into the constitutional appraisal and in case fiscal integration proposals are conceptually modified. In the alternative, the compatibility assessment illustrated a variety of feasible reform steps that are compatible with the current national constitutional space. These attainable reform steps would be devised on the basis of the currently existing Treaty-framework, which guarantees the central involvement of national parliaments in the confirmation of any additional financial burden on the respective national state budget. The recent NGEU recovery strategy illustrates that sufficient legal space – also at the national constitutional level – exists to equip EU level with additional financial means if political actors reach an agreement. Given the identified constitutional hurdles that more far-reaching reform proposals are con fronted with as well as the current political tensions within the EU – which mostly relate to the distribution of the envisaged EU fiscal capacities and which constitutes a genuine political question that EU fiscal integration steps would have to answer[328] – it appears most realistic to employ this existing legal space in order to stabilize the Euro without potentially fuelling a new fundamental conflict between the EU and national constitutional authorities.

328. Haltern, 'Ultra-vires-Kontrolle im Dienst europäischer Demokratie' 823; Eriksen, *Contesting Political Differentiation: European Division and the Problem of Dominance* 249-250.

CHAPTER 9
Overall Conclusions and Outlook

A TACKLING THE DILEMMA: CONSTITUTIONAL CONCERNS AND EU FISCAL INTEGRATION

The economic implications of COVID-19 and the Russian war of aggression against Ukraine have amplified the urgency of stabilizing the Euro – an imperative that has been widely acknowledged since the Eurocrisis.[1] The resulting serious economic disruption and high inflation have pushed the Eurozone again into turbulent waters – thereby increasing the risk of a new, existential challenge for the single currency. Ultimately, this crisis could leave the Eurozone politically and economically more divided than ever – various national and EU interventions were submitted to pre-empt the feared additional fragilities within the Eurozone. Confronted with the economic consequences of COVID-19, the EU has adopted a EUR 750 billion recovery strategy. Its endorsement in 2021 illustrates the political capability of committing substantial financial means to joint EU action within the existing national constitutional framework. However, the economic prospect in light of the continuing Russian war of aggression against Ukraine remains uncertain for the Eurozone and it puts the long-term stabilization of the single currency back on the political agenda.

Furthermore, while NGEU constitutes a major achievement, it provides only temporary relief and will require structural follow-up in order to lead to a lasting stabilization of the Eurozone. In addition, the negotiations that culminated in this recovery strategy displayed the inherent challenge in the current design of the EU finances, as Member States retain exclusive final control. Here, Member States remained primarily driven by domestic political interests instead of following a shared EU vision on how to remedy the unfolding economic disruption most effectively,[2]

1. Ruffert, 'The Future of the European Economic and Monetary Union: Issues of Constitutional Law' 33-34.
2. Khan and Peel, '"Frugal Four" Fight to Protect EU Budget Rebates'; Alcidi and Gros, 'Next Generation EU: A Large Common Response to the COVID-19 Crisis' 203.

which is not surprising as the EU's recovery strategy is financed through national state budgets. The apparent shortcomings of the EU financing system, which incentivizes Member States to pursue domestic financial interests, have once again pushed the proposed EMU-reforms and fiscal integration steps into the limelight as a potential solution. The envisaged increase in EU supervision over national budgeting,[3] the creation of an additional fiscal capacity at EU level[4] and the establishment of a Ministry of Finance[5] could fundamentally transform the current EU financing thereby making Eurozone decision-making politically less contentious across Member States.

However, the structural reforms required to achieve a (politically) more resilient Euro are confronted with intensifying national constitutional opposition. The consequence appears to be the difficult dilemma from which this book departed, and which suggests that EU fiscal integration is both indispensable to stabilize the Euro yet legally impossible to achieve in light of increasing national constitutional resistance. The research dismantled this dilemma by investigating the legal-constitutional feasibility of EU fiscal integration steps. Through the comparative evaluation of a sample of national constitutional concerns formulated against EU fiscal integration proposals and the compatibility assessment of these proposals with the charted, de-constructed national constitutional space, this book refutes the absoluteness of this dilemma (B). It has demonstrated that the current legal framework allows for fiscal integration, if Member States' parliaments are centrally involved in the decision-making (C).

Subsequently, the book introduced two transformative propositions that create additional constitutional space for far-reaching EU fiscal integration steps. According to the first proposition, national constitutional limits to EU fiscal integration proposals could be read to entail a degree of *constitutional flexibility*, which can be located and activated through specific methods (D). According to the second proposition, EU fiscal integration proposals can defuse central national constitutional concerns by altering their narrative and embracing national parliaments as central actors in the administration of Eurozone fiscal capacities (E). These propositions represent achievable transformative ideas rooted in the current legal-political discussion, yet they contribute to reviving the seemingly deadlocked national constitutional debate on EU fiscal integration. The resulting nuanced overview provides the opportunity to reflect on the future interaction between national constitutional law and EU integration in core state policy areas (F).

3. Commission, *Reflection Paper on the Deepening of the Economic and Monetary Union* 24; Juncker et al., *The Five Presidents' Report: Completing Europe's Economic and Monetary Union* 8; cf. as well: Lionello, *The Pursuit of Stability of the Euro Area as a Whole: The Reform of the European Economic Union and Perspectives of Fiscal Integration* 170.
4. Commission, *Reflection Paper on the Deepening of the Economic and Monetary Union* 25-26; Juncker et al., *The Five Presidents' Report: Completing Europe's Economic and Monetary Union* 15; Bibow, 'Making the Euro Viable: The Euro Treasury Plan' 4; cf. as well: Craig and Markakis, 'EMU Reform' 1426.
5. Commission, *Completing Europe's Economic and Monetary Union: A European Minister of Economy and Finance*; Commission, *Reflection Paper on the Deepening of the Economic and Monetary Union* 27; Juncker et al., *The Five Presidents' Report: Completing Europe's Economic and Monetary Union* 14, 18; Marzinotto, Sapir and Wolff, 'What Kind of Fiscal Union? (2011)' 5.

B CHARTED COMPARATIVE CONSTITUTIONAL SPACE FOR EU FISCAL INTEGRATION

Through the comprehensive comparative assessment, the book established that national constitutional concerns over EU budgetary and fiscal integration steps surface in a range of constitutional systems regardless of their general approach to EU integration. The book distinguished between more flexible[6] as well as more rigid constitutional systems[7] and subsequently assessed, based on two representative examples, the system's respective potential to accommodate EU fiscal integration. Interestingly, the core constitutional concerns under the more flexible Finnish and the more rigid German constitutional system coincide. Notably, the Finnish Constitutional Law Committee identified conflicts between integrating budgetary or fiscal competences and Finnish sovereignty, parliamentary control over the state budget as well as Finnish democracy.[8] Similarly, the German Constitutional Court established its *overall budgetary responsibility* limit based on the principle of democracy and the need for central parliamentary control over budgetary decisions.[9] When comparing both constitutional approaches, it can thus be substantiated that the normative constitutional basis employed by national constitutional authorities when addressing EU budgetary and fiscal integration steps overlaps. This comparative conclusion can be confirmed by the findings on the French, Polish and Spanish *constitutional identity limits*, which similarly protect budgetary and fiscal competences based on national sovereignty, democracy or parliamentary-related institutional arguments. Despite this overlap, the attached constitutional consequences and strategies to address these concerns vary significantly in flexible or rigid constitutional systems.

Notably, in Finland, the constitutional concerns against EU fiscal integration steps mainly result in procedural obstacles. In light of the constitutional relevance of EU fiscal integration steps, the Finnish Constitutional Law Committee will likely require that the Finnish Parliament approves the necessary conferral of powers by a qualified two-thirds majority according to section 94(2)(2) Finnish Constitution.[10] In addition, the Committee will likely insist on comprehensive parliamentary involvement in the national preparation of EU secondary law based on section 96 Finnish

6. Heringa, *Constitutions Compared: An Introduction to Comparative Constitutional Law* 9; Grewe, 'Methods of Identification of National Constitutional Identity' 43.
7. Heringa, *Constitutions Compared: An Introduction to Comparative Constitutional Law* 7-8; Dixon, 'Constitutional Amendment Rules: a Comparative Perspective' 102; Wendel, 'Lisbon Before the Courts: Comparative Perspectives' 123.
8. Leino and Salminen, 'The Euro Crisis and Its Constitutional Consequences for Finland: Is There Room for National Politics in EU Decision-Making?' 458-459; Ojanen, 'The EU at the Finnish Constitutional Arena' 247.
9. Calliess, '70 Jahre Grundgesetz und europäische Integration: "Take Back Control" oder "Mehr Demokratie wagen"?' 688.
10. *Commission's Draft EU Recovery Plan and MFF Planning* 12; *On the Establishment of a European Monetary Fund* 3-4; *Second Assessment Draft ESM-Treaty (II.)* 2; cf. as well: Mutanen, *Towards a Pluralistic Constitutional Understanding of State Sovereignty in the European Union? The Concept, Regulation and Constitutional Practice of Sovereignty in Finland and Certain Other EU Member States* 306-307.

Constitution.[11] However, the Committee refrained from imposing substantive limits to the parliamentary power to pursue EU integration steps in the past. The absence of substantive limitations to EU integration ambitions seems to derive from the Finnish model of a constitutional review conducted by a parliamentary committee,[12] the constitutional history of Finland[13] as well as the strong focus on parliamentary sovereignty.[14] Although the qualified majority threshold could render EU fiscal integration politically challenging, the Finnish constitutional order does not impose substantive legal-constitutional obstacles to such integration ambitions.

In contrast, the German Constitutional Court established its *overall budgetary responsibility* doctrine as an absolute limit to the powers of the German legislator.[15] Based on this doctrine, the Court demands that central budgetary decisions remain permanently under the control of the German Parliament, which translates into procedural and substantive requirements for the conferral of fiscal competences to EU level. Procedurally, the Court insists that the conferral of fiscal powers is strictly limited in volume and is specific to the pursued objectives. For larger financial commitments, the Court requires that the German Parliament remains actively involved in its administration and that it retains the competence to determine how the available funding is distributed.[16] Notably, it requires that EU commitments do not undermine German budgetary autonomy, which sets an abstract constitutional limit on the prospect of fiscal integration. Different to Finland, the resulting German constitutional limit cannot be overcome by the legislator.

Comparing both constitutional approaches, suggests that substantive constitutional limits, which are formulated as *constitutional identity* concerns in Germany, constitute the strictest material obstacles to EU fiscal integration. Based on this observation, the research investigated whether the absolute conception of the German *constitutional identity* limit is a particularity or whether *constitutional identity* limits in other EU Member States have a comparable limiting effect on the proposed EU fiscal integration steps. The conducted *micro-comparison* of the French, Polish and Spanish *constitutional identity limits* substantiated the observed overlap of protected constitutional principles. Notably, all three assessed limits identified budgetary and fiscal

11. Tomuschat, 'Lisbon: Terminal of the European Integration Process? The Judgment of the German Constitutional Court of 30 June 2009'; cf. as well: Leino and Salminen, 'The Euro Crisis and Its Constitutional Consequences for Finland: Is There Room for National Politics in EU Decision-Making?' 452.
12. De Visser, *Constitutional Review in Europe: A Comparative Analysis* 26.
13. Lavapuro, Ojanen and Scheinin, 'Finland: Intermediate Constitutional Review in Finland: Promising in Theory, Problematic in Practice' 220.
14. Ojanen, 'The EU at the Finnish Constitutional Arena' 254.
15. *Final Decision on the Ratification of the Own Resources Decision (NGEU)* paras 134-135; cf. as well: Ohler, 'Rechtliche Maßstäbe der Geldpolitik nach dem Gauweiler-Urteil des EuGH' 1002.
16. *Final OMT-Judgment* para. 214; *ESM-Treaty and Fiscal Compact (interim relief)* para. 107; cf. as well: Reestman, 'Legitimacy Through Adjudication: The ESM Treaty and the Fiscal Compact Before the National Courts' 259.

competences as particularly important parliamentary prerogatives protected by national sovereignty and democracy.[17] In addition, the research detected that the examined *constitutional identity limits* are mainly conceptualized as competence-centric limitations that exclude certain core state powers from the scope of supranational cooperation. The apparent underpinning assumption is that the conferral of budgetary and fiscal competences in itself can be sufficient to trigger *constitutional identity* concerns, given the traditional importance of these competences for national sovereignty and democracy.[18] National authorities seem similarly concerned that the conferral of these competences could alter national political decision-making through a modification of EU cooperation in case discretionary, political powers are allocated to the EU.[19] However, despite these serious constitutional concerns, the research revealed that the French, Polish and Spanish *constitutional identity* limits can ultimately be overcome by the constitution-amending legislator, in contrast to the German *constitutional identity limit.* Nevertheless, the requirements imposed to enact constitutional amendments and the surrounding national practice reveal that the attainability of constitutional amendments is uncertain in Poland[20] and Spain.[21] Hence, although the French, Polish and Spanish limits can be distinguished from the German *constitutional identity limit* based on their nature and general conception, the practical limiting effect of the Polish and Spanish *constitutional identity limit* is comparable to the German one given the seemingly low likelihood of successful constitutional amendments.

The evaluation of national *constitutional identity limits* illustrates the central position that national constitutional authorities occupy in determining the relationship between national constitutional law and EU integration steps. Strikingly, it is through

17. *France: Entwurf eines Gesetzes zu dem Beschluss des Europäischen Rates vom 25. März 2011 zur Änderung des Artikels 136 des Vertrags über die Arbeitsweise der Europäischen Union hinsichtlich eines Stabilitätsmechanismus für die Mitgliedstaaten, deren Währung der Euro ist (Drucksache 17/9047)* para. 21; Reestman, 'Legitimacy Through Adjudication: The ESM Treaty and the Fiscal Compact Before the National Courts' 265; *Spain:* Martín Y Pérez de Nanclares, 'Constitutional Identity in Spain: Commitment to European Integration Without Giving up the Essence of the Constitution' 279; *Poland: Challenges Against Article 136 (3) TFEU and ESM-Treaty* section 7.7.; Bainczyk, 'Folgen einer mangelnden Anpassung der polnischen Verfassung nach dem Vertrag von Lissabon im Lichte des Urteils des polnischen Verfassungsgerichtshofes zum Beschluss des Europäischen Rates zur Änderung von Art. 136 AEUV' 314.
18. Puntscher Riekmann and Wydra, 'Representation in the European State of Emergency: Parliaments Against Governments?' 567.
19. *Germany: Final Decision on the Ratification of the Own Resources Decision (NGEU)* paras 134; cf. as well: Wendel, 'Exceeding Judicial Competence in the Name of Democracy: The German Federal Constitutional Court's OMT Reference' 273-274; *France: Lisbon Treaty* para. 8; Vranes, 'Constitutional Foundation of, and Limitations to, EU Integration in France' 539; *Spain: Treaty Establishing a Constitution for Europe* section II.2.; Castillo de la Torre, '*Tribunal Constitucional* (Spanish Constitutional Court), Opinion 1/2004 of 13 December 2004, on the Treaty Establishing a Constitution for Europe' 1175; *Poland: Treaty of Lisbon* sections III.2.2. and III.2.3.; Wróbel, 'Die Grenzen der europäischen Integration im Lichte jüngerer Entscheidungen des polnischen Verfassungsgerichts' 500.
20. Cf. requirements in Article 235 (6) Polish Constitution; cf. as well: Bainczyk, 'Folgen einer mangelnden Anpassung der polnischen Verfassung nach dem Vertrag von Lissabon im Lichte des Urteils des polnischen Verfassungsgerichtshofes zum Beschluss des Europäischen Rates zur Änderung von Art. 136 AEUV' 321.
21. Bustos Gisbert, 'National Constitutional Identity in European Constitutionalism: Revisiting the Tale of the Emperor's New Clothes in Spain?' 85-86.

the jurisprudence of the Constitutional Court that the German *eternity clause* could emerge as a strict limit to EU fiscal integration.[22] Similarly, the French, Polish and Spanish *constitutional identity limits* are primarily inventions of national constitutional authorities.[23] This shows that EU integration is not only dependent on national parliaments and governments but that in light of *national constitutional identity* reservations, the attainability of EU integration increasingly depends on domestic constitutional authorities that adjudicate the compatibility of EU integration with national constitutional law. Given the resulting pivotal position that national constitutional authorities occupy, the sound functioning of these authorities is of vital interest to the EU. Therefore, the highlighted adverse constitutional development in Poland[24] triggers serious concerns regarding the continued reliability as well as the persistence of the established Polish jurisprudence - and with it concerns regarding the actual constitutional restrictions deriving from the Polish *constitutional identity limit* for EU fiscal integration steps. Aside from the Polish case, the important role of national constitutional authorities in determining the scope for EU integration steps necessitates a high(er) degree of attention at EU level to the national constitutional reasoning when devising EU integration.

C CONSTITUTIONALLY ATTAINABLE EU FISCAL INTEGRATION STEPS

The conducted compatibility assessment revealed that the charted national constitutional space allows for the implementation of several EU fiscal integration steps, provided that these are strictly limited in size, preserve the central control of national parliaments over budgetary and fiscal matters and ensure that core political decisions - that concern the collection and the distribution of money - remain at the national level. Based on these national constitutional requirements, it was concluded that the proposed allocation of new, tax-based 'own resources', the creation of an additional budgetary capacity under Article 311 TFEU, the establishment of further emergency instruments modelled on the ESM- or NGEU-structure, further supervisory tools with non-binding character and even the creation of an EU Ministry of Finance are generally compatible with the charted national constitutional space and thus constitutionally attainable, albeit presumably requiring qualified parliamentary support in both Germany as well as Finland - and thus likely also in other EU Member States.

22. Rademacher, 'Die "Verfassungsidentität" als Grenze der Kompetenzübertragung auf die Europäische Union?' 144; Ohler, 'Rechtliche Maßstäbe der Geldpolitik nach dem Gauweiler-Urteil des EuGH' 1002.
23. *France: Compatibility of the Maastricht Treaty with the French Constitution after Constitutinal Amendments ('Maastricht II')* para. 19; cf. as well: Millet, 'Constitutional Identity in France: Vices and - Above All - Virtues' 150-151; *Spain: Treaty Establishing a Constitution for Europe* section II.2.; cf. as well: Ferreres Comella, *The Constitution of Spain: A Contextual Analysis* 57; *Poland: Treaty of Lisbon* section III.2.1.; cf. as well: Śledzińska-Simon and Ziółkowski, 'Constitutional Identity in Poland: Is the Emperor Putting on the Old Clothes of Sovereignty' 244.
24. Sadurski, *Poland's Constitutional Breakdown* 2-3, 206-207; Mattias Wendel, 'Mutual Trust, Essence and Federalism: Between Consolidating and Fragmenting the Area of Freedom, Security and Justice after LM' (2019) 15 European Constitutional Law Review 17, 18.

Overall, this suggests that decisive reform steps can be taken such as the initiation of a Eurozone budget or the allocation of new revenue without triggering rigid constitutional opposition. Yet, it also appears that the resulting reform potential would be limited to the current EU-Treaties. In turn, this would not permit the type of long-term-oriented innovations of the Eurozone which are deemed necessary by more far-reaching integration proposals.[25] These more far-reaching proposals centrally aim at the conferral of discretionary competences to EU level to enable the Eurozone to take political decisions independently from continuous national parliamentary approval, which sits uneasily with the current conception of national democracy, national sovereignty and national parliamentary prerogatives. Consequently, under a conventional *face-value* application of these national constitutional limits, a fundamental alteration of the EMU remains highly precarious with possibly adverse implications for the viability of the Euro. Therefore, the book introduced two transformative propositions to ease the apparent conflict between ambitious EU fiscal integration reform needs and limiting national constitutional concerns.

D TRANSFORMING NATIONAL CONSTITUTIONAL LIMITS THROUGH *CONSTITUTIONAL FLEXIBILITY*

The first transformative proposition is to locate flexibility in national constitutional approaches against EU fiscal integration steps. The book established that seemingly rigid national constitutional approaches contain, on closer inspection and with sufficient judicial goodwill, a degree of *constitutional flexibility*. It was substantiated that this *constitutional flexibility* could enable national authorities to construe national constitutional approaches to EU integration in a more open but still effective manner, thereby potentially facilitating additional EU level fiscal integration. Given that the German *constitutional identity limit* emerged as the most rigid substantive restriction to EU fiscal integration, the research employed three different methods to identify such *constitutional flexibility* within the German constitutional approach. These methods include the consistent application of the constitutional framework (I), the identification and application of domestic *best practices* (II), as well as the increased focus on the added benefit of EU (fiscal) integration for the national constitutional order (III). The book applied these methods in an exemplifying fashion to the German *constitutional identity limit*, but the employed methods can be extended to other constitutional systems to similarly locate and activate sources of *constitutional flexibility*.

I Consistent Application of the National Constitutional Framework

The first method employed to generate *constitutional flexibility* is the consistent application of the applicable constitutional framework. The *micro-comparison*

25. Cf. Juncker et al., *The Five Presidents' Report: Completing Europe's Economic and Monetary Union* 15; or the Bruegel-proposal, cf. Marzinotto, Sapir and Wolff, 'What Kind of Fiscal Union? (2011)' 5, 7; cf. as well: Lionello, *The Pursuit of Stability of the Euro Area as a Whole: The Reform of the European Economic Union and Perspectives of Fiscal Integration* 226-227.

demonstrated the existence of a constitutional double standard in the jurisprudence of the German Constitutional Court at the disadvantage of EU integration measures. Notably, this double standard can be detected in the application of the established constitutional standing requirements, which makes it comparably easier to proceed against EU measures before the Constitutional Court.[26] It can equally be detected in the application of the *eternity clause*, which is rarely employed *internally* and yet is a focal point in the constitutional assessment of EU-related matters. It was demonstrated that this practice undermines the *ultima ratio* function that the *eternity clause* traditionally has in the German constitutional order.[27] And it can equally be identified in the conception of *overall budgetary responsibility*. Notably, it was established that the core premise of this important EU-related doctrine - namely that the German Parliament takes all central budgetary and fiscal decisions - can be challenged.

In light of these three instances, the research proposed a three-stepped *constitutional roadmap* illustrated in Figure 9.1. This *roadmap* outlines how adherence to a consistent interpretation of the applicable national constitutional framework can reduce future conflicts between German constitutional law and EU (fiscal) integration steps.

Figure 9.1 Roadmap to Locate Flexible Constitutional Space in Germany

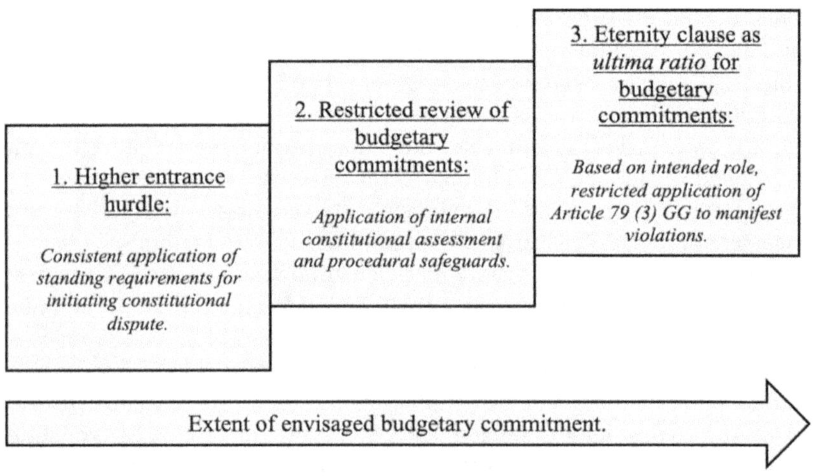

The book maintains that the consistent application of the German constitutional framework is a constitutional imperative under the rule of law and legal certainty

26. Gärditz, 'Beyond Symbolism: Towards a Constitutional Actio Popularis in EU Affairs? A Commentary on the OMT Decision of the Federal Constitutional Court' 190-197; Klein and Sennekamp, 'Aktuelle Zulässigkeitsprobleme der Verfassungsbeschwerde' 949.
27. Möllers and Redcay, 'Das Bundesverfassungsgericht als europäischer Gesetzgeber oder als Motor der Union?' 425-426; Mayer, 'Rashomon in Karlsruhe: A Reflection on Democracy and Identity in the European Union' 763; Schorkopf, 'Case Nos. 2 BvE 2/08, 2 BvE 5/08, 2 BvR 1010/08, 2 BvR 1022/08, 2 BvR 1259/08, and 2 BvR 182/09: 123 BVerfGE 267 (2009)' 263.

considerations, but it is also required to respect the constitutionally enshrined division of powers and the constitutional duty to support European cooperation. Finally, the consistent application of constitutional provisions is equally required under EU law itself as national authorities are required to engage in sincere cooperation with the EU and its institutions.[28]

II Creating Constitutional Flexibility Through Domestic Best Practices

Second, building on the observation that constitutional concerns against EU fiscal integration steps derive from similar underpinning constitutional principles, the comparative setting allowed for the identification of constructive *best practices*. These *best practice* examples include the Finnish parliamentary mandating system according to which the Finnish Parliament participates in the *ex ante* preparation of EU decisions in a comprehensive and constitutionally secured fashion that is politically respected.[29] These examples also include the constitutional review conducted by the Finnish Constitutional Law Committee which incorporates factual benefits stemming from EU cooperation into the constitutional assessment thereby resulting in a constructive conception of Finnish sovereignty,[30] and which is employed in a comparable manner by the Polish Constitutional Tribunal.[31] The book demonstrates how these *best practice* examples can address and partly dispel German constitutional concerns that stem from *overall budgetary responsibility*.

The exemplary involvement of the Finnish Parliament in EU decision-making and the Constitutional Law Committee's recognition of this constitutionally secured parliamentary participation can address the German procedural requirements under *overall budgetary responsibility*. It appears that given the interplay of constitutional rules and the institutional acceptance of parliamentary involvement in preparing EU decisions, the Finnish Parliament evolved into a central domestic authority that can impact Council and European Council decision-making. The Finnish example further illustrates that such effective participation does not necessarily require a legally binding parliamentary vote[32] but that political mandates can work as effectively in guaranteeing parliamentary control over such EU decisions. Hence, even once competences are

28. Christian Calliess and Anita Schnettger, 'The Protection of Constitutional Identity in a Europe of Multilevel Constitutionalism' in Christian Calliess and Gerhard Van der Schyff (eds), *Constitutional Identity in a Europe of Multilevel Constitutionalism* (Cambridge University Press 2019) 361.
29. Tomuschat, 'Lisbon: Terminal of the European Integration Process? The Judgment of the German Constitutional Court of 30 June 2009' 4-5; cf. as well: Ojanen, 'The Europeanization of Finnish Law' 169.
30. As highlighted, cf. Mutanen, *Towards a Pluralistic Constitutional Understanding of State Sovereignty in the European Union? The Concept, Regulation and Constitutional Practice of Sovereignty in Finland and Certain Other EU Member States* 328-332.
31. *Challenges Against Article 136 (3) TFEU and ESM-Treaty* section 6.4.2.; cf. as well: Czaputowicz, 'Sovereignty in Theories of European Integration and the Perspective of the Polish Constitutional Tribunal' 32.
32. De Visser, *Constitutional Review in Europe: A Comparative Analysis* 27-28; Leino and Salminen, 'The Euro Crisis and Its Constitutional Consequences for Finland: Is There Room for National Politics in EU Decision-Making?' 459-460.

conferred at EU level, the Finnish Parliament retains vital influence on supranational decisions secured through the constitutional framework. The German Constitutional Court could similarly embrace the opportunities stemming from Article 23(3) GG by considering parliamentary involvement in EU decisions and by more consistently relying on the provision to establish not only parliamentary control over governmental action at EU level but to employ it as a forceful constitutional basis to provide the German Parliament with its own genuine role in EU matters. Put differently, instead of being an accessory to the government, parliament could obtain stronger and independent political influence on EU decisions, as exemplified in Finland. Concretely, the application of the Finnish *best practice* example could ease German constitutional concerns in relation to the required comprehensive parliamentary involvement at EU level, expressed in relation to the EFSF- and the ESM-Treaty.[33] Instead of requiring specific procedural arrangements under the respective EU agreements, the Court could focus on the possibilities deriving from Article 23(3) GG. For example, the required continuous parliamentary involvement under the ESM-Treaty to evaluate financial risks could be safeguarded by the *best practice* use of parliamentary mandating systems. Parliament could then forward its views to the German Government, which would consider these politically binding – with the option of parliament to proceed against any divergence from its position. The result would be an enhanced standing of the German Parliament in EU matters and the consequential emergence of a political culture that protects parliamentary involvement in EU matters, as apparent in Finland.

An additional advantage of the Finnish model is that the Grand Committee can communicate positions on behalf of parliament, after receiving the relevant views of other parliamentary committees.[34] This allows for the speedy handling of EU affairs by the Finnish Parliament. This contrasts with the current German model, which prescribes that decisions with budgetary and fiscal implications have to be taken by the plenary given the overall importance of the affected competences as well as given the parliamentarians' right to equally participate in all relevant parliamentary affairs.[35] Yet, employing the available explicit constitutional option in Article 45(2) GG to increasingly delegate EU matters to the responsibility of the European Committee could ensure the more efficient involvement of the German Parliament. Such delegation is democratically secured in two regards. First, the constitutional legislator included the possibility of delegating responsibilities in EU affairs to the European Committee. And second, the initial conferral of powers is ratified by the German Parliament. Therefore, the empowerment of the parliamentary committee seems less contentious and could secure speedy national parliamentary involvement. Overall, if the German Constitutional Court were to accept that the current system under Article 23(3) GG could provide a workable route for parliamentary involvement in EU matters, this might also relax the substantive democracy concerns raised towards EU fiscal integration.

33. *ESM-Treaty and Fiscal Compact (interim relief)* para. 107; *Participation of Members of German Parliament in the EFSF* paras 109-111.
34. Miller, 'Finnish Judges and the European Union: An American Perspective' 503; Ojanen, 'The Impact of EU Membership on Finnish Constitutional Law' 555.
35. *Participation of Members of German Parliament in the EFSF* paras 131, 136.

An additional *best practice* element is the inclusion of factual benefits of supranational cooperation in the constitutional assessment of EU integration steps. According to the Finnish Constitutional Law Committee, EU integration steps do not only challenge Finnish sovereignty but can also factually increase sovereign competences through shared decision-making at EU level.[36] Similarly, the Polish Constitutional Tribunal submitted that the 'modern' interpretation of national sovereignty warranted supranational cooperation in order to attain national constitutional objectives.[37] Building on these examples, the book illustrates how the German Constitutional Court could create additional flexibility under its substantive requirements of *overall budgetary responsibility* notably by filtering various factual benefits into the constitutional appraisal. A readiness to follow this reasoning could be detected in the German constitutional assessment of the ESM-Treaty where the Court concluded that not establishing the ESM would have resulted in hardly predictable financial risks.[38] Following the Finnish and Polish *best practice* examples, the inclusion of factual benefits could be further extended, as will be substantiated now.

III Immediate and Indirect Benefits of EU Cooperation

A final tool employed to locate and activate *constitutional flexibility* is to better incorporate immediate and indirect benefits of EU cooperation into the national constitutional assessment of EU integration. Building on the various EU integration theories,[39] it can be ascertained that Member States pursue specific objectives when acceding to the EU. These vary from mainly trade and economic considerations[40] to political and societal goals that Member States aim to attain.[41]

Regardless of the specific national reasons for EU accession, these theories suggest that EU membership offers a range of incentives that may outbalance the inherent costs that supranational integration brings with it.[42] These incentives prevail after accession – they are visible economically through permanent access to the

36. Mutanen, *Towards a Pluralistic Constitutional Understanding of State Sovereignty in the European Union? The Concept, Regulation and Constitutional Practice of Sovereignty in Finland and Certain Other EU Member States* 328-332; Ojanen, 'The EU at the Finnish Constitutional Arena' 245.
37. Czaputowicz, 'Sovereignty in Theories of European Integration and the Perspective of the Polish Constitutional Tribunal' 32.
38. *ESM-Treaty and Fiscal Compact (interim relief)* para. 167.
39. Liesbet Hooghe and Gary Marks, 'Grand Theories of European Integration in the Twenty-First Century' (2019) 26 Journal of European Public Policy 1113, 1114-1118; Sergio Fabbrini, 'The Euro Crisis Through Two Paradigms: Interpreting the Transformation of the European Economic Governance' (2017) 18 European Politics and Society 318, 322-324.
40. Particularly within intergovernmentalism, cf. Hooghe and Marks, 'Grand Theories of European Integration in the Twenty-First Century' 1114; Fabbrini, 'The Euro Crisis Through Two Paradigms: Interpreting the Transformation of the European Economic Governance' 322-323.
41. For example, in neo-functionalism, cf. Hooghe and Marks, 'Grand Theories of European Integration in the Twenty-First Century' 1114; Fabbrini, 'The Euro Crisis Through Two Paradigms: Interpreting the Transformation of the European Economic Governance' 323-324.
42. With a comprehensive overview on costs-benefits analyses for the 2004 Enlargement, cf. Susan Senior Nello, 'EU Enlargement and Theories of Economic Integration' in Amy Verdun and Alfred Tovias (eds), *Mapping European Economic Integration* (Palgrave Macmillan UK 2013) 178-183.

internal market but are also apparent in the relative increase in national powers by pooling sovereign competences at EU level, thereby enhancing the national position in negotiating international trade agreements as Union of 27.[43] This suggests that the domestic reasons for accession to the EU and the anticipated benefits do not merely vanish once membership is achieved, but these reasons transform into continuous grounds of justification for membership. Although national constitutional systems signal their ability to consider the benefits stemming from EU integration, apparent from EU law friendliness doctrines in some Member States,[44] a comprehensive assessment of EU benefits resulting from a specific conferral is not conducted. To that end, the research outlined examples of immediate and indirect benefits that EU integration entail which could counter-balance national constitutional concerns.

As substantiated in Chapter VIII, this could entail that the constitutional appraisal not only focuses on the volume of a proposed financial commitment but that it equally considers direct financial benefits stemming from such commitment. Here, the Commission's concept of 'operating budgetary balance' provides useful guidance.[45] Following current EU financing rules, Germany contributed a substantial EUR 25.8 billion to the EU budget in 2019. However, when including the direct return through EU funds into the equation, the operating budgetary balance indicated 'only' a minus of EUR 14.3 billion.[46] It thus revealed that the Member States' financial commitments towards the EU are not one-directional but that direct financial returns stem from them. Thus, when considering EU fiscal integration proposals, the German constitutional assessment should not merely focus on the financial commitment that is required but it should equally pay attention to the 'return' that flows back to Germany. Furthermore, these EU benefits also occur indirectly. The research highlighted that the German GDP would be at least 0.5 % lower without the Euro[47] and that Eurozone membership thus increased fiscal decision-making space in Germany.

Ultimately, this suggests that EU integration in fiscal matters is not only reducing national fiscal decision-making abilities but that through the resulting cooperation, additional fiscal space can be tapped that would otherwise not be available to the Member States. This highlights that the current focus of the constitutional review based on a reduction of own competences is not sufficient to adequately reflect the impact that supranational cooperation has on the national constitutional order. Incorporating the outlined EU benefits would render the national constitutional assessment more balanced and connect it to the highlighted EU integration theories which conceptualize incentives for countries to join the EU.

43. Dieter Grimm, 'The Role of National Constitutions in a United Europe' in Dieter Grimm (ed.), *Constitutionalism: Past, Present, and Future* (Oxford University Press 2016) 289-292.
44. *Germany:* Thym, 'Europäische Integration im Schatten souveräner Staatlichkeit: Anmerkungen zum Lissabon-Urteil des Bundesverfassungsgerichts' 559; *France:* Ziller, 'European Union Law in the Jurisprudence of French Supreme Courts: Europe-Friendliness with a French Touch' 776; *Poland:* Górski, 'European Union Law Before National Judges: the Polish Experience – Adept Multicentric Vision or Creeping Hierarchical Practice' 132.
45. Darvas, 'A New Look at Net Balances in the European Union's Next Multiannual Budget' 3.
46. For the data, cf. Commission, *EU expenditure and revenue 2014-2020 (dataset).*
47. Petersen, Böhmer and Stein, 'How Germany Benefits from the Euro in Economic Terms (Policy Brief # 2013/01)' 6.

E TRANSFORMING THE DESIGN OF FISCAL INTEGRATION PROPOSALS

The second transformative proposition relates to the conception of EU fiscal integration. The compatibility assessment of the EU fiscal integration steps with the charted national constitutional space revealed that limited reforms are constitutionally feasible. In light of a more flexible conception of national constitutional limits and the resulting additional national constitutional space, even more ambitious EU fiscal integration proposals could possibly be attainable. However, the proposed transformation largely depends on the receptiveness of national constitutional authorities. Therefore, the book introduces a second transformative proposition to trigger a re-conceptualization of EU fiscal integration proposals as well.

This proposition departs from the idea of connecting EU fiscal integration and particularly EU revenues with achievements that can be directly attributed to EU cooperation instead of relying on Member States' national contributions.[48] It thus connects to the previous point of more comprehensively incorporating EU benefits into the national constitutional appraisal of EU fiscal integration steps, thereby rendering such reform ambitions less contentious. In essence, EU fiscal integration proposals are designed around the conferral of competences from the national to EU level. Notably, the creation of the proposed Eurozone budget is constructed as a limit of national competences for the sake of EU decision-making which requires the transfer of powers or funds from the Member States to the EU. In a comparable manner, the creation of an EU Ministry of Finance and increased budgetary supervision are construed as limitations of national competences. Obviously, this design choice conflicts with the competence-centric conception of national *constitutional identity limits*, which aim to preserve core competences at the national level.

Hence, EU fiscal integration should be devised from the perspective of the 'added benefit' that it entails as well as the fiscal opportunities that it might create. The underpinning idea is that the EU would be financed by or operate through revenue that it creates itself and subsequently employ this revenue to stabilize supranational cooperation in the long run. From a national constitutional perspective, such a design would address the concerns that the EU is limiting budgetary competences at the national level, as these competences would stem from EU level itself and would therefore not be under the direct control of the Member States in the first place. Consequently, it can be submitted that sourcing the financial advantages generated from the EU does not reduce the traditional budgetary competences enjoyed by national parliaments. In fact, these financial benefits are complementary to the nationally generated financial benefits. It could even be added that as long as EU cooperation results in more fiscal benefits than it requires to sustain itself, EU fiscal integration steps increase the available national fiscal decision-making space. From an EU perspective, the proposed design would provide the advantage that EU finances would be less dependent on national contributions.[49] Taken together, this second

48. Fabbrini, 'Fiscal Capacity' 129.
49. Crowe, 'The European Budgetary Galaxy' 433.

proposition would change the debate surrounding EU fiscal integration steps and steer the focus towards added benefits created by envisaged supranational integration, instead of centring around the reduction of national constitutional competences, which are protected by national *constitutional identity limits*.

However, determining these fiscal opportunities in a detailed manner – for example, in the case of Germany, the financial benefits resulting from low-interest rate payments on state bonds or the advantages of the Euro as an important global currency – and translating them into EU fiscal integration steps exceeds the framework of this book. Given that EU cooperation traditionally entails the elimination of costs and liberation of trade, these EU benefits might not yet constitute genuine sources of revenue at any administrative level.

F EU COOPERATION AS A NATIONAL CONSTITUTIONAL DUTY IN THE TWENTY-FIRST CENTURY

The book comprehensively demonstrates how these two innovative transformative propositions help escape the apparent dilemma between EU fiscal integration ambitions and national constitutional concerns. It was illustrated how outright substantive constitutional opposition against EU fiscal integration could be overcome by embracing EU membership and including the resulting supranational benefits in the domestic constitutional assessment. Nevertheless, the book equally highlighted that budgetary and fiscal competence are considered across all examined constitutional orders central parliamentary prerogatives connected to national sovereignty and democracy.[50] Therefore, EU fiscal integration triggers much wider constitutional questions of how national democracies and nation-states can effectively function in an ever more integrated European Union which affects ever more core constitutional concerns. Thus, while the proposed transformative ideas address the short-term need to create additional fiscal capacities at EU level in line with national constitutional requirements, a wider process of reflection is required as to how core national constitutional concerns can be accommodated in the design of EU integration in a constitutionally sound, effective and mutually respectful way. Ultimately, this might require a paradigm shift in national constitutionalism, which exceeds the limits of this concluding outlook. Yet, building on the made observations, one conceptual and one institutional point of reflection will be submitted to contribute to such a wider constitutional reflection process.

On a conceptual level, it was shown how EU fiscal integration ambitions could trigger a broader re-conception process within the national constitutional culture about the added benefits of EU cooperation for national constitutional values. It was illustrated that the EU legal order offers the supranational stabilization of constitutional principles, such as democracy and the rule of law. The immediate benefits can be witnessed in the EU interventions regarding Hungary and Poland.[51] Similarly, supranational cooperation enhances the protection of fundamental rights, boosts economic

50. Lionello, *The Pursuit of Stability of the Euro Area as a Whole: The Reform of the European Economic Union and Perspectives of Fiscal Integration* 222.
51. Sadurski, *Poland's Constitutional Breakdown* 2-3.

prosperity and contributes to objectives such as environmental protection or digitalization which are all of immediate national constitutional relevance. Therefore, EU cooperation is much more than an intrusion into the national constitutional space – it is in fact a means to accomplish constitutional goals and fulfil constitutional obligations in the globalized world of the twenty-first century where international priorities are no longer determined in Washington DC, Berlin, Paris or Rome but increasingly at tables in Beijing, New Delhi or Brasilia. In this new global setting, European cooperation secures international influence that Member States alone could hardly exercise, and it enables Member States to defend national constitutional values at the global stage by integrating them into the supranational DNA, as the case in Article 2 TEU. Against this background, it can be argued that EU cooperation no longer only signifies a constitutional opportunity for Member States but that it in fact transforms into a constitutional obligation in order to effectively protect constitutional principles in our modern world. From that perspective, EU cooperation can be seen as collective empowerment on the world stage and an opportunity for national constitutional orders to determine jointly how this cooperation can best protect shared national constitutional principles in a shifting global context.

On an institutional level, the book indicated that various national constitutional concerns relate to the conferral of politically important competences to the EU and the subsequent insufficient involvement of national parliaments in the administration of these competences. The research illustrated that the Finnish constitutional system of parliamentary involvement in EU matters and the surrounding institutional acceptance of these systems might partly address these concerns. Yet, the debate on EU fiscal integration also offers the opportunity to re-think the institutional involvement of national parliaments in EU decision-making more generally, which was discussed in some proposals on fiscal integration that envisage the creation of a Eurozone assembly.[52] These institutional reform ideas connect to earlier proposals that argued for the establishment of a *European Senate*.[53] A *European Senate* could guarantee that national parliaments are better informed on EU policies, that they can subsequently play a more decisive role in policy-making at EU level and thereby equally better involve the citizens in EU decisions.[54] Building on these proposals, the research proposes the establishment of a *Eurozone Forum of National Parliamentary Delegates* as an initial institutional innovation for the Eurozone. This *Forum* would be exclusively composed of national parliamentary delegates and thus integrate the national parliamentary level better into EMU decision-making, which could address the identified concerns of national constitutional authorities regarding EU fiscal integration and the required

52. Ruffert, 'The Future of the European Economic and Monetary Union: Issues of Constitutional Law' 59-60.
53. Gerhard van der Schyff and Gert-Jan Leenknegt, 'The Case for a European Senate: A Model for the Representation of National Parliaments in the European Union' (2007) 62 Zeitschrift für öffentliches Recht (ZöR) 237, 238; or a *congress of parliaments*, cf. Philipp Kiiver, *The National Parliaments in the European Union: A Critical View on EU Constitution-Building*, vol. 50 (European Monographs, Kluwer Law International 2006) 133-134.
54. Schyff and Leenknegt, 'The Case for a European Senate: A Model for the Representation of National Parliaments in the European Union' 238.

degree of national parliamentary control over budgetary and fiscal decision-making. The *Forum* should tentatively consist of five *Delegates* per Member State, which are determined by the national parliaments themselves. The determined *Delegates* should equally be members of the national parliamentary EU Committees, in order to guarantee a high degree of EU expertise and to better integrate EU level discussions with national parliamentary discussions – which are either prepared or even fully conducted by the respective national EU Committees. The specifics of how national *Delegates* are selected should be determined by national law – for example, within the *rules of procedures* of national parliaments. These *Eurozone Delegates* could come together in the proposed *Forum* to discuss the national parliamentary perspective on EU budgetary and fiscal matters in a supranational setting. Initially, this *Forum* could take an informal ad hoc format, following the example of the European Council which similarly only developed over time into a formal EU institution.[55]

To pre-empt legal concerns regarding possible interference with the EU's institutional structure, the *Forum* would not be assigned decision-making powers but instead operate in a coordinating capacity. The regular joint debates of the *Forum* would be integrated into the national parliamentary work and occur before the national parliament reaches a final decision on the matter. The decisions taken by the *Eurozone Forum* would be declaratory and not replace national decision-making. National parliaments are merely invited to take the deliberations of the *Eurozone Forum* – as presented by the national *Delegates* – into due account. Despite only operating on an informal basis and taking declaratory decisions, the creation of a *Eurozone Forum* could counter-balance the criticized dominance of national executive actors at EU level and offer a comprehensive institutional framework – beyond the current *informal* exchange of views at the Conference of Parliamentary Committees for Union Affairs of Parliaments of the European Union (COSAC) gatherings – to supranationally align national parliamentary priorities within the Eurozone. It would equally offer national parliaments the opportunity to more effectively use their prerogatives under the EU-Treaties – for example by coordinating the initiation of the yellow and orange card procedure. In the long run, the proposed *Eurozone Forum* could be formally integrated into the EU's institutional framework and it might be assigned genuine decision-making powers. Ultimately, this would make national parliaments less dependent on national governments in EU matters and firmly integrate them into the EU's institutional structure.

As it stands, EU integration is a process of continuous amendments, challenges and transformation. Increasingly, this process conflicts with traditional characteristics of the national constitutional space, which explains the emergence of *national constitutional identity* limits as a new type of constitutional defence mechanism. Through these limits, national constitutional authorities attempt to contain EU integration and preserve national constitutional structures in light of ever-deepening integration. Although it was illustrated that national constitutional systems can be receptive

55. Luuk Van Middelaar, *The Passage to Europe: How a Continent Became a Union* (Yale University Press 2013) 179-180.

towards the various benefits that stem from supranational cooperation, this receptiveness is increasingly limited as EU integration advances towards the core of national systems: their *constitutional identity*. EU fiscal integration ambitions squarely fit into this trend, as they propose a shift of core constitutional and political competences from the national to the supranational level. Naturally, this proposed shift is met with national constitutional resistance displayed in the various constitutional proceedings in the Member States assessed within this book. Overcoming these national constitutional challenges against EU fiscal integration – but also against EU cooperation in core state areas generally – might require initiating a new chapter in national and supranational constitutionalism. After all, EU integration and national constitutional law are not opponents but can and should be mutually reinforcing allies in a globalized world.

Bibliography

Books and Monographs

Albert R, *Constitutional Amendments: Making, Breaking, and Changing Constitutions* (Oxford University Press 2019).f

Bell J, *French Legal Culture* (Butterworths 2001).

Berger A, *Anwendungsvorrang und nationale Verfassungsgericht*, vol. 113 (Jus Internationale et Europaeum, Mohr Siebeck 2015).

Bumke C and Voßkuhle A, *German Constitutional Law: Introduction, Cases, and Principles* (Oxford University Press 2019).

Caldwell PC, *Popular Sovereignty and the Crisis of German Constitutional Law: The Theory and Practice of Weimar Constitutionalism* (Duke University Press 1997).

Cloots E, *National Identity in EU Law* (Oxford University Press 2015).

Craig P, *The Lisbon Treaty: Law, Politics, and Treaty Reform*, vol. Revisited (Oxford University Press 2013).

Craig P and de Búrca G, *EU Law Text, Cases, and Materials* (6th edn, Oxford University Press 2015).

De Visser M, *Constitutional Review in Europe: A Comparative Analysis* (Hart Publishing 2015).

Eichengreen B, *European Monetary Unification: Theory, Practice, and Analysis* (MIT Press 1997).

Epping V, *Grundrechte* (6th edn, Springer Verlag 2015).

Eriksen EO, *Contesting Political Differentiation: European Division and the Problem of Dominance* (Palgrave Macmillan - Springer 2019).

Fabbrini F, *Economic Governance in Europe: Comparative Paradoxes and Constitutional Challenges* (Oxford University Press 2016).

Ferreres Comella V, *The Constitution of Spain: A Contextual Analysis* (Hart Publishing 2013).

Finer SE, Bogdanor V and Rudden B, *Comparing Constitutions* (Clarendon Press 1995).

Foster N and Sule S, *German Legal System and Laws* (4th edn, Oxford University Press 2010).

Fuller LL, *The Morality of Law* (Revised Edition edn, Yale University Press 1969).

Fürst W and Hellmuth G, *Grundgesetz – Das Verfassungsrecht der Bundesrepublik Deutschland in den Grundzügen* (Studienbücher Rechtswissenschaft, 3rd edn, Verlag W. Kohlhammer 1982).

Gordillo LI, *Interlocking Constitutions: Towards an Interordinal Theory of National, European and UN Law* (Hart Publishing 2012).

Granat M and Granat K, *The Constitution of Poland: A Contextual Analysis* (Hart Publishing 2019).

Gundel J, *Die Einordnung des Gemeinschaftsrechts in die französische Rechtsordnung*, vol 42 (Schriften zum Europäischen Recht, Duncker & Humblot 1997).

Heringa AW, *Constitutions Compared: An Introduction to Comparative Constitutional Law* (4th edn, Intersentia Ltd 2016).

Hesse K, *Grundzüge des Verfassungsrechts der Bundesrepublik Deutschland* (C.F. Müller 1993).

Hinarejos Parga A, *The Euro Area Crisis in Constitutional Perspective* (Oxford University Press 2015).

Husa J, *The Constitution of Finland: A Contextual Analysis* (Hart Publishing 2011).

Jokela J, *Finland and the Eurozone Crisis* (Palgrave Macmillan 2014).

Ketterer L, *Zustimmungserfordernis beim Europäischen Stabilitätsmechanismus* (Freiburger Rechtswissenschaftliche Abhandlungen, Mohr Siebeck 2016).

Kiiver P, *The National Parliaments in the European Union: A Critical View on EU Constitution-Building*, vol. 50 (European Monographs, Kluwer Law International 2006).

Kiss C, *Constitutional Democracy in Eastern Europe: The Role of Constitutional Courts in Democratic Consolidation in Post-Communist Hungary and Poland* (ProQuest Dissertations Publishing 2005).

Lionello L, *The Pursuit of Stability of the Euro Area as a Whole: The Reform of the European Economic Union and Perspectives of Fiscal Integration* (Springer 2020).

Markakis M, *Accountability in the Economic and Monetary Union: Foundations, Policy, and Governance* (Oxford Studies in European Law, Oxford University Press 2020).

Meiers F-J, *Germany's Role in the Euro Crisis: Berlin's Quest for a More Perfect Monetary Union* (Springer 2015).

Mutanen A, *Towards a Pluralistic Constitutional Understanding of State Sovereignty in the European Union? The Concept, Regulation and Constitutional Practice of Sovereignty in Finland and Certain other EU Member States* (Hansaprint Oy 2015).

Newton MT and Donaghy PJ, *Institutions of Modern Spain: A Political and Economic Guide* (Cambridge University Press 1997).

Raunio T and Tiilikainen T, *Finland in the European Union* (Frank Cass Publishers 2003).

Richter A, *Funktionswandel im Mehrebenensystem? Die Rolle der nationalen Parlamente in der Europäischen Union am Beispiel des Deutschen Bundestags* (Herbert Utz Verlag 2016).

Rompuy Hv, *Europe in the Storm: Promise and Prejudice* (Davidsfonds Uitgeverij nv 2014).

Sadurski W, *Poland's Constitutional Breakdown* (Oxford University Press 2019).

Schlaich K and Korioth S, *Das Bundesverfassungsgericht – Stellung Verfahren, Entscheidungen* (11th edn, C.H. Beck 2018).
Simon S, *Grenzen des Bundesverfassungsgerichts im europäischen Integrationsprozess*, vol. 253 (Jus Publicum, Mohr Siebeck 2016).
Steiner E, *French Law: A Comparative Approach* (Oxford University Press 2018).
Tappe H and Wernsmann R, *Öffentliches Finanzrecht* (2nd edn, C.F. Müller 2019).
Tresselt W, *Die Vertreter der Länder im Rat der Europäischen Gemeinschaft* (Books on Demand (BoD) 2006).
Troitino DR, *European Integration: Building Europe* (Nova Publishers 2013)
Tuori K and Tuori K, *The Eurozone Crisis: A Constitutional Analysis* (Cambridge University Press 2014).
Union E, *European Union Public Finance* (Publications Office of the European Union 2014).
Van Middelaar L, *The Passage to Europe: How a Continent Became a Union* (Yale University Press 2013).
Vanberg G, *The Politics of Constitutional Review in Germany* (Cambridge University Press 2005).
Zippelius R, *Juristische Methodenlehre* (JuS Schriftreihe, 11th edn, C.H. Beck 2012).

Book Sections

Ahumada Ruiz M, 'The Spanish Constitutional Court' in Jakab A, Dyevre A and Itzcovich G (eds), *Comparative Constitutional Reasoning* (Cambridge University Press 2017).
Allemand Fdr, 'European Economic Constitution: From Soft to Hard Policy Coordination?' in Hofmann HCH, Pantazatou K and Zaccaroni G (eds), *The Metamorphosis of the European Economic Constitution* (Edward Elgar Publishing Limited 2019).
Baranger D, 'The Apparition of Sovereignty' in Kalmo H and Skinner Q (eds), *Sovereignty in Fragments: The Past, Present and Future of a Contested Concept* (Cambridge University Press 2010).
Becker P, 'Haushaltspolitik' in Weidenfeld W and Wessels W (eds), *Jahrbuch der Europäischen Integration 2017* (Nomos 2017).
Bell J, 'Court Institutions' in Bell J, Boyron S and Whittaker S (eds), *Principles of French Law* (2nd edn, Oxford University Press 2008).
Beukers T, 'The Eurozone Crisis and the Autonomy of Member States in Economic Union: Changes and Challenges' in Koutrakos P and Snell J (eds), *Research Handbook on the Law of the EU's Internal Market* (Edward Elgar Publishing Limited 2017).
Biernat S and Kawczyńska M, 'The Role of the Polish Constitution (Pre-2016): Development of a Liberal Democracy in the European and International Context' in Albi A and Bardutzky S (eds), *National Constitutions in European and Global Governance: Democracy, Rights, the Rule of Law* (T.M.C. Asser Press 2019).
Bignami F, 'Introduction: EU Law, Sovereignty, and Populism' in Bignami F (ed.), *EU Law in Populist Times: Crises and Prospects* (Cambridge University Press 2020).
Boyron S, 'Constitutional Law' in Bell J, Boyron S and Whittaker S (eds), *Principles of French Law* (2nd edn, Oxford University Press 2008).

Bustos Gisbert R, 'National Constitutional Identity in European Constitutionalism: Revisiting the Tale of the Emperor's New Clothes in Spain?' in Saiz Arnaiz A and Alcoberro Llivina C (eds), *National Constitutional Identity and European Integration* (Intersentia Ltd 2013).

Calliess C, 'Constitutional Identity in Germany: One for Three or Three in One?' in Calliess C and Van der Schyff G (eds), *Constitutional Identity in a Europe of Multilevel Constitutionalism* (Cambridge University Press 2019).

Calliess C and Schnettger A, 'The Protection of Constitutional Identity in a Europe of Multilevel Constitutionalism' in Calliess C and Van der Schyff G (eds), *Constitutional Identity in a Europe of Multilevel Constitutionalism* (Cambridge University Press 2019).

Chalmers D, Jachtenfuchs D and Joerges C, 'The Retransformation of Europe' in Chalmers D, Jachtenfuchs D and Joerges C (eds), *The End of the Eurocrats' Dream: Adjusting to European Diversity* (Cambridge University Press 2016).

Claes M, 'National Identity: Trump Card or up for Negotiation?' in Saiz Arnaiz A and Alcoberro Llivina C (eds), *National Constitutional Identity and European Integration* (Intersentia Ltd 2013).

Craig P and Markakis M, 'EMU Reform' in Amtenbrink F and Herrmann C (eds), *The EU Law of Economic and Monetary Union* (Oxford University Press 2020).

Czuczai J, 'Accession to the EU, But to Which EU? The Legal Impact of the Constantly Evolving EMU Acquis on the EU Enlargement Process' in Adam S et al. (eds), *The European Union in the World: Essays in Honour of Professor Marc Maresceau* (Martinus Nijhoff Publishers 2014).

Dannemann G, 'Comparative Law: Study of Similarities or Differences?' in Reimann M and Zimmermann R (eds), *The Oxford Handbook of Comparative Law* (2nd edn, Oxford University Press 2019).

Dawson M, Enderlein H and Joerges C, 'Introduction: The Governance of the Transformation of Europe's Economic, Political, and Constitutional Constellation Since the Euro-Crisis' in Dawson M, Enderlein H and Joerges C (eds), *Beyond the Crisis: The Governance of Europe's Economic, Political, and Legal Transformation* (Oxford University Press 2015).

De Sadeleer N, 'The New Architecture of European Economic Governance' in Philipsen N and Xu G (eds), *The Role of Law and Regulation in Sustaining Financial Markets* (Routledge 2015).

Delledonne G, 'A Legalization of Financial Constitutions in the EU? Reflections on the German, Spanish, Italian and French Experiences' in Adams M, Fabbrini F and Larouche P (eds), *The Constitutionalization of European Budgetary Constraints* (Hart Publishing 2014).

Dietlein J, 'Art. 79 GG: Änderungen des Grundgesetzes' in Epping V and Hillgruber C (eds), *Beck Online Kommentar zum Grundgesetz* (45th edn, C.H. Beck 2020).

Díez-Nicolás J, 'Spaniards' Long March Towards Europe' in Royo Sn and Manuel PC (eds), *Spain and Portugal in the European Union: The First Fifteen Years* (Frank Cass and Company Limited 2003).

Dixon R, 'Constitutional Amendment Rules: A Comparative Perspective' in Ginsburg T and Dixon R (eds), *Comparative Constitutional Law* (Edward Elgar Publishing Limited 2011).

Dyevre A, 'The *Melki* Way: The *Melki* Case and Everything You Always Wanted to Know about French Judicial Politics (But Were Afraid to Ask)' in Claes M et al. (eds), *Constitutional Conversations in Europe* (Intersentia 2012).

Dyevre A, 'The French Constitutional Council' in Jakab A, Dyevre A and Itzcovich G (eds), *Comparative Constitutional Reasoning* (Cambridge University Press 2017).

Elvira A, 'Spain' in Fusaro C and Oliver D (eds), *How Constitutions Change: A Comparative Study* (Hart Publishing 2011).

Epping V, 'Art. 87a GG – Streitkräfte' in Epping V and Hillgruber C (eds), *Beck Online Kommentar zum Grundgesetz* (45th edn, C.H. Beck 2020).

Fabbrini F, 'Fiscal Capacity' in Fabbrini F and Ventoruzzo M (eds), *Research Handbook on EU Economic Law* (Edward Elgar Publishing Limited 2019).

Ferreres Comella V, 'La Constitución española ante la cláusula de primacía del Derecho de la Unión Europea – Un comentario a la Declaración 1/2004 del Tribunal Constitucional' in Closa Montero C (ed.), *Constitución Española y Constitución Europea – Análisis de la Declaración del Tribunal Constitucional (DTC 1/2004, de 13 de Diciembre)* (Centro de Estudios Políticos y Constitucionales 2015).

Garoupa N, Solanes Mullor J and Violante T, 'Constitutional Courts and National Parliaments in Spain and Portugal' in Fernandes JM and Leston-Bandeira C (eds), *The Iberian Legislatures in Comparative Perspective* (Routledge 2019).

Ginsburg T and Dixon R, 'Introduction' in Ginsburg T and Dixon R (eds), *Comparative Constitutional Law* (Edward Elgar Publishing Limited 2011).

González Pascual M, 'Welfare Rights and Euro Crisis: The Spanish Case' in Kilpatrick C and De Witte B (eds), *Social Rights in Times of Crisis in the Eurozone: The Role of Fundamental Rights' Challenges*, vol. 2014/05 (EUI Working Paper LAW, EUI 2014).

Górski M, 'European Union Law Before National Judges: the Polish Experience: Adept Multicentric Vision or Creeping Hierarchical Practice' in de Witte B et al. (eds), *Judicial Review and Cooperation Series, National Courts and EU Law: New Issues, Theories and Method* (Edward Elgar Publishing Limited 2016).

Grabenwarter C, 'National Constitutional Law Relating to the European Union' in von Bogdandy A and Bast J (eds), *Principles of European Constitutional Law* (2nd edn, Hart Publishing and C.H. Beck 2009).

Grewe C, 'Methods of Identification of National Constitutional Identity' in Saiz Arnaiz A and Alcoberro Llivina C (eds), *National Constitutional Identity and European Integration* (Intersentia Ltd 2013).

Grimm D, 'The Role of National Constitutions in a United Europe' in Grimm D (ed.), *Constitutionalism: Past, Present, and Future* (Oxford University Press 2016).

Hailbronner M and Martini S, 'The German Federal Constitutional Court' in Jakab A, Dyevre A and Itzcovich G (eds), *Comparative Constitutional Reasoning* (Cambridge University Press 2017).

Heintschel von Heinegg W and Frau R, 'Art. 23 GG – Mitwirkung bei Entwicklung der EU' in Epping V and Hillgruber C (eds), *Beck Online Kommentar zum Grundgesetz* (45th edn, C.H. Beck 2020).

Heintschel von Heinegg W and Frau R, 'Art. 24 GG – Kollektives Sicherheitssystem' in Epping V and Hillgruber C (eds), *Beck Online Kommentar zum Grundgesetz* (45th edn, C.H. Beck 2020).

Herdegen M, 'Art. 79 GG' in Maunz T and Düring G (eds), *Grundgesetz-Kommentar* (92nd edn, C.H. Beck 2020).

Hume M, 'Macroeconomic Imbalances in the Euro Area: Can They Be Managed?' in Campos NF, De Grauwe P and Ji Y (eds), *Economic Growth and Structural Reforms in Europe* (Cambridge University Press 2020).

Iso-Markku T, 'Finland: Pro-European Arguments Prevail Despite the Rise of Euroscepticism' in Bukovskis K (ed.), *Euroscepticism in Small EU Member States* (Zinātne 2016).

Jacobsohn GJ, 'The Formation of Constitutional Identities' in Ginsburg T and Dixon R (eds), *Comparative Constitutional Law* (Edward Elgar Publishing Limited 2011).

Jarass HD, 'Art. 23 GG – Europäische Union' in Jarass HD and Pieroth B (eds), *Grundgesetz für die Bundesrepublik Deutschland – Kommentar* (9th edn, C.H. Beck 2007).

Jokela J, 'Finland: Towards a More Cautious Europeanization' in Bretherton C and Mannin M (eds), *The Europeanization of European Politics* (Palgrave Macmillan 2013).

Kern B and Eggers C, 'Art. 174 AEUV – Ziele, Regionen und benachteiligte Gebiete' in Grabitz E, Hilf M and Nettesheim M (eds), *Das Recht der Europäischen Union – Kommentar* (70th edn, C.H. Beck 2020).

Kube H, 'Art. 105 GG – Steuergesetzgebungskompetenz' in Epping V and Hillgruber C (eds), *Beck Online Kommentar zum Grundgesetz* (45th edn, C.H. Beck 2020).

Kube H, 'Art. 110 GG' in Maunz T and Düring G (eds), *Grundgesetz-Kommentar* (92nd edn, C.H. Beck 2020).

Länsineva P, 'Fundamental Principles of the Constitution of Finland' in Nuotio K, Sakari M and Huomo-Kettunen M (eds), *Introduction to Finnish Law and Legal Culture* (University of Helsinki 2012).

Lavapuro J, 'Constitutional Review in Finland' in Nuotio K, Sakari M and Huomo-Kettunen M (eds), *Introduction to Finnish Law and Legal Culture* (University of Helsinki 2012).

Lavapuro J, Ojanen T and Scheinin M, 'Finland: Intermediate Constitutional Review in Finland: Promising in Theory, Problematic in Practice' in Bell J and Paris M-L (eds), *Rights-Based Constitutional Review: Constitutional Courts in a Changing Landscape* (Edward Elgar Publishing Limited 2016).

López Castillo A, 'La Unión Europea "en constitución" y la Constitución estatal en (espera de) reformas – A propósito de la DTC 1/2004 de 13 de diciembre' in Closa Montero C (ed.), *Constitución Española y Constitución Europea – Análisis de la Declaración del Tribunal Constitucional (DTC 1/2004, de 13 de Diciembre)* (Centro de Estudios Políticos y Constitucionales 2015).

Maduro MP, 'Foreword: Fiscal Capacity and Constitutional Reform in the EMU' in Adams M, Fabbrini F and Larouche P (eds), *The Constitutionalization of European Budgetary Constraints* (Hart Publishing 2014).

Martín Y Pérez de Nanclares J, 'Constitutional Identity in Spain: Commitment to European Integration Without Giving up the Essence of the Constitution' in Calliess C and van der Schyff G (eds), *Constitutional Identity in a Europe of Multilevel Constitutionalism* (Cambridge University Press 2019).

Michaels R, 'The Functional Method of Comparative Law' in Reimann M and Zimmermann R (eds), *The Oxford Handbook of Comparative Law* (2nd edn, Oxford University Press 2019).

Mik C, 'State Sovereignty and European Integration: Public International Law, EU Law and Constitutional Law in the Polish Context' in Walker N (ed.), *Sovereignty in Transition* (Hart Publishing 2003).

Millet F-X, 'Constitutional Identity in France: Vices and – Above All – Virtues' in Calliess C and Van der Schyff G (eds), *Constitutional Identity in a Europe of Multilevel Constitutionalism* (Cambridge University Press 2019).

Nettesheim M, 'Die "haushaltspolitische Gesamtverantwortung" in der Rechtsprechung des BVerfG' in Brandt P (ed.), *Verfassung und Krise*, vol. 16 (Berliner Wissenschafts-Verlag (BWV) 2015).

Ojanen T, 'The Europeanization of Finnish Law' in Luif P (ed.), *Österreich, Schweden, Finland: Zehn Jahre Mitgliedschaft in der Europäischen Union* (Böhlau Verlag 2007).

Ojanen T, 'The Europeanization of Finnish Law: Observations on the Transformations of the Finnish Scene of Constitutionalism' in Nuotio K, Sakari M and Huomo-Kettunen M (eds), *Introduction to Finnish Law and Legal Culture* (University of Helsinki 2012).

Ojanen T, 'Constitutional Amendment in Finland' in Contiades X (ed.), *Engineering Constitutional Change: A Comparative Perspective on Europe, Canada and the USA* (Routledge 2013).

Ojanen T, '§ 296: Grundrechte in Finland' in Merten D and Papier H-J (eds), *Handbuch der Grundrechte in Deutschland und Europa: Band X (Grundrechte in West-, Nord- und Südeuropa)* (C.F. Müller 2018).

Ojanen T and Salminen J, 'Finland: European Integration and International Human Rights Treaties as Sources of Domestic Constitutional Change and Dynamism' in Albi A and Bardutzky S (eds), *National Constitutions in European and Global Governance: Democracy, Rights, the Rule of Law* (T.M.C. Asser Press 2019).

Paris M-L, 'France: The French System of Rights-Based Review: From Exceptionalism to Parochial Constitutionalism' in Bell J and Paris M-L (eds), *Rights-Based Constitutional Review: Constitutional Courts in a Changing Landscape* (Edward Elgar Publishing Limited 2016).

Pérez Tremps P, 'National Identity in Spanish Constitutional Court Case-Law' in Saiz Arnaiz A and Alcoberro Llivina C (eds), *National Constitutional Identity and European Integration* (Intersentia Ltd 2013).

Raunio T, 'The Finnish Eduskunta and the European Union: The Strengths and Weaknesses of a Mandating System' in Hefftler C et al. (eds), *The Palgrave*

Handbook of National Parliaments and the European Union (Palgrave Macmillan 2015).

Reestman J-H, 'Legitimacy Through Adjudication: The ESM Treaty and the Fiscal Compact Before the National Courts' in Beukers T, de Witte B and Kilpatrick C (eds), *Constitutional Change Through Euro-Crisis Law* (Cambridge University Press 2017).

Requejo Pagés JL, 'The Spanish Constitutional Tribunal' in von Bogdandy A, Huber PM and Grabenwarter C (eds), *Constitutional Adjudication: Institutions*, vol. III (The Max Planck Handbook in European Public Law, Oxford University Press 2020).

Rideau J, 'The Case-Law of the Polish, Hungarian and Czech Constitutional Courts on National Identity and the "German Model"' in Saiz Arnaiz A and Alcoberro Llivina C (eds), *National Constitutional Identity and European Integration* (Intersentia Ltd 2013).

Rodríguez ML, 'Labour Rights in Crisis in the Eurozone: The Spanish Case' in Kilpatrick C and De Witte B (eds), *Social Rights in Times of Crisis in the Eurozone: The Role of Fundamental Rights' Challenges*, vol. 2014/05 (EUI Working Paper LAW, EUI 2014).

Rossi LS, 'A New Revision of the EU Treaties after Lisbon?' in Rossi LS and Casolari F (eds), *EU after Lisbon: Amending or Coping with the Existing Treaties?* (Springer 2014).

Royo Sn and Steinberg F, 'Using a Sectoral Bailout to Make Wide Reforms: The Case of Spain' in Chang M, Steinberg F and Torres F (eds), *The Political Economy of Adjustment Throughout and Beyond the Eurozone Crisis: What Have We Learned?* (Routledge 2019).

Ruffert M, 'The Future of the European Economic and Monetary Union: Issues of Constitutional Law' in Bignami F (ed.), *EU Law in Populist Times: Crises and Prospects* (Cambridge University Press 2020).

Ruiz Almendral V, 'The European Fiscal Consolidation Legal Framework: Its Impact on National Fiscal Constitutions and Parliamentary Democracy' in Beukers T, De Witte B and Kilpatrick C (eds), *Constitutional Change Through Euro Crisis Law* (Cambridge University Press 2017).

Sadurski W, 'Constitutional Crisis in Poland' in Graber MA, Levinson S and Tushnet M (eds), *Constitutional Democracy in Crisis?* (Oxford University Press 2018)

Saiz Arnaiz A and Alcoberro Llivina C, 'Why Constitutional Identity Suddently Matters: A Tale of Brave States, a Mighty Union and the Decline of Sovereignty' in Saiz Arnaiz A and Alcoberro Llivina C (eds), *National Constitutional Identity and European Integration* (Intersentia Ltd 2013).

Schneider C, 'Exkurs: Die Rolle des Haushaltsausschusses des Bundestages bei Aufstellung und Vollzug des Haushalts: ein Praxisbericht' in Gatzer W and Schweisfurth T (eds), *Öffentliche Finanzwirtschaft in der Staatspraxis* (BWV – Berliner Wissenschafts-Verlag 2015).

Scholz R, 'Art. 23 GG' in Maunz T and Düring G (eds), *Grundgesetz-Kommentar* (92nd edn, C.H. Beck 2020).

Scholz R, 'Art. 45 GG' in Maunz T and Düring G (eds), *Grundgesetz-Kommentar* (92nd edn, C.H. Beck 2020).

Sefton T, 'Distributive and Redistributive Policy' in Goodin RE, Moran M and Rein M (eds), *The Oxford Handbook of Public Policy* (Oxford University Press 2008).

Senior Nello S, 'EU Enlargement and Theories of Economic Integration' in Verdun A and Tovias A (eds), *Mapping European Economic Integration* (Palgrave Macmillan UK 2013).

Śledzińska-Simon A and Ziółkowski M, 'Constitutional Identity in Poland: Is the Emperor Putting on the Old Clothes of Sovereignty' in Calliess C and Van der Schyff G (eds), *Constitutional Identity in a Europe of Multilevel Constitutionalism* (Cambridge University Press 2019).

Solanes Mullor J and Torres Pérez A, 'The Constitution of Spain: The Challenges for the Constitutional Order under European and Global Governance' in Albi A and Bardutzky S (eds), *National Constitutions in European and Global Governance: Democracy, Rights, the Rule of Law* (Asser Press 2019).

Suksi M, 'Finland' in Dawn O and Fusaro C (eds), *How Constitutions Change: A Comparative Study* (Hart Publishing 2011).

Tuori K, '§ 98: Verfassungsgerichtsbarkeit in Finnland' in von Bogdandy A, Grabenwarter C and Huber PM (eds), *Handbuch Ius Publicum Europaeum: Band VI (Verfassungsgerichtsbarkeit in Europa: Institutionen)* (C.F. Müller 2016).

Tuori K and Raitio J, 'Finland' in Neergaard; U, Jacqueson; C and Danielsen JH (eds), *The Economic and Monetary Union: Constitutional and Institutional Aspects of the Economic Governance Within the EU (The XXVI FIDE Congress in Copenhagen)*, vol. 1 (DJØF Publishing Copenhagen 2014).

Van den Bogaert S and Cuyvers A, 'Of Carrots and Sticks: What Direction to Take for Economic and Monetary Union?' in Steunenberg B, Voermans W and Van den Bogaert S (eds), *Fit for the Future? Reflections from Leiden on the Functioning of the EU* (Eleven International Publishing 2016).

Van Middelaar L, 'Taking Decisions or Setting Norms? EU Presidencies Between Executive and Legislative Power in a Crisis-Driven Union' in Steunenberg B, Voermans W and Van den Bogaert S (eds), *Fit for the Future? Reflections from Leiden on the Functioning of the EU* (Eleven International Publishing 2016).

Walter C, 'Art. 93 GG' in Maunz T and Düring G (eds), *Grundgesetz-Kommentar* (92nd edn, C.H. Beck 2020).

Wiederin E, 'Die Gesetzeskraft der Entscheidungen des Bundesverfassungsgerichts' in Brenner M, Huber PM and Möstl M (eds), *Der Staat des Grundgesetzes – Kontinuität und Wandel: Festschrift für Peter Badura zum siebzigsten Geburtstag* (Mohr Siebeck 2004).

Wyrozumska A, 'Poland' in Shelton D (ed.), *International Law and Domestic Legal Systems: Incorporation, Transformation, and Persuasion* (Oxford University Press 2011).

Ziller J, 'Sovereignty in France: Getting Rid of the Mal de Bodin' in Walker N (ed.), *Sovereignty in Transition* (Hart Publishing 2003).

Journal Articles

Abdellatif L et al., 'Transparency of Law Making and Fiscal Democracy in the Middle East' (2019) 43 Public Sector Economics 49.

Alaez Corral B and Arias Castaño A, 'The Role of the Spanish Constitutional Court in the Judicial Review of Parliamentary Legislation' (2009) 15 European Public Law 597.

Alcidi C and Gros D, 'Next Generation EU: A Large Common Response to the COVID-19 Crisis' (2020) 55 Intereconomics - Review of European Economic Policy 202.

Álvarez L, 'Die spanische Dogmatik der Verfassungstreue - Geschichte einer fehlgeschlagenen Rezeption des deutschen Verfassungsdenkens' (2010) 70 Zeitschrift für ausländisches öffentliches Recht und Völkerrecht (ZÄRV) 433.

Andor L, 'SURE: EU Capacity for Stabilising Employment and Incomes in the Pandemic' (2020) 55 Intereconomics - Review of European Economic Policy 139.

Auel K and Raunio T, 'Debating the State of the Union? Comparing Parliamentary Debates on EU Issues in Finland, France, Germany and the United Kingdom' (2014) 20 The Journal of Legislative Studies 13.

Aust HP and Meinel F, 'Entscheidungsmöglichkeiten des BVerfG - Tenor, Systematik und Wirkungen' (2014) 54 Juristische Schulung (JuS) 25.

Azoulai L and Ronkes Agerbeek F, '*Conseil constitutionnel* (French Constitutional Court), Decision No. 2004-505 DC of 19 November 2004, on the Treaty Establishing a Constitution for Europe' (2005) 42 Common Market Law Review 871.

Bainczyk M, 'Das Ratifizierungsverfahren des Vertrages von Lissabon in Polen' (2009) 44 Europarecht (EuR) 145.

Bainczyk M, 'Die erste Vorabentscheidungsfrage des polnischen Verfassungsgerichtshofs an den EuGH' (2017) 52 Europarecht (EuR) 121.

Bainczyk M, 'Die praktische Anwendung des Unionsrechts in Polen: Anmerkung zum Urteil des EuGH v. 7.3.2017, Rs. C-390/15 (RPO), und zum Beschluss des polnischen Verfassungsgerichtshofes v. 17.5.2017, Akz. K 61/13' (2017) 52 Europarecht (EuR) 725.

Bainczyk M, 'Folgen einer mangelnden Anpassung der polnischen Verfassung nach dem Vertrag von Lissabon im Lichte des Urteils des polnischen Verfassungsgerichtshofes zum Beschluss des Europäischen Rates zur Änderung von Art. 136 AEUV' (2017) 52 Europarecht (EuR) 306.

Bainczyk M and Ernst U, 'Urteil des polnischen Verfassungsgerichtshofs vom 11. 05. 2005 AZ.K 18/04' (2006) 41 Europarecht (EuR) 236.

Bara Y-E et al., 'A Contribution to the Work on the Strengthening of the Euro Area' (2017) Trésor-Economics.

Baranger D, 'The Language of Eternity: Judicial Review of the Amending Power in France (Or the Absence Thereof)' (2011) 41 Israel Law Review 389.

Barcz J, 'Polish Policy in the Context of the Euro Area Reform' (2013) 16 Yearbook of Polish European Studies 69.

Bartl M, 'The Way We Do Europe: Subsidiarity and the Substantive Democratic Deficit' (2015) 21 European Law Journal 23.

Beaud O, 'Le Conseil constitutionnel sur la souveraineté et ses approximations' (2018) 20-21 Jus Politicum - Revue de droit politique 143.

Beck H and Wentzel D, 'Eurobonds: Wunderwaffe oder Sprengsatz für die Europäische Union?' (2011) 91 Wirtschaftsdienst - Zeitschrift für Wirtschaftspolitik 717.

Beichelt T, 'Recovering Space Lost? The German Bundestag's New Potential in European Politics' (2012) 21 German Politics 143.

Bibow J, 'Making the Euro Viable: The Euro Treasury Plan' (2015) Levy Economics Institute Working Paper Collection.

Blachèr P and Protière G, 'Le Conseil Constitutionnel, Gardien de la Constitution Face aux Directives Communautaires' (2007) 69 Revue francaise de Droit constitutionnel 123.

Bobek M, 'Landtová, Holubec, and the Problem of an Uncooperative Court: Implications for the Preliminary Rulings Procedure' (2014) 10 European Constitutional Law Review 54.

Bogdandy Av and Schill S, 'Die Achtung der nationalen Identität unter dem reformierten Unionsvertrag: Zur unionsrechtlichen Rolle nationalen Verfassungsrechts und zur Überwindung des absoluten Vorrangs' (2010) 70 Zeitschrift für ausländisches öffentliches Recht und Völkerrecht (ZÄRV) 701.

Bon P, 'La Identidad Nacional o Constitucional, una Nueva Noción Jurídica' (2014) 100 Revista Española de Derecho Constitucional 167.

Bonnie A, 'The Constitutionality of Transfers of Sovereignty: the French Approach' (1998) 4 European Public Law 517.

Borger V, 'The ESM and the European Court's Predicament in Pringle' (2013) 14 German Law Journal 113.

Boyron S, 'The French Constitution and the Treaty of Amsterdam: A Lesson in European Integration' (1999) 6 Maastricht Journal of European and Comparative Law 169.

Brandt W, 'Verfassungsrecht in Polen: Verfassungsbeschwerde und Rechtsprechung des polnischen Verfassungsgerichtshofes zu Fragen der EU-Mitgliedschaft' (2009) 44 Europarecht (EuR) 131.

Brauneck J, 'Rettet die EU den Rechtsstaat in Polen?' (2018) 37 Neue Zeitschrift für Verwaltungsrecht (NVwZ) 1423.

Brouard S, 'The Politics of Constitutional Veto in France: Constitutional Council, Legislative Majority and Electoral Competition' (2009) 32 West European Politics 384.

Burchardt D, 'Die Ausübung der Identitätskontrolle durch das Bundesverfassungsgericht: Zugleich Besprechung des Beschlusses 2 BvR 2735/14 des BVerfG vom 15.12.2015 ("Solange III"/"Europäischer Haftbefehl II")' (2016) 76 Zeitschrift für ausländisches öffentliches Recht und Völkerrecht (ZÄRV) 527.

BVerfG, 'Kein Rechtsschutz des Bürgers gegen Auflösung des Bundestages' (1983) 36 Neue Juristische Wochenschrift (NJW) 383.

Cahill M, 'Ever Closer Remoteness of the Peoples of Europe? Limits on the Power of Amendment and National Constituent Power' (2016) 75 Cambridge Law Journal 245.

Calliess C, 'Der Kampf um den Euro: Eine "Angelegenheit der Europäischen Union" zwischen Regierung, Parlament und Volk' (2012) 31 Neue Zeitschrift für Verwaltungsrecht (NVwZ) 1.

Calliess C, 'The Future of the Eurozone and the Role of the German Federal Constitutional Court' (2012) 31 Yearbook of European Law 402.

Calliess C, 'Bausteine einer erneuerten Europäischen Union: Auf der Suche nach dem europäischen Weg: Überlegungen im Lichte des Weißbuchs der Europäischen Kommission zur Zukunft Europas' (2018) 37 Neue Zeitschrift für Verwaltungsrecht (NVwZ) 1.

Calliess C, '70 Jahre Grundgesetz und europäische Integration: "Take Back Control" oder "Mehr Demokratie wagen"?' (2019) 38 Neue Zeitschrift für Verwaltungsrecht (NVwZ) 684.

Calliess C, 'Konfrontation statt Kooperation zwischen BVerfG und EuGH? Zu den Folgen des Karlsruher PSPP-Urteils' (2020) 39 Neue Zeitschrift für Verwaltungsrecht (NVwZ) 897.

Casey J, 'The Spanish Constitutional Court' (1990) 25 Irish Jurist 26.

Castillo-Ortiz P, 'The Illiberal Abuse of Constitutional Courts in Europe' (2019) 15 European Constitutional Law Review 48.

Castillo de la Torre F, '*Tribunal Constitucional* (Spanish Constitutional Court), Opinion 1/2004 of 13 December 2004, on the Treaty Establishing a Constitution for Europe' (2005) 42 Common Market Law Review 1169.

Charpy C, 'The Status of (Secondary) Community Law in the French Internal Order: The Recent Case-Law of the *Conseil Constitutionnel* and the *Conseil d'Etat*' (2007) 3 European Constitutional Law Review 436.

Charpy C, 'Droit constitutionnel et droit communautaire: Le statut constitutionnel du droit communautaire dans la jurisprudence (récente) du Conseil constitutionnel et du Conseil d'État' (2009) 80 Revue Française de Droit Constitutionnel 795.

Claes M, 'Luxembourg, Here We Come? Constitutional Courts and the Preliminary Reference Procedure' (2015) 16 German Law Journal 1331.

Claes M and Reestman J-H, 'The Protection of National Constitutional Identity and the Limits of European Integration at the Occasion of the *Gauweiler* Case' (2015) 16 German Law Journal 917.

Comments E, 'Editorial Comments: Tinkering with Economic and Monetary Union' (2018) 55 Common Market Law Review 1.

Cremer W, 'Lissabon-Vertrag und Grundgesetz' (2010) 32 JURA – Juristische Ausbildung 296.

Crespy A and Schmidt V, 'The Clash of Titans: France, Germany and the Discursive Double Game of EMU Reform' (2014) 21 Journal of European Public Policy 1085.

Crowe R, 'The European Budgetary Galaxy' (2017) 13 European Constitutional Law Review 428.

Czapliński W, 'Recent Constitutional Jurisprudence Concerning the European Union: Some Remarks on 2010 Judgments of the Polish Constitutional Court' (2011) 12 ERA Forum 197.

Czaputowicz J, 'Sovereignty in Theories of European Integration and the Perspective of the Polish Constitutional Tribunal' (2014) 17 Yearbook of Polish European Studies 15.

Czarny P, 'Der Streit um den Verfassungsgerichtshof in Polen 2015-2016' (2018) 64 Osteuropa Recht (OER) 5.

Daiber B, 'Das Integrationsverantwortungsgesetz in der Praxis des Deutschen Bundestages' (2012) 43 Zeitschrift für Parlamentsfragen 293.

Darvas Z, 'A New Look at Net Balances in the European Union's Next Multiannual Budget' (2019) Bruegel Working Paper.

Dawson M and De Witte F, 'Constitutional Balance in the EU after the Euro-Crisis' (2013) 76 The Modern Law Review 817.

De Areilza Carvajal JM, 'La Inserción de España en la Nueva Unión Europea: La Relación entre la Constitución Española y el Trato Constitucional (Comentario a la DTC 1/2004, de 13 de diciembre de 2004)' (2005) 73 Revista Española de Derecho Constitucional 365.

de Vries T, 'Bedrohungen für die Unabhängigkeit der Justiz in Polen: Teil 1' (2018) 27 Wirtschaft und Recht in Osteuropa (WiRO) 105.

De Witte B, 'The European Union's COVID-19 Recovery Plan: The Legal Engineering of an Economic Policy Shift' (2021) 58 Common Market Law Review 635.

Deffaa W, 'New Impetus for EU Taxation Policy' (2011) 46 Intereconomics – Review of European Economic Policy 287.

Dermine P, 'The Commission's December Package 18 Months Later' (2019) Maastricht Law – Faculty of Law Working Paper Series 7.

Dubout É, '"Les règles ou principes inhérents à l'identité constitutionelle de la France": une supra-constitutionalité?' (2010) 83 Revue francaise de Droit constitutionnel 451.

Dyevre A, 'The German Federal Constitutional Court and European Judicial Politics' (2011) 34 West European Politics 346.

Emmert F and Petrović S, 'The Past, Present, and Future of EU Enlargement' (2014) 37 Fordham International Law Journal 1349.

Engels A, 'Die Integrationsverantwortung des Deutschen Bundestags' (2012) 52 Juristische Schulung (JuS) 210.

Eriksen EO and Fossum JE, 'Bringing European Democracy Back In: Or How to Read the German Constitutional Court's Libson Treaty Ruling' (2011) 17 European Law Journal 153.

Estella de Noriega A, 'A Dissident Voice: The Spanish Constitutional Court Case Law on European Integration' (1999) 5 European Public Law 269.

Fabbrini F, 'The Euro-Crisis and the Courts: Judicial Review and the Political Process in Comparative Perspective' (2014) 32 Berkeley Journal of International Law 101.

Fabbrini F, 'Austerity, the European Council, and the Institutional Future of the European Union: A Proposal to Strengthen the Presidency of the European Council' (2015) 22 Indiana Journal of Global Legal Studies 269.

Fabbrini S, 'The Euro Crisis Through Two Paradigms: Interpreting the Transformation of the European Economic Governance' (2017) 18 European Politics and Society 318.

Falkner G, 'How Pervasive Are Euro-Politics? Effects of EU Membership on a New Member State' (2000) 38 Journal of Common Market Studies 223.

Faraguna P, 'Taking Constitutional Identities Away from the Courts' (2016) 42 Brooklyn Journal of International Law 491.

Ferreres Comella V, 'The Spanish Constitutional Court: Time for Reforms' (2008) 3 Journal of Comparative Law 22.

Fischer MG and Ladiges M, 'Evakuierungseinsätze der Bundeswehr künftig ohne Parlamentsvorbehalt' (2016) 35 Neue Zeitschrift für Verwaltungsrecht (NVwZ) 32.

Franzius C, '70 Jahre Grundgesetz und Europa: Passt das zusammen?' (2019) 54 Europarecht (EuR) 365.

Galetta D-U, 'European Union Law in the Jurisprudence of Italian High Courts: Is the Counter-Limits Doctrine a Dog That Barks but Does Not Bite?' (2015) 21 European Public Law 747.

Gärditz KF, 'Beyond Symbolism: Towards a Constitutional Actio Popularis in EU Affairs? A Commentary on the OMT Decision of the Federal Constitutional Court' (2014) 15 German Law Journal 183.

Garoupa N, Gomez-Pomar F and Grembi V, 'Judging under Political Pressure: An Empirical Analysis of Constitutional Review Voting in the Spanish Constitutional Court' (2011) 29 The Journal of Law, Economics, and Organization 513.

Geis M-E and Meier H, 'Grundfälle zum Organstreitverfahren, Art. 93 I Nr. 1 GG, §§ 13 Nr. 5, 63ff. BVerfGG' (2011) 51 Juristische Schulung (JuS) 699.

Ginter C and Narits R, 'The Perspective of a Small Member State to the Democratic Deficiency of the ESM' (2013) 38 Review of Central and East European Law 54.

Gött H, 'Die ultra vires-Rüge nach dem OMT-Vorlagebeschluss des Bundesverfassungsgerichts' (2014) 49 Zeitschrift Europarecht (EuR) 514.

Granat K, 'Kontrolle des EU-Sekundärrechts durch den polnischen Verfassungsgerichtshof: Anmerkung zum Beschluss des polnischen Verfassungsgerichtshofs vom 16. November 2011, SK 45/09' (2013) 48 Europarecht (EuR) 205.

Grawert R, 'Homogenität, Identität, Souveränität: Positionen jurisdiktioneller Begriffsdogmatik' (2012) 51 Der Staat 189.

Groß T, 'Erlaubt das Grundgesetz einen Austritt aus der EU?' (2018) 53 Europarecht (EuR) 387.

Hahn J-U, 'Die Mitwirkungsrechte von Bundestag und Bundesrat in EU-Angelegenheiten nach dem neuen Integrationsverantwortungsgesetz' (2009) 20 Europäische Zeitschrift für Wirtschaftsrecht (EuZW) 758.

Haltern U, 'Ultra-vires-Kontrolle im Dienst europäischer Demokratie' (2020) 39 Neue Zeitschrift für Verwaltungsrecht (NVwZ) 817.

Hamann A, 'Sur un "sentiment" de souveraineté' (2018) 20-21 Jus Politicum - Revue de droit politique 187.

Hautamäki V-P, 'Novel Rules in the Finnish Constitution: The Question of Applicability' (2007) 52 Scandinavian Studies in Law 133.

Heber C, 'Europarechtliche Grenzen für den Wiederaufbaufonds' (2021) 56 Europarecht (EuR) 416.

Herbst T, 'Legale Abschaffung des Grundgesetzes nach Art. 146 GG?' (2012) 45 Zeitschrift für Rechtspolitik (ZRP) 33.

Herrmann C, 'Die Bewältigung der Euro-Staatsschulden-Krise an den Grenzen des deutschen und europäischen Währverfassungsrechts' (2012) 23 Europäische Zeitschrift für Wirtschaftsrecht (EuZW) 805.

Hild A, Herz B and Bauer C, 'Structured Eurobonds: Limiting Liability and Distributing Profits' (2014) 52 Journal of Common Market Studies 250.

Hilpold P, 'Next Generation EU und die "Einnahmensouveränität": Das EU-Eigenmittelsystem vor dem BVerfG - Zugleich Bespr. von BVerfG 6.12.2022 - 2 BvR 547/21, 2 BvR 798/21' (2023) 34 Europäische Zeitschrift für Wirtschaftsrecht 169.

Hinarejos A, 'The Euro Area Crisis and Constitutional Limits to Fiscal Integration' (2012) 14 Cambridge Yearbook of European Legal Studies 243.

Hinarejos A, 'Fiscal Federalism in the European Union: Evolution and Future Choices for EMU' (2013) 50 Common Market Law Review 1621.

Höbel S, 'Polish and German Constitutional Jurisprudence on Matters of European Community Law: A Comparison of the Constitutional Courts' (2007) 3 Croatian Yearbook of European Law and Policy 515.

Hoecke MV, 'Methodology of Comparative Legal Research' (2015) Law and Method 1

Hooghe L and Marks G, 'Grand Theories of European Integration in the Twenty-First Century' (2019) 26 Journal of European Public Policy 1113.

Jaakkola J, 'A Democratic Dilemma of European Power to Tax: Reconstructing the Symbiosis Between Taxation and Democracy Beyond the State?' (2019) 20 German Law Journal 660.

Jager J and Hafner KA, 'The Optimum Currency Area Theory and the EMU: An Assessment in the Context of the Eurozone Crisis' (2013) 48 Intereconomics - Review of European Economic Policy 315.

Jaggi S, 'Revolutionary Constitutional Lawmaking in Germany: Rediscovering the German 1989 Revolution' (2016) 17 German Law Journal 579.

Jankovic S, 'Polish Democracy under Threat? An Issue of Mere Politics or a Real Danger?' (2016) 9 Baltic Journal of Law & Politics 49.

Kainer F, 'Aus der nationalen Brille: Das PSPP-Urteil des BVerfG' (2020) 31 Europäische Zeitschrift für Wirtschaftsrecht (EuZW) 533.

Kersten J, 'Parlamentarismus und Populismus' (2018) 58 Juristische Schulung (JuS) 929

Kirchhof P, 'Die Rechtsarchitektur der Europäischen Union' (2020) 73 Neue Juristische Wochenschrift (NJW) 2057.

Klein O and Sennekamp C, 'Aktuelle Zulässigkeitsprobleme der Verfassungsbeschwerde' (2007) 60 Neue Juristische Wochenschrift (NJW) 945.

Klotz C, 'Die Machtbalance zwischen Politik und verfassungsgerichtlicher Rechtsprechung' (2012) 45 Zeitschrift für Rechtspolitik (ZRP) 5.

Koncewicz TT, 'Of Institutions, Democracy, Constitutional Self-Defence and the Rule of Law: The Judgments of the Polish Constitutional Tribunal in Cases K 34/15, K 35/15 and Beyond' (2016) 53 Common Market Law Review 1753.

Koncewicz TT, 'The Capture of the Polish Constitutional Tribunal and Beyond: Of Institution(s), Fidelities and the Rule of Law in Flux' (2018) 43 Review of Central and East European Law 116.

Konertz P, 'Historische und philosophische Grundlagen der Rechtsordnung im Überblick: Am Beispiel von BGB, GG und StGB' (2019) 59 Juristische Schulung (JuS) 201.

König T and Hug S, 'Ratifying Maastricht: Parliamentary Votes on International Treaties and Theoretical Solution Concepts' (2000) 1 European Union Politics 93.

Kottmann M and Wohlfahrt C, 'Der gespaltene Wächter? Demokratie, Verfassungsidentität und Integrationsverantwortung im Lissabon-Urteil' (2009) 69 Zeitschrift für ausländisches öffentliches Recht und Völkerrecht (ZÄRV) 443.

Kowalik-Bańczyk K, 'Should We Polish It Up? The Polish Constitutional Tribunal and the Idea of Supremacy of EU Law' (2005) 6 German Law Journal 1355.

Kröger K, 'Die Entstehung des Grundgesetzes' (1989) 42 Neue Juristische Wochenschrift (NJW) 1318.

Krygier M, 'The Challenge of Institutionalisation: Post-Communist "Transitions", Populism, and the Rule of Law' (2019) 15 European Constitutional Law Review 544.

Kühn Z, 'Ultra Vires Review and the Demise of Constitutional Pluralism: The Czecho-Slovak Pension Saga, and the Dangers of State Court's Defiance of EU Law' (2016) 23 Maastricht Journal of European and Comparative Law 185.

Ladiges M, 'Grenzen des wehrverfassungsrechtlichen Parlamentsvorbehalts' (2010) 29 Neue Zeitschrift für Verwaltungsrecht (NVwZ) 1075.

Lang A, 'Ultra Vires Review of the ECB's Policy of Quantitative Easing: An Analysis of the German Constitutional Court's Preliminary Reference Order in the PSPP Case' (2018) 55 Common Market Law Review 923.

Larik J, 'Prêt-à-Ratifier: The CETA Decision of the French *Conseil constitutionnel* of 31 July 2017' (2017) 13 European Constitutional Law Review 759.

Lastra RM and Louis J-V, 'European Economic and Monetary Union: History, Trends, and Prospects' (2013) 32 Yearbook of European Law 57.

Lavapuro J, Ojanen T and Scheinin M, 'Rights-Based Constitutionalism in Finland and the Development of Pluralist Constitutional Review' (2011) 9 International Journal of Constitutional Law 505.

Łazowski A, 'Case Note: Accession Treaty – Polish Constitutional Tribunal: Conformity of the Accession Treaty with the Polish Contitution – Decision of 11 May 2005' (2007) 3 European Constitutional Law Review 148.

Łazowski A, 'Half Full and Half Empty Glass: The Application of EU Law in Poland (2004-2010)' (2011) 48 Common Market Law Review 503.

Leino-Sandberg P and Ruffert M, 'Next Generation EU and Its Constitutional Ramifications: A Critical Assessment' (2022) 59 Common Market Law Review 433.

Leino P and Salminen J, 'The Euro Crisis and Its Constitutional Consequences for Finland: Is There Room for National Politics in EU Decision-Making?' (2013) 9 European Constitutional Law Review 451.

Lorz RA and Sauer H, 'Verfassungsändernde Mehrheiten für die Stabilisierung des Euro?: Mehrheitserfordernisse bei der Zustimmung zum Fiskalpakt, zum ESM-Vertrag und zur Änderung des AEUV' (2012) 47 Europarecht (EuR) 682.

Louis J-V, 'The Economic and Monetary Union: Law and Institutions' (2004) 41 Common Market Law Review 575.

Ludwigs M, 'Der Ultra-vires-Vorbehalt des BVerfG: Judikative Kompetenzanmaßung oder legitimes Korrektiv' (2015) 34 Neue Zeitschrift für Verwaltungsrecht (NVwZ) 537.

Ludwigs M, 'Die Krisenpolitik der EZB zwischen Verfassungs- und Unionsrecht' (2017) 70 Neue Juristische Wochenschrift (NJW) 3563.

Madsen MR, Olsen HP and Šadl Uk, 'Competing Supremacies and Clashing Institutional Rationalities: The Danish Supreme Court's Decision in the Ajos Case and the National Limits of Judicial Cooperation' (2017) 23 European Law Journal 140.

Magnon X, 'Commentaire de Décisions: Décision n° 2017-749 DC du 31 juillet 2017, Accord économique et commercial global entre le Canada, d'une part, et l'Union européenne et ses États membres, d'autre part' (2018) 113 Revue française de droit constitutionnel 173.

Martínez-Herrera E and Miley TJ, 'The Constitution and the Politics of National Identity in Spain' (2010) 16 Nations and Nationalism 6.

Matczak M, 'Poland's Rule of Law Crisis: Some Thoughts' (2019) 11 Hague Journal on the Rule of Law 407.

Maugüé C, 'Le Conseil Constitutionnel et le droit supranational' (2003) 2 Le Seuil 53.

Mayer FC, 'Der Vertrag von Lissabon im Überblick' (2010) 50 Juristische Schulung (JuS) 189.

Mayer FC, 'Rashomon in Karlsruhe: A Reflection on Democracy and Identity in the European Union' (2011) 9 International Journal of Constitutional Law 757.

Mayer FC, 'Rebels Without a Cause? Zur OMT-Vorlage des Bundesverfassungsgerichts' (2014) 49 Europarecht (EuR) 473.

Mayer FC and Heidfeld C, 'Eurobonds, Schuldentilgungsfonds und Projektbonds: Eine dunkle Bedrohung?' (2012) 45 Zeitschrift für Rechtspolitik 129.

Mayer FC and Heidfeld C, 'Verfassungs- und europarechtliche Aspekte der Einführung von Eurobonds' (2012) 65 Neue Juristische Wochenschrift (NJW) 422.

Mayer FC, Lenski E and Wendel M, 'Der Vorrang des Europarechts in Frankreich: zugleich Anmerkungen zur Entscheidung des französischen Conseil d'Etat vom 8. Februar 2007 (Arcelor u.a.)' (2008) 43 Europarecht (EuR) 63.

Meinel F, 'The Constitutional Miracle on the Rhine: Towards a History of West German Constitutionalism and the Federal Constitutional Court' (2016) 14 International Journal of Constitutional Law 277.

Melin P, 'Die Rolle der deutschen Bundesländer im Europäischen Rechtsetzungsverfahren nach Lissabon' (2011) 46 Europarecht (EuR) 655.

Miller MC, 'Finnish Judges and the European Union: An American Perspective' (2016) 24 Michigan State International Law Journal 495.

Möllers TMJ and Redcay K, 'Das Bundesverfassungsgericht als europäischer Gesetzgeber oder als Motor der Union?' (2013) 48 Europarecht (EuR) 409.

Morlok M and Kühr H, 'Wahlrechtliche Sperrklauseln und die Aufgaben einer Volksvertretung' (2012) 52 Juristische Schulung (JuS) 385.

Murkens J, 'Identity Trumps Integration: The Lisbon Treaty in the German Federal Constitutional Court' (2009) 48 Der Staat 517.

Nägele C, 'German Constitutional Law Cases 2012-2015' (2016) 22 European Public Law 439.

Nettesheim M, 'Die Integrationsverantwortung: Vorgaben des BVerfG und gesetzgeberische Umsetzung' (2010) 63 Neue Juristische Wochenschrift (NJW) 177.

Nettesheim M, '"Euro-Rettung" und Grundgesetz: Verfassungsgerichtliche Vorgaben für den Umbau der Währungsunion' (2011) 46 Europarecht (EuR) 765.

Nettesheim M, 'Verfassungsrecht und Politik in der Staatsschuldenkrise' (2012) 65 Neue Juristische Wochenschrift (NJW) 1409.

Neuman GL, 'The Brakes That Failed: Constitutional Restriction of International Agreements in France' (2012) 45 Cornell International Law Journal 257.

Oeter S, 'Bundesstaat, Föderation, Staatenverbund: Trennlinien und Gemeinsamkeiten föderaler Systeme' (2015) 75 Zeitschrift für ausländisches öffentliches Recht und Völkerrecht (ZÄRV) 733.

Ohler C, 'Rechtliche Maßstäbe der Geldpolitik nach dem Gauweiler-Urteil des EuGH' (2015) 34 Neue Zeitschrift für Verwaltungsrecht (NVwZ) 1001.

Ojanen T, 'The Impact of EU Membership on Finnish Constitutional Law' (2004) 10 European Public Law 531.

Ojanen T, 'EU Law and the Response of the Constitutional Law Committee of the Finnish Parliament' (2007) 52 Scandinavian Studies in Law 203.

Ojanen T, 'The EU at the Finnish Constitutional Arena' (2013) 4 Tijdschrift voor Constitutioneel Recht 242.

Oliver P, 'The French Constitution and the Treaty of Maastricht' (1994) 43 International & Comparative Law Quarterly 1.

Pache E, 'Das Ende der europäischen Integration? Das Urteil des Bundesverfassungsgerichts zum Vertrag von Lissabon, zur Zukunft Europas und der Demokratie' (2009) 36 Europäische Grundrechte-Zeitschrift (EuGRZ) 285.

Pagoulatos G, 'EMU and the Greek Crisis: Testing the Extreme Limits of an Asymmetric Union' (2020) 42 Journal of European Integration 363.

Paris M-L, 'Europeanization and Constitutionalization: The Challenging Impact of a Double Transformative Process on French Law' (2010) 29 Yearbook of European Law 21.

Payandeh M, 'Constitutional Review of EU Law after Honeywell: Contextualizing the Relationship Between the German Constitutional Court and the EU Court of Justice' (2011) 48 Common Market Law Review 9.

Payandeh M, 'The OMT Judgment of the German Federal Constitutional Court: Repositioning the Court Within the European Constitutional Architecture' (2017) 13 European Constitutional Law Review 400.

Perez Ayala A, 'La Unión Europea y el Proceso de Revisión Constitucional en Francia (1992-2008)' (2009) 75-76 Revista de Derecho Político 409.

Pernice I, 'Multilevel Constitutionalism and the Treaty of Amsterdam: European Constitution-Making Revisited?' (1999) 36 Common Market Law Review 703.

Pfeiffer TM, 'Zur Verfassungsmäßigkeit des Gemeinschaftsrechts in der aktuellen Rechtsprechung des französischen Conseil constitutionnel' (2007) 67 Zeitschrift für ausländisches öffentliches Recht und Völkerrecht (ZÄRV) 469.

Pfersmann O, 'Concrete Review as Indirect Constitutional Complaint in French Constitutional Law: A Comparative Perspective' (2010) 6 European Constitutional Law Review 223.

Pieroth B, 'Das Demokratieprinzip des Grundgesetzes' (2010) 50 Juristische Schulung (JuS) 473.

Pilz S, 'Ein Schatzamt für die Eurozone? – Überlegungen zu den Vorschlägen des Europäischen Parlaments und der Kommission zu einer Reform der Wirtschaftsunion' (2017) 28 Europäische Zeitschrift für Wirtschaftsrecht (EuZW) 637.

Plaza C, 'The Constitution for Europe and the Spanish Constitutional Court' (2006) 12 European Public Law 353.

Pollard D, 'France's Conseil Constitutionnel: Not Yet a Constitutional Court?' (1988) 23 Irish Jurist 2.

Półtorak N and Dudzik S, '"The Court of the Last Word": Competences of the Polish Constitutional Tribunal in the Review of European Union Law' (2012) 15 Yearbook of Polish European Studies 225.

Polzin M, 'Constitutional Identity, Unconstitutional Amendments and the Idea of Constituent Power: The Development of the Doctrine of Constitutional Identity in German Constitutional Law' (2016) 14 International Journal of Constitutional Law 411.

Preuss U, 'The Implications of "Eternity Clauses": The German Experience' (2012) 44 Israel Law Review 429.

Puntscher Riekmann S and Wydra D, 'Representation in the European State of Emergency: Parliaments Against Governments?' (2013) 35 Journal of European Integration 565.

Rademacher T, 'Die "Verfassungsidentität" als Grenze der Kompetenzübertragung auf die Europäische Union?' (2018) 53 Europarecht (EuR) 140.

Raunio T, 'Refusing to Be Sidelined: The Engagement of the Finnish *Enduskunta* in Foreign Affairs' (2016) 39 Scandinavian Political Studies 312.

Rech W, 'Some Remarks on the EU's Action on the Erosion of the Rule of Law in Poland and Hungary' (2018) 26 Journal of Contemporary European Studies 334.

Reestman J-H, 'France: *Conseil Constitutionnel* on the Status of (Secondary) Community Law in the French Internal Order – Decision of 10 June 2004, 2004-496 DC' (2005) 1 European Constitutional Law Review 302.

Reestman J-H, 'The Franco-German Constitutional Divide: Reflections on National and Constitutional Identity' (2009) 5 European Constitutional Law Review 374.

Reestman J-H and Besselink LFM, 'Editorial: On the Lissabon-Urteil: Democracy and a Democratic Paradox' (2009) 5 European Constitutional Law Review 341.

Reimer F, 'Vertrauensfrage und Bundestagsauflösung bei parlamentarischer Anscheinsgefahr' (2005) 45 Juristische Schulung (JuS) 680.

Rochère JDdl, 'Conseil constitutionnel (French Constitutional Court), Decision No. 2004-496 of 10 June 2004, Loi Pour La Confiance Dans L'Économie Numérique (Ecommerce)' (2005) 42 Common Market Law Review 859.

Rosas A, 'Finland: Finland's Accession to the European Union: Constitutional Aspects' (1995) 1 European Public Law 166.

Roženský V, 'Mandatory Expenditure and the Flexibility of Fiscal Policy in the Czech Republic (in Czech: Mandatorní Výdaje A Flexibilita Fiskální Politiky V Čr)' (2012) 60 Politická ekonomie 40.

Ruffert M, 'Europarecht: Vorlagebeschluss des BVerfG zum OMT-Programm – Die Europarechtswidrigkeit des Kaufs von Staatsanleihen durch die EZB im Rahmen des OMT-Programms ist vom EuGH zu prüfen' (2014) 54 Juristische Schulung (JuS) 373.

Ruffert M, 'Europarecht für die nächste Generation: Zum Projekt Next Generation EU' (2020) 39 Neue Zeitschrift für Verwaltungsrecht (NVwZ) 1777.

Ruffert M, 'Europarecht und Verfassungsrecht: NextGenerationEU – Der Eigenmittelbeschluss zur Verwirklichung des Programms NextGenerationEU ist nicht offensichtlich unionsrechtswidrig' (2023) 63 Juristische Schulung (JuS) 277.

Ruffert M, Grischek F and Schramm M, 'Europarecht im Examen: Grundfragen und Organisationsstruktur' (2019) 59 Juristische Schulung (JuS) 974.

Rupp HG, 'Judicial Review of International Agreements: Federal Republic of Germany' (1977) 25 The American Journal of Comparative Law 286.

Sadurski W, 'Polish Constitutional Tribunal under PiS: From an Activist Court, to a Paralysed Tribunal, to a Governmental Enabler' (2019) 11 Hague Journal on the Rule of Law 63.

Salo S and Rydgren J, 'Politicisation of the Eurozone Crisis in Finland: Adaptation Toward the Radical Right?' (2018) 34 Journal of International and Comparative Social Policy 234.

Sauer H, 'Verfassungsvergleichung durch das Bundesverfassungsgericht – Zur Bedeutung der Verfassungsvergleichung für die Auslegung des Grundgesetzes' (2010) 18 Journal für Rechtspolitik 194.

Schäfer H-B and Bigus J, 'Consequences of Different Eurobonds Proposals' (2016) 12 Review of Law & Economics 523.

Schäfers D, 'Einführung in die Methodik der Gesetzesauslegung' (2015) 55 Juristische Schulung (JuS) 875.

Scheuer A and Schmitt H, 'Sources of EU Support: The Case of Germany' (2009) 18 German Politics 577.

Schoeller MG, 'Preventing the Eurozone Budget: Issue Replacement and Small State Influence in EMU' (2020) Journal of European Public Policy 1.

Schönberger C, 'Die Europäische Union zwischen "Demokratiedefizit" und Bundestaatsverbot – Anmerkungen zum Lissabon-Urteil des Bundesverfassungsgerichts' (2009) 48 Der Staat 535.

Schorkopf F, 'Case Nos. 2 BvE 2/08, 2 BvE 5/08, 2 BvR 1010/08, 2 BvR 1022/08, 2 BvR 1259/08, and 2 BvR 182/09 – 123 BVerfGE 267 (2009)' (2010) 104 The American Journal of International Law 259.

Schorkopf F, 'Die Europäische Union auf dem Weg zur Fiskalunion – Integrationsfortschritt durch den Rechtsrahmen des Sonderhaushalts "Next Generation EU"' (2020) 73 Neue Juristische Wochenschrift (NJW) 3085.

Schratzenstaller M, 'The EU Own Resources System: Reform Needs and Options' (2013) 48 Intereconomics – Review of European Economic Policy 303.

Schratzenstaller M and Krenek A, 'Tax-Based Own Resources to Finance the EU Budget' (2019) 54 Intereconomics – Review of European Economic Policy 171.

Schröder UJ, 'Das Demokratieprinzip des Grundgesetzes' (2017) 49 Juristische Arbeitsblätter (JA) 809.

Schwarze J, 'Die verordnete Demokratie: Zum Urteil des 2. Senats des BVerfG zum Lissabon-Vertrag' (2010) 45 Europarecht (EuR) 108.

Schwerdtfeger A, 'Europäisches Unionsrecht in der Rechtsprechung des Bundesverfassungsgerichts: Grundrechts-, ultra-vires- und Identitätskontrolle im gewaltenteiligen Mehrebenensystem' (2015) 50 Europarecht (EuR) 290.

Schyff GVd, 'Exploring Member State and European Union Constitutional Identity' (2016) 22 European Public Law 227.

Schyff Gvd and Leenknegt G-J, 'The Case for a European Senate: A Model for the Representation of National Parliaments in the European Union' (2007) 62 Zeitschrift für öffentliches Recht (ZöR) 237.

Sluis Mvd, 'A Euro Area Budget: Another Seedling?' 2019) Maastricht Law – Faculty of Law Working Paper Series 18.

Sokolov E, 'Wege zur Partizipation für Inländer: Volksbegriff und Einbürgerung im Lichte des Demokratieprinzips' (2016) 35 Neue Zeitschrift für Verwaltungsrecht (NVwZ) 649.

Spieker LD, 'Breathing Life into the Union's Common Values: On the Judicial Application of Article 2 TEU in the EU Value Crisis' (2019) 20 German Law Journal 1182.

Spieker LD, 'Framing and Managing Constitutional Identity Conflicts: How to Stabilize *Modus Vivendi* Between the Court of Justice and Constitutional Courts' (2020) 57 Common Market Law Review 361.

Steinbach A, 'All's Well That Ends Well? Crisis Policy after the German Constitutional Court's Ruling in Gauweiler' (2017) 24 Maastricht Journal of European and Comparative Law 140.

Steinbach A, 'Insurance-Type Cooperation Mechanisms under EU Law' (2017) 27 Swiss Review of International and European Law 19.

Steinbach A and Grund S, 'Der EU-Corona-Aufbaufonds: nächste Etappe in die Fiskal- und Transferunion?' (2023) 76 Neue Juristische Wochenschrift (NJW) 406.

Steuerle CE, 'America's Related Fiscal Problems' (2010) 29 Journal of Policy Analysis and Management 876.

Terhechte JP, 'Souveränität, Dynamik und Integration: Making up the Rules as We Go Along? – Anmerkungen zum Lissabon-Urteil des Bundesverfassungsgerichts' (2009) 20 Europäische Zeitschrift für Wirtschaftsrecht (EuZW) 724.

Thiele A, 'Friendly or Unfriendly Act? The "Historic" Referral of the Constitutional Court to the ECJ Regarding the ECB's OMT Program' (2014) 15 German Law Journal 241.

Thiele A, 'Der Austritt aus der EU: Hintergründe und rechtliche Rahmenbedingungen eines "Brexit"' (2016) 51 Europarecht (EuR) 281.

Thiele A, 'Die Integrationsidentität des Art. 23 Abs. 1 GG als (einzige) Grenze des Vorrangs des Europarechts' (2017) 52 Europarecht (EuR) 367.

Thym D, 'Europäische Integration im Schatten souveräner Staatlichkeit: Anmerkungen zum Lissabon-Urteil des Bundesverfassungsgerichts' (2009) 48 Der Staat 559.

Tiilikainen T, 'Finland: An EU Member State with a Small State Identity' (2006) 28 Journal of European Integration 73.

Tomuschat C, 'Lisbon: Terminal of the European Integration Process? The Judgment of the German Constitutional Court of 30 June 2009' (2010) 70 Zeitschrift für ausländisches öffentliches Recht und Völkerrecht (ZÄRV) 251.

Torres Pérez A, 'Constitutional Dialogue on the European Arrest Warrent: The Spanish Constitutional Court Knocking on Luxembourg's Door; Spanish Constitutional Court, Order of 9 June 2011, ATC 86/2011' (2012) 8 European Constitutional Law Review 105.

Tridimas T and Xanthoulis N, 'A Legal Analysis of the Gauweiler Case: Between Monetary Policy and Constitutional Conflict' (2016) 23 Maastricht Journal of European and Comparative Law 17.

Urbaneck P, 'Die Zulässigkeitsprüfung im Verfassungsrecht' (2014) 54 Juristische Schulung (JuS) 896.

Vinx L, 'The Incoherence of Strong Popular Sovereignty' (2013) 11 International Journal of Constitutional Law 101.

Voßkuhle A, 'Grundwissen – Öffentliches Recht: Der Grundsatz des Vorbehalts des Gesetzes' (2007) 47 Juristische Schulung (JuS) 118.

Voßkuhle A, 'Verfassungsgerichtsbarkeit und europäische Integration' (2013) 32 Neue Zeitschrift für Verwaltungsrecht (NVwZ) 27.

Voßkuhle A, 'Der Wandel der Verfassung und seine Grenzen' (2019) 59 Juristische Schulung (JuS) 417.

Voßkuhle A and Kaiser A-B, 'Grundwissen: Öffentliches Recht – Demokratische Legitimation' (2009) 49 Juristische Schulung (JuS) 803.

Vranes E, 'Constitutional Foundation of, and Limitations to, EU Integration in France' (2013) 19 European Public Law 525.

Vranes E, 'German Constitutional Foundations of, and Limitations to, EU Integration: A Systematic Analysis' (2013) 14 German Law Journal 75.

Wasserfallen F, 'Political and Economic Integration in the EU: The Case of Failed Tax Harmonization' (2014) 52 Journal of Common Market Studies 420.

Weber A, 'Die Reform der Wirtschafts- und Währungsunion in der Finanzkrise' (2011) 22 Europäische Zeitschrift für Wirtschaftsrecht 935.

Weiler JHH, 'The "Lisbon Urteil" and the Fast Food Culture' (2009) 20 The European Journal of International Law 505.

Weiß W, 'Die Integrationsverantwortung der Verfassungsorgane' (2018) 58 Juristische Schulung (JuS) 1046.

Wendel M, 'Lisbon Before the Courts: Comparative Perspectives' (2011) 7 European Constitutional Law Review 96.

Wendel M, 'Comparative Reasoning and the Making of a Common Constitutional Law: EU-Related Decisions of National Constitutional Courts in a Transnational Perspective' (2013) 11 International Journal of Constitutional Law 981.

Wendel M, 'Exceeding Judicial Competence in the Name of Democracy: The German Federal Constitutional Court's OMT Reference' (2014) 10 European Constitutional Law Review 263.

Wendel M, 'Kompetenzrechtliche Grenzgänge: Karlsruhes *Ultra-vires*-Vorlage an den EuGH' (2014) 74 Zeitschrift für ausländisches öffentliches Recht und Völkerrecht (ZÄRV) 615.

Wendel M, 'Mutual Trust, Essence and Federalism: Between Consolidating and Fragmenting the Area of Freedom, Security and Justice after LM' (2019) 15 European Constitutional Law Review 17.

Wendel M, 'The Fog of Identity and Judicial Contestation: Preventive and Defensive Constitutional Identity Review in Germany' (2021) 27 European Public Law 465.

Wood S, 'Germany and the Eastern Enlargement of the EU: Political Elites, Public Opinion and Democratic Processes' (2002) 24 Journal of European Integration 23.

Wouters J, 'Revisiting Art. 2 TEU: A True Union of Values?' (2020) 5 European Papers 255

Wright S, 'The French *Conseil Constitutionnel* under an Evolving Constitution' (2017) 23 European Public Law 245.

Wróbel A, 'Die Grenzen der europäischen Integration im Lichte jüngerer Entscheidungen des polnischen Verfassungsgerichts' (2013) 13 ERA Forum – Journal of the Academy of European Law 491.

Würtenberger T and Kunz E, 'Die Mitwirkung der Bundesländer in Angelegenheiten der Europäischen Union' (2010) 42 Juristische Arbeitsblätter (JA) 406.

Wyplosz C, 'The Six Flaws of the Eurozone' (2016) 31 Economic Policy 559.

Wyrzykowski M, 'Experiencing the Unimaginable: the Collapse of the Rule of Law in Poland' (2019) 11 Hague Journal on the Rule of Law 417.

Ziller J, 'The German Constitutional Court's Friendliness Towards European Law: On the Judgment of *Bundesverfassungsgericht* over the Ratification of the Treaty of Lisbon' (2010) 16 European Public Law 53.

Ziller J, 'European Union Law in the Jurisprudence of French Supreme Courts: Europe-Friendliness with a French Touch' (2015) 21 European Public Law 765.

Zwingmann B, 'The Continuing Myth of Euro-Scepticism? The German Federal Constitutional Court Two Years after *Lisbon*' (2012) 61 International & Comparative Law Quarterly (ICLQ) 665.

Newspaper Articles and Online Sources

Arnold M and Romei V, 'Eurozone Economy Shrinks by Fastest Rate on Record' *Financial Times* (London 30 April 2020), https://www.ft.com/content/dd6cfafa-a56d-48f3-a9fd-aa71d17d49a8, accessed 5 April 2023.

Bank TW, 'GDP (Current US$): Euro Area' (*The World Bank*, 2020), https://data.worldbank.org/indicator/NY.GDP.MKTP.CD?end=2019&locations=XC&start=2006&view=chart, accessed 5 April 2023.

Barber T, 'Eurozone Reform Deadlock Reflects Deep Malaise Over Integration: The Fiscal Stalemate Derives in Part from the Frictions in Franco-German Relations' *Financial Times* (London 26 December 2019), https://www.ft.com/content/8ffa04c6-1815-11ea-8d73-6303645ac406, accessed 5 April 2023.

Chassany A-S, Chazan G and Khan M, 'Impatient Macron Pushes Merkel Hard on Eurozone Reform' *Financial Times* (London 16 March 2018), https://www.ft.com/content/8c521504-2904-11e8-b27e-cc62a39d57a0, accessed 5 April 2023.

D'Alfonso A and Stuchlik A, *A Fiscal Capacity for the Euro Area?* (European Parliament 2016).

Deloy C, 'General Elections in Hungary: Viktor Orban Easily Sweeps to Victory for the Third Time Running in the Hungarian Elections' (*Foundation Robert Schuman*, 10 April 2018), https://www.robert-schuman.eu/en/doc/oee/oee-1765-en.pdf, accessed 5 April 2023.

Delpla J and von Weizsäcker J, 'The Blue Bond Proposal (2010)' Bruegel Policy Brief, https://www.bruegel.org/wp-content/uploads/imported/publications/1005-PB-Blue_Bonds.pdf, accessed 5 April 2023.

Fasone C, 'Constitutional Courts Facing the Euro Crisis: Italy, Portugal, and Spain in a Comparative Perspective (2014)' EUI Working Papers (Max Weber Programme), https://cadmus.eui.eu/bitstream/handle/1814/33859/MWP_WP_2014_25.pdf?sequence=1&isAllowed=y, accessed 5 April 2023.

Großner C and Lawton S, 'Merkel and Macron Roll Out €500 Billion COVID-19 Recovery Initiative' *EURACTIV* (Schiphol 19 May 2020), https://www.euractiv.com/section/economy-jobs/news/merkel-and-macron-roll-out-e500-billion-covid-19-recovery-initiative/, accessed 5 April 2023.

Kammer A, 'Europe Must Address a Toxic Mix of High Inflation and Flagging Growth' (2022), https://www.imf.org/en/Blogs/Articles/2022/10/23/europe-must-address-a-toxic-mix-of-high-inflation-and-flagging-growth, accessed 5 April 2023.

Khan M and Peel M, '"Frugal Four" Fight to Protect EU Budget Rebates' *Financial Times* (London 18 August 2020), https://www.ft.com/content/55f6796e-4a9f-43b2-8d94-da0804d1f83b, accessed 5 April 2023.

Leino P and Salminen J, *Constitutional Change Through Euro Crisis Law: 'Finland'* (European University Institute – Law Department Project, 2014).

Leino-Sandberg P, 'Who Is Ultra Vires Now? The EU's Legal U-Turn in Interpreting Article 310 TFEU' (*Verfassungsblog*, 18 June 2020), https://verfassungsblog.de/who-is-ultra-vires-now-the-eus-legal-u-turn-in-interpreting-article-310-tfeu/, accessed 5 April 2023.

Leino-Sandberg P, 'Between European Commitment and "Taking the Law Seriously"' (*Verfassungsblog*, 2021), https://verfassungsblog.de/between-european-commitment-and-taking-the-law-seriously/, accessed 5 April 2023.

Marzinotto B, Sapir A and Wolff GB, 'What Kind of Fiscal Union? (2011)' Bruegel Policy Brief, https://www.bruegel.org/2011/11/what-kind-of-fiscal-union/, accessed 5 April 2023.

Oscar A, Gerrit K and Nickel C, 'One Year since Russia's Invasion of Ukraine: The Effects on Euro Area Inflation' (2023), https://www.ecb.europa.eu/press/blog/date/2023/html/ecb.blog20230224~3b75362af3.en.html, accessed 5 April 2023.

Pancevski B and Norman L, 'France, Germany Propose €500 Billion EU Pandemic Recovery Fund' *The Wall Street Journal* (New York City 18 May 2020), https://www.wsj.com/articles/france-germany-propose-500-billion-eu-pandemic-recovery-fund-11589826351, accessed 5 April 2023.

Petersen T, Böhmer M and Stein Hv, 'How Germany Benefits from the Euro in Economic Terms (Policy Brief # 2013/01)' (*Bertelsmann Stiftung*, 2013), https://www.bertelsmann-stiftung.de/fileadmin/files/BSt/Presse/imported/downloads/xcms_bst_dms_37730_37731_2.pdf, accessed 5 April 2023.

Rakic D, 'Monetary Policy Issues in the Context of the War in Ukraine (Briefing ECON in focus)' (2022), http://www.europarl.europa.eu/RegData/etudes/BRIE/2022/703361/IPOL_BRI(2022)703361_EN.pdf, accessed 5 April 2023.

Streeck W and Mertens D, 'An Index of Fiscal Democracy (2010)' MPIfG Working Paper, https://www.mpifg.de/pu/workpap/wp10-3.pdf, accessed 5 April 2023.

Suvanto A and others, *Improving the Resilience of Europe's Economic and Monetary Union (37b/2015)* (Finnish Ministry of Finance Publications, 2015).

Utrilla D, 'Insight: "The European Deal for Post-Pandemic Economic Recovery: Content and Meaning"' (*EU Law Live,* 21 July 2020), https://eulawlive.com/the-european-deal-for-post-pandemic-economic-recovery-content-and-meaning/, accessed 5 April 2023.

Walker A, 'Eurozone Suffers Double-Dip Recession as Pandemic Impact Continues' (2021), https://www.bbc.com/news/business-56940720, accessed 5 April 2023.

Zalan E, 'EU Set for Record Recession, Putting Euro at Risk' *EU-Observer* (Brussels 7 May 2020), https://euobserver.com/coronavirus/148283, accessed 5 April 2023.

Official Documents

(BMWi) FMfEAaE, *Facts about German Foreign Trade* (German Government 2019).

Bundeskanzlerin, *Press Release 173/20: A French-German Initiative for the European Recovery from the Coronavirus Crisis* (Presse- und Informationsamt der Bundesregierung 18 May 2020).

Bundestages WDdD, *Zum Erfordernis eines qualifizierten Mehrheitsbeschlusses des Bundestages hinsichtlich des Zustimmungsgesetzes zum Eigenmittelbeschluss der EU (WD 4 – 3000 – 055/20)* (German Parliament 2020).

Commission E, *Green Paper on the Feasibility of Introducing Stability Bonds (COM (2011) 818)* (European Commission 2011).

Commission E, *Communication from the Commission to the European Parliament and the Council: A Roadmap Towards a Banking Union (COM (2012) 510)* (European Commission 2012).

Commission E, *Completing Europe's Economic and Monetary Union: A European Minister of Economy and Finance* (European Commission 2017).

Commission E, *Reflection Paper on the Deepening of the Economic and Monetary Union* (European Commission 2017).

Commission E, *White Paper on the Future of Europe: Reflections and Scenarios for the EU27 by 2025* (European Commission 2017).

Commission E, *Commission Staff Working Document: Impact Assessment: Accompanying the Document for Proposal for a Regulation of the European Parliament and of the Council on the Establishment of a European Investment Stabilisation Function (COM (2018) 297)* (European Commission 2018).

Commission E, *Communication from the Commission to the European Parliament, the European Council, the Council, the European Economic and Social Committee and the Committee of the Regions: A Modern Budget for a Union That Protects, Empowers and Defends The Multiannual Financial Framework for 2021-2027 (COM (2018) 321)* (European Commission 2018).

Commission E, *EU Expenditure and Revenue 2014-2020 (Dataset)* (DG Budget data 2020)

Council E, *Conclusions Special Meeting of the European Council (17, 18, 19, 20 and 21 July 2020): EUCO 10/20* (General Secretariat of the Council 2020).

Diputados SCdl, *Dictamen de la Comisión de Asuntos Exteriores (110/000176): Decisión del Consejo de 26 de mayo de 2014 sobre el sistema de recursos propios de la Unión Europea (2014/335/UE, EURATOM), adoptada en Bruselas el 26 de mayo de 2014* (Boletín Oficial de las Cortes Generales 2015).

Eurogroup, *Term Sheet on the Budgetary Instrument for Convergence and Competitiveness* (Eurogroup 2019).

Europe MftDo, *Draft Treaty on the Democratization of the Governance of the Euro Area ('T-Dem')* (2020).

FDP GPFoCCa, *Entwurf eines Gesetzes zu dem Beschluss des Europäischen Rates vom 25. März 2011 zur Änderung des Artikels 136 des Vertrags über die Arbeitsweise der Europäischen Union hinsichtlich eines Stabilitätsmechanismus für die Mitgliedstaaten, deren Währung der Euro ist (Drucksache 17/9047)* (German Parliament 2012).

FDP PFoCCu, *Drucksache 17/9046: Gesetzentwurf der Fraktionen der CDU/CSU und FDP: Entwurf eines Gesetzes zu dem Vertrag vom 2. März 2012 über Stabilität, Koordinierung und Steuerung in der Wirtschafts- und Währungsunion* (German Parliament 2012).

Finance GFMo, *Bundeshaushalt 2019* (German Government 2019).

Government G, *Unterrichtung durch die Bundesregierung: Finanzplan des Bundes 2018 bis 2022 (Drucksache 19/3401)* (German Government 2018).

Juncker J-C et al., *The Five Presidents' Report: Completing Europe's Economic and Monetary Union* (European Commission 2015).

Meeting F-GM, *Erklärung von Meseberg: Das Versprechen Europas für Sicherheit und Wohlstand erneuern* (German Government 2018).

Summit E, *Statement of the Euro Summit, 14 December 2018 (EURO 503/18)* (General Secretariat of the Council 2018).

Bundestages WDdD, *Reichweite der Wesentlichkeitslehre: Grenzfälle der Wesentlichkeit (WD 3 – 3000 – 043/15)* (Deutscher Bundestag, 2015).

Monti M et al., *Future Financing of the EU: Final Report and Recommendations of the High Level Group on Own Resources December 2016* (EU High Level Group on Own Resources (HLGOR), 2016).

Commission Decision on Establishing an Independent Advisory European Fiscal Board (COM 2015/1937).

Commission Proposal for a Regulation of the European Parliament and of the Council on the establishment of a European Monetary Fund (COM (2017) 827).

Commission Proposal for a Regulation of the European Parliament and of the Council on the Governance Framework for the Budgetary Instrument for Convergence and Competitiveness for the Euro Area (COM (2019) 354).

Commission Proposal for a Regulation of the European Parliament and of the Council establishing a Recovery and Resilience Facility (COM (2020) 408).

European Parliament Resolution of 20 November 2012 with Recommendations to the Commission on the Report of the Presidents of the European Council, the European Commission, the European Central Bank and the Eurogroup 'Towards a Genuine Economic and Monetary Union' (2012/2151(INI)) (2012).

Bank TW, 'GDP (Current US$): Euro Area' (*The World Bank*, 2020), https://data.worldbank.org/indicator/NY.GDP.MKTP.CD?end=2019&locations=XC&start=2006&view=chart, accessed 5 April 2023.

Commission E, 'European Economic Forecast: Spring 2020' (*Publication Office of the European Union*, 2020), https://ec.europa.eu/info/sites/info/files/economy-finance/ip125_en.pdf, accessed 5 April 2023.

Commission E, 'SURE: Supporting Member States to Help Protect People in Work and Jobs' (*European Commission*, 2020), https://ec.europa.eu/info/sites/info/files/economy-finance/sure_factsheet.pdf, accessed 5 April 2023.

Finance GFMo, 'Haushaltsrechnung des Bundes für das Haushaltsjahr 2012' (*German Government*, 2013), https://www.bundesfinanzministerium.de/Content/DE/Standardartikel/Themen/Oeffentliche_Finanzen/Bundeshaushalt/Haushalts_und_Vermoegensrechnungen_des_Bundes/2013-06-13-haushaltsrechnung-des-bundes-2012.pdf?__blob=publicationFile&v=1, accessed 5 April 2023.

Ministres FCd, 'Annex au Project de Loi de Finances pour 2021 (Jaune Budgétaire): Relations Financières avec l'Union Européenne' (*French Conseil des Ministres*, 2020), https://www.budget.gouv.fr/documentation/file-download/6871, accessed 5 April 2023.

Moens De Fernig M, 'Factsheet: The Polish Sejm' (*European Parliament – Directorate-General for the Presidency*, 2018), http://www.epgencms.europarl.europa.eu/cmsdata/upload/0398faee-9664-4eb0-8e1b-ac615ab65a49/Factsheet_PL_-_Sejm.pdf, accessed 5 April 2023.

Parliament F, 'HE 248/2014 on the Government Proposal to Parliament on the Adoption of the Council Decision on the System of the European Union's Own Resources (2014/335 / EU, Euratom)' (*Finnish Parliament*, 2014), https://www.finlex.fi/fi/esitykset/he/2014/20140248#idp446520544, accessed 5 April 2023.

Publications EO, 'Government Finance Statistics' (*Eurostat*, 2020), https://ec.europa.eu/eurostat/statistics-explained/pdfscache/1137.pdf, accessed 5 April 2023.

Table of Constitutional Decisions and Case-Law

1951

Survivor's Pension I 1 BvR 220/51 (German Federal Constitutional Court), 67

1955

Law on Direct (Financial) Support 1 BvL 13/52, 1 BvL 21/53 (German Federal Constitutional Court), 60

1966

Party-Financing I 2 BvF 1/65 (German Federal Constitutional Court), 87

Introduction of the EU's System of Own Resources Decision 70-39 DC (French Conseil Constitutionnel), 275

1970

Wiretapping I 2 BvF 1/69, 2 BvR 629/68 und 308/69 (German Federal Constitutional Court), 79

1973

Frontini Judgment of 27. December 1973 – No. 183 (Italian Constitutional Court), 11

Treaty Concerning the Basis of Relations Between the Federal Republic of Germany and the German Democratic Republic 2 BvF 1/73 (German Federal Constitutional Court), 61

1974

Solange I-Decision BvL 52/71 (German Federal Constitutional Court), 11

1976

Direct Election of the European Parliament Decision 76-71 DC (French Conseil Constitutionnel), 136

1977

Concerning the Introduction of an Isoglucose Levy Decision 77-90 DC (French Conseil Constitutionnel), 275

1978

Peaceful Use of Nuclear Energy in Germany 2 BvL 8/77 (German Federal Constitutional Court), 90

1979

Nuclear Plant Mülheim-Kärlich 1 BvR 385/77 (German Federal Constitutional Court), 67

1982

Non-Contributory Health Insurance 1 BvR 602/78 (German Federal Constitutional Court), 67

1983

Dissolution of the German Parliament 2 BvQ 4/82 (German Federal Constitutional Court), 70

1984

Committee of Enquiry in the Flick-Matter 2 BvE 11, 15/83 (German Federal Constitutional Court), 72
Deployment of Nuclear Weapons 2 BvE 13/83 (German Federal Constitutional Court), 74
Granital Judgment of 8 June 1984 (Italian Constitutional Court), 11
Solange II-Decision 2 BvR 197/83 (German Federal Constitutional Court), 58

1987

Deployment of Chemical Weapons 2 BvR 624, 1080, 2029/83 (German Federal Constitutional Court), 90

1989

Public Debt Level 2 BvF 1/82 (German Federal Constitutional Court), 102

1990

Constitutionality of Establishing a Marketing Fund 2 BvL 12, 13/88, 2 BvR 1436/87 (German Federal Constitutional Court), 102
Right to Vote for Foreigners I 2 BvF 2, 6/89 (German Federal Constitutional Court), 86
Right to Vote for Foreigners II 2 BvF 3/89 (German Federal Constitutional Court), 85

1991

Spanish Rules on the Elections to the European Parliament Sentencia 28/1991 (Spanish Constitutional Tribunal), 160

1992

Compatibility of the Maastricht Treaty with the French Constitution after Constitutional Amendments ('Maastricht II') Decision 92-312 DC (French Conseil Constitutionnel), 138

Constitutional Review of the Maastricht Treaty Declaration 1/1992 (Spanish Constitutional Tribunal), 154

Review of Maastricht Treaty (Maastricht I) Decision 92-308 DC (French Conseil Constitutionnel), 9

1993

Interest-Rate Adjustment for Mortgage Awarded by the GDR 1 BvR 1509/91 (German Federal Constitutional Court), 67

Maastricht-Judgment 2 BvR 2134/92 and 2159/92 (German Federal Constitutional Court), 58

German Participation in NATO Actions 2 BvE 3/92, 5/93, 7/93, 8/93 (German Federal Constitutional Court), 73

1997

Revision of Amsterdam Treaty Decision 97-394 DC (French Conseil Constitutionnel), 129

1998

Bavarian Municipal Elections 2 BvR 1953/95 (German Federal Constitutional Court), 86

German Spelling Reform 1 BvR 1640/97 (German Federal Constitutional Court), 91

1999

Conditions for the Keeping of Laying Hens 2 BvF 3/90 (German Federal Constitutional Court), 91

2000

Casino-Regulation of the German Region of Baden-Württemberg 1 BvR 539/96 (German Federal Constitutional Court), 67

2001

NATO-Concept 2 BvE 6/99 (German Federal Constitutional Court), 74

2003

Obligatory Information Concerning Extra Public Charge 2 BvL 1, 4, 6, 16, 18/99, 2 BvL 1/01 (German Federal Constitutional Court), 102

2004

Digital Economy Decision 2004-496 DC (French Conseil Constitutionnel), 144

Treaty Establishing a Constitution for Europe Declaration 1/2004 (Spanish Constitutional Tribunal), 11, 128, 156, 159, 162, 164, 166, 167, 197, 198, 201, 249, 255, 277, 289, 321
Wiretapping II 1 BvR 2378/98 and 1 BvR 1084/99 (German Federal Constitutional Court), 79

2005

Poland's EU Membership K 18/04 (Polish Constitutional Tribunal), 168

2006

Copyright and Related Rights in the Information Society Decision 2006-540 DC (French Conseil Constitutionnel), 128–129
French Act Pertaining to the Energy Sector Decision 2006-543 DC (French Conseil Constitutionnel), 143

2007

Constitutional Complaint Against Protocol No. 4 to the European Agreement SK 54/05 (Polish Constitutional Tribunal), 173
Lisbon Treaty Decision 2007-560 DC (French Conseil Constitutionnel), 127
Statute on the Federal Supplementary Budget 2 BvF 1/04 (German Federal Constitutional Court), 102

2008

Adoption of the Lisbon Treaty PeVL 13/2008 vp (Finnish Constitutional Law Committee), 45
French Law on Genetically Modified Organisms Decision 2008-564 DC (French Conseil Constitutionnel), 128

2009

Copyright-Law Amendment I 1 BvR 213/08 (German Federal Constitutional Court), 67
Lisbon-judgment 2 BvE 2/08 (German Federal Constitutional Court), 9

2010

Act Pertaining to the Opening Up to Competition and the Regulation of Online Betting and Gambling Decision 2010-605 DC (French Conseil Constitutionnel), 128
Honeywell Judgment 2 BvR 2661/06 (German Federal Constitutional Court), 39
Mr Daniel W and Others Decision 2010-14/22 QPC (French Conseil Constitutionnel), 132
Mr Kamel D. Decision 2010-79 QPC (French Conseil Constitutionnel), 145
Treaty of Lisbon K 32/09 (Polish Constitutional Tribunal), 7

2011

Amendment of Article 136 (3) TFEU PeVL 6/2011 vp (Finnish Constitutional Law Committee), 31

Amendment to the EFSF (Increase in State Guarantee) PeVL 5/2011 vp (Finnish Constitutional Law Committee), 31

Constitutional Complaint Against Brussels I Regulation SK 45/09 (Polish Constitutional Tribunal), 177

Financial Support for Greece and EFSF 2 BvR 987/10, 2 BvR 1485/10, 2 BvR 1099/10 (German Federal Constitutional Court), 58

First Assessment Draft ESM-Treaty (I.) PeVL 1/2011 vp (Finnish Constitutional Law Committee), 31

N.S. and M.E. et al. v. Minister for Justice, Equality and Law Reform Joined Cases C-411/10 and C-493/10 (CJEU), 176

Preliminary Reference Concerning EAW (Melloni) AUTO 86/2011 (Spanish Constitutional Tribunal), 152

Protocol on the EFSF PeVP 11/2011 vp (Finnish Constitutional Law Committee), 31

Second Assessment Draft ESM-Treaty (II.) PeVL 22/2011 vp (Finnish Constitutional Law Committee), 31

2012

Additional Amendment to the EFSF PeVL 3/2012 vp (Finnish Constitutional Law Committee), 31

ESM-Treaty and Fiscal Compact (interim relief) 2 BvR 1390, 1421, 1438, 1439, 1440/12, 2 BvE 6/12 (German Federal Constitutional Court), 58

Final Assessment Draft ESM-Treaty (III.) PeVL 13/2012 vp (Finnish Constitutional Law Committee), 31

Final Assessment of Fiscal Compact (II.) PeVL 37/2012 vp (Finnish Constitutional Law Committee), 31

New Allocation of Seats in the German Parliament 2 BvF 3/11, 2 BvR 2670/11, 2 BvE 9/11 (German Federal Constitutional Court), 87

Participation of Members of German Parliament in the EFSF 2 BvE 8/11 (German Federal Constitutional Court), 58

Preliminary Assessment of Fiscal Compact (I.) PeVL 24/2011 vp (Finnish Constitutional Law Committee), 31

Pringle C-370/12 (CJEU).

Right to Participation for German Parliament at the Occasion of ESM-Treaty and Euro-Plus-Pact 2 BvE 4/11 (German Federal Constitutional Court), 58

2013

Challenge Against the Fiscal Compact K 11/13 (Polish Constitutional Tribunal), 173

Challenges Against Article 136 (3) TFEU and ESM-Treaty K 33/12 (Polish Constitutional Tribunal), 175

2014

Constitutional Complaint Melloni Sentencia 26/2014 (Spanish Constitutional Tribunal), 157

ESM-Treaty and Fiscal Compact 2 BvR 1390, 1421, 1438, 1439, 1440/12, 2 BvE 6/12 (German Federal Constitutional Court), 58

OMT-Reference 2 BvR 2728/13, 2 BvR 2729/13, 2 BvR 2730/13, 2 BvR 2731/13, 2 BvE 13/13 (German Federal Constitutional Court), 58

2015

Appointment of Constitutional Judges K 34/15 (Polish Constitutional Tribunal), 186
Relation Between International Law and the German Legal Order 2 BvL 1/12 (German Federal Constitutional Court), 88
Vereinten Dienstleistungsgewerkschaft (ver.di) 2 BvR 2292/13 (German Federal Constitutional Court), 67

2016

Catalan Independence Declaration Sentencia 259/2015 (Spanish Constitutional Tribunal), 166
Final OMT-Judgment 2 BvR 2728/13, 2 BvR 2729/13, 2 BvR 2730/13, 2 BvR 2731/13, 2 BvE 13/13 (German Federal Constitutional Court), 7, 58
Interim Relief Against Comprehensive Economic and Trade Agreement (CETA) 2 BvR 1368/16, 2 BvR 1444/16, 2 BvR 1482/16, 2 BvR 1823/16 and 2 BvE 3/16 (German Federal Constitutional Court), 71
Opposition Rights in the German Parliament 2 BvE 4/14 (German Federal Constitutional Court), 73, 74
Transatlantic Trade and Investment Partnership (TTIP) 2 BvR 1368/16, 2 BvR 1444/16, 2 BvR 1482/16, 2 BvR 1823/16, 2 BvE 3/16 (German Federal Constitutional Court), 71

2017

Comprehensive Economic and Trade Agreement (CETA) Decision 2017-749 DC (French Conseil Constitutionnel), 128
Constitutionality of Introductory Provisions to the Act on the Organisation of the Constitutional Tribunal and the Mode of Proceedings Before the Constitutional Tribunal K 1/17 (Polish Constitutional Tribunal), 186
Procedure to Prohibit the Political Party NPD 2 BvB 1/13 (German Federal Constitutional Court), 87
Quantitative Easing (PSPP) Reference 2 BvR 859/15, 2 BvR 1651/15, 2 BvR 2006/15, 2 BvR 980/15 (German Federal Constitutional Court), 2, 8

2018

Commission v. Poland C-619/18 R (CJEU), 78
Constitutional Challenge of German Migration Policy Initiated by the AfD 2 BvE 1/18 (German Federal Constitutional Court), 73
National Law Related to the Protection of Personal Data under the GDPR Decision 2018-765 DC (French Conseil Constitutionnel), 129
On the Establishment of a European Monetary Fund PeVL 12/2018 vp (Finnish Constitutional Law Committee), 47
Wightman C-621/18 (CJEU), 197

2020

Commission's Draft EU Recovery Plan and MFF Planning PeVL 16/2020 vp (Finnish Constitutional Law Committee), 2

Decision on the Unified Patent Court 2 BvR 739/17 (German Federal Constitutional Court)

EIB Proposal for EU COVID-19 Guarantee Fund PeVL 12/2020 vp (Finnish Constitutional Law Committee), 51

Protocol Concerning Possible EU COVID-19 Rescue Measures PeVP 34/2020 vp (Finnish Constitutional Law Committee), 270

Quantitative Easing (PSPP) Final Judgment 2 BvR 859/15, 2 BvR 1651/15, 2 BvR 2006/15, 2 BvR 980/15 (German Federal Constitutional Court), 8

2021

Interim Decision on the Ratification of the Own Resources Decision (NGEU) 2 BvR 547/21 (German Federal Constitutional Court), 99

Ratification of the Own Resources Decision (II.) PeVL 14/21 vp (Finnish Constitutional Law Committee), 2

2022

Final Decision on the Ratification of the Own Resources Decision (NGEU) 2 BvR 547/21; 2 BvR 798/21 (German Federal Constutional Court), 2

Index

A

Absolute limit/restriction, 20, 63, 78, 92, 95, 107, 117, 121, 143, 149, 164, 190, 191, 192, 194, 201, 231, 249, 253, 279, 294, 301, 312, 320
Actio popularis, 67, 71, 107
Archetype (of constitutional approaches), 10
Article 122 TFEU, 233, 238, 239
Article 175 TFEU, 216, 217, 233, 237, 238
Article 50 TEU, 91, 160, 179, 197, 252, 305, 306

B

Budgetary Instrument for Convergence and Competitiveness (BICC), 208, 215, 218, 232, 233, 238, 240, 310, 311
Budgetary/fiscal autonomy, 95, 97, 98, 99, 105, 107, 239, 240, 246, 265, 266, 269, 272, 273, 292, 294, 309, 320

C

Centralized approach, 211
CJEU, 7, 36, 46, 50, 81, 83, 100, 127, 144, 147, 197
Classic fiscal federalism model, 211
Commission White Paper on the future of Europe, 5, 208
Comparative framework, 10, 12, 13, 169
Competence-centric interpretation/state-centric interpretation, 10
Constitutional amendment, 11, 27, 29, 33, 34, 35, 44, 52, 54, 58, 63, 74, 76, 113, 125, 138, 141, 142, 149, 151, 159, 161, 165, 166, 167, 175, 178, 182, 184, 189, 192, 194, 198, 201, 248, 249, 250, 251, 253, 254, 255, 267, 268, 271, 276, 278, 279, 280, 288, 293, 299, 301, 312, 321
Constitutional consistency/Constitutional double standard, 14, 69, 71, 301, 310
Constitutional evolution, 52
constitutional flexibility, 13, 14, 15, 20, 23, 42, 55, 59, 107, 120, 211, 232, 247, 256, 301, 302, 304, 305, 306, 307, 309, 310, 313, 314, 318, 323, 324, 325, 326, 327, 328
  best practices, 325
  immediate and indirect benefits of EU cooperation, 327
Constitutional identity classification board, 123, 148, 167, 190, 192, 193, 194

Constitutional identity limits
comparative evaluation, 193, 194
comparative findings, 205
EU fiscal integration, 195, 196, 197, 198, 199, 200, 201, 202
institutional and procedural framework, 203, 204, 205
national constitutional space, 195, 196, 197, 198, 199, 200, 201, 202
Constitutional identity review, 82
Constitutional rigidity, 12
(Economic) convergence, 2, 4, 214, 215
Coordination approach, 211, 216, 229
COVID-19, 2, 4, 16, 218, 239, 272, 279, 304, 311, 317

D

Decentralized approach, 211
Derived legal order, 106, 148, 179, 183, 189

E

Economic and Monetary Union's (EMU), 1, 2, 3, 5, 33, 137, 139, 140, 141, 208, 213, 214, 224, 225, 226, 243, 248, 262, 270, 284, 285, 287, 288, 290, 295, 304, 311, 314, 323
EMU decision-making, 285, 331
EMU-architecture, 298
EMU-cooperation, 249
EMU-deficiencies, 4
EMU-framework, 244
EMU-policies, 290
EMU-powers, 284
EMU-reforms, 3, 4, 7, 15, 111, 124, 202, 211, 318
(National) enabling clause, 119, 133, 151, 194, 195, 252
Essential conditions for the exercising of national sovereignty, 129, 133, 134
Eternity clause (Article 79(3) GG), 9, 58, 63, 76, 77, 78, 82, 85, 90, 95, 101, 103, 107, 108, 109, 117, 191, 192, 195, 201, 236, 245, 256, 257, 261, 264, 271, 282, 287, 288, 292, 294, 295, 301, 324
EU added value/benefit, 305, 309, 313, 323, 329, 330
EU borrowing, 6, 49, 99, 221, 223, 270, 274, 276, 277, 278, 279, 281, 300, 313
EU cooperation
conferral of additional competences to, 62, 63, 64
constitutional oversight
individual, 66, 67, 68, 69, 70, 71
institutional actors, 72, 73, 74, 75
involvement of, 65, 66
participation of parliament, 64, 65
EU debts, 220, 221, 222, 223, 259, 269, 270, 271, 272, 273, 274, 275, 276, 277, 278, 279, 280, 282
EU emergency instruments, 214, 216, 217, 218, 223, 233, 234, 235, 236, 238, 239, 240, 241, 242, 243, 244, 245, 246, 247, 249, 250, 253, 257, 269, 304, 310, 311, 322
EU fiscal integration, 2
applicable procedural and institutional framework, 75, 76
charted comparative constitutional space for, 319, 320, 321, 322
compatibility of, 231, 232
budgetary capacity/instrument introduced by EU treaty amendment, 243
charted macro-comparative constitutional space, 233
charted micro-comparative constitutional space, 241
fiscal capacity/instrument based on existing treaty-framework, 233
interim conclusion, 243

national constitutional space, 232
competences to Eurozone Ministry, 290
consistent constitutional standard, 107, 108, 109
constitutional concerns, 317
constitutional flexibility
actual german contributions to EU budget, 301
best practices, 307
functioning Euro, 304
German constitutional approach, 306
net contribution of Germany, 303
procedural dimension of, 305
re-conception of national approach and EU benefits, 308
two-way street, 310
constitutional identity limit
interim conclusion of, 147
scope of application, 144, 145
substantive content by, 145, 146
constitutionally attainable, 322, 323
core constitutional limit to, 151, 152
deconstuction of
emergency budgetary instruments, 216, 217
enhanced supervision of national budgeting, 227, 228, 229
envisaged, 229
EU Ministry of Finance, 224, 225, 226, 227
Eurozone-budget, 214, 215, 216
possible funding sources, 223
treaty-based funding sources, 220, 221, 222
treaty-framework, 222, 223
democracy
delegation of public authority, 88, 89
elections, 86, 87
legitimizing object, 87, 88
resulting challenge for, 89, 90, 91, 92
Volkssouveränität, 85
EU cooperation for national constitutional duty, 330–333
EU debts and shared liabilities, 269
French constitutional approach
EU primary law, 127, 128
EU secondary law, 128, 129
genuine EU taxation competence, 263
German constitutional space, 106, 107
German sovereignty, 105
national sovereignty
AFJS, 137
constitutional basis of employed limit, 133, 134
EMU, 139
free movement, 137
institutional actor enforcing, 130, 131
longevity and absoluteness of, 142, 143
procedural framework, 131, 132
single currency, 139
substantive core proctected by, 134, 135, 136, 137, 138, 139, 140, 141, 142
Union citizenship, 137
overall budgetary responsibility
application of, 96, 97, 98, 99, 100
conclusion on, 101
possible double standard, 101, 102, 103, 104
requirements of, 94, 95, 96
underpinning democracy-theoretical considerations, 92, 93
Polish perspective
constitutional basis of, 174, 175
core constitutional limits, 170, 171
institutional actor enforcing the limit, 171, 172
longevity and absoluteness of, 183, 184
procedural framework, 172, 173, 174

rule of law at risk in Poland, 185, 186, 187, 188
substantive core protected by, 175, 176, 177, 178, 179, 180, 181, 182, 183
Structural-Institutional Dimension, 284
Tax-Based Own Resources, 259
tightened EU supervision, 296
underpinning mechanisms
constitutional identity review, 82
constitutional jurisprudence on, 83, 84
eternity clause, 76, 77, 78, 79
fundamental rights review, 79, 80
ultra vires review, 80, 81
EU Fiscal Union, 5
EU Five President Report, 5, 208, 224, 227, 310, 311
EU integration theories, 327, 328
EU law supremacy, 170, 172, 174, 189, 203
EU Minister of Finance, 210, 224, 225, 226, 227
EU Ministry of Finance, 2, 5, 213, 229, 300, 310, 313, 318, 322, 329
compatibility of proposals envisaging, 284, 286, 287, 288, 290, 291, 292, 293, 294, 295
creating administrative-executive capacity, 224, 225, 226, 227
EU Own Resources, 220, 259, 261, 262, 270, 273, 274, 278, 279, 303
EU revenue, 213, 254, 259, 261, 266, 280, 329
EU Six Pack, 19, 39
EU taxation, 220, 222, 223, 259, 263, 264, 265, 266, 267, 268, 275, 279, 282, 290, 292, 293, 309, 312
Eurobonds, 209, 222, 270, 271, 276, 277, 279, 312
Eurocrisis, 1, 3, 4, 19, 20, 21, 22, 23, 31, 35, 37, 38, 46, 47, 48, 50, 51, 55, 57, 58, 64, 68, 72, 75, 76, 84, 92, 96, 106, 107, 111, 115, 140, 149, 150, 151, 155, 156, 163, 164, 167, 175, 191, 192, 207, 227, 234, 240, 248, 261, 264, 304, 317
European Central Bank (ECB), 4, 7, 58, 95, 98, 99
European Law Friendliness, 76, 83, 328
European Senate, 331
European Stability Mechanism (ESM), 1, 19, 35, 37, 48, 63, 73, 94, 98, 101, 115, 124, 218, 226, 239, 240, 245, 270, 274, 327
Eurosceptical/Euroscepticism, 6, 22, 35, 116
Eurozone budget, 5, 33, 213, 218, 233, 247, 280, 310, 323, 329
Eurozone Fiscal Capacity, 4, 210, 213, 214, 215, 217
Eurozone Forum of National Parliamentary Delegates, 331
Ex Ante constitutional review, 38, 41, 111, 124, 126, 131, 148, 154, 172, 173, 236
Ex Post constitutional review/judicial scrutiny, 38, 41, 111, 124, 126, 131, 148, 154, 172, 173, 236
Exceptive enactment, 24, 27, 28, 33, 44, 54
External layer of constitutional protection, 78

F

Factual benefits (of EU integration), 43, 45, 118, 119, 313, 325, 327
Finnish Constitutional Law Committee, 2, 8, 19, 26, 27, 28, 111, 112, 113, 114, 117, 118, 119, 125, 269, 279, 285, 307, 313, 319, 325, 327
Finnish democracy, 51, 52, 53, 319
Finnish Government, 26
Finnish Parliament, 9, 19, 20, 22, 26, 27, 28, 30, 31, 32, 33, 34, 35, 36,

37, 38, 39, 40, 41, 42, 44, 47, 48, 49, 50, 51, 52, 53, 54, 55, 111, 112, 113, 114, 115, 118, 119, 234, 235, 260, 264, 270, 285, 286, 291, 311, 312, 319, 325, 326
Finnish sovereignty, 22, 25, 32, 38, 42, 43, 52, 54, 55, 113, 117, 118, 119, 260, 263, 264, 269, 270, 285, 286, 290, 291, 297, 307, 319, 325, 327
  evolutionary conception, 43, 44, 45, 46, 47, 48, 49, 50, 51
Fiscal compact, 19, 35, 63, 75, 115, 140, 141, 173, 204, 227, 228, 248, 287
Flexible constitutional approach, 12, 55
French Constitutional Council/Conseil Constitutionnel, 9, 124, 125, 126, 127, 128, 129, 130, 131, 132, 133, 134, 135, 136, 137, 138, 139, 141, 142, 143, 144, 145, 147, 148, 149, 195, 196, 198, 199, 200, 204, 241, 248, 249, 266, 267, 275, 276, 288, 292
French Parliament/Assemblée Nationale, 130, 131, 140, 266, 276

G

German constitution
  origin of, 59, 60
German democracy, 8, 20, 68, 82, 85, 87, 88, 89, 91, 92, 97, 105, 106, 107, 110, 116, 247, 255, 265, 269, 301, 306, 308
German Federal Constitutional Court/Bundesverfassungsgericht, 19, 57, 59, 60, 66, 67, 68, 69, 70, 71, 73, 74, 75, 76, 88, 96, 98, 100, 101, 102, 103, 104, 105, 107, 108, 111, 112, 119, 125, 195
German Federal Council/Bundesrat, 61, 66, 87, 203, 237
German Parliament/Bundestag, 61, 64, 65, 68, 70, 72, 73, 74, 82, 84, 86, 87, 88, 89, 90, 91, 92, 93, 94, 95, 96, 97, 98, 99, 100, 101, 102, 103, 106, 108, 115, 116, 117, 119, 121, 191, 192, 198, 199, 200, 203, 205, 235, 236, 237, 238, 239, 240, 244, 245, 246, 247, 254, 255, 261, 265, 271, 272, 273, 274, 287, 291, 294, 297, 302, 304, 305, 306, 312, 320, 324, 326
German sovereignty, 84, 91, 105, 106
German ultra vires review, 39, 58
Globalized context/Globalization, 8, 15, 22, 45, 118, 180, 189, 307, 310, 331, 333

H

High Level Group on Own Resources (HLGOR) Report/Monti-Report, 5, 220, 222, 259, 260, 309, 311

I

Implied ultra vires, 39
Integration approach, 211, 214, 229
(German) integration responsibility, 83, 84, 237, 286

J

Joint liabilities, 220
Judicial reluctance, 107, 191
"Just return" debate, 220, 259, 280

K

Kompetenz-Kompetenz, 106, 118, 176, 189, 190, 249, 252, 289, 305

M

Macroeconomic imbalances/shocks, 2, 3, 4, 5, 304
Masters of the Treaty, 106
Modern interpretation of sovereignty, 15, 183
Mutable constitutional approach, 12

N

National constitutional identity, 11, 14, 117, 118, 121, 122, 129, 143, 152, 180, 188, 193, 195, 198, 199, 200, 203, 205, 231, 241, 243, 255, 263
National constitutional limits, 323, 324, 325, 326, 327, 328
  micro-comparison, 323
Next Generation EU (NGEU), 2

O

Operating budgetary balance, 302, 303, 304, 328
Overall budgetary responsibility, 64, 68, 84, 92, 106, 107, 108, 115, 116, 117, 119, 191, 192, 198, 199, 238, 239, 240, 244, 246, 247, 254, 255, 256, 259, 261, 262, 265, 266, 272, 273, 274, 280, 287, 288, 291, 292, 294, 297, 298, 301, 302, 305, 306, 308, 311, 312, 319, 320, 324, 325, 327
  Bundesverfassungsgericht, 96
  conclusion on, 101
  possible double standard
    constitutional scrutiny of German budget, 101, 102, 103, 104
  procedural dimension of, 305
  requirements of, 94, 95, 96
  underpinning democracy-theoretical considerations, 92, 93

P

Polish Constitutional Tribunal, 168, 169, 170
Polish Parliament/Sejm, 172, 182, 184, 185, 186, 187, 189, 190, 204, 251, 268, 278, 294
Polish sovereignty
  constitutional identity limit of, 181
Preliminary reference, 81
Procedural constitutional limit, 102
PSPP-judgment, 7
Public Sector Purchase Programme (PSP), 2

R

Re-distributive policy/redistribution, 6, 99
Red-line limits, 11, 12, 301
Rigid constitutional approach, 10, 12, 14, 20
Rule of law crisis, 172
Russian War of Aggression, 5, 16, 304, 317

S

Shared liabilities, 259, 269, 270, 271, 272, 273, 274, 275, 276, 277, 278, 279, 280, 282
Spanish constitutional identity limit
  constitutional basis of, 156, 157
  institutional actor enforcing the limit, 153, 154
  procedural framework, 154, 155, 156
  substantive core protected by, 157, 158, 159, 160, 161, 162, 163, 164
Spanish Constitutional Tribunal, 149, 152, 157, 160, 161, 162, 164, 167, 195, 197, 198, 199, 201, 242, 251, 268, 277
Spanish Parliament, 242, 249, 250, 293

Spanish Senate, 249, 250
Spanish sovereignty, 152, 157, 158, 159, 160, 163, 166, 167, 197, 198, 249, 268, 277
Spanish substantive core, 163, 164
Stable constitutional approach, 10
Substantive constitutional limit, 20, 169, 320
Surveillance model, 211

U

Ultima ratio function, 324
Ultra vires review, 80, 81, 82, 83, 84, 170, 237

EUROPEAN MONOGRAPH SERIES

1. Lammy Betten (ed.), *The Future of European Social Policy,* 1991 (ISBN 90-654-4585-4).
2. Annemarie Loman, Kamiel Mortelmans, Harry H.G. Post & Stewart Watson, *Culture and Common Law: Before and After Maastricht,* 1992 (ISBN 90-654-4638-9).
3. John A.E. Vervaele, *Fraud against the Community: The Need for European Fraud Legislation,* 1994 (ISBN 90-654-4634-6).
4. Philip Raworth, *The Legislative Process in the European Community,* 1993 (ISBN 90-654-4690-7).
5. Jules Stuyck, *Financial and Monetary Integration in the European Economic Community,* 1993 (ISBN 90-654-4718-0).
6. Jules Stuyck & A.J. Vossestein (eds), *State Entrepreneurship, National Monopolies and European Community Law,* 1993 (ISBN 90-654-4773-3).
7. Jules Stuyck & A. Looijestijn-Clearie (eds), *The European Economic Area EC-EFTA,* 1994 (ISBN 90-654-4815-2).
8. Rosita B. Bouterse, *Competition and Integration: What Goals Count?,* 1995 (ISBN 90-654-4816-0).
9. René Barents, *The Agricultural Law of the EU, 2nd Edition,* 2022 (ISBN 978-94-035-4411-3).
10. Nicholas Emiliou, *Principles of Proportionality in European Law: A Comparative Study,* 1996 (ISBN 90-411-0866-1).
11. Eivind Smith, *National Parliaments as Cornerstones of European Integration,* 1996 (ISBN 90-411-0898-X).
12. Jan H. Jans, *European Environmental Law,* 1996 (ISBN 90-411-0877-7).
13. Síofra O'Leary, *The Evolving Concept of Community Citizenship: From the Free Movement of Persons to Union Citizenship,* 1997 (ISBN 90-411-0878-5).
14. Laurence W. Gormley (ed.), *Current and Future Perspectives on EC Competition Law,* 1983 (ISBN 90-411-0691-X).
15. Simone White, *Protection of the Financial Interests of the European Communities: The Fight against Fraud and Corruption,* 1998 (ISBN 90-411-9647-1).
16. Morten P. Broberg, *Broberg on the European Commission's Jurisdiction to Scrutinise Mergers*, 4th Edition, 2013 (ISBN 978-90-411-3339-7).
17. Doris Hildebrand, *The Role of Economic Analysis in the EC Competition Rules: The European School,* 2nd Edition, 2002 (ISBN 90-411-1706-7).
18. Christof R.A. Swaak, *European Community Law and the Automobile Industry,* 1999 (ISBN 90-411-1140-9).

19. Dorthe Dahlgaard Dingel, *Public Procurement: A Harmonization of the National Judicial Review of the Application of European Community Law,* 1999 (ISBN 90-411-1161-1).
20. John A.E. Vervaele (ed.), *Compliance and Enforcement of European Community Law,* 1999 (ISBN 90-411-1151-4).
21. Martin Trybus, *European Defence Procurement Law: International and National Procurement Systems as Models for a Liberalized Defence Procurement Market in Europe,* 1999 (ISBN 90-411-1167-0).
22. Helen Staples, *The Legal Status of Third Country Nationals Resident in the European Union,* 1999 (ISBN 90-411-1277-4).
23. Damien Geradin (ed.), *The Liberalization of State Monopolies in the European Union and Beyond,* 1999 (ISBN 90-411-1264-2).
24. Katja Heede, *European Ombudsman: Redress and Control at Union Level,* 2000 (ISBN 90-411-1413-0).
25. Ulf Bernitz & Joakim Nergelius (eds), *General Principles of European Community Law,* 2000 (ISBN 90-411-1402-5).
26. Michaela Drahos, *Convergence of Competition Laws and Policies in the European Community,* 2002 (ISBN 90-411-1562-5).
27. Damien Geradin (ed.), *The Liberalization of Electricity and Natural Gas in the European Union,* 2001 (ISBN 90-411-1560-9).
28. Gisella Gori, *Towards an EU Right to Education,* 2001 (ISBN 90-411-1670-2).
29. Brendan P.G. Smith, *Constitution Building in the European Union,* 2001 (ISBN 90-411-1695-8).
30. Friedl Weiss & Frank Wooldridge, *Free Movement of Persons within the European Community,* 2nd Edition, 2007 (ISBN 978-90-411-2545-3).
31. Ingrid Boccardi, *Europe and Refugees: Towards an EU Asylum Policy,* 2002 (ISBN 90-411-1709-1).
32. John A.E. Vervaele & André Klip (eds), *European Cooperation Between Tax, Customs and Judicial Authorities,* 2001 (ISBN 90-411-1747-4).
33. Wouter P.J. Wils, *The Optimal Enforcement of EC Antitrust Law: Essays in Law and Economics,* 2002 (ISBN 90-411-1757-1).
34. Damien Geradin (ed.), *The Liberalization of Postal Services in the European Union,* 2002 (ISBN 90-411-1780-6).
35. Nick Bernard, *Multilevel Governance in the European Union,* 2002 (ISBN 90-411-1812-8).
36. Jill Wakefield, *Judicial Protection through the Use of Article 288(2) EC,* 2002 (ISBN 90-411-1823-3).
37. Sebastiaan Princen, *EU Regulation and Transatlantic Trade,* 2002 (ISBN 90-411-1871-3).
38. Amaryllis Verhoeven, *The European Union in Search of a Democratic and Constitutional Theory,* 2002 (ISBN 90-411-1872-1).
39. Paul L.C. Torremans, *Cross Border Insolvencies in EU, English and Belgian Law,* 2002 (ISBN 90-411-1888-8).

40. Malcolm Anderson & Joanna Apap (eds), *Police and Justice Cooperation and the New European Borders,* 2002 (ISBN 90-411-1893-4).
41. Christin M. Forstinger, *Takeover Law in EU and USA: A Comparative Analysis,* 2002 (ISBN 90-411-1919-1).
42. Antonio Bavasso, *Communications in EU Antitrust Law: Market Power and Public Interest,* 2003 (ISBN 90-411-1974-4).
43. Fiona G. Wishlade, *Regional State Aid and Competition Policy in the European Union,* 2003 (ISBN 90-411-1975-2).
44. Gareth Davies, *Nationality Discrimination in the European Internal Market,* 2003 (ISBN 90-411-1998-1).
45. René Barents, *The Autonomy of Community Law,* 2003 (ISBN 90-411-2251-6).
46. Gerhard Dannecker & Oswald Jansen (eds), *Competition Law Sanctioning in the European Union,* 2004 (ISBN 90-411-2100-5).
47. Nauta Dutilh (ed.), *Dealing with Dominance: The Experience of National Competition Authorities,* 2004 (ISBN 90-411-2211-7).
48. Stefaan van den Bogaert, *Practical Regulation of the Mobility of Sportsmen in the EU Post Bosman,* 2005 (ISBN 90-411-2327-X).
49. Katalin Judit Cseres, *Competition Law and Consumer Protection,* 2005 (ISBN 90-411-2380-6).
50. Philipp Kiiver, *The National Parliaments in the European Union: A Critical View on EU Constitution Building,* 2006 (ISBN 978-90-411-2452-4).
51. Alexander Turk, *The Concept of Legislation in European Community Law,* 2006 (ISBN 978-90-411-2472-2).
52. Dimitrios Sinaniotis, *The Interim Protection of Individuals before the European and National Courts,* 2006 (ISBN 978-90-411-2498-2).
53. M. Holoubek & D. Damjanovic, M. Traimer (eds), *Regulating Content: The European Regulatory Framework for the Media and Related Creative Sectors,* 2006 (ISBN 978-90-411-2597-2).
54. Anneli Albi & Jacques Ziller (eds), *The European Constitution and National Constitutions: Ratification and Beyond,* 2006 (ISBN 978-90-411-2524-8).
55. Gustavo E. Luengo, *Regulation of Subsidies and State Aids in WTO and EC Law: Conflicts in International Trade Law,* 2007 (ISBN 978-90-411-2547-7).
56. Eniko Horvath, *Mandating Identity: Citizenship, Kinship Laws and Plural Nationality in the European Union,* 2007 (ISBN 978-90-411-2662-7).
57. Rass Holdgaard, *External Relations Law of the European Community: Legal Reasoning and Legal Discourses,* 2007 (ISBN 978-90-411-2604-7).
58. Jill Wakefield, *The Right to Good Administration,* 2007 (ISBN 978-90-411-2697-9).
59. Dimitry Kochenov, *EU Enlargement and the Failure of Conditionality: Pre- accession Conditionality in the Fields of Democracy and the Rule of Law,* 2008 (ISBN 978-90-411-2696-2).
60. Despina Mavromati, *The Law of Payment Services in the EU: The EC Directive on Payment Services in the Internal Market,* 2008 (ISBN 978-90-411-2700-6).

61. Anne Meuwese, *Impact Assessment in EU Lawmaking,* 2008 (ISBN 978-90-411-2720-4).
62. Ulf Bernitz, Joakim Nergelius & Cecilia Cardner (eds), *General Principles of EC Law in a Process of Development,* 2008 (ISBN 978-90-411-2705-1).
63. Johan van de Gronden (ed.), *The EU and WTO Law on Services: Limits to the Realisation of General Interest Policies within the Services Markets?,* 2008 (ISBN 978-90-411-2809-6).
64. Alina Tryfonidou, *Reverse Discrimination in EC Law,* 2009 (ISBN 978-90-411-2751-8).
65. Mikael Berglund, *Cross-Border Enforcement of Claims in the EU: History Present Time and Future,* 2014 (ISBN 978-90-411-4564-2).
66. Theodore Konstadinides, *Division of Powers in European Union Law: The Delimitation of Internal Competence between the EU and the Member States,* 2009 (ISBN 978-90-411-2615-3).
67. Mattias Derlén, *Multilingual Interpretation of European Union Law,* 2009 (ISBN 978-90-411-2853-9).
68. René Barents, *Directory of EU Case Law on the Preliminary Ruling Procedure,* 2009 (ISBN 978-90-411-3150-8).
69. Yan Luo, *Anti-dumping in the WTO, the EU and China: The Rise of Legalization in the Trade Regime and Its Consequences,* 2010 (ISBN 978-90-411-3207-9).
70. Patrick Birkinshaw & Mike Varney (eds), *The European Union Legal Order after Lisbon,* 2010 (ISBN 978-90-411-3152-2).
71. Thomas Gr. Papadopoulos, *EU Law and Harmonization of Takeovers in the Internal Market,* 2010 (ISBN 978-90-411-3340-3).
72. Bas van Bockel, *The* Ne Bis In Idem *Principle in EU Law,* 2010 (ISBN 978-90-411-3156-0).
73. Veljko Milutinović, *The 'Right to Damages' under EU Competition Law: From* Courage v. Crehan *to the White Paper and Beyond,* 2010 (ISBN 978-90-411-3235-2).
74. Amandine Garde, *EU Law and Obesity Prevention,* 2010 (ISBN 978-90-411-2706-8).
75. Leonard Besselink, Frans Pennings & Sacha Prechal (eds), *The Eclipse of the Legality Principle in the European Union,* 2011 (ISBN 978-90-411-3262-8).
76. Sacha Garben, *EU Higher Education Law: The Bologna Process and Harmonization by Stealth,* 2011 (ISBN 978-90-411-3365-6).
77. Dimitry Kochenov (ed.), *EU Law of the Overseas: Outermost Regions, Associated Overseas Countries and Territories, Territories Sui Generis,* 2011 (ISBN 978-90-411-3445-5).
78. Pablo Ibáñez Colomo, *European Communications Law and Technological Convergence: Deregulation, Re-regulation and Regulatory Convergence in Television and Telecommunications,* 2012 (ISBN 978-90-411-3829-3).
79. Elise Muir, *EU Regulation of Access to Labour Markets: A Case Study of EU Constraints on Member State Competences,* 2012 (ISBN 978-90-411-3823-1).
80. Tim Corthaut, *EU Ordre Public,* 2012 (ISBN 978-90-411-3232-1).

81. Oana Ştefan, *Soft Law in Court: Competition Law, State Aid and the Court of Justice of the European Union*, 2013 (ISBN 978-90-411-3997-9).
82. Francesco Rossi dal Pozzo, *Citizenship Rights and Freedom of Movement in the European Union*, 2013 (ISBN 978-90-411-4660-1).
83. Jens Hartig Danielsen, *EU Agricultural Law*, 2013 (ISBN 978-90-411-3280-2).
84. Ulf Bernitz, Xavier Groussot & Felix Schulyok (eds), *General Principles of EU Law and European Private Law*, 2013 (ISBN 978-90-411-4683-0).
85. Michelle Everson, Cosimo Monda & Ellen Vos (eds), *European Agencies in between Institutions and Member States*, 2014 (ISBN 978-90-411-2843-0).
86. Stefan Leible & Matthias Lehmann (eds), *European Contract Law and German Law*, 2014 (ISBN 978-90-411-2588-0).
87. Piero Leanza & Ondrej Pridal, *The Right to a Fair Trial: Article 6 of the European Convention on Human Rights*, 2014 (ISBN 978-90-411-4855-1).
88. Patrick J. Birkinshaw, *European Public Law: The Achievement and the Brexit Challenge*, 3rd Edition, 2020 (ISBN 978-90-411-9751-1).
89. George Cumming, *Expert Evidence Deficiencies in the Judgments of the Courts of the European Union and the European Court of Human Rights*, 2014 (ISBN 978-90-411-4123-1).
90. Vesna Rijavec, Tomaž Keresteš & Tjaša Ivanc (eds), *Simplification of Debt Collection in the EU*, 2014 (ISBN 978-90-411-4854-4).
91. Nina Półtorak, *European Union Rights in National Courts*, 2015 (ISBN 978-90-411-5863-5).
92. Kyriaki-Korina Raptopoulou, *EU Law and Healthcare Services: Normative Approaches to Public Health Systems*, 2015 (ISBN 978-90-411-5013-4).
93. Torsten Frank Koschinka & Piero Leanza, *Preliminary Injunctions: Germany, England/Wales, Italy and France*, 2015 (ISBN 978-90-411-5833-8).
94. Vesna Rijavec, Tomaž Keresteš & Tjaša Ivanc (eds), *Dimensions of Evidence in European Civil Procedure*, 2016 (ISBN 978-90-411-6662-3).
95. Stefan Leible (ed.), *General Principles of European Private International Law*, 2016 (ISBN 978-90-411-5955-7).
96. Patrick J. Birkinshaw & Andrea Biondi (eds), *Britain Alone!: The Implications and Consequences of United Kingdom Exit from the EU*, 2016 (ISBN 978-90-411-5832-1).
97. René Barents, *Remedies and Procedures before the EU Courts*, 2nd Edition, 2020 (ISBN 978-94-035-1140-5).
98. Luca Prete, *Infringement Proceedings in EU Law*, 2017 (ISBN 978-90-411-6900-6).
99. Robert van den Hoven van Genderen, *Privacy Limitation Clauses: Trojan Horses under the Disguise of Democracy*, 2017 (ISBN 978-90-411-8599-0).
100. Mariusz Krzysztofek, *Post-Reform Personal Data Protection in the European Union: General Data Protection Regulation (EU) 2016/679*, 2017 (ISBN 978-90-411-6237-3).
101. Gianni Lo Schiavo, *The Role of Financial Stability in EU Law and Policy*, 2017 (ISBN 978-90-411-8230-2).

102. Emmanuel Guinchard & Marie-Pierre Granger (eds), *The New EU Judiciary: An Analysis of Current Judicial Reforms*, 2017 (ISBN 978-90-411-6834-4).
103. Kirsten Henckel, *Cross-Border Transfers of Undertakings: A European Perspective,* 2017 (ISBN 978-90-411-9227-1).
104. Vesna Rijavec, Wendy Kennett, Tomaž Keresteš & Tjaša Ivanc, *Remedies Concerning Enforcement of Foreign Judgements: Brussels I Recast,* 2018 (ISBN 978-90-411-9416-9).
105. Albert Sanchez-Graells & Constant De Koninck, *Shaping EU Public Procurement Law: A Critical Analysis of the CJEU Case Law 2015–2017*, 2018 (ISBN 978-94-035-0160-4).
106. Andrea Biondi, Patrick J. Birkinshaw & Maria Kendrick, *Brexit: The Legal Implications*, 2019 (ISBN 978-90-411-9540-1).
107. Mariusz Krzysztofek, *GDPR: General Data Protection Regulation (EU) 2016/679: Post-Reform Personal Data Protection in the European Union*, 2019 (ISBN 978-94-035-0594-7).
108. Giovanni Bassani, *The Legal Framework Applicable to the Single Supervisory Mechanism: Tapestry or Patchwork?,* 2019 (ISBN 978-94-035-0872-6).
109. Piotr Staszczyk, *A Legal Analysis of NGOs and European Civil Society*, 2019 (ISBN 978-94-035-1251-8).
110. Patrizio Messina, *Finance for SMEs: European Regulation and Capital Markets Union – Focus on Securitization and Alternative Finance Tools*, 2019 (ISBN 978-94-035-0161-1).
111. Jacques H.J. Bourgeois (ed.), *EU Framework for Foreign Direct Investment Control*, 2020 (ISBN 978-94-035-1883-1).
112. Ulf Bernitz, Xavier Groussot, Jaan Paju & Sybe de Vries (eds), *General Principles of EU Law and the EU Digital Order*, 2020 (ISBN 978-94-035-1165-8).
113. Aleksandra Drożdż, *Protection of Natural Persons with Regard to Automated Individual Decision-Making in the GDPR*, 2020 (ISBN 978-94-035-2045-2).
114. Mariusz Krzysztofek, *GDPR: Personal Data Protection in the European Union*, 2021 (ISBN 978-94-035-3270-7).
115. Katarzyna Gromek-Broc (ed.), *Public Law in a Troubled Era: A Tribute to Professor Patrick Birkinshaw*, 2023 (ISBN 978-94-035-3576-0).
116. Guido Alpa, *Solidarity: A Normative Principle*, 2023 (ISBN 978-94-035-3596-8).
117. Frederik Behre, *Fixing the Euro Within the National Constitutional Guardrails: A Comparative Assessment of the National Constitutional Space for EU (Fiscal) Integration*, 2023 (ISBN 978-94-035-3586-9).